A FIELD GUIDE TO
Gettysburg

A FIELD GUIDE TO
Gettysburg

Experiencing the Battlefield through Its History, Places, & People

CAROL REARDON & TOM VOSSLER

The University of North Carolina Press *Chapel Hill*

Publication of this book was supported in part by a generous gift from
Eric Papenfuse and Catherine Lawrence.

Designed by Kimberly Bryant and set in Quadraat types by Rebecca Evans.
Manufactured in the United States of America

The paper in this book meets the guidelines for permanence and durabil-
ity of the Committee on Production Guidelines for Book Longevity of the
Council on Library Resources. The University of North Carolina Press has
been a member of the Green Press Initiative since 2003.

Library of Congress Cataloging-in-Publication Data
Reardon, Carol.
A field guide to Gettysburg : experiencing the battlefield through
its history, places, and people / Carol Reardon and Tom Vossler.
pages cm
Includes bibliographical references and index.
ISBN 978-0-8078-3525-8 (pbk : alk. paper)
1. Gettysburg National Military Park (Pa.)—Tours. 2. Gettysburg,
Battle of, Gettysburg, Pa., 1863. I. Vossler, Tom. II. Title.
E475.56.R43 2013
973.7'349—dc23   2013002824

17 16 15 14 13 5 4 3 2 1

TO THE MEMORY OF OUR CIVIL WAR ANCESTORS

Captain Henry V. Fuller, 64th New York—killed in the Wheatfield, July 2, 1863

Sergeant Robert Clever, 155th Pennsylvania

Corporal Henry Brandes Jr., 64th and 160th New York

Corporal George Clever, 155th Pennsylvania

Private Henry Heers, 189th New York

Private James Higginbotham, 19th Virginia—missing in action during Pickett's Charge

AND TO THE MEMORY OF OUR BATTLEFIELD MENTOR

Jay Luvaas

Contents

A FIELD GUIDE TO
Gettysburg

The Gettysburg Campaign

When war came to Gettysburg in the summer of 1863, it unleashed its destructive power on a community entirely unprepared for it. As popular early twentieth-century novelist Mary Johnston wrote of the small market town: "It should have been all peace, that rich Pennsylvania landscape—a Dutch peace—a Quaker peace. Market wains and country folk should have moved upon the roads, and a boy, squirrel-hunting, should have been the most murderous thing in the Devil's Den. Corn-blades should have glistened, not bayonets; for the fluttering flags the farmers' wives should have been bleaching linen on the grass; for marching feet there should have risen the sound of the scythe in the wheat; for the groan of gun-wheels upon the roads the robin's song and the bob white's call."[1]

But war came, unwelcome and unbidden. In June 1863 General Robert E. Lee's Confederate Army of Northern Virginia marched north into the Keystone State from Virginia, and the Union Army of the Potomac followed in pursuit. The campaign culminated in three days of violent confrontation—July 1, 2, and 3, 1863—as the two armies clashed on the fields, in the woodlots, and on the ridges and hills of the county seat of Adams County, home to nearly 2,400 souls. When the Battle of Gettysburg ended, the names of approximately 53,000 soldiers—nearly one of every three men who fought there—filled the long lists of the dead, wounded, captured, and missing. Thus the clash became the costliest single military engagement on North American soil, one that inspired President Abraham Lincoln to deliver his most enduring statement of national values: the Gettysburg Address.

What brought the two armies to this small Pennsylvania town? In the spring of 1863, Confederate President Jefferson Davis faced a rapidly deteriorating military situation. Major General U. S. Grant had laid siege to the key Mississippi River port at Vicksburg, penning in Confederate Lieutenant General John C. Pemberton's 30,000 troops. If both Vicksburg and the Confederate garrison at Port Hudson, Louisiana, fell under Union control, the Confederacy would be cut in two. In central Tennessee, Union Major General William S. Rosecrans had begun to execute a slow, relatively bloodless maneuver campaign designed to push Confederate General Braxton Bragg back to and beyond the key railroad center at Chattanooga. On the south Atlantic coast, Major General David Hunter and Commodore Samuel Du-Pont launched a joint army-navy operation against the Confederate stronghold at Charleston. In the Virginia Tidewater, a Federal garrison of some 20,000 men held Suffolk, and Davis harbored serious concerns about the safety of Richmond. With so much bad news arriving from so many quarters, Davis called Lee to Richmond

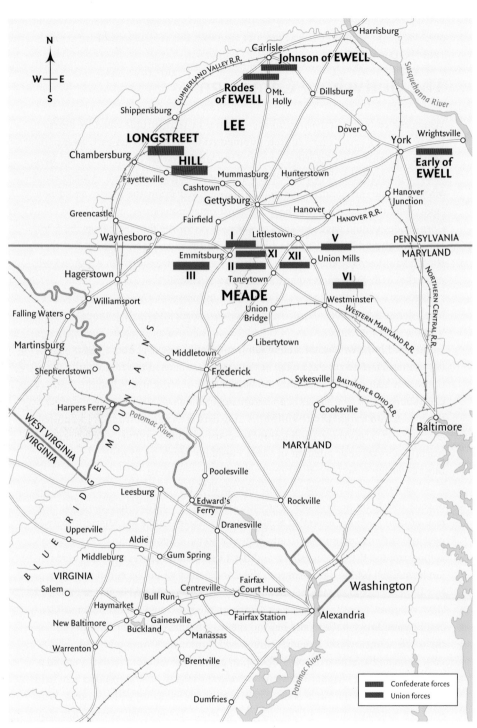

The Gettysburg Campaign

twice in mid-May 1863 to discuss the courses of action still open to the Confederacy.[2] While no minutes of these meetings survive, the dire military situation must have added a significant note of urgency to their considerations.

Even before the military situation had begun to deteriorate, however, Lee had begun to design an offensive operation for his Army of Northern Virginia. In early April he advised Secretary of War James A. Seddon that "should General Hooker's army assume the defensive, the readiest method of relieving pressure on General [Joseph E.] Johnston [ordered to aid Pemberton at Vicksburg] and General Beauregard would be for this army to cross into Maryland."[3]

Lee also expressed a second reason for considering a northward advance. If his army marched into Pennsylvania, he asserted, "the [Shenandoah] Valley could be swept of [Union Brigadier General Robert] Milroy and the army [of the Potomac, the major Union army in the eastern theater, commanded by Major General Joseph Hooker] opposite me be thrown north of the Potomac. I believe greater relief would in this way be afforded to the armies in middle Tennessee and on the Carolina coast than by any other method."[4] It also might resolve Lee's increasingly severe logistical issues. Milroy's 6,500-man garrison at Winchester severely limited Confederate access to the valley's rich harvests. As Lee wrote to his wife in mid-April: "This year I hope will establish our supplies on a firm basis." But hoping would not be enough. He needed to act.[5]

Jefferson Davis (USAMHI)

During his mid-May deliberations with Davis and Seddon, Lee continued to favor an offensive operation against Hooker's army. Clearly, he hoped to take the Army of Northern Virginia north of the Potomac once again. His reverse at Antietam in September 1862 did not deter him from preparing for a second effort. Indeed, while in winter camp in February 1863, Lee had directed Jedediah Hotchkiss, Stonewall Jackson's topographical engineer, to draw up a map of the valley of Virginia "extending to Harrisburg, PA and then on to Philadelphia—wishing the preparation to be kept a profound secret."[6] Not all of the senior Confederate political officials who engaged in the strategic debate in Richmond supported Lee's notions—including, at times, Davis himself. In the end, however, Lee's views held sway.

On June 3 General Lee issued his initial orders for the Army of Northern Virginia's movement north into Maryland and then into Pennsylvania. He hoped to get a head start before Hooker could discover his intentions, but the Union commander learned of his march by June 5. Union cavalry, probing for Lee's whereabouts, surprised and nearly routed Major General J. E. B. Stuart's Confederate horsemen at Brandy Station on June 9. Despite the scare, Lee forged ahead with his ambitious plans. He moved north flushed with confidence. His men had come to revere him;

as one Georgian told his comrades when passing Lee on the march north: "Boys, there are ten thousand men sitting on that one horse."[7]

As Lee moved north, Hooker saw an opportunity to launch a quick strike to the south against a lightly defended Richmond. Abraham Lincoln, however, reminded him that "Lee's army and not Richmond, is your sure objective point."[8] Thus Hooker gave up his plan and began a more active pursuit of the Army of Northern Virginia. But Lee's men moved quickly. By June 20 Brigadier General Albert G. Jenkins's cavalry, scouting ahead of Lieutenant General Richard S. Ewell's main column, reached Chambersburg, Pennsylvania, and two days later Confederate infantry entered the Keystone State near Greencastle. On June 23, Lee ordered Stuart to "harass and impede as much as possible" the progress of Hooker's army if it attempted to cross the Potomac. If Hooker still managed to cross, Lee expected Stuart to "take position on the right of our column as it advanced" to protect its flank closest to the Union forces.[9] Stuart certainly bothered the Union army and caused great consternation

in Washington, but he ultimately chose a northward course during that crucial final week of June that stayed to the right of both Lee and Hooker. Thus Lee had to make decisions in the absence of timely information that he always relied upon Stuart to provide.

Nonetheless, for the next week, Ewell's men fanned out throughout south-central Pennsylvania to the outskirts of Harrisburg with orders to procure supplies. On June 21 Lee had issued General Order 72 to outline the only acceptable processes for his quartermaster, commissary, ordnance, and medical staffs to obtain items deemed to be military necessities. He also made clear his expectation that his soldiers would respect private property. Still, Jenkins's cavalry and Ewell's infantry freely enjoyed the bounty of the region. Reports of his men's excesses troubled Lee.

Abraham Lincoln (USAMHI)

On June 27—the day after a Confederate brigade marched through Gettysburg on its way to York and the Susquehanna River bridges—he issued General Order No. 73 to chastise his soldiers for their "instances of forgetfulness" and to remind them of the "duties expected of us by civility and Christanity."[10] Still, wagon trains brimming with foodstuffs and other goods already had begun to return south.

Pennsylvanians responded to the arrival of Lee's army in many ways. Many in Lee's path simply fled with all they could carry. Some Pennsylvania Democrats actually believed that their political affiliation would protect them. On June 9 the Lincoln administration had established the Department of the Susquehanna to organize local defense—and Governor Andrew Curtin, in fact, had called out the state's emergency forces—but such efforts proved entirely insufficient. Just west of Gettysburg on June 26, the 26th Pennsylvania Emergency Regiment deployed against some of Ewell's men, but they scattered in panic after exchanging just a few shots.

Indeed, Lee's men continued to display an aggressiveness that confounded Hooker. Convinced that he faced a foe that greatly outnumbered him, on June 27 the Union commander sent an ultimatum to President Abraham Lincoln and the general in chief of the U.S. Army, Major General Henry W. Halleck: either extend his authority to strengthen his numbers or accept his resignation.[11] His superiors chose the latter. Major General George G. Meade—then the commander of the Army of the Potomac's V Corps—wrote to his wife that on June 28 before dawn, "I was aroused from my sleep by an officer from Washington entering my tent, and after waking me up, saying he had come to give me trouble. . . . He then handed me a communication to read; which I found was an order relieving Hooker from the command and assigning me to it."[12]

When Meade went to meet with Hooker, the deposed general left camp quickly without providing his successor with a detailed assessment of the military situation. Meade did not know the whereabouts of the various corps of the Army of the Potomac. Nor did he know much about the location of Lee's force. Nonetheless, he successfully made the transition from corps commander to army commander in short order. He made a few administrative changes, communicated directly with General Halleck and President Lincoln, fielded unending requests for information and supplies from regional political and military officials, and began to consider his first steps against Lee. Halleck made clear to Meade his expectations: "You will, therefore, maneuver and fight in such a manner as to cover the capital and also Baltimore. . . . Should General Lee move upon either of these places, it is expected that you will either anticipate him or arrive with him so as to give him battle."[13]

Despite the defensive tone of these instructions, Meade fully understood he had "to find and fight the enemy." Thus he issued orders for the Army of the Potomac to resume its northward advance the very next day—June 29. Still not certain about Lee's location and intentions, however, Meade developed a contingency plan to concentrate his army along Pipe Creek in Maryland, just south of the Pennsylvania line, in case his advance met strong resistance. Meade's critics later used his Pipe Creek circular of June 30 as proof of his unwillingness to fight, but his concluding sentence suggests something different: "Developments may cause the Commanding General to assume the offensive from his present positions."[14]

Encamped near Chambersburg, Lee learned of Meade's accession to command the day after the appointment. Although he suspected Meade might approach his duties cautiously, Lee nonetheless issued orders on June 29 for the Army of Northern Virginia to concentrate at Cashtown, east of the Blue Ridge and seven miles northwest of Gettysburg. He specifically warned his corps commanders not to give battle with Meade's approaching forces until the whole of the Confederate army could provide ready support. By June 30, most of Lieutenant General A. P. Hill's Third Corps already had reached Cashtown. Lieutenant General James Longstreet remained west of the Blue Ridge, but his First Corps could close on Cashtown in less than a day. Lieutenant General Richard S. Ewell issued orders to march from his camps around Carlisle early on July 1 and head for Cashtown.

From Cashtown on June 30, Hill sent forward a North Carolina brigade from Brigadier General Henry Heth's division to reconnoiter toward Gettysburg. Its commander reported that Union cavalry had entered the town from the south and fanned out to cover the western approaches to Gettysburg. Indeed, the highly capable Buford had deployed his troopers across the entire road network to watch the eastern, northern, and western approaches to Gettysburg. The Union cavalryman guessed that the Confederates would come back in the morning. He was right.

How to Use This Book

The best way to explore Gettysburg's rich battle history is to spend time out on the battlefield itself. This field guide—with thirty-five tour stops, each offering a detailed account of a specific element of the three-day engagement—is designed to help you discover for yourself the action, the heroism, and the tragedy that unfolded in and around this modest Pennsylvania town during the first days of July 1863.

Each stop begins with an orientation section that introduces the central features of the landscape and offers an overview of the most prominent visual landmarks to prepare you to understand what occurred at that site. This section also identifies a specific location from which you can best experience the action described in the narrative. (Because of the complexity of certain battle situations, some stops have more than one position at which to stand and assess the action.) An accompanying photograph will allow you to confirm that you have found the correct spot. As you use this guide to move through the battlefield, you will become an "active learner," following the clear, informative instructions to know where to look, which way to turn, and how to find the essential visual cues to help you appreciate the battle as it unfolds around you.

Trying to cover all thirty-five stops in a single day may present a rather daunting prospect. Thus this book is divided into key segments of the battle with natural thematic breaks, allowing you to choose to do as much or as little at one time as you wish.

After the orientation section places you in the best position to follow the action, each stop is organized around six important questions. The kind of information you will find under each question, and the sources on which that information is based, are described below as a way to introduce you to the battlefield and to the armies that made it famous.

Question 1: What Happened Here?

The first major section of each stop provides a basic narrative to explain the events that took place at that site. To inject a sense of immediacy, this section draws heavily—but not exclusively—upon a wide variety of source material generated in 1863 just before, during, and soon after the battle itself. Typical sources include after-action reports by officers in both armies that were later published in the three-part volume 27 of the *War of the Rebellion: Official Records of the Union and Confederate Armies;* newspaper accounts penned by both Northern and Southern war correspondents; and letters, diaries, and reports from the battlefield written both by soldiers and civilians caught up in the fight or its aftermath. In short, this section is designed to

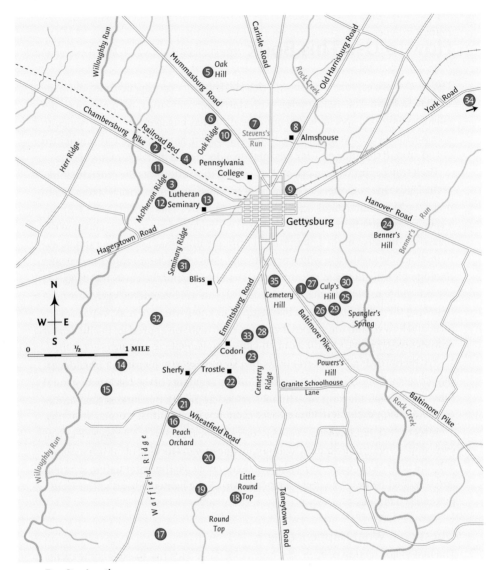

Tour Stop Locations

explain what happened but also to provide insight into the ways in which the participants and eyewitnesses themselves explained it.

Your journey starts with the town of Gettysburg itself. Very few Northerners or Southerners recognized its name before the three-day battle here made it famous. While settlers started building houses and laying out roads in the 1760s, the borough of Gettysburg's formal incorporation occurred later in 1786. It was named for James Gettys, acknowledged as its founder. As Theodore Ditterline, a local resident, wrote in the very first guidebook published in 1863 for the hordes of visitors descending on the small town: "Gettysburg, the county seat of Adams County, Pa., . . . has a beautiful and picturesque location, and is situated in the centre of an extensive basin, in a region delightfully diversified with hills and valleys. At about the distance of ten miles west of the town rises the bold outline of the South Mountain, running in a direction from northeast to southwest. Half a mile west of the town, and extending southward for miles, in a line parallel with the Blue Ridge, is Oak Ridge, which, to the northward of the town, extends across the roads leading to Carlisle and Harrisburg."[1] Indeed, Gettysburg sat at the juncture of ten different roads, radiating in all directions from the town square—a factor that helps to explain why the two armies clashed here.

The railroad came to Gettysburg in 1858, and a new courthouse the following year secured the town's status as an up-and-coming political administrative center. Like most towns of its size in Pennsylvania, Gettysburg supported two newspapers, one affiliated with the Republican Party and the other with strong Democratic leanings. As the business hub of a farming region, Gettysburg provided all the services required to support an agriculture-based economy. Blacksmiths, grocers, tinsmiths, potters, carpenters, and carriage makers all made good livings in Gettysburg. Inns and taverns met the needs of visitors passing through. Banks and attorneys handled the details of property transfers and business matters of all sorts. Churches of many denominations attracted active congregations. Two institutions of higher learning—the Lutheran Theological Seminary, founded in 1826, and Pennsylvania College, established in 1832—as well as free public schools and a "Female Institute" inspired a young graduate of the last establishment to praise her town for its "refined, intelligent and enterprising society." As Tillie Pierce, another young resident, later noted: "From year to year, [Gettysburg] pursued the even and quiet tenor of an inland town, with nothing to vary the monotony but the annual exercises of the above-named institutions." When the visitors left, the town settled into "more irksome quietude."

In 1860 Gettysburg's population numbered 2,390, including several hundred African American residents, most of them freeborn and clustered on the southwest side of town along Washington Street and its cross streets. When the Civil War broke out, loyal residents demonstrated their support for the Union in patriotic public displays and parades; still, the town knew that several of its residents held

Southern sympathies, and secession divided several Gettysburg families that tried to maintain contact with kinsmen in Virginia. Gettysburg sent several companies of its sons into the army, and it became the training ground for the 10th New York Cavalry over the winter of 1861–62. Rumors of invading Confederates swept through Gettysburg's streets during the Maryland Campaign in the fall of 1862.

By the summer of 1863, the nearness of war did not strike Gettysburgians as unusual. Still, it came as a shock when Confederates brushed away a local defense regiment and marched through the town square on June 26. After demanding a long list of supplies from the town fathers, they marched on toward York. At first, Gettysburg's residents sighed with relief. Indeed, they felt immeasurably better on June 30, when Brigadier General John Buford's Union cavalrymen arrived. As Tillie Pierce explained: "I had never seen so many soldiers at one time. They were Union soldiers and that was enough for me, for I then knew we had protection, and I felt they were our dearest friends. . . . My sister started to sing the old war song 'Our Union Forever.' As some of us did not know the whole of the piece we kept repeating the chorus." Daniel Skelly, another local teenager, concurred that he felt safer with cavalrymen around, certain that "the Confederate army would never reach Gettysburg." He noted that "on the night of the 30th [of June,] the people of Gettysburg settled down in their homes with a sense of security they had not enjoyed for days and with little thought of what the morrow had in store for them."[2] A few hours later, the leading elements of Lee's army clashed with Buford's troopers west of town, opening the battle.

Many of the war correspondents who arrived at Gettysburg to cover the action noted the importance of the relative openness of the terrain surrounding the town, a significant change from the battlegrounds on which the Union's Army of the Potomac and the Confederacy's Army of Northern Virginia previously clashed. L. L. Crounse of the *New York Times* noted: "The country is generally open and rolling, affording great opportunities for the use of artillery. There is not much timber." A Richmond newspaper described the battlefield in this way: "Unlike every previous battle of the war, the movements of the two armies were not hidden by forests and dense thickets. The country was broken and rolling, and in a high state of cultivation. On every side were wheat and cornfields, surrounded by stone fences, and dotted here and there by groves and clumps of timber. The movements of each army were visible from every part of the field, and the game of battle as thus played on a clear board, is said to have been of absorbing interest to such as had time to watch it."[3]

Question 2: Who Fought Here?
The organization of armies and the various component units often confuse visitors to Gettysburg and those just starting their study of the Civil War. You should take heart in realizing that the Civil War generation shared those feelings. One Virginia journalist, in an early report from Gettysburg, confessed: "Military nomenclature is

so strange to me, and the repetition of brigades, of divisions, and the regiments of brigades, with the names of their several commanders, hurried through by the reciter who is familiar with them, confuses my attention."[4] Nonetheless, you will find it useful to familiarize yourself with basic army organization, just as this reporter ultimately did.

At Gettysburg, the Union's Army of the Potomac confronted the Confederacy's Army of Northern Virginia. On June 30, 1863, the Army of the Potomac carried approximately 112,735 men on its rolls; of this number, approximately 93,921 soldiers were present under arms and available to participate in the battle. On that same date, the Army of Northern Virginia carried approximately 80,202 as present, with 71,699 present under arms and ready for battle. Both armies used the same basic table of organization.

Begin by understanding that Civil War armies included three different kinds of combat soldiers: the infantry, the foot soldiers who comprised the greatest proportion of each force; the artillery that provided fire support with their cannons; and the cavalry, the mounted horsemen who screened their army's movements, performed reconnaissance duties to gather information on the location and intentions of enemy forces, and, when called upon, accepted battle—mounted or dismounted—against enemy forces to protect their own army or to defend key terrain.

A Civil War army's smallest building block usually centered on a unit that numbered about 100 soldiers and was commanded by a captain. Infantrymen called this unit a company; cavalrymen often called it a company or a troop; artillerymen called it a battery. Companies often included sets of brothers; fathers and sons; friends; classmates; business associates; and members of the same church, social club, or occupation. The bonds within a company could be quite strong. On the battlefield, you will see many monuments and tablets along both armies' battle lines recounting the service of artillery batteries. These were the only company-sized units to fight in the battle as identifiable independent commands.

Infantry and cavalry companies rarely served independently. Instead, they served as components of the next-higher level of organization: the regiment, which was usually commanded by a colonel. The great majority of the many small and midsized monuments that cover the battlefield represent a regiment. A regimental designation contains at least three elements: a numerical designation, the name of a state (or, simply, "United States" to designate a unit from the U.S. Regular Army), and its branch of service. Thus the 24th Michigan Infantry was the twenty-fourth regiment raised in the Wolverine State for Federal service, and its members served as foot soldiers. Some regiments include "Volunteers" in their designation, but at the time of the Battle of Gettysburg, this was not really necessary; neither army contained units overwhelmingly composed of draftees. Many regiments included multiple companies raised in a single large city or a cluster of small towns within a county or region in their home states, and the survivors often included that information on their monuments; just as in companies, strong bonds linked family and friends on the home front to regiments in which their soldiers served. A regiment with full ranks contained a little over 1,000 men, but death, disease, desertion, and medical discharges had reduced these units at Gettysburg to strengths generally ranging from 250 to 400 men available for duty. Nearly any Civil War soldier asked to identify his unit would respond with his regiment; it was his military "home."

In the Union Army of the Potomac, typically four regiments—but sometimes more—comprised a brigade, commanded by either a colonel or a brigadier general—the latter of whom wore shoulder straps bearing a single star. In general, a Union brigade contained regiments from different states; for instance, Colonel Strong Vincent's brigade on Little Round Top included regiments from Maine, Michigan, New York, and Pennsylvania. Brigades in the Confederate Army of Northern Virginia generally contained five regiments, which in nearly all cases came from a single state and often were commanded by a brigadier general who also came from that state or had a close association with it. Thus the brigade of Brigadier General Richard B. Garnett, a Virginian, contained five Virginia regiments. West Point graduates became the primary exception to this rule; they received assignments to any command requiring the strong hand of a trained leader.

In the Union Army of the Potomac, three brigades made up a division, commanded by a brigadier general or a major general, who wore two stars on his shoulder straps. In the Confederate Army of Northern Virginia, most divisions included four brigades and served under the command of a major general. Thus, beginning at the division level, Confederate units tended to be numerically stronger than their Union equivalents.

In the Union Army of the Potomac, the highest level of organization was the Army Corps, commanded by a major general. The Army of the Potomac included seven corps of infantry and a cavalry corps. The I, II, V, VI, XI, and Cavalry Corps each had three divisions; the III and XI Corps included only two. Since March 1863, each corps in the Army of the Potomac also had a geometric shape designated as its corps badge. The I Corps used a circle; the II Corps, a three-leafed clover, or trefoil; the III Corps, a diamond; the V Corps, a Maltese cross; the VI Corps, a Greek cross; the XI Corps, a crescent; and the XII Corps, a star. You will see these markings on regimental monuments and other markers on the battlefield.

Lee entered into the summer campaign season with a newly reorganized army, occasioned by the death in May of Lieutenant General Thomas J. "Stonewall" Jackson at Chancellorsville. Up to that time, Lee divided the Army of Northern Virginia into two large corps of infantry, each supported by artillery; Jackson commanded one and Lieutenant General James Longstreet the other. Unable to identify an acceptable successor to Jackson, Lee restructured his army into a force that contained three corps. Longstreet retained command of the First Corps, while two newly promoted lieutenant generals, Richard S. Ewell and Ambrose Powell Hill, received command of the Second and Third Corps, respectively. Major General J. E. B. Stuart commanded Lee's cavalry division.

In practice, Union generals alternated freely between Roman numerals and words to designate individual army corps. General John F. Reynolds's command, then, might be designated as the I Corps or the First Corps. The Confederate Army of Northern Virginia tended to use words rather than numbers of any sort or simply referred to the corps by the commander's name. To make it easier to separate Union from Confederate corps in this text, all corps designated with Roman numerals refer to units in the Union army, unless they appear in a direct quotation.

The strengths of the various organizations provided in this section reflect those compiled by John W. Busey and David G. Martin in their thoroughly researched *Regimental Strengths and Losses at Gettysburg*.[5]

Question 3: Who Commanded Here?

At Gettysburg and for every Civil War battle, success or failure depended heavily both on the sound decisions made by senior commanders and the ability of their subordinates to execute them. This section will include thumbnail biographies of some of the more interesting leaders featured at each stop. Basic biographical material on Gettysburg's major commanders is readily available in many sources, of course, and the authors have relied upon such standards as Ezra J. Warner's *Generals in Blue* (1964) and *Generals in Gray* (1959) and Stewart Sifakis's *Who Was Who in the Civil War* (1988) for such information. For now, we will begin with the rival army commanders.

Major General George Gordon Meade (1815–72) became commander of the Union's Army of the Potomac upon the relief of Major General Joseph Hooker on June 28, 1863, just three days before the start of the Battle of Gettysburg. Born in Cadiz, Spain, the son of a prosperous American merchant, Meade grew up in Philadelphia and considered himself a Pennsylvanian. He graduated from the U.S. Military Academy in 1835, finishing nineteenth in his class of fifty-six members. He served on active duty only briefly and resigned his commission in 1836. Civilian life did not appeal to Meade, however, and in May 1842 he reentered the U.S. Army as a second lieutenant of topographical engineers. For most of his antebellum career, he built lighthouses and breakwaters, but he also served in Mexico, where, as a *New York Herald* correspondent noted when introducing the new commander to the paper's readership, Meade's conduct during the war "was marked by determination and bravery, and at the battle of Palo Alto he was particularly distinguished."

Meade won a brevet to first lieutenant for his service in Mexico, but when the Civil War broke out, he had advanced in rank only to captain. With the active support of Pennsylvania governor

Major General George G. Meade, U.S.A. (USAMHI)

Andrew G. Curtin, he quickly received a promotion to brigadier general of volunteers on August 21, 1861, and became a brigade commander in the Pennsylvania Reserve division. He suffered a serious hip wound at Glendale during the Seven Days Battles, but he returned in time to lead a division of the Pennsylvania Reserves into the Bloody Cornfield at Antietam. At Fredericksburg, Meade's men broke through a gap in Lee's line south of the city, and he pulled back only for lack of support against a fierce Confederate counterattack. Now a major general of volunteers, he commanded the V Corps at Chancellorsville. Meade numbered among Hooker's corps commanders in that battle who pushed the army commander to step down after an artillery shell stunned him and left him temporarily incapacitated. Nonetheless, Meade did not seek army command for himself. When he received appointment to that position on June 28, he simply wrote his wife: "This, so help me God, I will do."

Meade's selection came as a surprise to some; Major Generals John F. Reynolds of the I Corps, John Sedgwick of the VI Corps, and Henry W. Slocum of the XII Corps all outranked him by date of seniority. He had no time to put together his own command team and had no choice but to rely upon Hooker's staff, including some who were openly hostile to him; fortunately, he also could count upon the professional soldiers of Hooker's staff and on the services of his son, George Meade Jr., who served on his father's staff as an aide-de-camp.

Although Meade won great praise as the victor of Gettysburg, critics denounced him for a perceived failure to follow up and destroy the defeated Army of Northern Virginia; even President Lincoln expressed his dismay. Meade became the target of special hearings convened in the spring of 1864 by the Joint Committee on the Conduct of the War to answer charges—laid out in a newspaper diatribe by "Historicus," long believed to be his III Corps commander, Major General Daniel E. Sickles, or one of his close associates—that accused Meade of desiring to retreat from Gettysburg without a fight. In the end, the committee terminated the hearings, and Meade remained in command of the Army of the Potomac until the end of the war. He labored largely in obscurity, however, after the promotion of Lieutenant General Ulysses S. Grant and Grant's decision to take the field with Meade's army to take on the Army of Northern Virginia. Meade nonetheless remained in the U.S. Army after the Confederate surrender at Appomattox, won promotion to the permanent rank of major general, U.S. Army—though he always resented that Grant's confidants William T. Sherman and Philip H. Sheridan received that rank before he did—and died on active duty in November 1872.

Meade's horse, "Old Baldy," who had suffered a wound at Gettysburg, participated in the general's funeral procession. Meade is buried in Laurel Hill Cemetery in Philadelphia. A general far more likely to inspire respect than love or admiration in his troops, he had a sharp temper and admitted often to difficulty in controlling it. Lieutenant Colonel Theodore Lyman, a staff officer, declared him a "thorough soldier, and a mighty clear-headed man. . . . I never saw a man in my life who was so characterized by straightforward truthfulness as he is. He will pitch into himself in a moment, if he thinks he has done wrong; and woe to those, no matter who they are, who do not do right!" General Meade's son, who remained in the U.S. Army until 1874, became his father's most stalwart defender during a variety of postwar controversies. In 1882 he published a pamphlet taking on some of his father's critics titled *Did General Meade Desire to Retreat at the Battle of Gettysburg?*, answering the question unequivocally in the negative. He later compiled and edited his father's Civil War letters as the two-volume *The Life and Letters of George Gordon Meade, Major General, United States Army*, a work finally completed by the general's grandson and namesake in 1912. His family remembered him as a "loving husband, a professional soldier in the highest sense, and a man who never truckled to the public."[6]

General Robert E. Lee (1807–70), born in Virginia to Revolutionary War hero "Light-Horse Harry" Lee and Ann Hill Carter Lee, followed his father into military service, starting as a cadet at the U.S. Military Academy in 1825. He graduated four years later second in the class of 1829 without a single demerit remaining on his record—it was possible then for cadets to be awarded "merits" to cancel out demerits against them—and received a brevet commission as a second lieutenant of engineers. Two years later, he married Mary Ann Randolph Custis and began a family that ultimately included seven children; "Arlington," the Custis manor and the future site of the famous Arlington National Cemetery, became his home. He served on a variety of engineering projects that included coastal fortifications and navigation improvements around St. Louis, Missouri. In the Mexican War, he served with distinction on General Winfield Scott's staff on the march from Vera Cruz to Mexico City, often reconnoitering well to the front at high personal risk; his actions led to brevet promotions through the rank of colonel and won him high esteem throughout the army. He served as superintendent of the U.S. Military Academy at West Point from 1852 through 1855; his oldest son, Custis, graduated first in the class of 1854.

General Robert E. Lee, C.S.A. (USAMHI)

In 1855 Lee transferred from the engineers to accept a promotion to lieutenant colonel of the 2nd U.S. Cavalry in west Texas. He held that rank in late 1859, when abolitionist John Brown and his party raided Harpers Ferry and the Federal arsenal there. Lee, who was on leave at Arlington, took command of the effort to secure the arsenal and capture Brown, a mission he accomplished with a detachment of U.S. Marines and the assistance of a young cavalry lieutenant named J. E. B. Stuart. After Fort Sumter, General Scott—with President Lincoln's approval—had tendered to Lee the command of the field forces of the U.S. Army. Lee, however, refused; on April 20, 1861, he resigned his commission and soon after accepted the command of all the military forces of Virginia. He became a general in the Confederate army on June 14, 1861. Lee's early career in Confederate service did not fill many Southerners with confidence. His first command in western Virginia ended in failure, and the Union navy established a strong foothold at Port Royal in South Carolina while Lee commanded that coastal district. As military adviser to Jefferson Davis, he succeeded to command of the Army of Northern Virginia on June 1, 1862, after General Joseph E. Johnston fell seriously wounded at Fair Oaks, outside Richmond.

Although initially derided as "Granny Lee" and the "King of Spades" for the earthworks he ordered constructed around Richmond, Lee soon demonstrated his aggressive nature during the Seven Days Battles, pushing Major General George B. McClellan's larger Army of the Potomac away from the gates of the Confederacy's capital city. For the next thirteen months, Lee enjoyed a nearly unbroken string of victories; only the strategic reverse after the tactical draw at Antietam marred his record. During the spring of 1863, Lee suffered what he deemed a heavy cold; some medical specialists suspect he may have suffered an attack of angina. In any case, at fifty-six, Lee was suffering health problems as he entered Pennsylvania. He did not lack confidence, however. Although he entered active operations without his lamented lieutenant Stonewall Jackson, Lee felt confident that his army simply could not be defeated.

The results of the Battle of Gettysburg did not go Lee's way, of course, but he fought on until the war's end. Afterward, he refused to be interviewed about Gettysburg and left no personal memoirs. After he died in October 1870 in Lexington, Virginia, while serving as president of Washington College (now Washington and Lee University), his friends and fellow Virginians worked for several decades to promote an image of Lee as the spotless "Marble Man." In an effort to remove any stain or blemish on Lee's military record, they began to twist the historical narrative of the Battle of Gettysburg in ways that still influence our views today. General Edward Porter Alexander, one of Lee's most capable subordinates and a man who never shied away in later years from meting out praise or criticism as he deemed appropriate, concluded: "I think that military critics will rank Gen. Lee as decidedly the most audacious commander who lived since Napoleon, & I am not at all sure that even Napoleon in his whole career will be held to have overmatched some of the deeds of audacity to which General Lee committed himself in the 2 years & 10 months during which he commanded the Army of Northern Va."[7]

Question 4: Who Fell Here?
After Gettysburg, the names of approximately 53,000 soldiers ended up on the long Union and Confederate casualty lists awaited with dread in hundreds of hometowns across the North and the South. Neither army established a systematic way to deliver these sad tidings to families back home. Many people learned of their loved one's fate from long—and invariably incomplete and often inaccurate—lists reprinted from big-city newspapers. Others learned from letters written directly to small-town newspapers by a regimental adjutant or some other responsible corre-

spondent who sent the bad news directly to the source most likely to be able to deliver it expeditiously. Still others received information in personal letters written by friends or surviving family members. Some never learned anything at all. From July 1 through July 3, 1863, a combined total of over 7,000 soldiers died on the field of battle. Perhaps another 4,000 to 5,000 died of their Gettysburg injuries over the weeks and even months to come. Thousands more fell wounded, and many more became prisoners of war, some ultimately filling graves at Fort Delaware in the North, Andersonville in Georgia, or other horrific camps. Other soldiers simply disappeared, the final entry of their military records noting only that they remained "missing in action at Gettysburg."

This section will provide a summary of the losses inflicted in the fighting at each stop. In many cases, the numbers will reflect brigade losses. In some situations, however, an examination of casualties taken down to the regimental level provides an even clearer appreciation of the intensity of the fighting at certain stops. Indeed, in specific cases, a further breakdown of regimental casualties into the individual categories of killed, wounded, and missing better illuminates the nature of the struggle. The numbers in this section once again reflect the findings in John W. Busey and David G. Martin's *Regimental Strengths and Losses at Gettysburg.*

Each stop also includes several vignettes to personalize the experience of death in ways that numbers simply cannot. Most avid students of Gettysburg already know the tragic story of Sergeant Amos Humiston of the 154th New York, mortally wounded in the brickyard fight and identified from the photograph of three small children found in his dead hand in a lot off Stratton Street (Stop 9). Every account of the repulse of Pickett's Charge includes passing commentary on the last minutes of Lieutenant Alonzo Cushing, as he fired a final round from one of his cannons before he fell dead (Stop 33). But the stories of the final sacrifice of thousands more of Gettysburg's fallen remain untold. The Compiled Service Records of Union and Confederate soldiers held at the National Archives contain a treasure trove of information about the individual fates of thousands of Gettysburg's neglected fallen; you will find many of their stories recounted here.

Gettysburg's tragic story reached well beyond the battlefield. Some soldiers' files contained comparatively little on their own last moments, but the records containing pension applications submitted by their widows or mothers speak volumes about the aftermath of battle. Survivors of Union enlisted men generally could receive only an $8 monthly stipend. Nonetheless, to obtain even that pittance, applicants faced a burdensome and complicated administrative process. Enlistment dates and death dates had to be confirmed by the U.S. Army or state adjutant general; if records went missing or files remained incomplete, then affidavits from a regimental officer still in the field had to be obtained. A widow had to prove the validity of her marriage—not always easy in a day before marriage licenses. If she had children to claim as dependents, she had to prove that she and the deceased soldier were the lawful parents without the advantage of birth certificates. A mother generally had to prove that her deceased son had contributed heavily to her support while he was in the army, and often for a period of time before he enlisted, to win approval of the funds. The legacy of the Gettysburg dead extends far beyond the Soldiers' National Cemetery. Survivors of Confederate soldiers, of course, did not have a pension system to call on for financial support. The best they might do was to submit a claim to the Confederate War Department for any back pay or allowances still owed to their fallen soldier. Hundreds of bereaved mothers, fathers, and widows did just that, and their experiences entirely match the struggles that their Northern counterparts faced.

Question 5: Who Lived Here?

The Battle of Gettysburg swept over the town and across at least thirty-eight individual family farms and numerous isolated out lots belonging to town residents who used them for wood supplies, grazing, and building stone. Every resident felt the impact of the passage of the armies in some way, and their experiences, too, add to the Gettysburg story.

This section identifies the owners of the spots where the greatest carnage took place and, in many cases, explores the families' postbattle efforts to return to life as they once knew it. Until well into the 1880s, many of Gettysburg's residents—indeed all Pennsylvanians in the southern border counties that suffered from Confederate military operations in 1862, 1863, and 1864—took advantage of multiple opportunities to file damage claims. The Commonwealth of Pennsylvania hired agents to oversee parts of the process, and the Federal government wrote strict rules for obtaining compensation. Probably the most difficult claims to win were those submitted to the U.S. Army's quartermaster general. A number of Gettysburg residents filed such claims in the late 1870s and early 1880s, most of which were rejected. Those who could show clearly that Union troops took certain supplies—usually hay to feed horses—and used them specifically for their own purposes proved to be the most likely to win any award. Owners of property damaged as a consequence of the actual fighting rarely received any compensation at all. This opportunity to explore one aspect of the challenges facing the residents of Gettysburg who endured the painful legacy of battle long after the armies had marched away offers a generally underappreciated element of the region's experience.

Question 6: What Did They Say about It Later?

As one veteran reported after the silver reunion of the Battle of Gettysburg in 1888, "the great majority" of veterans who had returned "had come to dedicate their monuments, to see again the field upon which they had won undying glory, to find the places where their comrades had died, to go over the ground again with those who had stood by their sides in the bloody combat, and to show to their wives and children just where all these things of which history is full had occurred, and to explain the share they had in making that history."[8] In published reunion speeches, monument dedications, and veterans' periodicals, in the first postwar generation of history books through those being written today, the men who fought here and those who study them still have much to say about what soldiers in both armies did here, how they did it, why they did it, and what we should learn from it all.

Until the mid-1880s, most of the popular interest in Gettysburg centered on controversies relating to command issues. The Meade-Sickles controversy and the rise of the "Lee cult" that shifted blame for the defeat from General Lee to his second in command, General Longstreet, became major themes in most Gettysburg literature. The voice of the private soldier rarely made itself heard early on. Indeed, the editor of a Union veterans' newsletter wrote:

> The veterans themselves are to a certain extent responsible for the lack of popular appreciation of the terrible character of [their military] service. When they meet together in Reunions, at Campfires, or elsewhere, they never dwell on the awful storms, the frightful strain of the marches, the terrible discomforts of every hour, the sickening perils, the gnawing anxieties, the anguish of defeat, the crushing sorrows of mangled and slain comrades. Soldier-like, they put these unhappy things as far out of sight as possible, and talk of the fun, the excitement, the larks of soldier, until their hearers are inclined to think that three years' service in the army was merely a prolonged picnic.[9]

Beginning especially in the 1880s and flourishing for several more decades, Civil War veterans rediscovered their voices. They now demanded battle laurels owed them and their comrades, and the importance of being remembered for grand deeds became far more important in many cases than preserving a true record of how they accomplished them. Few soldiers entered into the literary fray in regimental histories and veterans' newsletters with conscious intent to defile the historical record. Few veterans delivering memorial addresses or monument dedication speeches did so fully intending to lie to promote their own unit's reputation at the expense of others. But few could let perceived slights or insults stand, and in expressing their justifiable pride in their accomplishments, they also introduced inaccuracies, whether they be errors of omission, errors of commission, or exaggerations of fundamental truths in ways that led to inaccuracies of all sorts.

Major Edwin B. Wight of the 24th Michigan, at the dedication of his regiment's memorial in Herbst's Woods, explained just how this process occurred:

> Recall, if you can, any engagement of the war and positively state, of your own knowledge, that you passed through some particular field (a wheat field, for instance) when you were ordered forward to charge the enemy's position. You did pass through the open; so much you remember, but the nature of the field you

never once considered. You took possession of a strip of woodland, as a bit of shelter from the skurrying shot, but the character of the fruit or forest trees did not impress itself upon your memory. Some hill or ridge was near; you occupied it as a natural vantage-ground for present or later conflict—but how it sloped or what were its surroundings, you had no time to note. You charged the enemy or were charged by them; but just how you advanced or how you met the onset, you were too busy then to enter in your mental memorandum book.

Then, of course, "some military or civilian report mentioned a wheat field, a peach orchard, an Oak Hill or a Seminary Ridge and thenceforth you adopted the names in your attempted descriptions of the battle. But while the battle raged, your horizon range was limited. The lines of your Regiment or possibly of your Brigade covered all the field that your vision seemed able to compass and accurately note. And even then, in the excitement of the struggle, many little incidents occurred in your immediate vicinity of which you were not cognizant." Wight concluded with a useful warning that still commands reflection: "Volumes have been written, with the Battle of Gettysburg as sole and only topic, but the whole story has not been told. Much of the planning and more of the doing has been omitted."[10]

No modern-day work about Gettysburg can begin to fill that void, but it behooves all those who respect not just the content of history but also its methods and intellectual rigor to consider carefully these postwar examples of controversies, differing perspectives, and interpretations about various episodes of the battle or their greater meaning; personal vignettes of both reliable and dubious provenance; and historians' ongoing debates. All of these factors shape history and our own views of it. After all, the wartime generation itself warned the citizenry at large to be wary of everything it read about the battle. As one Virginia editor reminded readers in the immediate aftermath of Gettysburg: "Correspondents—especially telegraphic correspondents—with the best intentions are often led astray. They are obliged, in the absence of official intelligence, to depend on the evidence of persons far from the scene of action, who are often but imperfectly informed themselves, and sometimes on mere rumor."[11] His advice is as relevant today as it was in 1863.

■ As this book guides you through the sweeping battle scenes and the smaller, often poignant human dramas that unfolded on these grounds in early July 1863, we hope you will gain a better appreciation for the complexities of mid-nineteenth-century combat from the perspectives of both the senior leaders and the privates in the ranks. We also hope that you will come to appreciate the challenges facing historians who seek to uncover an ideal called historical "truth" in the midst of Gettysburg's myriad voices and assessments.

Helpful Hints for Touring the Battlefield

Access to the Battlefield. The grounds of Gettysburg National Military Park are open to the public with no access fee. Entry points to some portions of the battlefield, however, do pass through gates. From April 1 through October 31, those gates open at 6:00 A.M. and close at 10:00 P.M. daily. Winter visiting hours on the battlefield are a bit abbreviated; from November 1 through March 31, the park gates open at 6:00 A.M. and close at 7:00 P.M. daily.

The Roads. Some of the roads you will travel on during this tour are public highways, accessible to drivers twenty-four hours a day. The National Park Service and local municipalities consider the following to be public roads: Buford Avenue, Reynolds Avenue, Wadsworth Avenue, Doubleday Avenue, Howard Avenue, West Confederate Avenue, Millerstown Road, Wheatfield Road, and Granite School House Road. Please observe posted speed limits closely; National Park Service and municipal law-enforcement officers routinely patrol these roads.

Other roads you will travel on are avenues specifically built for visitors to tour the battlefield. A number of these are one-way roads that are clearly marked as such. The driving directions from one tour stop to the next will remind you when you are driving or turning onto one-way roads. When you drive on one-way roads, the rule is to pull over to the right to park, pause, or observe and allow other drivers to pass you on your left. Do not block traffic.

Note: always park on pavement. As an acceptable alternative at some stops, you may park on the right shoulder of the road if it is graveled. Do not park—or drive across—grassy areas on the side of the road; you may be trespassing on private property.

During periods of severe weather, some park roads may close temporarily. If in doubt, check the Gettysburg National Military Park website at www.nps.gov/gett.

Tour Stops. Our field guide is organized into thirty-five separate stops. In your travels around the battlefield, you will notice signage that marks the National Park Service Auto Tour route and its sixteen stops. Following the driving directions in this guide, you will use these very visible tour-stop signs as reference points to help guide you from stop to stop or to help you find parking. In some cases, the stops in this guide and the National Park Service tour stops coincide, but be alert that the stop numbers of the tours likely will be different. In many cases, the stops in this guide take you to locations that are not part of the National Park Service tour, so do not become disconcerted if you see no park signs there.

Touring Etiquette. The battlefield can be a crowded place at times, particularly at the most popular sites, such as Little Round Top. To make the tour as pleasant as possible for all visitors, follow these basic rules:

- Do not crowd other groups already on the field. If this guide directs you to stand on a specific spot on the field and other people are there, please be patient. They will move along soon.
- The monuments on the battlefield are not only excellent interpretive tools for studying the battle but also memorials to the soldiers who fought here. Some are over 120 years old and thus are historical artifacts in their own right. Treat the monuments with respect. Do not climb or sit on them.
- Over 400 cannons can be found on the battlefield today, and they should be treated with the same respect accorded to the monuments. Sitting on cannons for photographs or climbing on the old guns may seem harmless enough, but such actions could endanger visitors and cause damage to an irreplaceable artifact.
- It should go without saying that relic hunting on the battlefield violates federal law. Signs are posted, and the National Park Service will prosecute. Similarly, the natural landscape of the battlefield is protected by federal law; do not remove or disturb plants or wildlife or remove rocks that are part of historic fence lines.
- Many historic homes still dot the battlefield today. During this tour, you will learn about the families who lived in some of them and the challenges they faced during and after the battle. Today, some of the homes are privately owned. Others are owned by the federal government and occupied by the families of National Park Service staff. In either case, please respect both the property and the privacy of the families who occupy these homes.

Please don't do this! (USAMHI)

Restrooms on the Battlefield. The National Park Service maintains restrooms on the battlefield at the following sites: (1) near Stop 2 of this guide, across Chambersburg Road from the memorials to Generals Buford and Reynolds; (2) adjacent to the picnic area on South Confederate Avenue just before you reach Stop 17; (3) at the Round Top parking area on the way to Stop 18 (these are portable toilets); (4) at the intersection of Sedgwick Avenue and Wheatfield Road, after you leave Stop 18 (these are portable toilets); (5) near the Pennsylvania monument at Stop 23; and (6) near Spangler's Spring at Stop 29. The National Park Service generally closes these facilities when the park operates on its winter schedule from November 1 through March 31. Year-round modern facilities are located at the National Park Service Visitor Center and at the northeast corner of the Soldiers' National Cemetery.

Picnic Areas. There are two established picnic areas on the battlefield. One is on South Confederate Avenue just prior to arriving at Stop 17. The other picnic area is adjacent to the bus parking lot at the National Park Service Visitor Center. Additional picnic tables are available on the periphery of the visitor center parking lot number 1. Picnicking at other sites on the battlefield is prohibited.

STOP 1. THE KEY TERRAIN OF CEMETERY HILL

Orientation

These instructions assume you are about to begin your battlefield tour from either the center of the town of Gettysburg or from the National Park Service visitor center at 1195 Baltimore Pike. From the center of town (the traffic circle), drive south on Baltimore Street (Route 97) 0.7 miles to the top of Cemetery Hill. Alternatively, if you are starting your tour from the visitor center, take the eastern exit from the visitor center complex to Baltimore Pike (Route 97). At the traffic light, turn left and drive 0.7 miles north to the top of Cemetery Hill. In either case, your landmark will be a tall, light-blue-colored water tower on the hill on the east side of Baltimore Street. There usually is ample parking space at the metered spaces along the west side of Baltimore Street adjacent to the Soldiers' National Cemetery.

After parking your car, walk to the very crest of Cemetery Hill. Stand across Baltimore Street from the gatehouse, the entrance to Evergreen Cemetery, the local burial ground and a structure that predates the battle. You can see the Soldiers' National Cemetery, where many of Gettysburg Union dead now rest, to your right front; it extends behind Evergreen Cemetery as you now view it. The equestrian statue of Major General Winfield Scott Hancock, his hand reaching out toward the high ground of Cemetery Hill, should be behind you.

The gatehouse of Evergreen Cemetery.

What Happened Here?

Since so many of the decisions made during the battle of Gettysburg center on the possession or capture of "the high ground," it is important to begin with an appreciation of the key terrain to which the generals referred. In 1873 Gettysburg's first "official historian," John B. Bachelder, published one of the first guidebooks for visitors to the battlefield. About this location, he wrote:

> No person can stand on Cemetery Hill, and from its commanding summit survey the field on which the Army of the Potomac and the Army of Northern Virginia met to decide the fate of human liberty, without being impressed with the remarkable beauty of the landscape view, and its peculiar fitness for a great battlefield. . . . The whole scene is grand and imposing. Broad fields, stretching away

The Road Network from the Key Terrain of Cemetery Hill

in the distance; diversified by gentle undulations, and flanked by commanding heights, with contiguous valleys, affording a natural *covered way* for the movement of troops; deep forests, and sheltering groves, with streams of water; and beyond all, towering in the distance, clothed in azure blue, a picturesque mountain range completes a landscape of rare beauty and magnificent proportions.[1]

Bachelder's pastoral description does not represent the current vista from this height, of course, but from this position, you still can see hints of the geographical elements that made this hill so important to a professional soldier.

First, the road passing across your front—now Baltimore Street, but then known as the Baltimore Pike—crossed the eastern crest of the hill in 1863, just as it does today, and entered Gettysburg from the southeast. Beyond your current line of sight, but crossing your front on the western crest of Cemetery Hill on the far side of the Soldiers' National Cemetery, is Taneytown Road, which approaches Gettysburg from the south. Both the Baltimore Pike and Taneytown Road intersect at an angle with Emmitsburg Road that skirts the bottom of Cemetery Hill's western slope and approaches Gettysburg from the south-southwest; within the current town limits of Gettysburg, Emmitsburg Road is called Steinwehr Avenue, named for the Union general initially charged with preparing defenses on this hill. These three roads brought the Army of the Potomac to Gettysburg—the Northern forces approached the battlefield from the south—and the Baltimore Pike and Taneytown Road served as its main lines of communication, supply, reinforcement, and, if needed, retreat.

Now face to your left and look down the hill to the south. In 1863 the crest of Cemetery Hill had little tree cover. Although a small grove of trees grew on the southern slope of the hill back then, it did not obstruct the open panoramic view now spread out in front of you; the vista suggests why the two armies sought control of this elevation. (You can find a similarly open view if you turn to your left once again and walk up to the artillery line that faces to the east; you do not need to do this now, however, since you will visit that location when you return here for Stop 27.) The trees you see today on the crest of the hill, many planted purposefully as ornamentals as an element of late nineteenth-century cemetery design, now prevent a full appreciation of the view available to Union commanders, and commercial expansion now blocks the view to the north toward the town. Thus we simply cannot enjoy the remarkably clear view that so impressed many participants in the conflict who came to this hill over the first three days of July 1863.

Face the gatehouse once more. A number of generals who served at the Battle of Gettysburg commented on the importance or utility of Cemetery Hill and appreciated its significance in the conduct of the battle. When Major General Oliver O. Howard, commanding officer of the Army of the Potomac's XI Corps, arrived here just before noon on July 1, he examined the "general features of the country" and "came to the conclusion that the only tenable position for my limited force was the ridge to the southeast of Gettysburg now so well known as Cemetery Ridge. The highest point at the cemetery commanded every eminence within easy range. The slopes toward the west [straight ahead] and south [left] were gradual, and could be completely swept by artillery." Howard immediately established his headquarters "near the cemetery, and on the highest point north [right] of the Baltimore pike," not far from this position.

When the division of Brigadier General Adolph von Steinwehr of the XI Corps arrived, he received orders from Howard to occupy this hill. As von Steinwehr reported after the battle, "Cemetery Hill is the commanding point of the whole position, and its occupation by our troops had a decisive influence upon the further progress and final result of the battle." He arrived while the battle raged north and west beyond the town, well beyond your current line of sight to your front and right. Thus he "placed the First Brigade, Col. Charles R. Coster, on the northeast end of the hill" that is to your right and rear. Then "the Second Brigade, Col. Orland Smith, took a position toward the northwest"—to your front and right in today's Soldiers' National Cemetery. When the XI Corps finally fell back through the town, von Steinwehr reported that their survivors took up positions on this hill. "Our position now was quite strong," he reported, "the infantry being placed partly behind stone fences and forming with our batteries a front fully able to resist an attack of even greatly superior forces." XI Corps artillerymen especially enjoyed the outstanding field of fire this elevation offered them. Indeed, Major Thomas Osborn, the XI Corps chief of artillery, asked for additional batteries from the army's Artillery Reserve to strengthen his line because his "position was finely adapted to its use."[2]

War correspondents also noted the importance of this elevation. Indeed, a number of them observed the battle of July 2 and July 3 from Howard's Cemetery Hill headquarters, and they thanked him profusely for the opportunity with highly complimentary commentary about his performance during the fight. Whitelaw Reid of the *Cincinnati Gazette* divided this hilltop into two separate hills divided by the Baltimore Pike (in front of you), but his conclusions about the importance of this height sound much like those expressed by the generals: "Resting on the left-hand side of the Baltimore pike [the opposite side from where you now stand] is the key to the position, Cemetery Hill. This constitutes our extreme front, lies just south of Gettysburg [to your right], overlooks and completely commands the town. . . . Just across the Baltimore pike [here where you stand], another hill, almost as high, and

An 1880s view to the north and west from East Cemetery Hill's open summit. (USAMHI)

crowned like the Cemetery with batteries" fills the front. Combat artist and journalist Edwin Forbes noted the military importance of this area, but he also noticed the most prominent man-made feature here: the gatehouse itself. "To the left of the turnpike," he wrote, "near the entrance of the Gettysburg cemetery stood a two-story brick building with an archway through the center which gave entrance to a small graveyard of a few acres." Inside the cemetery on July 1, before the battle raged here most fiercely, reporter Charles Carleton Coffin of Boston noticed unusual activity: squads of soldiers removing ornamental headstones from their pedestals and laying vertical marble slabs on the ground. Coffin learned that General Howard himself had ordered this be done "to protect his soldiers from splintering stone . . . if enemy shells fell among the graves, and to save the markers from being defaced."[3]

We will consider the actual fighting here at Stops 24 and 27, but it is essential that you go into your tour with an understanding of the reasons why this hill loomed so large in the decision-making processes of the senior commanders on both sides.

Who Fought Here?

The XI Corps of the Army of the Potomac under Major General Oliver O. Howard will hold Cemetery Hill through most of the battle, although elements of the I and II Corps and the Artillery Reserve will support efforts here on several occasions.

Who Commanded Here?

Major General Oliver Otis Howard (1830–1909), a native of Maine and an 1850 graduate of Bowdoin College, also graduated from the U.S. Military Academy at West Point in 1854, ranking fourth in a class of forty-six. His West Point classmates serving at Gettysburg included Confederate Generals J. E. B. Stuart and William Dorsey Pender. Before the Civil War, Howard served much of his time as an instructor at West Point. He resigned his Regular Army commission on June 7, 1861, to accept a U.S. Volunteer commission as colonel of the 3rd Maine Infantry. He fought at First Bull Run as the commander of a four-regiment brigade. At the Battle of Fair Oaks during the Peninsula Campaign, he suffered severe wounds that resulted in the amputation of his right arm. He quickly returned to duty, however, and at Second Bull Run commanded the rear guard that covered the retreat of the Union army back to its Washington, D.C., defenses. At Antietam, he succeeded to division command upon the wounding of Brigadier General John Sedgwick. Promoted to major general at the end of November 1862, Howard continued to command a division at Fredericksburg in December. A month before the Battle of Chancellorsville, he assumed command of the XI Corps. His command performed poorly in that battle, due in part to Howard's failure to protect its right flank despite multiple warnings of the approach

Major General Oliver O. Howard, U.S.A. (USAMHI)

of Stonewall Jackson's flanking force. A man of strong religious and temperance views and a noted abolitionist, Howard was not well liked by the large number of ethnic Germans belonging to XI Corps regiments. In the fall of 1863, he oversaw the transfer of his XI Corps out of the Army of the Potomac to Chattanooga in the western theater of operations. The following year, he commanded the IV Corps in the Atlanta Campaign and in 1865 the Army of the Tennessee in the Carolina Campaign. After the war, Howard became the first commissioner of the Freedmen's Bureau, and he helped to establish an institution of higher learning for former slaves that grew into today's Howard University in Washington, D.C. During the 1870s and 1880s, he served in the Indian Territory, became the superintendent of West Point, and, after his promotion to major general in the Regular Army in 1886, commanded the Division of the East until his retirement in 1894. General Howard died of natural causes in Burlington, Vermont, in 1909. He was Gettysburg's last surviving corps commander.

Brigadier General Baron Adolph Wilhelm August Friedrich von Steinwehr (1822–77) was born in the German duchy of Brunswick, where his father and grandfather preceded him in military service. He also was raised to be a soldier, attending the Brunswick military academy and accepting a commission as a lieutenant in ducal service. In 1847 he took a one-year leave of absence and came to the United States to seek a commission in the U.S. Army to serve in the Mexican War. He failed to obtain one, but he married into an Alabama family, and, after a brief return to Brunswick with his new wife, he returned to the United States and settled on a farm in Connecticut. Upon the outbreak of the Civil War, he was appointed colonel of the 29th New York Infantry but served in reserve in the Battle of First Bull Run. He subsequently commanded a brigade in the Shenandoah valley and an infantry division in the defenses of Washington during the Second Bull Run and Maryland Campaigns of 1862 and in the field during the Chancellorsville and Gettysburg Campaigns of 1863. Transferred with his corps to the western theater of operations after Gettysburg, he commanded his division at Chattanooga and in the relief of Knoxville. Subsequently, in an army reorganization, he lost command of his division and was assigned instead to lead a brigade, an assignment that he refused. Mustered out in July 1865, von Steinwehr became a celebrated geographer and cartographer, taught at Yale University, and worked for the federal government. Von Steinwehr died in Buffalo, New York, in February 1877 and is buried in Albany, New York. A primary commercial street in the town of Gettysburg close to Cemetery Hill where von Steinwehr served is named for him.

Who Fell Here?

You will learn more about those who fell in defense of Cemetery Hill in July 1863 during your exploration of the combat action here when you return for Stop 27.

Who Lived Here?

In 1853, nine years before the battle, the town's religious leaders met to consider a shared problem: many of the small church cemeteries within the town limits of Gettysburg had little room left for future burials. To solve the problem, they soon incorporated the "Ever Green Cemetery Association" and raised the funds required to purchase a seventeen-acre lot from George Shryock and Conrad Snyder on this hilltop just south of town. The fund drive proved successful, and the first burial, that of Mary M. Beitler, took place on November 1, 1854. Construction on the gatehouse began in 1855, and the contractors completed the job for $1,025.

In 1856 the cemetery board hired German immigrant Peter Thorn to serve as cemetery caretaker, and he, his wife Elizabeth, their three sons—Fred, George, and John—and Elizabeth's parents lived in the gatehouse. Peter was not present for the Battle of Gettysburg; he had mustered into Company B of the 138th Pennsylvania Infantry as a corporal in August 1862 and now served on Maryland Heights near Harpers Ferry. He had returned home on leave during winter encampment, and as the rival armies approached Gettysburg, Elizabeth was in her sixth month of pregnancy. General Howard ordered the Thorn family to leave the gatehouse before the fighting for their own safety. After the war, like most local residents who lost property in the battle, Peter Thorn submitted at least two damage claims, one for $405 and the other for $355. For his claim submitted to the U.S. Army's quartermaster general, he was approved for partial compensation and received a check for the sum of $41.50 to cover two tons of hay and four bushels of corn.[4] Both Peter and Elizabeth died in 1907 and are buried in Evergreen Cemetery.

Before the establishment of Ever Green Cemetery (it was commonly called "Evergreen Cemetery" by the 1880s), residents referred to the elevation, especially the area on the east side of the Baltimore Pike on which you now stand, as Raffensperger Hill, named for Peter Raffensperger, a farmer who owned some of this land.

What Did They Say about It Later?

In his memoirs, noted Confederate artilleryman Edward Porter Alexander recalled his first thoughts about this height: "Just beyond the town & over looking it, stands Cemetery Hill. It forms part of a ridge, presenting the most beautiful position for an army, which I have seen occupied."[5]

A bit of controversy erupted after the war among Union officers and their partisans over who deserved credit for selecting Cemetery Hill to serve as anchor for the Army of the Potomac's defensive line. General Howard staked the claim in his official report. Indeed, he received the thanks of Congress for selecting the position. As he later recalled, when he arrived at Gettysburg on July 1, "as was my habit in coming to a new field, I began to examine the positions with a view of obtaining the best location in that vicinity for my troops." To that end, he "rode rapidly to the highest point of the Cemetery Ridge. Here was a broad view which embraced the town, the Seminary, the College, and all the undulating valley of open country spread out between the ridges. There was a beautiful break in the ridge to the north [east] of me, where Culp's Hill abuts against the Cemetery, and touches the creek below. It struck me that here one could make a strong right flank. Col. [Theodore A.] Mysenburg was my Adjutant-General. He will remember my words: 'This seems to be a good position, Colonel,' and his own prompt and characteristic reply: 'It is the only position, General.'"[6]

In 1875, however, controversy flared up when several published sources suggested others might deserve credit for that decision. Joseph G. Rosengarten, a former staff officer of Major General John F. Reynolds of the Army of the Potomac's I Corps claimed in the Philadelphia Times's popular "Annals of the War" series that his corps commander and cavalryman John Buford deserved to share the credit. As he argued: "It was Buford who first attracted Reynolds's attention to the concentration of roads that gave Gettysburg its strategic importance, and it was Reynolds who first appreciated the strength and value of Cemetery Hill and the plateau between that point and Round Top." Samuel P. Bates, a noted historian of his era and author of one of the first book-length studies of the Battle of Gettysburg—after recognizing Cemetery Hill as "the boldest and most commanding ground upon the central portion of the line" where the rest of the battle was fought—gave the credit to the slain I Corps commander alone, asserting that "Reynolds had noticed the great advantage it presented, and had designated it as the position on which to hold his reserves, and as a rallying-point in case he was forced back from the more advanced position in front of the town where he had made his stand." The last word—for now, perhaps—came from historian Edwin B. Coddington, whose detailed study of the Gettysburg Campaign still ranks as a "must-read" for students of Gettysburg. Dismissing the evidence in the Reynolds case as "flimsy," he stated that "it was Howard—and it could have been no one else—who decided to keep his reserve force there and prepare it for occupation by an even larger number of men. . . . The placing of the reserves on Cemetery Hill, and not in the town or some other place, testified to the importance he attached to it as a possible stronghold and to his lack of confidence in the Union position [north and west of town]."[7]

Cemetery Hill became one of the first pieces of land to be purchased with an eye to preserving the battlefield. The first observation tower to grace the battlefield crowned its summit. These heights also hosted reunions and annual meetings of the Grand Army of the Republic beginning in the early 1880s. As one veteran who visited noted, "No part of the battlefield receives more attention than East Cemetery Hill. Everybody visits Roundtop, but everybody loses interest when it is learned that Roundtop did not receive as much attention as its height seemed to warrant during the battle."[8]

The unobstructed view from East Cemetery Hill into the town of Gettysburg, 1880s. (USAMHI)

Driving directions to the next stop: From the parking lot, drive 0.6 miles north on Baltimore Street to the traffic circle in the center of town. Three-quarters of the way around the traffic circle, bear right onto Chambersburg Street (Route 30 West). At the third traffic light on Chambersburg Street, bear to the right onto Buford Avenue, a continuation of Route 30 West. Buford Avenue becomes Chambersburg Road at the edge of town; 0.9 miles from where you turned onto Buford Avenue, turn left onto Stone Avenue. Take an immediate right into the parking lot in front of the small stone building that serves as an information station and restroom facility and park your vehicle.

The First Day of Battle

July 1, 1863

1

The Meeting Engagement

STOP 2. THE CAVALRY FIGHT

Orientation

Cross Chambersburg Road with caution and stand near the statue of Brigadier General John Buford, commander of the Union cavalry here when the fighting opened. You are standing on the western branch of McPherson's Ridge, the high ground that served as the Union cavalry's final line of resistance against the advance of the lead elements of General Robert E. Lee's Army of Northern Virginia. Follow General Buford's gaze and locate the red roof of a barn about three-quarters of a mile away. The barn sits on Herr's Ridge, the main Confederate position for much of the first day's fight. Much of the narrative that follows concerns preliminary battle action that took place early on July 1 between your current position and Knoxlyn Ridge, about one mile beyond Herr's Ridge and well outside the national park boundary.

What Happened Here?

Face west, the same direction that Buford's statue is gazing. At approximately 7:00 A.M. on Knoxlyn Ridge nearly two miles ahead of you, pickets from the 8th Illinois Cavalry spotted a column of Confederate infantry marching east on the Chambersburg Road toward them. When Lieutenant Marcellus Jones arrived in response to his troopers' alert, he borrowed a sergeant's carbine and fired a few rounds at the shadowy figures. Thus Jones claimed credit for firing the first shots of the Battle of Gettysburg. (If you wish, you may drive to the first-shot monument at the intersection of Chambersburg Road and Knoxlyn Road; there is no parking on-site, however.) Couriers quickly informed General Buford of the impending threat as he moved actively between here and his observation post in the cupola of the seminary building on the tree line over your left shoulder.

The Confederates marching down the Chambersburg Road toward this position belonged to the division of Brigadier General Henry Heth of Lieutenant General A. P. Hill's Third Corps of the Army of Northern Virginia. Heth had no cavalry to scout ahead of his column. Thus, upon Jones's first shots, the Tennesseans and Alabamians of Brigadier General James J. Archer's brigade, Heth's advance unit, deployed from a marching column to a line of skirmishers to test the resistance ahead. It was a time-consuming action but a prudent one in the absence of reliable intel-

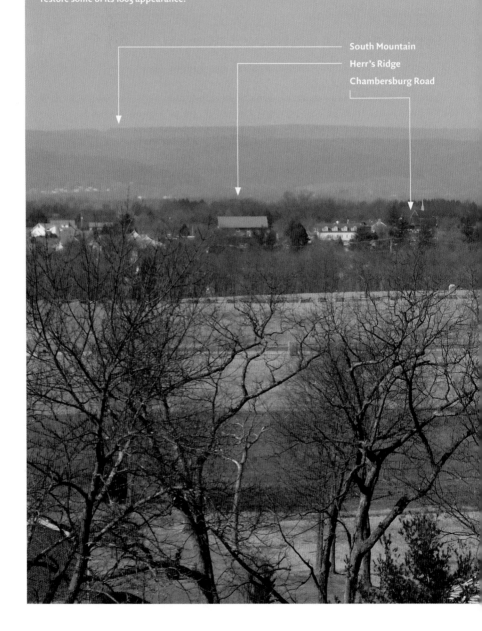

Union General John Buford's view from the cupola of the Lutheran Seminary of the Confederate approach march along Chambersburg Road and the opening phases of the meeting engagement between his cavalrymen and General Heth's Confederate infantry early on July 1, 1863. Long obscured by the mature oak grove surrounding Schmucker Hall—the historic Old Dorm—this vista was restored in late February 2013 as part of the rehabilitation of the seminary grounds to restore some of its 1863 appearance.

South Mountain

Herr's Ridge

Chambersburg Road

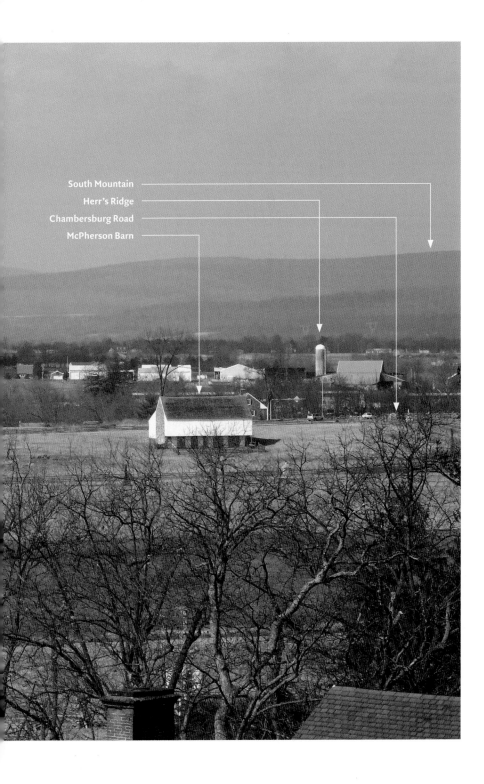

South Mountain
Herr's Ridge
Chambersburg Road
McPherson Barn

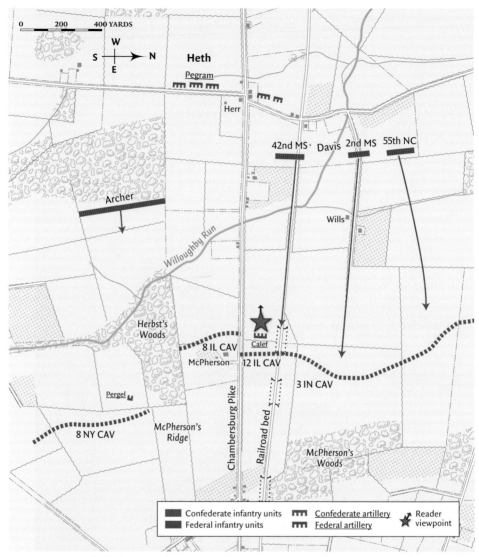

The Last Stand of Buford's Cavalry

ligence about the enemy's strength or intentions. "I was ignorant what force was at or near Gettysburg," Heth reported after the battle. The 5th Alabama Battalion and the 13th Alabama Infantry Regiment took the lead.

The Chambersburg Road between Knoxlyn Ridge and the position where you currently stand traverses a series of low ridges, each one offering the Union troopers a defensible position from which to fire a few shots. As Colonel William Gamble, Buford's brigade commander on this front, reported: "Our skirmishers, fighting under cover of trees and fences, were sharply engaged, did good execution, and retarded the progress of the enemy as much as could possibly be expected." Their stout resistance forced the Confederates to halt and deploy a heavy line of skirmishers in advance of their marching column and bring up artillery to harass the troopers, actions that further delayed their advance. This underappreciated series of firefights across the ridges and valleys that began about two miles ahead of your position permitted the Union cavalrymen to trade space for the time needed for the leading elements of the infantry—the main body of the Union Army of the Potomac—to arrive on the field.

Here, astride McPherson's Ridge and extending to the right and left, Buford posted Gamble's tired troopers for a final stand. He also posted here four of the six cannons belonging to Lieutenant John Calef's Battery A, 2nd U.S. Artillery, two on each side of the road; look around the base of Buford's statue to find the clearly marked barrel of the cannon that fired the first Union artillery round of the battle. Buford's troopers did not have long to wait. By about 9:30 A.M., General Heth began to deploy his Confederate infantry on Herr's Ridge, clearly marked by the silo and red-roofed barn three-quarters of a mile in front of you. The batteries of Major William J. Pegram's artillery battalion also wheeled into position on that ridge, far outnumbering Calef's four guns.

After a brief artillery exchange, Heth's infantry advanced from Herr's Ridge toward you. On the right (north) side of the Chambersburg Road, the 2nd and 42nd Mississippi from Brigadier General Joseph R. Davis's brigade brushed away Buford's skirmishers along the banks of Willoughby Run—the stream that flows from right to left under the bridge at the base of the hill in front of you—and attacked up through the open fields directly toward and to the right of your present posi-

The vista between your
current position and Herr's
Ridge after the war. (USAHMI)

tion. Archer's Alabamians and Tennesseans also crossed the creek and attacked up through the woods to the left (south) of the Chambersburg Road.

The first clash of arms here on the western slopes of the ridge itself, however, lasted only a few minutes. Still, as Lieutenant Colonel S. G. Shepard of the 7th Tennessee reported, "We were not over 40 or 50 yards from the enemy's line when we opened fire. Our men fired with great coolness and deliberation and with terrible effect, as I learned next day by visiting the ground." While Buford's cavalrymen, armed with single-shot, breech-loading carbines, enjoyed a more rapid rate of fire than the Southern infantrymen's muzzle-loading rifles, the Confederates' numerical superiority now clearly gave them an important advantage. But they did not enjoy it for long. As the Indiana, Illinois, New York, and Pennsylvania cavalrymen pulled back toward this ridge line and the Herbst woodlot to your left, they heard a most welcome sound: the cadence of drums denoting the arrival of Union infantry.

Buford's men had bought enough time for Major General John F. Reynolds and his I Corps of the Army of the Potomac to reach the battlefield. General Reynolds's equestrian monument behind you salutes his timely arrival at this key juncture. The troopers' stand also made it possible for Buford to pass a stream of useful information to General George G. Meade at his headquarters in Taneytown, Maryland. At this point, neither Lee nor Meade had committed to fighting a battle at Gettysburg, but Buford made clear to the Union commander that he faced a deteriorating situation, and not just along the Chambersburg Road. At 10:10 A.M., just before Reynolds's I Corps arrived, Buford wrote: "The enemy's force (A. P. Hill's) are advancing on me at this point, and driving my pickets and skirmishers very rapidly. There is also a large force at Heidlersburg that is driving my pickets at that point from that direction [northeast]. General Reynolds is advancing, and is within 3 miles of this point with his leading division. I am positive that the whole of A. P. Hill's force is advancing."[1] Reynolds and his first division arrived minutes later and, in Gamble's words, "relieved the cavalry brigade in its unequal contest with the enemy."

The clash between Buford's Union cavalry and Heth's Confederate infantry that culminated here on McPherson's Ridge illustrates a "meeting engagement." These first contacts between hostile forces often occur without positive orders to attack, break off quickly or (as occurred here at Gettysburg) develop into a much larger fight, and prove difficult for commanders on either side to control.

Who Fought Here?

C.S.A.: Two brigades of Brigadier General Henry Heth's division of Lieutenant General A. P. Hill's Third Corps of the Army of Northern Virginia served here: Brigadier General James J. Archer's 1st, 7th, and 14th Tennessee, 13th Alabama, and 5th Alabama Battalion, approximately 1,197 men; and Brigadier General Joseph R. Davis's 2nd and 42nd Mississippi and 55th North Carolina, approximately 1,707 men. The infantry assault was supported by the Fredericksburg (Va.) Artillery, the Crenshaw

(Va.) Battery, the Letcher (Va.) Artillery, the Pee Dee (S.C.) Artillery, and the Purcell (Va.) Artillery of Major William J. Pegram's battalion.

U.S.: One brigade of Brigadier General John Buford's cavalry division, commanded by Colonel William Gamble—3rd Indiana, 8th Illinois, 12th Illinois, and 8th New York Cavalry regiments, numbering approximately 1,600 troopers—served here. They were supported by the six 3-inch ordnance rifles of Lieutenant John Calef's Battery A, 2nd U.S. Artillery, a battery of "horse artillery."

Who Commanded Here?

Brigadier General John Buford (1826–63), a native of Kentucky, spent his early teenage years in Illinois. He graduated from the U.S. Military Academy at West Point in 1848, ranking sixteenth in a class of thirty-eight. Buford likely knew two of his opponents in this fight, Confederate Generals A. P. Hill and Henry Heth, who graduated from West Point one year ahead of him. Prior to the Civil War, Buford became a veteran campaigner against Native American tribesmen in the West, serving in Texas, New Mexico, and Kansas. He also participated in the U.S. Army's Mormon expedition in Utah in 1857–58. John Buford held the rank of captain when the Civil War broke out. An innovator and motivator of the highest order, he evaluated the full range of roles and missions his cavalry might have to execute and trained and armed his men to carry them out. At Thoroughfare Gap during the Second Manassas Campaign in August 1862, he dismounted his small force and, with the fire of their breech-loading carbines, held back a much superior force of Lee's army. Both General Meade and General Reynolds, to whom he also reported during this advance, trusted his ability to evaluate threats, gather intelligence, keep them informed, and take no action that would close off options. Colonel Theodore Lyman of General Meade's staff provided an interesting physical description of John Buford: "A compactly built man of middle height with a tawny mustache and a little triangular gray eye, whose expression is determined, not to say sinister. . . . He is a very soldierly looking man. He is of good disposition but not to be trifled with."[2] As General O. O. Howard wrote of Buford, "He specifically distinguished himself during the war for boldness in pushing up close to his foe; for great dash in his assaults, and, at the same time shrewdness and prudence in the presence of a force larger than his own." Buford died of typhoid fever in December 1863. Lieutenant Aaron Jerome,

Brigadier General John Buford, U.S.A. (USAMHI)

one of Buford's signal officers, feared that as a consequence, history would overlook his good work here on July 1. In October 1865 Jerome wrote to Major General Winfield S. Hancock—who had just returned from a trip to Gettysburg—and made a special plea: "Excuse me, Gen., but it will be difficult to find a parallel in history to the resistance made by a small force of Cavalry against such odds of Infantrymen. . . . Will you not General, endeavor to bring General Buford's name more prominently forward? Everyone knows that he 'in his day' was first and foremost."[3]

Lieutenant General Ambrose Powell Hill (1825–65), commander of the Third Corps of the Army of Northern Virginia, ranked as the senior Confederate commander on the field as the battle began on July 1. A Virginia native, Hill graduated from West Point in 1847. A veteran of military campaigns in Mexico and against the Seminole Indians, he proved to be an aggressive fighter. Resigning from the Regular Army as a first lieutenant on March 1, 1861, he joined the Confederates with the rank of colonel. He commanded a brigade at First Manassas

Lieutenant General Ambrose Powell Hill, C.S.A. (USAMHI)

in 1861 and at Yorktown and Williamsburg on the Virginia peninsula in 1862 before receiving command of an infantry division. After fighting in the Seven Days Battles, his division served at Cedar Mountain and Second Manassas and in the capture of Harpers Ferry. Leading his division from Harpers Ferry to Antietam in a forced march on September 17, 1862, Hill led the counterattack that blunted the final Federal attack during the battle of Antietam and saved the day for the Confederate forces. His division saw considerable action during the Fredericksburg and Chancellorsville Campaigns, and he briefly assumed command of Stonewall Jackson's Corps following that general's mortal wounding at Chancellorsville until he himself fell wounded and left the field. At the end of May 1863, Hill was given command of the newly formed Third Corps of the Army of Northern Virginia. Plagued by the aftereffects of a social disease that he contracted while a cadet, Hill frequently fell ill and performed inconsistently on the battlefield. At Gettysburg, he certainly put in a lackluster performance. A. P. Hill was killed in action on April 2, 1865, by Federal troops at the end of the siege of Petersburg. The U.S. Army's Fort A. P. Hill in Virginia is named in his honor.

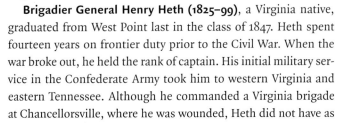

Brigadier General Henry Heth (1825–99), a Virginia native, graduated from West Point last in the class of 1847. Heth spent fourteen years on frontier duty prior to the Civil War. When the war broke out, he held the rank of captain. His initial military service in the Confederate Army took him to western Virginia and eastern Tennessee. Although he commanded a Virginia brigade

Brigadier General Henry Heth, C.S.A. (USAMHI)

at Chancellorsville, where he was wounded, Heth did not have as much combat experience as his contemporaries in divisional command. He did not seem to understand his commander's intent not to bring on a battle until the Army of Northern Virginia had concentrated, and if he did understand it, he proved incapable of breaking off the fight on July 1 once it started. Heth was wounded in the fighting that day. Although some of his subordinates expressed dissatisfaction in his leadership at Gettysburg and during the retreat to Virginia, he continued to command Confederate troops for the remainder of the war until the Confederate surrender at Appomattox in April 1865. When Heth died in 1899, he was eulogized as a man with a "disposition as gentle as a woman; in character he was courteous and chivalric. He had no enemies." He possessed "noble qualities, manifest at all times and under all circumstances" and represented the finest kind of "unselfish friend" and "wise counselor."[4]

Who Fell Here?

The mobility of cavalry generally worked against the kind of stand-and-fight clashes that exact high casualties from attackers and defenders alike. As a consequence, the casualties during this opening clash were light. Gamble's brigade of Buford's division did most of the fighting in this area, and it suffered 99 troopers killed, wounded, and missing; Calef's battery lost an additional 12 men. Confederate casualties were also light, but since these same units continued to fight throughout the day, it is not possible to determine how many of their losses occurred in the opening clashes with Buford's cavalry. You will learn more about the casualties of the brigades of Archer and Davis on July 1 at later stops where they suffered their greatest losses.

Individual vignettes. In the years after the war, both Southerners and Northerners placed great importance on identifying the first soldier on each side to fall at Gettysburg. By tradition, Private Henry C. Rison—often misspelled as "Raisin"—a soldier in the 7th Tennessee Infantry of Archer's brigade who had enlisted in Nashville on May 20, 1861, became the first Confederate to die on July 1. In reality, a bullet fractured the thigh of the private at some point that day. Too badly injured to remove back to Virginia, he became a prisoner of war on July 5. Inconsistencies in his records obscure his ultimate fate. Some say that he lingered until August 1 or perhaps August 5, when he died and was buried in section 1, grave 40, of the temporary cemetery at Camp Letterman, the main U.S. Army hospital that operated east of Gettysburg from July through mid-November 1863. If so, then Rison's remains likely were disinterred in June 1872 and taken south, perhaps to Gettysburg Hill in Hollywood Cemetery in Richmond. Other records suggest that he died at the U.S. Army hospital at Chester, Pennsylvania, on either August 1 or August 15. Thus the name of the first Confederate to die at Gettysburg remains unknown, and the circumstances of the death of Henry Rison are equally uncertain.[5]

Controversy also surrounds the identity of the first Union soldier to fall at Gettysburg. In the years after the war, veterans of the 12th Illinois Cavalry asserted that either Corporal Gabriel B. Durham of Company I or Private Ferdinand Ushuer of Company C fell first; shrapnel from rounds fired by Captain Marye's Fredericksburg Artillery of Pegram's Battalion felled both men. Veterans of the 3rd Indiana Cavalry named Private John E. Weaver of Company A as the first soldier to suffer a fatal injury, although he did not die of his leg wound and subsequent amputation until August 3 at Camp Letterman. Veterans of the 9th New York that fought against the advance of Lieutenant General Richard S. Ewell's Confederates marching south to the battlefield from Carlisle claimed that the attention heaped on Buford's fight obscured an important truth: their Corporal Cyrus W. James of Company G fell first, hit during a skirmish several miles north of town while delaying Ewell's advance.[6]

Who Lived Here?

McPherson's Ridge is named for Edward M. McPherson, owner of the farm on which sits the large barn to your left across Chambersburg Road. Fire destroyed the farmhouse in 1895, and the outbuildings have been removed; the barn, however, looks substantially the same today as it did in 1863, thanks to modern preservation work. McPherson was the former chief clerk of the U.S. House of Representatives and a former Republican congressman turned out of office in the midterm elections of 1862. Three months prior to the battle, McPherson had moved to Washington and assumed duties as deputy commissioner of internal revenue, part of a new office designed to collect the nation's first federal income tax as required by the law enacted on August 2, 1861. At the time of the battle, tenant farmer John Slentz and his family lived on the McPherson farm. Prior to the start of the battle, the Slentz family fled to town to seek refuge and remained there until the battle was over. In a letter dated August 10, 1863, Slentz informed absentee landlord McPherson that the bodies of dead soldiers are "still laying there yet and they won't let any be raised till the 1st of October. I would give ten hundred dollars if I had it if I was back on your place and fixed as I was on the 29th of June. I had a fair prospect for a good summer crop but all is gone."[7]

What Did They Say about It Later?

Many Civil War regiments formed regimental associations after the war and produced a unit history of their wartime experiences. In the unit history of the 8th Illinois Cavalry, the following was recorded:

> Early the next morning, July 1st, our pickets brought word that the enemy was advancing in force. Captain [Amasa E.] Dana was in command of the picket line on the Chambersburg road where they first made their appearance; and here, as in many other of the great battles, the Eighth Illinois received the first fire and shed the first blood. . . . The long line of the enemy came in full view, and their batteries rained upon our men showers of shot and shell, but our brave boys stood firm and fell back only when ordered. The Eighth New York, on our left, was wavering some, but the Third Indiana, on the right never flinched. . . . It began to be warm work. Sergeant [Charles] Goodspeed, of Company H, was wounded and taken

to the depot where a temporary hospital had been established, and soon after [Private John] Williams, of Company M, had his arm shattered by a ball, which required amputation.

General Buford told me that he never saw so daring and successful a thing as was done by one of the Eighth Illinois men. As the cavalry skirmishers fell back, one man, either not hearing the command or determined not to yield, at first stood his ground, then lay down in the grass until the enemy's line was nearly upon him, when he arose and cried out at the top of his voice, "Come on—we have them." Whether the rebels were astonished at his madness, or thought he was an officer leading on a host, we know not, but their line faltered.[8]

Lieutenant Jerome's concern that the stand of Buford's men might be forgotten possessed some merit. The first book-length historical study of the Battle of Gettysburg—Samuel Penniman Bates's 336-page *The Battle of Gettysburg*, published in 1875—gave the cavalry action only four very general paragraphs that included few tactical details.[9] The pattern held true in many histories of the battle, a delightful exception being Colonel James K. P. Scott's *The Story of the Battle of Gettysburg*, published in 1927. Michael Shaara's *The Killer Angels* (1974) and Sam Elliott's portrayal of Buford in the movie *Gettysburg* (1993) both have played a large role in increasing both popular and scholarly awareness of the role of the cavalry in the opening phases of the battle on July 1.

Driving directions to the next stop: Return to your vehicle and drive forward out of the parking lot, turning right onto Chambersburg Road (Route 30). Take the next immediate right turn onto a one-way road (Stone Avenue). Follow Stone Avenue 0.5 miles to the stop sign at Reynolds Avenue. Turn left and drive a short distance to the sign on your right marking National Park Service Auto Tour Stop 1, where you will park.

STOP 3. THE DEATH OF REYNOLDS

Orientation

Cross the road to the informational waysides. To your left front, you will see the square, pointed monument on a mound of earth near the tree line that marks the approximate site where Major General John F. Reynolds, commander of the Army of the Potomac's I Corps and the senior Union general then on the battlefield, fell to enemy fire. Walk partway down the slope toward the monument, facing it and the woodlot behind it.

This woodlot belonged to the Herbst farm; sometimes, history books still refer to it incorrectly as McPherson's Woods for the more well-known farm in the open field to your right front. The woods to your front became the site of bloody fighting twice on July 1, shortly after 10:00 A.M. and again later in the afternoon. Before 10:00 A.M., New York and Indiana cavalrymen held these woods only lightly, with support from two cannons from Lieutenant Calef's battery under the command of Sergeant Charles Pergel on the crest of the ridge over your left shoulder. At this stop, you will explore only the morning fight; you will return later to examine the much more intense afternoon fight.

The monument in the center marks the death site of Major General John F. Reynolds.

What Happened Here?

From Herr's Ridge, a mile ahead of you, the battle line of Brigadier General James J. Archer's Alabamians and Tennesseans crossed Willoughby Run, entered these woods, and advanced toward your present location. Buford's troopers and Calef's two detached guns continued to resist here, but Confederate numbers had begun to tell. At approximately 10:15 A.M., the arrival of the two brigades of Brigadier General James Wadsworth's division of Reynolds's I Corps remedied the imbalance. As Reynolds deployed Brigadier General Lysander Cutler's brigade of New York and Pennsylvania regiments to relieve the cavalrymen astride Chambersburg Road to your right (you will learn more about this at Stop 4), the head of Brigadier General Solomon Meredith's Iron Brigade—the 2nd, 6th, and 7th Wisconsin, 19th Indiana, and 24th Michigan—reached the open fields to your left rear.

Major General Abner Doubleday, Reynolds's senior subordinate, had ridden ahead of his own division. While Reynolds strengthened the Union position on the Chambersburg Road, Doubleday, according to his report, identified the Herbst woodlot (in front of you) as possessing "all the advantages of a redoubt, strengthening the center of our line, and enfilading the enemy's columns should they advance in the open spaces on either side." Deeming the woods to be "the key of the position," he sent four regiments of the Iron Brigade to its defense, holding back only the 6th Wisconsin as a reserve. As Doubleday recalled, when he urged the men to hold it "to the last extremity," they responded: "'If we can't hold it, where will you find men who can?'" It fell to Colonel Lucius Fairchild's 2nd Wisconsin to form a line of battle (behind you) and press directly ahead into Herbst's Woods to confront Archer's men.

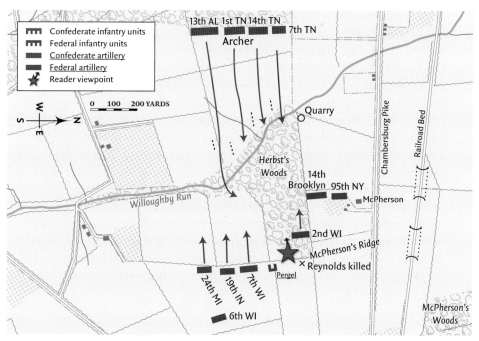

The Death of Reynolds

As the 2nd Wisconsin deployed, General Reynolds arrived on the scene, returning from deploying Cutler's men, and now he urged on the Iron Brigade to repulse Archer's troops, already visible through the trees ahead. They could not act too quickly. As one of the Alabamians wrote shortly thereafter, the entire brigade had heard Archer's command to charge Pergel's two guns, and "every man responded with becoming courage."[1] Already, Confederate bullets had begun to exact a toll in the 2nd Wisconsin's ranks. A round then hit General Reynolds behind the ear. He had directed the fight only for about thirty minutes, and now he lay dead. Command on the field immediately fell to Doubleday.

Generally unaware of their corps commander's fall, the 2nd Wisconsin began to press forward into the woods. The 7th Wisconsin fell in to the left of the 2nd, and the 19th Indiana and 24th Michigan extended the Iron Brigade's line even farther to your left. The Iron Brigade received orders, as Colonel Henry Morrow of the 24th Michigan reported, to "advance at once, no order being given or time allowed for loading guns." Morrow's men tried to do so, but a staff officer ordered the colonel "to move forward immediately without loading, which I did." As the rest of the Iron Brigade advanced through the open fields to your left to stop Archer's right flank and center, the 2nd Wisconsin entered these woods and hit the left of Archer's line. The midwesterners' field officers dismounted and led them on foot. After the regiment had advanced about fifty yards into the woods, a bullet shattered Colonel Fairchild's left elbow, and Lieutenant Colonel George H. Stevens fell mortally wounded; Major John Mansfield suddenly found himself in command of the 2nd Wisconsin.

The Iron Brigade's line soon overlapped the right flank of Archer's brigade, and now the Alabamians and Tennesseans found themselves caught in a cross fire. As Lieutenant Colonel S. G. Shepard of the 7th Tennessee reported, "Our position was at once rendered untenable, and the right of our line [to your left front] was forced back." When the 2nd Wisconsin pressed harder against Archer's left, the entire line fell back across Willoughby Run. The Iron Brigade followed in hot pursuit. In the open fields west of the creek to your left front but beyond your current line of sight, a close hand-to-hand struggle ensued. After enjoying a generally successful morning advance, the Confederates now suffered a decisive reverse. As a member of the 13th Alabama advised a Richmond editor soon after the battle, "Here we were, surrounded nearly on all sides, but our brave little Brigadier ordered his men to fight to the last, and never did one of the Brigade surrender until the enemy was within ten or fifteen paces of the General."[2] Indeed, many of Archer's men now became prisoners of the Iron Brigade, and Private Patrick Maloney of the 2nd Wisconsin captured the general himself.[3] Archer became the first general officer in the Army of Northern Virginia to be captured on the field of battle since General Lee had taken command thirteen months earlier.

The fight west of Willoughby Run—by necessity ignored in battlefield interpretation because it took place on previously inaccessible, privately owned land—will no doubt be studied in greater detail in the future. Gettysburg National Military Park took possession of this ground in 2011; at the time of publication, there is no timeline in place for the opening of trails, the placement of interpretive markers, or parking. Nonetheless, the fight provided one of the earliest newspaper accounts of the Battle of Gettysburg that could be linked to a specific incident. As early as July 3, a Harrisburg paper reported (with considerable exaggeration): "General Archer and his whole staff were taken. About fifteen hundred of the enemy's men thus fell into our hands, and went to the rear. Small regiments were the order in this brigade; and when an Alabama Colonel was asked where the rest of his regiment was, he responded laconically, 'Gone to hell, sir.'"[4] Lieutenant Colonel Shepard, by contrast, reported the loss of only seventy-five prisoners.

After Archer's capture, the fighting here quieted, the forces parted, and the Iron Brigade recrossed Willoughby Run and re-formed its line on the high ground deep in the Herbst woodlot to your front. You will revisit the woodlot and the Iron Brigade's regimental monuments at Stop 12 to examine the afternoon fight of July 1.

Who Fought Here?

C.S.A.: Archer's Tennessee and Alabama brigade, which you met at Stop 2, served here.

U.S.: The famous Iron Brigade—one of several Northern commands that claimed this title, but clearly the most famous of them—won its special designation in September 1862 at the Battle of South Mountain during the Antietam Campaign. Their black felt, high-crowned, Hardee hats, the headgear of the Regular U.S. Army dress uniform, set them apart from most of the volunteer regiments, which sported wide-brimmed hats or kepis. The soldier on the monument to the 24th Michigan wears the distinctive headgear; you can see it when you stop there for Stop 12. Here at Gettysburg, the Iron Brigade numbered approximately 1,829 men, with the 24th Michigan's 496 soldiers making it the largest regiment in the brigade.

Who Commanded Here?

Major General John Fulton Reynolds (1820–63), the senior Union general upon his arrival, reached the field at midmorning on July 1 and immediately began to assess the situation unfolding around him. The authorized commander of the Army of the Potomac's I Corps, Reynolds also commanded the entire left wing of the army—the I, III, and XI Corps—as it advanced northward from Maryland into Pennsylvania. A native of Lancaster, fifty miles east of Gettysburg, Reynolds graduated from the U.S.

Military Academy with the class of 1841. His classmates included Confederate Richard B. Garnett, who would share Reynolds's own fate at Gettysburg. Following graduation, Reynolds saw service on the Atlantic coast and in Texas. He served in the Mexican War, during which he received two brevet promotions for gallantry. In 1860 he served as commandant of cadets and instructor in tactics at West Point. Upon the outbreak of the Civil War, Reynolds was appointed a brigadier general of volunteers and began a lengthy association with the Pennsylvania Reserves. He led one of its brigades on the Virginia peninsula in 1862, and he commanded an infantry division at Second Bull Run. At Fredericksburg in December 1862, he led the I Corps, and one of his divisions under Major General George G. Meade—now commanding the entire Army of the Potomac—made the only penetration of the Confederate line. After making initial deployments of his leading division here on McPherson's Ridge on July 1, Reynolds was killed in action. He is buried in his hometown of Lancaster.

Major General Abner Doubleday (1819–93), a native of upstate New York, graduated from West Point in the class of 1842 with several other major figures in the Gettysburg story, including Richard H. Anderson, Lafayette McLaws, and James Longstreet. Doubleday's paternal and maternal grandfathers served in the Conti-

nental army during the American Revolution. His father was an American veteran of the War of 1812. In April 1861 Captain Doubleday was the second in command of the Federal garrison at Fort Sumter in the harbor of Charleston, South Carolina. With the onset of the war, Doubleday enjoyed rapid promotion. Before Gettysburg, he saw action as a brigade and division commander at Second Bull Run, Antietam, Fredericksburg, and Chancellorsville. When he arrived at Gettysburg, Doubleday commanded the 3rd Division of Reynolds's I Corps, and he assumed corps command when Reynolds was killed. However, on July 2, General Meade relieved Doubleday of command and put in his place Major General John Newton, Doubleday's West Point classmate. Doubleday received no more active field assignments during the war, but he remained in the army until his retirement in 1873. Abner Doubleday died in New Jersey in 1893 and is buried in Arlington National Cemetery. Traditionally, he has been credited with inventing baseball, even though there is contradictory evidence to support the claim. Nonetheless, Doubleday Field, where cadets play baseball at West Point, is named in his honor, as is the baseball diamond at the Major League Baseball Hall of Fame at Cooperstown, New York.

Major General Abner Doubleday succeeded Reynolds in command. (USAMHI)

Brigadier General James J. Archer (1817–64), a Maryland native, graduated from Princeton University in 1835 and later studied law at the University of Maryland. He served as an infantry captain during the war with Mexico, earning a brevet promotion to major for gallantry at Chapultepec before honorably mustering out of service in 1848. That same year, Archer was wounded in a duel with future Union General Andrew Porter. Archer's "second" in the duel was Lieutenant Thomas J. Jackson, later famous as "Stonewall." Archer resumed his legal profession before reentering the Regular Army in 1855 at the rank of captain. In 1861 he resigned his commission and entered Confederate service as colonel of the 5th Texas Regiment. Promoted to brigadier general in June 1862, he took command of what became known as the Tennessee brigade in the Army of Northern Virginia. A veteran regiment and brigade commander, Archer saw action in every battle from the Seven Days in 1862 to Gettysburg in July 1863. His men nicknamed him the "little gamecock" for his slight build and fierce attitude in battle. Archer and an undetermined number of his soldiers were captured in the Willoughby Run fight. Along with many other Confederate officers captured at Gettysburg, Archer was confined as a prisoner of war at Johnson's Island, Ohio. He remained there for a year before being exchanged. Archer returned to Confederate service in the summer of 1864 as brigade commander. However, his confinement had ruined his health, and he died in Richmond in October 1864. His remains lie in Hollywood Cemetery in Richmond.

Brigadier General James J. Archer, C.S.A., captured on July 1. (USAMHI)

Who Fell Here?

Archer's command suffered its greatest loss at Gettysburg in this action. It went into action with approximately 1,197 men in ranks. The 13th Alabama lost 214 of its 308 men killed, wounded, and missing; the 5th Alabama Battalion lost 48 of its 135 men; the 1st Tennessee lost 178 of its 281 men; the 7th Tennessee lost 116 of its 249 men; and the 14th Tennessee lost 127 of its 220 men—for a total loss of 684 Confederate soldiers. However, it is important to remember that Archer's brigade—under the command of the 13th Alabama's Colonel B. D. Fry—also participated in the July 3 assault best known as "Pickett's Charge," and some of the men enumerated here fell in that action. It is often difficult to separate casualties suffered on that day from those inflicted by the Iron Brigade or Buford's cavalrymen on July 1.[5] This episode only opened a long and bloody day for the Iron Brigade; their casualties will be described in detail after a closer look at their hardest action at Stop 12.

Individual vignettes. Civil War memoirs and regimental histories frequently include presentiments of death shared between comrades on the eve of battle. Orderly Sergeant Cornelius Weaver of the 2nd Wisconsin recalled one such exchange that took place early on July 1.

We had not been long upon the march before Sergeant Joseph O. Williams of my company . . . came forward and fell in alongside of me at the head of the column, and opened up a conversation by saying that he did not feel quite right, that he felt as though something was going to happen to him, and that he should not get through the day. I laughed at him and told him he was foolish to feel so blue, there seemed to be no trouble ahead for the day, but if there should be, that he would come out all right as he always had done.

As regimental historian George H. Otis recorded: "Sergt. Williams of I company came to see me with a handful of articles and said that he believed he would be the first one shot in the battle. He said he felt it and could not shake it off. He asked me to take charge of the trinkets. I argued with him, hoping to turn his mind in another direction, but all to no avail. He insisted that 'his time had come.' Sure enough he was at about the first shot, instantly killed."[6]

Private Jacob W. Pickett enlisted in Company G, 13th Alabama Infantry, on July 19, 1861, in Montgomery. He represents the thousands of enlisted men about whom Civil War record keeping reveals very little. Pickett seems to have spent parts of 1862 in hospitals, including a stint between February and March 1863 in the 3rd Alabama Hospital in Richmond. Early on July 1, one bullet hit him in the right arm and a second bullet crashed into his left leg. Taken to a Confederate field hospital, he could not be carried south with the more lightly wounded, and as a consequence, he became a Union prisoner on July 5. His surgeons transferred him to Camp Letterman, the U.S. Army's general hospital east of Gettysburg, on July 24, but he did not survive the short trip. He died of his wounds on July 28.[7]

Who Lived Here?

Most of this action took place on the 110-acre farm of John Herbst. In June 1864 he submitted a damage claim. He wrote that on July 1, "the rebels took possession of the place; that he came out of the cellar and was met by a rebel soldier or officer of low grade who told him he was ordered to burn the buildings on account of 'the Yankees' having been firing from them, that he had set fire to the Barn and insisted on burning the House also, but found that there were wounded men, one of whom was a Union soldier and two rebels who had been carried into the house, and who begged him not to burn it, one of them being too badly wounded to be removed, he did not burn the House." The barn put to the torch measured eighty feet by forty-five feet and included "two threshing floors with stabling in the basement." Herbst also lost a four-horse threshing machine, a reaper and mower, eight sets of horse equipment, a windmill, a wheelbarrow, a cultivator, two plows, and a "corn-fork," plus foodstuffs. He ultimately filed for damages amounting to $2,689.36 and was approved for a settlement for $2606.75.[8]

What Did They Say about It Later?

The war correspondent's dilemma: telling the story first, or telling the story accurately. The *Richmond Sentinel* of July 7, 1863, noted that great inconsistency surrounded the initial Northern reports of General Reynolds's death. His fall, noted the editor, "is mentioned no less than six times" in the July 4 issue of the *New York Tribune*, and none of the reports seemed to agree. This is the kind of problem that historians regularly encounter. What did those initial reports say?

P. G. Chapman's dispatch in the *New York Herald* of July 3, 1863, reported: "General Reynolds, seeing that he could not use his artillery to advantage, rode out to an eminence a short distance from the road to find a place to plant a battery, when he received a volley from some sharpshooters posted in a thicket close at hand. His horse became unmanageable, wheeled and reared, and at the same time a ball struck the General in the back of the neck, passing downward, severing the spinal column, and killing him instantly."

The July 4 *Baltimore American* suggested that the general died in the midafternoon rather than the midmorning, reporting that "at three o'clock the enemy massed his entire forces, and endeavored to turn our right wing. Gen. Reynolds advanced to meet them. . . . In this charge Maj. Gen. Reynolds fell mortally wounded, and died soon after being conveyed to Gettysburg."

The *New York Tribune* of July 6, 1863, reported that Reynolds "was struck by several balls and died instantly without saying a word. His acting Adjutant-General, Captain Bond, was at this side and caught him in his arms to prevent his falling from his horse."

The *New York Herald* of July 7, 1863, included a notice that "Gen. Reynolds was mortally wounded early in the battle, when he was placing his men. To conceal the casualty he rode off the field some distance before he dismounted, when a surgeon was called, but he soon died."

The *Franklin Repository* of Chambersburg published on July 22 that while Reynolds and two aides were selecting positions for his troops, "The enemy at that moment poured in a cruel musketry fire upon the group of officers; a bullet struck Gen. Reynolds in the neck, wounding him mortally. Crying out, with a voice that thrilled the hearts of his soldiers 'Forward! For God's sake, forward!' he turned for an instant, beheld the order obeyed by a line of shouting infantry, and falling into the arms of Captain Wilcox, his aide, who rode beside him, his life went out with the words, 'Good God, Wilcox, I am killed.'"

History or Memory? Some Confederates developed their own take on the incident. In his postbattle report, General Heth asserted: "One of the first shells fired by Pegram['s battalion] mortally wounded Major-General Reynolds, then in command of the force at Gettysburg."[9] Few Confederate infantrymen challenged that assertion until much later. Early in the twentieth century, former Sergeant Ben Thorpe of the 55th North Carolina confessed to a group of visitors from Lancaster, Pennsylvania—Reynolds's hometown—that he, in fact, had shot the general. One of his officers had spotted an officer on horseback posting a battery and ordered Thorpe, a sharpshooter, to bring him down. It was a long-range shot and required three attempts, but he did so. An article about Thorpe's claim appeared in November 7, 1902, in the *Lancaster Intelligencer*, and the tale gained credence through repeated retellings. Thorpe faced no serious challenge until E. T. Boland, a member of Company F of the 13th Alabama, went to the 1913 golden anniversary reunion and offered his own reminiscence of the event: "I and John Hendrix, of my company were about 80 or 100 yards from where Gen. Reynolds's monument is now located a few paces from the woods. A squad of officers or soldiers dashed in just where the monument stands. John Hendrix fired and one of them fell. He asked me if I saw him empty that saddle." Boland wanted to go on record because "it has been claimed that a North Carolina soldier killed him. There were no such troops on the field" at that time, he insisted.[10]

Shades of many of these early reports still color our understanding of Reynolds's death today.

Driving directions to the next stop: Return to your vehicle and drive forward on Reynolds Avenue to the intersection with Chambersburg Road. Drive straight across the intersection and, just over the modern bridge, park in the designated parking spots just beyond the statue of General James Wadsworth with his raised arm pointing toward the fields on your left.

STOP 4. THE FIGHT AROUND THE RAILROAD CUT

You will be exploring two different actions at this stop.

Orientation

Park near General Wadsworth's statue. To position yourself for the first of the two actions, walk back toward the bridge that crosses over the historic railroad cut. Just before you reach the bridge, you will see the monument to the 147th New York Infantry on your left. Carefully cross to the other side of the park road and face toward the open field, with the 147th New York's monument behind you. The railroad tracks can be found in the low cut to your left, and you may be able to spot the base of General Reynolds's equestrian monument on the high ground to your left front.

In the late 1850s, the Pennsylvania Railroad planned to extend a line of track from Harrisburg to Hanover, with a spur to Gettysburg and points westward. The panic of 1857, however, stalled the project. While the bed for an extension west of Gettysburg lay ready, the company had laid no tracks there at the time of the battle. The railroad bed, not appearing on any map, presented both Union and Confederate forces with challenges and opportunities. Some maps refer to the area where you are standing right now as the "middle cut." The "western cut" carves through west McPherson's Ridge straight ahead of you where the banks are steepest, and the "eastern cut" slices through Seminary Ridge near the cluster of white buildings behind you.

The site of the stand of the 147th New York, with the railroad cut to the left.

Position 1: The Opening Volleys

What Happened Here?

Continue to face the open field with the railroad cut on your left. Before the first Confederate infantry advanced upon McPherson's Ridge, the strongest part of the defensive line of Colonel William Gamble's cavalry brigade astride the Chambersburg Road had stopped at the lip of the western cut ahead of you; only his skirmishers extended northward onto the ground in your immediate front. Troopers from the 6th and 9th New York Cavalry Regiments from Colonel Thomas Devin's brigade continued the Army of the Potomac's cavalry screen along the ridge to your distant right front, where you can see a sparse line of monuments.

When Brigadier General Joseph R. Davis's brigade made its first advance, which you explored at Stop 2, it did so on such a broad front that his leftmost regiment, the 55th North Carolina, tangled with Devin's skirmishers. Davis's rightmost regiment, the 42nd Mississippi, advanced directly toward where you are standing, and the 2nd Mississippi filled the center of the brigade line. During Davis's first advance, the combined effect of the four guns of Lieutenant John Calef's horse artillery bat-

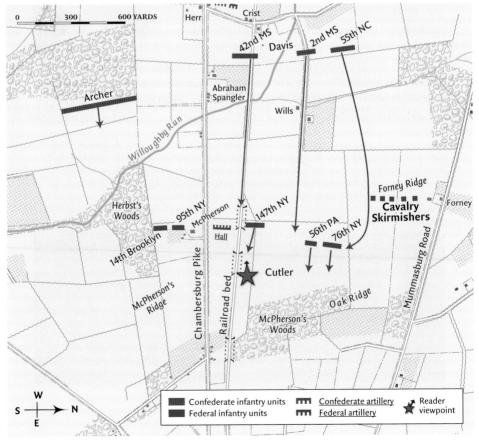

The Stand of Cutler's Brigade North of the Railroad Cut—Position 1

The 6th Wisconsin reached the right edge of the railroad cut here and helped to capture several hundred Mississippians. (USAMHI)

tery, the volume of fire put out by the carbines of Gamble's troopers, and threats by Devin's New York cavalrymen to turn the 55th North Carolina's left flank proved sufficient to repulse him. Davis pulled his line back to Herr's Ridge to reorganize for another push. When he launched his second attempt, however, Buford's cavalry had withdrawn and Reynolds's infantry replaced them.

Brigadier General James Wadsworth—you parked near his statue—commanded Reynolds's lead division, and Brigadier General Lysander Cutler led the brigade at the head of its line of march; the Iron Brigade you met at Stop 3 followed close behind. Perhaps because neither Wadsworth nor Cutler was a professional soldier, Reynolds remained on the field to help them deploy their troops here. Calef's battery departed with Buford, so Reynolds replaced it with Captain James Hall's 2nd Maine Battery, its six guns entirely filling the space between the Chambersburg Road and the lip of the western cut near Reynolds's statue to your left front. Two of Cutler's regiments—the 14th Brooklyn and 95th New York—formed their line by the McPherson barn on the other side of the Chambersburg Road to protect Hall's left flank. Cutler's 76th New York, followed by the 56th Pennsylvania and—after a brief bit of confusion—the 147th New York, crossed to this side of the Chambersburg Road and over the railroad cut. The 147th New York took position on the knob of ground ahead of you and the 56th Pennsylvania and 76th New York extended Cutler's line along the slight ridge that extends to its right, up toward Devin's cavalry monuments that you located earlier.

They had not formed their lines completely when Davis launched his second attack. Indeed, as a soldier in the 147th New York related in a letter to his hometown newspaper shortly after the battle, "We . . . reached the foot of the hill"—the low ground right at your feet—"and formed in line of battle under shelter of the ridge in front of us." They prepared to receive the enemy's attack in the wheat field at the top of the rise, but they did not know exactly where Davis's men were until "they fired a volley into our ranks," and they "could only tell even then by the way the wheat was moved in front of us by the bullets." This was the 147th New York's first major combat, so the author remembered the event in quite personal terms: "On the first fire while we were advancing Hiram Stowel[l] and Celestine Berkley [Celestin Bircklee] were killed instantly for I saw them fall. Then Fred. Rife, one of the finest men I ever saw."[1]

To your right front, the 76th New York and 56th Pennsylvania, as Cutler reported, just as quickly became "engaged with a vastly superior force of the enemy, advancing in two lines, at short range, in front and on my right flank."[2] Davis readily admitted in his report that the "engagement soon became very warm."[3] It did not take long, however, for Davis's 55th North Carolina to wrap around Cutler's right flank in the fields to your far right front. The 76th New York now found itself in a desperate situation. As First Lieutenant C. A. Watkins wrote home a few weeks after the fight: "The 76 being the advance of the Corps, of course were on the extreme right, and subject to the cross fire from the enemy who had succeeded in flanking us. Our gallant boys now return their fire with interest and the enemy arose from their cover in a wheat field [to your front] and charged upon us, supposing we were raw militia."[4] But Cutler's men could not stand the cross fire for long. Major Andrew Grover of the 76th New York fell dead, and both his regiment and the 56th Pennsylvania received orders to fall back. They withdrew to McPherson's Woods, the woodlot on the northern extension of Seminary Ridge behind you, often incorrectly labeled on maps as "Sheads's Woods."

The "Ploughboys" of the 147th New York, however, stayed in position directly ahead of you when the 76th New York and the 56th Pennsylvania pulled back. A courier arrived with withdrawal orders, but Lieutenant Colonel F. C. Miller already had fallen with a severe wound before he could act on them. Thus on the knoll ahead of you, Major George Harney and the Ploughboys continued to hold their ground against the frontal attacks of Davis's Mississippians and at the same time prepared to defend its right flank against the surging 55th North Carolina.

To confront this new threat, Major Harney bent back—the military term was "refused"—the companies on the right of his line until they were perpendicular to their original line, thus transforming the 147th New York's straight battle line into an L-shaped formation. Its right flank now confronted the North Carolinians, while its center and left continued to face the Mississippians to their front. The New Yorkers fell in droves on the knoll in front of you, but they continued to hold the line, even as the Mississippians pushed down through the western cut around their left flank and the 55th North Carolina threatened to wrap around the 147th New York's right flank and rear. Finally, Major Harney gave an order of his own design: "In retreat, double time, run." The surest avenue toward safety took the men across the railroad cut, across the Chambersburg Road, and in the direction of the seminary over your left shoulder. As one of their number wrote back to his hometown newspaper, "about 30 rods down the cut the rebs had throw up a barricade of rails, and as many of them as could stand behind that used their powder and balls to the best of their ability, and many of our men perished before they could get out. . . . How any of us escaped that trap alive, I cannot tell."[5] The stand of the 147th New York cost the regiment a full 77.9 percent of its strength.

Captain Hall of the 2nd Maine Battery did not seem to appreciate the New Yorkers' efforts. Instead, he reported his surprise at seeing "my support falling back without an order having been given me to retire." Hall, "feeling that if the position was too advanced for infantry it was equally so for artillery," pulled his battery off western McPherson's Ridge, losing horses and taking fire most of the way.[6] McPherson's Ridge north of the Chambersburg Road had fallen into Confederate hands.

Who Fought Here?

C.S.A.: The 1,707 men of the 2nd and 42nd Mississippi and 55th North Carolina of Brigadier General Joseph R. Davis's brigade of Heth's division in A. P. Hill's Third Corps participated in this action; Davis's fourth regiment, the 11th Mississippi, did not participate in the July 1 fighting.

U.S.: The approximately 1,007 men of the 76th and 147th New York and 56th Pennsylvania of Brigadier General Lysander Cutler's brigade held the Union line here, in support of Captain Hall's 117 men in the 2nd Maine Battery.

Who Commanded Here?

Brigadier General Lysander Cutler (1807–66), born in Worcester County, Massachusetts, became a schoolmaster and subsequently engaged in a variety of business activities. He also gained experience in a number of civic positions that included trustee of Tufts College, director of a railroad, and state senator. Although not a Mexican War veteran, Cutler gained some military experience as a colonel in the Maine militia. In the late 1850s, he moved to Milwaukee, Wisconsin, where he worked as an investigator for a mining company and established a business as a grain dealer. At the outset of the Civil War, the fifty-six-year-old businessman was commissioned colonel of the 6th Wisconsin Infantry. Cutler led this regiment in the Second Battle of Bull Run in August 1862, where he fell severely wounded in the right thigh. He missed the Battle of Antietam in September but was again in command at Fredericksburg, and he was commissioned a brigadier general dating from November 29, 1862. In the spring of 1863, he took command of the second brigade of James Wadsworth's I Corps division and served with distinction at Gettysburg. In the reorganization of the Army of the Potomac in March 1864, Cutler received command of a brigade in the V Corps. When General Wadsworth fell during the Battle of the Wilderness, Cutler assumed command of the division. At the Battle of Globe Tavern in August 1864, a shell fragment sliced into Cutler's face. Badly disfigured, he left field command and spent the remainder of the war administering the draft in Jackson, Michigan. Cutler died of a stroke in July 1866. He is buried in Forest Home Cemetery in Milwaukee.

Brigadier General Joseph Robert Davis (1825–96), born in Woodville, Mississippi, received his education in Nashville, Tennessee, and at Miami University of Ohio, ultimately becoming a Madison County lawyer and Mississippi state senator. Like his famous uncle, Confederate President Jefferson Davis, he took an active

role in the state militia. Davis entered Confederate service in the spring of 1861 as a captain in the 10th Mississippi Regiment. He subsequently became an aide-de-camp to his uncle with the rank of colonel. President Davis attempted to get Joseph promoted to brigadier general, but the Confederate Senate initially rejected his nomination amid charges of nepotism. Finally, after much wrangling, the nomination won approval, with Davis's new rank to date from September 1862. He was given command of an infantry brigade, serving on limited duty in and around Richmond and in southeast Virginia until the late spring of 1863, when his unit received a posting to Heth's division in A. P. Hill's Third Corps in the Army of Northern Virginia. After Gettysburg, Davis continued to serve in the Army of Northern Virginia, seeing action at Spotsylvania Court House, Cold Harbor, and the siege of Petersburg. Joe Davis surrendered at the end of the war with the Army of Northern Virginia at Appomattox Court House in April 1865. After the war, he returned to Mississippi and resumed his law practice in Biloxi, where he died in 1896.

Brigadier General Joseph R. Davis, C.S.A. (USAMHI)

Who Fell Here?

Since Davis's brigade also engaged in the next action at this stop, their losses are detailed below.

The 76th New York lost 234 of its 375 men when the 55th North Carolina outflanked it; the 56th Pennsylvania lost 130 of its 252 men in the same action. In its stand on the knoll, the 147th New York lost 296 of its 380 men in its first major combat action. Hall's 2nd Maine Battery lost 18 of its 117 artillerymen.

Individual vignettes. The 147th New York came from Oswego, New York, and the newspapers often carried the most comprehensive news of the dimensions of their community's losses. As one article published shortly after the battle began reported:

"Wednesday, July 1st, 1863, will ever remain a memorable day with the whole of Oswego, for on that day some of her best blood perished by rebel bullets, and left the bodies of many of her sons dead upon the fields around the town of Gettysburg."

The town of Oswego delegated two respected local men—O. J. Harmon and Philo Bundy—to go to Gettysburg, report back on the condition of the men of the 147th New York, and inform the townspeople of any needs the community might meet. Oswego-area newspapers printed many of Harmon and Bundy's telegrams for public information. On July 24, 1863, Harmon wrote a letter with special information for Mrs. Carolina L. Church. He had visited with her husband, Private Jonathan B. Church of Company F, who suffered a severe thigh wound that had not responded to treatment; amputation seemed likely. But, as Harmon wrote, "It was a great comfort to me and will be to you to know the happy condition of mind your husband was in. . . . He expresses perfect resignation to the divine will, whatever it might be; though he desired much to see his wife and family." Harmon ended with a note of reassurance, however, adding: "You have made a noble offering to your country, and you cannot lose your reward." Unfortunately, Private Church died of his wounds. He is buried in grave C-85 in the New York plot of the Soldiers' National Cemetery.[7]

Private James C. Knott, 55th North Carolina Infantry, C.S.A., was killed in action here. (Clark)

Private James C. Knott was a thirty-two-year-old farmer from Granville County, North Carolina, when he voluntarily enlisted in Company K, 55th North Carolina, on May 6, 1862. The recruiting officer who signed him up was Maurice T. Smith, who later became lieutenant colonel of his regiment. Knott signed on for a term of service designated as "for the war." Perhaps the $50 bounty he received on enlistment and the one-month authorized absence after his muster-in on May 30—denoted on his records as a "wheat furlough"—made his decision to enlist a bit easier. Private Knott was killed in action on July 1 at Gettysburg, along with his recruiter, Lieutenant Colonel Smith. On April 28, 1864, Mary J. Knott, the private's widow, filed a claim with the Confederate government for the settlement of her husband's military accounts.[8]

What Did They Say about It Later?

The "First Shot" Squabble in the I Corps. For nearly twenty years after the battle, most Northern veterans seemed content to agree with President Lincoln's assessment that their victory at Gettysburg possessed enough glory for all to share. By the 1880s, however, that spirit largely had evaporated, and the quest for battle laurels began in earnest. As you have seen, the cavalrymen argued over credit for firing the first shot of the battle. Veterans of infantry commands believed they had every right to become involved in this discussion as well. As Colonel J. W. Hofmann of the 56th Pennsylvania in Cutler's brigade claimed: "It is generally understood that unless a battle be one confined to the cavalry arm, it is not opened until the infantry become engaged."[9]

Within Cutler's brigade, Lieutenant M. M. Whitney of the 76th New York made clear his position: "I do not wish to fight the battles over again, nor do I wish to claim laurels undeserved," but he added, "nor will I permit one of our well earned feathers to be plucked from our helmet." He advised doubters to speak with any one of Buford's troopers "who will satisfy him that our regiment was the first that lifted the burden of death and responsibility from their tried position."[10] H. H. Lyman, onetime adjutant of the 147th New York, conceded that the 76th New York might have a legitimate claim, but it should "be qualified by the fact that Serg't. H. H. Hubbard, 147th N.Y., in command of the provost-guard of 18 men, formed the extreme right of the 76th's line."[11] Colonel Hofmann claimed from the start that his 56th Pennsylvania, "to its officers and men—not to any individual officer or man," fired the first volley of the battle. In time, veterans of other I Corps commands, including the Iron Brigade and Colonel Roy Stone's Pennsylvania Bucktails, attempted to claim the "first shot" laurels for themselves.

A Search for Respect. In 1888 J. V. Pierce, a captain in the 147th New York during the battle, served as dedication speaker for the regiment's Gettysburg battlefield monument. It concerned him that the previous year, General Daniel E. Sickles had written off the first day's battle as "a preliminary skirmish." He begged his audience's indulgence as he devoted much of his address to correcting the long list of "errors in the histories which affect the credit and honor of the One hundred and forty-seventh New York"—most of which ignored the regiment or portrayed them as either overwhelmed or in need of rescuing. "Had our regiment flinched for one moment, or allowed the three Confederate regiments to have marched over the field unopposed," Pierce noted, "Hall's battery and the left of the line would have been taken in flank and rear, with results no man can appreciate."[12]

Position 2: The Fight for the Railroad Cut

From your current position, turn to your left and walk across the bridge over the railroad cut. When you get to the other end of the bridge (the end closest to the traffic light), simply cross the park road to the other side. Face toward the traffic light. Chambersburg Road should run across your front. Look to your right and locate the monument crowned by the statue of a Zouave—a soldier wearing a uniform loosely patterned on those worn by French North African troops—that represents the 14th Brooklyn of Cutler's brigade. Now look to your left into the low ground to the right of the tracks right below you and locate the monuments to the 6th Wisconsin of the Iron Brigade and the 95th New York of Cutler's brigade that stand almost side by side.

What Happened Here?

The repulse of Cutler's line presented Davis's men with an opportunity. If they could take control of the railroad cut here, they might use its cover to launch attacks against the right flank and rear of the Iron Brigade line engaged in the Herbst woodlot to your right front. Alert to the crisis, Wadsworth ordered Cutler's 95th New York and the 14th Brooklyn near the McPherson barn to cross over to this side of the Chambersburg Road to stop the Confederates from taking possession of this railroad bed. The 14th Brooklyn advanced to the lip of the cut to your right, and the 95th New York hit it around the middle cut where you now stand. At nearly the same time, General Doubleday saw—or at least he claimed he saw—the brewing crisis and ordered the Iron Brigade's 6th Wisconsin, still in reserve near the Seminary buildings across the road, to attack; they advanced toward the stretch of the railroad bed to your left.

As enlisted man Henry Matrau wrote to his aunt, when the 6th Wisconsin "came up to the scene of action we were ordered 'forward in line, double quick march, load as you run.' It was sharp work." Even before they crossed the Chambersburg Road, they opened fire on Davis's men, some of whom already had passed through the railroad bed and pushed into the fields to your left and below you. Lieutenant

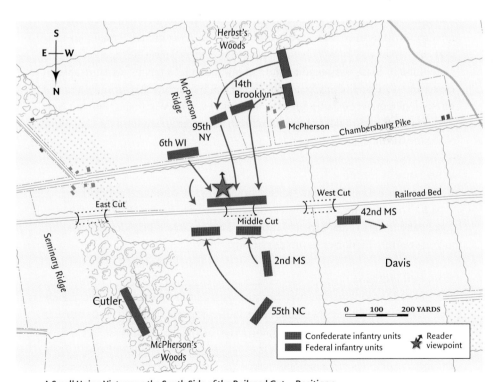

A Small Union Victory on the South Side of the Railroad Cut—Position 2

Colonel Rufus Dawes ordered a volley that checked Davis's advance and sent the Confederates running back to seek shelter in the railroad bed to your right and left. From that protected position, Dawes recalled, "they opened a murderous fire upon us." From his view in the ranks, Matrau agreed, noting that Davis's men poured "a

perfect storm of bullets into us & our men were falling in every direction."[13] Still, in short order, the New Yorkers and the Wisconsin troops cleared the fences and charged toward your position across the strip of ground between the road to the cut. In their reports, both Dawes and Colonel Edward B. Fowler of the 14th Brooklyn claim credit for initiating the advance. In the end, however, all three regiments arrived at the edge of the cut where their monuments now sit, aiming their rifles toward the masses of Confederate soldiers crowded into the low ground of the railroad bed. Resistance collapsed quickly. As Dawes reported, "the rebels began throwing down their arms in token of surrender." Hundreds of Mississippians and North Carolinians became Union prisoners; only those fortunate to be near the western cut to your right escaped to safety. When a detachment of Wisconsin soldiers sealed off the eastern end of the railroad bed to your left, some soldiers of the 55th North Carolina found themselves trapped. Although Lieutenant Joseph J. Hoyle of the Tar Heel regiment escaped capture, he wrote to his wife a week later: "I might say truly that I was in the very Jaws of death."[14] Dawes took special pleasure in reporting that Major John A. Blair, commanding the 2nd Mississippi, "upon my demand, surrendered his sword and regiment to me."[15] The 6th Wisconsin also captured the 2nd Mississippi regiment's battle flag. The success of the 6th Wisconsin, the 95th New York, and the 14th Brooklyn at the railroad cut temporarily stabilized the Union line along the Chambersburg Road.

Lieutenant Colonel Rufus R. Dawes, 6th Wisconsin Infantry, U.S.A. (USAMHI)

Who Fought Here?

C.S.A.: Davis's Mississippi and North Carolina brigade continued to fight here.

U.S.: The Union troops involved in this fight included the Iron Brigade's 6th Wisconsin and the 95th New York and 14th Brooklyn of Cutler's brigade, all belonging to Wadsworth's division of Reynolds's I Corps.

Who Fell Here?

The 2nd and 42nd Mississippi and the 55th North Carolina also participated in Pickett's Charge on July 3, but they suffered a significant proportion of their Gettysburg casualties in their July 1 fight. During the entire battle, the 2nd Mississippi lost 232 of its 492 men, the 42nd Mississippi lost 265 of its 575 men, and the 55th North Carolina lost 220 of its 640 men, but it is not always easy to separate the July 1 casualties from those of July 3.

In the fight at the railroad cut, the 6th Wisconsin lost 168 of its 344 men, while the 14th Brooklyn lost 217 of its 318 men and the 95th New York lost 114 of its 241 men. Each of these regiments would face fire again later in the battle, but the overwhelming proportion of their losses occurred in this location.

Individual vignettes. Corporal James Kelly served in Company B of the 6th Wisconsin. During the fight around the railroad cut, he took a bullet in the chest, and the round lodged itself there. Lieutenant Colonel Rufus Dawes, his commanding officer, wrote about the circumstances of Kelly's wounding: "I could tell a thousand stories of [my soldiers'] heroism: One young man, Corporal James Kelly of company 'B,' shot through the breast, came staggering up to me before he fell and opening his shirt to show the wound, said 'Colonel, won't you write to my folks that I died a soldier.'"[16] But there was no glory in Kelly's final days. The bullet lodged in a location that practically eliminated any chance of removing it. Kelly developed empyema, the accumulation of an excessive amount of pus, between his lungs and his chest wall, causing great pain and making it increasingly difficult to breathe. Fifteen days after Kelly received his wound, surgeon A. W. Preston of the 6th Wisconsin performed a process called "tapping" on him in an effort to remove the buildup of pus and fluid. *The Medical and Surgical History of the Civil War* recorded only four documented cases of applying this measure to an injury of this sort; three of the four cases ended in death.[17] Kelly died on July 21, and he is buried in the Soldiers' National Cemetery in grave A-18 of the Wisconsin plot.

Joshua Martin Adkins, a single, twenty-two-year-old merchant from Flewellin's Cross Roads, Mississippi, went to nearby Grenada and enlisted in Company D of the 42nd Mississippi Infantry on May 14, 1862. His enrolling officer was Hugh R. Miller, who became the colonel of the regiment and led it on the march into Pennsylvania. On the forms for Adkins's period of enlistment, it stated simply "for the war." At the very start of his service, he became the second sergeant of his company, but he did sufficiently well—his records show no prolonged absences for sickness or detached duty—that he began to draw pay as company first sergeant in March 1863. Sergeant Adkins was killed in action near the railroad cut on July 1, hit by a bullet. His colonel died two days later in Pickett's Charge.[18]

Who Lived Here?

Most of the fighting in this immediate area occurred on Edward McPherson's property. The farm in the open fields in the middle distance beyond and to the right of the stand of the 147th New York belonged to James Jack Wills, a local attorney and businessman. He was the father of attorney David Wills, who played such a large part in the establishment of the Soldiers' National Cemetery after the battle. James Jack Wills made a name for himself as a "farmer whose thrift and industry brought him great prosperity," and he served his community as county commissioner and justice of the peace. Wills lived in town during the Battle of Gettysburg and let his farm to a tenant named William Job. As the property owner, Wills filed for substantial damage claims after the battle, amounting to a sum that exceeded $1,000.[19]

What Did They Say about It Later?

Rivalries in the I Corps. Just like the squabble over credit for firing the first shots of the infantry fight, the veterans of the 14th Brooklyn and the 6th Wisconsin argued for years about their specific roles in the action at the railroad cut. Colonel Fowler perhaps started it when he wrote in his battle report that "the Sixth Wisconsin gallantly advanced to our assistance." Dawes challenged that notion from the start and continued his effort to place the 6th Wisconsin in the forefront of the fight. In 1885 he wrote: "It is due to the 6th Wisconsin for me to say that the regiment led the charge and by its dash forward substantially accomplished the results. . . . I have explained this exact because Colonel Fowler has claimed to have ordered me to charge. He had no command over me, and I did not know his regiment was there until I saw them come up and pour a volley into the cut upon the rebels who had already begun to surrender." The Brooklynites stuck to their claim, but even as late as late as 1910, George Fairfield of the 6th Wisconsin still felt the need to make clear his position: "Horace Greeley says the 14th Brooklyn did most of the capturing, but those Zouaves never came up on our left until after the surrender was completed and Col. R. R. Dawes had their flag."[20]

Driving directions to the next stop: Return to your vehicle and drive forward 0.1 miles to the stop sign at the T intersection of Buford and Wadsworth Avenues. Turn left and follow this one-way road to the west and then to the north 0.6 miles to the intersection with Mummasburg Road. Drive straight across the intersection and park in the parking lot below the tall monument.

2

The Battle Is Joined and Expands

STOP 5. EWELL ENTERS THE FIGHT

Orientation

You have arrived on Oak Hill, an eminence that played a significant role in the fighting during the afternoon of July 1. After you leave your vehicle, follow the paved sidewalk along the car parking area to the right to the point where it abruptly ends. Then face to the right and look out across the broad expanse of open fields. The large Eternal Light Peace Memorial should be on the hill over your right shoulder.

The road crossing your front approximately seventy yards ahead of you is the wartime Mummasburg Road. The open fields in the middle distance are those over which Generals Cutler and Davis fought during the late morning; the dense woodlot to your left front, just beyond a prominent line of monuments, is McPherson's Woods, where Cutler's men had withdrawn earlier in the day. In the distance, you should be able to pick out the large barn of the McPherson farm that stood just on the south side of Chambersburg Road. The trees you see behind the barn are Herbst's Woods, the location of the Iron Brigade clash with General Archer's brigade near General Reynolds's death site.

The Eternal Light Peace Memorial.

What Happened Here?

Fresh off its advance to the outskirts of Harrisburg and a bit of refreshment at Carlisle, Lieutenant General Richard S. Ewell's Second Corps of the Army of Northern Virginia broke camp early on July 1 to rejoin General Lee near Cashtown. Near present-day Biglerville, six miles north of Gettysburg, Ewell received a message from Lieutenant General A. P. Hill about the early fighting along the Chambersburg Road. He immediately turned the head of Major General Robert E. Rodes's division directly south toward Gettysburg and sent word to Major General Jubal A. Early to advance his division on the Old Harrisburg Road and approach the town from the northeast. Ewell also informed Lee of his decision and proceeded on the under-

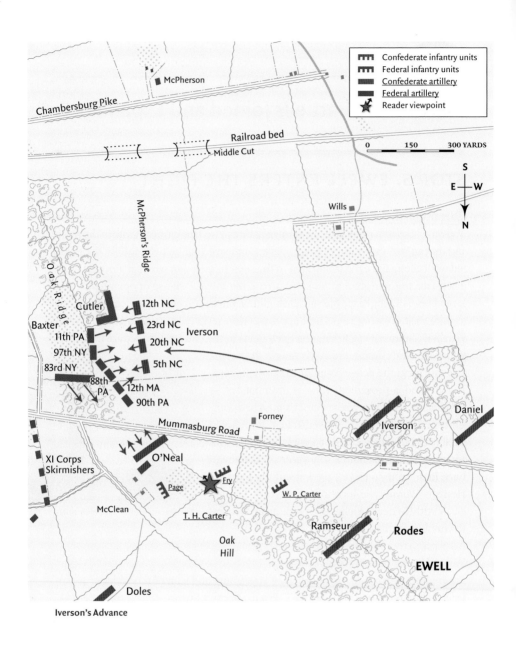

Iverson's Advance

McPherson

Chambersburg Pike

Railroad bed

Middle Cut

Wills

Confederate infantry units
Federal infantry units
Confederate artillery
Federal artillery
Reader viewpoint

0   150   300 YARDS

S
E —— W
N

McPherson's Ridge

Oak Ridge

Cutler
12th NC
Baxter
23rd NC   Iverson
11th PA
20th NC
97th NY
83rd NY   5th NC
88th
PA   12th MA
90th PA

Iverson

Daniel

Forney

Mummasburg Road   Iverson

XI Corps
Skirmishers   O'Neal

McClean   Page   Fry

W. P. Carter

T. H. Carter

Ramseur   **Rodes**

Oak
Hill

EWELL

Doles

standing that "in case we found the enemy's force very large, he [Lee] did not want a general engagement brought on till the rest of the army came up."

This position offered Ewell a number of advantages. First, the high ground gave him an outstanding artillery platform, and the batteries of Lieutenant Colonel Thomas H. Carter's battalion immediately wheeled into position on the southern and eastern faces of the hill here and to the left and rear of where you now stand. Second, Rodes's infantry had approached the battlefield in such a way that they seemed well positioned to launch an assault from this high ground to hit what appeared to be the right flank of the main Union battle line. At first, Ewell kept in mind Lee's caution against bringing on a fight, but then he witnessed the arrival of Union forces on the northern edge of Gettysburg, the low ground below you and to your left. These troops comprised two divisions of Major General Oliver O. Howard's newly arrived XI Corps, and Ewell observed signs that convinced him that they soon would attack his position. At that point, he decided that "it was too late to avoid an engagement without abandoning the position already taken up, and I determined to push the attack vigorously."

Lieutenant Colonel Thomas Hill Carter, C.S.A. (Wise)

Ewell ordered Rodes to attack. Rodes immediately determined to advance three of his five brigades from this area around Oak Hill against what he believed to be the right flank of the Union I Corps—the troops moving in McPherson's Woods to your left front. He expected Colonel Edward A. O'Neal's Alabamians to anchor the left flank of the attack, Brigadier General Alfred Iverson Jr.'s North Carolinians to be its center, and Brigadier General Junius Daniel's large North Carolina brigade—nearly 2,200 men strong—to "advance to support Iverson, if necessary; if not, to attack on his right as soon as possible."

Unfortunately for Rodes, his plan quickly fell apart. As he reported, his brigades, and even individual regiments, moved with alacrity "but not in accordance with my orders as to direction" and created great confusion. You will learn more about the fate of O'Neal's Alabamians at Stop 6 and the fate of Daniel's North Carolinians at Stop 11. The fields in front of you, however, became a slaughter pen for Iverson's Tar Heels (you will explore this action from the Union perspective at Position 2 of Stop 6).

Just to the left of McPherson's Woods, you should see a line of monuments representing the Union regiments that held that position—Oak Ridge—during the afternoon of July 1. When Iverson's men advanced toward the woodlot, however, they remained unaware of the presence of Brigadier General Henry L. Baxter's brigade just behind the crest of Oak Ridge. Baxter's command, part of Brigadier General John C. Robinson's division of Reynolds's I Corps, had just arrived from its reserve position near the seminary to anchor the right of the Union line on the Mummasburg Road.

He had established a strong position along the road and repelled O'Neal's first attack. But neither O'Neal nor anyone else alerted Iverson to Baxter's presence.

Thus, Iverson's men pushed forward into the green fields in front of you, unaware that Baxter then had ordered his men to change front to face these open fields. Usually the advance of skirmishers in front of the battle line would have revealed an enemy's presence, but Iverson did not give orders to send them forward; nor did he check to see if his regimental commanders tended to the matter. Baxter did not send out skirmishers, either, precisely for the purpose of concealing his line.

In the open fields to your left front on the far side of Mummasburg Road, nearly half of Iverson's men were killed or wounded when Baxter's men rose up from behind a stone wall at the crest, leveled their rifles, and fired volleys into the North Carolinians' ranks. As Iverson reported: "When I saw white handkerchiefs raised, and my line of battle still lying down in position, I characterized the surrender as disgraceful; but when I found afterward that 500 of my men were left lying dead and wounded on a line as straight as a dress parade, I exonerated, with one or two disgraceful individual exceptions, the survivors, and claim for the brigade that they nobly fought and died without a man running to the rear." Those who survived the initial volleys tried vainly to fight back; of Iverson's four regiments, however, only the 12th North Carolina, with the benefit of the slight protection offered by a low knoll, suffered less than 60 percent casualties. As General Rodes reported, Iverson's men "fought and died like heroes."[1] Private Henry Robinson Berkeley, a Virginia artilleryman who rode along the Mummasburg Road on July 2, recounted in his diary that day the effectiveness of those initial Union volleys: "I saw a sight which was perfectly sickening and heart-rending in the extreme. It would have satiated the most blood-thirsty and cruel man on God's earth. There were, [with]in a few feet of us, by actual count, seventy nine (79) North Carolinians laying dead in a straight line. I stood on the right and looked down their line. It was perfectly dressed. Three had fallen to the front, the rest had fallen backward; yet the feet of all these dead men were in a perfectly straight line. Great God! When will this horrid war stop?"[2]

Surprisingly, perhaps, the reports of Union officers about this action said little about the destruction their men had unleashed on Iverson's men. Colonel Charles Wheelock of the 97th New York said only: "Soon their second line appeared on our front. After firing several rounds, and finding them, as I thought, crippled, the order was given to charge." Captain Edmund Y. Patterson of the 88th Pennsylvania wrote only that, after changing position to face Iverson's men, "we immediately engaged the enemy, who were advancing on us. Having expended nearly all our ammunition, we charged upon the enemy, capturing a number of prisoners and the colors of the Twenty-Third North Carolina and the Sixteenth Alabama Regiments." Patterson erred in one regard; the 16th Alabama did not fight at Gettysburg.[3]

The soldiers in Iverson's ranks suffered in more than one way: some of their own countrymen branded them as cowards. Captain Benjamin Robinson of the 5th North Carolina sought to set the record straight. In a letter to Governor Zebulon Vance, he wrote: "In the hottest of the fire the enemy closed in upon our lines, pouring a murderous fire into our men, and in many cases bayonetted them, when some of the wounded cried out for quarter and raised their handkerchiefs as an appeal for mercy. This, Governor, has given rise to a report that the Regiment surrendered. That charge I denounce as an infamous falsehood and malicious slander. No surrender was authorized; no order was given for a cessation of the fire; our colors were brought in triumph from the field." He deplored the "ungenerous aspersions" cast upon "the pale bloody corpses of its noble men who lie sleeping on the hill sides near Gettysburg" that dishonored "the shrieks of its wounded on that field; [and] the mangled bodies of its officers and soldiers."[4]

Who Fought Here?

C.S.A.: Brigadier General Alfred Iverson Jr.'s 1,384-man brigade—the 5th, 12th, 20th, and 23rd North Carolina Infantry—of Rodes's Division in Ewell's Second Corps did the bulk of the infantry fighting in your front during the action described here; a few individual regiments, including the 3rd Alabama of O'Neal's brigade, also participated in this action. The artillery pieces emplaced on Oak Hill represent Lieutenant Colonel Thomas H. Carter's battalion that included the Jeff Davis (Miss.) Artillery, the King William (Va.) Artillery, the Morris (Va.) Artillery, and the Orange (Va.) Artillery.

U.S.: Brigadier General Henry L. Baxter's 1,452-man brigade in Brigadier General John C. Robinson's division of Reynolds's I Corps included the 12th Massachusetts; the 83rd and 97th New York; and the 11th, 88th, and 90th Pennsylvania Infantry.

Who Commanded Here?

Lieutenant General Richard Stoddert Ewell (1817–72) commanded the Second Corps of the Army of Northern Virginia. He graduated from West Point in the class of 1840 along with future Union generals William Tecumseh Sherman and George Henry Thomas. "Old Bald Top," as he was sometimes called, spent his entire antebellum service in the West and Southwest, winning a brevet for gallantry in the Mexican War. Never rising above the rank of a company grade officer in twenty years of service, Captain Ewell resigned his Regular Army commission in May 1861 and joined the Confederate army. He became a brigadier general in June 1861 and major general in January 1862. He fought with distinction at First Manassas and commanded a division of infantry in Jackson's Valley Campaign of

Lieutenant General
Richard S. Ewell,
C.S.A. (USAMHI)

1862 and during the Seven Days Battles on the Virginia peninsula. At the Battle of Groveton during the Second Manassas Campaign, he fell seriously wounded and suffered the amputation of a leg. Returning to duty with the Army of Northern Virginia in the late spring of 1863, he was promoted to the rank of lieutenant general and named to command the newly reorganized Second Corps after the death of Thomas J. "Stonewall" Jackson. Although his performance at the Battle of Gettysburg usually generates controversy, his actions in the early part of the campaign, particularly at the Battle of Second Winchester in June 1863, merit higher marks. After Gettysburg, Ewell continued in corps command until the Battle of Spotsylvania in the spring of 1864, after which his health limited his command opportunities. Still, he commanded the Richmond defenses until very late in the war. Captured at Saylor's Creek on April 6, 1865, General Ewell retired to his farm near Spring Hill, Tennessee, where he died in 1872. As Ewell brought his forces onto the field at Gettysburg, the editors of the *Southern Illustrated News* finalized the editing of their featured profile of the general, complete with a woodcut portrait. The editors sang Ewell's praises and hinted at even better things to come: "The capture of Winchester [two weeks earlier on the march into Pennsylvania] was one of the most magnificent achievements of the war, and places its author at once, in the foremost ranks of our generals. It is remarkable that Dr. Hancock sent to a cork-leg maker in Philadelphia, to whom, before the war, he had frequently sent orders, for a leg for General Ewell, adding that he need not send it on, for that the general would come for it himself very shortly. It seems, from present appearances, as though it might be so."[5]

Major General Robert Emmett Rodes (1829–64) holds the distinction of being the only division or corps commander in the Army of Northern Virginia who did not graduate from West Point. A Virginia Military Institute graduate and professor, he worked as an engineer for a railroad company at the outbreak of the war. He became a company commander in the 5th Alabama Infantry and soon rose to colonel of the regiment. Promoted to brigadier general in October 1861, Rodes took command of Ewell's old brigade and saw action on the Virginia peninsula, at South Mountain, and at Antietam. Appointed to division command in January 1863, Rodes and his men served in the forefront of Jackson's flank attack against the Union army at Chancellorsville, and he temporarily commanded the Second Corps upon the mortal wounding of Jackson. After Gettysburg, Rodes continued in division command through the Battles of the Wilderness, Spotsylvania, and Cold Harbor, and he took part in Major General Jubal A. Early's raid down the Shenandoah valley toward Washington in July 1864. General Rodes was killed in action at the Third Battle of Winchester on September 19, 1864.

Major General
Robert E. Rodes,
C.S.A. (USAMHI)

Brigadier General Alfred Iverson Jr. (1829–1911), son of a U.S. senator, got an early start on his military career, serving as a seventeen-year-old second lieutenant leading Georgia volunteers in the Mexican War. He received a direct commission as a first lieutenant into the Regular Army in 1855 but resigned in March 1861 to join the Confederate army as colonel of the 20th North Carolina Infantry. Prior to Gettysburg, Iverson commanded his regiment in the Seven Days Battles on the Virginia peninsula and at South Mountain and Antietam. He was promoted to brigadier general in November 1862 and took command of a brigade of infantry, which he led at Fredericksburg, Chancellorsville, and Gettysburg. Because of the large number of casualties sustained by his brigade on July 1 at Gettysburg, Iverson received a vote of no confidence from its survivors. General Lee removed him from command on July 16. In October 1863 Iverson received orders relieving him of duty with the Army of Northern Virginia and sending him to command state forces in Rome, Georgia. Iverson subsequently led a division of cavalry opposing General Sherman's advances during the Atlanta, Savannah, and Carolina Campaigns. Iverson became a citrus farmer in Florida after the war. He died in Atlanta in 1911 and is buried there in Oakland Cemetery.

Who Fell Here?

Iverson's regiments lost heavily here. The 5th North Carolina lost 289 of its 473 men. The protected 12th North Carolina lost proportionately fewer—79 of its 219 men. The 20th North Carolina lost 253 of its 372 men; and the 23rd North Carolina suffered worst of all, losing 282 of its 316 men—including Colonel Daniel Christie, who fell mortally wounded—for an 89.2 percent loss. Carter's artillery battalion lost 77 of its 385 men.

Individual vignettes. Captain George T. Baskerville, the valedictorian of his class at the University of North Carolina—he delivered his graduation address in Latin—had no military ambitions. He enlisted in the 23rd North Carolina, however, and his men elected him captain of Company I. The bond between the captain and his soldiers became so strong that he turned down promotions to remain with them. He fell mortally wounded on July 1 and died the next day. As a comrade recalled, Captain Baskerville's "devoted wife . . . crushed at the tidings of his death, took to her bed and never rose again. . . . Plighting their troth when children, marrying very early in life, their devotion to each other was complete. And when the sturdy oak was stricken down, the clinging vine fell with it."[6]

Captain George Baskerville, 23rd North Carolina, fell mortally wounded here. (Clark)

Leonidas Torrence went to Garysburg to volunteer for service in Company H of the 23rd North Carolina Infantry on July 18, 1861. He did not take to soldiering at first, falling ill and spending time in hospitals; a bout with typhoid over the winter of 1861–62 lingered for a while. He finally returned to the ranks, however, until he fell severely wounded at Antietam on September 17, 1862. He was given a furlough to recuperate from that injury and then received a promotion to corporal. After Baxter's Union troops fired their volleys from behind their stone wall, Corporal Torrence lay among the badly injured. A comrade wrote this letter to Leonidas's parents to break the bad news: "Leonidas was shot between the eye and ear and in the thigh. I think the ball that went in his head went near his brain. He did not know any thing for several hours. . . . When he was shot he was lying in a hollow in a very muddy place. All that were badly wounded and killed was shot in the same hollow. I was shot before the Regiment got to this place. Leonidas and I went into battle side by side. We promised each other if one got hurt to do all we could for him."[7] There was little Leonidas's friend could do for him, however. Litter bearers carried him to a hospital, but Corporal Torrence died of a fractured skull on July 7.

Who Lived Here?

The fields south of the Mummasburg Road directly opposite the Eternal Light Peace Memorial were owned by John Swope Forney, born in Gettysburg in 1830. In 1861 Forney married Mary E. Shriver, and in 1862 he purchased this farm along the Mummasburg Road. The house sat along the road near the intersection of Buford Avenue and Mummasburg Road to your right front. When the fighting started, the Forneys, with their six-month-old daughter, fled to the home of Mary's father, who lived farther away from town and away from the fighting. When the Forneys returned to the farm after the battle, they found that "everything about the place was completely destroyed by the battle except the house and barn which were riddled by shot and shell."[8] The house eventually fell into disrepair and was removed by the National Park Service to make the area more presentable for the dedication of the Eternal Light Peace Memorial in 1938. Many of the North Carolina soldiers killed in the fight described above were buried in trench graves in the fields of the Forney farm that became known as "Iverson's Pits."

What Did They Say about It Later?

Reassessing Iverson. Iverson's incompetence has become a standard element of the Gettysburg story. After the war, a historical sketch of the 23rd North Carolina includes this terse commentary:

> [O]ur brigade commander (Iverson) after ordering us forward, did not follow us in that advance, and our alignment soon became false. There seems to have been utter ignorance of the force crouching behind the stone wall. For our brigade to have assailed such a stronghold thus held, would have been a desperate

undertaking. To advance southeast against the enemy, visible in the [McPherson's] woods at that corner of the field, exposing our left flank to an enfilading fire from the stronghold was fatal. Yet this is just what we did. And unwarned, unled as a brigade, went forward Iverson's deserted band to its doom. Deep and long must the desolate homes and orphan children of North Carolina rue the rashness of that hour.

In a postscript, it was noted that "Iverson's part in the heroic struggle of his brigade seems to have begun and ended with the order to move forward and 'Give them hell.'"[9]

In a strictly military sense, as author Robert J. Wynstra recently has argued, Iverson was not solely to blame for the destruction of his brigade. He lays some of the fault on General Rodes. "After he arrived on the [Oak] hill, Rodes let two hours slip away before launching his assault against the Federal position on Oak Ridge," Wynstra notes. He attributes to Rodes some of the blame for "allowing Iverson to advance his brigade into the field without a screen of skirmishers" to cover his front. Additionally, Rodes may have been ill that day; a staff officer noticed that he seemed "flushed with fever" on July 1. Recent scholarship also has uncovered important underlying factors that set the stage for Iverson's quick downfall. Governor Zebulon Vance greatly influenced officer promotions and appointments in North Carolina brigades, and he was no friend of Iverson. The general's own brigade suffered from political and personal feuds among its regimental officers that created a fractious and inharmonious command climate on the best of days. Oftentimes, factors well beyond the battlefield shape the history we study in both obvious and subtle ways.[10]

The Eternal Light Peace Memorial. The origin of the Eternal Light Peace Memorial, the tall monument on Oak Hill, goes back to 1913, the fiftieth anniversary of the battle. Many of the veterans who attended the massive reunion at Gettysburg that year expressed a desire to construct a lasting symbol of the unity of the nation following the Civil War. Another twenty-five years passed before their dream became reality. Seven states made monetary contributions: Pennsylvania, Virginia, Wisconsin, Illinois, Tennessee, New York, and Indiana. On July 3, 1938, the seventy-fifth anniversary of the battle, President Franklin D. Roosevelt, in the presence of 1,800 Civil War veterans aged 88 to 112 years old, unveiled the monument. This was the last reunion of Civil War veterans, and people came from all parts of the country to witness the event. Estimates of the number of attendees at the dedication ceremony that day range from 250,000 to 400,000. Atop the forty-foot-high shaft is a natural gas–fed flame that symbolizes eternal peace. The eight-foot-high bas-relief figures of two women on the front of the memorial represent the peace and goodwill existing between the people of the North and the South, with an eagle representing the nation.[11]

Driving directions to the next stop: Return to your vehicle and pull out of the one-way parking lot to the stop sign at the intersection with Mummasburg Road. Drive straight across the intersection and park in the designated parking lot on the left just beyond the gray observation tower.

STOP 6. OAK RIDGE

You will visit two positions at this stop to learn about the efforts of Brigadier General Henry L. Baxter's brigade.

Position 1: Baxter versus O'Neal

Orientation

Stand near the unique tree-trunk monument (with a mother bird feeding her hatchlings still in the nest) of the 90th Pennsylvania Infantry near the observation tower. Face the two-lane road and look down the slope into the low ground on the other side of it. The road passing across your immediate front is Mummasburg Road, a wartime avenue. The Confederates of Ewell's Second Corps were positioned on Oak Hill, the high ground to your left front.

What Happened Here?

You are standing on the extreme right flank of the Union I Corps line as it was positioned in the early afternoon of July 1, shortly before Iverson's attack. Just after noon, when General Howard's XI Corps began to emerge from the town into the low ground in front of you, General Doubleday initially hoped that the reinforcements would come up to this high ground and "connect with the right of my line" to

The slope beyond the 90th Pennsylvania Infantry monument and the McClean farm.

confront the Confederates approaching from the west. The presence of Carter's batteries on Oak Hill, however, made it quite clear to the XI Corps troops that the high ground in question already had come under Confederate control. More important, the two XI Corps divisions Howard sent forward faced an even more dire threat approaching from the north. They had to hold back some of Rodes's men advancing toward the town along the Carlisle Road—look for traffic in the middle distance to locate this road—as well as Early's division nearing Gettysburg on the Old Harrisburg Road, beyond the Carlisle Road where you see the tall red-and-white tower. Once Howard's two divisions covered those two approaches, they ran out of troops to effect a link with the I Corps. The XI Corps left flank rested on the Mummasburg Road in the low ground to your right front, just beyond the single house sitting on the left of the road. The I Corps would have to fend for itself, and that explains how General Baxter's brigade deployed here.

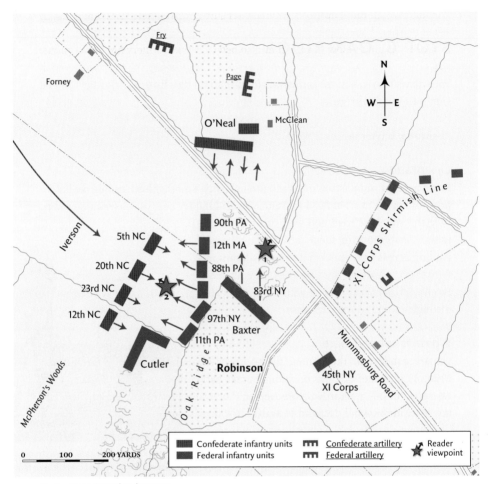

Baxter stops O'Neal and Iverson

When Doubleday realized that Ewell's Confederates had taken possession of Oak Hill, he initially considered pulling back toward the seminary, about half a mile behind you. He decided against that move, however, concerned that the open fields there left his men too vulnerable to Ewell's newly placed batteries. Therefore, he ordered Brigadier General John C. Robinson, holding his newly arrived I Corps division in reserve at the seminary, to send a brigade to close the gap with the XI Corps. Robinson sent Baxter's 1,452 men to extend the right flank of Cutler's brigade from McPherson's Woods to the Mummasburg Road. Thus they originally planned to take up a line that faced to the west. The stone wall behind you roughly parallels the intended location of Baxter's line; his soldiers would have faced the open fields on the other side of it.

Shortly after noon, however, when Baxter's men arrived here, they could readily see that a gap of about 400 yards separated them from the left flank of the XI Corps in the low ground below. Worse, they also began to take artillery fire from Colonel Carter's Confederate artillery and prepared for an infantry attack from an unanticipated direction. Baxter saw O'Neal's Alabama brigade advance directly toward the gap between the two Union corps, moving through the Moses McClean farm, its red barn clearly visible below you. Acting quickly, Baxter deployed his men along this side of the Mummasburg Road facing northward toward the charging Alabamians on the McClean property. From this position, his regiments fired effective volleys into O'Neal's ranks. As Captain Robert E. Park of the 12th Alabama recorded in his diary: "We passed the woods and a wheat field [in front of you], where Private Rogers, our Baptist preacher, had his knee shattered by a minié ball."[1] Baxter made little reference to the efficient reaction of his brigade to the unexpected threat, however, noting only that "indications being that we should be attacked on our right flank, I at once changed front" to meet it.

Baxter's men also benefited from the active participation of four companies of the 45th New York under the command of Captain Francis Irsch. The 45th New York belonged to Major General Carl Schurz's division of the XI Corps, the command that held the left flank of the XI line in the low ground off to your right front. The New Yorkers advanced to the McClean farm buildings, took a number of Alabamians as prisoners, and contributed significantly to the ultimate repulse of O'Neal. In the meantime, the 45th New York's remaining six companies under Lieutenant Colonel Adolphus Dobke attempted to lessen—if they could not close—the gap between the two corps. He did not have enough men to forge a link.

Colonel O'Neal downplayed the importance of his contact with Baxter's brigade. He merely wrote that he "found the enemy strongly posted and in heavy force, and, after a desperate and bloody fight of about half an hour, we were compelled to fall back." He did not inform Rodes or any other senior commander about the nature or location of the opposition he had met. Through his inaction, he contributed to the slaughter of Iverson's North Carolina brigade.

Position 2: Baxter versus Iverson

Orientation

Now return to the parking area but cross to the other side of the road and locate the monument to the 12th Massachusetts Infantry. This regiment was nicknamed the "Webster Regiment," and you will see a bust of Daniel Webster on its front; Fletcher Webster, Daniel's son, served as the regiment's first colonel until his death in battle at Second Bull Run in August 1862. To the left of the 12th Massachusetts monument you will see another stone tribute saluting the 88th Pennsylvania Infantry.

Behind both monuments you will find unimproved earthen paths that lead about 100 paces out into the open field. Follow either path to the small stone marker on the spot where the 88th Pennsylvania captured a North Carolina battle flag. Once at the marker, look out into the open field; the Eternal Light Peace Memorial on Oak Hill should be to your right.

What Happened Here?

Shortly after O'Neal's repulse, Iverson began his attack. His North Carolinians advanced over Oak Hill and through the Forney orchard and farm—its replanted trees can be seen across the valley from you—and marched diagonally across your front heading toward McPherson's Woods on your left. The 3rd Alabama became detached from O'Neal's command and attached itself to Iverson's right flank. Baxter's regiments redeployed from the Mummasburg Road to meet this new threat.

Turn around and face toward the line of the monuments where the earthen path started. Baxter's men now left their original positions where they stopped O'Neal and formed a new line on the reverse slope of this ridge—Oak Ridge—that parallels the line of monuments you now see. Confederate troops advancing across the low ground in these fields could not see the Union soldiers as long as they determined to remain concealed. Many of Baxter's men took cover behind a rock wall on that high ground. When Iverson's men were approximately as close to that wall as you are to the line of monuments, Baxter's troops rose up and fired directly into their line. The North Carolinians' left flank—where you now stand—suffered especially high losses.

These volleys seriously depleted the ammunition supply of Baxter's men, but that did not stop them from taking decisive action after staggering Iverson's front ranks. As Colonel Charles Wheelock of the 97th New York reported, "the order was given to charge." Suffering almost no casualties in this sudden advance, Wheelock's regiment "brought out as prisoners 213 officers and men of the Twentieth North Carolina Regiment, with their colors. We took more prisoners than we had men in our regiment."[2] The marker at this stop, as you can see, marks the point where the 88th Pennsylvania also captured a flag, one of the most prized trophies in Civil War combat.

On a day that ultimately ended with a costly Union withdrawal, it was still possible for localized success. The fight of Baxter's brigade on Oak Ridge in the early afternoon of July 1 ranks among such small victories. But Baxter's men did not enjoy their success for long. You will revisit this position at Stop 10 to explore the collapse of the right flank of I Corps later in the afternoon of July 1.

Who Fought Here?

C.S.A.: Engaged here were Colonel Edward A. O'Neal's 1,688-man brigade of Rodes's division of Ewell's Second Corps, including the 3rd, 5th, 6th, 12th, and 26th

Alabama Infantry; and Brigadier General Alfred Iverson's North Carolina brigade (detailed at the previous stop) and artillery from Carter's artillery battalion.

U.S.: Brigadier General Henry L. Baxter's brigade of Robinson's division of Reynolds's I Corps—including the 12th Massachusetts; the 83rd and 97th New York; and the 11th, 88th, and 90th Pennsylvania Infantry Regiments—served here. Four companies of the 45th New York of Brigadier General Alexander Schimmelfennig's brigade in Major General Carl Schurz's division of Howard's XI Corps also participated in the fight at the McClean farm.

Who Commanded Here?

Brigadier General Henry L. Baxter (1821–73), born in Delaware County, New York, moved at the age of ten with his family to Michigan. In 1849 he went to California, where he stayed for three years before returning to Michigan and the lumber business. At the outbreak of the Civil War, he won election to the captaincy of a company in the 7th Michigan Infantry. In July 1862 he became lieutenant colonel of the regiment. Baxter suffered a severe wound during the Peninsula Campaign. Returning to duty in time for Fredericksburg, he was again wounded leading the assault boat crossing of the Rappahannock River on December 11, 1862, his left shoulder shattered by a bullet. He returned to active service as a brigadier general in March 1863. In the spring of 1864, while still in com-

Brigadier General Henry L. Baxter, U.S.A. (USAMHI)

mand of a brigade, Baxter again fell wounded during the Battle of the Wilderness. He mustered out of service in August 1865 and returned to Jonesville, Michigan, and the lumber business.

Colonel Edward Asbury O'Neal (1818–90), a native of Madison County, Alabama, graduated from LaGrange College in 1836. He practiced law in Florence, Alabama. One of the state's leading secessionists, he enlisted in the 9th Alabama Infantry Regiment upon the outbreak of the war and was soon elected major and then lieutenant colonel. In 1862, now a colonel, O'Neal commanded the 26th Alabama Infantry in the Peninsula Campaign and fell wounded at Seven Pines. He was again wounded at Boonsboro in the Maryland Campaign and led an infantry brigade at Chancellorsville and Gettysburg. Prior to the Gettysburg Campaign, General Lee had recommended O'Neal for a brigadier generalship, which was approved. After O'Neal's poor showing at Gettysburg, however, Lee never delivered the commission, and the Confederate Congress retracted its confirmation. In early 1864 Colonel O'Neal and the 26th Alabama went home on recruiting duty and left the Army of Northern Virginia. O'Neal saw action in the Atlanta Campaign and finished his wartime service in North Alabama gathering up deserters. After the war, O'Neal resumed his law practice in Alabama and won election as governor in 1882 and 1884. He died at Florence, Alabama, in November 1890 and is buried there.

Who Fell Here?

C.S.A.: You learned the fate of Iverson's brigade at the last stop. O'Neal's Alabama brigade, 1,688 strong, fought again on July 3 at Culp's Hill—you will meet them again at Stop 30—but the majority of its casualties fell in the fight in the McClean farmyard attempting to penetrate the gap between the right of the I Corps and the left of the XI Corps. The 3rd Alabama lost 91 of its 350 men; the 5th Alabama lost 209 of its 317 men; the 6th Alabama lost 160 of its 382 men; the 12th Alabama lost 83 of its 317 men; and the 26th Alabama lost 130 of its 319 men. The 3rd Alabama became detached from O'Neal early in the action and fell in with Iverson's brigade; most of its casualties fell on July 1.

U.S.: Since they fought on the defensive and enjoyed the protection of stone walls part of the time, Baxter's regiments did not suffer a high number of killed or wounded. The 12th Massachusetts lost 57 of its 261 men; the 83rd New York lost 24 of its 199 men; the 97th New York lost 48 of its 236 men; the 11th Pennsylvania lost 67 of its 270 men; the 88th Pennsylvania lost 59 of its 274 men; and the 90th Pennsylvania lost 53 of its 208 men. Later in the afternoon, however, when this position collapsed, regimental casualty totals swelled with the names of soldiers who were captured or simply went missing. In this way, the 12th Massachusetts would lose an additional 62 men; the 83rd New York, 58 men; the 97th New York, 78 men; the 11th Pennsylvania, 60 men; the 88th Pennsylvania, 51 men, and the 90th Pennsylvania, 40 men. In all, Baxter lost 44.7 percent of his brigade at Gettysburg. The 45th New York of the XI Corps lost 224 of its 375 men, but only a few of them fell during this initial skirmishing; 178 of those lost were classified as captured or missing, mostly in the collapse of the XI Corps line and the retreat through Gettysburg later on the afternoon of July 1.

Individual vignettes. When Francis James Price left his home in England and emigrated to the United States, his future seemed limitless. He settled near Greensburg in western Pennsylvania, became a plasterer by trade, and on Christmas Day 1855 married Margaret Emily Hawk. They soon started a family. Thomas George Price entered the world on Christmas Eve in 1856, and Edward Charles Price was born on February 9, 1858. When the Civil War began, Francis, now aged thirty-two—though his gray hair likely made him appear older—enlisted as a private in Company K of the 11th Pennsylvania Infantry on November 23, 1861. When he left home, Margaret was pregnant, and on May 26, 1862, she gave birth to Maggie Catherine Price. On July 1 on Oak Ridge, Private Price was killed in action. At home in Greensburg, the new widow applied immediately for a pension. Complications arose when the adjutant general could find no evidence of her husband's enlistment and had to obtain confirmation of his service from regimental records. When Margaret attempted to provide proof of her marriage, she discovered that the Lutheran minister in Greensburg who had performed the ceremony had kept no official records; he had to be deposed in person to verify that he indeed had married the couple. Already burdened with sorrows, the family received a second hard blow when little Maggie died on December 5, 1863. Finally, in July 1864, Margaret Emily Price won approval for the payment of an $8 monthly stipend, and two years later she received an additional $2 each month for each of her two surviving sons until they reached the age of sixteen. Margaret remarried in 1881 and gave up her pension, but after her second husband—a nonveteran—died, she reapplied for and received her pension in 1902 as the widow of Private Francis James Price.[3]

Private John Preskitt of Company F, 12th Alabama Infantry, of O'Neal's brigade, enlisted in Tuskegee on June 12, 1861. Initially, the rigors of military life wore on him greatly. Illness sent him to army medical facilities on several occasions, including a three-month stay at Richmond's Chimborazo Hospital over the winter of 1861–62. Preskitt was then captured at the Battle of South Mountain in September 1862 and later paroled. Back with his regiment for the Gettysburg Campaign, he went into action with his regiment on July 1. His company commander, Captain Robert E. Park, wrote in his diary of the private's fate: "Poor John Preskitt was mortally wounded and died. He died saying 'All is right.'" On July 2, Park, who himself had fallen wounded, added: "Limped inside the barn and saw Preskitt's body, and urged a decent burial [by] the ambulance corps. He leaves a very helpless family."[4]

Who Lived Here?

The land over which O'Neal's brigade advanced centered upon the white house and red barn of the farm below you. The farm was owned by Moses McClean, who was a prominent attorney in Adams County. During the mid-1840s, he served in the U.S. House of Representatives as a Democratic congressman, representing the district that included Adams County. McClean and his family lived in town on Baltimore Street during the battle and rented the farm to David H. Beams. During the battle, Beams himself was away from home, serving with the 165th Pennsylvania Infantry. When O'Neal's brigade advanced across the farm on July 1, Harriet Beams and her three-year-old child left for a place of safety. Confederate troops occupied the house during the battle, and when Harriet subsequently returned, she found that all of their possessions were either destroyed or stolen. Today, the house, barn, and adjoining acreage are owned by the National Park Service; park staff live in the house, while the barn is used for storage.[5]

What Did They Say about It Later?

When the veterans returned to dedicate their monuments, most celebrated national reunion. A few others, however, chose instead to recall why they had fought and touted the superiority of the Union cause over that of the Confederacy.

At the dedication of the 88th Pennsylvania monument on September 11, 1889, former Lieutenant Colonel George Wagner served as the speaker. He concluded his speech this way:

> Gettysburg! A name, before the eventful days of July 1863, known only to the people of this locality, but then made famous and renowned to all parts of the earth—a name that will be celebrated to the most distant ages of the world—a name that will be forever historic, made so by the brave men who here stood in the defense of their country's laws and flag. Where are these men? Some lie dead beneath your feet; the bones of others lie bleaching upon many other southern battle-fields; others have fallen a prey to disease or age, whilst but a remnant of the grand old Army of the Potomac is left to participate in the reunion of this day. Gettysburg! The slaughter on your fields was not in vain; from your green slopes the tide of rebellion ebbed and shrank, until, month by month, it sank lower and lower, and finally disappeared.[6]

Driving directions to the next stop: Pull out of the parking lot and turn left at the Y intersection, following the road down the hill. At the next stop sign at the intersection with Mummasburg Road and the railroad crossing, turn right and drive 0.3 miles to the T intersection with Howard Avenue on your left. Turn left onto Howard Avenue and drive 0.2 miles to the second grouping of cannons on your right and park at the monument to Lieutenant William Wheeler's 13th New York Battery.

STOP 7. THE ARTILLERY DUEL ON THE XI CORPS LINE

Orientation

After leaving your vehicle, stand behind either of the two center cannons and look in the direction they are pointing.

What Happened Here?

At about noon on July 1, Major General Oliver O. Howard's XI Corps arrived in Gettysburg. Since Howard was senior to General Doubleday, he took over command of all Union troops in contact with enemy forces. Ordering Doubleday to hold his I Corps on McPherson's Ridge, Howard made two important decisions about the deployment of his own XI Corps. First, he ordered Brigadier General Adolph von Steinwehr to have his division erect defenses on the key terrain—and potential rallying point—of Cemetery Hill, which you visited at Stop

The view into the field from the center cannons of Lieutenant Wheeler's 13th New York Battery.

1. Second, he sent his other two divisions under Major General Carl Schurz and Brigadier General Francis C. Barlow north through the town to this area. As the more senior in rank, Schurz took command.

As you learned at Stop 6, Howard initially planned to deploy these two divisions on Doubleday's right flank, extending his line west of town onto Oak Hill, the high ground to your left front. When Schurz and Barlow emerged from the town, however, the Confederates already held Oak Hill in force. Moreover, Colonel Devin's cavalry scouts reported to Schurz the presence of enemy forces heading south toward Gettysburg on both the Carlisle Road, visible to your right front, and the Old Harrisburg Road, located near the red and white tower to your far right. Thus, as Schurz reported to Howard after the battle, after reporting this new information, "I received an order from you to remain in the position I then occupied and to push my skirmishers forward as far as possible."

Schurz intended for his own division—now temporarily under the command of Brigadier General Alexander Schimmelfennig—to defend the ground between the Mummasburg Road, coming down the slope to your left, and the Carlisle Road to your near right. He expected his own line to link with that of Barlow's division, which he assigned to defend the approaches to Gettysburg between the Carlisle Road and the Old Harrisburg Road farther to the right of your current position. You

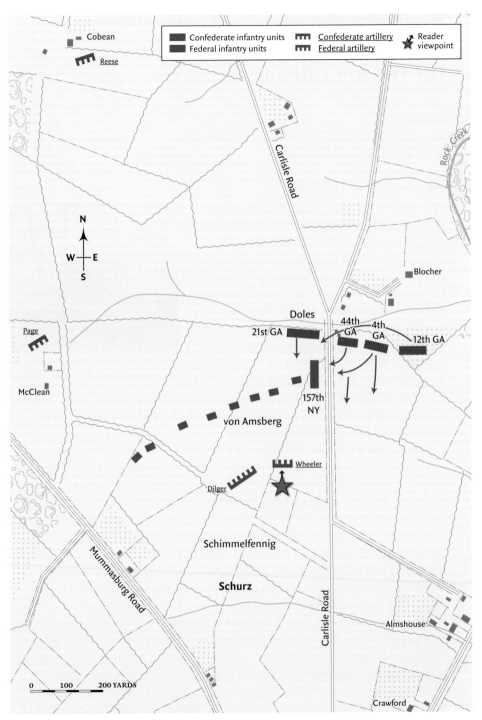

The Fighting between Mummasburg and Carlisle Roads

will learn the fate of Barlow's division at Stop 8. Here you will consider the action of Schimmelfennig's division and, especially, two batteries of XI Corps artillery that supported it.

A typical division in the Army of the Potomac contained three brigades, but each of the three divisions in the XI Corps had only two brigades. When Schimmelfennig took over division command, he turned over his brigade to Colonel George von Amsberg. Now he ordered von Amsberg to throw out a heavy skirmish line—not a fully developed line of battle—between the McClean farm buildings to your left front and the Carlisle Road. The 45th New York held the left of the line closest to the Mummasburg Road, and that explains how they came in contact with O'Neal's Alabamians when they launched the attack you explored at Stop 6. The 61st Ohio, the 74th Pennsylvania, and the 82nd Illinois extended the line eastward toward your position, ending at the Carlisle Road to your right. Schimmelfennig's second brigade, that of Colonel Wladimir Krzyzanowski, remained in reserve at the northern edge of town (behind you).

Von Amsberg's regiments found themselves engaged in heated skirmishing almost from the very start. They confronted Major Eugene Blackford's battalion of Alabama sharpshooters of Rodes's division. The Alabamians already had fought for several hours, skirmishing with Devin's troopers and covering Rodes's advance onto the battlefield. They had taken part, as well, in O'Neal's fight at the McClean barn. Blackford did not consider von Amsberg's force a great threat. As he reported, "There was no movement by any force heavier than a double line of sharpshooters, whom our men invariably drove back, charging them once in gallant style."

If the infantry fight in this sector did not develop into a particularly intense engagement, the artillery duel between two XI Corps batteries posted here in the low ground and the Confederate batteries of Carter's battalion on Oak Hill demonstrated the skill of the gunners on both sides. The six Napoleons of Captain Hubert

Oak Hill from the Mummasburg Road, with the McClean farm in the middle distance. (USAMHI)

Dilger's Battery I, 1st Ohio Light Artillery, reached the field first, and its monument and representative cannons are posted along the park road to your left. Lieutenant William Wheeler's 13th New York Battery arrived about thirty minutes later and took up a position on Dilger's right, near this location. As Wheeler wrote to his family shortly after the battle, Dilger's battery "had only smooth bores," so "he was no match for his opponent and was getting cut up badly, so I was ordered forward to help him . . . and soon showed the enemy that they had [a] three-inch rifled battery to contend with, and they had to shut up entirely."

Dilger made quick use of Wheeler's presence, determining to use the rifled guns' fire to cover the forward movement of his Napoleons. He wanted to move farther forward into the fields to your left front to close the range between his smoothbores and the Confederate guns on Oak Hill. "As soon as he got in position," Wheeler recounted, "a dreadful fire was opened on him, and I had the chief benefit of this as I moved after him; all the shots fired too high for him fell into my Battery."[1] Dilger's gunnery from his advanced position seriously damaged at least one of Carter's batteries, Captain R. C. M. Page's Morris Artillery of Virginia. "His loss here was heavy," reported Carter, with "2 men killed, 2 mortally wounded, 26 more or less badly wounded, and 17 horses killed and disabled." Still, Page's men bore up "with unflinching courage" until ordered to retire. One section of two guns advanced to within "800 to 1,000 yards" of Dilger's battery to silence it, but, as the Ohio battery commander reported, "I finally succeeded in silencing them, with a loss of five carriages, which they had to leave on the ground, after several efforts to bring them to the rear with new horses."[2]

Captain Hubert "Leather-breeches" Dilger, U.S.A. (USAMHI)

Dilger had authority to post Wheeler's guns as well as his own, and when he advanced, the New York battery remained close by on his right. As Wheeler tried to keep up, he wrote, his battery "came suddenly on a very substantial fence which the men could not tear down, and we had to wait, under a very heavy fire, until axes could be brought from the caissons" to cut a hole through it. During their wait, Wheeler's New Yorkers continued to take fire from Carter's batteries. One shell made a strong impression on Wheeler: "I saw an infantry man's leg taken off by a shot, and whirled like a stone through the air, until it came against a caisson with a loud whack." Once through the fence and into position, however, "we were again too much for the opposing battery, and were getting along finely."[3] Both Dilger and Wheeler fired from multiple positions during the afternoon.

There is no doubt that the fire of these Union artillery batteries inflicted significant damage on both the Confederate artillery and infantry. Dilger and Wheeler fired at O'Neal's Alabama brigade in the area of the McClean farm, and Captain Robert E. Park of the 12th Alabama noted its effects in his diary entry for July 1, 1863: The "Alabama brigade, under Col. E. A. O'Neal, was shelled fiercely. Capt. Jas. T. Davis, of Co. 'D,' was killed near me, and his brains scattered upon me. He was a brave, good man. Another shell exploded in my company and wounded Corporal J. H. Eason and Private Lucius Williams, while we halted on a hilly woods" (Oak Hill, ahead of you).[4]

The most intense infantry action at this stop occurred in the fields to your front. General Rodes ordered Brigadier General George P. Doles to advance his Georgia brigade southward along the Carlisle Road toward your location in an effort to link with the right flank of Early's column approaching on the Old Harrisburg Road by the tower off to your right. Although Schurz had expected his right flank to connect with Barlow's left, Barlow's actions (examined further at Stop 8) had opened a gap between the two XI Corps divisions. As a consequence, Doles's advance could hit either Schurz's right flank or Barlow's left, and initially it appeared he headed for Schurz's line here. As they neared the Union line, however, the Georgians moved on an oblique, crossing over to the east side of the road, away from your position, and toward Barlow's left flank. Krzyzanowski's reserve brigade received orders to move forward to fill that gap, but it had not yet gone into position. Only Colonel Philip P. Brown's 157th New York of von Amsberg's brigade was in position to attack Doles and slow his advance.

The men of the 157th New York started out gamely enough. An initial volley exchanged with the 21st Georgia seemed to make the enemy troops melt away. But the rest of Doles's men—the 4th, 12th, and 44th Georgia—continued to angle their line of march off to your right toward Barlow's left flank, crossing to the other side of the Carlisle Road. The 157th New York attempted to re-form its line parallel to the road to fire into the open flank the Georgians presented to them, but, as Captain Charles van Slyke wrote to the editor of his hometown newspaper, they were "espied by the Rebel Commander who immediately changed his front toward the regt, and poured in such a tremendous fire of balls, that many fell to breathe no more." He assured the editor that the 157th New York "returned the fire, and with interest, as the number of the rebels who fell testified," but then the fight took an unanticipated turn that the New Yorkers would never forget. As Marlow D. Wells described it for his father a week after the battle, they had advanced into "a large wheat field, where the grain stood up to our shoulders." They had not gone far when "the enemy raised up from the ground and poured into us an awful fire of shot and shell." Indeed, the 157th had walked into a deadly cross fire. With the 4th, 12th, and 44th Georgia to their front, the soldiers of the 157th now learned to their horror that the 21st Georgia had not retreated at all; its men simply had hidden in the tall grass and grain and now rose up to fire into their left flank. The heavy fire from multiple directions quickly destroyed the 157th New York. Lieutenant Colonel George Arrowsmith fell dead, five other officers went down dead or mortally wounded, and dozens of their men fell with them.[5] Brown's men continued to put up a fight until ordered to pull back to the division line.

As the clash on this side of the Carlisle Road died down, the fighting on Barlow's line grew in intensity. You will pick up the narrative at Stop 8.

Who Fought Here?

C.S.A.: Colonel O'Neal's Alabama brigade (including Major Blackford's sharp-shooter battalion) and Lieutenant Colonel Carter's artillery battalion—both of which played major roles at previous stops—comprise the Confederate forces most actively involved in this sector.

U.S.: General Schimmelfennig's brigade—under the command of Colonel von Amsberg while Schimmelfennig acted as temporary commander of Schurz's XI Corps division—had approximately 1,683 men in line on 1 July. The command included the 82nd Illinois, the 45th and 157th New York, the 61st Ohio, and the 74th Pennsylvania Infantry. Captain Hubert Dilger's Battery 1, 1st Ohio Light Artillery, had 127 men in ranks, while Lieutenant William Wheeler's 13th New York Battery counted 110 men.

Who Commanded Here?

Major General Carl Schurz (1829–1906) immigrated to the United States from Germany in 1852 following the failed revolution of 1848. After a three-year stay in Philadelphia, he settled in Wisconsin in 1856 and became involved in the antislavery cause.

He became a vigorous campaigner for the election of Abraham Lincoln in 1860, and in April 1862 the president commissioned him a brigadier general. Schurz commanded a division in the Shenandoah valley in the corps commanded by John Fremont and then served under fellow German immigrant Franz Sigel. Promoted to major general in March 1863, he commanded his division at Chancellorsville and Gettysburg. Schurz, like Howard, transferred to the western theater of operations with his troops in the fall of 1863. After the Battle of Chattanooga and a falling out with Major General Joseph Hooker, Schurz commanded a recruiting depot in Nashville, Tennessee, but he spent most of his time in the fall of 1864 campaigning for the reelection of President Lincoln.

Major General Carl Schurz, U.S.A. (USAMHI)

After the war, Schurz returned to politics, serving one elected term in the U.S. Senate and also serving as secretary of the interior during the Grant administration. He maintained his social, literary, and political pursuits, exercising a large influence on every presidential election from 1860 to 1904. Carl Schurz died in New York City on May 14, 1906, and is buried at Sleepy Hollow Cemetery in Tarrytown, New York.

Brigadier General George Pierce Doles (1830–64) was born in Milledgeville, Georgia, and became a businessman and commander of a militia company there before the war. In 1861 his company became part of the 4th Georgia Infantry and received an assignment to active duty near Norfolk, Virginia. Doles was elected colonel of the regiment in May 1862, and his regiment joined the Army of Northern Virginia in time for the Seven Days Battles in the late spring of 1862. In September 1862 Doles drew positive comment for his conspicuous leadership at the Battle of South Mountain and then succeeded to brigade command at Antietam after the brigade commander was wounded. He subsequently retained his command and received a promotion to brigadier general in November 1862. George Doles was known as one of the best brigadier generals in the Army of Northern Virginia, showing great promise until a Federal sharpshooter killed him near Bethesda Church on June 2, 1864. He was buried in his hometown of Milledgeville.

Who Fell Here?

C.S.A.: O'Neal's casualties were given at Stop 6 and Carter's casualties at Stop 5.

U.S.: Fighting on an extended skirmish line generally proves less costly than standing on a traditional firing line. Thus, except for the 157th New York, the regiments in this sector did not suffer greatly in killed and wounded. The 82nd Illinois lost only 23 of its men; the more active 45th New York lost 46 men; the 61st Ohio lost 42 men; and the 74th Pennsylvania lost 50 men. Not surprisingly, the 157th New York lost 193 men killed and wounded. These regiments would be caught up in the unraveling of the Union line later in the afternoon of July 1, and their losses in captured and missing reflect the chaos they endured: the 82nd Illinois lost 89 men captured or missing; the 45th New York lost 178 men; the 157th New York lost an additional 114 men; the 61st Ohio lost 12 men; and the 74th Pennsylvania lost 60 men. Dilger had no men missing, while Wheeler could not account for three of his artillerymen.

Individual vignettes. Adjutant Joseph F. Henery of the 157th New York was born in Quebec, Canada, on June 22, 1841, and moved with his family to Massachusetts while he was still a child. After the fight on July 1, he could not be found. Nobody saw him fall, so the first casualty reports in his hometown newspaper listed him with the missing. In actuality, he had taken a bullet in the knee, and because he could not move, he simply lay on the field for several days, waiting for help. At first, doctors held out hope for his recovery, and he became a great favorite of the nurses, especially Mrs. Beckie L. Price of Phoenixville, Pennsylvania, "one of the noble Christian women of our land." Henery's conditioned worsened, however, and surgeons removed his leg

Adjutant Joseph F. Henery,
157th New York Infantry,
fell mortally wounded here.
(USAMHI)

on July 22; he did not rally from the operation and died two days later. His family recovered his remains, which were interred, with elaborate ceremony, in a Catholic cemetery in Oneida, New York.[6]

Private William R. Butler enlisted in Company H, 4th Georgia Infantry, on April 26, 1861, in Milledgeville, Georgia. His enrolling officer was his future brigade commander, George P. Doles. Butler apparently had plenty of friends in his company; they elected him corporal on June 3, 1861. Like many soldiers from the Deep South, Butler did not thrive in the colder winters of Virginia, spending time in the hospital for chills and fever and even developing a touch of rheumatism. He endured a major disappointment in the spring of 1862. Regiments such as the 4th Georgia that initially enlisted for one year now had to "reorganize" and sign on "for the war." Reorganization required new elections, and Butler lost his corporal stripes as a result. Thus he was serving in the ranks as a private when he was mortally wounded somewhere along the Carlisle Road on July 1, and he died two days later.[7]

Who Lived Here?

Much of the fire that Dilger and Wheeler faced came from Oak Hill, but the Jeff Davis Artillery under Captain William Reese also caused the Union gunners much trouble. Posted on the Samuel Cobean farm on the west side of the Carlisle Road, Reese's guns sat approximately 1,500 yards from the Union batteries. A lively duel pitted the rival gunners against each other, and Cobean's farm suffered as a consequence. Cobean had much to lose: he was the eleventh-wealthiest person in Cumberland Township, with real estate worth over $8,000 and personal property valued at $2,500 more. In addition to his house, barns, and outbuildings, he had an especially large well that local citizen J. F. McKentrick used to bring water to wounded soldiers of both armies in the days after the fighting in the area had ended.[8] To the left of Dilger's and Wheeler's guns, along the Mummasburg Road, lay the farm of David A. Heagey (sometimes rendered as "Hagy"). The skirmishers of the 45th New York advanced into the grain fields and the orchard of the Heagey farm as they engaged O'Neal's brigade and Blackford's sharpshooters at the McClean farm. On October 21, 1868, David Heagey filed a claim with the state of Pennsylvania for damages to his personal property during the battle. The claim listed $100 in lost "meat" and $120 in lost "beds and clothing." Payment was authorized by the state, but records show no evidence that Heagey ever received any money.[9]

What Did They Say about It Later?

"Dread scenes must rise before our eyes as heroic action illumines every place; therefore, Gettysburg is resplendent," intoned the orator at the dedication of the 157th New York's monument. Many of its survivors gathered here in September 1886 to right an injustice. They still smarted from the legacy of Chancellorsville, after which the "northern press, anxious for any possible reason to explain the cause of defeat, charged the Eleventh Corps with cowardice, and even officers and men of other corps jeeringly spoke of it as 'the flying crescent.'" Still "writhing under the unjust charge of cowardice the Eleventh Corps came on to Gettysburg," and on July 1 the 157th New York lost 309 men killed, wounded, or missing. "Thirty-three fell in line of battle, marking the extreme advance of the battalion with dead men," the speaker noted, without also pointing out that when combined with the mortally wounded, the regiment's death toll at Gettysburg actually numbered fifty-three. Still, he asserted, "We question whether any regiment, in open field in battle line, has a more glorious spot to honor. We doubt whether any regiment has a more glorious roll."[10] Interestingly, while a number of regiments placed two markers on the battlefield—a primary one at the site of their hardest fighting and another at a secondary or tertiary position held on another day of the battle—the 157th New York is one of a small number of regiments to place multiple markers on the same day's battlefield. Its first marker, paid for by the veterans themselves and placed near Mummasburg Road, marks their first position while in reserve; their second—and larger—marker, paid for with state money, rests close to Carlisle Road on the main XI Corps battle line just south of its bloody fight with Doles's Georgians. A third small marker sits farther north from this second one, at the edge of Carlisle Road near the point of the regiment's most advanced position.

Driving directions to the next stop: Return to your vehicle and drive forward 0.1 miles to the intersection with Carlisle Road. Drive straight across the intersection and go 0.2 miles. Park on the right side of the road in the designated spaces near the Old Alms House Cemetery and walk to the top of the knoll in front of you.

3 The Union Line Collapses

STOP 8. BARLOW'S KNOLL

You will consider two separate actions while you are at this stop.

Position 1: The Fight at Barlow's Knoll

Orientation

Stand beside the cannon on the right of Lieutenant Bayard Wilkeson's battery and look in the direction that it is pointing. General Barlow's statue should be behind you. The main road to your right is Old Harrisburg Road. The trees in your immedi-

Cannons of Lieutenant Bayard Wilkeson's battery.

ate front were not there in such density at the time of the battle. Directly behind them—currently out of view—is the Josiah Benner farmstead where some of Barlow's skirmishers deployed. On the other side of Old Harrisburg Road, approximately one-half mile ahead to your right front, is a little-visited Jones Battalion Avenue along a ridge of ground where Lieutenant Colonel Hilary P. Jones's Confederate artillery unlimbered

and opened fire on your present position. In the distance to your left, you can see the high ground of Oak Hill and Oak Ridge. In the low ground in the middle distance to your left, you can see Carlisle Road.

What Happened Here?

As you learned at Stop 7, General Howard ordered two of his XI Corps divisions under Major General Carl Schurz and Brigadier General Francis C. Barlow—with Schurz in command—to come north of town, where Schurz prepared to defend the northern approaches to Gettysburg. While Brigadier General Alexander Schimmelfennig took over Schurz's duties and held the Union line between the Mummasburg Road and the Carlisle Road to your left, Schurz ordered Barlow to watch for Early's approach down the Old Harrisburg Road to your right.

To carry out his mission, Barlow initially placed his division on a slight ridge near the edge of town behind you, where he could connect with Schimmelfennig's troops. He grew uneasy, however, about a knob of ground in his front—the high ground on which you now stand. He worried that Early might place artillery on it. His next decision surprised Schurz, who reported: "I discovered that General Barlow had moved forward his whole line, thus losing on his left the connection" with Schimmelfennig. Schurz "immediately gave orders to re-establish the connection" by advancing Schimmelfennig's right wing and sent off to Howard for at least one brigade to reinforce his line. Help could not arrive too quickly. Early's men already had deployed for their attack down the Old Harrisburg Road, and the Georgians of Brigadier General George P. Doles's brigade of Rodes's division began to push down the Carlisle Road toward the gap Barlow's advance had created.

When Barlow moved his two brigades forward, he focused on the defense of his right flank near the Old Harrisburg Road. He sent out skirmishers to the Josiah Benner farm, beyond the tree line in front of you. He then deployed most of Colonel Leopold von Gilsa's brigade as a reinforced skirmish line—not a fully developed battle line—at the base of the knoll below you; the men took position along the steep banks of Rock Creek, flowing from left to right across your front. The right of the 54th New York touched the Old Harrisburg Road. Two companies of the 153rd Pennsylvania held the skirmish line's center—the rest of the regiment fell in line here on top of the knoll—and the 68th New York held the left of the skirmish line in the low ground in the trees in front of you. Four Napoleons from Battery G, 4th U.S. Artillery, commanded by nineteen-year-old Lieutenant Bayard Wilkeson, rolled into position where you now stand to strengthen Barlow's line. Barlow then put Brigadier General Adelbert Ames's brigade into position to support Wilkeson's guns; the men deployed along a line that roughly follows the park road over your left shoulder. Confederate artillery frequently disrupted Barlow's deployment. Lieutenant Wilkeson soon fell mortally wounded when a shell from Jones's guns nearly severed his right leg; he tied a tourniquet around his limb and amputated it himself, but he died later that night. A short time later, a shell also decapitated Lieutenant Colonel Douglas Fowler of the 17th Connecticut in Ames's brigade.

Early gave Barlow no more opportunities to complete his preparations. He launched Brigadier General John B. Gordon's Georgia brigade directly toward the knoll. As Gordon described his attack, "Moving forward under heavy fire over rail and plank fences, and crossing a creek whose banks were so abrupt as to prevent a passage excepting at certain points, this brigade rushed upon the enemy with a resolution and spirit, in my opinion, rarely excelled." The skirmishers at the Benner farm fell back under pressure, but for a brief time, von Gilsa's heavy skirmish line at the base of the slope in front of you and to your right—now reinforced by the rest of the 153rd Pennsylvania—held.

Now turn to your left and face Carlisle Road. While Barlow's men fought Gordon here, Doles's Georgians had advanced down the far side of Carlisle Road toward Schurz's division. Their fight with the 157th New York only slowed them down briefly. They continued their oblique movement, angling across your front from right to left toward the gap between Schimmelfennig and Barlow, coming closer and closer to Barlow's unprotected left flank. Schurz had ordered forward his reserve brigade under Colonel Wladimir Krzyzanowski to fill that gap, and the brigade just now arrived where it was most needed.

Position 2: Krzyzanowski Moves Forward

Orientation

Walk back toward your car, but before leaving for the next stop, take a short walk farther down the park road to the point where it makes a nearly ninety-degree turn to the right. The line of monuments along the left of the road on the way down to the

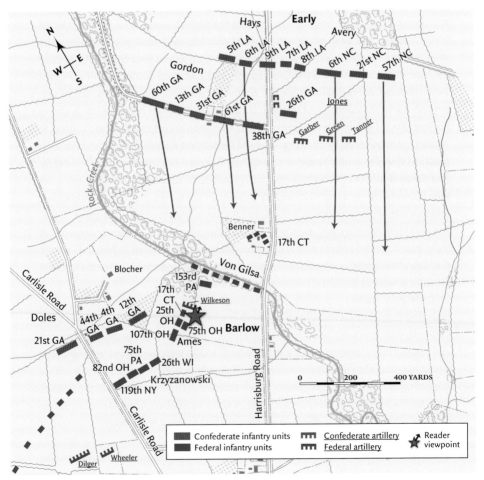

The Collapse of the Union Right Flank

bend salutes Ames's Ohio regiments, which continued to battle with Gordon's men. Once you turn at the bend, look down the row of monuments that extends down the left side of the park road to Carlisle Road ahead of you; they mark the approximate battle positions of the regiments of Krzyzanowski's brigade. Walk down to the obelisk for the 26th Wisconsin and turn to face the fields to the north; the park road should pass right in front of you.

What Happened Here?

When he responded to Schurz's orders to protect Barlow's open left flank, Krzyzanowski led his men into the open fields to your left. Once Doles's men re-formed their ranks after fighting the 157th New York, they again pushed forward—no longer toward a gap but directly toward Krzyzanowski's command. The fighting in the fields to your left and front grew in intensity. As Major Benjamin Willis of the 119th New York reported, "Here we withstood an enemy more than threefold our number, receiving volleys of musketry in swift succession, and suffering severely from a destructive fire of shot and shell." But the intensity of Doles's attacks won the day. As Doles reported, "Our effort was successful." The enemy was driven back "with heavy loss in killed and wounded, and a large number of prisoners sent to our rear." Doles had not exaggerated. By July 4 Northern newspapers reported that "every regimental commander of Colonel Krzyzanowski's brigade was killed or wounded. The 82nd Ohio, Colonel [James S.] Robinson, lost eighteen officers. The 26th Wisconsin lost all but one of its officers. This regiment last fall joined General [Franz] Sigel at Fairfax, with nearly the maximum number, and then appeared splendid. It has been in two fights—Chancellorsville and Gettysburg—and came out with less men than are required to form a company."[1]

Colonel Wladimir Krzyzanowski, U.S.A. (USAMHI)

Despite the gallant stand of Krzyzanowski's men, the XI Corps's time had run out. Astride the Old Harrisburg Road beyond the knoll you just visited, Brigadier General Harry T. Hays's Louisiana brigade began its advance. Colonel Isaac Avery's North Carolinians came in on Hays's left, extending the Confederate line across to the other side of the road. Greatly outnumbered and under increasing pressure from front and flank, von Gilsa's line finally broke. Individual soldiers stopped to fire a shot or two, and von Gilsa himself tried to rally the men, but when Wilkeson's guns also left, it was clear that Barlow's line had begun to crumble.

The departure of von Gilsa's men left Ames's brigade vulnerable to attack from front, right flank, and rear. Under growing pressure from Gordon's Georgians, Hays's Louisianians, and even some of Doles's men, Ames's line finally gave way, too. He reported: "The whole division was falling back with little or no regularity, regimental organizations having become destroyed."[2] As Barlow tried in vain to stem the tide of retreating soldiers, he fell seriously wounded. In a short time, Krzyzanowski, and then Schurz and Schimmelfennig, realized the time had come to leave the field. As Captain William H. Harrison of the 31st Georgia wrote home just after the battle: "Met, fought, whipped, routed and captured almost double our numbers. We killed dead on the field 480 Yankees. . . . We took near two thousand prisoners including their wounded, drove them over a mile, captured two or three stands of colors, wounded and took prisoner nearly all of the officers including the Genl. (Barlow). . . . Our loss was as follows: killed between 40 and 50, wounded between 250 and 300, including a good many slightly, who are with us yet."[3]

At the northern edges of the town, guns from XI Corps batteries fired blasts of canister to cover the withdrawing infantry. Some units, such as the 17th Connecticut, "deployed in the streets, and fired several volleys into the ranks of the enemy, which thinned their ranks and retarded their advance."[4] Still, most of the survivors of Schurz's and Barlow's divisions hurried through the unfamiliar streets of Gettysburg toward their predetermined rallying point on Cemetery Hill. With unit cohesion gone, hundreds more of them—by twos and by tens—became prisoners of Early's and Rodes's victorious troops.

The first newspaper accounts of this fight praised the "German" XI Corps for putting up a good fight. "The division fought bravely, and lost heavily; the brigade of Colonel von Gilsa holding its position firmly, and that of General Ames doing well," wrote New York war correspondent J. H. Vosburg.[5] Most of the regimental reports say nothing of a rout but use measured language like that of Captain John M. Lutz of the 107th Ohio, who wrote simply: "The enemy approaching in heavy force, the regiment was ordered to the south end of the town."[6] But the XI Corps did not escape entirely the dark shadows of Chancellorsville and ethnic slurs of the era. In short order, their critics charged, the Germans who "ran" in May "ran again" on July 1. In fairness to the XI Corps, their casualty rates—especially the high numbers of killed and wounded on both sides—demonstrate clearly the tenacity of the combatants of both forces.

Who Fought Here?

C.S.A.: Brigadier General John B. Gordon's 1,813-man brigade of Early's division of Ewell's Second Corps included the 13th, 26th, 31st, 38th, 60th, and 61st Georgia Infantry; Brigadier General Harry T. Hays's 1,295-man brigade of Early's division included the 5th, 6th, 7th, 8th, and 9th Louisiana Infantry; and Colonel Isaac Avery's smaller 1,244-man brigade of Early's division included the 6th, 21st, and 57th North Carolina Infantry. Lieutenant Colonel Hilary P. Jones's 290-man artillery battalion included the Charlottesville (Va.) Artillery, the Courtney (Va.) Artillery, the Louisiana Guard (La.) Artillery, and the Staunton (Va.) Artillery.

Brigadier General George P. Doles's 1,323-man brigade of Rodes's division of Ewell's Second Corps included the 4th, 12th, 21st, and 44th Georgia Infantry.

U.S.: Brigadier General Adelbert Ames's 1,337-man brigade of Brigadier General Francis C. Barlow's division of Howard's XI Corps included the 17th Connecticut and the 25th, 75th, and 107th Ohio Infantry. Colonel Leopold von Gilsa's 936-man brigade of Barlow's division contained the 41st, 54th, and 68th New York and the 153rd Pennsylvania Infantry; the 41st New York of this brigade did not participate in the July 1 battle.

Colonel Wladimir Krzyzanowski's 1,420-man brigade of Major General Carl Schurz's division of Howard's XI Corps included the 119th New York, the 82nd Ohio, the 75th Pennsylvania, and the 26th Wisconsin Infantry; the 58th New York has a monument along the brigade line, but it did not participate in the fighting here.

Who Commanded Here?

Brigadier General Francis Channing Barlow (1834–96), a Harvard University graduate, was born in Brooklyn, New York, and raised in Brookline, Massachusetts. Barlow worked as a lawyer in New York, but when the Civil War broke out, he enlisted as a private for three months in the 12th New York Infantry. Upon the expiration of his enlistment, he continued in service as the lieutenant colonel of the 61st New York Infantry. In 1862 he participated in McClellan's Peninsula Campaign and the Battle of Antietam, where he was wounded in action. He was promoted to brigadier general after Antietam. Returning to duty in the spring of 1863, he commanded an XI Corps brigade at Chancellorsville and assumed division command just five weeks prior to Gettysburg. Because of the wound he received at Gettysburg, Barlow did not rejoin the Army of the Potomac until the following spring, participating in Grant's

Brigadier General Francis C. Barlow, U.S.A., fell seriously wounded here. (USAMHI)

Overland Campaign as an infantry division commander in General Hancock's II Corps. He performed especially distinguished service in the II Corps assault on the "mule shoe" at Spotsylvania on May 12, 1864. At the onset of the Union investment of Petersburg, Barlow went on sick leave and did not return to the army until shortly before the Confederate surrender at Appomattox Court House in April 1865. Promoted to major general in May 1865, Barlow resigned from the army the following November. Upon leaving the army, Barlow returned to his law practice in New York and entered politics. He was a founding member of the American Bar Association and, as attorney general of the state of New York, initiated the prosecution of the infamous "Tweed Ring" in New York City. He continued to practice law until his death in New York City in January 1896.

Barlow's wounding became one of the enduring human-interest stories in Gettysburg lore. Shot in his left side between his arm pit and his thigh, he could not get back to the Union lines before Gordon's men overran his lines. Gordon himself aided and comforted Barlow briefly before directing that he be moved to a place where he could die more comfortably. Though Gordon thought Barlow had died, the New Yorker recovered. In 1864 a Confederate cavalry brigade commander named James B. Gordon fell near Richmond, and Barlow assumed he had been his benefactor at Gettysburg. Many years after the war, Barlow and Gordon met by chance in Washington, D.C., and each inquired of the other if he was related to the deceased Civil War general of the same name. When they discovered that they, in fact, were the two men who had met on the field under the difficult circumstances of the first day of Gettysburg, they enjoyed an especially happy reunion.[7]

Major General Jubal Anderson Early (1816–94), a Virginia native, graduated from West Point in the class of 1837. He saw action against the Seminole Indians and served as a major of volunteers in the Mexican War. Then he left the army to practice law in Virginia and enter politics. He became a member of the house of delegates and voted against secession in the Virginia convention of April 1861, but he did his duty as he saw it after Virginia seceded. He entered the Confederate army as a colonel of the 24th Virginia Infantry, which he led at First Manassas; he was then promoted to brigadier general. He took part in all of the engagements of the Army of Northern Virginia from 1862 to 1864 as an infantry brigade and division commander and was promoted to major general to rank from January 1863. In the summer of 1864, Early, now a lieutenant general, commanded Ewell's Second Corps in the Shenandoah valley, led a raid into Maryland, and skirmished close to the defenses of Washington before being forced back into Virginia. His cavalry conducted wide-ranging raids and burned the town of Chambersburg, Pennsylvania. Defeated by Union Major General Philip H. Sheridan at Winchester, Fisher's Hill, and Cedar Creek, Early finally gave up control of the Shenandoah valley in late 1864. Following the Confederate surrender in April 1865, Early spent time in Mexico before returning to Virginia. He became active in the Southern Historical Society and spent most of his later life trying to destroy the military reputation of rival corps commander Lieutenant General James Longstreet.

Brigadier General John Brown Gordon (1832–1904) emerged from civilian life in Georgia to become a lieutenant general and corps commander by war's end. Starting as a company commander in the 6th Alabama Infantry and participating in the Battle of First Manassas, he subsequently became regimental commander and led at that level through the Battle of Antietam, where he was severely wounded in the face. Promoted to brigadier general in November 1862, he served as a brigade commander at Chancellorsville and Gettysburg. In the spring of 1864, he established an excellent record in the Overland Campaign and fought well in the Shenandoah valley under Early's command. He was promoted to major general in May 1864. In the spring of 1865, Gordon commanded one-half of the infantry of the Army of Northern Virginia

Brigadier General John B. Gordon, C.S.A. (USAMHI)

as it began its retreat from Petersburg on the road to Appomattox Court House. After the war, Gordon settled in Atlanta and served the state of Georgia as a three-term U.S. Senator and also as governor. His statue adorns the grounds of the state capitol. He died at Miami, Florida, and is buried in Atlanta.

Who Fell Here?

C.S.A.: While many accounts of this fight have made it sound like the Confederate troops had an easy time handling the XI Corps, the numbers tell a different story. In Gordon's brigade, the 13th Georgia lost 137 of its 312 men; the 26th Georgia lost 32 of its 315 men; the 31st Georgia lost 65 of its 252 men; the 38th Georgia lost 133 of its 341 men; the 60th Georgia lost 59 of its 299 men; and the 61st Georgia lost 111 of its 288 men. In sum, Gordon's brigade lost 29.6 percent of its strength. Hays's and Avery's brigades suffered a far greater percentage of their losses at Gettysburg in the action at East Cemetery Hill on July 2; their casualties will be considered in detail at Stop 27.

Jones's artillery battalion lost 12 of its 290 men.

In Doles's brigade, the 4th Georgia lost 52 of its 341 men, and Lieutenant Colonel D. R. E. Winn was killed; the 12th Georgia lost 53 of its 327 men; the 21st Georgia lost 38 of its 287 men; and the 44th Georgia lost 74 of its 364 men, and Lieutenant Colonel Samuel P. Lumpkin was mortally wounded. The brigade loss totaled 16.6 percent.

U.S.: Despite the lingering impression that the XI Corps ran without a fight, the numbers of killed and wounded tell as important a story as the number of men captured.

The casualties for von Gilsa's and Ames's brigades will be summarized at Stop 27, after their tough fight on July 2 at East Cemetery Hill.

In Krzyzanowski's brigade, which put up an especially tough fight, the 119th New York lost 140 of its 262 men, including 59 prisoners; the 82nd Ohio lost 181 of its 312 men, including 79 prisoners; the 75th Pennsylvania lost 110 of its 208 men, including 3 prisoners, and Colonel Francis Mahler was killed; and the 26th Wisconsin lost 217 of 443, including 62 prisoners.

Individual vignettes. Joseph S. Haden, twenty-three years old and a private in the 13th Georgia in Gordon's brigade, took a bullet in the pelvis as he advanced against the XI Corps lines. The march north to Pennsylvania must have been hard on him, and his weakened condition made it difficult for him to rally from such a severe wound. He likely received initial treatment at a farm close to where he fell, but he soon found himself in the seminary hospital. On August 2, the doctors there transferred Haden to Camp Letterman on the east side of Gettysburg. Dr. J. A. Newcombe, a surgeon who attended him, noted that the bullet had gone completely through Haden without injuring his bladder or any major artery, eliminating the need for major surgery. However, the doctor observed that Haden's "general health was much impaired" and the discharge from his wound was "offensive and ichorus" (watery). He improved for a few days in mid-August, but on August 21 he began a rapid decline. On that day, his doctor described his countenance as "pinched" and his skin as "icteroid" (yellowish). The hemorrhage from his wounds could not be controlled, and he entirely lost control of his bowels. Private Haden died on August 30.[8]

Sergeant Samuel Comstock, Company H, 17th Connecticut, fell badly wounded in the hip or thigh near Barlow's Knoll on July 1. Private Justus M. Silliman, another member of the regiment who fell wounded that day, could not find his friend at first. "I am quite anxious about Sam and would like to know how he fares," he wrote to his family. Within a few days, the two soldiers both came under doctors' care at the XI Corps hospital at the George Spangler farm south of town. The Christian Commission arrived, and Silliman seemed pleased to report that "Sam has been supplied with a shirt and drawers by them." By July 15 many of the wounded had left Gettysburg for larger hospitals, but Comstock could not be moved. Silliman stayed with him. "Sam is doing well though is quite weak and tired of lying so long in one position," Silliman noted that day, adding that "he is in comfortable quarters and has good attention, though thousands of our wounded died solely for want of timely care." The Comstock family sent a supply of wine and other goods, and Silliman reported that "Sam enjoys the wine very much. . . . [H]e has regular rations of whisky prescribed but take[s] the wine instead which is much pleasanter and more beneficial." Comstock's leg remained suspended in a sling, and he had to remain immobilized, but his spirits remained strong. On September 26, however, Private Silliman wrote: "I have just returned from visiting Sam. . . . He is failing rapidly and is liable to drop away at any moment, he seemed disinclined to talk and wished to sleep." He died the next day. True to the end, Silliman arranged for his friend's remains to be embalmed and requested a pass to accompany the body home. Sergeant Comstock was buried in New Canaan, Connecticut, on October 11, 1863.[9]

Who Lived Here?

As you stand on Barlow's Knoll, 550 yards ahead of you is the David Blocher farm, which includes a red brick house and white Pennsylvania bank barn. Farther to the west, near the intersection of Table Rock Road and Carlisle Road just beyond your line of sight to your left front, was the home of David's father John. The Blocher blacksmith shop stood nearby. What we today call Barlow's Knoll was originally called Blocher's Knoll. Doles's Confederate brigade attacked through the Blocher family holdings to hit Krzyzanowski's brigade. In 1998 the Friends of the National Parks at Gettysburg, a battlefield preservation group, purchased the remaining 23.6 acres of the Blocher farm and removed a nonhistoric 1970s steel-clad barn. The property, with historical easement, was then donated to the National Park Service, which resold the property to a private owner in 1999.[10]

Just across Rock Creek, adjacent to Old Harrisburg Road and behind the tree line north of Barlow's Knoll, rests the Josiah Benner Farm. The farm covered 123 acres at the time of the battle. The 17th Connecticut Infantry posted its skirmish line near the house and barn. Parts of Early's division, chiefly Gordon's brigade, crossed this farm in their attacks against Barlow's Knoll. The Benner family fled to a safe area as the fighting began. Upon their return to the farm, they found that the house and barn had been converted into a temporary hospital and were filled with wounded Confederate soldiers; wounded Union General Francis Channing Barlow was also being treated there. Recently, the National Park Service obtained possession of the Benner farm.[11]

The cemetery near where you parked was part of the complex known as the Adams County Almshouse. Established in 1818, the institution provided care for the poor, disabled, or insane of the county. The almshouse buildings were dismantled in the 1960s.[12]

What Did They Say about It Later?

In the aftermath of victory, the XI Corps did not take much immediate criticism for the rapid collapse of its line north of Gettysburg or its disordered retreat through the town. That came later, especially from critics—many in the I Corps—who blamed the XI Corps's withdrawal for the dissolution of the entire Union line.

During the postwar years, XI Corps veterans stood up for their own command. E. C. Culp of the 25th Ohio in Ames's brigade responded to the I Corps critics by assuring them that he did not mean to insult them. "The First Corps was as good as the Eleventh—no better," he wrote, adding: "There were probably cowards in both. I saw stragglers from both corps, and in about the same proportion. I saw officers of the First Corps running away from nothing, and I saw an officer of the Eleventh Corps (Judge C. P. Wickham, now upon the bench in Ohio, then a Captain in the 55th Ohio) run his sword into an officer of the Eleventh Corps, who was acting in a cowardly manner." He made his challenge to critics of the XI Corps in a forthright manner: "Is it not better to try and bring out facts for future history, and let up on this silly twaddle of cowardice?"[13]

On Wednesday, September 14, 1887, Ohio veterans met at Gettysburg for one comprehensive ceremony to dedicate all their monuments. Colonel James S. Robinson of the 82nd Ohio of Krzyzanowski's brigade recalled with pride the stand of his men at the spot where his regiment's monument now stood.

The men stubbornly contested every inch of ground. Our position was in every respect untenable. We were not permitted even to build a temporary barricades out of the numerous fence rails that incumbered our movements. We were in the valley while the neighboring hills to the front and right of us were covered by the guns of the enemy. The first intimation I had of the advance of the enemy on my right flank was a volley of musketry from that quarter, decimating the ranks of my command. . . . No troops could have fought better than the Eleventh Corps soldiers that came under my observation. They yielded only to the superior force of the enemy. They fought at a great disadvantage, but they fought well.[14]

Even their former foes gave them credit for a good stand. As Private G. W. Nichols of the 61st Georgia in Gordon's brigade later wrote: "We met the enemy at Rock Creek. We attacked them immediately, but we had a hard time moving them. We advanced with our accustomed yell, but they stood firm until we got near them. Then they began to retreat in fine order, shooting at us as they retreated. They were harder to drive than we had ever known them before."[15]

Driving directions to the next stop: Return to your vehicle and drive along this one-way road 0.3 miles to the stop sign at the intersection with Old Harrisburg Road (business Route 15). Turn right toward the town and, just after the road bends at 0.5 miles, make an immediate left onto Stratton Street. Go two blocks, turn left onto Coster Avenue (Stevens Street will be on your right), and park along the road.

STOP 9. COSTER AVENUE

Orientation

Walk into the open field along the line of monuments and find the marker to the 154th New York. Face northward, with the colorful painted mural behind you.

What Happened Here?

Well before the XI Corps line north of Gettysburg gave way under pressure from Early and Doles, General Schurz called for reinforcements. As he later reported to General Howard: "I dispatched one of my aides to you, with the request to have one brigade of the Second Division [von Steinwehr's division on Cemetery Hill] placed upon the north side of the town. . . . My intention was to have that brigade in readiness to charge upon any force the enemy might move around my right." That initial request was denied, but as the XI Corps's situation deteriorated, von Steinwehr—with Howard's assent—finally ordered forward the small 1,217-man brigade of Colonel Charles R. Coster. The men of the 27th and 73rd Pennsylvania and the 134th and 154th New York ceased work on Cemetery Hill's defenses, called in their pickets, and advanced to the support of their comrades in arms.

Coster found Schurz shortly after Barlow's line had collapsed. Schurz then ordered him to deploy his brigade "north and east of Gettysburg . . . to check the advance of the enemy." The 73rd Pennsylvania remained in the town square, leaving Coster with just three regiments numbering approximately 900 men to face the enemy. Schurz guided Coster here to this position, to the northern end of Stratton Street (a north-south avenue one block east of the square), and into open fields

The 154th New York monument and mural.

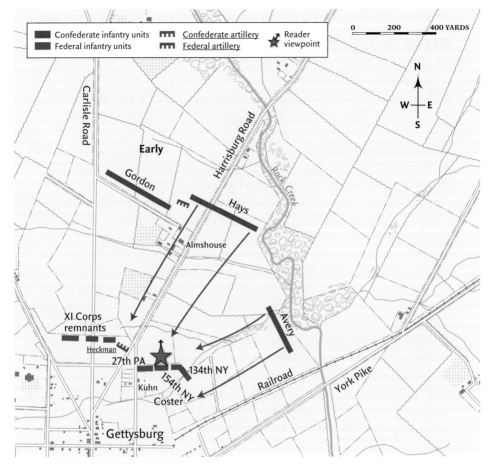

The Brief Fight at Kuhn's Brickyard

here to the right of the road. The 27th Pennsylvania held the left of the line closest to Stratton Street at the stop sign to your left; the 154th New York held the center here; and to your right, the 134th New York anchored the other end of Coster's line.

The position was not naturally a strong one. Stevens's Run flows to your right and rear. The kilns of Kuhn's brickyard lay behind you, and fenced enclosures for live-stock around the Kuhn property created obstacles to forming a respectable defensive line. And there were far worse drawbacks: the terrain forward of their position actually rose up ahead of them, the ground off to your left beyond Stratton Street included a ridge that blocked their view of potential threats to Coster's left flank, and the land to the right of the 134th New York sloped off to the east and south. Coster's men enjoyed few advantages of position. They only enjoyed the slight protection offered by a stout rail fence positioned somewhere in this area and some minor additional support from quickly organized (and equally quickly scattered) fragments of Barlow's and Schurz's commands and the fire of Captain Lewis Heckman's Battery K, 1st Ohio Light Artillery, off to their left—which, by the commander's own report, "expended 113 rounds of ammunition, mostly canister," in thirty minutes.

Before Coster had completed his preparations, Hays's brigade attacked. The Louisiana troops hit Coster's left and center, advancing directly at your current position and to your left. At first, Coster's men stood to their task, firing volley after volley into the advancing Confederate ranks. Finally, however, Avery's North Carolina brigade curled around the flank of the 134th New York in low open ground to your right, now obscured by the tree line. The 6th North Carolina led that charge, and, although the New Yorkers tried hard to redeploy to meet them, the Tar Heels' final rush made it impossible to stand longer. As Major Samuel M. Tate of the 6th North Carolina reported, his brigade "advanced to charge the enemy behind fences. It was rapidly done (and, as is our usual fortune, immediately in our front was a stone fence), and the enemy driven before us through the town."[1] Once the 134th New York broke, the 154th New York and the 27th Pennsylvania tried to pull back and re-form to your left on Stratton Street. A final push by Hays's men hit the 27th Pennsylvania in the flank, ending further resistance. Coster's survivors pulled back toward Cemetery Hill in some disorder.

As a war correspondent concluded: "Col. Coster and his men did all that brave men could do; but it was so late when they were called out that it was scarcely worthwhile for them to be slaughtered by the artillery and infantry force to which they were exposed."[2] For a fairly contained action that receives little attention in the broader flow of the first day's fight at Gettysburg, the Coster Avenue fight resulted in significant casualties for both the Union and Confederate units that fought there. While Coster's men returned to Cemetery Hill and took up new positions well integrated into the XI Corps line, both Hays and Avery played even more significant roles in the July 2 fight—and did so with ranks far more weakened than perhaps their senior leaders appreciated.

Who Fought Here?
C.S.A.: Hays's and Avery's brigades were introduced at Stop 8.

U.S.: Colonel Charles R. Coster's 1,217-man brigade of von Steinwehr's division in Howard's XI Corps included the 27th and 73rd Pennsylvania and the 134th and 154th New York. Captain Lewis M. Heckman's Battery K, 1st Ohio Light Artillery, that supported the brigade's left flank numbered 100 men.

Who Commanded Here?
Colonel Charles Robert Coster (1838–88) succeeded to the command of this small brigade after its permanent commander, Colonel Adolphus Buschbeck, fell wounded at Chancellorsville. Coster was from New York City and started his army

Colonel Charles R. Coster, U.S.A. (USAMHI)

service as a private in the 7th New York Militia. He soon received a direct commission into the 12th U.S. Infantry as a first lieutenant, followed rapidly by promotion to captain in the same regiment. With the Regulars, he saw action in 1862 at Yorktown and at Gaines's Mill, where he was wounded. He returned to duty with a colonel's commission and command of the 134th New York Infantry in Buschbeck's brigade. Shortly after Gettysburg, when the XI Corps went west, Coster resigned his commissions and spent the rest of the war as provost marshal of New York's 6th District, administering the draft.

Who Fell Here?

C.S.A.: The casualties of Hays's and Avery's brigades will be summarized at Stop 27, East Cemetery Hill, the site of their heaviest losses.

U.S.: In Coster's brigade, the 27th Pennsylvania lost 111 of its 283 men, including 76 prisoners; the 134th New York lost 252 of its 400 men, including 59 prisoners; and the 154th New York lost 200 of its 239 men, including 178 prisoners. Perhaps the most famous enlisted man killed in this battle, Sergeant Amos Humiston—whose photo of his children helped to identify his remains and launch an orphanage for the children of fallen soldiers—was among the dead of the 154th New York. The 73rd Pennsylvania of Coster's brigade did not participate in this action. Heckman's battery lost 15 of its 110 men, including 2 prisoners.

Private William N. Earl, 134th New York, was killed in the fighting here. (USAMHI)

Individual vignettes. During the fighting of July 1, Sergeant Merrit B. Pendley, Company E, 6th North Carolina Infantry, received a bullet in the right hip joint, slightly fracturing the head of his femur. The round had passed through his "pocket book" and remained in his body. The thirty-six-year-old sergeant was too badly injured to be taken back to Virginia, and he remained in a field hospital until August 7, when the surgeons transferred him to Camp Letterman. Surgeon D. R. Good reported that "the patient's general health has been very good, though he has suffered constant and severe pain from the injury and cannot endure the least motion of the limb." But Pendley suffered little from inflammation or swelling, and he enjoyed "a generous diet." On August 22, the attending surgeon wrote that the "patient is comfortable so long as his limb is not moved, and is doing well." Just five days later, however, Pendley took a turn for the worse. His leg began to swell. While he briefly seemed to improve, he began to suffer from diarrhea, and by September 12 the doctors saw signs of blood poisoning and then gangrene. Pendley died at about 10:00 P.M. on September 17. The doctors performed a postmortem examination and determined that infections around the site of the shattered femur head had caused Pendley's death.[3]

Ebenezer Heath enlisted as a private in Company F of the 154th New York on August 25, 1862, and worked himself up to the rank of sergeant. On July 1 at Gettysburg, while engaged in the firefight near the brickyard, a Confederate bullet hit him in the side, seriously wounding him. He died of that injury on July 27. His widow, Lucy J. Williams Heath, began the application process for a widow's pension in mid-September 1863. To validate her claim as Sergeant Heath's widow, she needed to provide testimony from the justice of the peace of Clymer, New York, who had married them in 1855. She, like all applicants for a widow's or mother's pension, had to affirm that "she has not in any manner been engaged in or aided or abetted the rebellion in the United States." Her monthly pension of $8.00 was approved on August 30, 1864.[4]

Who Lived Here?

At the time of the battle, the town of Gettysburg did not extend out beyond where you are standing. The expanse of open space and the nearby water supply of Stevens's Run provided an ideal location for John P. Kuhn's brickyard. Kuhn and his family resided in a two-story brick house on Stratton Street. His brickyard enterprise stretched out toward the open fields here. His property was described as "a pentagonal lot of a few acres, enclosed by a post-and-rail fence." It included a wooden barn, the large kilns shaped like beehives, and the large "barrel and tall center pole of the pug mill (where clay was kneaded)," along with molds used to shape the bricks and pallets to hold the finished products off the damp ground to help them dry.[5] Kuhn would submit a substantial damage claim after the war.

What Did They Say about It Later?

Interestingly, while three regiments fought here, only one chose to place its primary monument here. On July 1, 1890, the veterans of the 154th New York Infantry dedicated their regimental monument at the site of their bloody stand. Colonel Daniel B. Allen recalled:

> We stopped the enemy and were holding them in our front, but their line so far overlapped the One hundred and thirty-fourth on our right that they swung around almost in their rear, and had such an enfilading fire upon them and our whole line, that that regiment was compelled to give way, and I immediately gave orders for my regiment to fall back. . . . The ground directly in rear of the position which we had occupied was cut up into village lots surrounded by board fences, so that retreat was greatly impeded in that direction. Then men being almost entirely surrounded by the enemy, who outnumbered them more than five to one and were right in their midst, many of our men were compelled to surrender.[6]

During the Civil War Centennial of the 1960s, a group of Gettysburg boys who lived in the area of Coster Avenue and North Stratton Street organized the "Coster Cadets" and participated in the local pageant to celebrate the 100th anniversary of the battle.[7]

Driving directions to the next stop: Turn around and return to Stratton Street. Turn right, and at the stop sign, turn left onto East Lincoln Avenue. At the traffic light, continue straight ahead, and at the second stop sign—in the heart of the Gettysburg College campus—turn right. After two blocks, you will find yourself in the open fields lining Mummasburg Road once more. Just across the railroad tracks, turn left onto Robinson Avenue. Go up the hill, turn left at the stop sign, and park on the right in the gravel patch near the tall monument to the 83rd New York Infantry.

STOP 10. RAMSEUR'S ATTACK

You will visit two positions at this stop.

Position 1: Ramseur's Attack

Orientation

Walk on the park road back toward the observation tower. Stop at the bronze statue of Brigadier General John C. Robinson, commander of the I Corps division that fought on Oak Ridge. Stand in front of the monument and look in the same direction that Robinson is looking.

What Happened Here?

At your previous visit to this general location at Stop 6, you learned about Brigadier General Henry Baxter's repulse of O'Neal's Alabamians in the low ground to your front and then the decimation of Iverson's North Carolina brigade in the fields to your left. After these two actions, Baxter's men had begun to run low on ammunition. General Robinson, Baxter's division commander, saw that the Confederates continued to threaten this position and sent for his other brigade, that of Brigadier General Gabriel R. Paul. When called, Paul's men stopped erecting breastworks for the defense of Seminary Ridge one-half mile behind you and came up quickly to support Baxter.

The tall oak trees behind General Robinson's monument are the remnants of an open oak grove that covered this immediate area almost down to Mummasburg Road in the low ground in front of you. When Paul's regiments arrived, the right flank initially formed a battle line in the edge of the grove closest to the road. They fired toward Confederate skirmishers in the fields of the McClean farm and on the slopes ahead of you, while the center and left of the brigade curled around to the left to confront still more attackers threatening the Union position from the general direction of Oak Hill—the high ground to your left front—as well as from the open fields to your left.

Paul's men on the right flank enjoyed some initial success. Colonel Gilbert Prey of the 104th New York reported that when his men initially charged forward to the Mummasburg Road itself, "some 35 or 40 prisoners were taken, but having neither officers nor men to spare to take charge of them, I directed them to pass to the rear and join some already taken by the Thirteenth Massa-

The view of the 83rd New York Infantry monument and beyond.

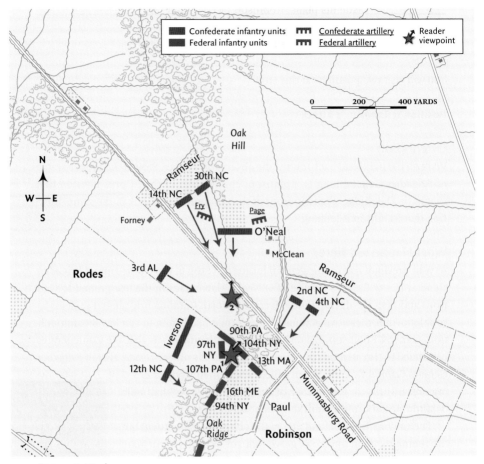

Ramseur's Attack

chusetts." Prey's men then took fifteen or twenty more prisoners before breaking off contact.

They did not have to wait long for the Confederates to return. The four North Carolina regiments in Brigadier General Stephen Dodson Ramseur's brigade—Rodes's last remaining uncommitted unit held in reserve—were more likely to be deployed individually as needed rather than ordered forward in brigade strength. This, in fact, seemed to be their fate. Ramseur received orders to "send two regiments to the support of Colonel O'Neal, and with the remaining two to support Iverson." Although assigned a supporting role, when he discovered "three regiments of Iverson's command almost annihilated," Ramseur took a more active leadership role, rounding up men scattered from Iverson's and O'Neal's units, adding them to his own force, and organizing an attack.

As Ramseur made his plans, Robinson faced a tough tactical challenge of his own. He had to continue to hold the line against the remnants of Iverson's command in the open fields to your left as well as prepare for whatever Ramseur might pull together from Oak Hill. Thus Robinson cobbled together a line that initially included a mixture of Baxter's and Paul's regiments. Two of Paul's regiments held the right of the new line. They formed up on the edge of the oak grove to your right and faced toward Mummasburg Road below you. The monuments you can see over your right shoulder as you look down the hill represent those two regiments; the color-bearer on top of the 13th Massachusetts toward the bottom of the slope marks the anchor of Paul's right flank, while the 104th New York's marker sits halfway up the slope, its line extending across your immediate front. Through the energetic action of Major Alfred Sellers, the 90th Pennsylvania of Baxter's brigade redeployed from facing west toward Iverson to face the Mummasburg Road roughly on the left of the 104th New York. The rest of Paul's regiments fell into line with Baxter's men along the stone wall where they had crushed Iverson's brigade in the open fields off to your left. In a very short time, however, most of Baxter's men—now out of ammunition—pulled back to McPherson's Woods behind you. Robinson confronted Ramseur's fresh brigade with Paul's men, some scattered elements of Baxter's command, and a vulnerable V-shaped line that had one arm facing the Mummasburg Road, the other arm facing the remnants of Iverson's brigade, and its apex pointing toward Oak Hill.

Now look to your left front toward Oak Hill. Ramseur divided his brigade into two separate elements, as ordered, but he still managed to coordinate those two elements toward a single common objective: clearing this ridge of Union troops. His 14th and 30th North Carolina—with the active cooperation of the 3rd Alabama that had fought for a time with Iverson—advanced off Oak Hill along the west (left) of the ridgeline toward your position. Baxter's 90th Pennsylvania and then the left flank of Paul's 104th New York took the brunt of that attack. At roughly the same time, Ramseur's 2nd and 4th North Carolina and some of O'Neal's men attacked over the open eastern slopes of Oak Hill and the McClean farm fields (ahead of you) to hit the right of Paul's line, where the 104th New York and 13th Massachusetts paralleled the Mummasburg Road. As Lieutenant Colonel N. Walter Bachelder reported, a wide interval separated his 13th Massachusetts from the 104th New York, and "we were not able to properly support each other."[1] Still, they put up a fight. As Captain Robert Park of the 12th Alabama, one of O'Neal's men who stayed in the fight, recorded in his diary, the "balls were flying thick and fast around us, and whizzing past and often striking some one near. Capt. Hewlett and Lieut. Bridges and Private Lester were wounded near me. While urging my men to fire and keep cool, I received a ball in my hip. It was a wonder, a miracle, I was not afterward shot a half dozen times, but a merciful Providence preserved me."[2]

In holding the right of Paul's brigade line, the 13th Massachusetts and the 104th New York suffered high losses. As Private Charles Barber of the 104th New York wrote to his wife a few days later, "We went in with 235 men and have less than fifty left. Not a single captain and just one Lieutenant is left in our whole regiment. Company A went in with thirty men and now we have only seven here and not a single officer of any kind except one Sergent."[3] General Paul, trying to rally his two regiments against mounting pressure, suffered a horrific face wound that blinded him for life.

Despite a valiant effort by Robinson's two brigades, his time quickly ran out. In the low ground below, the XI Corps line unraveled, and its troops now streamed off the battlefield, making Robinson's right flank—and the flank of the entire I Corps—increasingly vulnerable. Still, he stayed in place until receiving orders to withdraw, orders that "were not received until all other troops . . . had commenced moving to the rear." Nonetheless, his division "held its ground until outflanked right and left, and retired fighting."[4]

Position 2: The Last Stand of the 16th Maine Infantry

Orientation

Walk forward, past the observation tower to the point where the park road intersects with Mummasburg Road. On the way, observe the unique flank markers shaped like tree stumps that mark the rough location of the 90th Pennsylvania's stand at the apex of Robinson's line. Continue to the intersection and find the low, flat memorial marking the last stand of Colonel Charles W. Tilden's 16th Maine Infantry.

What Happened Here?

Colonel Charles Tilden,
16th Maine Infantry, U.S.A.
(USAMHI)

The 16th Maine's Lieutenant Colonel Augustus B. Farnham, Tilden's second in command, reported that to buy time for the rest of the division to move out, "We were then ordered, alone, by General Robinson, to take possession" of a hill "which commanded the road, and hold the same as long as there was a man left." That hill is where you now stand. The 16th Maine took this position "and held the same until, finding the enemy in such force, and rapidly advancing on us, and seeing no support coming to our aid, we fell back." Several times, the men from Maine rallied and held for a few additional minutes. Finally, when it was clear that they stood alone on the ridge, Colonel Tilden ordered a retreat, "but not in time to reach the main body of the brigade." Many of the men of the 16th Maine—and Colonel Tilden himself—became prisoners of the Confederates when they exited McPherson's Woods (behind you) and became trapped in the area of the eastern railroad cut.[5]

They shared that fate with hundreds of Baxter's and Paul's men who also found themselves caught between surging Confederates closing in on Gettysburg from both west and north.

Who Fought Here?

C.S.A.: The 1,027-man brigade of Brigadier General Stephen Dodson Ramseur of Major General Robert E. Rodes's division of Ewell's Second Corps included the 2nd, 4th, 14th, and 30th North Carolina Infantry. You met Iverson's brigade at Stop 5 and O'Neal's at Stop 6.

    U.S.: The 1,537-man brigade of Brigadier General Gabriel R. Paul of Brigadier General John C. Robinson's division of Reynolds's I Corps included the 16th Maine, the 13th Massachusetts, the 94th and 104th New York, and the 107th Pennsylvania Infantry.

Who Commanded Here?

Brigadier General Gabriel R. Paul (1813–86), a Regular Army officer of long service, did excellent service as a brigade commander during the Civil War. Born in St. Louis, Missouri, and a grandson of an officer in Napoleon's army, Paul graduated from West Point with the class of 1834. His antebellum service included action against the Seminole Indians in Florida and active duty during the Mexican War, for which he was awarded a brevet promotion to major for gallant service at the storming of Chapultepec. He was regularly appointed to major in April 1861, and in December he became colonel of the 4th New Mexico Infantry. In the spring of 1862, he was promoted to brigadier general and brought east to command brigades at Fredericksburg and Chancellorsville. The rifle ball that wounded Paul here on July 1 entered his right temple and passed out through his left eye, blinding him for life. Most Northern newspaper accounts in the week after the battle simply listed General Paul's name among those killed in action. Three weeks later, however, the *New York Herald* reported the general's real fate—and future prognosis—in far greater detail: "A round ball, evidently from a hunting rifle, in the hands of a sharpshooter, penetrated the right side of the head, near the temple, and, passing near the brain, severed the optic nerve, and passed out through the left eye. The wound is an ugly and dangerous one, but the physicians not only look for a recovery, but hope to restore the sight in one or both eyes."[6] That did not happen, of course, but nonetheless, Paul remained on active duty, doing administrative tasks until he retired from active service as a brigadier general in the Regular Army in February 1865. General Paul died in Washington, D.C., in May 1886 and is buried in Arlington National Cemetery.

Brigadier General Gabriel R. Paul, U.S.A., after his disfiguring wound. (USAMHI)

Brigadier General Stephen Dodson Ramseur (1837–64), a North Carolina native, graduated from West Point in 1860 and was commissioned a second lieutenant of artillery. He resigned in April 1861 and entered Confederate service as captain of the Ellis Artillery, a Raleigh, North Carolina, battery. In the spring of 1862, he and his unit saw service on the Virginia peninsula before he was elected colonel of the 49th North Carolina Infantry, a regiment he led with distinction during the Seven Days Battles. Wounded severely at Malvern Hill and promoted to brigadier general in November 1862, Ramseur returned to field duty in 1863 in time for Chancellorsville and continued to command his brigade until June 1864, seeing especially significant action at Spotsylvania Court House. Promoted to major general the day after his twenty-seventh birthday on June 1, he participated in his 1864 raid into Maryland and march on Washington. When Early's command was forced back into the Shenandoah valley, Ramseur saw action at Third Winchester and then took over the command of Rodes's division when that officer fell in battle. On October 19, 1864, at the Battle of Cedar Creek, Ramseur was shot through both lungs. Taken into Union lines, he died the next day surrounded by friends and West Point classmates in the Union army. Married less than a year, he had received word the day before he was mortally wounded of the birth of a daughter. General Ramseur's remains were taken home to North Carolina for burial.

Brigadier General Stephen Dodson Ramseur, C.S.A. (USAMHI)

Who Fell Here?

C.S.A.: In Ramseur's brigade, the 2nd North Carolina lost 67 of its 243 men; the 4th North Carolina lost 69 of its 196 men; the 14th North Carolina lost 64 of its 306 men; and the 30th North Carolina lost 75 of its 278 men—for a brigade loss of 26.8 percent.

U.S.: Paul's brigade lost heavily in prisoners, many of whom were captured in the area of the railroad cut during the final retreat. In its brave stand, the 16th Maine lost 232 of its 298 men, including its colonel and 163 men taken prisoner; the 13th Massachusetts lost 185 of its 284 men, including 101 prisoners; the 94th New York lost 240 of its 411 men, including 175 prisoners; the 104th New York lost 194 of its 286 men, including 92 prisoners; and the 107th Pennsylvania lost 165 of its 255 men, including 98 prisoners. The brigade loss amounted to 66.8 percent.

Individual vignettes. Captain Oliver H. Lowell, commander of Company D of the 16th Maine, fell mortally wounded along the Mummasburg Road. The Confederates put some of the Union prisoners to work carrying their wounded to field hospitals, and Corporal Luther Bradford found Lowell still lying where he fell. As the regimental historian reported, "Although conscious, he was speechless. He was carried to a vacant room in the seminary, on the first floor. Before Bradford could find a surgeon, he, with others, was marched to the rear some two miles. Corporal Bradford adds, that when he found Captain Lowell he had been robbed of all valuables, and the absence of papers, and a small diary torn up and scattered, made it impossible for strangers to identify the body, hence his burial place is unknown."[7]

Private Jacob A. Massey of Company A, 4th North Carolina Infantry, in Ramseur's brigade participated in the attack on this position. He took a bullet in the left thigh that fractured the femur. Massey was taken to a field hospital, and surgeons amputated his left leg on July 3. As a result, he stayed behind when so many other Confederate wounded made the rough wagon trip back to Virginia. Amputations close to the trunk of the body invariably showed a high mortality rate, but Massey seemed to hold his own for a while. When the Union army medical staff decided to consolidate medical care into the large general hospital at Camp Letterman, Massey was taken there and admitted on either August 4 or 6. The area around his wound began to develop abscesses, however, and signs of pyemia became apparent by August 28. The doctors prescribed "tonic and stimulants," likely whiskey. Massey also suffered from "obstinate diarrhea." He finally gave up his struggle on September 2.[8]

Who Lived Here?
Review the material on the Forney and McClean farms at Stops 5 and 6.

What Did They Say about It Later?
Many of Baxter's and Paul's survivors recalled with special vividness their retreat through the town and back to their rallying point on Cemetery Hill. The regimental historian of the 13th Massachusetts of Paul's brigade provided the following account:

> While some of the boys fell back along the railroad cut, others went directly through the town to the hill. Those who went through the town were obliged to run the gauntlet of side streets, already filled with the men of Ewell's corps, who were endeavoring, with artillery and musketry, to prevent our escaping. We saw at once that we had stayed at the front a little too long for our safety. . . . Over fences, into yards, through gates, anywhere an opening appeared, we rushed with all our speed to escape capture. The streets swarmed with the enemy, who kept up an incessant firing, and yelling, "Come in here, you Yankee_____!" . . . There was no time to consider; we must keep moving and take our chances; so on we went until at last, completely blown, we reached the hill. . . . In spite of our efforts ninety-eight of the Thirteenth were captured.[9]

The survivors of the 16th Maine held especially enduring memories. In ceremonies dedicating its two monuments on Oak Ridge, Adjutant Abner Small recalled the final moments of the regiment's last stand here:

The rebels fired upon us from all sides. . . . They swarmed down upon us, they engulfed us, and swept away the last semblance of organization which marked us as a separate command. To fight longer was useless, was wicked. For this little battalion of heroes, hemmed in by thousands of rebels, there was no succor, no hope. Summoned to surrender, Colonel Tilden plunged his sword into the ground and broke it short off at the hilt, and directed the destruction of the colors. A rebel officer sprang to seize the flag, when the men, once more and for the last time, closed around the priceless emblems, and in a moment of fury rent the staves in twain and threw the pieces at the officer's feet. Eager hands from every direction seized the banners and tore them piece by piece beyond reclaim or recognition—but now to be held doubly dear. To-day, all over Maine, can be found in albums and frames and breast-pocket-books gold stars and shreds of silk, cherished mementoes of that heroic and awful hour. And so the Sixteenth Maine was the last regiment that left the extreme front on the 1st of July—if four officers and thirty-six men can be called a regiment.[10]

Driving directions to the next stop: Return to your vehicle and drive forward on Doubleday Avenue 0.4 miles to the stop sign at Reynolds Avenue. Turn left onto Reynolds Avenue and drive 0.2 miles to the traffic light at Chambersburg Road. Turn right and drive 0.1 miles, then turn left at Stone Avenue and drive into the small lot where you parked for Stop 2.

STOP 11. BUCKTAILS VERSUS TAR HEELS ON McPHERSON'S RIDGE

Orientation

From the parking lot of the guide station, cross Stone Avenue toward McPherson's barn and walk toward the 149th Pennsylvania monument, the memorial topped by the seated infantryman near the edge of Chambersburg Road. Proceed about ten paces beyond the monument, then face to the left. Chambersburg Road should run across your front. In the far distance, you should see the Eternal Light Peace Memorial on Oak Hill. General Reynolds's equestrian monument should be across the road to your left front. The McPherson barn should be behind you.

What Happened Here?

When you last visited this area during Stop 2 to cover the opening cavalry fight, the combat action ebbed and flowed from left (west) to right (east) across your front. When the 147th New York made its stand on the knoll just on the other side of the railroad cut—marked by the line of trees about 100 yards in front of you—it faced to the left, too. Only the 14th Brooklyn and the 95th New York followed your current line of sight as they moved from the McPherson farmyard behind you to the railroad cut to your front and right front. After all that late-morning fighting here in the Chambersburg Road corridor, however, a brief lull began at about noon.

The view from Chambersburg Road north to the Eternal Light Peace Memorial on Oak Hill.

During that time, Doubleday's own division finally arrived on the battlefield. Since Doubleday now served as acting I Corps commander after Reynolds's death, his senior brigade commander, Brigadier General Thomas A. Rowley, stepped up to division command. Rowley sent one of his two fresh brigades—the 143rd, 149th, and 150th Pennsylvania under Colonel Roy Stone—here to fill the gap in the I Corps line between the Chambersburg Road and the Iron Brigade in Herbst's Woods behind you; the space opened up when the 14th Brooklyn and the 95th New York moved to attack Davis's Confederates in the railroad cut.

If you look at the cap worn by the soldier sitting atop the 149th Pennsylvania's monument to your left, you will see a bronzed deer tail attached to it. Early in the war, each potential recruit for the 13th Pennsylvania Reserves was expected to demonstrate his prowess with a rifle by presenting the tail of a deer that he shot. Many successful recruits stuck it on their caps, and in a short time they became known as the "Pennsylvania Bucktails." The regiment developed a good reputation on the battlefield, and a number of its junior officers and sergeants decided to improve their chances for promotion by raising companies of their own using the Bucktails as a model. Two new regiments, the 149th and 150th Pennsylvania, incorporated many of these new companies into their ranks, and since their officers still wore their old headgear, the soldiers in the ranks copied them and called themselves "bucktails." The rest of the army needed to be convinced, however; until the 149th and 150th proved themselves in battle, veteran soldiers tended to refer to the two new regiments as the "Bogus Bucktails." Gettysburg offered the first chance for the two new regiments—and the 143rd Pennsylvania, which did not claim the "bucktail" designation—to demonstrate what they could do in battle.

The arrival of Ewell's Second Corps on Oak Hill gave these Pennsylvanians that opportunity. Initially, all three of Stone's regiments faced westward (to your left) toward Herr's Ridge—marked by the red-roofed barn—where the morning's attacks against McPherson's Ridge began. However, the first hostile fire Stone's men took came from the batteries of Lieutenant Colonel Thomas H. Carter's artillery battalion on Oak Hill, which opened an accurate fire on the McPherson farmyard. As Stone reported, the guns "opened a most destructive enfilade of our lines" which "made my position hazardous and difficult in the extreme." It did not take long for Stone to order the 143rd and 149th Pennsylvania to form a new line. Instead of facing west toward Herr's Ridge, he had them redeploy into ditches and along the fence line paralleling the Chambersburg Road and face toward Oak Hill to the north, as you now do. By so doing, he hoped to reduce the size of the target his brigade offered to Carter's gunners. The 150th Pennsylvania, closer to the tree line behind you and protected by the farm buildings, continued to face to the west. But none of Stone's men enjoyed much of a respite from the artillery fire. The Confederate guns on Herr's Ridge opened fire again, and their well-placed rounds—when combined with those from Oak Hill—caught Stone's men in a lethal cross fire. Sergeant William R. Ramsey of the 150th Pennsylvania left this lively account of the shelling in his diary: "While the shells were flying dangerously close to the recumbent line, John S. Weber of our company (F), stood up and yelled: 'come, boys, choose your partners! The ball is about to open! Don't you hear the music?'" He adds: "Poor 'Dutchy' (Weber's nickname in the company)! He danced to another tune before night."[1]

The artillery fire proved so damaging to Stone's line that he ordered the color guard of the 149th Pennsylvania to take the regimental colors to the north side of the Chambersburg Road and display them on top of a prominent pile of rails stacked up by Buford's cavalrymen earlier in the day; this would place the colors in the open field to your left front, just beyond General Buford's statue. The waving flags diverted the attention of the Confederate gunners, who shifted their fire to that conspicuous target and gave Stone's lines a bit of relief.

The respite did not last long. After Iverson launched his attack through the open fields that are in front of the Eternal Light Peace Memorial, Brigadier General Junius Daniel's North Carolina brigade of Rodes's division prepared to step off as well. Daniel had received orders to "protect the right of the division, and to support Iverson's right." When Iverson advanced, however, Daniel did not move forward with him. When he finally reached the field, Daniel realized that Iverson had changed direction without informing him of his exact location. Worse, Iverson's open right flank clearly had drawn the attention of Stone's brigade. Soldiers from the 143rd and 149th Pennsylvania posted here along the Chambersburg Road had begun to fire long-range shots at Iverson's men. To protect Iverson and the rest of the division as ordered, Daniel now realized that he faced a complex tactical problem. If he moved forward on Iverson's right flank as ordered and advanced on the Union line in McPherson's Woods—the woodlot visible just beyond the bridge over the railroad cut to your right front—his own right flank would be vulnerable to the fire of the 143rd and 149th Pennsylvania, and at a much closer range.

To carry out his original mission and neutralize the threat to his right flank, Daniel decided to divide his brigade into two elements. He sent the 43rd and 53rd North Carolina into action on Iverson's right against the McPherson's Woods position. He then deployed the 32nd and 45th North Carolina and the 2nd North Carolina Battalion almost perpendicular to his other two regiments and directed them to advance against Stone's line here. Over the next hour, Daniel attacked his dual targets three times. From this position, you will follow the more challenging of his two efforts: his fight against Stone.

Look straight ahead once more and locate the knoll just on the other side of the railroad cut where the 147th New York made its stand on the morning of July 1. In the low ground behind that knoll, just out of your sight, Daniel deployed the 32nd North Carolina, the 45th North Carolina, and the 2nd North Carolina Battalion from left to right from your position. He ordered them to advance up over the knob and attack the two Pennsylvania regiments here. In anticipation of just such an assault, Stone

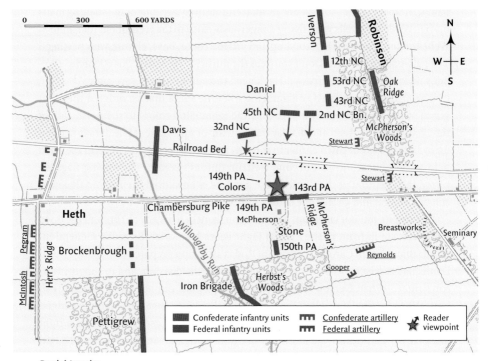

0 | 300 | 600 YARDS

Iverson

Robinson

N
W — E
S

12th NC
53rd NC   Oak
43rd NC   Ridge

Daniel

45th NC   2nd NC Bn.

32nd NC   McPherson's
Davis   Woods

Railroad Bed   Stewart

149th PA
Colors   143rd PA   Stewart

Chambersburg Pike   149th PA

Heth   McPherson   Breastworks   Seminary

Stone

Willoughby Run   150th PA   Reynolds

Brockenbrough

Pegram

Cooper

McIntosh

Herr's Ridge

Herbst's
Iron Brigade   Woods

Pettigrew

| Confederate infantry units | Confederate artillery | Reader viewpoint |
| Federal infantry units | Federal artillery | |

Daniel Attacks

ordered the 149th Pennsylvania to go "forward to occupy a deep railroad cutting about 100 yards from the road," and the regiment obeyed with enthusiasm. When Daniel's men "came to a fence within pistol-shot" of the 149th Pennsylvania's new line in the cut, the Union troops unleashed "a staggering volley; reloading as they [Daniel's men] climbed the fence, and waiting till they came within 30 yards." Then Stone's men "gave them another volley, and charged, driving them back over the fence in utter confusion." The affair did not go all Stone's way, of course. As Captain J. A. Hopkins of the 45th North Carolina reported: "We were ordered to charge, in which a very gallant one was made, driving the enemy [skirmishers] back." Daniel drew his men back into the low ground on the other side of the knoll, while Stone's troops returned to the ditches on the south side of the Chambersburg Road.

Daniel's second attack followed in short order. When the Southern artillery paused for the advance, some of the Pennsylvanians attempted to return to the railroad cut. This time, according to Daniel, the 45th North Carolina and the 2nd North Carolina Battalion "advanced at a charge, driving the enemy from the cut in confusion, killing and wounding many and taking some prisoners."[2] Some even reached the fences on the north side of the Chambersburg Road before the Pennsylvanians stopped them. The exchanges of close-range volleys took a high toll on both sides,

This painting depicts the 149th Pennsylvania lining Chambersburg Pike to fire on Daniel's North Carolinians. When you stand at your orientation point, you are standing among the soldiers on the left side of this illustration. (Chamberlin)

especially among the officers. Daniel nearly gained the upper hand on this occasion, however, by changing the mission of the 32nd North Carolina, his right-flank regiment. Instead of attacking on the same line with his other two regiments, he ordered Colonel Edmund Brabble to move slightly to the west (your left), cross through the railroad cut, and advance into the open field that is just beyond Buford's statue, remaining largely out of the line of sight of the Pennsylvanians deployed here. Daniel intended for Brabble's men to wheel and flank Stone's men. The 150th Pennsylvania deployed amid the McPherson farm buildings behind you spotted the 32nd North Carolina, however, and they charged across the open fields over your left shoulder, crossed the Chambersburg Road near and beyond the stone building of the modern guide station to your left, and pushed Brabble back into the railroad cut. A simultaneous advance by the 149th Pennsylvania and an effective cover fire provided by the 143rd Pennsylvania to your right seemed to secure the Chambersburg Road line against the advance of Daniel's Tar Heels once more.

But Daniel came back a third time. This time, however, he decided to concentrate on one target rather than two. He shifted the 45th North Carolina and the 2nd North Carolina Battalion away from Stone's front to reinforce the attack of his 43rd and 53rd North Carolina at McPherson's Woods. Those latter regiments had not made much headway in their own efforts, due in great part to the oblique fire of the Napoleons of Lieutenant James Stewart's well-served Battery B, 4th U.S. Artillery, posted on Oak Ridge south of the railroad cut (just in front of the red-roofed white buildings of the modern motel on the opposite side of Chambersburg Road). Daniel

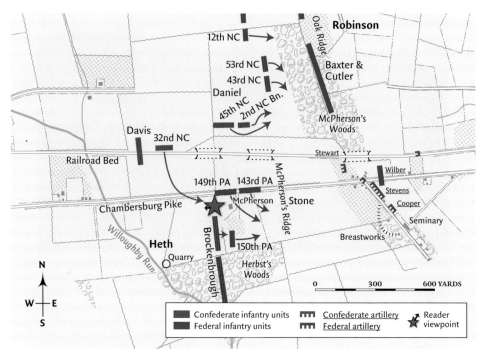

Brockenbrough Attacks

believed that a more forceful attack by four of his units on the north side of the rail-road cut might make better progress than continuing the attack here.

Daniel could afford to do this because at that very moment, Heth's division launched its afternoon attacks from Herr's Ridge. One of Heth's brigades—the Virginians of Colonel John M. Brockenbrough—headed from the area of the red-roofed barn to your left straight for Stone's brigade, completely outflanking the line of the 149th and 143rd Pennsylvania here along the road. Daniel's only contribution to this final push was his decision to leave the 32nd North Carolina in position in the low ground beyond Buford's statue to cooperate with Brockenbrough in the effort to break Stone's line and capture the artillery supporting this position. Appreciat-ing that its greater threat now came from the west rather than the north, the 149th Pennsylvania finally left this position along the road and redeployed along the line of Stone Avenue, the park road over your left shoulder.

Walk back to Stone Avenue and stand in front of the metal sign with the name of the road on it. Face toward Herr's Ridge. Once aligned in this direction, the 149th and 150th Pennsylvania could face Brockenbrough directly. Brockenbrough's bri-gade numbered fewer than 1,000 men—it had been badly battered at Chancel-lorsville—but they were fresh. They advanced up the slope toward where you are standing with a momentum that the exhausted Pennsylvanians could not match.

Brockenbrough's men pushed Stone's troops back into the McPherson farmyard behind you. Some of the 150th Pennsylvania made a fight of it around a small quarry with steep walls, taking advantage of a natural obstacle to slow down the Virginians. (The remnants of the quarry sit close to the east bank of Willoughby Run just inside the tree line in the low ground to your left front.) In time, however, the Pennsylvanians slowly gave way. But few in the army would call them "Bogus Bucktails" after their fights against Daniel and Brockenbrough here at the McPherson farm.

You will learn more about the last stand of Stone's men and the rest of the I Corps at Stop 13.

Who Fought Here?

C.S.A.: The 2,161-man brigade of Brigadier General Junius Daniel of Major General Robert Rodes's division of Ewell's Second Corps included the 32nd, 43rd, 45th, and 53rd North Carolina Infantry Regiments and the 2nd North Carolina Infantry Battalion. The 972-man brigade of Colonel J. M. Brockenbrough of Heth's division in Hill's Third Corps included the 40th, 47th, and 55th Virginia Infantry Regiments and the 22nd Virginia Infantry Battalion. Carter's battalion on Oak Hill and Pegram's battalion on Herr's Ridge created the artillery cross fire that made McPherson's Ridge such a dangerous place to be in the early afternoon of July 1.

U.S.: The 1,317-man brigade of Colonel Roy Stone of Major General Abner Doubleday's division of Reynolds's I Corps included the 143rd, 149th, and 150th Pennsylvania Infantry in their first substantial combat action of the war. Stewart's Battery B, 4th U.S. Artillery; Cooper's Battery B, 1st Pennsylvania Artillery; and Reynolds's Battery L, 1st New York, provided essential fire support.

The monument to John Burns, the Gettysburg town constable who picked up his flintlock musket and came out to the firing line on July 1, sits on Stone Avenue in the line of the 150th Pennsylvania. Burns asked Major Thomas Chamberlin if he could fight with that regiment. Chamberlin referred him to Colonel Langhorn Wister, who asked him if he could shoot. Burns, as Chamberlin explained, said, "'Oh, yes,' and a smile crept over the old man's face which seemed to say, 'If you knew that you had before you a soldier of the War of 1812, who fought with Scott at Lundy's Lane, you would not ask such a question.'" Burns fought here with the 150th Pennsylvania and the Iron Brigade—and may well have fired off a round or two with a few other units—until he fell wounded and was removed back to town.[3]

Who Commanded Here?

Colonel Roy Stone (1836–1905), born in Plattsburg, New York, was an engineer and lumberman before the Civil War. He was appointed major in the 13th Pennsylvania Reserves in June 1861. In August 1862 Stone recruited and received command of the 149th Pennsylvania Infantry. In February 1863 he rose to brigade command. Stone was shot in the hip during the action just described. His men took him to the McPherson barn, which functioned as a makeshift medical station. Captured and paroled by the Confederates, Stone went home to recuperate from his wounds and returned to the command of his brigade in the spring of 1864. At the Battle of the Wilderness, he suffered severe injuries when his horse fell on him. In the fall of 1864, he commanded the volunteer training depot at Camp Curtin near Harrisburg, Pennsylvania. He tendered his resignation at the end of January 1865 and mustered out of service in early March of that year. Stone received a brevet promotion to brigadier general of volunteers for his leadership at Gettysburg. He later returned to military service as a brigadier general of volunteers in 1898 during the Spanish-American War. In 1893 he established the Office of Road Inquiry in the Department of Agriculture, the precursor of the modern Federal Highway System.

Brigadier General Junius Daniel (1828–64) was born in Halifax, North Carolina, and graduated from West Point in 1851. He served seven years in the U.S. Army, five of those years at Fort Albuquerque, New Mexico; he served temporarily under the command of Captain Richard S. Ewell in skirmishes with the Apache Indians. Daniel resigned his commission in 1858 to manage his father's plantation in Louisiana. Upon the secession of North Carolina, he became colonel of the 14th North Carolina Infantry and led it during the Seven Days Battles. In September 1862 he was promoted to brigadier general and spent that winter with his command in North Carolina. In the spring of 1863, his brigade became part of Rodes's division of Ewell's Second Corps. After Gettysburg, Daniel continued in brigade command until May 12, 1864, when he was killed in action at Spotsylvania. His widow remained active in Confederate veteran activities well into the twentieth century.

Brigadier General Junius Daniel, C.S.A. (USAMHI)

Who Fell Here?

C.S.A.: In Daniel's brigade, the 32nd North Carolina lost 181 of its 454 men; the 43rd North Carolina lost 187 of its 572 men; the 45th North Carolina lost approximately 219 of its 570 men; the 53rd North Carolina lost at least 211 of its 322 men; and the 2nd North Carolina Battalion lost 199 of its 240 men—for a brigade loss of 46.2 percent. While Daniel's brigade suffered its largest loss at Gettysburg in these attacks, an unknown percentage of these casualties would fall at Culp's Hill on the morning of July 3, which you will visit at Stop 30. Brockenbrough's brigade suffered comparatively light casualties. The 40th Virginia lost 65 of its 254 men; the 47th Virginia lost 54 of its 209 men; the 55th Virginia lost 65 of its 268 men; and the 22nd Virginia Battalion lost only 31 of its 237 men—for a brigade loss of 22 percent. Some of these losses, however, would occur during the brigade's brief participation in the July 3 attack known as Pickett's Charge.

U.S.: In Stone's brigade, the 143rd Pennsylvania lost 253 of its 465 men; the 149th Pennsylvania lost 336 of its 450 men; and the 150th Pennsylvania lost 264 of its 400 men. The brigade thus lost 64.8 percent of its strength. Stewart's battery lost 36 of its 123 men; Cooper lost 12 of his 106 men; and Reynolds lost 17 of his 124 men, although it should be noted that all three batteries served in several additional actions after this one. Captain Reynolds lost an eye in this action.

Individual vignettes. Corporal Joseph D. Hammel, Company D, 149th Pennsylvania Infantry, was a proud member of his regiment's color guard. During the fighting, he took a bullet in the right hip that buried itself in the pelvic bone. At first, Hammel received treatment at a field hospital, but on July 14 surgeons sent him to the Camden Street Hospital in Baltimore. Upon Hammel's admission, Surgeon E. G. Waters reported that "his general condition was good." Waters urged Hammel to "submit to an operation for the removal of the bullet, but he declined, and nothing more was done at the time." On August 27, Hammel suffered a "great constitutional disturbance, and intense pain in the vicinage of the ball." When Waters visited him that morning, Hammel "implored me to extract the missile, which was done accordingly," along with several pieces of the surrounding bone. In the process of operating, however, Waters noted signs of infection. Hammel struggled to rally from the operation. On August 29 he "slept indifferently, notwithstanding a full dose of morphia." He showed little improvement or appetite, although he took "beef essence with milk-punch, as ordered" and "gets his tonic, with eight ounces of whiskey, daily." On September 8, Waters noted that Hammel "had become suddenly and universally jaundiced; much inclined to sleep . . . body bathed in sweat, as it has been for several days, necessitating frequent changes of clothing; remedies persevered in to no purpose, and he sank at 11 P.M." Waters's final comment: "I attribute this man's death to his obstinate refusal to have the bullet extracted soon after his admission."[4]

Austin Brockenbrough, from Tappahannock, Virginia, entered Confederate service as first lieutenant of Company D, 55th Virginia Infantry. A friend described him as "a young man of chivalrous spirit, frank, ingenuous and full of soul, but with a certain dignity and even something of hauteur of bearing." By the time of the Gettysburg Campaign, he had won promotion to captain, became the assistant adjutant and inspector general of Colonel J. M. Brockenbrough's brigade, and occasionally commanded its sharpshooter battalion. When the line of Stone's brigade finally began to give way under pressure from Daniel to the north and from Brockenbrough's brigade from the west, the young captain and another officer in his regiment "became contestants for the capture of one of the Federal colors." Both claimed the banner at the same time. Soon thereafter, a bullet hit Captain Austin Brockenbrough in the arm and chest, passing though both lungs. He asked for his brother Benjamin, serving with Stuart's cavalry, but he died the next day before his brother arrived to minister to him. The young officer was buried "on the turnpike, about halfway between Cashtown and Gettysburg," and after the war, his family reclaimed his remains and returned with them to Tappahannock.[5]

Who Lived Here?

Most of this action occurred on the McPherson farm, fully examined at Stop 2.

What Did They Say about It Later?

Controversy arose in postwar years over the identification of a color-bearer noted by British Lieutenant Colonel A. J. L. Fremantle of the Coldstream Guards in his famous diary of his visit to the Confederacy and its main armies. After observing the

Color Sergeant Samuel Peiffer, 150th Pennsylvania, U.S.A., killed in action here. (Chamberlin)

battle from Herr's Ridge with General A. P. Hill late on the afternoon of July 1, Fremantle wrote that Hill had credited the Union forces for fighting "with a determination unusual to them. He pointed out a railway cutting, in which they made a good stand; also, a field in the center of which he had seen a man plant the regimental color, round which the regiment had fought for some time with much obstinacy, and when at last it was obliged to retreat, the color-bearer retired last of all, turning round every now and then to shake his fist, at the advancing Rebels. General Hill said he felt quite sorry when he saw this gallant Yankee meet his doom."[6] But who was the gallant color-bearer?

To rally his command as the Confederate attackers from the west finally pushed the 150th Pennsylvania out of the McPherson farmyard, Lieutenant Colonel Henry S. Huidekoper ordered Sergeant Samuel Peiffer (sometimes rendered as "Phifer"), "a man of large stature and boundless courage," to take the color guard and move forward with the colors. He did as ordered without hesitation, and the regiment moved forward with him. Four color corporals fell dead or wounded. Then Peiffer went down with a mortal wound. Chamberlain asserted: "This is undoubtedly the incident which drew from A. P. Hill, who was approaching on the Chambersburg road, the expression of regret at the death of so brave a man, as detailed by an English officer in an article published soon after. . . . No other Union color-bearer could well have been visible to General Hill at the time."[7]

At the dedication address at the future site of the 143rd Pennsylvania's monument on September 11, 1889, however, the orator read the Fremantle quotation and then intoned:

> This regiment was the One hundred and forth-third, and the color-bearer Sergeant Ben Crippen, to whose heroic conduct the survivors of the One hundred

and forty-third are about erecting a monument upon the spot where he fell, to be chiseled from marble, life size, and in that defiant attitude in which he met his death. . . . The fate of the young soldier will stimulate the patriotism of future generations who will envy us the privilege we have enjoyed in our time, of receiving from the lips of the veterans the record of his experience, and contributing our mite to the erection of this memorial.[8]

Driving directions to the next stop: Return to your vehicle, drive out of the parking lot, and turn right onto Chambersburg Road. Take the immediate right turn onto Stone Avenue and follow it 0.3 miles and around the bend to the monument to the 24th Michigan Infantry (topped by a soldier) on your left and the low marker to the 26th North Carolina Infantry on your right. Park on the right side of the road in the designated parking spaces.

STOP 12. THE IRON BRIGADE TAKES A STAND

You will visit two main positions at this stop.

Position 1: The Iron Brigade versus Pettigrew's Brigade

Orientation

Stand beside the 24th Michigan monument, topped by an infantryman wearing the distinctive tall Hardee hat of the Regular U.S. Army, and follow the soldier's gaze into the woods. Except when dense vegetation obscures the view during the summer, you may be able to see Willoughby Run flowing from right to left in the low ground to your front.

What Happened Here?

Four regiments of the Iron Brigade held this position since re-forming here after their late-morning fight—explained at Stop 3—against Archer's brigade across Willoughby Run ahead of you. The 19th Indiana deployed to the left of the 24th Michigan, while the 2nd and 7th Wisconsin extended the brigade's line to the right of the Michiganders until it ended at the northwestern edge of Herbst's Woods. (The

The 24th Michigan monument.

detached 6th Wisconsin continued to operate away from the brigade, even after the end of its fight at the railroad cut.) Colonel Henry A. Morrow of the 24th Michigan considered this position "untenable" but "received answer that the position was ordered to be held, and must be held at all hazards." At about noon, the 150th Pennsylvania and the rest of Stone's brigade from Doubleday's old division—now commanded by Brigadier General Rowley—fell in on the 7th Wisconsin's right flank (you learned of that brigade's experiences at Stop 11). Rowley deployed his own brigade—now under Colonel Chapman Biddle—to the left and rear of the Iron Brigade to secure its left flank. You will visit Biddle's position shortly.

At approximately 2:00 P.M., after about a two-hour lull on its front—and with the sound of Stone's fight with Daniel clearly audible to its right—the Iron Brigade once again found itself under attack. The attackers, belonging to Brigadier General James Johnston Pettigrew's fresh North Carolina brigade of General Heth's division, crossed Willoughby Run and advanced up the slopes directly toward this line. As Morrow reported, "I gave direction to the men to withhold their fire until the enemy should come within short range of our guns. This was done, but the nature of the ground was such that I am inclined to think we inflicted but little injury on the enemy at this time. Their advance was not checked and they came on with rapid strides, yelling like demons."

Colonel Henry A. Morrow, 24th Michigan, U.S.A. (USAMHI)

In short order, the fighting along the entire Iron Brigade line grew heated, but some of the deadliest combat occurred right in this area, where fate pitted the 496 men of Detroit and Wayne County's 24th Michigan against the approximately 800 men of the 26th North Carolina, the largest regiment in Lee's entire army. As the men of Michigan stood their ground here, twenty-one-year-old Colonel Henry K. Burgwyn's Tar Heel regiment charged up the slope. Each time, the massed fire of Michigan rifles threw them back, but they rallied and rushed forward again. Heth contradicted Morrow's assessment of the effectiveness of the 24th Michigan's fire, reporting: "When the Twenty-sixth North Carolina Regiment encountered the second line of the enemy, his dead marked his line of battle with the accuracy of a line at a dress parade." Each time their colors fell—and the 26th North Carolina lost eleven color-bearers that day—another man picked them up and bore them forward. The Michigan men lost as heavily in defense as the Tar Heels did in the attack. It was no wonder. As Major John T. Jones of the 26th North Carolina reported, "The fighting was terrible—our men advancing, the enemy stubbornly resisting, until

Colonel Henry K. Burgwyn, 26th North Carolina, C.S.A., killed in action here. (Clark)

the two lines were pouring volleys into each other at a distance not greater than 20 paces." A bullet mortally wounded Colonel Burgwyn, but the attack continued.

The rest of the Iron Brigade also had its hands full. Walk up the road to your right a short distance until you reach the 2nd Wisconsin's monument (it is the next marker to your right) and note that the monument to the 7th Wisconsin sits just a bit farther ahead on the opposite side of the road. These two Wisconsin regiments contended mostly with the left flank of the 26th North Carolina and some of Brockenbrough's Virginians. Major John Mansfield of the 2nd Wisconsin admitted that the fight on his front "continued with great spirit for a time." Colonel William W. Robinson of the 7th Wisconsin reported, a bit more pointedly, that advancing Confederates "opened a galling fire." As he heard the firing intensify to his left, where the 19th Indiana and the 24th Michigan "were being badly cut up by superior numbers," his own regiment and the 2nd Wisconsin kept up "a rapid fire upon the enemy in front, but, I think, without doing him much injury, as he was protected by the hill and the timber." Robinson greatly underestimated the effectiveness of his regiment's fire.

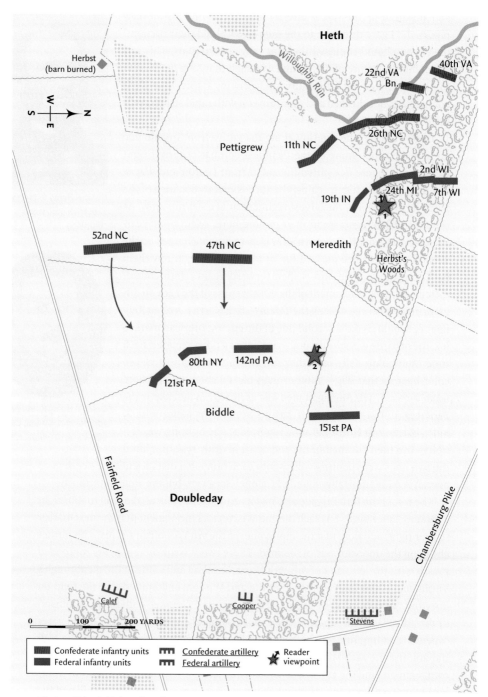

Heth

Herbst
(barn burned)

Willoughby Run

22nd VA
Bn.

40th VA

26th NC

Pettigrew   11th NC

2nd WI

19th IN   24th MI   7th WI

52nd NC

47th NC   Meredith

Herbst's
Woods

80th NY   142nd PA

121st PA

Biddle

151st PA

Fairfield Road

Doubleday

Chambersburg Pike

Calef

Cooper

Stevens

0   100   200 YARDS

Confederate infantry units   Confederate artillery   Reader
Federal infantry units   Federal artillery   viewpoint

The Iron Brigade Makes a Stand

Now walk back toward the 24th Michigan monument but continue past it to the memorial to the 19th Indiana on the low ground to the right of the road. Face the monument. The Hoosiers faced a tough foe in Colonel Collett Leventhorpe's 11th North Carolina. The Tar Heels enjoyed an advantage of position here, advancing toward the high ground visible through the trees to your left front to overlap the 19th Indiana's left flank and shoot down its line. The intensity of the attack forced the Hoosiers back into the woods behind you and onto the high ground visible over your left shoulder. Their move opened the left flank of the 24th Michigan to enfilading fire from the 11th North Carolina. Thus Colonel Morrow adjusted his lines, drawing back his right and center "a short distance in the rear" to continue to fight the 26th North Carolina in his front while also swinging back his left flank to face the 11th North Carolina and restore his connection to the 19th Indiana.[1] The 24th Michigan—and the Iron Brigade as a whole—had to pull back and form new lines in the woods behind you several different times as the pressure of the Tar Heel attacks took their toll. As Morrow described it: "We then fell back and rallied again, losing over one hundred men. Again we fell back and rallied, the men literally slaughtered as they tried to form."[2]

As Lieutenant John H. McGilvary of the 26th North Carolina wrote home to his parents on July 9 as he recovered in Winchester, Virginia, from three bullet wounds: "The battle was *grand, sublime, awful*. Neither language nor pen can describe the scene. The enemy was strewn in piles—some in rows just as literally *blue*. Our Brigade (Pettigrew's) that day was opposed to the Iron Brigade, never having been repulsed before (so I heard some of the prisoners say) but, said they, 'what men fought them that day' in a certain part of the line, being answered 'North Carolinians,' he said, 'I don't want to fight them again.'"[3]

Position 2: The Fight of Biddle's Brigade

Orientation
From the 19th Indiana monument, continue to walk (or drive) to the stop sign at the top of the hill. Stand near the stop sign and look back down the park road toward the low ground.

What Happened Here?
As the 11th North Carolina threatened the left flank of the 19th Indiana, General Rowley became concerned that a collapse by the Hoosiers might open a gap between the Iron Brigade's left flank and the right of Biddle's line. He advanced the 151st Pennsylvania of Biddle's brigade to prevent such a gap from opening. For the 151st Pennsylvania—a nine-month regiment due to muster out of service on July 23—July 1 at Gettysburg brought its first major combat experience. "The enemy greeted me with a volley which brought several of my men down, ere I had halted in

position," Lieutenant Colonel George F. McFarland reported. Since the Confederates were "partly concealed in the woods on lower ground [ahead of you] than we occupied, I did not order [my men] to fire a regular volley, but each man to fire as he saw an enemy on which to take a steady aim." The stand exacted a high cost from the "Schoolteachers' Regiment," so named for the significant number of teachers and students from the McAllisterville Academy and other educational institutions in central Pennsylvania who served in its ranks. Its monument is the large marker to your right front.

Now look to your left along the park road. Along with the statue of General Doubleday surveying the scene of the action, the line of monuments you see lining the crest represent the rest of the regiments in Biddle's brigade. Beginning with the cross-shaped monument and proceeding away from it, the memorials commemorate the 142nd Pennsylvania, the 80th New York, and the 121st Pennsylvania of Biddle's brigade, along with a smaller marker for guns from Cooper's Battery B, 1st Pennsylvania Light Artillery, that supported the brigade line.

Shortly after they arrived early in the afternoon, skirmishers from the 121st Pennsylvania marched over the fields to your left front and crossed over to the west side of Willoughby Run. They had orders to flush out Confederate sharpshooters from a barn on the Harman farm. The skirmishers pulled back to McPherson's Ridge, however, when they observed an increase in Confederate troop strength on their front. While enduring a severe artillery fire from Herr's Ridge, they returned to this ridgeline—and perhaps even a bit behind it to take advantage of the cover it offered—and prepared to receive an attack. The forces massing on their front represented the final two regiments of Pettigrew's brigade, the large 47th and 52nd North Carolina. When Biddle first saw them, he believed they amounted to "a division or more."

Before the North Carolinians advanced, they set ablaze the Harman barn. Then they crossed Willoughby Run and charged from the low ground toward the crest to your left. Biddle reported that he "saw the line of the enemy slowly approaching up the hill, extending far beyond our left flank. . . . As the enemy's faces appeared over the crest of the hill, we fired effectually into them." Most of his subordinates, however, reported a far more chaotic result. As the battle lines swayed back and forth across these fields, Colonel Robert Cummins of the 142nd Pennsylvania fell mortally wounded. Finally, most of Biddle's line, progressing from left to right, simply pulled back without orders to the wood line on Seminary Ridge behind you. Biddle's men suffered severely, but according to General Heth, the 47th and 52nd North Carolina were merely "subjected to a heavy artillery fire" and "suffered much less than the Eleventh and Twenty-sixth North Carolina Regiments." Indeed, the fire from Union batteries temporarily kept the Tar Heels from advancing any farther than the line of monuments at the crest of the ridge to your left. Heth said nothing about the Tar Heels' contact with Biddle's Union infantry, reporting only that the two regiments "behaved to my entire satisfaction."

The Old Dorm (Schmucker Hall),
Lutheran Theological Seminary

The Iron Brigade and Biddle's men fell back to hastily constructed breastworks in the open ground just in front of the Old Dorm of the Lutheran Seminary.

Now turn around and face toward the grounds of the Lutheran Theological Seminary on Seminary Ridge. You can see Schmucker Hall, also called the Old Dorm, the main building of the wartime seminary. Both Buford and Reynolds observed the battlefield from that location. Finally, by about 4:00 P.M., exhausted and badly bloodied, the Iron Brigade, along with Biddle's and Stone's survivors, began a fighting withdrawal to an open area on the slope in front of the Old Dorm. Over the course of the day, several different I Corps commands had piled up fence rails and other materials to establish a defensive breastwork there. Brigadier General James Wadsworth gave credit to the 7th Wisconsin for "bringing up the rear, and suffering heavily, with the whole of the command, from the fire from front and both flanks," but they did not receive a "stand to the last" order like that issued to the 16th Maine.[4] Once on the grounds of the Lutheran Seminary, the I Corps prepared to make one final stand. You will visit the site of that stand at Stop 13.

Who Fought Here?

C.S.A.: The large 2,584-man North Carolina brigade of Brigadier General J. Johnston Pettigrew of Heth's division, Hill's Third Corps, included the 11th, 26th, 47th, and 52nd North Carolina Infantry.

U.S.: You met Brigadier General Solomon Meredith's Iron Brigade previously at Stop 3. The 1,361-man brigade of Colonel Chapman Biddle of Doubleday's division (under Rowley) in Reynolds's I Corps included the 80th New York and the 121st, 142nd, and 151st Pennsylvania Infantry.

Who Commanded Here?

Colonel Chapman Biddle (1822–80) was born into a prominent Philadelphia family. An attorney by education and practice, he entered the army in 1862 as the colonel of the 121st Pennsylvania Infantry. The men of Biddle's brigade never forgot the personal courage of their commander on July 1:

> The coolness of Colonel Chapman Biddle, commanding the brigade, was remarkable. Throughout this tornado of fire he rode back and forth along the line of his brigade, and by his daring, by his apparent forgetfulness of his own danger, accomplished wonders with his four small regiments—cheering his men and urging them through that fiery ordeal, his words unheard in the roaring tempest, but, as well by gesture and the magnificent light of his countenance, speaking encouragement to the men on whom he well knew he could place every reliance. A modest unassuming gentleman in the ordinary walks of life, suddenly transformed into an illustrious hero, the admiration of friend and foe. Even his devoted horse seemed to partake of the heroism of the rider, as he dashed along the line between the two fires, daring the storm of death-dealing messengers that filled the atmosphere.[5]

Even though his brigade line finally withdrew under pressure from Pettigrew's North Carolinians, Biddle clearly understood the importance of personal leadership in ways that Iverson did not.

Who Fell Here?

C.S.A.: In Pettigrew's brigade, the 11th North Carolina lost 366 of its 617 men; the 26th North Carolina lost Colonel Burgwyn and 687 of its 843 men; the 47th North Carolina lost 217 of its 567 men; and the 53rd North Carolina lost 177 of its 553 men—for a brigade loss of 56.1 percent. Not all of these losses occurred in this fight, however. Pettigrew's brigade also would participate in Pickett's Charge on July 3; these casualty figures include both July 1 and July 3.

U.S.: In the Iron Brigade, the 19th Indiana lost 210 of its 318 men; the 24th Michigan lost 363 of its 496 men; the 2nd Wisconsin lost 233 of its 302 men; and the 7th Wisconsin lost 178 of its 364 men—for a total brigade loss (including the 6th Wisconsin's loss of 168 of its 344 men) of 63 percent.

In Biddle's brigade, the 80th New York lost 170 of its 287 men; the 121st Pennsylvania lost 179 of its 263 men; the 142nd Pennsylvania lost Colonel Robert Cummins (killed) and 210 more of its 336 men; and the 151st Pennsylvania lost 337 of its 467 men—for a brigade loss of 66 percent. The 80th New York would participate in the repulse of Pickett's Charge on July 3.

Individual vignettes. The regiments in Pettigrew's brigade suffered the loss of a significant number of their company-grade officers—captains and lieutenants—that could not be replaced easily. For the rest of the war, General Lee complained about his inability to find sufficient officers in these grades able and willing to maintain discipline in his ranks. Among those who fell on these fields was Lieutenant Edward Averett Rhodes of the 11th North Carolina. The lieutenant was born in 1841 in Galveston, Texas, where his North Carolina–born father served as U.S. consul before the Lone Star Republic became a state. Rhodes grew up in California; thus, "he owned no interest in the South, not a foot of land, not a slave." By age twelve, he had become "a fearless rider and an excellent shot," and he entered the Virginia Military Institute in July 1860. Rhodes went to Richmond with the rest of the corps of cadets in April 1861 to serve as a drillmaster, then he accepted a lieutenancy in the 11th North Carolina under Colonel Collett Leaventhorpe. On July 1 the colonel talked to Rhodes—whom he called "Eddie"—during the advance toward the Iron Brigade's line, and the lieutenant "remarked to me with a smile, 'We are marching in excellent line.'" A few minutes later, after Rhodes had picked up his regiment's fallen colors, a bullet hit him in the head, killing him almost instantly. He was buried side by side with two brother lieutenants—Thomas W. Cooper and J. B. Lowrie—who fell at nearly the same moment.[6] In addition to these three lieutenants, the 11th North Carolina also lost its major and ten additional lieutenants killed at Gettysburg.

No other Union regiment lost more officers killed or mortally wounded at Gettysburg than the 24th Michigan's eight company-grade officers; only one regiment—the 120th New York—equaled it. One of the Michigan officers who fell here on July 1 was William J. Speed, captain of Company D. A convincing speaker, Speed addressed public meetings during the regiment's recruiting drive; the regimental history recounts that, after a successful effort at Livonia Center, "as the announcements of the names of recruits were made, the young men tossed their hats in the air and the old men shouted for joy." Speed had just completed a term as city attorney in Detroit when the war broke out, and when the 24th Michigan left for the front, the Detroit Bar Association presented him with a sword. His legal background led to his appointment during the fall of 1862 to serve as division judge advocate for general court-martials. Still, he preferred to be with his men and participated in all the regiment's major battles, being absent from the unit for only about a month on sick leave. When the assaults of the 11th North Carolina pushed back the 19th Indiana, the movement opened the left flank of the 24th Michigan to a murderous cross fire. As acting major of the regiment, Speed rushed to the left flank and endeavored to carry out Colonel Morrow's orders to refuse the two leftmost companies to counter the fire from the Tar Heels. While executing the movement, as his regimental history asserts, "a Confederate bullet pierced his heart!" At a speech in Detroit on July 30, 1863, Morrow eulogized Captain Speed as "gallant and noted for his amiable

Lieutenant Edward A. Rhodes, 11th North Carolina, C.S.A., killed in action here. (Clark)

qualities. Well posted in military tactics, had he lived, he would have entered the regular army."[7]

Corporal Elkanah Sulgrove, described by friends in his hometown as an "industrious hard working young man," mustered in to Company F of the 19th Indiana Infantry on July 29, 1861, in Indianapolis. He became a good soldier, but he never forgot his mother back home in Indiana. Lucinda Potter had been widowed twice. Elkanah's father, Jacob Sulgrove, died when Elkanah was young. Soon thereafter, Lucinda had married a man named Potter, and he died in 1855. Elkanah was the oldest of Lucinda's four children from the two marriages. His captain testified that Elkanah routinely sent home three-quarters of his pay to support his mother and his youngest sibling; the captain himself made out the money orders. On July 1, in Herbst's Woods or on slopes of Seminary Ridge, a bullet killed Corporal Sulgrove instantly. Several of his company mates testified that they saw his body "lying on that battlefield." Since Lucinda's two middle sons were married, had families, and were themselves "in indigent circumstances," she found herself relying on the charity of neighbors for support. She applied for a mother's pension, but before it could be approved, Lucinda Potter, too, died, passing away in October 1864 of lung disease. Corporal Sulgrove's remains rest in grave A-7 of the Indiana plot.[8]

On March 20, 1862, three young men, all surnamed Coffey, volunteered for service in Company F, 26th North Carolina Infantry, for three years or the duration of the war. Thomas Milton Coffey, the oldest of the three, was twenty-seven; Cleveland Coffey was twenty-five; and William S. Coffey was eighteen. They were part of a large contingent of men from the extended Coffey family to serve in the 26th North Carolina. The three men turned into reliable soldiers; only Cleveland suffered any extended illness, being hospitalized for rheumatism from December 1862 to March 1863. The three share more than a surname and an enlistment date, of course. On July 1, 1863, all three fell to Iron Brigade bullets. Private Cleveland Coffey died of his wounds on July 3; Thomas Milton survived until August 12; and William, the youngest, lived until August 20.[9]

Who Lived Here?

Biddle's brigade contested the advance of the right of Pettigrew's brigade on farms owned by Emanuel Harman and John Herbst. You learned about the Herbst farm at Stop 3. The Harman farm was situated about 250 yards west of Willoughby Run, beyond the tree line to your left front. Structures on the farm included a large brick house topped with a cupola, a stone barn, a two-story brick washhouse, a smokehouse, and a corncrib. Teenager Amelia Harman was in the home with her aunt when the fighting started, and they observed firsthand the bloody action swirling around them. First, Union cavalry rode through the farmyard heading west toward the advancing lines of Confederate infantry. A Union officer ordered the ladies into the basement for their own safety. Advancing Confederate skirmishers forced back the cavalry, and the Confederate infantry in turn occupied the house and barn, using the upper levels as positions from which to fire into Biddle's line on the southern end of McPherson's Ridge. Soon Union skirmishers advanced forward of the brigade line, crossed Willoughby Run, and forced the Confederates out of the Harman buildings. Soon, however, nearly surrounded by Confederate infantry, they were forced to withdraw. The Confederate advance against Biddle's brigade crossed through the Harman farm property. As was the fate of the Herbst barn, soldiers of the 52nd North Carolina burned the Harman buildings so that Union sharpshooters could not use them again. Amelia and her aunt escaped the burning buildings, survived the fighting, and found refuge behind Confederate lines until the battle ended.[10]

What Did They Say about It Later?

On June 12, 1889, 126 veterans of the 24th Michigan—including 115 who actually fought at Gettysburg—gathered in the town square to march to the site of their new regimental monument. Major E. B. Wight delivered the dedicatory address. Describing their visit as a worthy pilgrimage, he observed: "Volumes have been written, with the Battle of Gettysburg as sole and only topic, but the whole story has not been told. Much of the planning and more of the doing has been omitted. The living may have given their version of what they did and what they witnessed there—but, oh—if the dead lips could be unsealed, what truer and larger testimony might be spread upon the pages of history."[11]

The advance of Pettigrew and Brockenbrough ended the most active involvement of Heth's division in the fighting of July 1. Jaquelin Marshall Meredith, the chaplain of the 47th Virginia in Brockenbrough's brigade, believed that he had never seen an account that did "simple justice to the brave and gallant division of General Harry Heth and its faithful commander, upon whom rested the responsibility of opening the battle." Of the action at Stops 11 and 12, he wrote:

> I saw the Virginians . . . driving the enemy in hand to hand fighting out of houses and barns of which they made forts. Here General Heth was wounded; here fell the brave Colonel Burgwin [sic], of North Carolina, and here I buried next day, on the highest point, under a lone tree, with the Church's solumn [sic] services, Captain [Austin] Brockenbrough, brother and aid of our brigade commander. . . . All honor is due General Heth and his noble division for pressing the enemy enabling Rodes and Pender and Early to secure a severely-fought battle.[12]

Driving directions to the next stop: Drive forward to the stop sign at Reynolds Avenue. Turn left and drive to the traffic light at the intersection with Chambersburg Road. Turn right and drive 0.2 miles to the east, back toward town, turning right onto Seminary Ridge Avenue. Drive forward and park in the vicinity of Schmucker Hall, the large red-brick building with the prominent cupola on the roof.

STOP 13. LAST STAND AT THE SEMINARY

Orientation

Schmucker Hall—also called the Old Dorm—was the main academic building of the wartime Lutheran Seminary. Generals Reynolds and Buford both observed some of the fighting from the cupola on its roof. It is now home to the Seminary Ridge Museum.

Begin your exploration of this site by walking back to the corner of Seminary Ridge Road and Chambersburg Road (Route 30). Look across the street and to the left at Mary Thompson's stone house. Although signs indicate that this building served as Robert E. Lee's headquarters, the general and his staff actually used a cluster of tents on the side of Chambersburg Road where you now stand; if you look to your left, you can spot the upturned bronze cannon that serves as a headquarters marker placed just beyond the nearby parking lot. Lee arrived on Herr's Ridge at about 2:00 P.M.; thus, the event you are about to explore was the only major part of the July 1 fight that he could have witnessed personally from start to finish.

Now turn around and retrace your steps along Seminary Ridge Road. When you reach the low marker to Captain Greenleaf T. Stevens's 5th Maine Battery next to a single Napoleon cannon on the right side of the road, face to the right (west) toward the open fields where the cannon is pointing. Realize that at the time of the fighting, the Charles Krauth house, the red-brick building over your left shoulder, was the only building on this part of Seminary Ridge. The recently replanted fruit trees on the slopes below you represent the orchard that stood here in 1863.

Schmucker Hall, the Old Dorm of the wartime Lutheran Seminary. Generals Buford and Reynolds viewed the battlefield from its cupola, and a Union signal team enjoyed an excellent view of the battle from that point, too.

What Happened Here?

Colonel Charles S. Wainwright, the commander of the I Corps's artillery brigade, offered a clear description of this ridgeline on July 1, 1863:

> Gettysburg Seminary is situated on a ridge about a quarter of a mile from the town [behind you], the ridge running nearly north and south. . . . It is crossed by the Cashtown [i.e., Chambersburg] turnpike [to your right] about 100 yards north of the seminary, and cut through by the railroad some 40 yards farther on [the east railroad cut, behind the motel buildings and restaurant to your right]. The west front of the seminary is shaded by a grove of large trees [to your left front], and the whole top of the ridge on both sides is more or less crowned with open woods through its entire length. Beyond this ridge [in front of you] the ground falls gradually to the west, and rises again [onto eastern and then western McPherson's Ridge].

As the brigades of Biddle and Stone and the Iron Brigade continued to resist on McPherson's Ridge ahead of you, they began to waver under the pressure of growing Confederate numbers. Finally, General Doubleday ordered them to pull back to Seminary Ridge.

During the course of the day, several commands—notably Baxter's and Paul's brigades—had begun to pile up fence rails and other materials to build impromptu breastworks on the slope in front of Schmucker Hall. Those defenses did not extend to your immediate front, however. On this segment of the ridge closest to the Chambersburg Road, Colonel Charles Wainwright cobbled together a formidable line of artillery.

He took such a risk with his guns largely due to a misunderstanding. As he reported: "Having heard incidentally some directions given to General Doubleday about holding Cemetery Hill, and not knowing that there was such a place, while the seminary was called indiscriminately cemetery and seminary, I supposed the latter was meant." Thus he ordered Captain James H. Cooper of Battery B, 1st Pennsylvania Light Artillery, "to take a good position in front of the professor's house on this ridge" (the Krauth house behind you). Although Wainwright's batteries had been scattered all over the field—often on the orders of generals who never informed him of their decisions—the colonel still managed to amass twelve Napoleons from Stevens's 5th Maine and Lieutenant James Stewart's Battery B, 4th U.S. Artillery, and at least three 3-inch ordnance guns of Cooper's battery on a line that extended from the left of your current position to the railroad bed across Chambersburg Road to your right; indeed, three of Stewart's Napoleons remained in place on the north side of the rail bed, well placed to enfilade any Confederate advance that came through the cut, advanced along the pike, or charged through the open fields and orchard ahead of you.

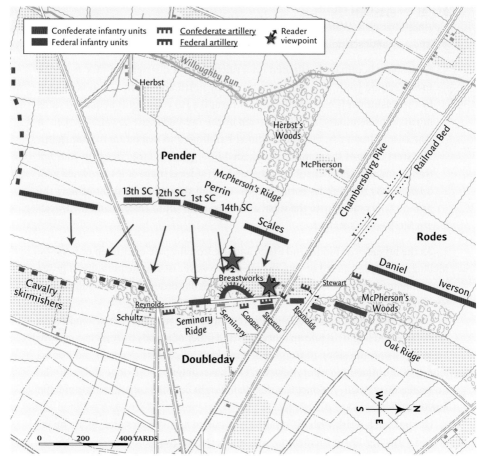

Legend within map:
- Confederate infantry units
- Federal infantry units
- Confederate artillery
- Federal artillery
- Reader viewpoint

Map labels: Willoughby Run, Herbst, Herbst's Woods, Pender, McPherson, McPherson's Ridge, Chambersburg Pike, Railroad Bed, 13th SC, 12th SC, Perrin, 1st SC, 14th SC, Scales, Rodes, Cavalry skirmishers, Breastworks, Reynolds, Schultz, Stewart, Daniel, Iverson, McPherson's Woods, Seminary Ridge, Cooper, Stevens, Reynolds, Seminary, Oak Ridge, Doubleday, 0 200 400 YARDS

Last Stand of the I Corps at the Seminary

It would not be long until those guns found targets. Major General William Dorsey Pender's division of Hill's Third Corps had followed Heth's troops from Cashtown that morning and now closed on the battlefield to relieve the bloodied brigades. They arrived on Herr's Ridge while Daniel's North Carolinians and Stone's Pennsylvanians still battled on McPherson's Ridge ahead of them.

To see how Pender's attack unfolded, walk from your current position along Wainwright's artillery line back toward Schmucker Hall. When you reach that building, walk through the parking lot across the street from it to the trailhead of the walking path in the low ground at the edge of the open fields. You should be able to see the line of monuments to Biddle's brigade along the park road on McPherson's Ridge to your front. The Iron Brigade and some of Biddle's men fell back to this general location, while many of Stone's men pulled back to Wainwright's guns to your right and rear. The rest of Biddle's line extended to your left.

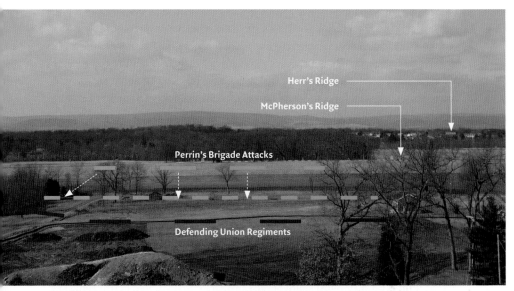

Herr's Ridge

McPherson's Ridge

Perrin's Brigade Attacks

Defending Union Regiments

Union signalmen stationed in the cupola of the Old Dorm had an unobstructed view of the advance of Perrin's South Carolinians from McPherson's Ridge in the middle distance toward the exhausted soldiers of the Union I Corps posted behind fence rails and other obstructions in the open ground just in front of this building.

The Union troops gained a few minutes to organize their new line. Pettigrew's and Brockenbrough's men of Heth's division had pushed them off McPherson's Ridge successfully, but then Heth fell wounded, and his attack lost its momentum. They did not press their assaults past the ridgeline ahead of you. Pender ordered his men to pass over Heth's exhausted men and press forward.

From your left to your right, Brigadier General James H. Lane's North Carolinians, alert to potential threats by Union cavalry against the right flank of Pender's assault, advanced mostly south of the Fairfield Road, just out of sight to your far left. Colonel Abner M. Perrin's South Carolinians advanced directly toward the strongest portion of the Union infantry line, the breastworks located near your current position. Brigadier General Alfred M. Scales's North Carolinians advanced to your right front, heading generally toward Wainwright's massed guns (behind you and to your right). North of the Chambersburg Road—indeed, north of the eastern railroad cut—a few of Daniel's and Iverson's North Carolinians joined in the attack, hitting the remnants of Cutler's, Paul's, and Baxter's brigades in McPherson's Woods across the road and behind the red-roofed white motel buildings to your far right. Despite the exhaustion of nearly six hours of fighting, the Union defenders at first held their ground against their comparatively fresh Confederate attackers. The hardest fighting occurred here, where Perrin attacked, and to your right front, where Scales attacked.

Wainwright's artillery plowed gaping holes in Scales's ranks; Stewart's guns north of the Chambersburg Road did especially effective work, hitting the North Carolinians with accurate enfilading fire. Scales fell wounded early on, and all his regimental colonels fell; the survivors came out of the fight under the command of a lieutenant colonel. As Scales reported, "The brigade encountered a most terrific fire of grape and shell on our flank, and grape and musketry [from Stone's Pennsylvanians] in our front. Every discharge made sad havoc in our line, but still we pressed on." Scales's men never reached the I Corps line, however, stopping in the low swale to your right front.

Here, in front of and around the Old Dorm of the seminary, Perrin's South Carolinians advanced against the Union breastworks. The 14th South Carolina in your immediate front and left front suffered severely; thirty-four of thirty-nine men in Company K fell to Union bullets. As Colonel Perrin reported, "The Fourteenth Regiment was staggered for a moment by the severity and destructiveness of the enemy's musketry. It looked to us as though this regiment was entirely destroyed." Oblique fire from Biddle's brigade and even some of Buford's troopers—especially those of the 8th Illinois Cavalry—just south of the Fairfield Road disrupted Perrin's advance. The advance of Lane's men south of the Fairfield Road helped to quiet the cavalry threat. On your immediate front, Perrin ordered his 12th and 13th South Carolina to oblique to the right (your left) to confront Biddle's line and silence the threat to his flank from both Biddle's men and the Union cavalry.

The 1st South Carolina seemed to be moving obliquely along with the 12th and 13th South Carolina, but then it swung around and outflanked Biddle's men. Just as had occurred on McPherson's Ridge, Biddle's line collapsed from left to right, the 121st Pennsylvania giving way first and the 80th New York, the 142nd Pennsylvania, and the 151st Pennsylvania following in sequence. The end came quickly. As Major Alexander Biddle of the 121st Pennsylvania reported: "The rebels, advancing on our left flank, soon turned the position, and our regimental colors, with the few men left with them, moved out of the hospital grounds through the town."[1] Lieutenant Colonel George F. McFarland, whose 151st Pennsylvania "Schoolteachers' Regiment" had lost so heavily on McPherson's Ridge, now fell with two serious leg wounds that required amputation of portions of both legs.

With the left flank of the Union line collapsing, Perrin made one final push against the barricade and broke the last Union resistance by the Iron Brigade and some of Biddle's men. As a reporter recounted: "At this moment the field presented a true war picture. Across the fields to the right came the rebels' line, with colors which fluttered in the pleasant breeze; in the centre were two farm houses, outhouses, and [the Herbst and Harman] barns in flames, and on the left the column of cavalry in retreat, while beyond all the rays of the sun beat down through the showery clouds and gilded every object with a peculiarly golden light."[2]

As the I Corps infantry left Seminary Ridge, Wainwright withdrew his guns as deliberately as possible, some stopping only a few yards from their previous position or as far as the recoil of their last shot had taken them. "Our brigade of batteries suffered heavily," wrote Lieutenant George Breck of Battery L, 1st New York Artillery, who also explained his own unit's experience: while "in the act of falling back, the enemy pressing closely to the front, . . . a body of them suddenly appeared close on the right and opened a destructive fire, shooting down the gun carriage horses, and the horse Lieut. Wilber was riding. It was impossible to save the piece. Col. Wainwright was along with it at the time, and says that everything was done to save it but to no avail."[3] Some of Stone's Pennsylvanians tried to help the batteries leave the field.

As Perrin's South Carolinians encircled both the north and south ends of the Old Dorm, lightly wounded Union soldiers being treated in the makeshift aid station there tried to make their escape from its halls. Some of the Union troops ran eastward into Gettysburg's streets and alleyways, while others skirted the town through open fields to the southeast. All headed for Cemetery Hill, the designated rallying point. The victorious Confederates followed, of course, and Perrin's 1st South Carolina hoisted its battle flag in the Gettysburg town square.

Who Fought Here?
C.S.A.: The 1,882-man brigade of Colonel Abner M. Perrin of Pender's division in Hill's Third Corps included the 1st, 12th, 13th, and 14th South Carolina Infantry and the 1st South Carolina (Orr's) Rifles. The 1,734-man brigade of Brigadier General James H. Lane of Pender's division in Hill's Third Corps included the 7th, 18th, 28th,

East side of the Gettysburg Lutheran Seminary, 1863. These fields would have teemed with supply wagons on July 1 as fighting raged on the other side of the building. (USAMHI)

33rd, and 37th North Carolina Infantry. The 1,351-man brigade of Brigadier General Alfred H. Scales of Pender's division in Hill's Third Corps included the 13th, 16th, 22nd, 34th, and 38th North Carolina Infantry.

U.S.: You have been introduced to Biddle's and Stone's brigades, as well as to the Iron Brigade, at previous stops.

Who Commanded Here?

Major General William Dorsey Pender (1834–63), born in Edgecombe County, North Carolina, graduated from West Point in 1854 with future Confederate General J. E. B. Stuart and Union General Oliver O. Howard. His antebellum service took him mostly to the Pacific coast, where he skirmished with Native American tribesmen. In March 1861 First Lieutenant Pender resigned his commission in the U.S. Army and went into Confederate service as colonel of the 3rd (later 13th) North Carolina Infantry. In June 1862 he was promoted to brigadier general for gallant service at the Battle of Seven Pines and given command of a brigade in A. P. Hill's division. He suffered three wounds in battle before Gettysburg. Promoted to major general in May 1863, he assumed command of his newly organized infantry division on May 30, 1863. As he marched with his division north to Pennsylvania, he knew that his young wife in North Carolina did not favor the invasion because she felt the Lord would not bless the Southern cause for taking the offensive beyond its own territory. But as a professional soldier, he believed that a whole-hearted offensive could offer the most prudent defense. While Pender's men won a great victory on July 1, on July 2 he was wounded in the leg by a shell fragment. During the difficult retreat back into Virginia, the injury became infected and his leg had to be amputated. Pender did not recover and died near Staunton, Virginia, on July 18.

Major General William Dorsey Pender, C.S.A. (USAMHI)

Colonel Abner Monroe Perrin (1827–64), like Confederate Lieutenant General James Longstreet, was born in the Edgefield District of South Carolina. He fought in the Mexican War as an infantry lieutenant in the Regular Army. He subsequently studied law in South Carolina and was admitted to the bar in 1854. He entered Confederate service in the summer of 1861 as a captain in the 14th South Carolina Infantry. Perrin went to Virginia with his regiment in the spring of 1862, seeing action in the Seven Days Battles, Cedar Mountain, Second Manassas, Harpers Ferry, Antietam, and Fredericksburg. Promoted to colonel in February 1863, he led the regiment at Chancellorsville and assumed command of the brigade when its commander, Brigadier General Samuel McGowan, was wounded. He continued in command of the brigade through Gettysburg. Promoted to brigadier general in September 1863, he took command of Wilcox's Alabama brigade in the early spring of 1864. In May, just prior to the battle of Spotsylvania Court House, he declared: "I shall come out of this fight a live major general or a dead brigadier general."[4] Once the fighting started, Perrin led his men forward to reinforce the Confederate lines at "the Mule Shoe"; there, he was shot from his horse, his body pierced with seven rifle balls. Brigadier General Perrin was buried in the Confederate Cemetery in Fredericksburg, Virginia.

Who Fell Here?

C.S.A.: Although most histories give little attention to this final attack of the day, Pender's losses suggest that it deserves more examination than it generally receives. In Perrin's brigade, the 1st South Carolina lost 111 of its 328 men; the 12th South Carolina lost 132 of its 366 men; the 13th South Carolina lost 130 of its 390 men; and the 14th South Carolina, the regiment that appeared to be annihilated, lost 209 of its 428 men. Orr's Rifles did not participate in this action but lost 11 men during the battle. Perrin's brigade loss reached 31.5 percent.

In Lane's brigade, the 7th North Carolina lost 159 of its 291 men; the 18th North Carolina lost 88 of its 346 men; the 28th North Carolina lost 237 of its 346 men; the 33rd North Carolina lost 132 of its 368 men; and the 37th North Carolina lost 176 of its 379 men—for a brigade loss of 45.7 percent.

In Scales's brigade, the 13th North Carolina lost 179 of its 232 men; the 16th North Carolina lost 123 of its 321 men; the 22nd North Carolina lost 166 of its 321 men; the 34th North Carolina lost 104 of its 311 men; and the 38th North Carolina lost 130 of its 216 men—for a brigade loss of 50.1 percent.

Scales and Lane fought both on July 1 and in Pickett's Charge on July 3; these casualty figures reflect their combined losses for both days. It is likely that Scales suffered greater losses on July 1 and Lane on July 3.

Individual vignettes. Many members of the extended Ouzts family of the Edgefield District of South Carolina served in the 14th South Carolina Infantry. Two of them died in the assault against the heart of the final Union defensive line at the seminary. Private George Ouzts enlisted for the war on March 20, 1862, at the age of twenty. He stood only five feet tall. He was killed in action on July 1 in the assault. Private James Ouzts enlisted for the war in August 1861 and suffered a severe wound at Antietam that kept him hospitalized from September 1862 until April 1863. He fell mortally wounded in the assault of July 1 and died the next day. James's mother, Rebecca Ouzts, filed a claim in October 1864 for any monies owed her son upon his death, and she received a payment of $121.39.[5]

Second Lieutenant John B. Ford, Company G, 16th North Carolina, participated in the advance of Scales's brigade against Colonel Wainwright's massed artillery near the seminary. George Henry Mills, a member of Ford's company, described the officer's death on July 1: "We moved off at a quick step across a meadow and soon began to receive the attention of the foe, and many of our men being struck with minnie balls and shells, the men began to fall around me in my own company. Lt. John Ford fell on my right, John H. Bradley on the left." A piece of shell hit Mills in the thigh, and he headed for the rear. On the way, "I found Ford lying face down, and raising him up saw at once that he was dying. I asked him if I could do anything for him: he could not speak but motioned with his hand to be carried off the field, as the minnie balls and shells were falling thick about him. I called a couple of litter bearers that I saw in the woods nearby to come and take him to a safer place, but could not prevail on them to do so, and the poor man died where he was in a few minutes." Thus ended the life of a young man who had thrived in military life. Ford had enlisted as a private on May 9, 1861, at Rutherfordton, North Carolina, and his colonel promoted him to color-bearer with the rank of sergeant on July 25. He served with distinction and fell wounded in action at Fredericksburg. When he returned from a brief furlough, he found a promotion to second lieutenant waiting for him, the rank he held when he died.[6]

Private Duane S. Bush of Company A, 80th New York Infantry, was one of the last men of his regiment to fall before his regiment left the seminary grounds. A carpenter in civilian life, Bush enlisted on September 14, 1861, at the age of twenty-four. His death left his mother, Sarah, without any means of support; her husband, Benjamin, had died in 1860 and left her a widow with property valued at less than $400. Private Bush regularly sent home part of his pay to cover his mother's needs. After his death, she filed a claim for a mother's pension, which finally received approval in August 1864; she received a monthly sum of $8 retroactive to July 1, 1863, when Private Bush fell in battle. She continued to receive her monthly pension until her death in the spring of 1895.[7]

Who Lived Here?

The Lutheran Theological Seminary at Gettysburg was established in 1826. At the time of the battle, there were three main buildings on the campus. The Old Dorm, a three-story brick structure with a basement, housed the seminary students and classrooms. Two brick homes on the campus provided residences for the families of the chairman of the faculty, Samuel Simon Schmucker, and Professor Charles Philip Krauth. In his August 11, 1863, report to the seminary board of trustees, Schmucker reported that "the injury done to the institution is considerable. . . . The house I occupy was most damaged. . . . Thirteen cannon balls or shells pierced the walls, and made holes several of which were from 2 to 3 feet in length and nearly as broad; window frames were shattered to pieces, sash broken and the greater part of the glass in the house destroyed. The fences around the yard and garden were nearly all leveled. . . . The Seminary edifice (old dorm) was perforated by several balls, and large portions knocked out of the N. east gable corner. There being also a crack in the wall extending over two stories."[8] In a letter to his aunt six days after the battle ended, Professor Krauth wrote: "After the first day's fighting we had to leave the house, it was made a hospital for our wounded. We could not get to town but had to go into the country. . . . On Monday we returned. The wounded were removed from our house but the condition in which it was cannot be described. Much had been taken away. Much had been used for the wounded."[9]

What Did They Say about It Later?

The 14th South Carolina's Colonel Joseph Newton Brown pointedly evaluated the options open to Perrin's South Carolina brigade as it descended into the last valley leading up to the seminary: "To stop was destruction. To retreat was disaster. To go forward was 'orders.'"

The advance of Perrin's brigade from the high ground of McPherson's Ridge into the low ground leading to the seminary grounds brought with it a horrible realization. Colonel Brown explained this after the war:

It was the only battlefield in which all avenues of escape for our wounded were closed. There was nothing that the ambulance corps could do. The ground was swept at every point by the deadly minnie balls. The artillery fire is terrible, but the almost silent whirl of the minnie ball is the death-dealing missile in battle. Not a foot of ground presented a place of safety. The Union troops fired low, and their balls swept close to the ground on the dishlike field in their front. The terrible strife was over in a few minutes—fifteen, say twenty at most. Men never fell faster in this brigade, and perhaps never equally so, except in Orr's regiment at Gaines's Mill [which lost 59 percent of its strength in about thirty minutes].[10]

Driving directions to the next stop: From Schmucker Hall, drive south 0.2 miles on Seminary Avenue to the intersection with Middle Street. At the green light, drive straight across the intersection onto West Confederate Avenue for 1.7 miles, moving past the North Carolina memorial (National Park Service Auto Tour Stop 4), the Virginia memorial (National Park Service Auto Tour Stop 5), and the Florida memorial. Turn right at the edge of the woods onto Berdan Avenue. Drive straight back into the woods to the loop in the road and park.

Day One Conclusion

The Union retreat through the town of Gettysburg—and the Confederate pursuit, as well—descended into pure chaos. *New York Herald* correspondent H. H. Vosburg praised the women of Gettysburg, who came out "upon the sidewalks, with composed though anxious faces, and offered our soldiers everything needed in the way of refreshments. The shot were whistling meanwhile, but they appeared elevated by noble impulses above the sentiment of fear. . . . How we grieved to leave this interesting town in the possession of rebel soldiers."[1]

After the Union troops exited the town to Cemetery Hill beyond, however, the tenor of Northern accounts changed. Newspapers throughout the Union carried stories of Confederate atrocities against noncombatants. Rebel troops charging through town, firing "promiscuously at all who might be in the street," killed the "most pious, excellent and beloved" chaplain Horatio Howell of the 90th Pennsylvania Infantry on the steps of a church on Chambersburg Street. The report noted that "those committing these downright deliberate murders, seemingly exulted over the crimes."[2] By evening, hungry Confederates broke into homes and stores seeking food. A Philadelphia editor reported that "many atrocious acts were committed by some of the troops belonging to the Rebel army, some of them of a character too indelicate to mention. Among the many acts of vandalism prominent, was that of wantonly destroying, with axes and hatchets in hands, houses and furniture, robbing stores, and otherwise committing acts worthy of the dark ages."[3] Even some Southerners admitted to great lapses in discipline. Private John Stikeleather of the 4th North Carolina Infantry in Ramseur's brigade wrote: "Our officers used their utmost endeavor to prevent violence of any kind to them in person or property. But in many of their houses were wines and different kinds of liquor, and in all armies there are many men who will drink and will risk a good deal to get liquor and other spoils, such as were easily found that first night in Gettysburg."[4]

Late in the afternoon of July 1, General Lee issued an order to General Ewell to take the high ground south of Gettysburg "if practicable" and without bringing on a larger engagement. Ewell considered his options. In the end, he did not attack Cemetery Hill. "I could not bring artillery to bear on it," he reported, "and all the troops with me were jaded by twelve hours' marching and fighting." Moreover, asserted Ewell, "Cemetery Hill was not assailable from the town." He found too little maneuver space between the town and hill to deploy his men safely beyond the range of Union artillery for an advance. As a result, Ewell "determined with [Major General Edward] Johnson's division, to take possession of a wooded hill to my left [Culp's Hill], on a line with and commanding Cemetery Hill." But reports of possible Union skirmishers on his extreme left flank caused him to pause. Once Ewell investigated

General Hancock's Statue

East Cemetery Hill

New York Monument,
Soldiers' National Seminary

Although it is not certain that General Lee ever observed the Union line from the Old Dorm cupola—many commentators suggest that his uncertain health made it unlikely he could climb its steep steps—any Confederate observer posted there could witness clearly the chaos that reigned on the broad and open crest of Cemetery Hill in the late afternoon of July 1.

and dismissed that potential threat, "the night was far advanced."[5] Ewell made no further effort to take the high ground.

While Ewell contemplated his options for taking Cemetery Hill, Union generals on top of the eminence attempted to bring order out of chaos and organize a defense against exactly the kind of attack Lee had ordered Ewell to execute. At first, General Howard took charge. As he reported, he sent a staff officer to General Slocum, commander of the newly arrived XII Corps and Howard's senior, to ask him to advance his divisions and come in person to Cemetery Hill to take charge of the fight. Slocum refused to come. According to Howard, the general responded that "he did not wish to come up in person to the front and take the responsibility of that fight" based on a belief that such a step "was against the wish of the commanding general to bring on a general engagement at that point." Howard retained command on the hill. When Doubleday arrived with the remaining fragment of his I Corps, Howard ordered him "to occupy the ground to the west of the road [the Baltimore Pike], the Eleventh Corps being on its right. A portion of the troops was placed behind the hill in reserve."

At approximately 4:30 P.M., Major General Winfield Scott Hancock, commanding officer of the Army of the Potomac's II Corps, arrived on the scene. He did not bring his corps with him, but he bore authorization from Meade to assess the situation at Gettysburg and act in his stead. Hancock evaluated the potential battleground and immediately began to lay out a plan for a defensive position based on

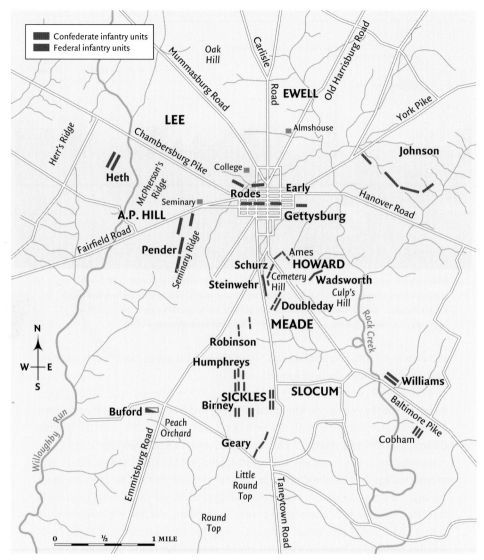

Troop Deployments at the End of Day One

Cemetery Hill and Culp's Hill. Howard outranked Hancock, however, and at first refused to acknowledge Hancock's authority to give orders in his presence. Even in his report, Howard noted that Meade likely gave Hancock "his instructions while under the impression that he was my senior." But Hancock's commanding personality asserted itself, and he took charge.

Neither Doubleday nor Howard seemed pleased by Hancock's arrival. Doubleday reported incorrectly that Hancock "rode up, and informed me he had been placed in command of both corps." Hancock ordered him to take his men in one direction and then, Doubleday noted, "immediately afterward, orders came from Major-General Howard who ranked Hancock to send the troops in another direction. This occasioned at the time some little delay and confusion." For his own part, Howard finally noted: "We agreed that that was no time for talking, and that General Hancock should further arrange the troops and place the batteries on the left of the Baltimore pike, while I should take the right of the same. In a very short time we put the troops in position, as I had previously directed, excepting that General Wadsworth's division was sent to occupy a height to the right and rear of our position" at Culp's Hill. After the exhausted troops deployed, "no very serious demonstrations were made against our new position," Doubleday reported, and "the hours passed away until sundown in comparative quiet."[6]

Hancock reported back to Meade on the strength of the defensive line now forming south of Gettysburg and assured his commander that it could be held with "good troops." Meade then decided to order the remainder of the Army of the Potomac to close on Gettysburg. He ordered his chief quartermaster to send forward the ammunition and medical supplies; food could follow later. Meade himself arrived around midnight. A staff officer commandeered a small farmhouse owned by the widow Lydia Leister, located on the Taneytown Road on the southern slopes of Cemetery Hill, to serve as army headquarters; Meade spent his first few hours on the battlefield talking to Buford, Hancock, and others who fought on July 1, did a brief reconnaissance of his line, and rested briefly before rising early to prepare for the day's action.

Quiet fell over the Confederate lines, too. Late in the afternoon, Lieutenant General James Longstreet arrived at Lee's headquarters with two divisions of his First Corps not far west on the Chambersburg Pike. After Longstreet congratulated Lee on his success on July 1, the two men exchanged ideas for the following day. Much to Longstreet's dismay, Lee already had decided to stay and fight. As Lee explained in his report:

> It had not been intended to deliver a general battle so far from our base unless attacked, but coming unexpectedly upon the whole Federal Army, to withdraw through the mountains with our extensive trains would have been difficult and dangerous. At the same time we were unable to await an attack, as the country was unfavorable to collecting supplies in the presence of the enemy, who could restrain our foraging parties by holding the mountain passes with local and other troops. A battle had, therefore, become in a measure unavoidable, and the success already gained gave hope of a favorable issue.

The decision made, the commander of the Army of Northern Virginia retired for the night.[7]

The Second Day of Battle

July 2, 1863

4

Lee, Meade, and the Challenges of High Command

STOP 14. PITZER'S WOODS

Orientation

Go to the center of the loop, stand in front of the low marker representing the 3rd Maine Infantry, and face the thick woods ahead of you. Monuments to various companies in the 1st United States Sharpshooters should be on your right and left. It may not be apparent to you during the summer months, but you are standing on a slight ridge that falls off to your right and left. It is important to remember that the trees and undergrowth here in 1863 were not nearly as dense as they are today.

What Happened Here?

During the morning and early afternoon of July 2, General Lee continued to form his main battle line along Seminary Ridge. To that end, Lieutenant General A. P. Hill extended his Third Corps to the south to occupy this portion of the ridge. Brigadier General Cadmus M. Wilcox's Alabama brigade, at the head of Major General Richard H. Anderson's division, led the advance. When the action featured here began, most of Wilcox's men were still several hundred yards north of this position—in short, straight ahead of you—but they were heading toward the position where you now stand.

Up until now, Wilcox's men had met no resistance, but the general had observed Union skirmishers on the Emmitsburg Road to your right and rear. Those skirmishers belonged to Major General David B. Birney's First Division of Major General Daniel E. Sickles's III Corps, and they noticed Wilcox's presence here in the tree line, as well. Wilcox put out skirmishers of his own, and a brisk firefight ensued. Birney reported that "at 12 m., believing from the constant fire of the enemy that a movement was being made toward the left, I received permission from Major-General Sickles to send 100 of [Colonel Hiram] Berdan's sharpshooters, with the 3rd Maine Regiment as a support, and feel the enemy's right."

Lieutenant Colonel Casper Trepp of the 1st United States Sharpshooters received the order to send out the reconnaissance. Following a senior officer's aide-de-camp, he conducted his detachment forward "in full view of the enemy"—a sore point with Trepp, who made clear that his men could have reached the point of contact with Wilcox's men "perfectly concealed from view of the enemy and with no loss

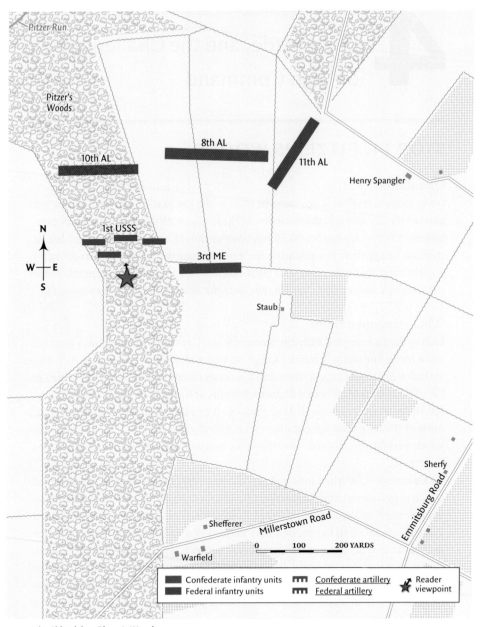

The Skirmish at Pitzer's Woods

of time." Adding to Trepp's aggravation, the advance stalled further when Colonel Moses B. Lakeman's 3rd Maine, sent to his support, halted on the Emmitsburg Road in open view. "For this violation of rules of secret expeditions we paid dearly," Trepp reported.

Trepp initially deployed his men parallel to the Emmitsburg Road, facing to the west (your left). He placed Companies D and E on the left of his line and Companies F and I on his right. He placed the 3rd Maine in a second line in support of the sharpshooters. Once he reached the wood line behind you, Trepp ceased his westward advance and swung around to face northwest, the direction you are now facing.

Wilcox had watched the approach of Trepp's reconnaissance and sent the 10th and 11th Alabama to confront them. He deployed the 11th Alabama in the open field visible through the trees to your right. Its battle line would have advanced toward West Confederate Avenue to your right and rear rather than directly toward this position. Facing fewer obstacles, the 11th Alabama got as much as 300 yards ahead of the 10th, which was still working its way through the woods in your immediate front. Look to your right. As the 11th Alabama came into clear view, as Wilcox reported, "this regiment received a heavy volley of musketry on its right flank and rear from the enemy, concealed [here where you stand] behind ledges of rock and trees in the woods on its right." The 11th Alabama soon fell back. The 10th Alabama continued to push forward, however, and soon clashed with Trepp's detachment and the 3rd Maine near this position. The sharpshooters continued to fight in dispersed fashion, taking advantage of all available cover, but the 3rd Maine formed traditional infantry battle lines. As Colonel Lakeman reported, his regiment returned the enemy fire "with a good will," but he also admitted that his men had "labored under a decided disadvantage. . . . The skirmishers were well secured behind trees, while my battalion filled the intervals" and took significant casualties.[1] Private Charles N. Maxwell of the 3rd Maine wrote in a letter later in July: "In ten minutes we had forty-five men out of one hundred and ninety shot down."[2]

Colonel Moses B. Lakeman, 3rd Maine Infantry, U.S.A (USAMHI)

The fighting in the woods along this line did not last long, perhaps less than thirty minutes. Still, the ferocity of this clash had given the sharpshooters and the men from Maine the intelligence that their superiors desired. Trepp soon received orders to withdraw his detachment and return to the skirmish line on the III Corps front.

Sickles now knew of the existence of a growing Confederate threat on his immediate front. At least one element of Lee's army now knew of the presence of a substantial Union force positioned farther south and west than previous reports had indicated. The action had no immediate impact on Confederate plans for July 2, but it helped General Sickles make a very important decision that dramatically altered Meade's intentions.

Who Fought Here?

C.S.A.: From Brigadier General Cadmus M. Wilcox's brigade of R. H. Anderson's division of A. P. Hill's Third Corps, the 10th and 11th Alabama Infantry served here.

U.S.: From Brigadier General J. H. H. Ward's brigade of Birney's division of Sickles's III Corps, four companies—approximately 100 men—of the 1st U.S. Sharpshooters and the 3rd Maine Infantry were involved here.

Who Commanded Here?

Brigadier General Cadmus Marcellus Wilcox (1824–90), a native of Wayne County, North Carolina, grew up in Tipton County, Tennessee. He entered West Point in 1842 and graduated in the class of 1846 with classmates Thomas J. "Stonewall" Jack-

son and George Edward Pickett. He received a brevet promotion for bravery in the Mexican War. He then served as a tactics instructor at West Point for five years and spent two years touring Europe while studying the organization and training of European armies. In 1859 Wilcox published a tactics manual entitled *Rifles and Rifle Practice*, which became a standard reference text for both armies during the Civil War. Captain Wilcox resigned his Regular Army commission in June 1861 and entered Confederate service as colonel of the 9th Alabama Infantry. Promoted to brigadier general in October 1861 and major general in August 1863, he participated in all of the major battles of the Army of Northern Virginia, commanding successively at the regimental, brigade, and division level. As Robert E. Lee's noted biographer Douglas Southall Freeman described Wilcox: "In all the Army's battles he had been de-

Brigadier General Cadmus M. Wilcox, C.S.A. (USAMHI)

pendable and by every campfire he had been the gentleman."[3] After the war, Wilcox settled in Washington, D.C., where he died in 1890. He was so highly respected that four former Union generals and four former Confederate generals served as pallbearers at his funeral.

Who Fell Here?

C.S.A.: According to Wilcox's report, the 10th Alabama lost 10 killed and 28 wounded, while the 11th Alabama lost 18 men wounded. Wilcox's brigade suffered far more heavily in combat actions late in the afternoon of July 2 and on July 3.

U.S.: The 1st U.S. Sharpshooters lost 49 of its 312 men at Gettysburg, many of them in this action. Over the course of July 2, the 3rd Maine lost 112 of its 210 men, but many of them fell in combat near the Peach Orchard later in the day. Private Maxwell's guess about the 3rd Maine's casualties here and Wilcox's estimate that both of these units combined lost "20 or 25 dead and twice that number wounded and prisoners" in the Pitzer's Woods action seem reasonable.

Individual vignettes. In a postwar memoir, Private Bailey George McClelen of Company D, 10th Alabama Infantry, recalled the fight in Pitzer's Woods:

> We deployed into line of battle on our first halt and before sending skirmishers in advance, Nathaniel Harrelson and Thomas Mackey of Co. "D" volunteered their services for our company's skirmishers. We did not advance but a short distance after our skirmishers preceded us until we were ordered to lie down and wait for further developments. . . . In short time the enemy moved our skirmishers back into retreat. Thomas Mackey before returning received a gunshot wound in one of his legs. . . . The enemy charged up and shooting at us all they could until they got within 30 or 40 yards of our line before we arose from the ground and gave them a sound volley. . . . We pursued them some distance and then fell back to be near where we were lying in line of battle. Only our brigade engaged the enemy in that morning's short battle. We were opposed by Maine troops and probably some other troops. Comrade William Carter was just to my left one man between us while lying under the enemy's missiles where he was killed before we arose. Comrade Silas Street also got killed while lying there. Comrade Clark Harmon got killed in the charge. I will say that Thomas Mackey died next day from his wounds after an amputation of his wounded leg.

Privates Thomas Mackey, Silas B. Street, Clark L. Harmon, and William F. Carter all enlisted in Company D, 10th Alabama Infantry, at Alexandria, Alabama, in June 1861 for the war. Their enlisting officer was their future colonel, John H. Forney. Private Street suffered a wound at Gaines Mill on June 27, 1862, but soon recovered to rejoin his company. Private Mackey proved to be a steady soldier, rarely absent from the ranks due to disease. Private Carter, on the other hand, fell sick enough to require hospitalization on several occasions for treatment of severe diarrhea. Private Clark Harmon's brother Thomas also served in Company D, 10th Alabama, and was killed in battle at Antietam; Clark took charge of the effort to claim the $100 in pay owed Thomas so he could send it home to his mother. All four of these soldiers, as Private McClelen rightly recalled, were killed in action or mortally wounded in Pitzer's Woods. Private Carter's mother filed a claim in April 1864 for any back pay owed her son; when all accounts were settled, she received the sum of $80.89. Private McClelen, the author of this account, who already had been wounded at Antietam, fell with a second wound later on July 2 and became a prisoner. He was exchanged in October 1863, received a promotion to lieutenant, and was transferred to a company nearer his home. He died on March 25, 1925.[4]

Captain Charles D. McLean, commanding officer of Company D, 1st United States Sharpshooters, fell at the head of his command in the fighting at Pitzer's Woods on July 2. On July 6, 1863, Lieutenant John Hetherington, who lived in McLean's New York hometown, recounted in a letter home to his mother the circumstances of the captain's death:

Many friends have fallen, *and those dearer*. . . . We had a hard fight, a very serious one for Co. D. Capt. Chas. D. McLean, of Co. D., was wounded very soon after we were ordered to fall back. We carried him some ways, but the rebels charged and we had to leave him. I told Peter Kipp to stay with him, and he done so. [W. Edwin] Marks and [Edwin E.] Nelson were helping carry them. Nelson was badly wounded in the groin; Marks was hit in the top of his boot; [Private James] Reed was taken prisoner, and [Private Smith] Haight was killed. . . . [On July 5, upon discovering that the Confederates had retreated,] it was with the throbbing heart and a quick step that I entered the rebel hospitals as we came to them to look for our Captain. . . . Those were anxious moments forming. Just as we halted who should come forward but Kipp—and from whom I learned the sad news (*must I write it?*) that he [Captain McLean] had his leg amputated and died on the morning of the 4th of July.

Kipp, recorded Hetherington, reported that "he never saw an amputation performed so quick or so well." Hetherington also admitted: "These are hard letters to write."[5]

Who Lived Here?

The woods in which you stand belonged to Samuel Pitzer, whose farm sat in the open fields in the low ground through the trees to your left (west). Although the farm sat behind the Confederate battle line on both July 2 and July 3 and saw no combat after the brief skirmish just described, the farm nonetheless suffered much collateral damage associated with the Confederate occupation. In a damage claim filed in October 1868, Samuel Pitzer claimed $1,286.64 for loss or damage to personal property during the battle, including a carriage, 130 chickens, six milk cows, a bull, three heifers, three young cattle, ten good sheep, two brood sows, four stock hogs, milled flour, and numerous other items associated with farm operations. Additionally, he claimed $1,147.52 for real estate damage to the farm, including $166.52 in broken fences, as well as additional damage to his corn, wheat, and oat crops. In 1871 the estate of Elizabeth Pitzer—who lived in the same house as Samuel at the time of the battle—was awarded $355.25 for her claim of lost or damaged property associated with the Confederate occupation of the farm.[6]

Ninety years after the battle, most of the Pitzer farm was purchased by President Dwight D. Eisenhower for incorporation into his adjacent 189-acre farm, which he and his wife, Mamie, had purchased in 1950. The Pitzer farm then became known simply as Farm #3.

What Did They Say about It Later?

Changing interpretations. The men of the 3rd Maine—and especially Colonel Hiram Berdan, the commander of the 1st U.S. Sharpshooters—always took pride in their efforts in this small skirmish. In a postwar account, a veteran of the 3rd Maine recalled that "when the order was received by our Colonel, Lakeman, he said, 'From a military standpoint it is an honor to be appreciated.' Then promptly gave the order, 'Forward, quick-step, march.'"[7]

With the passage of time, Berdan and other Union survivors changed an important detail in their accounts. The two Alabama regiments from Wilcox's brigade in A. P. Hill's Third Corps disappeared, replaced by Longstreet's First Corps. Berdan had begun to spin a different story, and it shaped this story written by one of his admirers about the silver reunion ceremonies at Gettysburg in 1888:

> An exceedingly important and interesting feature of the great Gettysburg celebration was the public recognition of the immense value of the reconnaissance made by Gen. Berdan in front of Gen. Sickles's line on the second day, and which developed the startling fact that Gen. Longstreet had massed a force of 26,000 infantry and 4,000 artillery and cavalry behind the cover of the woods for a crushing onslaught upon our left, then held by Gen. Sickles with 10,000 men. So well had Longstreet concealed his movements that our officers had no intimation of the gathering of the awful storm which the rebels sanguinely hoped would roll up our left like a scroll, sweep away our hold upon the all-important Round Tops, and send the disorganized remnants of the Army of the Potomac flying from the field.[8]

It did not help the cause of history that Longstreet bought into this interpretation and credited Berdan's men with delaying his assault a full forty minutes.

Most modern histories of the battle restore the Alabamians to their rightful place in this contest and reject Berdan's claims entirely. As historian Harry Pfanz asserted: "The only new information that Berdan's men could have provided was that the Confederates in some force were moving into the north end of Pitzer's Woods. Berdan might have assumed more and told a greater tale, but that is all his expedition uncovered and all he could rightly report. He could have seen nothing of Longstreet's corps, for it was out of his sight. His force might have delayed Wilcox's brigade in occupying its position on Anderson's right, but this was a meaningless achievement."[9]

Driving directions to the next stop: Return to your vehicle and drive back out to West Confederate Avenue. Turn right onto West Confederate Avenue and drive 0.3 miles to the prominent Louisiana monument on your left that features an angel holding a trumpet to her lips hovering over a fallen soldier. The metal tablet to Barksdale's Mississippi brigade sits on the right side of the road. Park in the marked spaces on the right side of the road and watch for traffic as you cross the road to the Louisiana monument.

STOP 15. LONGSTREET'S MAIN EFFORT HITS A SNAG

Orientation

Two marble benches rest just beyond the Louisiana monument. Take a position near the left bench; it will give you the best vista across the open fields to the east. Extending to the right and left along your front, you will see traffic moving on Emmitsburg Road. Millerstown Road curves in front of you until it intersects with Emmitsburg Road. At the intersection, you will see a knob of high ground crowned with an orchard and marked with monuments and cannons. This is the historic Sherfy Peach Orchard. The prominent red barn and red-and-yellow farmhouse to your immediate left front was home to the Joseph Sherfy family. Follow Emmitsburg Road to the left of the Sherfy farm and you will see the red barn of the Daniel Klingel farm. During the battle, two additional homes stood in clear view of this position. The John Wentz house sat directly ahead of you on the far side of Emmitsburg Road on the edge of the Peach Orchard. To the left of the Klingel farm, Peter Rogers's house stood on this side of Emmitsburg Road. In the far distance on your left front, you can see the high wooded ground of Cemetery Hill. The top of the unforested western slope of Little Round Top and the fully wooded crest of Round Top are on the skyline to your right.

The open fields beyond the Louisiana monument.

What Happened Here?

By 9:00 A.M. on July 2, Lee had finalized his battle plan for the day. He intended "to make the principal attack upon the enemy's left." At the time he drafted that order, based on Captain Samuel R. Johnston's reconnaisance, Lee believed the Union left rested along the Emmitsburg Road and likely no farther south than the Klingel farm to your left front. He ordered Lieutenant General James Longstreet with two of his First Corps divisions—those commanded by Major Generals Lafayette McLaws and John Bell Hood—to a position well south of Gettysburg to envelop the Union left, "which he was to drive in." When General Ewell heard the sound of Longstreet's artillery, Lee wanted him to use his Second Corps to probe the Union right at Culp's Hill and Cemetery Hill, even launching significant attacks if opportunities presented. Lee expected General A. P. Hill's Third Corps, deployed along Seminary Ridge in the Confederate center along a line roughly approximating the park road you have been following, to demonstrate in support of Longstreet and Ewell; Lee ordered the division of Major General Richard H. Anderson from Hill's Third Corps to cooperate with Longstreet's main effort.

General Longstreet did not like Lee's plan, although he did not say so in his official report; the heated controversy centering on his performance at Gettysburg did not flower fully until after Lee's death in 1870. For the record, he only wrote: "Fearing that my force was too weak to venture to make an attack, I delayed until General [E. M.] Law's brigade joined" the rest of Hood's division. When Law finally arrived near 11:00 A.M., Longstreet finally began his southward march from the area behind Herr's Ridge toward his attack position, with McLaws's division in the lead.

During the march, Brigadier General Joseph B. Kershaw's South Carolina brigade at the head of McLaws's division topped a slight rise and halted. As Kershaw reported, they had been directed "to move under cover of the hills toward the right . . . if cover could be found to conceal the movement." From the hilltop, they could see Little Round Top in the far distance and the activity of a Union signal station. Longstreet ordered McLaws's men to countermarch and utilize the cover provided by several intervening ridges to move toward the designated attack position without being seen by the Union signalmen. Hood's men followed.

At approximately 3:30, Kershaw reached the base of Seminary Ridge (behind you) and prepared to march up the Millerstown Road toward the crest of the ridge here. Longstreet provided no details about the attack plan in his after-action report, and McLaws did not file a report. Kershaw, however, offers insight into what was supposed to happen next: "Arriving at the [Pitzer] school-house, on the [Millerstown] road leading across the Emmitsburg road by the peach orchard . . . the lieutenant general commanding [Longstreet] directed me to advance my brigade and attack the enemy at that point, turn his flank, and extend along the cross-road, with my left resting toward the Emmitsburg road." In the main, this had been the plan that Lee, Longstreet, and McLaws had agreed upon when the First Corps broke camp

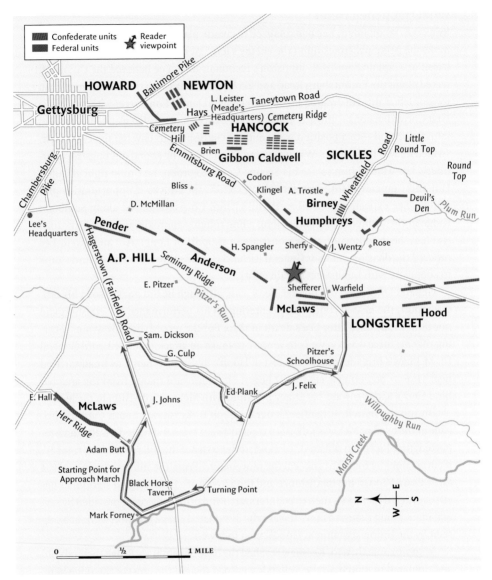

Longstreet's Countermarch

behind Herr's Ridge that morning. When McLaws reached the Emmitsburg Road, he planned simply to deploy his division perpendicular to it and advance astride it to the north (your left) to crush the flank of the Union line—then believed to be near the Klingel farm—and assault Cemetery Hill from the south. But as Kershaw's phrase "attack the enemy at that point" suggests, by the time McLaws's division crested Seminary Ridge near here, the military situation had changed dramatically.

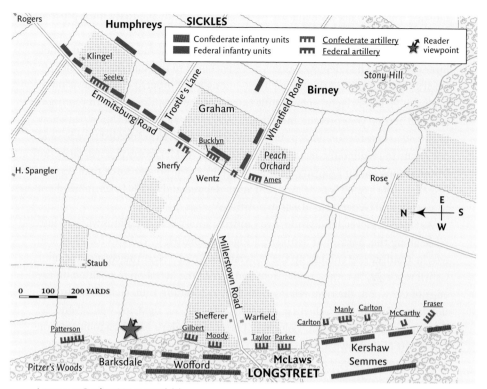

Longstreet Deploys McLaws's Division

Major General Daniel E. Sickles's III Corps now held the intersection of the Emmitsburg Road and the Millerstown Road at what McLaws described to his wife as "the *Peach orchard*, a small settlement with a very large Peach Orchard attached." It now bristled with soldiers and cannons. Clearly, Longstreet could not use this location as a jump-off point for his attack.

Longstreet realized that Lee likely would not alter his attack plan at this late hour. He also recognized he had an obligation to point out the changed circumstances to his commander. As he did so, he also ordered McLaws to deploy his division along the ridge line here, parallel to—rather than perpendicular to—the Emmitsburg Road and facing the Peach Orchard. McLaws placed Kershaw's South Carolinians into position in the tree line well beyond the stop sign at the intersection of the park road and Millerstown Road visible to your right; Brigadier General Paul J. Semmes's Georgians deployed several hundred yards behind Kershaw in the open fields on the reverse slope of Seminary Ridge. Immediately behind you, Brigadier General William Barksdale's Mississippi brigade went into position; several hundred yards behind it rested the Georgians of Brigadier General William T. Wofford's brigade. As McLaws wrote to his wife, Longstreet initially "sent word that he was satisfied there was but a small force of the enemy in front and that I must proceed at once to the assault."

Then—even though he did not quite yet understand fully the way in which Birney's division had deployed from the Peach Orchard through the Wheatfield to Devil's Den and toward the Round Tops—Longstreet ordered Hood's division to deploy to McLaws's right, significantly extending the First Corps line to your right and well beyond your present line of sight. Any attack against the Union flank now likely had to take the Round Tops into consideration, but Hood needed time to send out scouts to reconnoiter and assess the situation. As McLaws explained, since the Union troops facing Longstreet's men "were in much greater force than was expected . . . the assault was delayed, but again delayed and finally I was directed not to assault until General Hood was in position."

As Hood deployed his division, two Confederate artillery battalions wheeled into place along this portion of Seminary Ridge. Colonel H. C. Cabell's battalion had led the Confederate column up the Millerstown Road. "Near the crest of the hill," Cabell reported, "I turned to the right and placed the battalion in position on the edge of the wood, the right resting near the road leading from Gettysburg to Emmitsburg." That placed Cabell's guns on this ridge to your right and well beyond the stop sign at the intersection. Colonel E. Porter Alexander's battalion took position astride the Millerstown Road, some of his guns taking position near where you now stand. At approximately 4:00 P.M., as Alexander reported, "a spirited engagement" began.[1] The Confederate guns around you opened fire on Sickles's Emmitsburg Road line and the Sherfy Peach Orchard.

Even if the senior Confederate generals had not quite resolved all the problems confronting them, the battle finally had begun. The seeds had been sown as well for a much longer literary war between Longstreet and armies of Southern critics.

Who Fought Here?

Participating in this element of Lee's main effort were Major General Lafayette McLaws's and Major General John Bell Hood's divisions of Longstreet's First Corps, along with First Corps artillery. You will meet their component units as you visit the individual sites where they fought.

Who Commanded Here?

Lieutenant General James Longstreet (1821–1904), born in the Edgefield District of South Carolina, soon after his birth returned with his family to their plantation near Gainesville, Georgia. Longstreet entered West Point in 1838 and graduated in 1842 along with future Gettysburg comrades Lafayette McLaws and Richard H. Anderson. He was known to his classmates as "Old Pete" from "Peter," his family's nickname for him. Following graduation from West Point, Longstreet saw action on the frontier and in the Mexican War, during which he received two brevet promotions for gallantry. Major Longstreet resigned his commission in the Regular Army in June 1861, entered Confederate service as a brigadier general, and saw action at First Manassas. Promoted to major general in October 1861, he commanded a division in the Peninsula Campaign of the late spring and early summer of 1862 and a wing of the Army of Northern Virginia during Second Manassas and the Maryland Campaign. Promoted to lieutenant general in October 1862, he took command of the newly authorized First Corps that same month. At Fredericksburg in December, he held the critical defensive position at Marye's Heights. Thomas J. Goree of Longstreet's staff described his general as "a very fine officer, as brave as Julius Caesar. His forte though as an officer consists, I think, in the seeming ease with which he can handle and arrange large numbers of troops, as also with the confidence and enthusiasm with which he seems to inspire them."[2]

Lieutenant General James Longstreet, C.S.A. (USAMHI)

Longstreet and part of his corps served on detached duty in southeastern Virginia during the spring of 1863, thus missing Chancellorsville. His performance at Gettysburg remains one of the most controversial issues connected with the history of the battle. After Gettysburg, Longstreet and two of his divisions were detached from the Army of Northern Virginia and sent to the western theater of operations. He performed exceedingly well at the Battle of Chickamauga but failed in his efforts to retake Knoxville. During the winter of 1863, the senior leadership of his First Corps underwent great change as an increasingly toxic command climate forced several of his subordinates to demand transfers away from his command— among them McLaws. The First Corps returned to Lee's army in the late spring of 1864, and Longstreet fell seriously wounded at the Battle of the Wilderness on May 6, 1864. Lee's "old war horse" returned to the army in the fall of 1864 and remained in corps command until the surrender at Appomattox in April 1865. After Lee's death in 1870, a faction of former Confederate officers—sometimes called the "Lee cult"—attempted to shift the blame for the defeat at Gettysburg to Longstreet. He spent the last four decades of his life defending his personal conduct and professional reputation as a soldier, his lack of literary restraint sometimes making him his own worst enemy. He also joined the Republican Party and renewed his old friendship with Ulysses S. Grant. A frequent visitor to Gettysburg in his older years, he became a friend of General Sickles, against whom he fought here. His wartime memoirs, From Manassas to Appomattox, appeared in 1896. General Longstreet died at Gainesville, Georgia, in January 1904. His equestrian monument at Gettysburg was dedicated in 1998.

Major General Lafayette McLaws (1821–97), a native of Augusta, Georgia, graduated from West Point in 1842 along with his future corps commander James Longstreet. He spent his antebellum years on the western frontier, served in the Mexi-

Major General Lafayette McLaws, C.S.A. (USAMHI)

can War, and held the rank of captain in the 6th U.S. Infantry for almost ten years before resigning in March 1861 to enter Confederate service as colonel of the 10th Georgia Infantry. On at least one occasion during the war, as a general officer in Confederate service, he ran into soldiers from his old Federal command, who greeted him as "Captain McLaws."[3] Promoted to brigadier general in September 1861, he commanded an infantry brigade in the war's early campaigns, gaining a reputation for solid, if not particularly energetic, performance. Made a major general in May 1862, he rose to division command after the Seven Days Battles; he remained in divisional command at Gettysburg. After Gettysburg, McLaws's relationship with Longstreet soured badly. At Knoxville, "Old Pete" relieved him of command, allegedly for failing to make proper preparations for the failed attacked on Fort Sanders. Eventually exonerated by President Davis, McLaws received another command in Georgia and subsequently served under General Joseph E. Johnston in the Carolina Campaign against Sherman. He surrendered with Johnston at Bennett Place near Durham Station (later Durham), North Carolina, on April 26, 1865. After the war, McLaws went into the insurance business in Augusta, and he was collector of internal revenue and postmaster in Savannah. General McLaws died in Savannah in July 1897 and is buried there.

Who Fell Here?

You will find the casualty reports for these various units at the stops where the losses were incurred.

Who Lived Here?

To your right, along Millerstown Road, you can see two houses. The one closer to you is the Christian Shefferer farm. On the far side of the road sits a stone house, which, as of this writing, remains somewhat obscured by modern additions and a large garage. The original stone portion of the house belonged to African American property owner James Warfield. He, his wife Eliza, and at least seven children moved to Adams County from Uniontown in Carroll County, Maryland, shortly before the Battle of Gettysburg. He first appears on Cumberland Township tax records in 1863, taxed for thirteen acres of land. A sale notice in 1864 described the Warfield property as "a stone house and barn, a blacksmith shop and an excellent orchard." As with many adjacent property owners, James Warfield filed claims with the state and federal governments for property damage incurred during the battle. An abstract of award dated November 9, 1871, states that Warfield was entitled to $410: $55 for the loss of two head of cattle and three hogs, $100 for loss of household goods and kitchen furniture, $155 for damage to crops and fencing, and $100 for damage to buildings and land. The Warfield property is now owned by the federal government, and it is the intent of the National Park Service to restore the original stone portion of the house to its 1863 condition.[4]

What Did They Say about It Later?

General Longstreet later came under much criticism for his performance on July 2, but little of that negative evaluation emerged in the immediate aftermath of the battle. Only after Lee died in 1870 and his admirers began to erase all potential blemishes from his military record did James Longstreet become targeted. Longstreet had set himself up for the troubles that came his way. Right after the war ended, he sat for an interview with prominent Northern war correspondent William Swinton, who asked him specifically about Lee's performance in the Pennsylvania Campaign. Longstreet told Swinton that Lee "expressly promised his corps-commanders that *he would not assume a tactical offensive*, but force his antagonist to attack him." When Lee would not break off the engagement after July 1 and planned to attack on July 2, Longstreet had told Swinton that Lee seemed "to have lost that equipoise in which his faculties commonly moved, and determined to give battle."[5]

Most notable among Longstreet's critics was Confederate General Jubal A. Early, who, by the mid-1870s, secured his position as Lee's stoutest defender—and thus "Old Pete's" archenemy—with his pointed commentaries in the *Southern Historical Society Papers*. Harkening back to the Swinton interview, as well as many subsequent literary offerings, Early asserted that

> General Longstreet is of the opinion that he is a very deeply-aggrieved man, because he has not been permitted, without question, to pronounce that General Lee's strategy in the Gettysburg campaign was very defective; that General Lee had lost his mind when he determined to deliver battle at Gettysburg, or, to use the language in which the idea is conveyed, that he has "during the crisis of the campaign lost the matchless equipoise that usually characterized him and that whatever mistakes were made were not so much matters of deliberate judgment as the impulses of a great mind disturbed by unparalleled conditions"; that, he, himself, alone understood the requirements of the occasion, and if he had been allowed to control the operations of the army, a brilliant victory would have ensued.

Indeed, Early asserted that on July 2, 1863, "it is beyond all dispute that General Longstreet thwarted General Lee's purpose of attacking the enemy at as early an hour as practicable, by his reluctance and procrastination."[6]

Every time Longstreet responded to his critics, however, he only made things worse. In a provocative essay titled "The Mistakes of Gettysburg," he continued to offer pithy assessments of General Lee: "His remark, made just after the battle, 'It is all my fault,' meant just what it said. . . . [I]t was the utterance of a deep-felt truth, rather than a mere sentiment."[7] Longstreet remained so certain of his essential correctness that he did not hesitate to claim:

> I have written nothing that was not supported by abundant proof, advanced no opinions not clearly justified by the facts. As disastrous as the results of that battle were, and as innocent as I was of bringing them upon my people, I accepted my share of the disaster without a murmur. . . . I should probably have never written a line concerning the battle, had it not been for the attempt of the wordy soldiers to specifically fix upon me the whole burden of that battle—their rashness carrying them so far as to lead them to put false orders in the mouth of our great captain, and charge me with having broken them.[8]

Driving directions to the next stop: Return to your vehicle and drive forward to the stop sign ahead of you. Turn left onto Millerstown Road and drive 0.4 miles to the intersection with Emmitsburg Road. Drive straight across the intersection and just over the crest of the hill to your front (0.1 miles), turn right onto Birney Avenue. Park along the east side of the road.

STOP 16. THE SHERFY PEACH ORCHARD

Orientation

It is important to take the time here to orient yourself to the terrain and landmarks associated with the Union defense against the Confederate main effort on July 2 (the details of which you will explore at subsequent stops). Climb the steps to view the informational wayside near the monument to the 141st Pennsylvania in the northeast corner of the orchard. You will notice that the Peach Orchard sits on a knob of high ground, and the highest point is just ahead of you. From the wayside, walk about ten paces toward the statue of the artilleryman holding his ramrod, and then stop. This general area provides an excellent location from which to see all the key terrain features.

First, face toward the artilleryman and look beyond him, as the orientation photo shows below. From this perspective, you are looking to the west. The prominent tree line to your front is Seminary Ridge, the main Confederate battle line on July 2 and 3. Pitzer's Woods and the Louisiana Monument are both off to your right front. The road that crosses from left to right across your front is Emmitsburg Road. Notice that it runs along a slight ridge; the Peach Orchard itself sits on it. The road to your right was only a narrow farm lane at the time of the battle, but on the other side of the intersection across Emmitsburg Road, it became known as the Millerstown Road.

The view past the artilleryman statue toward Seminary Ridge.

Now turn to the right and face the expanse of open fields. You are facing north, and the artilleryman's statue should be to your left. From this position, you can see the key elements of General Meade's battle line as it began to develop. The high tree-covered ground in the distance is the key terrain of Cemetery Hill. The town of Gettysburg is beyond that hill. The elevation to the right of Cemetery Hill is Culp's Hill; you may be able to spot the top of its observation tower above the trees. The line of monuments to your far right front, including the large obelisk to the U.S. Regular Army and the white dome of the Pennsylvania monument, mark the crest of Cemetery Ridge. Meade's line, running from Culp's Hill across Cemetery Hill and south along Cemetery Ridge, resembled a large fishhook. Thus many studies of this battle refer to Meade's position as his "fishhook defense."

Emmitsburg Road on your left heads northeasterly into the Gettysburg town square. The red barn along the road to your left is the Joseph Sherfy farm; this is his orchard. The cluster of red and white farm buildings in the middle distance ahead of you is the Daniel Klingel farm. The large red barn of the Nicholas Codori farm is visible farther up Emmitsburg Road on the same side as the Klingel farm. Between your position and the domed Pennsylvania monument are the large red barn and white house of the Abraham Trostle farm, Sickles's headquarters during the afternoon of July 2.

Now turn to your right again. You are facing east, and the artilleryman's statue should be behind you. The tree line in your immediate front masks the lowest portion of Cemetery Ridge about one-half mile behind it. Meade's initial orders had required part of General Sickles's III Corps to hold that low ground, a situation that Sickles deplored. His left flank, however, was supposed to anchor the Union line on Little Round Top—the elevation just visible over the trees to your right front—at least until the V Corps arrived to take over that responsibility; you can see a large monument shaped like a castle on Little Round Top's cleared west face. The large tree-covered hill to its right is Round Top.

Turn to your right once more. You are facing south, and the artilleryman's statue should be to your right. You can see the trees marking the southern extension of Seminary Ridge to your right front. The white fences to your left front surround parts of the George Rose farm, the site of a Confederate field hospital and mass graves in the coming hours and days.

What Happened Here?

Now once again face to the west toward the artilleryman. Sherfy's Peach Orchard, where you now stand, presented both commanders with a tactical problem. The ridge along Emmitsburg Road hid the main Union line on Cemetery Ridge from the Confederates. At the same time, this knob of ground represented a potential threat to the Union line if Lee's artillery took possession of it. Buford's cavalry held

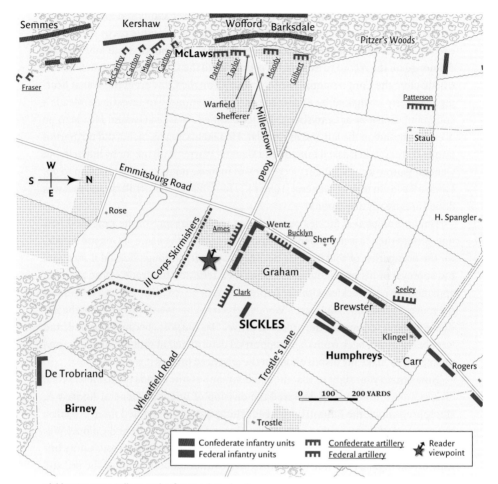

Semmes Kershaw Wofford Barksdale
Pitzer's Woods
McLaws
McCarthy Carlton Manly Calton
Parker Taylor Moody Gilbert
Fraser
Patterson
Warfield
Shefferer
Staub
Millerstown Road
W
S — N
E
Emmitsburg Road
Rose
H. Spangler
Ames Wentz Bucklyn Sherfy
III Corps Skirmishers
Graham
Seeley
Clark
Brewster
SICKLES
Klingel
Trostle's Lane
De Trobriand
Humphreys Carr Rogers
Wheatfield Road
Birney
0   100   200 YARDS
Trostle

Confederate infantry units   Confederate artillery   Reader viewpoint
Federal infantry units   Federal artillery

Sickles Creates a Salient at Sherfy's Peach Orchard

the Sherfy farm and its Peach Orchard early on July 2, but when the Union horsemen redeployed elsewhere, both armies left this high ground unoccupied.

This high ground also commanded the lowest part of Cemetery Ridge behind you where Meade had deployed the III Corps, and General Sickles grew increasingly concerned about it. At Chancellorsville, he had been ordered off a similar high knoll called Hazel Grove; as soon as he had left, Confederate artillery rolled into position on its summit and inflicted great damage to his III Corps as it withdrew. Sickles wished to avoid that situation again. He decided that moving his corps from the low ground of Cemetery Ridge (behind you) to the high ground along Emmitsburg Road here offered the best course of action. Late in the morning, he went to Meade's headquarters to request permission to make the move.

Sickles fell badly wounded later on July 2, so he never submitted a formal after-action report in July or August as the Army of the Potomac's other corps commanders did. Thus we cannot reconstruct his argument as he expressed it in July 1863. He did not go on the record to explain his actions until the spring of 1864, when he testified before the Congressional Joint Committee on the Conduct of the War at hearings—largely instigated by Sickles's own machinations—to investigate Meade's command decisions at Gettysburg. Sickles testified: "I asked General Meade to go over the ground on the left and examine it. He said his engagements did not permit him to do that. I then asked him to send General Warren with me, or by himself; but General Warren's engagements were such as to make it inconvenient for him to go. I then asked him to send General [Henry J.] Hunt, his chief of artillery, and that was done" in the early afternoon.

Hunt accompanied Sickles on a detailed reconnaissance of the proposed new line. Sickles then "asked for General Hunt's sanction, in the name of General Meade, for the occupation of that line. He declined to give it, although he said it met with the approval of his own judgment." Hunt then returned to Meade's headquarters, apparently leaving Sickles with the impression that he could expect orders to make the move. The skirmish at Pitzer's Woods helped to convince Sickles to take the initiative without waiting for the orders to arrive: "My outposts became engaged, and were being driven back from their supports. I determined to wait no longer . . . and proceeded to make my dispositions on the advanced line, as it is called."

Now turn to your right so that the artilleryman's statue stands to your left. When Sickles moved forward, he deployed the division of Brigadier General Andrew A. Humphreys along the Emmitsburg Road. Humphreys commanded three brigades, but only two of them—those of Brigadier General Joseph B. Carr and Colonel William Brewster—formed the division's main line of battle along the road. Carr's brigade on the right of the line established its position on both sides of the red and white Klingel farm buildings. If you look up Emmitsburg Road toward Gettysburg, you can locate a point beyond the Klingel farm where it dips down into low ground. Humphreys's right flank ended there, unsupported. When he advanced, Sickles maintained no link to Major General Winfield S. Hancock's II Corps, still back on Cemetery Ridge beyond the domed Pennsylvania monument. Brewster's brigade extended Humphreys's line southward toward your position but stopped well before it reached the large red Sherfy farm buildings to your left front. Humphreys's third brigade, under Colonel George Burling, served as the III Corps reserve and, for now, remained close to Sickles's headquarters at the Trostle farm, ready to respond to any emergency.

Since Humphreys's division did not reach the Peach Orchard where you now stand, Sickles ordered Brigadier General Charles K. Graham's Pennsylvania brigade of Major General David B. Birney's division to extend the III Corps line through the Sherfy farm property. Graham deployed most of his regiments along Emmitsburg

Road nearly to the intersection, and at least two of them at times used the farm lane—today's park road in front of you—to face toward the low ground behind you.

Now face to the west toward Seminary Ridge once more. The artilleryman on his pedestal should be in front of you. The battery he represents, however, had not yet arrived on the field. The artillery brigade of the III Corps included only five batteries. Sickles's chief of artillery could spare only three to strengthen this part of the III Corps line.

The commander of Sickles's other division, General Birney, faced a particularly tough challenge. Sickles already had taken Graham's brigade away from him to strengthen the Emmitsburg Road line. He apparently trusted Birney to deploy his other two brigades wisely to confront any threat aimed at the Round Tops. During the joint committee hearings, Sickles only said: "I found out that the enemy were moving up to the attack in great force. . . . Fortunately my left [under Birney] had succeeded in getting into position on Round Top and along the commanding ridge to which I have referred; and those positions were firmly held by the 3d Corps."[1]

Now turn to the east so that the artilleryman's statue stands behind you. In fact, Sickles had offered a poor description of Birney's deployments. None of Birney's troops held either of the Round Tops. While Graham's Pennsylvanians held the Peach Orchard on "the commanding ridge," Birney had attempted to block some approaches to the Round Tops by parceling out his other two brigades as far as he could stretch them. He placed the brigade of Colonel Regis de Trobriand in a wheatfield—just beyond the first tree line to your front—and Brigadier General J. H. Hobart Ward's brigade along a low ridge that terminated on a distinctive cluster of large rocks later known as Devil's Den, several hundred yards in front of Little Round Top and not visible from this position.

Birney lacked sufficient troops to confront the enemy with a continuous battle line; his line included wide gaps—one stretched from here at the Peach Orchard to the western edge of the Wheatfield where de Trobriand's men waited. Only a thin skirmish line of Michigan and Maine troops provided security across Birney's broken front. You will visit the sites of Birney's most intense combat at Stops 19, 20, and 21.

As General Meade reported after the battle, "About 3 P.M., I rode out to the extreme left, to await the arrival of the Fifth Corps and to post it, when I found that Major-General Sickles, commanding the Third Corps, not fully apprehending the instructions in regard to the position to be occupied, had advanced or rather was in the act of advancing, his corps some half a mile or three-quarters of a mile in front of the line of the Second Corps, on the prolongation of which it was designed his corps should rest."[2] Meade quickly examined the position and, as Sickles recalled, "remarked to me that my line was too extended, and expressed his doubt as to my being able to hold so extended a line." The salient (the angled section of the line) here at the Peach Orchard especially worried Meade, since Confederates could attack Graham's position from the west or the south. In the end, Sickles admitted the correctness of Meade's assessment, but he argued "that, if supported, the line could be held; and, in my judgment, it was a strong line, and the best one." Finally, however, Sickles gave in, stating that, if Meade disapproved of the line, "it was not yet too late to take any position he might indicate."

Soon thereafter, at about 4:00 P.M., the bursting of artillery shells announced the start of the afternoon's action on this part of the line. Meade told Sickles to remain in place; he would send the V Corps to support the III Corps. Sickles needed the reinforcements, but he did not seem overly concerned. As he testified: "I could look to General Hancock for support on my right flank," and Meade "authorized me to to send to General Hunt . . . for as much artillery as I wanted." Among the most amazing sentences in Sickles's testimony immediately followed: "I then assured him of my entire confidence in my ability to hold the position; which I did."[3]

You will learn more about the fighting here at the Peach Orchard salient at Stop 21.

Who Fought Here?

Over the next seven stops, you will learn more about the component commands of Sickles's III Corps and all the Union troops that came to his support, as well as the individual Confederate brigades of Longstreet's First Corps and Major General Richard H. Anderson's division of A. P. Hill's Third Corps.

Who Commanded Here?

Major General Daniel Edgar Sickles (1819–1914), one of the most controversial figures in the Gettysburg story, was born in New York City and studied law at New York University. He soon entered the realm of politics and became a stalwart member of the Tammany wing of the Democratic Party. He became a New York state senator and served in the U.S. House of Representatives from 1857 until 1861. He gained national notoriety in 1859 for shooting and killing his wife's lover, Philip Barton Key II—the son of Francis Scott Key, the composer of the lyrics to the "Star-Spangled Banner." During the murder trial, Sickles's defense attorney (and future secretary of war), Edwin M. Stanton, gained an acquittal on the grounds of temporary insanity—reputedly the first successful use of that defense in American legal history. At the start of the Civil War, Sickles offered his services to the Lincoln administration, and he obtained a commission as colonel of the 70th New York Infantry in June 1861. Authorized to recruit a regiment of infantry for the war, he enlisted enough men for a brigade of five regiments and received an appointment as a brigadier general of volunteers in September 1861. His five regiments became known as New York's Excelsior Brigade. He led his brigade on the Virginia peninsula in the late spring and early summer of 1862 at Seven Pines and during the Seven Days Battles, and he commanded a division at Antietam and Fredericksburg. Promoted to major general in November 1862, he commanded the III Corps at Chancellorsville and Gettysburg. Seriously wounded on July 2 at Gettysburg, Sickles suffered the amputation of his right leg, thus ending his active field service. In 1864 Sickles instigated the Joint Committee on the Conduct of the War's investigations into Meade's conduct during the Gettysburg battle, accusing the general of desiring to retreat from Gettysburg rather than stand and fight. He never gave up his crusade against his commanding officer and, in time, was awarded the Medal of Honor for his actions at Gettysburg. Sickles was again elected to Congress and served from 1893 to 1895, during which time he drafted the legislation that established Gettysburg National Military Park. Sickles was the longtime chairman of the New York State Monuments Commission until he was forced out in 1912 in the midst of a financial scandal. Daniel Edgar Sickles died at his residence in New York City in May 1914 at the age of ninety-four. He is buried at Arlington National Cemetery.

Major General Daniel E. Sickles, U.S.A., lost his leg to a Confederate cannonball on July 2. (USAMHI)

Who Fell Here?

Casualty figures for the various components of the major Union and Confederate commands on July 2 will be considered at each battle stop.

Who Lived Here?

Across the park road from the artilleryman's statue, you can see a stone foundation marking the location of the John Wentz house. At the time of the battle, Wentz and his wife, Mary—both in their seventies—lived there with their daughter, Susan. Their son, Henry, had worked for a Gettysburg carriage maker, but Henry had moved to Martinsburg, Virginia, in the 1850s to take up the same occupation there. Henry joined the Virginia militia, and once the war started, he was mustered into the Confederate army. Henry came to Gettysburg in 1863 as an ordnance sergeant in Captain O. B. Taylor's Virginia Battery. His unit went into action not far from his childhood home. Historian William Storrick recorded the following story: "During the night of the third day, Henry was anxious to know whether or not his father was well. He went to the house and found his father unhurt but asleep in the basement. Rather than waking him up, John wrote a note which simply said 'Good bye and God Bless You' and pinned it to his father's coat lapel. Then he returned to his unit to prepare for the withdrawal from Gettysburg."[4] Today, the outline of the stone foundation is all that remains of the Wentz house.

Two hundred yards north of the foundation of the Wentz house and on the opposite side of the road are the buildings of the Sherfy farm. Fifty years old at the time of the battle, Joseph Sherfy had purchased the property in 1842 and built the two-story brick home that still stands today. The barn, however, is not original. The Reverend Sherfy—he was a deacon in the Church of the Brethren—and his wife, Mary, raised three boys and three girls. Sherfy's orchard had become famous even before the battle; the quality of its peaches made it a landmark on the official 1858 map of Adams County. When the battle began on July 1, Sherfy sent the children to safety but stayed to provide water to Union troops as they marched along the Emmitsburg Road. On the morning of July 2, Joseph, his wife, and her mother were ordered off the farm to wait out the battle in a safer location.[5] Joseph and his son Raphael returned to the home on July 6, and the rest of the family followed the next day. The family "witnessed a scene of destruction and desolation. The barn was in ashes; the house, while still standing, was riddled with shot and shell; the fencing was down and much of it gone and the shrubbery and peach trees were nearly destroyed. In the ashes of the barn the charred bodies of 14 men were found who had been wounded and had taken refuge there."[6] In a claim filed after the war, damages to the farm were estimated at almost $2,500.

What Did They Say about It Later?

Sickles's decision to move to this ridgeline ranks among the most controversial in the entire Gettysburg Campaign. It not only triggered a congressional hearing; it also pitted the partisans of Sickles against those of General Meade in vitriolic exchanges that continue to color how we view the July 2 fighting even today.

Over the years, the Meade-Sickles controversy has generated its own body of literature. Sickles found many ways to keep his name and his perspective of the battle in the public eye. During the fall of 1863, a member of his command formed the III Corps Association, designed for mutual support in a spirit of fraternity. It grew in importance—and found a unifying mission—after March 1864, when Meade issued orders disbanding the III Corps and consolidating its regiments with Hancock's II Corps. Sickles's men never forgave Meade for that act, and with Sickles's encouragement, they began to spread the interpretation of July 2's events to which their corps commander had testified at the joint committee's hearings. Several early battle histories, including Samuel P. Bates's *The Battle of Gettysburg* (1875), the first book-length "history" of the fight, drew heavily upon joint committee testimony and took a distinctly anti-Meade tone. Sickles found allies outside the III Corps as well. General Abner Doubleday, whom Meade had relieved of command on July 1, contributed *Chancellorsville and Gettysburg* to Charles Scribner's "Campaigns of the Civil War" series and took a swipe at Meade by finding Sickles's move to be "disastrous in some respects," but even more "propitious as regards its general results, for the enemy had wasted all their strength and valor in gaining the Emmetsburg [sic] road, which after all was of no particular benefit to them. They were still outside our main line. They pierced the latter it is true, but the gallant men who at such heavy expense of life and limb stood triumphantly on that crest were obliged to retire because the divisions which should have supported them remained inactive." At least while Sickles and his partisans controlled the narrative, there would be those who agreed with

Doubleday's conclusion that "Meade was considerably startled by the fact that the enemy had pierced our center."[7]

But Meade had his defenders, as well. Meade's son, who served on his father's staff here, issued a reply to Doubleday. General Humphreys, a professional soldier to the core who later became Meade's chief of staff, rejected any allegiance to his former III Corps commander and added his own *Gettysburg to the Rapidan: The Army of the Potomac, July, 1863 to April, 1864*, to the Scribner's series. He made clear from his first chapter that he championed Meade as a prudent and practical soldier. Artillery chief Henry Hunt, who wrote the primary article on July 2 at Gettysburg for *Century Magazine*'s influential "Battles and Leaders" series in the mid-1880s, made clear that he did not approve of Sickles's line, although some of Sickles's friends often announced that he had supported the III Corps advance. He also rejected as baseless Doubleday's charges, asserting that "General Meade was on the ground active in bringing up and putting in reinforcements, and in doing so had his horse shot under him."[8]

Most modern studies of the Battle of Gettysburg portray Meade in a far more positive light than much of the literature produced by the war generation itself, and Sickles's reputation has suffered accordingly. But the debate continues.

Driving directions to the next stop: Return to your vehicle and drive straight ahead and then to the right around the south side of the trees in the Peach Orchard, viewing the monuments as you go. They represent some of the Union defenders you will learn about at Stop 21. At the stop sign, turn left (south) onto Emmitsburg Road and follow it south for 0.6 miles, turning half-left onto South Confederate Avenue. Drive on South Confederate Avenue 0.4 miles. Just past the prominent Alabama monument on your right, pull off to the left at National Park Service Auto Tour Stop 7, park, and face the informational wayside.

STOP 17. LONGSTREET'S MAIN EFFORT BEGINS

Orientation

You are now on Warfield Ridge, a southeastern extension of Seminary Ridge. For the most comprehensive view of the important terrain features identifiable at this site, walk to the black-and-white metal tablet to Captain James Reilly's Rowan Artillery, a North Carolina battery in Major Mathis W. Henry's artillery battalion, located just over your left shoulder. Walk about ten additional paces past that tablet toward the Alabama monument, then face to the right for a panoramic view of the area's open fields and hills; the battery marker should be on your right.

The first elevation to your right front, unnamed at the time of the battle, is sometimes called Bushman's Hill today. The much larger wooded hill behind it is Round Top. Farther in the distance to your right front is the open western slope of Little Round Top. Look closely in the middle distance directly in front of you to find the distinctive cluster of rocks that marks Devil's Den. On busy days, you are most likely to locate that popular spot by traffic or parked cars. The white buildings in the low ground ahead of you belong to the John Slyder farm; the brown farm buildings to your left front are part of the Michael Bushman farm. A tributary of Plum Run drains the low ground near the Slyder farm, and since many of the soldiers who fought in this area had marched many miles on a warm day—it was 81 degrees at 2:00 P.M.—they could not fail to notice a source of water.

Hood's division attacked over these open fields and hills from here on Warfield Ridge.

What Happened Here?

By approximately 4:00 P.M. on July 2, Major General John Bell Hood's four brigades had deployed in line of battle behind where you are standing. The Alabamians of Brigadier General Evander M. Law, the brigade for which Longstreet had waited before moving into position for this attack, took up its position on the crest behind you. Several hundred yards behind you on the reverse slope of the ridge rested Brigadier General Henry L. Benning's Georgia brigade. To your left, beyond the prominent point of woods that projects out into the fields on your left front, Brigadier General Jerome B. Robertson's Texas Brigade took position. A few hundred yards behind them, Brigadier General George T. Anderson's Georgians waited. Two of the four batteries of Major Mathis W. Henry's battalion attached to Hood's division deployed here along Warfield Ridge, as well.

This stop presents an unusual historical challenge. In 1888 General Law summarized it clearly when he wrote that "concerning the operations of Lee's extreme right wing, extending to the foot of Round Top, little or nothing has been written on the Confederate side." He attributed this dearth of source material produced in 1863 in part to Longstreet's personal attention to McLaws's division of his own First Corps and the supporting division of R. H. Anderson from Hill's Third Corps. Law also cited Hood's early wounding and his own later inability to write a divisional report during the "active and constant movement of our army for some weeks after the battle."[1] Longstreet's report summarized the operation of Hood's division in a few generic sentences, and Hood never did write a report, lamenting as late as 1875 to Longstreet that, because of his wounds and his military responsibilities, "the admirable conduct of my division at Gettysburg, I have left unrecorded." Thus much of the narrative at this stop, of necessity, must rest on postwar sources, when reputations rose and fell and national memory began to solidify around specific interpretations of controversial actions.

As Hood moved to McLaws's right to extend Longstreet's line southeasterly, he sent forward some of his "picked Texas scouts" to locate the Union left flank. As Hood recalled, "They soon reported to me that it rested upon Round Top Mountain," but that "the country was open, and that I could march through an open woodland pasture around Round Top, and assault the enemy in flank and rear; that their wagon trains were parked in the rear of their line [along the Taneytown Road], and were badly exposed to our attack in that direction." Hood's scouts also had discovered the deployment of Birney's division at Devil's Den, in the Wheatfield, and in the Peach Orchard. An attack on those positions and over the rugged terrain of the Round Tops—"with immense boulders of stone, so massed together as to form narrow openings, which would break our ranks and cause the men to scatter"— might only be done "at a most fearful sacrifice of as brave and gallant soldiers as ever engaged in battle."

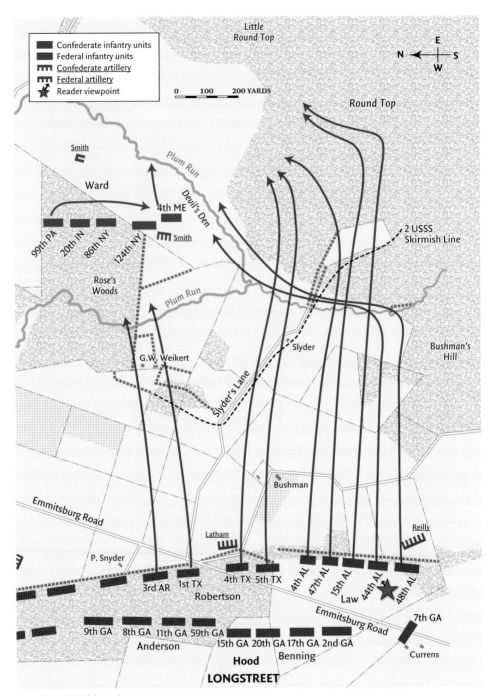

Little
Round Top

Round Top

Legend:
- Confederate infantry units
- Federal infantry units
- Confederate artillery
- Federal artillery
- Reader viewpoint

0   100   200 YARDS

N ← E / S / W

Smith

Plum Run

Ward

Devil's Den

4th ME

Smith

99th PA 20th IN 86th NY 124th NY

2 USSS
Skirmish Line

Rose's
Woods

Plum Run

G.W. Weikert

Slyder

Bushman's
Hill

Slyder's Lane

Emmitsburg Road

Bushman

P. Snyder

Latham

Reilly

3rd AR 1st TX   4th TX 5th TX   4th AL 47th AL 15th AL 44th AL 48th AL

Law

Robertson

Emmitsburg Road

7th GA

9th GA   8th GA 11th GA 59th GA   15th GA 20th GA 17th GA 2nd GA

Currens

Anderson   Benning

Hood
LONGSTREET

Hood's Division Advances

Hood reported his opinion to Longstreet "that it was unwise to attack up the Emmetsburg [sic] road, as ordered," stating a preference instead for attacking Round Top "in flank and rear." Longstreet rejected his suggestion, explaining only that "'General Lee's orders are to attack up the Emmetsburg road.'" Hood made a second appeal and received the same reply. Hood then made a third appeal through an especially trusted staff officer, suggesting that Longstreet "had better come and look" for himself. Rebuffed again, Hood recalled: "After this urgent protest against entering the battle at Gettysburg, according to instructions—which protest is the first and only one I ever made during my entire military career—I ordered my line to advance and make the assault."[2]

The Alabamians of Law's brigade stepped off first. Advancing from the tree line behind you and over the position where you now stand, the left flank regiments— the 4th and 47th Alabama—marched into the low ground ahead of you. To their right, Law's other three regiments—the 15th, 44th, and 48th Alabama—initially advanced over Bushman's Hill on your right front and moved toward the more challenging rocky slopes of Round Top.

Skirmishers from the 2nd U.S. Sharpshooters posted around the Bushman farm and the white buildings of the Slyder farm in front of you contested Law's advance. As Colonel Homer Stoughton later reported, Hood's men "advanced a line of battle covering our entire front and flank. While they were advancing, the Second [U.S. Sharpshooter] Regiment did splendid execution, killing and wounding a great many." The sharpshooters held their position until Confederate skirmishers pushed his right flank, "when I ordered my men to fall back, firing as they retired."

Colonel William C. Oates, commanding the 15th Alabama— Law's center regiment at the start of the attack—reported on the effectiveness of the sharpshooters' resistance: "I encountered the enemy's sharpshooters posted behind a stone fence, and sustained some loss thereby." As Stoughton's men pulled back up the slopes of Round Top, the 15th, 44th, and 48th Alabama continued their advance up the eminence. As Colonel James Sheffield of the 48th Alabama reported, he found "the worst cliffs of rocks there could have been traveled over." Then, as Union artillery in Devil's Den began to harass his advance, Law pulled the 44th and 48th Alabama off his right flank and redirected them over the open fields in your front toward the bothersome cannons. That shift moved Colonel Oates's 15th Alabama from the center of Law's brigade line to his right flank. With the 4th and 47th Alabama still on his left, Oates continued to advance in the direction of Round Top.

After Law's men stepped off, the men of Robertson's Texas Brigade began their advance, crossing the fields on your left front, heading into the Bushman farm.

Colonel Homer Stoughton,
2nd U.S. Sharpshooters,
U.S.A. (USAMHI)

General Hood himself watched his old command begin its assault. Within twenty minutes, however, Hood fell, hit badly in the arm by a piece of shell.

The consequences of Hood's wounding became apparent almost immediately. General Robertson, commanding the Texas Brigade, realized very quickly that he faced a challenge. "I was ordered to keep my right well closed on Brigadier-General Law's left, and to let my left on the Emmitsburg Pike," he reported. But as soon as his men advanced, he saw "that my brigade would not fill the space between General Law's left and the pike named, and that I must leave the pike, or disconnect myself from General Law on my right." Without Hood's guidance, Robertson ultimately chose to close on Law's left, believing, since "the attack on our part was to be general," that McLaws's men could close on the road. His decision, however, disrupted in the advance of the Texas Brigade and "caused some separation of my regiments."[3] You will learn more about the consequences of this confusion over the next few stops.

Who Fought Here?

C.S.A.: Brigadier General Evander M. Law's 1,933-man Alabama brigade of Hood's division in Longstreet's First Corps included the 4th, 15th, 44th, 47th, and 48th Alabama Infantry. They received direct artillery support from Reilly's Rowan Artillery and Latham's Branch Artillery from Major Mathis W. Henry's battalion.

U.S.: Engaged here were the 169 men of the 2nd U.S. Sharpshooters, serving as skirmishers, from Ward's brigade in Birney's division of Sickles's III Corps.

Who Commanded Here?

Major General John Bell Hood (1831–79), a native Kentuckian, graduated from West Point as a member of the class of 1853. He resigned his first lieutenancy in April 1861. A superb combat commander, he quickly rose to brigadier general by March

1862 and led the Texas Brigade in person in the breakthrough of the Union line at Gaines Mill during the Seven Days Battles. His men idolized him. When soldiers of the 4th Texas presented him with a horse, they said, "In you, sir, we recognize the soldier and the gentleman. In you we have found a leader who we are proud to follow—a commander whom it is a pleasure to obey." "In a word, General," others promised, "'you stand by us and we will stand by you.'"[4] As a major general and division commander, Hood led a thunderous counterattack at Antietam that restored Lee's line and drove the Union forces back into the Bloody Cornfield. At Gettysburg, he protested his orders but executed them nonetheless, until a wound to his arm knocked him out of action. He returned to his command for the Battle at Chickamauga, where another wound cost him a leg. He won promotion to lieutenant general and suc-

Major General John B. Hood, C.S.A., fell seriously wounded on July 2. (USAMHI)

ceeded General Joseph E. Johnston during the fight against Sherman's army for Atlanta. With the temporary rank of full general, Hood tried to relieve Georgia of the Union presence by advancing into west Tennessee toward Nashville, but his campaign ended in failure when his army practically dissolved at Nashville in December 1864. He lived in New Orleans after the war but died, along with his wife and one child, when a yellow fever epidemic swept through the city in 1879. His military memoir, *Advance and Retreat*, offers much insightful information about Hood's campaigns and his dealings with the war's major figures.

Brigadier General Evander McIver Law (1836–1920), born in South Carolina, graduated fourth in his class of fifteen cadets from the South Carolina Military Academy in 1856, excelling in oratory, constitutional law, and English literature. Only in conduct did McIver (pronounced "McKeever") fall short, ranking fourteenth in his class. When the Civil War broke out, he was elected lieutenant colonel of the 4th Alabama Infantry and fell wounded in the opening phases of the Battle of First Manassas. His colonel was killed in the battle, so after Law returned, he won election to fill that vacancy. He won promotion to brigadier general in October 1862. At Gettysburg, his Alabama brigade kicked off Longstreet's main effort against the Union left flank on Little Round Top on July 2. When General Hood fell wounded, Law rose to division command. He left the Army of Northern Virginia after receiving a second wound at Cold Harbor in June 1864 and led cavalry against Sherman's forces in 1865. As one of his veterans remembered him, "General Law in his prime was one of the handsomest of men, as straight as an arrow, with jet black beard, and of dashing appearance. The grace of his manner was flawless." Perhaps more telling, his men continued to refer to themselves as "Law's Brigade" for more than a year after another officer succeeded to its command.[5]

Brigadier General Evander M. Law, C.S.A. (USAMHI)

Who Fell Here?

The casualties for the 4th, 15th, and 47th Alabama in Law's brigade will be reported at the Little Round Top stop; the casualties for the 44th and 48th Alabama will be reported at Devil's Den. The Rowan Artillery lost 6 men; Latham's Branch Artillery lost 3 men.

The 2nd U.S. Sharpshooters lost 43 of their 169 men over the course of the entire battle.

Individual vignettes. In a letter to his wife on July 9, 1863, Private John C. West described one of the first casualties that the 4th Texas suffered in the advance: "Lieutenant Joe Smith, son of Captain Jack Smith, on Hog Creek was killed. We had just climbed a stone fence and crossed a branch and little marsh. Lieutenant Smith had wet his handkerchief in the branch and tied it around his head. It was extremely hot. It was about 3 o'clock in the afternoon, and we had double-quicked across an open field for nearly 500 yards. He was killed in twenty feet of me, just after we crossed the branch—shot through the head, the bullet passing through the folds of his handkerchief on both sides. He was a splendid officer and we miss him very much." Joe C. Smith enlisted in Company E, 4th Texas Infantry, on July 13, 1861, in Waco. He was appointed sergeant almost immediately. Except for a brief illness during the summer of 1862, he served without any extended absences. He won promotion to first sergeant of his company on July 4, 1862. His election as second lieutenant in his company at some point over the next several months—his records provide three different dates—clearly demonstrates that he won the respect of his fellow soldiers.[6]

Sergeant Henry L. Richards of Company F, 2nd U.S. Sharpshooters, enlisted at age thirty-seven in Portsmouth, New Hampshire. Usually an even-tempered man, he drew the attention of his company first sergeant, Wyman White, on the march into Pennsylvania: "Sergeant Richards of our company, who was generally very careful about finding fault or grumbling, no matter how uncomfortable things might be, gave the person that said we were in Pennsylvania this answer, 'G__ D__ your Pennsylvania. The Rebels ought to destroy the whole state if you can't afford better roads. This road is worse than Virginia roads.' Such an outburst from our beloved Sergeant was something very strange indeed. . . . His losing his temper and speaking out his feelings was a bad omen." On July 5, White recalled, "we received news of Sergeant Richards's death. He was killed while we were opposing Longstreet's great charges to capture Little Round Top on the second of July. He died on the amputating table July 3rd and we were informed that he died from an overdose of ether." Residents of his hometown of Auburn, New Hampshire, petitioned the town fathers to rename Auburn Street as "Richards' Avenue" in his honor because "the trees on the Avenue which will in future bear his name, were set out by his own hand, and nursed by his care."[7]

Who Lived Here?

The stone house and white-painted buildings located between where you are standing and Devil's Den were part of the John Slyder farm. Slyder purchased a seventy-five-acre tract of land along the western base of Round Top in 1849. A September 1863 sale notice described it as "a comfortable stone house ceiled above, answering for the purposes of two stories; double log barn with sheds all around, a two-story carpenter shop, blacksmith shop, and all necessary outbuildings; a well of water near the house, and a thriving orchard of good fruit." Soon after the battle, the Slyder family moved to Ohio.[8] Today, the farm and property are owned by the National Park Service. During the filming of the movie Gettysburg in 1992, several scenes were shot on the farm, and the house was used for General Lee's headquarters.

What Did They Say about It Later?

In his postwar memoir, Sergeant Wyman White of the 2nd U.S. Sharpshooters explained very specifically where he fought on July 2: "I was near the Snyder's [Slyder's] House, having a position in an angle of a stone wall just between the house and barn." He then described Hood's advance as it left your present position and advanced toward the Slyder farm:

> Just in front of where I was, the land was open and, as they were mostly dressed in butternut colored clothes they had the appearance of a plowed field being crossed in mass formation until they got within good fighting distance to our line, when they broke into line of battle formation three lines deep. Our line being only a skirmish line, that means five paces distance between the men, we were obliged to fall back or be either killed or taken prisoner. The enemy force in our front was at least ninety men to our one. Still they noticed that there was some opposition to their charge for we were armed with breech loaders and, as we took the matter very coolly, many a brave Southern threw up his arms and fell. But on they came, shouting and yelling their peculiar yell.[9]

Driving directions to the next stop: Drive straight ahead along South Confederate Avenue for 1.2 miles to the summit of Little Round Top. Proceed over the crest of Little Round Top and try to park toward the far end of the parking area where the road begins its descent. If you find the designated parking spots full, drive down the northern face of the hill, park on the right side of the road, and walk back up the road to the top of the hill to the first asphalted path to the summit that leads to the statue of Brigadier General Gouverneur K. Warren.

5 Longstreet Attacks

STOP 18. LITTLE ROUND TOP

This stop requires a bit of walking to three separate positions for a full understanding of this important action.

Orientation

Regardless of where you park, begin your tour of this important site by walking up to the open western face of the hill. Use the path next to the large bronze tablet describing the action of Brigadier General Stephen H. Weed's V Corps brigade. When you reach the top, locate the statue of Brigadier General Gouverneur K. Warren standing on a nearby rock, his gaze fixed toward the left. You are standing on the northwest slope of Little Round Top.

About twenty feet to the left of Warren's statue, you will see a broad, flat rock, nearly even with the ground surrounding it. Stand on this rock for an excellent view of the details of the July 2 battlefield and much more.

The view from the northwest slope of Little Round Top from the broad, flat rock described in the orientation.

Look out over the valley below you. In the middle distance almost directly in front of you, locate the top of the observation tower on the main Confederate line on Seminary Ridge; it stands not far from the Louisiana monument at Stop 15. Most of the fighting that pitted Hood's and McLaws's Confederates against Sickles's III Corps—and the thousands of Union reinforcements sent to its aid—took place on the ground between the tower and your current position.

Continue your terrain appreciation by looking to your left. The high wooded elevation is Round Top, and some of Law's Alabamians climbed to its crest as they advanced upon Little Round Top, where you now stand; the fight to hold this hill took place off to your left, and you will visit that site next. Now look once more into the valley below. Plum Run flows from right to left through low marshy ground; many books refer to the Plum Run valley as the "Valley of Death." Locate Crawford Avenue, the park road that runs through the valley toward Devil's Den, the conspicuous pile of boulders to your left front. The major combat action of July 2 in this area started at Devil's Den, at that moment the left flank of Birney's division of Sickles's III Corps and of the entire Army of the Potomac. In a slight break with historic chronology required by the road network, you will explore Meade's preferred anchor for the left flank of his line here on Little Round Top before you visit Devil's Den, where the first major combat action of July 2 occurred.

Now locate Houck's Ridge, the ridge of high ground rising up on the far side of Crawford Avenue below you. The scattering of monuments visible at the tree line on Houck's Ridge in front of you represent regiments in the two brigades of U.S. Regular infantry from the V Corps that came to the support of Birney's original III Corps defenders in the bloody Wheatfield. You cannot see the full expanse of the Wheatfield from this position, but you can see its northeast corner to your right front, just beyond the point where the Houck's Ridge tree line ends. Except during the summer, you also may be able to see the trees and monuments marking the location of Sherfy's Peach Orchard beyond the Wheatfield on a line between your current position and the observation tower.

Little Round Top also provides the best overview of the larger battlefield, and it is well worth the time to locate other key features important to understanding the battle.

Stand far forward on your large flat rock, face to the right, and look far beyond General Warren's statue. You are looking up the main Union line on Cemetery Ridge, clearly marked by a number of conspicuous monuments, especially the large dome of the Pennsylvania memorial. Follow that line of markers to the heavily wooded elevation on the horizon. That high ground is Cemetery Hill, the key to the Union position. The town of Gettysburg rests just beyond Cemetery Hill. If you are standing sufficiently far forward, you may also spot another large wooded hill to the right of Cemetery Hill with the roof of an observation tower clearly visible. This is Culp's Hill. You are once again viewing Meade's "fishhook" defensive

The view north from Little Round Top, following the shank of Meade's fishhook defense to Cemetery Hill, the high ground in the center distance. (USAMHI)

line, the right flank resting on Culp's Hill, proceeding to Cemetery Hill, and then extending southward along Cemetery Hill to your current position on Little Round Top. General Meade had intended for Sickles's III Corps initially to fill that part of the fishhook extending from here on Little Round Top toward—but not nearly as far as—the white-domed Pennsylvania monument; when the V Corps arrived, Meade planned to assign to it the responsibility of anchoring the Union left flank on this high ground, and the consolidated position of Sickles's III Corps only would have included the lowest part of Cemetery Ridge immediately ahead of you.

Now face front toward the Plum Run valley again. You already have examined Sickles's advanced line along Emmitsburg Road. Now you gain greater perspective on the disruption his advance caused for Meade's plans. Look across the open fields in the middle distance in your right front. You should be able to spot white fences, red barns, and traffic along the Emmitsburg Road ridgeline where Sickles posted Humphreys's division of the III Corps—its right flank unconnected to the left flank of Hancock's II Corps posted near the Pennsylvania memorial to your right. You will explore the collapse of Sickles's line across those open fields—and the Union effort to seal a near breach of their lines—in future stops.

To add one more useful bit of perspective about the size of this battlefield, look once again toward the far edge of the open fields to your right front and locate the red barn topped with three white spires. On the tree line behind that barn on a clear day, you should be able to locate a white church steeple. Extend your right arm and place the left side of your index finger beside the church steeple. On the same level as the steeple on the right side of your index finger, you should see a dark, heavily forested elevation with a conspicuous white dot in the center. That small white dot is the Eternal Light Peace Memorial you visited at Stop 5.

Position 1: Warren Spots the Danger

Orientation
Remain on the rock and look toward the Longstreet tower directly ahead of you.

What Happened Here?
During the midafternoon of July 2, Little Round Top remained largely unoccupied by Union forces. The XII Corps had moved from its morning camps on Little Round Top's eastern slopes to its permanent position on Culp's Hill. Sickles's men, who briefly encamped around the hill earlier in the day, had moved forward to the advanced III Corps line. The newly arrived V Corps had not yet moved to Little Round Top to take up its assignment for the defense of the extreme left flank of Meade's fishhook line. The only Union troops here when Longstreet started his assault included a small signal team and General Warren, Meade's chief engineer.

After the battle, Captain Lemuel B. Norton, the Army of the Potomac's chief signal officer, attributed an important discovery to his station on Little Round Top. He reported that "at about 3:30 P.M., the signal officer discovered the enemy massing upon General Sickles' left, and reported the fact to General Sickles and to the general commanding."

Warren did not file an official report of his activities at Gettysburg but, just the same, the testimony of others made him one of the central figures of the Little Round Top story. As part of his duty as chief engineer, he served as an extra set of trained eyes for Meade. At about 3:30 on July 2, Warren looked through his binoculars in the direction that his monument faces today and saw a sight that stunned him. He spotted activity in the tree line of Warfield Ridge (to your far left front where you may see the white Alabama monument). He sent an orderly to a nearby section of artillery with instructions to fire a few rounds in the direction of Warfield Ridge. The shots caused the Confederate infantry on the ridge to turn toward the sound, and sunlight glinted off their rifle barrels. Warren had spotted Hood's division in line of battle and realized that it extended well beyond the left flank of Sickles's line posted at Devil's Den below. If the Confederates advanced, unoccupied Little Round Top lay open to capture.

Warren knew he had to take the initiative to defend Little Round Top. He first sent an aide to Sickles for help, but he was informed that he could expect no help from the III Corps. He then saw Brigadier General James A. Barnes's division of the V Corps marching west on the Wheatfield Road—the park road heading out toward Emmitsburg Road to your right front. Warren sent Lieutenant Ranald Mackenzie— a future cavalry commander of note in the postwar West—to divert one of Barnes's brigades to Little Round Top. According to many accounts, Mackenzie tried and failed to convince two of Barnes's brigade commanders to bring their commands to Little Round Top before Colonel Strong Vincent agreed to do so. General Barnes, however, reported it quite differently: "General Warren, of the staff of General Meade, came up, riding rapidly from the left, and, pointing out the position of the elevation known as the Round Top, not far off and toward the left, urged the importance of assistance in that direction. General [George] Sykes [commander of the V Corps] yielded to his urgent request, and immediately directed Colonel [Strong] Vincent, commanding the Third Brigade, to proceed to that point."[1]

Who Commanded Here?

Brigadier General Gouverneur Kemble Warren (1830–82) grew up in Cold Spring, New York, right across the Hudson River from West Point. He graduated from the U.S. Military Academy in 1850, finishing second in his class. During the years before the Civil War, he received assignments in the topographical engineers and taught mathematics at West Point. He became one of the very first West Point graduates to see combat during the Civil War at Big Bethel, Virginia, on June 10, 1861, while serving as lieutenant colonel of the 5th New York Infantry. He rose to colonel and commanded an infantry brigade through the major campaigns of 1862 and received a promotion to brigadier general on September 26, 1862. He later became chief engineer of the Army of the Potomac, and in this role, he stood on Little Round Top on July 2 and saw Longstreet about to launch an assault against the unprotected height on which General Meade had planned to anchor his fishhook defense. Warren's actions on Little Round Top on July 2 demonstrated clearly how a senior leader in the heat of crisis should recognize a threat, assess its danger, form a workable plan, and follow it through to execution. A century later, his decision making on July 2 became a standard example of sound command initiative used in U.S. Army leadership manuals.

What Did They Say about It Later?

The debate over who gave the orders—and who refused to accept the initiative to defend Little Round Top—became quite heated in the postwar years. The majority settled on Warren or one of his aides acting on the chief engineer's authority. William Swinton, among the most astute and analytical of the Northern war correspondents, wrote that "General Warren assumed the responsibility of detaching from the force the brigade of Vincent and this he hurried up to hold the position." General Abner Doubleday, in his *Chancellorsville and Gettysburg*, noted in 1882 that Warren "rode down the slope, over to Barnes, took the responsibility of detaching Vincent's brigade and hurried it back to take post on Little Round Top" and then sent a staff officer to inform General Meade of his action. In the noted "Battles and Leaders of the Civil War" series, Union artillery commander General Henry J. Hunt stated that "the enemy was already advancing when, noticing the approach of the Fifth Corps, Warren rode to meet it, caused Weed's and Vincent's brigades and Hazlett's battery to be detached from the latter and hurried them to the summit."[2]

In 1888, however, Oliver Willcox Norton—who had served on Vincent's staff—suggested a quite different scenario. "I have always felt that General Vincent by his soldierly comprehension of the situation, and the promptness of his action, saved to our army the field of Gettysburg that day, and I think sufficient credit has never been given him," he argued. As Norton recalled it, Vincent stopped one of General Sykes's staff officers and asked him his mission. The officer replied that he had orders for Barnes. "Barnes ought to have been where Vincent was, but I do not recall seeing him any time during the day, after the early morning," Norton wrote. "I was under the impression that Barnes was not in condition to command a division on the field of battle, and that Vincent knew it, but military etiquette would prevent his speaking of that to the staff officer." When Vincent learned that Sykes had given orders to Barnes to send a brigade to Little Round Top, Norton continued, "without an instant's hesitation, Vincent said, 'I will take the responsibility myself of taking my brigade there.'" As Norton made clear, "Vincent received no orders from Genl. Warren, and Swinton and Doubleday attribute to Warren in error, almost the identical language used by Vincent."

Warren's own comments are enlightening. In 1872 he wrote to Porter Farley, a veteran of the 140th New York in General Weed's brigade: "If I detached Vincent's brigade I don't recollect it. General Barnes' report to General Sykes I think says something of the sort was done by me, which was Swinton's authority. . . . Perhaps it was Reese or Mackenzie acting under my orders who did it." Still, he noted, "the authority I assumed was on the responsibility of my judgment, and I would not have hesitated to take any troops I could get hold of, to maintain ourselves on the hill."[3]

Position 2: Vincent's Right Wing

Orientation
Now, leaving General Warren behind you, follow the asphalt path across the crest of Little Round Top. You will pass the guns of Lieutenant Charles E. Hazlett's Battery D, 5th U.S. Artillery, which arrived later in the fight. Continue along the asphalt path to its far end where you will see the prominent castle-like monument of the 44th New York Infantry. Stand in its archway facing the distinctive cluster of boulders—the famous Devil's Den—in the valley below.

What Happened Here?
Vincent's brigade included four regiments. From right to left, after some shuffling of positions, they deployed as follows: the 16th Michigan—their simple and un-adorned monument sits alone on a boulder on the low shelf of ground to your im-

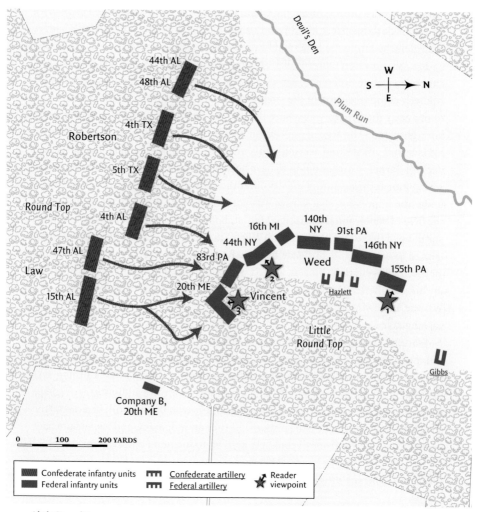

Little Round Top

mediate left front; the 44th New York, which extended the Michiganders' line to the left; Vincent's own 83rd Pennsylvania, on the New Yorkers' left flank over your left shoulder; and Colonel Joshua Lawrence Chamberlain's 20th Maine, holding the left flank of the brigade—and the new left flank of the Army of the Potomac—in a position well over your left shoulder, which you will visit shortly. Colonel James C. Rice of the 44th New York described the position of Vincent's brigade as "nearly that of a quarter circle, composed mostly of high rocks and cliffs on the center, and becoming more wooded and less rugged as you approached to the left. The right [ahead of you] was thrown forward somewhat to the front of the ledge of rocks, and was much more exposed than other parts of the line. A comparatively smooth ravine extended along the entire front, perhaps 50 yards from our line."[4] The ravine is much more heavily wooded today.

As Vincent's brigade deployed to meet the Confederate assault, Law's Alabamians continued to press toward Little Round Top (approaching from your left as you stand in the archway). The rough terrain had disrupted their advance, as you have learned, and only three of Law's five Alabama regiments—the 15th, 47th, and 4th, from left to right as they advanced toward your position—had continued to push forward. (Law's other two regiments—the 44th and 48th Alabama—played main roles in the fighting at Devil's Den, your next stop, but participated later in the action here.) In the confusion that split the Texas Brigade, the 4th and 5th Texas had continued to close on the left flank of Law's three Alabama regiments heading up the heights here. They would approach this position from your left front, advancing toward the shelf of rocks where the 16th Michigan's monument sits.

Indeed, after some skirmishing on the slopes of Round Top (to your left), the major fighting for Little Round Top began when the 4th and 5th Texas assaulted the regiments from Michigan and New York. The Texans reached the field of battle quite winded. As Lieutenant Colonel King Bryan of the 5th Texas reported, they had advanced "about three-fourths of a mile from our starting point, which distance was passed over by our line at a double quick and a run." At first, Vincent's right flank held. Bryan attributed the Texans' inability to advance farther "to the rocky nature of the ground over which we had to pass, the huge rocks forming defiles through which not more than 3 or 4 men could pass abreast, thus breaking up our alignment and rendering its reformation impossible." The soldiers in the ranks entirely concurred with the colonel. As Private John C. West wrote to his brother on July 27, "There were places full ten or fifteen feet perpendicular around which we were compelled to go, and the entire ascent would have been difficult to a man entirely divested of gun and accouterments. It was a mass of rock and boulders amid which a mountain goat would have revelled."[5]

Now leave the archway and walk around to the left side of the 44th New York monument to view the informational wayside showing how the Union soldiers utilized Little Round Top's rocks for defense. You are now standing behind the battle line of the 44th New York; the troops themselves formed farther down the slope in front of you. Except when the trees are in full foliage, you also may see Colonel Vincent's statue atop the monument to the 83rd Pennsylvania through the trees on your left front. Soon after the Texans attacked the 16th Michigan, the 4th Alabama and some of the Texans also advanced up the base of these slopes to hit the New Yorkers and Pennsylvanians in line below you and to your left. Like the Texans, the men of the 4th Alabama verged on exhaustion. As members of the last brigade to arrive before the July 2 fight, all of Law's men already had marched nearly twenty-five miles on this day with little time to rest or rehydrate. Although the 4th Alabama pressed its attack, Lieutenant Colonel L. H. Scruggs reported that, "owing to the exhausted condition of the men and the roughness of the mountain side, we found it impossible to carry this position." Lieutenant Colonel Freeman Conner of the 44th New York reported that the Confederates advanced "until the first line came within about 40 yards of our line," when "we opened a heavy fire upon them, which was continued until they were compelled to retreat."[6]

Despite the promising start, a crisis soon developed on the right of Vincent's brigade. As Colonel Norval A. Welch of the 16th Michigan reported after the battle, "someone (supposed to be [Brigadier] General [Stephen H.] Weed or [V Corps Commander] Major-General [George] Sykes) called from the extreme crest of the hill to fall back nearer the top, where a much less exposed line could be taken up." Welch asserted that "this order was not obeyed, except by single individuals," and he blamed Lieutenant William Kydd for an "entirely unwarrantable assumption of authority" for ordering the regiment's colors to fall back.

Nonetheless, the Michigan line did waver, and the Texans hit its right flank and swarmed into the flat open ground below you and to your right front. The Confederate attack put Vincent's entire line at risk. As he tried to rally the men and organize a defense of his weakening flank, Colonel Vincent fell with a mortal wound.

At that moment, however, deliverance came with the timely arrival of Colonel Patrick H. O'Rorke's 140th New York from General Weed's brigade. No controversy surrounded their deployment to Little Round Top: General Warren sent them there. In a letter to a local newspaper right after the battle, one survivor of the regiment described their arrival on the hill:

> Old General Warren, our former Brigadier, rode up and commanded our Brigade to move by the flank and follow him. We did so on the double quick. He led us up a steep, rocky cliff, and did not halt, until out of breath, we reached the top, where the bullets flew around us like hail. We had not much time for reflection, however, for very soon the Rebels were nearly to the top of the hill before us. . . . We reached there just in time to front them, and show them the muzzles of our guns. But here was a sad mistake committed. Our generals did not take the precaution to have our men load before we came into the contest, and so we were delayed a few moments in loading.[7]

Then, with the advantage of downhill momentum, O'Rorke's men pitched into the attackers and sent them reeling back to the bottom of the hill.

The charge of the 140th New York had secured the right of Vincent's line, but O'Rorke did not live to savor the victory. Eyewitness accounts of his death generally agree that the bullet that hit him in the neck killed him almost instantly. The arrival of the rest of Weed's brigade solidified Union control of the open western face of Little Round Top, and the arrival of Hazlett's battery added useful artillery support. But the victory exacted a high cost. In addition to O'Rorke and Vincent,

General Weed fell mortally wounded, and as Lieutenant Hazlett bent over to catch the general's final instructions, a bullet crashed into his skull and killed him.

Who Fought Here?

C.S.A.: Troops from Law's brigade included the 4th and 48th Alabama; troops of the 44th Alabama also likely participated. Troops from Robertson's brigade included the 4th and 5th Texas.

U.S.: Colonel Strong Vincent's brigade of Barnes's division in Sykes's V Corps included the 16th Michigan, the 44th New York, and the 83rd Pennsylvania Infantry. Colonel O'Rorke's 140th New York belonged to Brigadier General Stephen H. Weed's brigade, Ayres's division, Sykes's V Corps. The rest of Weed's brigade included the 146th New York and the 91st and 155th Pennsylvania, which took up positions across the western face of Little Round Top after the charge of the 140th New York and engaged with Confederate skirmishers toward the end of the action. Lieutenant Charles E. Hazlett's Battery D, 5th U.S. Artillery, provided direct artillery support.

Lieutenant Charles E. Hazlett, U.S.A., fell dead near his battery while attempting to catch the last words of mortally wounded Brigadier General Stephen Weed. (USAMHI)

Who Commanded Here?

Colonel Strong Vincent (1837–63), born at Waterford, Pennsylvania, near Erie, graduated from Harvard in 1859. He studied law, passed the bar examination within a year, and opened a practice in Erie. When the Civil War started, he began his military service as a first lieutenant and adjutant of a three-month regiment. When that unit's term of service ended, he reenlisted and became lieutenant colonel of the 83rd Pennsylvania, fated to become a hard-fighting regiment that suffered extremely high casualties over the course of the war. At Gaines Mill, Vincent was absent sick; when both the colonel and the major of the 83rd Pennsylvania were killed in action there, he rose to regimental command. On July 2 Vincent commanded the four-regiment brigade that arrived on

Colonel Strong Vincent, U.S.A., fell mortally wounded here. (USAMHI)

Little Round Top in response to Warren's emergency call for troops to defend the hill. His partisans later claimed that he took his brigade to Little Round Top on his own authority, not in response to any specific order from Warren or anyone else. In any case, the troops arrived on "Vincent's Spur" with about fifteen minutes to spare. In the fighting between Vincent's men and the Alabamians and Texans of Hood's brigade, Vincent fell mortally wounded. He died on July 5, and his remains rest at Erie Cemetery. He received a postbattle promotion to brigadier general, effective July 3, 1863, but he likely never knew of it. Strong Vincent High School in Erie is named for him.

Who Fell Here?

C.S.A.: In Law's brigade, 87 of the 346 men in the 4th Alabama fell here. Most of the losses in the 44th and 48th Alabama occurred at Devil's Den. In Robertson's Texas Brigade, 112 of the 415 soldiers in the 4th Texas fell here, along with 211 of the 409 men in the 5th Texas.

U.S.: In Vincent's brigade, 60 of the 263 men in the 16th Michigan fell, along with 111 of the 391 men in the 44th New York and 55 of the 295 men who served in the 83rd Pennsylvania. Colonel Vincent fell mortally wounded and died on July 5. His brigade lost 26.3 percent of its strength. In Weed's brigade, 132 of 447 men of the 140th New York fell, and Colonel O'Rorke died. The rest of Weed's brigade suffered lightly, with the 146th New York losing 28 men, the 91st Pennsylvania losing 19 men, and the 155th Pennsylvania also losing 19 men. Weed fell mortally wounded and died on July 3. His brigade lost 13.5 of its strength. Battery D, 5th U.S. Artillery, lost Lieutenant Hazlett, killed, and 12 additional men.

Individual vignettes. The military careers of John Taylor Darwin and Rufus B. Franks of Company I of the 4th Alabama seemed to follow fairly parallel paths. Both men enlisted on April 26, 1861, in Huntsville, initially for one year of service and later extended to a period of "for the war." Darwin's star rose steadily, and he earned a promotion to sergeant early in 1862 and became company first sergeant on December 1, 1862. He fought in most of the regiment's battles beginning with First Manassas, missing only the 1862 Maryland Campaign while home on furlough after a brief hospital stay. Franks, a student, received a promotion to corporal in early 1862 and became Company I's fifth sergeant late in the year. For reasons his records do not explain, however, he was reduced to ranks at some point in the two months before Gettysburg, and he came to Pennsylvania a private. In a speech in Birmingham on May 5, 1900, Captain W. C. Ward—who had served as a private in the 4th Alabama at Gettysburg—recounted the last moments of his two comrades:

> In the din of battle we could hear the charges of canister passing over us with the noise of partridges in flight. Immediately to the right, Taylor Darwin, Orderly Sergeant of Company I, suddenly stopped, quivered, and sank to the earth dead, a ball having passed through his brain. There was Rube Franks, of the same company, just returned from his home in Alabama, his new uniform bright with color, the envy of all his comrades, his gladsome face beaming as if his sweetheart's kiss had materialized on his lips, calling to his comrades; "Come on, boys; come on! The Fifth Texas will get there before the Fourth! Come on, boys; come on!" He shortly afterwards met the fatal shot.[8]

Private Sanford O. Webb of Rochester, New York, mustered into Company G of the 140th New York on September 13, 1862. When he enlisted, he left behind his fifty-five-year-old widowed mother, Lydia, in nearby Penfield to care for his invalid younger brother, Jesse. The Webbs enjoyed few luxuries in life, especially after Sanford's father died in 1858. Sanford had two older brothers, but since they had families of their own, they contributed nothing to the support of their mother and two younger brothers. Sanford and Jesse worked as farmhands around the neighborhood until Jesse fell ill. Local farmers later testified that they often paid Sanford partially in "such articles of consumption as were needed by the mother, including wood," as well as groceries and the use of a cow. He regularly sent home part of his pay, but that stopped when a Confederate bullet instantly killed Private Webb on Little Round Top on July 2. Lydia Webb began the application process for a mother's pension on July 15 and, in time, was awarded the monthly sum of $8 for her son's service. Private Webb's comrades never forgot his sacrifice, however. In 1892, in recounting the fight on Little Round Top, Samuel Hazen included this mention of a comrade in Company G with whom he served: "The first man I saw fall was Sanford Webb, of Co. G. He was touching my left elbow, and fell near the summit of Little Round Top, within four feet of and in front of the rock which has a tablet on in memory of Gen. Vincent."[9] Private Webb is buried in the Soldiers' National Cemetery in grave B-135 of the New York plot.

What Did They Say about It Later?

The performance of the 16th Michigan periodically became the subject of controversy among Vincent's survivors. Occasional charges and countercharges—some public, others private—swirled around the performance of its commander. While Colonel Welch had blamed one of his lieutenants for pulling the regiment out of line and back to the crest of the hill without orders, others suggested that Welch himself was responsible and, in fact, left the line entirely for a brief period. Shortly after the war, one veteran wrote to the Michigan adjutant general that "Colonel Welch commanded the 16th at Gettysburg, but during the hottest part of the battle in the P.M. towards night, the colonel left with the colors for some reason." The fine details, of course, are unrecoverable today, but they illustrate very well the difficulty of reconstructing an activity as complex as combat.[10]

Interestingly, there are two stone tributes on Little Round Top that allege to designate the spot where Colonel Vincent received his mortal wound. You can find a rock carving dedicated to him on the flat top surface of a large boulder on the opposite side of the 44th New York's monument from the informational wayside where you have been standing. The other tribute, a marble marker emblazoned with the Maltese cross of the V Corps, can be found affixed to a boulder farther down the slope of Little Round Top to the left front of the informational wayside. Oliver Willcox Norton, who served on Vincent's staff and later wrote extensively—and not always objectively—about the fight for Little Round Top, initially asserted that Vincent fell while urging the 140th New York into the fight. Later, he wrote that Vincent fell while attempting to stabilize his right flank as the 16th Michigan collapsed. Ultimately, he admitted that "no living man can point out the exact spot where Vincent stood when he was shot."[11]

Position 3: The Fight of the 20th Maine Infantry

Orientation

Now retrace your steps back toward Hazlett's battery, pause at the monument to Colonel O'Rorke's 140th New York, and consider the danger of the openness of the west face of Little Round Top here. Well illuminated by late afternoon sun, any conspicuous figure here made a tempting target for sharpshooters in Devil's Den—now in Confederate hands—who might seek a target. Of course, no one can say for certain whether or not a specific Northern soldier fell into a Southerner's sights, but in addition to Vincent, O'Rorke, Weed, and Hazlett, many other officers were killed on this hill. Warren himself suffered a minor wound serving on Little Round Top.

Now turn to your right and follow the first paved path that leads down to the parking area. Rather than return to your vehicle, however, walk down the park road to your right against the flow of traffic. You will see an asphalted path angling off to your left, marked by signs denoting the position of the 20th Maine. Follow that path down to the regimental monument. At that point, stand behind the stone wall that overlooks a small parking area in the low ground in front of you; the 20th Maine's monument should be on your left. The stone wall behind which you stand was not here at the time the 20th Maine made its stand; a small metal sign on the park road to your right, placed at Chamberlain's insistence, makes clear that the walls were constructed on the evening of July 2, after his regiment had secured the position. Remember, the park roads you see did not exist in 1863, and the vegetation was more open.

What Happened Here?

You are now standing in the approximate initial position of the 20th Maine on the extreme left flank of the Army of the Potomac at about 4:30 P.M. on July 2. While the 83rd Pennsylvania, the 44th New York, and the 16th Michigan extended the line of Vincent's brigade across the road to your right, Chamberlain sent Captain Walter G. Morrill's Company B approximately 100 yards to your left "to extend from my left flank across this hollow as a line of skirmishers, with directions to act as occasion might dictate, to prevent a surprise on my exposed flank and rear." The men from Maine heard the fighting on the right of the brigade line and waited for their own fight to begin. Finally, the 47th Alabama advanced down the slope of Round Top (in front of you) and toward your present position. "The action was sharp and at close quarters," Chamberlain reported, and the Alabamians returned to make several additional attempts to break the 20th Maine's line. Sergeant William T. Livermore of the 20th Maine's color guard recorded in his diary that the Alabamians "came to within four or five rods, covering themselves behind big rocks and trees, and kept up a murderous fire, which was returned by us."[12]

Then, as Chamberlain reported, "an officer from my center informed me that some important movement of the enemy was going on in his front beyond that of the line with which we were engaged." From a nearby rock, the colonel saw "a considerable body of the enemy moving by the flank in rear of their line engaged . . . toward the front of my left," taking up a position from which to assault the 20th Maine's open left flank. Chamberlain had spotted Colonel William C. Oates's 15th Alabama Infantry.

Chamberlain had to respond to the new crisis quickly. As he reported, "I immediately stretched my regiment to the left" and, placing Color Sergeant Andrew Tozier to plant the regimental colors at a boulder somewhere near where you now stand, he bent back—or "refused"—his left wing "so that it was nearly at right angles with my right, thus occupying about twice the extent of our ordinary front." "My officers and men understood my wishes so well," Chamberlain observed, "that this movement was executed under fire, the right wing keeping up fire, without giving the enemy any occasion to seize or even to suspect their advantage."

Retrace your steps up the asphalt path until you are standing even with the 20th Maine's right flank marker—engraved with a large R—near the stone wall to your left. Now turn to the right off the asphalt path and walk carefully over the rough ground toward the cluster of large rocks about fifty feet away. Near there, you will find the left flank marker—engraved with a large L to designate a possible location of the end of the 20th Maine's new refused line. (The actual location is impossible to discern today because of terrain changes caused by the construction of long-abandoned Chamberlain Avenue, traces of which you can still see when you look into the low ground below the left flank marker.) Stand at the 20th Maine's left flank marker and look into that low ground. The 20th Maine primary monument should now be on your right.

Colonel Chamberlain had just adjusted his lines when Oates's Alabamians advanced. "We were not a moment too soon," the Maine colonel reported. The 20th Maine repulsed Oates's first charge, but they returned "with a shout" and "pushed up to within a dozen yards of us" before pulling back again. The 47th Alabama continued to press against Chamberlain's right, while Oates pushed against his left. Chamberlain reported that "squads of the enemy broke through our line in several places, and the fight was literally hand to hand." By now, Chamberlain's men rummaged through the pockets and cartridge boxes of dead and wounded friends and foes alike for more ammunition; some even swapped their Enfield rifles, "which we found did not stand service well," for better weapons discarded on the battlefield. The few rounds remaining to each man proved unnerving.

Worse, Oates's men clearly prepared to make another assault. "It did not seem possible to withstand another shock like this coming on," Chamberlain reported. "Thus, I ordered the bayonet. The word was enough." Although the actual genesis of this next action remains a controversial issue, the colonel explained the advance of his left wing that followed: "Holding fast by our right, and swinging forward our left, we made an extended 'right wheel,' before which the enemy's line broke, and fell back, fighting from tree to tree, many being captured, until we had swept the valley and cleared the front of nearly our entire brigade." Captain Morrill's Company B "added much to the effect of the charge." Indeed, Colonel Oates reported that two entire regiments "were moving upon my rear and not 200 yards distance." The exhausted Alabamians, who had marched nearly twenty-five miles that day even before entering the battle, now retreated to avoid "capture or destruction." They broke and ran for the safety of the Confederate rear area. As Chamberlain reported, some of his elated soldiers "declared they were 'on the road to Richmond.'"[13] The stand of the 20th Maine had secured the left of Vincent's Little Round Top line. Thus the Union left flank had held.

Who Fought Here?

C.S.A.: From Law's brigade, the 15th and 47th Alabama Infantry were engaged here.

U.S.: From Vincent's brigade, Barnes's division, Sykes's V Corps, the 20th Maine Infantry, served here.

Colonel Joshua Lawrence
Chamberlain, 20th Maine,
U.S.A. (USAMHI)

Who Commanded Here?

Colonel Joshua Lawrence Chamberlain (1828–1914), of Brewer, Maine, received a classical education at Bowdoin College and theological training at Bangor Theological Seminary. He taught at Bowdoin, but when he tried to enlist in the Union Army early in the war, he was denied permission by the school. He did receive a leave of absence, allegedly to study abroad, and Chamberlain used the release time to enlist, becoming lieutenant colonel of the 20th Maine Infantry. He learned the soldier's art from his colonel, West Point–educated Adelbert Ames, whose promotion to brigadier general opened an opportunity for Chamberlain's advancement to regimental command about a month before Gettysburg. On Little Round Top, Chamberlain remained visible to his men; showed decisiveness; demonstrated initiative; and found ways to overcome the challenges of rough terrain, low ammunition, and unknown enemy strength in a situation in which he had no options but to stay and fight it out. Chamberlain received the Medal of Honor for his stand on Little Round Top. Before the war ended, he suffered six wounds; the effects of the one he received at Petersburg in June 1864 ultimately contributed to his death in 1914. But in his long life after Gettysburg and the Civil War, he continued to serve in the public good as governor of Maine and president of Bowdoin College, and he became a prolific writer of important and still-useful studies of the campaigns in which he participated. His description of Gettysburg as the "vision place of souls" has become iconic.

Colonel William Calvin Oates (1833–1910) commanded the 15th Alabama Infantry at Little Round Top. A native of Pike County, Alabama, he became captain of Company G in July 1861. He saw action in 1862 in the Shenandoah Valley Campaign, at the Seven Days Battles on the Virginia peninsula, and at Cedar Mountain, Antietam, and Fredericksburg. He was named colonel to rank from April 28, 1863, but the Confederate Congress failed to confirm the promotion; he officially became a major on that date. After serving at Chickamauga and Knoxville, he returned to Virginia with the rest of Longstreet's First Corps for the Overland Campaign in May 1864. He lost an arm in battle outside Richmond in the late summer of 1864. After the war, Oates became a U.S. congressman and governor of Alabama. He also served briefly as a U.S. brigadier general of volunteers during the Spanish-American War. He wrote an interesting personal memoir entitled *The War between the Union and the Confederacy and Its Lost Opportunities* (1905). He also returned to Gettysburg early in the twentieth century intent on erecting a memorial to his brother who fell mortally wounded on Little Round Top, but he could not obtain permission to do so.

Who Fell Here?

C.S.A.: In Law's brigade, the 15th Alabama lost 171 of its 499 men, and the 47th Alabama lost 44 of its 347 men.

U.S.: In Vincent's brigade, the 20th Maine lost 125 of its 386 men.

Individual vignettes. Lieutenant Barnett H. Cody of Company G, 15th Alabama Infantry, showed a natural talent for soldiering. When his company first organized, he was appointed a sergeant. He performed his duties so well that in April 1863, Colonel Oates recommended Cody for a "valor and skill" promotion to second lieutenant; he did not need to stand for election as so many officers did. On July 2, in the attack against the 20th Maine, a bullet hit Cody in the left groin. When the Alabamians retreated, they had to leave Cody behind. He was taken to the field hospital of the Second Division of the V Corps. Peritonitis set in, and Cody died, although surviving records disagree on the date; he died on July 22, 23, or 25 in Gettysburg. After the war, Oates wrote about the young lieutenant:

> Cody, a boy about eighteen years old, the best officer I ever saw of his age, except Major [Joseph W.] Latimer, of the artillery, fell near my brother [Lieuten-

ant John A. Oates], mortally wounded. When we retreated they, with most of our wounded and eighty-four men who were not, were taken prisoners, and the wounded were removed to the Federal field hospital, where they were as well cared for as wounded soldiers in the hands of an enemy ever are. Cody lived twenty-one and my brother twenty-three days. A Miss Lightner, a Virginia lady and Southern sympathizer, nursed them to the last, and Doctor Reid, of the One Hundred and Fifty-fifth Pennsylvania Regiment, did all that he could for them and had them decently buried when they died.[14]

Sergeant William S. Jordan of Company G, 20th Maine Infantry, was only eighteen years old when a bullet penetrated his left lung on July 2. He was taken to a V Corps hospital behind the lines, and assistant surgeon B. Howard attempted to "hermetically seal" the wound. This controversial practice sealed up the wound tightly without removing the bullet and with little changing of dressing or packing unless hemorrhage or some other condition required it. While many of the surgeons serving with the Third Division of the II Corps adopted it, the practice was, according to one contemporary study, "regarded with disfavor by the majority of the medical officers of this Army." At Gettysburg, Dr. J. S. Billings observed "six cases, in which the hermetically sealing process had been practiced by Dr. Howard. . . . An assistant surgeon was left by Dr. Howard to take charge of the cases, and carry out his peculiar mode of treatment, and a written order was given by Dr. Letterman that these cases should not be interfered with. All of these men died within eighteen days." Sergeant Jordan developed pyemia on July 20, and he died of his wound four days later. An autopsy was performed after his death that revealed "the left side of the chest was found filled with pus, displacing the heart." Sergeant Jordan is buried in the Soldiers' National Cemetery in grave C-13 of the Maine plot.[15]

Who Lived Here?

At the time of the Civil War, Ephraim Hanaway, a farmer and stonemason, owned the western face of Little Round Top. He had purchased about thirty acres on the hill's western face in 1858 and used his out lot as a source of wood and stone; he had timbered much of his property just the previous year, making his property an important military position for its cleared fields of fire. Jacob Weikert owned 102 acres of land here that included Little Round Top's eastern face. Weikert had purchased the property in 1840, and he and his wife, Sarah, settled down to cultivate their land and raise their thirteen children. Their stone house sat along the Taneytown Road some 650 yards southeast of the summit of the hill. On July 2 and July 3, a large number of wounded filled the house, the barn, and the carriage house. The family departed hurriedly at the behest of Union officers. Surgeon Billings, reaching the house shortly thereafter, reported: "I found it unoccupied and bearing evident traces of the hasty desertion of its inmates. A good fire was blazing in the kitchen stove, a large quantity of dough was mixed up, the bake-pans were greased; in short, everything was ready for use. I immediately set my attendants at work baking bread and heating large boilers of water." The wounded soon began to arrive, and, a short time later, the Weikerts and Tillie Pierce, a local teenager who fled her home in town for the presumed safety of the farm, returned to help. As the wounded arrived in greater and greater numbers, Tillie later wrote, "Beckie Weikert, the daughter at home, and I went out to the barn to see what was transpiring there. Nothing before in my experience had ever paralleled the sight we then and there beheld. There were the groaning and the crying, the struggling and dying, crowded side to side, while attendants sought to aid and relieve them as best they could."[16] Jacob Weikert claimed damages after the war in excess of $1,800. The farm is privately owned today.

What Did They Say about It Later?

Michael Shaara's Pulitzer Prize–winning novel, The Killer Angels (1975), and Gettysburg, the 1993 movie based on the book, have turned Colonel Chamberlain and the 20th Maine into larger-than-life figures. During the immediate aftermath of the battle and for years after the war, however, the survivors of the 20th Maine did not agree on just what occurred on the slopes of Little Round Top during the late afternoon of July 2, especially when it came to their final charge that repulsed Oates's Alabamians. Three different interpretations follow; compare them with Colonel Chamberlain's report quoted above.

First, Sergeant William T. Livermore later recorded this diary entry: "We were ordered to charge them when there were two to our one. With fixed bayonets and with a yell we rushed on them, which so frightened them, that not another shot was fired on us. Some threw down their arms and ran but many rose up, begging to be spared. . . . After chasing them as far as prudent, we 'rallied around the colors' and gave three hearty cheers, then went back to our old position, with our prisoners."

Second, Corporal Elisha Coan of the color guard, in a postwar memoir, wrote the following:

Lt. [Holman] Melcher conceived the idea of advancing the colors so that our line would cover our wounded & dead so that they could be removed to the rear and he asked Col. C[hamberlain] for the privilege of advancing his Company for that purpose. Col. C. hesitated for the step would be a hazardous one, for the enemy had a strong position behind the rocks 3 rods in front of us. But our line was melting away like ice before the sun, and something must soon be done or all would be lost. . . . Other officers joined Melcher in urging a forward movement and Col. C. gave his consent. Immediately Melcher passed to the front of his company & placing himself in front of the colors ordered his men forward. Other officers followed his example. . . . Then Col. C. gave the order "Forward."[17]

Finally, Major Ellis Spear explained it this way:

> On the left of the colors there were men wounded by the earlier fire and left in front as the line readjusted itself among the rocks. They were calling upon their comrades to get them back out of the fire. Comrades will understand that that involved cessation of fire on the part of the men attempting it and danger and disturbance to the line at a critical moment. But some enterprising and undaunted fellow said, "It's a damned shame to leave the boys there; let's advance and cover them." And those in the immediate vicinity joined the cry of "Forward!" Then the wounded would be in the rear and in reach of the stretcher-bearers. The shout was heard and movement seen to right and left further than the explanation of the original purpose of the movement, [and many more joined in the advance].[18]

Driving directions to the next stop: Drive down the northern face of Little Round Top on Sykes Avenue. At 0.2 miles, turn left onto Wheatfield Road and follow it to the west 0.2 miles, turning left onto Crawford Avenue and the Valley of Death. Proceed 0.5 miles through Devil's Den, bypassing the turn onto Warren Avenue. Follow the road to the upper west side of the hill. Park on the right side of the road just beyond the cannons and the prominent statue of an artilleryman holding a rammer, which represents the 4th New York Artillery Battery. The brigade marker to Robertson's brigade will be on your left. (Note: sharp turns in the road prohibit the movement of buses and large campers through Devil's Den. If you are driving such a vehicle, follow the directions above, except, rather than turning left onto Crawford Avenue from Wheatfield Road, continue driving west a short distance across the single-lane Plum Run Bridge and turn left onto Ayres Avenue, which runs along the eastern end of the Wheatfield. Park on the graveled shoulder of Ayres Avenue after making the loop through the row of identical monuments to the U.S. Regular Army's infantry regiments, then walk forward to the intersection with Sickles Avenue just beyond the 5th New Hampshire monument. Walking to the left on Sickles Avenue will take you to the start of Stop 19 [Devil's Den]. Walking to the right on Sickles Avenue will take you to the start of Stop 20 [the Wheatfield]).

STOP 19. THE FIGHT FOR DEVIL'S DEN

Orientation

To complete this stop, you will take a walking tour that makes a circle around Devil's Den and covers several different parts of the fight. The walk will start and end near your vehicle, if you followed the driving directions for automobiles.

Position 1: Ward Deploys for Action

Stand at the informational wayside placed between two cannons beside the 4th New York Battery monument. Face in the same direction that the artilleryman atop the monument seems to be looking.

Devil's Den, the unique rock formation behind you composed of diabase boulders, served as a picnic ground for Gettysburg residents in more peaceful times. Several explanations have been offered for its unusual name. Some have argued that it got its name from a Native American chieftain whose tribe roamed south-central Pennsylvania during colonial days. Others have posited that the name came from a large black snake that used to sun itself on its massive boulders. In any case, it lived up to its name fully in the late afternoon of July 2, 1863. The most detailed modern study uncovered no prebattle usage of the term "Devil's Den" but found an almost immediate popularization of the name afterward.[1]

The informational wayside at Devil's Den looking toward the Confederate line.

What Happened Here?

Initially, Devil's Den played no part in General Meade's defensive plan. If his fish-hook line developed as the Union commander intended, Devil's Den likely would have become little more than an advanced position to provide cover for Union skirmishers and sharpshooters protecting Little Round Top. Sickles's advance to the Emmitsburg Road line, however, left him with insufficient strength to deploy troops on Little Round Top itself. Thus Brigadier General John Henry Hobart Ward's brigade of Birney's division posted here became the protectors of Little Round Top as well as the left flank of Sickles's command—and, temporarily at least, the left flank of the entire Army of the Potomac. The skirmish line of the 2nd U.S. Sharpshooters extending into the open fields to your left represented the only organized Union resistance south of Devil's Den when Hood's division launched the Confederate main effort at about 4:00 P.M. on the afternoon of July 2.

Initially, the men of the 4th Maine of Ward's brigade held the ground to your immediate left, while the 124th New York deployed to your immediate right and extended to the tree line beyond its regimental monument crowned by the statue of Colonel A. VanHorn Ellis. Enlisted men manhandled four 10-pounder Parrott cannons from Captain James Smith's six-gun 4th New York Battery up over the rocks to protect against a Confederate advance from your front or left. As you will learn, the guns located here do not reflect their actual position during much of the fight. Smith placed his other two Parrotts in the Plum Run valley, the low ground on the other side of Devil's Den behind you. You will see their position shortly. The other regiments in Ward's brigade extended this line well into the trees to your right. The 1st and 2nd U.S. Sharpshooters also belonged to Ward's brigade, but they are not part of this battle line.

Position 2: The Fight in the Gorge

Orientation

Turn around and follow the footpath behind Smith's battery that leads through the rockiest part of Devil's Den, carefully walking down the steps to the parking area below. When you reach the park road, turn left and walk the short distance to the stop sign. Look down the park road beyond the stop sign. Captain Smith's other two cannons wheeled into position about where the road curves, aimed toward your location to cover the open ground behind you. The height to your right is Little Round Top; Round Top is the heavily forested elevation over your right shoulder. Plum Run—visible to your right where the bridge crosses over it—drains this low ground that became known generally as the "Valley of Death." To your right front in the low ground, note the monument to the 40th New York Infantry topped by a soldier lying prone with his rifle.

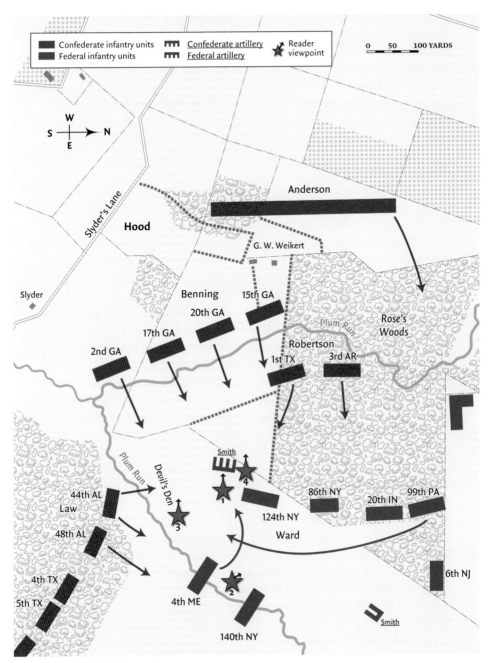

The Fight for Devil's Den

Now turn around and carefully walk back along the park road as it passes through the parking areas. To your right, on a boulder, you will see the obelisk commemorating the 4th Maine Infantry, the first of Ward's regiments to clash with Hood's men here. Observe the rocky gorge to your left. After you have passed all the parking areas and just before the road makes its first sharp bend to the right, stop and face forward toward the extensive expanse of scrubby ground dotted with small trees and large boulders. You should see the white buildings of the Slyder farm in the distance straight ahead of you.

What Happened Here?

The gorge became the site of the first major fighting on the Union left flank on July 2. When Hood's division advanced from Warfield Ridge—the high tree line in the distance—they marched down the slope and into the open fields around the Slyder house. When the rough terrain, the harassment of Union sharpshooters, and the fire of Smith's battery threw Law's brigade into disorder during its advance toward the Round Tops, Law pulled two of his regiments—the 44th and 48th Alabama—away from his badly disorganized right flank and shuttled them to the left of his line where the ground was more open. This was a complicated maneuver, and the two regiments ended up marching directly toward the rocky gorge, the 48th Alabama advancing toward your left front and the 44th Alabama heading toward your current position. Colonel William F. Perry of the 44th Alabama reported: "General Law informed me that he expected my regiment to take a battery which had been playing on our line from the moment the advance began"—no doubt Smith's 4th New York.

The fighting in the gorge grew heated very quickly. As Perry led his regiment into "a valley destitute of trees and filled with immense bowlders between them" and "not more than 300 paces in breadth," his men "received a deadly volley at short range, which in a few seconds killed or disabled one-fourth their numbers." That fire came from Colonel Elijah Walker's 4th Maine, Ward's left flank regiment. When skirmishers from the 2nd U.S. Sharpshooters warned of the Alabamians' approach, Ward had redeployed the 4th Maine from its initial position on top of the highest rocks of Devil's Den—near your orientation position—to a new line almost perpendicular to it and facing the gorge. Your current perspective is much like that of the soldiers of the 4th Maine as they watched the Alabamians approach.

Fighting continued to ebb and flow in this quarter, even as elements of Robertson's Texas Brigade began its own assault off to your right. You will visit that location shortly, but as the Texans mounted their attack, the Alabamians once more clashed violently with the 4th Maine here in the gorge. The men from Maine saw them coming. As Adjutant Charles F. Sawyer of the 4th Maine reported, the men in his regiment shot five to eight rounds before the Alabamians returned fire. As Colonel Perry explained, his men, "without an order from me, and availing themselves of the shelter which the rocks afforded . . . returned the fire" and then, despite their

Graphic evidence of
the bloody fighting in
Devil's Den. (USAMHI)

"extreme exhaustion," advanced when ordered. Finally, the Alabamians withdrew to the wood line on the other side of the gorge ahead of you, but only temporarily.

Position 3: Benning's Attack

Now proceed up the winding road until you reach the black-and-white iron tablet for Brigadier General Henry L. Benning's Georgia brigade on your left. You will notice that it sits on a knob of high ground. Stand on the top of the knoll so that the marker is behind you.

Ironically, Benning's men should not have been here at all. His orders called for him to follow Law's Alabamians. When Benning began his advance, smoke and trees confused him, and when he saw what he believed to be part of Law's brigade, he followed it. But, as he admitted, "in truth, it was Robertson's, Law's being farther to the right. This I did not discover until late in the fight, a wood on the right concealing from me most of Law's brigade." Thus, instead of following Law to Little Round Top, Benning brought his men to Devil's Den.

What Happened Here?

The knoll on which you stand divided Benning's four regiments into two elements. The 2nd and 17th Georgia headed into the rocky gorge to your left. As Benning described it: "The ground was difficult—rocks in many places presenting, by their precipitous sides, insurmountable obstacles, while the fire of the enemy was very heavy and very deadly. The progress was, therefore, not very rapid but it was regular and uninterrupted." Stout Union resistance continued to come from the 4th Maine, but now they finally received some additional support. The 40th New York from de Trobriand's brigade—you saw their monument earlier on this walk—and the 6th New Jersey from Colonel George Burling's brigade both originally had deployed in the Wheatfield, but they had hurried over to the swampy Plum Run valley, now over your left shoulder, to help the 4th Maine cover the gorge. "I immediately ordered my men to charge," reported the commanding officer of the 40th New York after the battle, "when with great alacrity they pushed forward at a double-quick, crossing a marsh up their knees in mud and water." Lieutenant Colonel William T. Harris, commanding the 2nd Georgia, fell dead.

Up on the highest summit of Devil's Den behind you, Ward ordered Major John W. Moore's 99th Pennsylvania to detach from the right of the brigade line and take up a new position on the left, on the high ground near Smith's battery. Ward intended for Moore to face toward the west (your right), the direction from which the Texans threatened. But when the 99th Pennsylvania arrived, the fighting in the gorge demanded immediate attention. Thus Moore deployed facing south toward the gorge. He reported that from his position "overlooking a deep ravine interspersed with large bowlders of rock," the fighting was "fierce." The fire of the 99th Pennsylvania, along with that of the 4th Maine, the 40th New York, and the 6th New Jersey, caught the Confederates in a deadly cross fire, but Benning's men, with the help of some of the 44th and 48th Alabama, held their ground and even inched forward.[2]

Position 4: The Texans Attack

Orientation

Now cross the park road and explore the informational wayside that explains the use of Devil's Den as a sharpshooters' nest. Then, proceed up the road to the crest of Devil's Den where you parked your car, walk past the monument of the 4th New York Battery where you started this walk, and stop near the informational waysides in front of the monument to the 124th New York topped by Colonel Ellis's statue. Cross the road and follow one of the unimproved paths down to a stone wall that marks one side of a piece of ground known simply as "the triangular field."

What Happened Here?

Recall that when the Texas Brigade advanced, it split in half. The 4th and 5th Texas, following orders to stay on Law's left flank, went on to fight at Little Round Top. The 1st Texas and 3rd Arkansas, in an effort to follow General Robertson's initial orders to maintain contact with the Emmitsburg Road, entered the fight for Devil's Den here.

Robertson's men had suffered greatly from the canister of Smith's cannons during their advance, but in the low ground to your front, they found temporary sanctuary; the barrels of Smith's guns—now pushed forward to the wall—could not be depressed sufficiently for their fire to reach them there. Behind the protection of another leg of the triangular field's stone wall at the base of the hill, the men of the 1st Texas unleashed an intense musketry that silenced Smith's guns, dispersed a thin skirmish line manned by the 124th New York, and then launched an assault up the hill where the rest of Colonel Ellis's men—nicknamed the "Orange Blossoms" after Orange County, New York—awaited them. The fighting on this hillside became both intense and confusing. A deteriorating situation in the woods to your right, where the 3rd Arkansas met stiff resistance from the rest of Ward's regiments, disrupted the ranks of the 1st Texas below you, and the Texans wavered. The 124th New York chose this moment to counterattack. With Major James Cromwell in the lead and Colonel Ellis on the regiment's left flank, the New Yorkers charged down this hill with a yell and sent the 1st Texas reeling. But Cromwell fell dead, Ellis fell dead, and the New Yorkers lost momentum. Moreover, by advancing so ardently, the 124th New York had left its left flank unprotected. During a lull in the fighting in the gorge, some of the men of the 44th Alabama surged through the fields below Benning's knoll to your left and opened a brisk fire on the New Yorkers, staggering them and sending them reeling back to the top of the hill here to reorganize.

While the 124th New York reformed, the men of the 1st Texas took advantage of their disarray and suddenly advanced up through the triangular field with little fanfare—and against little Union resistance—to capture Smith's four guns near the wall. When he saw Confederate infantry among the Union guns, Colonel Walker pulled his 4th Maine away from its position covering the gorge, faced it to the right, and charged through the rocks, coming from over your left shoulder. The men from Maine linked up with the remnant of the 124th New York and the 99th Pennsylvania and retook Smith's guns. Colonel Walker fell wounded in the effort, but Smith's guns and the crest of Devil's Den still remained in Union hands.

But Ward's time had begun to run out. While the Alabamians and Georgians continued to push the Union defenders in the gorge, Ward consolidated the rest of his regiments along the crest of Devil's Den behind you and stretching into the trees to your right. When the Texans returned for another push, they came in greater strength, now backed by the 15th and 20th Georgia from Benning's brigade. The 20th Georgia lost Colonel John A. Jones in its advance up the hillside, but it claimed credit for the recapture of three of Smith's guns that the 1st Texas had taken—and then lost—earlier in the day. The 1st Texas, the 3rd Arkansas, and the fresh 15th Georgia from Benning's brigade moved through the trees and rocks to your right front toward Ward's 86th New York and 20th Indiana; Colonel John Wheeler of the 20th Indiana already had fallen dead in that tree line.

Finally, after about ninety minutes of hard fighting from start to finish, Ward ordered his men to withdraw to the northern slopes of Little Round Top. The 40th

New York and the 6th New Jersey down in the Plum Run valley had made a fight of it, but when Ward's men left the crest of Devil's Den, they, too, pulled out. Devil's Den fell into Confederate hands, with Texas, Alabama, and Georgia flags flying here unchallenged.

Who Fought Here?

C.S.A.: From Law's brigade of Hood's division, Longstreet's First Corps, came the 44th Alabama and 48th Alabama. From Robertson's brigade of Hood's division, Longstreet's First Corps, came the 1st Texas and the 3rd Arkansas. Benning's brigade of Hood's division, Longstreet's First Corps, included the 2nd, 15th, 17th, and 20th Georgia Infantry.

    U.S.: Ward's brigade of Birney's division, Sickles's III Corps, included the 20th Indiana, the 4th Maine, the 86th and 124th New York, and the 99th Pennsylvania Infantry. From de Trobriand's brigade of Birney's division, Sickles's III Corps, came the 40th New York Infantry. From Burling's brigade of Humphreys's division, Sickles's III Corps, came the 6th New Jersey Infantry. Smith's 4th New York Battery came from the III Corps Artillery Brigade.

Who Commanded Here?

Brigadier General John Henry Hobart Ward (1823–1903), born in New York City, followed an unusual path to high command. He enlisted as a private in the U.S. Army at age eighteen and continued to serve until he reached the rank of sergeant major in the 7th U.S. Infantry. He served in combat during the Mexican War, suffering a wound at Monterrey. He left service after that conflict but maintained a link to the military life by finding work in the New York militia system. At the start of the Civil War, he became colonel of the 38th New York Infantry. After more than a year in regimental command, he rose to brigadier general in October 1862, and he commanded his brigade ably—and often, as at Devil's Den, under challenging circumstances. Popular with his men, Ward liked "very much the soldiers' amusements," organized them for his men on holidays, and invited all the III Corps generals to attend. As one soldier recalled, the events included "all kinds of races; mule-race, foot-race, sack-race, a greased pole, a huge turning cage (like a squirrel's cage) on which we need to gain ground on horseback to obtain a prize, etc." Such entertainment only went so far, of course. During the Overland Campaign, his men did not grouse when he was relieved of command in the middle of the Battle of Spotsylvania, having been accused of misconduct and intoxication at the Wilderness a few days earlier. Probably because of his previous good conduct, he was not publicly humiliated by a court-martial; he received, instead, an honorable discharge on July 18, 1864. General Ward lived quietly as a clerk in the offices of the superior and supreme courts of New York until his death, which resulted from injuries incurred when he got hit by a train.[3]

Brigadier General Jerome Bonaparte Robertson (1815–91), born in Woodford County, Kentucky, did not let the unfortunate circumstances of his youth hold him back. Orphaned and left penniless, he apprenticed as a hatter, studied medicine, served in the army of the Republic of Texas and later in both houses of the Texas legislature, became a noted Indian fighter, and maintained an active medical practice. An ardent supporter of secession, he helped to raise a company for the 5th Texas Infantry, entered Confederate military service as its captain, and later became the regiment's lieutenant colonel and then colonel. He received his promotion to brigadier general on November 1, 1862. In command of the Texas Brigade at Gettysburg, he fell wounded but recuperated in time to accompany Longstreet's First Corps to Georgia and Tennessee in the fall of 1863. Late that year, after unfounded charges were preferred against him for his seeming lack of aggressiveness during the East Tennessee Campaign, he transferred to a new command in Texas. One of his men later wrote that not a single member of the unit blamed him for his decisions: "On the contrary, the brigade heartily approved of his course, and its survivors are yet grateful to him for the firm stand he took and for the interest and fatherly solicitude he always manifested in the well-being of his men."[4]

Brigadier General Henry Lewis Benning (1814–75), a Georgia native, enjoyed an outstanding legal career during the antebellum years, including six years of service as an associate justice of Georgia's state supreme court. He took an active interest in Democratic politics and served as the vice president of the 1860 Baltimore Convention that nominated Stephen A. Douglas for the presidency. An ardent states' rights advocate but a reluctant secessionist, Benning nonetheless committed to defend the Confederacy, entering military service as colonel of the 17th Georgia Infantry. He won promotion to brigadier general on January 17, 1863. A solid commander but not always attuned to detail, he brought his men to the wrong place at Gettysburg. Still, after the battle an acquaintance wrote: "Genl Benning won laurels for himself in the Gettysburg fight. His men, I hear are delighted with him, and the men of the other Brigades in the Division cheered him as he passed along." Benning was wounded at the Wilderness in May 1864, but he returned to the army for the final campaign and the surrender at Appomattox Court House. Benning returned to Georgia and the practice of law after the war. The U.S. Army's Fort Benning in Georgia is named in his honor.[5]

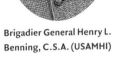

Brigadier General Henry L. Benning, C.S.A. (USAMHI)

Who Fell Here?

C.S.A.: In Law's brigade, the 44th Alabama lost 94 of its 363 men, while the 48th Alabama lost 103 of its 374 men—for a brigade loss, including losses suffered by units fighting on Little Round Top, of 25.9 percent. In Robertson's brigade, the 1st Texas lost 97 of its 426 men, while 182 of the 479 men in the 3rd Arkansas fell—for a brigade loss, including casualties taken on Little Round Top, of 34.8 percent. In Benning's brigade, 102 of the 348 men in the 2nd Georgia fell, including its commanding officer, Lieutenant Colonel Harris. The 15th Georgia lost 171 of its 368 men—many in a skirmish on July 3—while the 17th Georgia lost 103 of its 350 men. The 20th Georgia lost Colonel Jones and 136 more of its 350 men. The total brigade loss reached 36.2 percent.

U.S.: In Ward's brigade, the 20th Indiana lost Colonel Wheeler and 155 more of its 401 men. Colonel Walker's 4th Maine, 287 men strong, lost most of its 144 casualties in the fight at the gorge. The 86th New York lost 66 of its 287 men, while the 124th New York Orange Blossoms lost Colonel Ellis, Major Cromwell, and 88 more of their 238 men. The 99th Pennsylvania lost 110 of its 277 men. The brigade loss reached 35.7 percent. The 40th New York of de Trobriand's brigade lost 150 of its 431 men in the gorge. The 6th New Jersey of Burling's brigade, in a more protected position, still lost 41 of its 207 men. Smith's 4th New York Battery lost 13 of its 126 men.

Individual vignettes. On July 7, Edgeworth Bird wrote home to his wife, Sallie, back in Georgia. "Since you heard from me, our army has seen pretty rough times," he noted early on. Then he moved on to the distressing news he hesitated to relate. "Our loss of noble men is terrible," he began.

> In our own Brigade Col. Jones of 20th Ga., Lt. Col. Wm. Harris of 2nd Ga. were killed. I helped bury Col. Harris, a half brother to Ben Harris. Ev Culver, Joe Dickson, John Laughlin, Munt Harrison, of Co. K were killed. Lyons of Co. E the only one killed [in his company]. Lt. Hardwick of Co. K mortally wounded. Tom Culver and Doc Pierce shot through the calf of the leg, doing well and now with us in a spring waggon. Jimmy Reynolds lost his left arm. Jimmy Medlock wounded in the side by a shell. Jimmy Middlebrooks, Jasper Boyer, Doc McCook, and several others of our Hancock boys missing.

Privates Everard Culver, Joseph C. Dickson, and John Laughlin, all of Company K, 15th Georgia Infantry, died in battle on July 2. Bird reported that Culver's family "were very distressed that poor Ev's body could not be recovered from the hands of the enemy for burial." Dickson suffered a leg wound, and he died after amputation. Private Montgomery Harrison, described as "quiet, unassuming," also fell that day, as did Private B. F. Lyons. Second Lieutenant William H. Hardwick was wounded on July 2 and only survived until July 25. Second Lieutenant Thomas Culver of Company K, 15nd Georgia, survived his Gettysburg wound but was killed in action at the Battle of the Wilderness on May 6, 1864. Private Lovick Pierce Jr. survived his wound, and even a bout of gangrene; he returned to his regiment and fought on until Appomattox. Private James R. Reynolds, considered "an excellent soldier," was captured, his arm was amputated, and he was exchanged in August 1863. Private James E. Medlock received a slight wound from artillery fire; he returned to the ranks and served until the end of the war. Private James T. Middlebrook was captured and held at Point Lookout, Maryland, until February 1865. Private Jasper Boyer was captured after suffering a serious head wound; he was exchanged in March 1864 and spent the rest of the war in a hospital in Macon. Private Dawson McCook's records do not indicate that he was captured at Gettysburg.[6]

John A. Toothaker enlisted in Rockland, Maine, as a private in Company K of the 4th Maine Infantry on June 15, 1861. Toothaker left behind his fifty-five-year-old widowed mother, Abigail, in Belfast, Maine; his father had died at sea in 1852. The young man had become the sole support of his mother, who lived in a small home valued on the local tax roles at $225. She had little furniture because she had been forced to sell much of it, piece by piece, over the years to cover living expenses. Toothaker faithfully sent home $10 of his army pay each month for her support, a self-imposed obligation that became a bit easier when he won a promotion to sergeant. Sergeant Toothaker was mortally wounded on July 2 in the fighting in the rocky gorge. He was taken to a III Corps hospital, where Mrs. Charles A. L. Sampson cared for him until he died on July 20. Abigail T. Toothaker began the application process for a mother's pension on August 3, 1863. For unknown reasons, the approval process in this case took much longer than usual, even though she provided all required proof of her marriage to Thomas Toothaker, his death, and John's birth. Apparently, some confusion surrounded the circumstances of her son's death, since she had to procure an affidavit from Mrs. Sampson, attesting to the fact that Sergeant Toothaker had been her patient in Gettysburg in July 1863 and died there of a wound received in battle. The excessive delay caused Abigail Toothaker serious financial burden. Unable to pay her taxes on her small house, she had to apply for tax relief; fortunately, the town fathers of Belfast approved an abatement of her taxes for 1863 and 1864. Finally, in May 1866 Abigail Toothaker received the welcome news of the approval of her $8 monthly pension.[7]

Who Lived Here?

At the time of the battle, no one except livestock actually lived in the area of Devil's Den and Houck's Ridge, the name given to the tree-covered high ground extending north from the rocky outcropping. It provided grazing land at best or simply lay fallow. In 1848 John Houck and Samuel McCreary acquired this tract from Jacob Benner, who had bought it three years earlier from the estate of Jacob Sherfy. Houck and McCreary, two Gettysburg merchants, simply used the land as an out lot for its wood supply; neither man lived there or showed any interest in improving the land. Indeed, in April 1861 Houck bought out McCreary and became the sole owner of the forty-seven-acre tract. Basically rectangular in shape, Houck's tract was bordered on the north by a farm road, today's Wheatfield Road. The eastern boundary followed the western base of the Round Tops, adjoining property owned by Ephraim Hanaway. The southern end of the rectangle sat near the confluence of two intermittent streams, Plum Run and Rose Run, that flowed through the gorge. On the west side, Houck's property was bordered by the enclosed triangular field owned by George W. Weikert and, as one progressed to the north, by the woods and then the wheatfield owned by George Rose.[8]

What Did They Say about It Later?

The quest for battle laurels never ceased as long as the war generation remained willing to fight for them. Nearly forty years after the battle, Colonel W. F. Perry of the 44th Alabama noted about Devil's Den that "the storming and capture of this formidable position by the Southern troops was the opening act of the second day's battle of Gettysburg. Three bodies of troops have laid claim to the honor of the achievement: Benning's brigade of Georgians, the Fourth [actually First] Texas of Robertson's Brigade, and the Forty-Fourth Alabama Regiment of Law's Brigade. The commissioners of the Gettysburg National Military Park, unable or unwilling to discriminate, seem to have settled the dispute by dividing the honor among the claimants." Naturally, he supported the claim of his own command, "even at the risk of incurring the charge of egotism." He based his claim on an insistence that his men repulsed the 4th Maine at first contact, when Major George W. Cary, "flag in hand, bounded up the cliff, and landed on the crest ahead of the line. The gunners [of Smith's Battery], stationed where they could see what was coming, made their escape; while the infantry support of the battery, apparently taken by surprise, surrendered without resistance. They constituted the right wing of the Fourth Maine Regiment. I soon afterwards met one of the surrendered officers, who complimented in the highest terms, the gallantry of Maj. Cary and his men." The 4th Maine listed at least seventy-four men as "missing," but, as was common in such advocacy claims made well after the fact, the evidence to support the rest of Perry's assertion is more suspect. As did many soldiers in both armies, he felt the need to do so "for the sake of the truth of history, and as an act of justice to a body of men that, in all the qualities of true soldiership, had few, if any, superiors in the Army of Northern Virginia."[9]

Private James O. Bradfield of the 1st Texas offered a far more generous assessment.

> We moved quietly forward down the steep decline, gaining impetus as we reached the more level ground below. The enemy had already opened fire on us, but we did not stop to return it. "Forward—double quick," ran out, and then Texas turned loose. Across the valley and over the little stream that ran through it, they swept, every man for himself. . . . The enemy stood their ground bravely, until we were close on them, but did not await the bayonet. They [the skirmishers of the 124th New York] broke away from the rock fence as we closed in with a rush and a wild rebel yell, and fell back to the top of the ridge [your current position], where they halted and formed on their second line. . . . As we were moving on up the hill, an order came to halt. No one seemed to know whence it came, nor from

whom. It cost us dearly, for as we lay in close range of their now double lines, the enemy poured a hail of bullets on us, and in a few minutes a number of our men were killed or wounded. We saw that this would never do and so, without awaiting orders, every man became his own commander and sprang forward toward the top of the hill at full speed. By this time, Benning's brigade, which had been held in reserve, joined us and together we swept on to where the Blue Coats stood behind the sheltering rocks to receive us. Just here, and to our left . . . occurred one of the wildest, fiercest struggles of the war—a struggle such as it is given to few men to pass through and live. . . . This continued for some time, but finally, our fire grew so hot that brave as they were, the Federals could no longer endure it, but gave way and fled down the slope, leaving us in possession of the field. The Lone Star flag crowned the hill, and Texas was there to stay. Not alone, however, for just to our right stood Benning—"Old Rock"—that peerless old hero than whom no braver man ever lived. Striding back and forth in front of his line, he was calling to his gallant Georgians: "Give them h_ll, boys—give them h_ll," and the "boys" were giving it to them according to instructions.[10]

Driving directions to the next stop: Drive straight ahead 0.3 miles through the woods of Houck's Ridge into the open area of Rose's Wheatfield. Park in the turnout on the right of the road near the National Park Service wayside exhibit and the sign designating Park Service Auto Tour Stop 9.

STOP 20. THE BLOODY WHEATFIELD

You will visit two positions at this stop.

Position 1: The Fight of the Original Defenders

Orientation

After parking, exit your vehicle and walk down Sickles Avenue to the T intersection with the park road coming in from the left. When you reach it, face to the left and look down the intersecting park road toward the line of monuments at the tree line.

What Happened Here?

You are standing in the Wheatfield, owned by George Rose at the time of the battle. The fighting here ranks high among the most complex elements of the entire Battle of Gettysburg. The rapidly shifting ebb and flow of the fighting all around the field, the frequent attacks and counterattacks that crossed through it from several different directions, and the significant number of Union and Confederate brigades that fought here all tend to make this series of independent and sometimes simultaneous actions difficult to comprehend.

When General Sickles advanced his III Corps, General Birney's division deployed from the Peach Orchard well beyond the trees to your right, through this wheatfield, and to Devil's Den through the trees to your left front. Birney had insufficient

The Rose farm as viewed from near the T intersection in the Bloody Wheatfield.

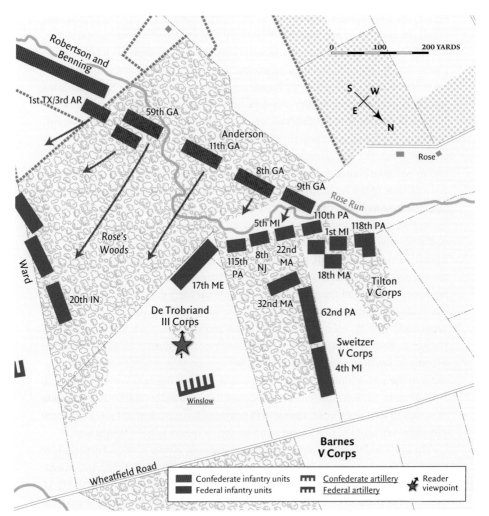

The Opening Phases of the Fight in the Wheatfield

manpower to form a continuous battle line, so he parceled out his troops to defend against the most likely avenues of attack. For now, ignore the two monuments closest to you on the left of the road ahead. Instead, focus your attention on the line of monuments crossing your front closest to the tree line ahead of you. These monuments represent the Wheatfield's first defenders.

This wheatfield formed the center of Birney's very thin divisional line. Initially, Colonel Regis de Trobriand's brigade held this field. Most of his regiments took position in the open ground to your right front to block the most obvious potential Confederate avenue of approach: the open ground to the south and southwest leading into the field from the Rose farm buildings. De Trobriand deployed the 17th

Maine, the 5th Michigan, and the 110th Pennsylvania into that area. His largest regiment, the 40th New York, formed its line on the high ground to your right and rear, now obscured by the tree line; the New Yorkers faced to the right (west) toward the Sherfy Peach Orchard. His final regiment, the 3rd Michigan, served as skirmishers across Birney's front. The six Napoleon cannons of Captain George Winslow's Battery D, 1st New York Artillery, took position on the crest of the hill behind you.

Even before the first Confederate attack on this position, de Trobriand's dispositions underwent three important changes. First, in response to the growing crisis at Devil's Den, the 40th New York left its position on the high ground to your right rear to go to the Plum Run valley; it took no part in the fight here. Second, when the 3rd Arkansas of the Texas Brigade attacked Ward's line near Devil's Den, de Trobriand could see its open left flank as it advanced from right to left in the woods to your front. He moved the 17th Maine from the open ground to your right front to the stone wall at the tree line. As Lieutenant Colonel Charles B. Merrill reported, "The line was formed behind a stone wall, which afforded a strong position. We opened fire upon the enemy, then within 100 yards of us. The contest became very severe." Merrill's regiment contributed greatly to the ability of Ward's left flank to maintain its line. Third, the movement of the 17th Maine to the stone wall opened a small gap in de Trobriand's line. To fill it, the 8th New Jersey and 115th Pennsylvania from Colonel George C. Burling's brigade, the III Corps reserve, arrived to fill it. Thus the monuments you see from left to right against the tree line to your front—the tall monument to the 17th Maine crowned with the soldier firing over a stone wall; the 115th Pennsylvania; the 8th New Jersey; and, if you move forward to look beyond the point of woods to your right front, the 110th Pennsylvania—represent not merely the first defenders but also the first Union reinforcements to arrive in the Wheatfield.

The first Confederate attack came from the woods to your front and especially to your right front, as four regiments of Brigadier General George T. Anderson's Georgia brigade launched their initial assault against de Trobriand's men. As Major H. D. McDaniel of the 11th Georgia described it, Anderson's men "dislodged them from the woods, the ravine, and from a stone fence running diagonally with the line of battle." After only a brief resistance, the 8th New Jersey and 115th Pennsylvania fell back. The Jerseymen fell all the way back to the wood line along the Wheatfield Road over the crest behind you; the commander of the 115th Pennsylvania gave in to pleas from Winslow and his officers to defend the battery and fell in on its right flank over your right shoulder. The gap in de Trobriand's line created by the departure of these two regiments required the 17th Maine, now "outflanked and exposed to a murderous fire from the enemy's re-enforcements," to bend back the right of its line "under a heavy fire from the advancing foe." If you follow the line of the stone wall to the right, you can see the fence line where the Maine soldiers rebuilt their right flank. After a while, the regiment pulled back into the Wheatfield, but it did not stay out of the fight for long. Additional Union reinforcements had begun to arrive.

Note that from where you now stand, you cannot see the Peach Orchard to your right or Devil's Den to your left. Thus the troops posted to your front and right front no doubt felt quite isolated. Under the pressure of Anderson's attack, the timely arrival of two additional brigades from Brigadier General James Barnes's division of the V Corps—those of Colonel Jacob Bowman Sweitzer and Colonel William S. Tilton—provided a welcome infusion of additional defenders. The two brigades went into position on the tree-covered knoll rising up to your right where Sickles Avenue disappears into the tree line. Most after-action reports refer to that ground simply as the "rocky hill" or the "stony hill." Two of Sweitzer's three regiments—the 62nd Pennsylvania and the 4th Michigan—held the high ground to your right and right rear, where the 40th New York had been deployed, and faced to the west (your right) toward the Peach Orchard. Sweitzer's 32nd Massachusetts fell in line with Tilton's regiments and formed on the southern crest of the "rocky hill" to your right front to confront directly the attack of Anderson's Georgians. As Tilton reported: "No sooner was the line formed than the foe attacked our front. The onslaught was terrible and my losses heavy—so much so that I was somewhat doubtful if our line could withstand it." Colonel George L. Prescott of the 32nd Massachusetts felt no such qualms. When told to prepare to retire, he retorted: "I don't want to retire; I am not ready to retire; I can hold this place." Anderson's men pulled back to the shelter of the woods. As Captain George Hillyer of the 9th Georgia wrote to his father on July 11: "If it had not been for the shelter of rocks and trees behind which we fought, not one of us would have escaped. I changed the front of the three left companies so as to face the enemy every way, and we held the enemy at bay until the flank was relieved by the coming up of McLaws' division."[1] The added fire of the 32nd Massachusetts and Tilton's brigade helped de Trobriand's original defenders to stop Anderson's advance briefly.

The Union advantage proved to be short-lived. When Anderson's men advanced once more, the Union defenders discovered that they faced not only an assault against their front from the Rose woods but also a growing threat from the west (your right). As Captain Hillyer had observed, McLaws's division now began to enter the fight. His first brigade to advance, the South Carolinians under Brigadier General Joseph B. Kershaw, headed toward the Rose farm. Kershaw reported his next move: "I determined to move upon the stony hill, so as to strike it with my center." Tilton saw the South Carolinians advance, "reconnoitered in person," and discovered "the enemy in large force coming from the direction of Rose's house, with the evident design of outflanking me." Tilton then "immediately retired." Sweitzer also withdrew, but he kept his men in line of battle in the Trostle woods behind you, prepared to reenter the fight if needed. The departure of Tilton and Sweitzer left only de Trobriand's original defenders in the Wheatfield against the combined strength of Anderson's Georgians and the 3rd, 7th, and 15th South Carolina from Kershaw's brigade.

Position 2: Reinforcements Pour In

Orientation

Now turn around and walk up to the guns of Winslow's battery. Stand beside the leftmost gun and look back down toward your previous position.

What Happened Here?

Before Kershaw's men could press their advantage and seize the rocky hill to your right front, the four brigades of General John C. Caldwell's division in Hancock's II Corps arrived from their position on Cemetery Ridge to stabilize the Union line in the Wheatfield. "I moved forward rapidly, a portion of the time at double-quick," Caldwell reported, since "the Third Corps was said to be hard pressed." De Trobriand's exhausted regiments pulled back when Caldwell's men began their advance.

Caldwell first deployed Colonel Edward E. Cross's brigade, ordering it to cross the Wheatfield toward the stone wall—and Anderson's Georgians—ahead of you. The line of monuments to your left represents the regiments in the right and center of Cross's line. Cross's men advanced so aggressively, reported Colonel H. Boyd McKeen of the 81st Pennsylvania, that "prisoners were taken by the brigade before the enemy had time to spring from their hiding places to retreat." Early in the heated action, Cross—who earlier in the day had predicted his own death—fell mortally wounded.

Caldwell then sent Brigadier General Samuel K. Zook's brigade to clear the high ground and tree line to your right that extends down to the "rocky hill." In that action against Kershaw's South Carolinians, Zook, too, fell mortally wounded.

Caldwell then sent Colonel Patrick Kelly's Irish Brigade through the center of the Wheatfield and directly against Kershaw's South Carolinians. The Irishmen, numbering only 532 engaged, charged from behind you over the ground where you now stand toward the "rocky hill." As Lieutenant James J. Smith of the 69th New York reported, "We moved forward until we met the enemy, who were posted behind large bowlders of rock, with which the place abounded." At first, the Irish Brigade's efforts met with success, Smith noted, adding that "after our line delivered one or two volleys, the enemy were noticed to waver." A soldier from the 63rd New York wrote to a friend on July 30: "As small as we were, the enemy found out to their cost that the same determined bravery was left in the three hundred they always found existed in the breasts of the three thousand Irishmen of that gallant brigade when they encountered them in deadly conflict on the Peninsula, and met them, face to face, on the bloody field at Antietam."[2]

Finally, Caldwell ordered the fourth of his brigades, that commanded by Colonel John R. Brooke, to advance through the middle of the Wheatfield and into the Rose woods to your front. As Brooke reported: "Pressing forward, firing as we went, we

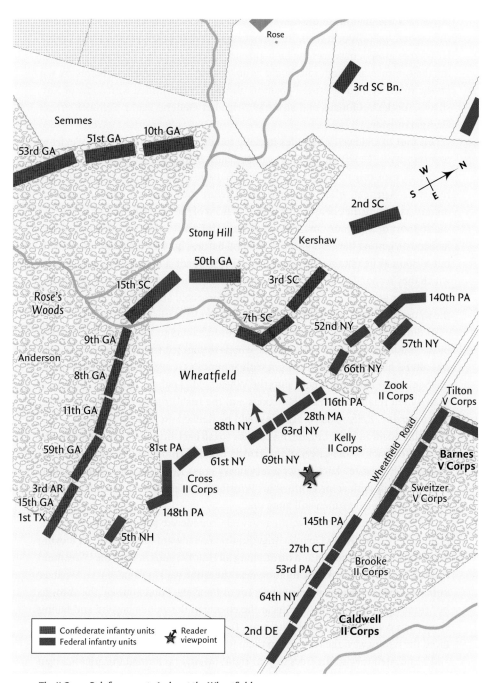

Rose

3rd SC Bn.

Semmes

53rd GA 51st GA 10th GA

Stony Hill

2nd SC

Kershaw

50th GA

15th SC

Rose's
Woods

3rd SC

7th SC

140th PA

52nd NY

57th NY

9th GA

66th NY

Anderson

8th GA

Wheatfield

Zook
II Corps

Tilton
V Corps

116th PA

11th GA

88th NY

28th MA

63rd NY

Kelly
II Corps

Barnes
V Corps

59th GA

81st PA

61st NY

69th NY

3rd AR

Cross
II Corps

Sweitzer
V Corps

15th GA

1st TX

148th PA

145th PA

5th NH

27th CT

Brooke
II Corps

53rd PA

64th NY

Caldwell
II Corps

Confederate infantry units   Reader
Federal infantry units   viewpoint

2nd DE

The II Corps Reinforcements Arrive at the Wheatfield

229

drove back the first line of the enemy, capturing a great number, and then charging the second line, drove it from its almost impregnable position on a rocky crest." Heavy tree growth obscures the high ground of Brooke's stand from your view during the summer, although you should be able to see it easily when the leaves are not on the trees. In their advanced position, Brooke's men clashed with some of Kershaw's South Carolinians and also met Brigadier General Paul J. Semmes's fresh Georgia brigade.

All four of Caldwell's brigades initially fought the Confederates in their front to a standstill. To stiffen his line further, Caldwell approached Colonel Sweitzer, whose V Corps brigade still remained in the Trostle woods behind you. As Sweitzer reported, "A general officer I had never seen before rode up to me, and said his command was driving the enemy in the woods in front of the wheat-field; that he needed the support of a brigade, and desired to know if I would give him mine." Sweitzer insisted on getting the permission of General Barnes, his own division commander, but as soon as he obtained it—and after Barnes "made a few patriotic remarks, to which they responded with a cheer"—the 32nd Massachusetts, the 62nd Pennsylvania, and the 4th Michigan returned into the Wheatfield and took up positions near the same stone wall that the 17th Maine had defended earlier in the action.

It did not take long, however, for the Confederates to reorganize for another push. As Anderson pushed through the woods to your left front, Brooke's men gave way after a hard twenty-minute fight with Semmes's Georgians—mortally wounding Semmes—and pulled back into the Wheatfield. At about the same time, Kershaw's men finally bested Zook's troops and the Irish Brigade to your right front. When Colonel Kelly realized his line could be flanked on both ends—"a very disagreeable position"—he ordered his brigade to fall back firing. Thus all of Caldwell's men pulled back to the safety of the Trostle woods behind you. As the general reported: "My men fell back under a very heavy cross-fire, generally in good order, but necessarily with some confusion." Winslow's battery left the Wheatfield then, as well, but Sweitzer's men still hung on.

Adding even more energy to the renewed Confederate advance, Brigadier General William T. Wofford's Georgia brigade advanced toward the Wheatfield, moving astride the road behind you and threatening all Union troops in both the Wheatfield and the Trostle woods. While fighting near the stone wall in front of you, Sweitzer noticed "considerable firing diagonally toward our rear" and believed the shots to be "from our troops aimed over us at the enemy in the woods beyond and falling short." His color bearer remarked to him: "Colonel, I'll be___ if I don't think we are faced the wrong way; the rebs are up there in the woods behind us, on the right"— and he pointed toward the trees to your right. Sweitzer reformed the 4th Michigan and the 62nd Pennsylvania to face those trees. The new threat did not take long to develop. Wofford's men, with some of Kershaw's troops, now advanced so quickly upon them, as Sweitzer explained, that "the Fourth Michigan and Sixty-second Pennsylvania had become mixed up with the enemy, and many hand-to-hand conflicts occurred." A Confederate soldier bayonetted Colonel Harrison H. Jeffords of the 4th Michigan to death as he attempted to protect his colors. Sweitzer's men headed out of the Wheatfield, too.

As the Wheatfield emptied of Union survivors of the combined attacks of Anderson, Semmes, Kershaw, and Wofford, Colonel Sidney Burbank's and Colonel Hannibal Day's two small brigades from Brigadier General Romeyn B. Ayres's V Corps division—the only Regular Army infantry on the battlefield—approached the Wheatfield through the trees to your left. Burbank's men took the lead, its battle line first marching toward you and then pivoting to their left to attack the Rose woods in front of you. Quickly caught in the cross fire of the four Confederate brigades, Burbank's men fell in droves and began a controlled withdrawal back the way they came, "as rapidly and in as good order as the nature of the ground would permit." Day's men had stayed in the tree line to your left, but Wofford's men, advancing down the Wheatfield road behind you, hit them and sent them reeling, too. The Regulars pulled back toward the north slope of Little Round Top, beyond the trees to your left.

With the withdrawal of the Regulars, the hardest fighting in the Wheatfield ended. As Wofford's men—the freshest of the four attacking brigades—continued to press their attack, the exhausted soldiers in the brigades of Kershaw, Anderson, and Semmes halted on the tree-lined ridge to your left just vacated by the U.S. Regulars. A few advanced from there with Wofford's men into the Plum Run valley, where the Georgians briefly captured several guns from Lieutenant Aaron F. Walcott's Battery C, 3rd Massachusetts Artillery. Brigadier General Samuel W. Crawford, commander of the Pennsylvania Reserve division in the V Corps, looked out upon his front "covered with fugitives from all divisions, who rushed through my lines and along the road to the rear. Fragments of regiments came back in disorder and without their arms, and for a moment all seemed lost." He ordered Colonel William McCandless's fresh brigade to counterattack. As Captain Hillyer reported, after three and a half hours of fighting, the Confederates made "a gallant attempt to storm the batteries, but the enemy being again heavily re-enforced, we were met by a storm of shot and shell, against which, in our worn-out condition, we could not advance."[3] With Colonel David Nevin's brigade from the newly arrived VI Corps adding weight to the Reserves's charge, the Confederate advance finally stopped.

When the action finally ended at about 6:30 P.M., the Confederate troops fell back to the rocky hill and the trees on the western edge of the Wheatfield to your right. McCandless's Pennsylvania Reserve brigade took position in the trees to your left. The Wheatfield itself became a horrific no-man's-land covered thickly with the dead and wounded of both armies.

Who Fought Here?

C.S.A.: All the Confederate infantry participating in the action here belonged to Lieutenant General James Longstreet's First Corps. Brigadier General George T. Anderson's Georgia brigade from Hood's division, including the 8th, 9th, 11th, and 59th Georgia, started the fighting at the stone wall. Only the 3rd, 7th, and 15th South Carolina from Brigadier General Joseph B. Kershaw's South Carolina brigade fought at the rocky hill. The 10th, 50th, 51st, and 53rd Georgia of Brigadier General Paul J. Semmes fought in the Rose Woods against Brooke's brigade and near the stone wall. Brigadier General William Wofford's brigade included the 16th, 18th, and 24th Georgia, along with Cobb's Legion and Phillips's Legion. Kershaw, Semmes, and Wofford belonged to McLaws's division.

U.S.: Here in the Wheatfield, more than at any other location of its size on the battlefield, General Meade kept his promise to bring the rest of the army to support General Sickles. Eleven different Union brigades participated in this fight. Look carefully at the monuments scattered throughout the Wheatfield. You should spot the diamond symbol of Sickles's original III Corps defenders from de Trobriand's and Burling's brigades; the Maltese cross designating regiments from the brigades of Tilton and Sweitzer, as well as the U.S. Regulars of Colonels Day and Burbank and McCandless's Pennsylvania Reserves, all of the V Corps; and the trefoil—the three-leafed clover—of Caldwell's four brigades under Cross, Zook, Brooke, and the Irish Brigade, all from the II Corps.

Who Commanded Here?

The fighting in the Wheatfield is notable chiefly for the lack of a consistent guiding hand above brigade level.

Brigadier General George Thomas "Tige" Anderson (1824–1901), a Georgia native, left Emory College to become a lieutenant in the Georgia cavalry and served in the Kearney Expedition during the Mexican War. He discovered an affinity for military life and in 1855 obtained a direct commission into the Regular Army. He served only three years and resigned in 1858 as a captain, but he parlayed that military experience into the colonelcy of the 11th Georgia Infantry in 1861. His personal bravery at Antietam in part led to his promotion to brigadier general on November 1, 1862. Although he fell wounded in the fighting at the Wheatfield at Gettysburg, he returned to the army in time for the Overland Campaign and continued to serve as a brigade commander through the end of the war. After the war, he lived in Atlanta and in Anniston, Alabama, taking up such varied positions as railroad freight agent, chief of police in both cities, and tax collector. As one soldier recalled Anderson's demeanor in battle, he "walked up and down the line with his hands folded behind him, as unconcerned as if he had been strolling in his front yard at home. Every eye was on him, and at intervals one of his boys would clap his hands and say: 'Did you see that shell brush his coat tail?' Bursting shells did not cause him to 'bat his eyes.' Brave Old Tige, how his boys loved him!"[4]

Brigadier General Joseph Brevard Kershaw (1822–94), a native of Camden, South Carolina, had only one year of prior military service—as a lieutenant in the Palmetto Regiment in the Mexican War—when he entered the Confederate army in 1861 as colonel of the 2nd South Carolina Infantry. Present at Fort Sumter, he served at First Manassas and in nearly all the major campaigns of the Army of Northern Virginia throughout the entire war. He received a promotion to brigadier general on February 13, 1862, and commanded a brigade through 1863, including at Gettysburg. He became a major general on May 18, 1864, and served in division command during the last year of the war until he was captured at Saylor's Creek on April 6, 1865, just a few days before Appomattox. Ezra J. Warner, the compiler of *Generals in Gray* (1959), described Kershaw as "a striking example of the citizen-soldier, who with little military background, developed into a wholly dependable, although not spectacular," midlevel commander. One of Kershaw's own soldiers seemingly validated this observation: at Chancellorsville, General Lee "gave Genl Kershaw and his command a very high compliment. Having ordered McLaws to send a brigade to a certain point, McL told him he would send Semmes. Lee told him, 'No, send Kershaw. He will go and do what is told him.'"[5]

Brigadier General Joseph B. Kershaw, C.S.A. (USAMHI)

Brigadier General John Curtis Caldwell (1833–1912), a native of Vermont, graduated from Amherst College and became a teacher. A principal at an academy in Maine when the Civil War broke out, Caldwell entered military service as colonel of the 11th Maine Infantry. He rose to brigadier general on April 28, 1862, and performed steadily and reliably but without imagination or great energy. By the time of the Battle of Gettysburg, he commanded a division in Hancock's II Corps and marched with it to the Wheatfield. Caldwell generally disappears from the historical narrative after that; it remains unclear how he directed his fight after he sent his four brigades into action. Wounds to his superiors temporarily made him II Corps commander at battle's end, but he did not

Brigadier General John C. Caldwell, U.S.A. (USAMHI)

retain that position for long. Indeed, during the Army of the Potomac's reorganization in March 1864, Caldwell even lost his division command and received no more significant field assignments. He served as one of the eight general-officer honor guards who escorted the remains of President Lincoln from Washington, D.C., to Springfield, Illinois, in 1865. Caldwell spent his postwar years practicing law in Maine and holding a variety of government appointments until his death in 1912.

Colonel Philippe Regis Denis de Keredern de Trobriand (1816–97) was born in France. Ezra J. Warner's compilation of Union generals' biographies describes his life as one devoted to pursuing "on several continents, the varied occupations of lawyer, poet, author, soldier, and bon vivant." He married a New York heiress, became a naturalized U.S. citizen, and started his American military career as colonel of the 55th New York Infantry. He did not seem to suffer any negative repercussions from commanding a regiment that had to be disbanded before its term of service officially ended because of its high desertion rate and colorful and controversy-filled history. He served in brigade command in the III Corps for a year as a colonel—including in the Wheatfield at Gettysburg, where, as he wrote to his wife on July 4, "as it was the first time I led the brigade into a fight, I did much more than I did before. I was always with my men, principally with the 5th Michigan, a regiment of Lions."[6] He finally received his promotion to brigadier general in January 1864. When the III Corps was consolidated with the II Corps in March 1864, he retained brigade command and served to the end of the war. During the demobilization of the U.S. Army after the war years, de Trobriand received a colonel's commission in the Regular Army, but he no longer seemed quite so committed to his duties; instead of returning to his regiment, he went to France to write a quite interesting book about his four years of service in the Army of the Potomac. He spent much of the rest of his life splitting his time between New Orleans and Long Island.

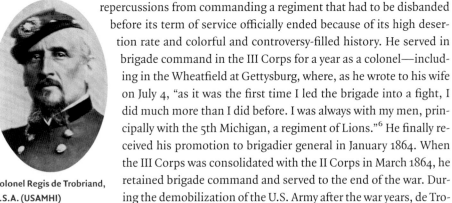

Colonel Regis de Trobriand, U.S.A. (USAMHI)

Who Fell Here?

On the ground around you, an estimated 6,000–7,000 men were killed, wounded, or captured. From the III Corps, de Trobriand's three regiments that fought here lost 295 of approximately 671 engaged men. Burling's two regiments left the line soon after first contact and lost only 71 of their 321 men. Winslow lost 18 cannoneers. From the V Corps, Tilton went into the fight with only about 665 men and lost 125 of them, for a brigade loss of 19.1 percent; Sweitzer's three regiments lost 420 of their 1,011 men. The battle devastated the two brigades of U.S. Regular infantry, with Colonel Burbank losing 447 of his 954 men for a 46.7 percent loss; Day—in the second line—suffered 381 casualties among his 1,557 soldiers for a 24.3 percent loss. McCandless's four regiments of 1,257 men fought on both July 2 and July 3 but suffered the majority of their 155 casualties on July 2, for a 12.5 percent loss; the attached 11th Pennsylvania Reserves lost 47 more. All four of General Caldwell's II Corps brigades went into battle severely undermanned and suffered substantially: Cross's brigade lost 219 of its 853 men, plus Cross; Zook's brigade lost 357 of its 975 men, plus Zook; Kelly's Irish Brigade lost 198 of its 532 men; and Brooke's brigade lost 389 of its 851 men. In total, Caldwell's division lost 38.7 percent of its strength.

Since only four Confederate brigades fought in the Wheatfield, they suffered a higher percentage of losses. Anderson's four regiments numbered approximately 1,495 men—the 7th Georgia was detached—and lost 720. The initial strength of Kershaw's three regiments in this fight was 1,275 men, of which he lost 429. Semmes was just one of the 391 casualties inflicted on his brigade of 1,335 men. Wofford's men entered the fight toward the end and thus lost a comparatively small 326 of his 1,632 men.

Individual vignettes. Captain Robert M. Forster, 148th Pennsylvania, did not answer the first call to arms in 1861 after Fort Sumter. As a married man with three small children, he continued to farm and to serve as postmaster of Farm School, Pennsylvania—the future Penn State University. When Lincoln issued his call for "300,000 more" in the summer of 1862, however, Forster could not resist the call to duty and became captain of a company that included a number of Farm School students he had recruited when they came in to pick up their mail. A private in Forster's Company C described how his rifle had malfunctioned during the battle and Captain Forster had told him to find another: "I threw it down, ran along the line, got one in Company I. When I came back the Captain was dead; the blood was running down his cheek. I picked up his cap and laid it on his head, but did not think of getting what was in his pockets. Sergt. John Benner, the color bearer brought off his sword and belt." On July 6, 1863, a brother officer sent this letter to Mark Halfpenny back in Centre County: "It is with feelings of the most profound sorrow that I take this, the very first spare moment, to give you the sad intelligence of the death of your brother-in-law, Capt. Robert M. Forster, who fell, while gallantly leading his company into the action of Thursday evening [July 2] near Gettysburg, pierced through the head with a musket ball. His death was, of course, instantaneous." Halfpenny retrieved his brother-in-law's remains, buried initially on the Hummelbaugh farm near the grave of Confederate General Barksdale, and reinterred them in a small cemetery near a settlement that later became State College, Pennsylvania, where he rests with his wife.[7]

Private William Messer Pritchett was born in Anderson County, South Carolina, but enlisted in Atlanta, Georgia, on July 3, 1861, for the war. He served in Company D of the 11th Georgia Infantry of Anderson's brigade. When the young farmer enlisted, he was twenty-five years old; stood five feet, seven inches tall; and had black eyes, "sleek" hair, and a fair complexion. His file depicts a reliable soldier, one who only rarely left ranks due to sickness, as he did briefly in the late summer of 1862 due to a nagging ear infection. Private Pritchett fell lightly wounded in combat at the Battle of Malvern Hill on July 1, 1862. One year and one day later, he was killed in action at the Wheatfield. On August 28, 1863, his father, William, submitted a claim for any monies still owed his late son. The actual amount the grieving father received remains unclear, but Pritchett still had $50 coming to him as the unpaid portion of a $100 bounty he had been promised.[8]

Private William H. Devoe of the 57th New York Infantry mustered into military service in Utica on September 24, 1861, for a three-year term of enlistment. He was forty-four years old. He did not fall in battle in the Wheatfield, but this fight, nonetheless, caused his death in December 1863. His regimental history reported it this way:

> Three men from the Second Corps were shot while at Morrisville and later at Stevensburg, in December [1863], one from our own regiment. The commander of his company still retains the feeling of regret at being compelled to testify of his absence and arrest, though the prisoner himself confessed his guilt. We withhold his name, not because it would blur the annals of so worthy a regiment, but because of our own sorrow at so fatally a termination of wrong doing. He was not a "bounty-jumper" but one of the first enlistments, had passed through several battles and was reported missing after Gettysburg. It was truly a funeral procession when the regiment marched to his execution. He sat upon his coffin at the open end of the hollow square and at the command to fire, fell instantly dead.[9]

Who Lived Here?

George Rose owned this ground. You can see his house on the rise to your front. The house and outbuildings became a hospital, and the slopes around them became a graveyard for many soldiers that fell near here. Rose, a physician and gentleman farmer from Maryland, purchased this 230-acre farm from Jacob Sherfy in 1858. At the time of the battle, George's brother John and tenant Francis Ogden and their families worked the farm and lived together in the stone house. After the battle, George Rose, John Rose, and Francis Ogden each filed damage claims with the Federal government, the total sum exceeding $4,500. They received no payment. J. Howard Wert later recalled his visit to the farm after the battle:

> I was on the Rose farm and around the Rose buildings immediately after hostilities ceased. . . . A much disgusted man was Rose when he returned. His stock was gone, his furniture was gone. His house was filled with vermin, his supply of drinking water polluted with dead bodies; nothing left of his farm but the rocks and some of the soil. Nearly 100 Confederates were buried in his garden, some 175 behind the barn and around the wagon shed; the half of a body sent asunder by spherical case shot was in his spring whence came the drinking water. Graves were everywhere, one Confederate Colonel being buried within a yard of the kitchen door.[10]

What Did They Say about It Later?

For sheer carnage, few sites on the Gettysburg battlefield exceed those experienced in the Wheatfield. Indeed, some have called George Rose's farm the bloodiest farm in America.

Private William Stillwell, 53rd Georgia, of Semmes's brigade, wrote home in a letter on 10 July:

Our regiment lost heavy and more officers than I knew. Lieutenant Colonel [James W.] Hance was killed. Captain Bond from Butts County and several more not now remembered. Captain Brown was shot through the leg between the knee and ankle. Lieutenant Farrar through the thigh. Sile Walker, Gus Brannon, George Fields, James Fryer, and several more were wounded, all of whom were doing well except James Fryer, he died shortly. . . . I forgot to say that General [Paul J.] Semmes was wounded through the thigh. I helped to carry him off the field. He said I was a faithful man. . . . Molly, a few more battles and our regiment will be all gone. It isn't much larger now than our company was when it came out. Oh, the horror of war, who can tell, if this war lasts much longer there won't be any left.[11]

Lieutenant J. J. Purman, 140th Pennsylvania, Zook's brigade, was one of the wounded officers lying on the field on the night of July 2. He had taken a bullet in the leg during the day's fighting. "Never shall I forget that midsummer night," he later wrote. "The almost full moon was shining, with drifting clouds passing over her face. At intervals a cloud obscured the moon, leaving in deep darkness the wheat field with its covering of trampled and tangled grain, boulders and wounded and dead men, then passing off revealed a ghastly scene of cold, white upturned faces. . . . The night wore on with no sleep for me, its quiet broken occasionally by the cries and groans of the wounded." Purman struck up a conversation with a wounded Michigan sergeant. Then, in the darkness, Purman "heard a ball make that peculiar thud, and the Sergeant cried out, 'I'm struck again. My right hand was resting on my left arm and the ball passed through my hand and arm.'" Purman got up on his one sound leg and looked around, hearing nothing but "the crack of the rifles and the zip of the bullets in the wheat, or the well-known thud in the ground or the body of a wounded man. I had drawn my right leg up at the angle, exposing it somewhat when a ball struck me, passing through, between the knee and ankle. I shouted to the Michigander: 'I've got it again through the other leg.'" Purman called to a nearby Confederate soldier on the skirmish line for water, pleading: "I am twice wounded and am dying out here." The Confederate refused, arguing, "If I attempt to come out there, your sharpshooters will think I am trying to rob you and pick me off." Purman convinced him to try anyway. "When he reached me I drank and drank and thought it was the sweetest water I ever had tasted. He then poured some on my wounds and cut the boots off my legs. After this I began to feel that I had a chance for life."[12]

Driving directions to the next stop: Drive straight ahead on this one-way road 0.3 miles around "the Loop" to the stop sign at Wheatfield Road. Turn left onto Wheatfield Road (a two-way road) and drive 0.2 miles west to the T intersection with Sickles Avenue coming in from your right. Turn right onto Sickles Avenue and park in the designated parking spaces near the bullet-shaped 7th New Jersey monument and the sign designating National Park Service Auto Tour Stop 10.

STOP 21. THE SALIENT COLLAPSES

Orientation

After parking, walk across the road to the monument to Captain A. Judson Clark's New Jersey Battery B and stand next to the left cannon. Look in the direction the cannon points to view the terrain discussed in the first part of the following narrative. Now turn to your right and continue up the rise to the large monument saluting the 73rd New York Infantry, topped by bronze statues of two individuals, a soldier and a fireman. Visitation to this monument has increased significantly since the terrorist attacks of September 11, 2001. To orient yourself to this position, stand in front of the monument and face toward Emmitsburg Road, the same direction the two figures seem to be looking. The Peach Orchard is now to your left. Millerstown Road runs from Emmitsburg Road back toward Seminary Ridge, the main Confederate line in the tree line ahead of you. The red barn to your immediate right front along the road is part of the Joseph Sherfy farm. The large red barn and white house to the immediate right of the Sherfy farm and set well back from the road is the Henry Spangler farm. Now look to the right up Emmitsburg Road. The red and white farm buildings on the right side of Emmitsburg Road are part of the Daniel Klingel farm. The large red barn on the right side of the road well beyond the Klingel farm belongs to the Nicholas Codori farm. The tree-topped elevation appearing above the Codori farm is Cemetery Hill.

The view south from Clark's New Jersey Battery monument.

Now move to the rear of the monument. Emmitsburg Road should be behind you. Round Top is clearly visible to your right front, but Little Round Top to its left is obscured by trees near the Wheatfield. To your left front, you can identify the main Union position on Cemetery Ridge—the shank of Meade's fishhook defense—by the large white dome of the Pennsylvania monument and the line of monuments leading off to its left toward Cemetery Hill. To your left, the stop sign at the next intersection marks the location of the Trostle farm lane that ran from Emmitsburg Road to the Abraham Trostle farm, the cluster of farm buildings in the low ground on your left front.

What Happened Here?

Return once more to the front of the 73rd New York monument and face Emmitsburg Road. At approximately 2:00 P.M., Sickles advanced his III Corps to this ridge of ground. He deployed two brigades of Brigadier General Andrew A. Humphreys's division along the road to your right, mostly on the far side of the Trostle farm lane from here. Note that, despite the presence of the monument to the Excelsior Brigade near your car and the 73rd New York monument here, the designation of this area as "Excelsior Field" is a bit of a misnomer; most of Colonel William Brewster's New York regiments—the "Excelsior Brigade"—deployed and fought north of the Trostle farm lane. Humphreys's division did not reach the Sherfy farm and could not defend the high ground here and at the Peach Orchard to your left.

As a consequence, Brigadier General Charles K. Graham's Pennsylvania brigade of Birney's division held the sector of the III Corps line where you now stand. The 105th Pennsylvania anchored Graham's right flank on the Trostle farm lane. The 57th and 114th Pennsylvania held the Sherfy farm grounds to your front and right front; men from both regiments took up fighting positions in the Sherfy barn and house. The guns of Lieutenant John K. Bucklyn's Battery E, 1st Rhode Island Artillery, sat near the road to your left front. The 68th and 141st Pennsylvania initially deployed facing south toward the Rose farm on the narrow lane to your left that became the park's Wheatfield Road. Graham had deployed his 63rd Pennsylvania as skirmishers in the fields in front of you beyond the Sherfy farm buildings.

The first crisis to threaten the security of Graham's line came from the south, the ground you viewed before you walked to this position. Initially, Sickles had defended that area with only a thin line of Michigan skirmishers; the deployment of two of Graham's Pennsylvania regiments could not fill the large gap that existed between the orchard and the Wheatfield. Shortly before the Confederate advance began, however, General Hunt ordered up batteries from the Army of the Potomac's Artillery Reserve to strengthen Sickles's line. Lieutenant Colonel Freeman McGilvery brought up Captain Charles Phillips's 5th Massachusetts Battery; Captain John Bigelow's 9th Massachusetts Battery; Captain James Thompson's Battery C and F, 1st Pennsylvania Artillery; and Captain Patrick Hart's 15th New York Battery to

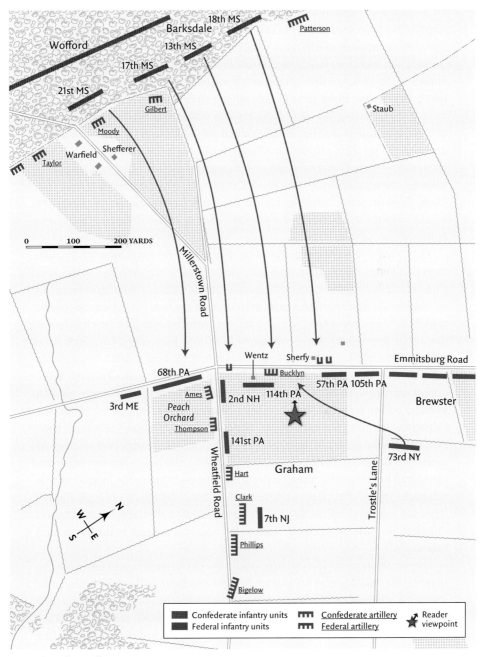

Wofford

Barksdale

18th MS

Patterson

13th MS

17th MS

21st MS

Gilbert

Moody

Staub

Shefferer

Warfield

Taylor

0   100   200 YARDS

Millerstown Road

Wentz

Sherfy

Emmitsburg Road

68th PA

Bucklyn

57th PA   105th PA

Ames

2nd NH

114th PA

Brewster

3rd ME

Peach Orchard

Thompson

141st PA

73rd NY

Wheatfield Road

Hart

Graham

N

W   E

S

Clark

7th NJ

Trostle's Lane

Phillips

Bigelow

■■■ Confederate infantry units   ▥ Confederate artillery   ★ Reader viewpoint
▬▬ Federal infantry units   ▥ Federal artillery

The Salient Collapses

241

fill the gap. If you look along the Wheatfield Road over your left shoulder and into Sherfy's Peach Orchard itself, you can spot the monuments and cannons that represent these batteries. When these guns opened up, Kershaw divided his brigade; the right half continued its advance toward the Wheatfield, but the left half wheeled to the left and advanced through the broad and open fields on the other side of the park road to silence these guns. McGilvery later reported, "I gave them canister and solid shot with such good effect that I am sure that several hundred were put hors de combat in a short space of time." Without any evidence of the work of a directing hand, the 3rd Michigan, the 141st Pennsylvania, the 3rd Maine, and the 2nd New Hampshire—each infantry regiment belonging to a different III Corps brigade—moved to the southern end of the Peach Orchard, the edge farthest away from you. Their added firepower helped to repulse the South Carolinians' attack. Kershaw's assault from the south failed to silence the guns or shatter Graham's line at the Peach Orchard salient.

The Union forces did not get to enjoy their victory for long, however. A much more dangerous threat came from the woods from Seminary Ridge to the west ahead of you, as Brigadier General William Barksdale's Mississippi brigade launched its assault. The 21st Mississippi advanced through the fields along the far (south) side of the Millerstown Road to your left front, directly toward the Peach Orchard. Just as the 141st Pennsylvania had moved to the southern edge of the orchard to face the threat presented by Kershaw, Colonel Andrew Tippin's 68th Pennsylvania redeployed to the western edge of the orchard, right on the road and directly in the path of the 21st Mississippi. "I ordered the men to reserve their fire until reaching a certain point," reported Tippin, "when a destructive fire was opened, the enemy halting and dropping behind a fence." The 21st Mississippi quickly reformed, however, and pushed forward. This time, they enjoyed the close support of artillery. As Lieutenant Colonel E. Porter Alexander reported, he ordered up two previously uncommitted batteries, and "these, arriving on the ground just as the infantry charge was made, joined in it." Tippin also noticed the rest of Barksdale's brigade advancing to his right—indeed, he saw the 17th, 13th, and 18th Mississippi charge toward this location—and he quickly decided to fall back to a position in the low ground behind you.

The departure of the 68th Pennsylvania from the western face of the Peach Orchard on the road doomed the four small regiments fighting Kershaw's men on its south side. They got caught in a cross fire coming from the 21st Mississippi on their right flank and from Kershaw's men in their front. These forces, combined with the fire of the Confederate batteries on Seminary Ridge, cracked the Union line. The 141st Pennsylvania may have been the last to leave the orchard knob: "I found myself alone," Colonel Henry J. Madill reported, "with a small regiment of about 180 men." Before they left the high ground at the orchard, the regiment lost "the color bearers and all of the color guard" among the 149 men the 141st Pennsylvania lost that day. As the 141st Pennsylvania departed, Thompson's battery pulled out of the Peach Orchard and joined the withdrawal. That convinced McGilvery to order the rest of his batteries to pull back across the fields behind you as well. Their departure and the fall of the Peach Orchard opened the way for Wofford's Georgians to advance down the farm road toward the Wheatfield; you have already seen the impact of their arrival in that action.[1]

The fall of the Peach Orchard also threatened Graham's line along the Emmitsburg Road here. As fighting swirled around the farm, Barksdale's men made short work of the Pennsylvanians. Even after the 73rd New York came to Graham's support—an action that explains the reason for the location of its monument here—the end came quickly and at high cost. The Mississippians crossed the Emmitsburg Road to your left front, wheeled to their left, and began to fire down the length of Graham's line. Graham himself fell wounded as he tried to rally his men, and he became a prisoner of Barksdale's troops. The Pennsylvanians withdrew toward the Trostle farm behind you. Both Barksdale's and Graham's brigades took nearly 50 percent casualties.

In the end, the events at the Peach Orchard and along Graham's front proved that Meade had been correct. Sickles's line could not hold. And Sickles's worst fear—Confederate artillery placed in Sherfy's Peach Orchard—came true when Graham's Pennsylvanians pulled off this high ground and batteries from Alexander's Confederate artillery battalion rolled into position.

Who Fought Here?

C.S.A.: Elements of Brigadier General Joseph B. Kershaw's brigade of McLaws's division of Longstreet's First Corps, including the 2nd and 8th South Carolina and the 3rd South Carolina Battalion, participated here. Brigadier General William Barksdale's brigade of McLaws's division of Longstreet's First Corps included the 13th, 17th, 18th, and 21st Mississippi Infantry.

U.S.: Brigadier General Charles K. Graham's brigade of Birney's division, III Corps, included the 57th, 63rd, 68th, 105th, and 141st Pennsylvania Infantry. Individual regiments from various commands of Sickles's III Corps that contributed to the fight here included the 73rd New York of Brewster's brigade, the 3rd Michigan of de Trobriand's brigade, the 2nd New Hampshire and 7th New Jersey of Burling's brigade, and the 3rd Maine of Ward's brigade.

Batteries from Sickles's III Corps included Battery E, 1st Rhode Island Artillery, and Battery B, New Jersey Artillery. Batteries from the Artillery Reserve included the 5th Massachusetts Battery; the 9th Massachusetts Battery; the 15th New York Artillery; Battery G, 1st New York Artillery; and Consolidated Batteries C and F, 1st Pennsylvania Artillery.

Who Commanded Here?

Brigadier General William Barksdale (1821–63), a native of Smyrna, Tennessee, moved to Mississippi to study law and edited the Democratic newspaper in Columbus in that state. He served in the Mexican War and was elected to the U.S. House of Representatives in 1852. He was present during Representative Preston Butler's famous caning of Senator Charles Sumner on the floor of Congress and, reputedly, held back some of those who attempted to stop the beating. He chose to serve the Confederacy in the military rather than in the political sphere, however, and became quartermaster general of Mississippi before accepting the colonelcy of the 13th Mississippi Infantry. He won promotion to brigadier general on August 12, 1862, and his brigade made a name for itself at Fredericksburg for opposing the Army of the Potomac's crossing of the Rappahannock River on December 11, 1862, two days before the bloody battle there. On July 2, 1863, at Gettysburg, his brigade smashed Sickles's salient at the Peach Orchard, but Barksdale himself fell mortally wounded and died the next day. His remains temporarily rested at the Hummelbaugh house on the Taneytown Road before being returned to Mississippi, where they rest in Greenwood Cemetery in Jackson. In 1893 W. Gart Johnson, a veteran of Company C, 18th Mississippi, offered his insights on General Barksdale: "He was a man of whom it could be truthfully said, 'Bold as a lion, yet gentle as a lamb.' He was not a military man, but was a pure type of genuine southern chivalry, a southern gentleman of the old school. Quick to resent and as quick to forgive; quick to punish disobedience in a subordinate, and as quick to ask forgiveness. . . . We loved Gen. Barksdale, because we knew he was proud of us, and would do anything in his power for our welfare."[2]

Brigadier General William Barksdale, C.S.A., killed in action on July 2. (USAMHI)

Brigadier General Charles K. Graham, U.S.A., wounded and captured on July 2. (USAMHI)

Brigadier General Charles Kinnaird Graham (1824–89), a native of New York City, served as a midshipman in the U.S. Navy during the Mexican War. He resigned at war's end, however, and studied both law and engineering. He became quite a noted engineer of public works, helping to lay out Central Park and working on construction projects in the Brooklyn Navy Yard. With several hundred of his dockworkers, he joined General Dan Sickles's Excelsior Brigade and started his army career as lieutenant colonel of the 74th New York Infantry. Graham's health kept him out of the field for the latter half of 1862 and much of early 1863, but he returned to the III Corps as a brigade commander in time for Chancellorsville. When the Peach Orchard fell to Barksdale's Mississippians, Graham fell wounded and became a prisoner. He was exchanged in November 1863, but he did not return to the Army of the Potomac. After the war, he returned to his civil engineering pursuits in New York City.

Who Fell Here?

C.S.A.: In Kershaw's brigade, 169 of 412 men in the 2nd South Carolina fell, along with 100 of 300 men in the 8th South Carolina and 46 of 203 men in the 3rd South Carolina Battalion. In Barksdale's brigade, 243 of the 13th Mississippi's 481 men fell, along with 270 of the 17th Mississippi's 468 men and 137 of the 18th Mississippi's 242 men. The 21st Mississippi lost 139 of its 424 men. The brigade's percentage loss reached 46.1 percent.

U.S.: In Graham's brigade, the 57th Pennsylvania lost 115 of its 207 men; the 63rd Pennsylvania, on skirmish duty, lost only 34 of its 245 men; the 68th Pennsylvania lost 152 of its 320 men; the 105th Pennsylvania lost 132 of its 274 men; the 114th Pennsylvania lost 155 of its 259 men; and the 141st Pennsylvania lost 149 of its 209 men—for a brigade loss of 48.8 percent. In supporting infantry regiments, the 3rd Michigan lost 45 of its 237 men, the 73rd New York lost 162 of its 349 men, the 2nd New Hampshire lost 193 of its 354 men, the 7th New Jersey lost Colonel Louis Francine and 113 more of its 275 men, and the 3rd Maine lost 122 of its 210 men, including some who fell earlier in Pitzer's Woods.

Sickles's two III Corps batteries in this action lost 50 of their 239 men. McGilvery's five Artillery Reserve batteries lost 100 of their 467 artillerymen. These numbers are disproportionately high rates of loss for artillery batteries.

Individual vignettes. On May 29, 1861, William R. Oursler, a Tennessee-born schoolteacher from Mount Pleasant, Mississippi, went to Corinth and mustered into military service as a private in Company F of the 17th Mississippi Infantry. Oursler went off with his regiment to Virginia, and, once encamped around Leesburg, he was joined there by his older brother Robert A. Oursler, a twenty-two-year-old farmer who had traveled from Mount Pleasant to enlist in the same company. Both brothers took to military life. William won election to fill a vacancy as Company F's first lieutenant on April 26, 1862. Although he endured many health problems, including a bout with typhoid fever, Robert, too, received a promotion, rising to sergeant on July 11, 1862. In the Battle of Fredericksburg, Lieutenant Oursler served as acting regimental adjutant; among the records he had to file was the one reporting his brother's wounding in that action. Sergeant Oursler obtained a furlough to go back to Mississippi to recuperate, but he returned in time for the campaign season of 1863. On July 2, 1862, both brothers took their places in the battle line of Company F of the 17th Mississippi and advanced with Barksdale's brigade against the Sherfy farm and Peach Orchard. Both of their records end with the same words: "Killed in action, July 2, 1863, at Gettysburg."[3]

Who Lived Here?

As you learned at Stop 16, Joseph Sherfy owned the Peach Orchard and the land surrounding the house and barn on the west side of Emmitsburg Road.

What Did They Say about It Later?

The survivors of Graham's brigade took special pride in having held Sickles's dangerous salient as long as they did. But they rarely gave their corps commander the kind of partisan support that survivors of other III Corps brigades heaped upon him.

The collapse of Sickles's Peach Orchard salient rendered untenable the 57th Pennsylvania's position at the Sherfy farm. At that regiment's monument dedication on September 11, 1889, Captain E. C. Strouss recalled: "No doubt the regiments stationed at this point could have beaten back the enemy, but we had not been long engaged when we learned that the enemy had broken through the angle at the Peach Orchard, and were swarming up the road in our rear. It was evident that if we remained at the house, we would all be captured, so we were obliged to fall back. We tried to warn our comrades, who had sought the cover of the house, and were firing from its doors and windows, but could not make them understand the situation, and all were captured." Worst of all, "of the fifty-five enlisted men who, on the 2d of July were captured at Gettysburg, forty-four died in southern prisons."

Perhaps that statistic—not unique to the 57th Pennsylvania—explains why the survivors of Graham's brigade were not likely to be counted among the Union veterans who embraced national reconciliation and reached across one of Gettysburg's stone walls to grasp the hand of a soldier who wore the gray. At the dedication of the 105th Pennsylvania's monument, Chaplain J. C. Truesdale avowed:

> This four year's fratricidal war was a dreadful thing, but for this Nation there was something worse than this war. The dissolution of the Union was worse; slavery was worse; and so, when the gage of battle was thrown down by those who were determined to have a government with slavery for its corner-stone, we said rather than these things, let us have
>   "War, dreadful war!
>   War on a hundred battle-fields;
>   War by land and by sea."
> We are sometimes charged with "waving the bloody shirt" when we talk about the war. Well, if stating the cause of the war—what it meant, what it was fought for, what it has accomplished—if that be "waving the bloody shirt," then, in the name of all the Union soldiers living and dead, I say "let it wave."[4]

Driving directions to the next stop: Drive straight ahead 0.1 miles to the stop sign at the intersection with United States Avenue. Turn right onto the one-way United States Avenue and drive 0.2 miles to the Trostle farm. Park in the designated parking spaces on the right of the road near the upturned cannon designating the site of the III Corps headquarters.

STOP 22. THE COLLAPSE OF THE EMMITSBURG ROAD LINE

Orientation

Follow the dirt path on the left side of the barn to the small marker at the top of the hill that marks the spot where General Sickles fell seriously wounded, struck in the right leg by a Confederate cannon ball. Face to the left (west) and view the Emmitsburg Road ridge, the high ground running across your front. The Abraham Trostle barn should be over your left shoulder.

To your left front and to the immediate left of the top of the observation tower are the monuments identifying Sherfy's Peach Orchard. The red Sherfy barn is visible to the right of the observation tower. The red and white farm buildings and their white fences directly in front of you are those of the Daniel Klingel farm. The section of white fencing to your right front marks the wartime location of the Peter Rogers

The site of General Sickles's wounding.

house, which no longer stands. The red barn to your right is part of the Nicholas Codori farm. Notice that you cannot see Seminary Ridge, the main Confederate line, from this perspective. You can clearly see the Union main line on Cemetery Ridge, the tree line behind you.

What Happened Here?

You are facing the line of Brigadier General Andrew A. Humphreys's division of Sickles's III Corps. Only two of Humphreys's three brigades deployed along the Emmitsburg Road. Immediately ahead of you is the line of Colonel William R. Brewster's New York Excelsior Brigade; the tall monument you see directly ahead salutes the stand of the 120th New York of that brigade. Brewster's men covered a fairly compact front that started at the Trostle farm lane—the park road (United States Avenue) to your left that begins at the top of the rise ahead of you—and extended to the right not quite to the Klingel farm. The brigade already had lost two of its regiments to detached duty before its fight here began. Lieutenant Francis W. Seeley's Battery K, 4th U.S. Artillery, supported this part of the line from a position near the Klingel farm; its marker today sits just to the left of the farm buildings ahead of you.

To Brewster's right, the brigade of Brigadier General Joseph B. Carr filled out the right of Humphreys's line from the immediate left of the Klingel farm to the end of the III Corps line between the right end of the white fencing and the Codori barn on your right front. Even with the addition of the 74th New York Regiment from Brewster's brigade and the deployment of the entire 1st Massachusetts as skirmishers, the right flank of Carr's brigade remained weak and vulnerable to attack. Sickles's advance had broken contact between his right flank and the left flank of Hancock's II Corps on Cemetery Ridge over your right shoulder. As Humphreys reported, he was "authorized to draw support, should I need it, from General Caldwell's division" of Hancock's II Corps, but when the crisis arose here, Caldwell already had departed for the Wheatfield. Humphreys did take advantage of his authority to draw upon the Artillery Reserve to post Lieutenant John K. Turnbull's Battery F and K, 3rd U.S. Artillery, in position in Carr's center near the left end of the white fence line at the Rogers farm to your right front. Carr's men welcomed Turnbull's arrival. As soon as the Confederate artillery opened fire, the shelling along Humphreys's line became particularly intense. Colonel Robert McAllister of the 11th New Jersey reported that "this artillery was no ordinary kind. It was very brisk and extremely fierce. Could I have divested myself of the thought that great numbers were being hurried into eternity, and great numbers more were being wounded and maimed, I should have exclaimed, 'Perfectly magnificent!'"[1]

Sickles had designated Humphreys's third brigade, commanded by Colonel George C. Burling, to serve as the corps reserve. Only its 5th New Jersey still remained in this sector, serving on the skirmish line in front of Brewster's brigade. Humphreys's men could count on no immediate support from its own corps. Ap-

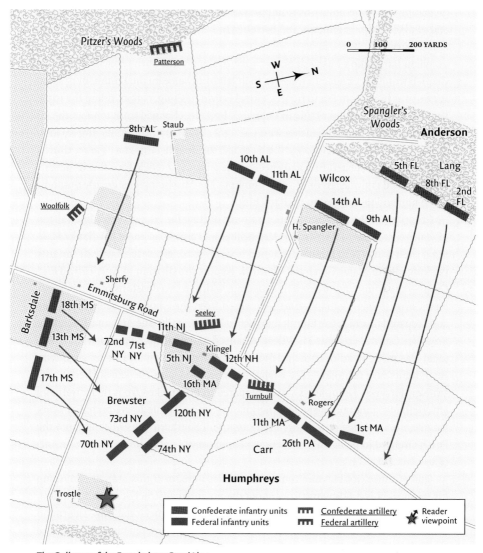

Pitzer's Woods

Patterson

0   100   200 YARDS

W
S — N
E

Spangler's
Woods

Anderson

8th AL   Staub

10th AL

11th AL

Wilcox

5th FL   Lang

8th FL

2nd
FL

Woolfolk

14th AL

9th AL

H. Spangler

Sherfy

Emmitsburg Road

Seeley

Barksdale

18th MS

11th NJ

72nd 71st
NY   NY

Klingel

13th MS

5th NJ   12th NH

17th MS

16th MA

Turnbull

Rogers

Brewster

120th NY

11th MA

1st MA

73rd NY

70th NY   74th NY

26th PA

Carr

Humphreys

Trostle

| | Confederate infantry units | | Confederate artillery | | Reader viewpoint |
| | Federal infantry units | | Federal artillery | | |

The Collapse of the Emmitsburg Road Line

preciating the vulnerability of Humphreys's line, however, Hancock advanced several of his II Corps regiments and batteries to be able to render aid to Humphreys if necessary.

When Barksdale's Mississippians broke Graham's line at the Peach Orchard to your left front, they began to wheel to their left to advance up the Emmitsburg Road across your front from left to right. Colonel Calvin A. Craig, commanding the 105th Pennsylvania on the right flank of Graham's brigade, changed front to meet the attack, moving his line from facing west (straight ahead) on the Emmitsburg Road to facing south (to your left) along "the by-road," the Trostle farm lane. There, Craig's regiment "again opened fire, and checked the advancing rebels for a few minutes." But his stand truly lasted only a few minutes. The Mississippians greatly outnumbered him and threatened to outflank him.

Craig's stand bought only a brief amount of time for Humphreys's line (ahead of you) to prepare to receive the Mississippians' attack on their left flank. Making it even worse for Humphreys's men was an imminent second threat: the first two brigades of Major General Richard H. Anderson's division of A. P. Hill's Third Corps—the command ordered to cooperate with the two divisions of Longstreet's First Corps in July 2's main effort—emerged from the woods on Seminary Ridge and prepared to attack the Emmitsburg Road line frontally. The Alabama brigade of Brigadier General Cadmus M. Wilcox advanced to the attack. "This forward movement was made in an open field," Wilcox reported, "the ground rising slightly to the Emmitsburg turnpike." The Alabamians brushed away the skirmishers of the 5th New Jersey as Humphreys's men prepared to be attacked from their front and left, perhaps simultaneously. Making matters worse, Confederate batteries firing from Seminary Ridge now enjoyed the support of Southern guns wheeling into the Peach Orchard in position to rake down Humphreys's entire line with accurate artillery fire.

One of those Confederate rounds hit Sickles here, near this marker, smashing his lower right leg. His worst fears about the potential destructiveness of Southern artillery in the Peach Orchard had become real in a very personal way. The round smashed the bone but did not quite sever the leg. Sickles ordered his staff to remove a door from the Trostle house and use it as a stretcher to carry him along his lines to rally his hard-pressed troops. An officer lit a cigar, and Sickles clamped it between his teeth, puffing on it heartily to convince his soldiers that he still lived. But Sickles's staff soon removed him to the hospital. Thus he did not witness the worst consequences of his earlier decisions.

For Brewster's New Yorkers and Carr's 11th New Jersey to the left of the Klingel farm (to your front), Barksdale's Mississippians offered the more immediate threat. Thus these regiments changed front from facing west on the Emmitsburg Road ahead of you to form a new line oriented to the southwest. Their new line started at the top of the hill and angled down the slope toward your left in the direction of the Trostle farm lane. The maneuver also permitted Humphreys to carry out orders he just had received from Birney, now acting corps commander, to "throw back my left, and form a line oblique to and in rear of the one I then held" to complete a line with Birney's division that would stretch to the Round Tops. The entire III Corps never managed to forge that new line, of course, but the maneuver Birney ordered coincidentally permitted Brewster's New York regiments to address the immediate threat to their left flank.

But Brewster's line could not focus entirely on the Mississippians. With measured step, Wilcox's Alabama brigade came closer and closer to the Klingel farm ahead of you. As Lieutenant Edmund DeWitt Patterson of the 9th Alabama described it: "Death had commenced his work in good earnest. The battle now rages furiously, but our lines move onward—straight onward."[2] The Alabamians' advance threatened the right flank of Brewster's new line and made especially perilous the position of the 11th New Jersey at the top of the ridge to the left of the Klingel house. As the skirmishers of the 5th New Jersey withdrew ahead of the Alabama advance, the rapidly deteriorating situation caused Lieutenant Seeley to pull his battery off the field and head for the rear. Only minutes later, Colonel David Lang's small Florida brigade advanced toward the rest of Carr's line on the Emmitsburg Road ridge to your right front.

When the Confederates hit, Humphreys's men resisted manfully. Colonel Lang reported that his Floridians met "a murderous fire of grape, canister, and musketry" when they first advanced. But it was not enough to stop them. The Floridians overran Turnbull's battery, its cannoneers "leaving four or five pieces of cannon in my front," Lang wrote, but carrying off the horses and limbers.

As Lang informed General E. A. Perry, his brigade commander still recuperating on medical leave: "About half way across the field the enemy had a line of batteries strongly supported by infantry. We swept over these, without once halting, capturing most of the guns and putting the infantry to rout with great loss. Indeed, I do not remember having seen anywhere before, the dead lying thicker than where the Yankee infantry attempted to make a stand in our front."[3] No wonder, perhaps, that Colonel John S. Austin of the 72nd New York referred to the day as "that memorable and ever-to-be-remembered July 2."

The withdrawal of the III Corps did not turn into an uncontrolled rout. Indeed, with some bravado, General Carr reported: "I could and would have maintained my position but for an order received direct from Major-General Birney, commanding the corps, to fall back. . . . At that time I have no doubt that I could have charged on the rebels and driven them in confusion, for my line was still perfect and unbroken, and my troops in the proper spirit for the performance of such a task."[4] Humphreys's officers managed a controlled return-fire to slow the charging Confederates.

Who Fought Here?

C.S.A.: You met Barksdale's Mississippians at the previous stop. Brigadier General Wilcox's brigade, part of which you met at Pitzer's Woods at Stop 14, belonged to R. H. Anderson's division of Hill's Third Corps and included the 8th, 9th, 10th, 11th, and 14th Alabama Infantry. Colonel David Lang's small brigade in R. H. Anderson's division, Hill's Third Corps, included the 2nd, 5th, and 8th Florida Infantry, the only Florida regiments in the Army of Northern Virginia.

U.S.: Colonel William Brewster's brigade, Humphreys's division, Sickles's III Corps, included the 70th, 71st, 72nd, 73rd, 74th, and 120th New York Infantry. Brigadier General Joseph B. Carr's brigade included the 1st, 11th, and 16th Massachusetts; the 12th New Hampshire; the 11th New Jersey; and the 26th Pennsylvania Infantry. From the III Corps artillery brigade came Battery K, 4th U.S. Artillery, and from the Artillery Reserve came Battery F and K, 3rd U.S. Artillery.

Who Commanded Here?

Brigadier General Andrew Atkinson Humphreys (1810–83) came from a family of naval architects; his grandfather drew the plans for the USS *Constitution*, known as "Old Ironsides." Humphreys opted to pursue an army career instead and graduated from West Point in 1831. He spent most of his antebellum career as an officer in the Corps of Topographical Engineers. In April 1862 he received a promotion to brigadier general and an assignment as chief topographical engineer of McClellan's Army of the Potomac. In the fall of 1862, he took command of a newly organized division composed of green troops raised during Lincoln's summer call for "300,000 more" three-year volunteers. His personal leadership and his martinet ways helped to impel his men across the fields leading to the base of Marye's Heights at Fredericksburg in December 1862, but they could not breach the Confederate line; a statue of Humphreys stands in the National Cemetery at Fredericksburg to salute the effort of his division there.

Major General Andrew A. Humphreys, U.S.A. (USAMHI)

When Meade took command of the Army of the Potomac on June 28, he asked Humphreys to serve as his chief of staff in place of Major General Daniel Butterfield. Humphreys demurred, however, suggesting that he stay with his division for the imminent battle. Meade agreed in the short term, but after Gettysburg, Humphreys won promotion to major general and moved to army headquarters. Lieutenant Colonel Theodore Lyman of Meade's staff described Humphreys as "an extremely neat man, and is continually washing himself and putting on paper dickeys. . . . He is an extremely gentlemanly man." But he also "has a tremendous temper, a great idea of military duty, and is very particular. When he does get wrathy, he sets his teeth and lets go a torrent of adjectives that must rather astonish those not used to little outbursts." When Hancock stepped down from II Corps command in late 1864 because of his Gettysburg wound, Humphreys succeeded him. After the war, he became the U.S. Army's chief engineer and held that post until his death.[5]

Major General Richard H. Anderson, C.S.A. (USAMHI)

Major General Richard Heron Anderson (1821–79), a native South Carolinian, graduated from the U.S. Military Academy in the class of 1842 as a brevet second lieutenant in the 1st Dragoons. He experienced a fairly typical antebellum military career, including Mexican War service. He resigned his commission as a captain in the 2nd Dragoons on May 3, 1861. Present at Fort Sumter, Anderson received a promotion to brigadier general on July 18, 1861, and succeeded General Beauregard in command of the post at Charleston. He sought reassignment to the field, however, and took command of a South Carolina brigade in the Army of Northern Virginia in early 1862. At Williamsburg, a friend later wrote, his "troops soon learned to admire the cool yet daring gallantry of their commander and to value his distinguished ability as a leader." He rose to major general in July 1862, suffered a wound in the Maryland Campaign, and held a divisional command through May 1864. When General Longstreet fell severely wounded at the Wilderness, Anderson received a temporary promotion to lieutenant general and commanded the First Corps. He commanded Richmond's defenses for a period. He died in 1879 and is buried in the Episcopal Churchyard in Beaufort, South Carolina.[6]

Who Fell Here?

C.S.A.: In Wilcox's brigade, the 8th Alabama lost 266 of its 477 men, the 9th Alabama lost 116 of its 306 men, the 10th Alabama lost 104 of its 311 men, the 11th Alabama lost 75 of its 311 men, and the 14th Alabama lost 48 of its 316 men, for a brigade loss of 45.1 percent.

In Lang's brigade, the 2nd Florida lost 101 of its 242 men, the 5th Florida lost 112 of its 321 men, and the 8th Florida lost 105 of its 176 men, for a brigade loss of 61.3 percent. Wilcox and Lang suffer heavy casualties on both July 2 (including a considerable number in the action described at the next stop) and July 3, when it played a supporting role in Pickett's Charge. These numbers represent their total losses from both days' action.

U.S.: Brewster's Excelsior Brigade lost 118 of the 288 men of the 70th New York, 91 of the 243 men of the 71st New York, 114 of the 305 men of the 72nd New York, 162 of the 349 men of the 73rd New York, 89 of the 255 men of the 74th New York, and 203 of the 383 men of the 120th New York—for a brigade loss of 42.4 percent. Carr's brigade lost 120 of the 321 men of the 1st Massachusetts, 129 of the 286 men of the 11th Massachusetts, 81 of the 245 men of the 16th Massachusetts, 92 of the 224 men of the 12th New Hampshire, 153 of the 275 men of the 11th New Jersey, and 213 of the 365 men of the 26th Pennsylvania—for a brigade loss of 46.0 percent.

III Corps artillery Battery K, 4th U.S. Artillery, lost 25 of its 113 men, while Battery F and K, 3rd U.S. Artillery, from the Artillery Reserve lost 24 of its 115 men. These are unusually heavy losses for an artillery battery in battle.

Individual vignettes. Regular Army units rarely got much attention in postwar accounts, since they had no strong regional or local identification that might promote reunions, regimental associations, published histories, and the erection of monuments. The survivors of Lieutenant John G. Turnbull's Battery F and K, 3rd U.S. Artillery, however, made sure that their comrades who died along the Emmitsburg Road confronting the attack of Wilcox's Alabamians and Lang's Floridians were not forgotten. As battery member Charles Hulin later wrote, the first round that hit among his guns "killed [Private Charles H.] Pinkham and [Private Jeremiah] Shehan, and took off the hind leg of Shehan's lead saddle-horse on the piece to which I had the honor to belong." Pinkham served with the battery on detached service from the 17th Maine Infantry; Shehan was an Irish immigrant, born in Cork. A number of years later, T. H. Little added that they had to retreat so quickly that they left four of their guns behind, but "a young cannoneer named [English-born Private John] Malone, discovered that one of the guns had not been fired. He walked back, inserted a friction tube and pulled the lanyard with a deadly fire upon the Confederates. He was shot and killed. Lieut. Turnbull, afterward Colonel in the army, had one bar taken off his shoulder straps by a bullet. Lieut. [Manning] Livingston, a nephew of Gen. [Henry W.] Halleck, was killed." Indeed, in addition to these men, Hulin pointed out that Irish-born Sergeant Robert Ayres; Bugler Thomas Whiteford; and Privates George C. Bentley, John Clifford (an Irishman), and Davis Murphy also were killed. He left out Private James H. Riddel, born in Augusta County, Virginia. "We are Regulars," Hulin pointed out, "and all of our dead save one—Bugler Whiteford—fill unknown graves." Bugler Whiteford rests in grave B-1 of the United States plot of the Soldiers' National Cemetery.[7]

Rudolphus Henry McClellan, a twenty-year-old farmer, enlisted in late 1861 in Monticello, Florida, and became a member of Company A, 5th Florida Infantry. His records provide a fairly detailed physical description of the young soldier: he stood five foot eleven and had blue eyes and light hair. His seventeen-year-old brother, William, enlisted at the same time. While Rudolphus won a promotion to corporal, the two young soldiers did not particularly thrive in military service. Both fell ill and had to be hospitalized multiple times. Rudolphus even obtained a furlough late in 1862 to restore his health. The year 1863 proved to be a devastating one for Henry McClellan, the boys' father, back in Monticello. In March, Private William McClellan succumbed to disease. On July 2 at Gettysburg, Corporal Rudolphus McClellan was mortally wounded in the attack on Humphreys's line along the Emmitsburg Road. He lingered a few days before dying on July 5. Back in Florida in December

1863, Henry McClellan repeated the process he had followed after William's death: he submitted an application for any pay owed to his son who fell at Gettysburg. The Confederate army settled Corporal Rudolphus McClellan's account by paying his father the sum of $135.20.[8]

Who Lived Here?

On the east side of the Emmitsburg Road, north of the Sherfy house, sat the farm of Daniel H. Klingel. In April 1863 Klingel acquired the house and farm property from Ludwig Essick, the original owner. The house was a two-story, six-room structure made of logs. His fifteen-acre property resembled a rectangle that was 180 yards wide, with the Emmitsburg Road as the western boundary, and 410 yards long, with the present-day United States Avenue as its southern boundary. On July 2, before the Confederate attack, Union officers urged Klingel to flee with his family to a place of safety. He allegedly responded: "If I must die, I will die at home." In due time, Klingel took his family to a friend's home near Rock Creek. By midday on July 2, Union troops filled the Klingel property, busily preparing to defend the line along the Emmitsburg Road. Men from the 16th Massachusetts Infantry went into Klingel's house to make firing slits between the logs. Surviving veterans described how they used the house as a fort after they "perforated the house in several places." He subsequently filed a damage claim for the loss of his household goods; a large number of pairs of shoes and shoe leather (in addition to farming, Klingel was also a shoemaker); and damage to his crops, buildings, and fields. In September 1863 he advertised the property for sale. In 1885 and 1887, the Gettysburg Battlefield Memorial Association bought portions of the Klingel farm and incorporated them into its holdings.[9] In 2011 the National Park Service completed a renovation of the Klingel property, recreating its 1863 appearance.

The Peter Rogers home sat across the Emmitsburg Road and to the north of the Klingel Farm, where the 1st Massachusetts monument sits today. Peter and his wife, Susan Kitzmiller Rogers, owned this farm at the time of the battle. Although his wife fled to a place of safety before the battle started, Peter may have stayed in his home during the fighting. Twenty-seven-year-old Josephine Miller, Susan's granddaughter whom Peter and Susan had adopted years earlier, stayed with him. During the afternoon of July 2, Josephine prepared food for the soldiers stationed around the house. As the fighting grew worse, she retired to the cellar and cared for the wounded collected there. Her exploits became something of battlefield legend. Thirty-five years after the battle, on the grounds of the Rogers farm, "Generals Longstreet, Sickles, Slocum, and Carr sat under a tree. . . . The talk here turned for a time upon reminiscences of Miss Rogers [sic]. General Carr told about how she turned out loaves from her oven, which the hungry soldiers devoured eagerly." The original Rogers House was removed in 1913 by subsequent property owners.[10]

THE TROSTLE FARM

The Trostle family received little compensation for the battle damage to their farm. (USAMHI)

The Trostle farm, where you are now standing, was owned by Peter Trostle, a resident of Straban Township east of Gettysburg. Peter had allowed his son Abraham and his family to reside on this farm since 1849 in exchange for a rent-to-own investment at the annual rate of $153.33. According to the 1860 census, Abraham and Catherine (Walter) Trostle lived here with at least nine children, ranging in age from fifteen years to five months. They added two additional children before July 1863.

Situated as it was between and within the battle lines of the second day of fighting, the farm suffered significant damage. Note the hole made by a cannon projectile in the south gable end of the barn and the destruction depicted in the photographs at the wayside exhibit. On September 4, 1874, Catherine Trostle, on behalf of Abraham, filed a federal claim for the loss of twenty-seven acres of wheat, nine of corn, eight of oats, thirty-two of grass, twenty tons of hay, three cows, one heifer, one bull, one large hog, and fifty chickens, as well as fifteen barrels of flour, two barrels of ham and shoulders, beds, bedding, clothing, and household goods. At least 6,400 fence rails were destroyed in the construction of earthworks or were burned for firewood. She also stated that neighbors William Patterson and George W. Trostle attested to the validity of the claim, which exceeded $3,000 in damages. There is no evidence that the Trostles ever received compensation for their losses. In 1899 the heirs of Abraham and Catherine Trostle sold the farm to the Gettysburg National Military Park Commission for $4,500.[11]

Driving directions to the next stop: Drive forward 0.4 miles to the stop sign at the T intersection with Hancock/Sedgwick Avenue. The farm buildings of the George Weikert farm will be on your immediate right. Turn left onto Hancock Avenue (a one-way road running north) and drive 0.3 miles to the large Pennsylvania monument and the sign designating National Park Service Auto Tour Stop 12. Park in the designated spaces on the right side of the road. (Restroom facilities are located in the stone building just to the east of the Pennsylvania monument.)

STOP 23. HOLDING THE CEMETERY RIDGE LINE

You will consider three different episodes at this stop.

Orientation

On Cemetery Ridge, locate the large, white-domed Pennsylvania monument. At the fork in the road just before reaching that monument, you will see the large monument to the 1st Minnesota Infantry topped by the bronze statue of a soldier running forward with a bayonetted rifle. Stand in front of that monument and look toward Emmitsburg Road, the direction the soldier is running.

You are standing on Cemetery Ridge, the main Union line on July 2 and 3 and the shank of Meade's fishhook defense. The Round Tops are visible to your left, Cemetery Hill is the heavily wooded high ground to your right, and you can see Culp's Hill and the top of its observation tower over your right shoulder. Turn around and look behind you. Note Taneytown Road, easily located by buildings and utility lines. Taneytown Road, along with Baltimore Street (then Pike) a few hundred yards beyond it, served as the Army of the Potomac's main lines of communication, supply, and reinforcement. Between those two roads encamped the army's supply trains and reserve artillery.

The 1st Minnesota
Infantry monument.

Now face Emmitsburg Road again. The brushy area in the low ground to your front follows the course of a branch of Plum Run, which flows from right to left. On Emmitsburg Road, the large, diamond-shaped monument to the 1st Massachusetts marks the site where the Rogers house stood at the time of the battle. Sickles's advanced right flank on Emmitsburg Road extended only a bit to the right of the Rogers house. The white log house and red barn on Emmitsburg Road to your immediate left front is the Daniel Klingel farm. The tree line beyond Emmitsburg Road ahead of you marks Seminary Ridge, the main Confederate line.

What Happened Here?

An important backstory. As Humphreys's division of Sickles's III Corps began to withdraw from its Emmitsburg Road line to your front and left front, very few Union troops occupied this portion of Cemetery Ridge. Brigadier General John Caldwell's division of Hancock's II Corps filled this position earlier in the day, but it had departed for the Wheatfield, well off to your left. A determined Confederate thrust through this gap would threaten the security of Taneytown Road and, possibly, sever the Union line.

Traditional interpretations of the action that took place in front of where you are standing focus almost solely on two units: the Alabama brigade of Brigadier General Cadmus M. Wilcox and the 262 men of the 1st Minnesota Infantry. According to the frequently repeated story, General Hancock of the II Corps saw this open stretch in the Union line on Cemetery Ridge, Wilcox's Alabamians charging directly for it, and only the 1st Minnesota close enough to stop them. It was a numerical mismatch, but to stave off disaster, Hancock rode up to Colonel William Colvill, the regimental commander, pointed to Wilcox's battle flags, and yelled, "Do you see those flags?" When Colvill nodded, Hancock bellowed, "Well, take them!" The 1st Minnesota attacked on the run, stopping the Alabamians along Plum Run in the low ground in front of you. When the fighting ended, only forty-seven Minnesota soldiers rallied under their banners. This classic account, however, ignores the sacrifices of thousands of other men who fought and died here.

Lieutenant Colonel Freeman McGilvery, for one, organized a massed battery from cannons retiring from Sickles's front near the Peach Orchard to cover the withdrawal of Humphreys's men. He established his gun line on a shelf of high ground about halfway between the Trostle farm and the crest of Cemetery Ridge. A correspondent for the *New York Herald* wrote that "our artillery worked with an energy and desperation almost superhuman, throwing in grape, canister and case shot," repulsing the Confederates at least four times "with terrible slaughter."[1] The guns that line Hancock Avenue today salute some of the batteries involved in this action, but they do not rest on the actual trace of July 2's "Plum Run line." Follow the fence line in your immediate front to the left until it meets the tree line near the George

Weikert farm—you can see the top of its buildings to your far left—and locate the single monument out in the field in front of that fence, well in advance of the line of monuments lining this road. That marker salutes Lieutenant Malbone Watson's Battery I, 5th U.S. Artillery, left-flank unit of McGilvery's quickly constructed artillery line. The monument was positioned incorrectly; it should sit well inside the tree line behind it. Still, the monument is useful for locating the low ridge where McGilvery posted his guns.

Position 1: The Counterattack of Willard's Brigade

Orientation
Remain in this position and look in the direction that the soldier with the bayoneted rifle is charging.

What Happened Here?
One part of the traditional story of this engagement is quite true: General Hancock had much to do with closing the gap in the Union line here. As soon as he heard of Sickles's wounding, Meade directed Hancock to assume command of both the II and III Corps and reinforce the III Corps line. Hancock personally accompanied Colonel George L. Willard's New York brigade, and near the George Weikert farm, he spotted some of the Confederates who had broken the III Corps line—Barksdale's Mississippians—pressing toward Cemetery Ridge. Hancock ordered Willard to stop them.

The 125th and 126th New York constituted Willard's first line, and they advanced with a will against Barksdale's 13th, 17th, and 18th Mississippi. As Lieutenant Colonel James M. Bull of the 126th New York reported, "The line advanced over declining ground, through a dense underbrush [to your front and left front] in as good order as the circumstances of the case would admit of." Barksdale's men, somewhat obscured by that scrub growth, then "fired upon the brigade as it advanced, which fire was returned by a portion of the brigade without halting. Many fell in the charge through the woods." Willard's men continued to advance, pushing the Confederates beyond the low ground, even fixing bayonets to do so. Indeed, with the added combat power of the 111th New York from the brigade's second line and the fire of McGilvery's guns, Willard's men pushed the Mississippians well back toward the Emmitsburg Road. Then, as Lieutenant Colonel Bull wrote home two weeks later, "a destructive cross fire from artillery on the left and infantry on the right, involving the certain destruction of this command," required Willard's men to pull back. As they withdrew, Bull explained, "the men fell by scores but the ranks were immediately closed up by the survivors."[2] A few minutes later, Willard fell dead, hit in the face by an artillery round; a rarely visited and somewhat obscured monument—dif-

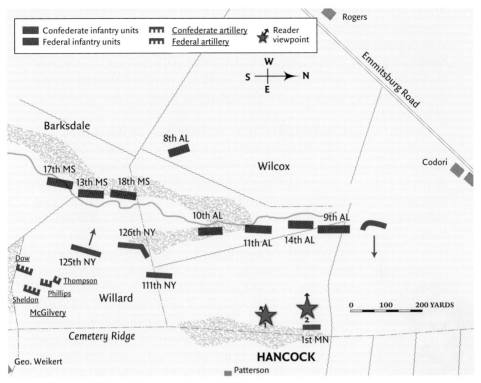

Confederate infantry units | Confederate artillery | Reader viewpoint
Federal infantry units | Federal artillery

Rogers

Emmitsburg Road

W
S ——→ N
E

Barksdale

8th AL

Wilcox

Codori

17th MS

13th MS 18th MS

10th AL

9th AL

126th NY

11th AL 14th AL

Dow

125th NY

Thompson

111th NY

Phillips

Sheldon

Willard

McGilvery

0   100   200 YARDS

Cemetery Ridge

1st MN

Geo. Weikert

HANCOCK

Patterson

Barksdale and Wilcox Push on toward Cemetery Ridge

ficult to spot, even though it stands in the scrub growth immediately in front of you—marks the spot of his death. But Willard's men had done what none of Sickles's units could do: they not only stopped Barksdale's attack, but they also stopped Barksdale, who fell mortally wounded in front of them.

Who Fought Here?

C.S.A.: You have met Barksdale's Mississippians at previous stops.

U.S.: Colonel George Willard's 1,508-man brigade from Brigadier General Alexander Hays's division of Hancock's II Corps. It included the 39th, 111th, 125th, and 126th New York. Willard's brigade went into action at Gettysburg bearing the unfortunate appellation of the "Harpers Ferry Cowards." During the Maryland Campaign of September 1862, Stonewall Jackson's troops surrounded Harpers Ferry, where this unit served. Despite their willingness to put up a fight, Colonel Dixon Miles, the post commander, raised the white flag of surrender. Gettysburg provided the first opportunity for Willard's brigade to clear its name.

Who Commanded Here?

The death of Brigadier General William Barksdale, whom you met at Stop 21, received much press coverage, as befitted a prominent antebellum politician. The *Baltimore Sun* reported: "He declared with his last breath that he was proud of the cause he died fighting for, proud of the means in which he had received his death wound; that the rebels were invincible, and although repulsed that day, they were sure of victory on the morrow."[3]

Colonel George L. Willard (1827–63) served in the Mexican War as an enlisted man and demonstrated sufficient gallantry in action to win a commission in the Regular Army. He accepted the colonelcy of the 125th New York in August 1862, and he served in brigade command at Gettysburg. During the fight with Barksdale's Mississippians and Wilcox's Alabamians in the Plum Run swale, he "was just emerging with his Brigade from some woods and bushes through which he had driven the enemy, when the fatal shell carried away a portion of his head and face." The city of Troy, New York, the town from which many of Willard's soldiers in the 125th New York came, hastily made preparations to honor him and to arrange for his funeral. As the *Troy Times* reported, "Colonel Willard was the embodiment of a true soldier—strict when on duty, cool amid danger, of oft-proven bravery, respected alike by subordinates and superiors." The editors did not spare their readers a grim description of the colonel's gory death. The *Times* reported that "Colonel Willard, while riding at the head of his brigade, was struck by a shell, which tore the angle of his mouth and shattered his chin and shoulder. He fell from his horse, which galloped into the rebel lines at full speed. The gallant rider was dead when taken from the ground." Colonel Willard's funeral was held at the home of his father-in-law, the Honorable Elias Plum of Troy.

Colonel George L. Willard, U.S.A. (USAMHI)

The casket had a glass top, most of which was covered in "a profusion of natural flowers. The upper part of the face looked quite natural, but the lower portion was covered to hide the wound which in an instant changed the heroic leader to a pale corpse."[4]

Who Fell Here?

Willard's brigade also fought on July 3, but it lost more heavily in this fight. In total, Willard's brigade lost at least 714 of its 1,508 men. The 111th New York lost 95 men killed or mortally wounded over the course of July 2 and 3, the second-highest number of deaths in a single regiment in the entire Union army at Gettysburg; add in the wounded and missing, and the unit lost 249 of its 390 men. The 125th New York lost Colonel Willard and 138 of its 392 men. The 126th New York lost its Colonel Eliakim Sherrill on July 3 and 230 more of its 455 men. The 39th New York, which did not take part in this charge but helped to save Watson's battery on McGilvery's artillery line, lost 95 of its 269 men. The brigade's total percentage loss reached 47.3 percent.

Individual vignettes. The deaths of General Barksdale and Colonel Willard represent all the soldiers who fell in this engagement.

Position 2: The Charge of the 1st Minnesota

Orientation

Move to your right to the informational wayside. Continue to look to the front but redirect your line of sight slightly to the right in the direction of the white fences and the diamond-shaped 1st Massachusetts monument at the site of the Rogers house on Emmitsburg Road. The 1st Minnesota's fight took place in the low ground halfway between your current position and Emmitsburg Road, not on a direct line that follows the gaze of the soldier on its monument.

What Happened Here?

Although Willard's New Yorkers finally stopped Barksdale, Wilcox continued to push Carr's brigade off the high ground near Emmitsburg Road to your front. As Wilcox reported, "When my command crossed the pike and began to descend the slope [toward the position where you now stand] they were exposed to an artillery fire from numerous pieces, both from the front and from either flank"—testimony to the effectiveness of McGilvery's Plum Run line. The 19th Massachusetts and the 42nd New York of the II Corps advanced to support Humphreys's right flank. In the open field beyond the scrubby growth to your right front, they waited until Carr's men passed over them, fired two volleys, then retreated immediately to avoid capture. Hancock then reported: "I met a regiment of the enemy, the head of whose column was about passing through an unprotected interval in our line. A fringe of undergrowth in front of the line offered facilities for it to approach very close to our lines without being observed. It was advancing firing, and had already twice wounded my aide." Hancock himself later reported that "the First Minnesota Regiment coming up at this moment, charged the regiment in handsome style."

Private Charles E. Baker, Company D, 1st Minnesota, was killed in action on July 2. (USAMHI)

Hancock did not report the details of his conversation with Colonel Colvill of the 1st Minnesota; he simply needed to plug the gap in the line as expeditiously as possible. Both Hancock—and to an unappreciated degree, General Meade himself—had begun to shift troops from quiet sectors to bolster this part of the Union line. While Hancock handled matters here, Meade had ridden over to Culp's Hill, and all but a single brigade of the XII Corps had begun to move toward this location. Elements of the I Corps, reorganized since their fight of the previous day, moved toward this position. But as the moment of crisis neared, no reinforcements had yet arrived to receive the Confederate assault. The 1st Minnesota had to face Wilcox's men alone.

As a letter written by "Sergeant" in late July recounted: "Now their cannon were pointed to us, and round shot, grape and shrapnel tore fearfully through our ranks, and the more deadly Enfield rifles were directed to us alone. Great heavens, how fast our men fell. . . . It seemed as if every step was over some fallen comrade. Yet no man wavers; every gap is closed up—and bringing down their bayonets, the boys press shoulder to shoulder and disdaining the fictitious courage proceeding from noise and excitement, without a word or cheer, but with silent, desperate determination, step firmly forward in unbroken line." The Minnesotans began to advance with a yell down through the fields immediately in front of you and down into the ravine where Plum Run flowed. Then, by several contemporary accounts, they received an order to halt. As they stood there, wrote Sergeant John Plummer to his brother, "the bullets were coming like hailstones and whittling our boys like grain before the sickle. 'Why don't they let us charge?' cried all of us. . . . 'Why do they stop us here to be murdered?' Everyone seemed anxious to go forward and some run way out ahead and beckoned for us to come on." They pressed on toward the ravine, where the Minnesotans fell in droves as the numerically superior Alabamians probed both flanks and attempted to shoot down the length of the regiment's line. Plummer expressed surprise to see a line of Alabamians "not fifty yards from us, standing out openly and loading and firing as deliberately as though they were in no danger whatever. Oh! There is no mistake but what some of those rebs are just as brave as it is possible for human beings to be."[5] As Captain Henry C. Coates, the senior unwounded officer, reported: "The fire we encountered was terrible, and, although we inflicted severe punishment upon the enemy, and stopped his advance, we there lost in killed and wounded more than two-thirds of our men and officers who were engaged." But the Minnesotans fought with uncommon ferocity. For his part, Wilcox began to pull his men out of what he considered to be a contest "so unequal."[6]

Who Fought Here?

You have met Wilcox's Alabama brigade at previous stops. The 1st Minnesota served in Brigadier General William Harrow's brigade of Brigadier General John Gibbon's division.

Who Commanded Here?

Major General Winfield Scott Hancock (1824–86), a native of Pennsylvania, graduated from the U.S. Military Academy ranked eighteenth in the twenty-five-member class of 1844. His antebellum career followed the typical course of solid Mexican

War service and frontier garrison assignments, and when the Civil War broke out, he served in California. He received a promotion to brigadier general on September 23, 1861, and during the Peninsula Campaign, he won an enduring nickname: "Hancock, the Superb." He rose to division command after Antietam and took over the II Corps of the Army of the Potomac after Chancellorsville; Hancock's presence is such a dominant feature of the Gettysburg story, it is not always easy to remember that it was his first battle as a corps commander. He performed his duties in an outstanding manner, taking the initiative to handle crises even if they were not necessarily within the limits of his authority; his detachment of Colonel Samuel S. Carroll's brigade to seal the breach of the XI Corps line on East Cemetery Hill on the evening of July 2 represents just one such effort. (You will learn more about this at Stop 27). Seriously wounded on July 3 during the repulse of Pick-

Major General Winfield S. Hancock, U.S.A. (USAMHI)

ett's Charge, Hancock did not return to active field duty until late in 1863. His injury never healed completely, and in late 1864, he had to give up the II Corps for departmental duties. After the war, he remained in the army but developed a deep interest in Democratic Party politics; he ran unsuccessfully for president in 1880. He died in 1886 and is buried in Norristown, near his Pennsylvania birthplace. As F. A. Walker noted in *General Hancock*, his 1894 biography of the general: "In every great career, whether civil or military, there is some one day which is peculiarly memorable; which, by reason in part of favorable opportunities or especially conspicuous position—in part, also, through some rare inspiration quickening the genius of the statesman or the warrior—becomes and to the end remains the crown of that career. . . . Such to Hancock was Gettysburg."[7]

Who Fell Here?

Brian Leehan, who has made a very detailed study of the 1st Minnesota's casualty list, admits that, "since the late nineteenth century, these figures have, literally, been carved in stone and cast in bronze and repeated endlessly in books, articles, and newspaper stories about the regiment. The figures are wrong." After comparing the methodologies used to reach these numbers—and other sets of figures that conflict with them—Leehan suggests that the figure 289, rather than the usually accepted 262, "is closer to the actual number of Minnesotans in the charge on July 2, 1863." But even that number, he admits, does not account for stragglers, men who may have fallen out of ranks from sunstroke—or fear—and a number of other factors large and small that influence troop strength.[8]

Individual vignette. Private Byron Welch, born Byron Welch Cobb, enlisted in Company I, 1st Minnesota Infantry, on April 28, 1861. The oldest of five children born to

Arial and Mary Ann Cobb in Colebrook, Connecticut, Welch left home and moved west in 1856. As he departed, this very determined young man made it clear to his friends and family that in the future, he only would answer to the name "Byron Welch," since his father had abandoned the family; the young man "would not carry a name which had been disgraced" in this way. Unfortunately, illness and misfortunes followed him. As he wrote home in 1858, "the ague has shaken me nearly to pieces," and he lost most of his $100 in gold to "board and Doctor's bills." Once he enlisted, however, he began to send money back to his mother in Connecticut, along with a promise that he would bring her to Minnesota to live with him. He never fulfilled that promise. A bullet killed him along Plum Run during the stand of his regiment on July 2. At first, his mother tried to rely upon her own resources; she owned a small house and a half acre of property and relied upon her skills as a nurse to support herself. Finally, in 1867, as she became increasingly infirm, she applied for a mother's pension and began collecting her $8 monthly stipend in early 1868. Private Byron Welch rests in grave B-11 of the Minnesota plot.[9]

Position 3: The Charges of Lang and Wright

Orientation

Now walk up the road to your right, past the large white Pennsylvania monument to where Pleasanton Avenue heads off to the right. Continue straight ahead on Hancock Avenue as it makes a wide curve and continues up Cemetery Ridge. You will soon reach a small, tree-covered knoll on the left of the road. Follow the mowed path at the far end of the knoll as you approach it to the pointed monument commemorating General Hancock's wounding on July 3. Stand in front of that marker and look out into the open ground toward Emmitsburg Road. The red buildings of the Nicholas Codori farm are in front of you.

What Happened Here?

As sunset neared, two final Confederate attacks ended the major fighting on the Cemetery Ridge line front. In the fields immediately in front of you, the 19th Maine essentially replayed the 1st Minnesota's experience, although against better odds. As Captain Charles E. Nash described it on July 29:

> The Nineteenth Maine was placed beside a battery [Lieutenant Evan Thomas's Battery C, 4th U.S. Artillery], to support it, and to hold its portion of the line, as the Third Corps had been driven back across the field, and was retiring in haste. The enemy was completely frantic with victory, and advanced impetuously. "Commence firing" was the command, when they were seventy yards distant, and almost instantly a deadly sheet of fire was poured into them. Through the thick smoke we could dimly see them advancing, but slowly and hesitatingly, for in the

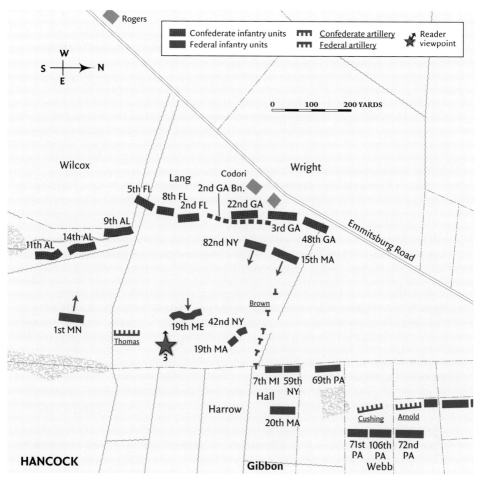

The Attacks of Lang and Wright

space of five minutes their strong line had melted away, and there were only a few daring spirits left to encounter. Our fire had been deadly; every shot had apparently done its duty. And when, with bayonets fixed, the command "Forward" was given, onward dashed all that was left of the Nineteenth.[10]

Colonel Lang of the Florida brigade reported that after taking heavy fire, which his men "handsomely replied to," he had to pull back to the road when Wilcox pulled back and left his flank unguarded. He regretted to report that, in addition to losing 300 of his men, "while retreating, the colors of the Eighth Florida Regiment were left upon the field, the color bearer and the color-guard (one sergeant and two corporals) being killed and wounded." All Colonel Francis Heath of the 19th Maine reported was that, "after firing about 10 rounds, I ordered an advance, and took quite a number of prisoners. I also retook four Napoleon guns that had been abandoned by some of our forces." He did not report that he lost close to 200 of his men in just a few minutes of close combat.

Now look into the open fields to your right front. Earlier in the day, Hancock had advanced Lieutenant Colonel James Huston's 82nd New York and Colonel George H. Ward's 15th Massachusetts to the Emmitsburg Road on the right of the Codori house to resist any effort to turn Humphreys's right flank. When the Confederate attack came, however, it came as a frontal assault by the Georgia brigade of Brigadier General Ambrose R. Wright.

Wright's men quickly overwhelmed the outnumbered men from New York and Massachusetts at the road. As Brigadier General William Harrow, their brigade commander, reported: "These two regiments, in the aggregate not more than 700 strong, and without support on their line, but partially protected by the rails of a fence which they had hastily taken down and piled in their front, gallantly sustained an unequal contest against greatly superior numbers" until Wright's Georgians outflanked their line. Adding to the confusion, the artillery supporting the Union line opened fire. Sergeant William J. Coulter of the 15th Massachusetts wrote soon after the battle: "Our artillery threw grape and canister, which, no doubt, was intended to go over our heads, but a good share of it struck our regiment. One discharge of canister from our own guns wounded the captain of Company E, the orderly sergeant and a private of my own company."[11] Both Huston and Ward lost their lives in the melee at the road. The 15th Massachusetts, according to Lieutenant Colonel George C. Joslin, "retired in some disorder being pressed so closely that we lost quite a number of prisoners, captured by the enemy." Captain M. R. Hall of the 48th Georgia, however, saw it differently: "We pushed them so rapidly that they broke and fled in great confusion, a large number of them running into our lines for safety." Several of Lieutenant T. Fred Brown's guns of Battery B, 1st Rhode Island Artillery, fell temporarily into Confederate hands.

Historians still disagree on exactly how far up Cemetery Ridge Wright's men advanced. Wright himself asserted that he reached the crest to the right of where you now stand, but the evidence for that claim is not incontrovertible. In any case, the Georgians retired under volleys from all three brigades of Brigadier General John Gibbon's division at the center of Hancock's II Corps line to your right. Two of Wright's regimental commanders were killed, and the colonel of the 48th Georgia suffered a severe wound. Brigadier General Alexander Webb, one of Gibbon's brigade commanders, reported that all his regiments opened up on Wright and that the enemy "halted, wavered, and fell back." His Pennsylvanians pursued and sent to the rear "about 250 prisoners, among whom were 1 colonel, 5 captains, and 15 lieutenants."[12]

When Anderson's two other brigades—Brigadier General Carnot Posey's Mississippians and Brigadier General William Mahone's Virginians—did not advance to the attack across the Emmitsburg Road to your far right front as expected, the Confederate main effort ground to a halt with the setting of the sun.

While the repulse of Wright's attack and nightfall ended the main fighting on this part of the Union line, it is important to remember that the 1st Minnesota's heroism is only one episode in a very complex response to a crisis situation. In addition to the units already introduced, Meade's efforts to bring to the field Brigadier General John W. Geary's XII Corps division from Culp's Hill, Robinson's and Doubleday's divisions of the I Corps, Caldwell's reformed II Corps division, and even some of Birney's and Humphreys's reorganized regiments speaks volumes about his clearmindedness at a crucial time. Many of these newly arrived regiments helped push Anderson's men back toward and then across the Emmitsburg Road, capturing flags and even recovering most of the cannons that had fallen into Confederate hands.

Who Fought Here?

C.S.A.: Brigadier General E. A. Perry's small 742-man Florida brigade, commanded by Colonel David Lang, included the 2nd, 5th, and 8th Florida. Brigadier General Ambrose R. Wright's 1,413-man Georgia brigade included the 3rd, 22nd, and 48th Georgia and the 2nd Georgia Battalion.

U.S.: Engaged here were Colonel Francis Heath's 19th Maine Infantry, the 15th Massachusetts, and the 82nd New York from Harrow's brigade, plus the 19th and 20th Massachusetts, the 7th Michigan, and the 42nd and 59th New York of Colonel Norman J. Hall's 922-man brigade. The 69th, 71st, 72nd, and 106th Pennsylvania of Brigadier General Webb's brigade participated toward the end of the action. Harrow, Hall, and Webb all served in Gibbon's division of Hancock's II Corps.

Who Commanded Here?

Brigadier General Ambrose Ransom Wright (1826–72), a Georgia native, devoted his antebellum years to the study of law and developed a strong interest in politics. During the 1860 presidential election, he supported the Constitutional Union ticket of Judge John Bell and Edward Everett, but this did not hold him back once Georgia seceded. He immediately obtained a commission as colonel of the 3rd Georgia Infantry on May 18, 1863. Promoted to brigadier general on June 3, 1862, he participated as a brigade commander in all of the major campaigns of the Army of Northern Virginia until reassigned to Georgia in November 1864. He suffered a serious wound during the 1862 Maryland Campaign. Wright resumed his law practice after the war ended, dabbled in newspaper ownership, and ran unsuccessfully for the U.S. Senate. He finally won a seat in the U.S. House of Representatives, but he

Brigadier General Ambrose R. Wright, C.S.A. (USAMHI)

died on December 21, 1872, before he could take his seat. At Gettysburg, his brigade broke the II Corps line along the Emmitsburg Road on July 2 and charged up the slopes of Cemetery Ridge near the clump of trees that Pickett's men made famous the following day. On July 3, when Confederate artilleryman Porter Alexander asked him his opinion of Pickett's chances, he replied: "Well, Alexander, it is mostly a question of supports. It is not as hard to get there as it looks. I was there yesterday with my brigade. The real difficulty is to stay there after you get there—for the whole infernal Yankee army is up there in a bunch."[13]

Colonel David Lang (1838–1927), a native Georgian who became a surveyor in Florida, enlisted as a private in the Gainesville Minutemen even before the firing on Fort Sumter. His original unit served only for one year, however, so when his enlistment ended, he returned home, raised a company for the 8th Florida Infantry, and in May 1862 won election as its captain. By July 1863 he had risen to the rank of colonel and took temporary command of the Army of Northern Virginia's small Florida brigade on several occasions. One of those opportunities came at Gettysburg. He described the experience to his cousin a week after the battle: "About 5 P.M. we were ordered to charge the enemy's positions, and away we dashed across an open field 1½ miles wide every foot of which was swept by the enemy's artillery and musketry." The next day, his men participated in a vain effort to support Pickett's Charge. In the aftermath of the fight, he reported his command's loss as "tremendous, of the whole number (700) which I carried in I now have 220 for duty." Lang served faithfully until Appomattox, then he returned to Florida, worked as a civil engineer, and, as the state of Florida's adjutant general, played an important role in the organization and modernization of its National Guard. Colonel Lang is buried in Tallahassee.[14]

Who Fell Here?

C.S.A.: The casualties for Lang's Florida brigade were listed at Stop 22. In Wright's brigade, the 3rd Georgia lost 219 of its 441 men; the 22nd Georgia lost Colonel Joseph Wasden and 170 more of its 400 men; the 48th Georgia lost 224 of its 395 men; and the 2nd Georgia Battalion lost its commanding officer, Major George W. Ross, and 82 of its 173 men—for a brigade loss of 49.3 percent.

U.S.: All of the Union regiments involved in this fight also took part in the repulse of Pickett's Charge on July 3. They suffered heavy casualties on both days. In Harrow's brigade, the 19th Maine lost 203 of its 439 men; the 15th Massachusetts lost Colonel George Ward on July 2 and 147 of its 239 men; and the 82nd New York lost Lieutenant Colonel James Huston on July 2 and 192 of its 335 men. When the casualties of the 1st Minnesota of Harrow's brigade are added to these numbers, the brigade loss at Gettysburg reached 57.1 percent. In Hall's brigade, the 19th Massachusetts lost 77 of its 163 men; the 20th Massachusetts lost 127 of its 243 men and Colonel Paul J. Revere, mortally wounded by a shell on July 2; the small 7th Michigan lost 65 of its 165

men; the 42nd New York lost 74 of its 197 men; and the 59th New York lost Lieutenant Colonel Max Thomann and 34 of its 152 men—for a brigade loss of 40.9 percent
over July 2 and 3. Webb's brigade suffered most of its casualties on July 3.

Individual vignette. Thomas M. Albert of Henry County enlisted in Company K of
the 22nd Georgia Infantry on August 31, 1861. An able soldier at the start, Albert
soon received a vote of confidence from his comrades, who on December 1, 1861,
elected him fifth sergeant of his company. Sergeant Albert's health declined precipi-
tously in the summer of 1862, however. On June 20 he entered a Richmond hospital
with severe dysentery. On July 8—with the hospitals overflowing with casualties
from the Seven Days Battles—Albert received a medical furlough back to Henry
County, with orders to check in weekly with a military surgeon; he returned to duty
on August 28 of that year. On July 2, Sergeant Albert was killed in action in the fighting along the Emmitsburg Road. He left behind his widowed mother, Emily, who on
May 28, 1864, submitted a claim for any remaining pay that might have been owed
to her son. The government delayed payment because no responsible authority in
the 22nd Georgia ever reported officially that Sergeant Albert had fallen in battle at
Gettysburg. Albert's records do not confirm that his mother ever received any payment due him for his service.[15]

Who Lived Here?

The fighting described at this stop occurred over three large tracts of land owned by
George Weikert, William Patterson, and Nicholas Codori. The seventy-eight-acre
farm of George Weikert, identified today by the stone house and wooden barn that
stands at the intersection of United States Avenue and Sedgwick Avenue, was acquired from Henry Bishop in 1851 for $1,645.00. The census of 1860 records the oc-
cupants of the property as George, age fifty-three; his wife, Ann, age fifty-two; and
six children ranging from twenty-three to nine years of age. By the time the battle
took place, the two eldest sons lived on properties adjacent to that of their father.
Compared to surrounding properties, the George Weikert farm did not suffer much
battle damage. In a claim filed in November 1871, he cited the loss of $15.00 worth
of hay and damage to crops, fences, and lands that totaled $1,141.00. There is no
record of compensation.

On April 5, 1849, William Patterson acquired thirty acres of property on the east
side of Taneytown Road, and on April 7, 1849, he bought a second parcel of approximately forty-eight acres on the west side of Taneytown Road extending westward to
the crest of Cemetery Ridge; the farm's northern boundary running east-west about
where the Pennsylvania monument sits today. Little information is known about
the Patterson family today, but it appears that William, like most of his neighbors,
was engaged in subsistence farming to support himself; his wife, Lydia; and their
eight children. Patterson sold off small parcels of his land to the Gettysburg Battle-

field Memorial Association. The 1899 sale involved the section of his land on the west side of Taneytown Road that became part of Gettysburg National Military Park.

Adjoining the Patterson property on its western boundary was the Nicholas Codori farm. The Codori farm was nearly 300 acres, a large tract for that time. The farm was bisected by the Emmitsburg Road, which ran for half a mile on a southwest-to-northeast axis through the center of the property. The section on the western side of the road was a wedge-shaped piece that stretched westward to Seminary Ridge and included the area where the Virginia Memorial—you will visit it at Stop 32—sits today.

According to naturalization records, Nicolas Codorus (later Nicholas Codori) was born in France in 1809. He and his brother George immigrated to the United States in 1828, eventually settling in Gettysburg. Nicholas petitioned to become a naturalized U.S. citizen in 1834. The following year, he married Elizabeth Martin, and they purchased a home in Gettysburg on York Street. The 1850 census lists Nicholas's occupation as a butcher. In 1854 he invested his savings in the purchase of the now-famous farm south of town, which they used as investment property occupied and farmed by a tenant. One account states that the farm was occupied at the time of the battle by John and Talithia Barrett Reiley. Another account states that the farm was occupied by Catherine Codori Staub, daughter of Nicholas's eldest brother, Anthony, while her husband John was away in the Union army. Damages to the farm over the two days of fighting were estimated to be over $3,000.

Over time, the Codori farm passed from ownership of the family to the U.S. government for incorporation into Gettysburg National Military Park. During the First World War, a training camp for the U.S. Army's newly formed U.S. Tank Corps was established on a substantial part of the Codori farm. Temporary barracks for some 10,000 enlisted men and 600 officers were erected near the house and barn. The camp was named Camp Colt in honor of nineteenth-century weapons designer Samuel Colt. The army's commander at Camp Colt was Captain Dwight D. Eisenhower.[16]

What Did They Say about It Later?

Private William Cowan McClellan, 9th Alabama, Wilcox's brigade, wrote home about his experiences along the Emmitsburg Road: "On the 2nd [of July] our army charged the powerful position of the enemy, took nearly all of their guns, by some means or other we had no Support, the consequence was a Brigade to the right of Wilcox gave way, this compelled Wilcox to fall back to keep the enemy from flanking him and coming up in his rear. Barksdale's Miss[issippi] Brigade was the one that gave way, so you may judge that it was a hot place."[17]

At the dedication of the monument to the 125th New York on October 3, 1888, Chaplain Ezra D. Simons made clear that after Gettysburg, nobody could ever again call Willard's brigade the "Harpers Ferry Cowards":

The sun was sinking low, and the heavens were ablaze with its splendors, in marked contrast with the lurid fires of death towards which we were marching. We were halted among the smoke in front of some swale—a new growth of trees—in which we could see, dimly, because of the smoke covering the field—men moving. . . . On we rushed with loud cries! On—with bullets whizzing by our ears, as if messengers from the cold-icy region of the dead—with shells screaming and cannon all tearing the air, like so many fields bent on destruction; now bursting among and around us; now ploughing the ground at our feet and laying many of our noble men low in death or bleeding with wounds; on, on, we rushed, through storm of fire and death, thundering above and darting around us like the thunder and lightning of Heaven.[18]

It had been a hard-fought battle, but the correspondent of the *New York Herald* already decided who had earned the credit for saving the day: "The promptness with which the great flank movement of Lee was met and checkmated reflects the highest credit upon the General commanding [Meade]. Indeed, the troops were handled with consummate ability the entire day, General Meade being in the field, often under a very heavy fire, holding everything under his own eye."[19]

Driving directions to the next stop: Return to your vehicle and drive forward, taking Pleasonton Avenue, the next road to your immediate right adjacent to the north side of the Pennsylvania monument. At the T intersection of Pleasonton Avenue and Taneytown Road, turn left and drive 0.9 miles over Cemetery Hill to the traffic light–controlled intersection with Steinwehr Avenue (Route 15 Business). Turn right onto Steinwehr Avenue and follow it to the next traffic light–controlled intersection with Baltimore Street (Route 15 North Business). Turn left onto Baltimore Street and drive 0.5 miles to the traffic circle in the center of town. Drive one-quarter of the way around the traffic circle and enter York Street (Route 30 East). Where the road splits at the second traffic light, follow the road straight ahead of you, which is Hanover Street (Route 116 East). Follow Hanover Street (which becomes Hanover Road) 0.7 miles out of town, across Rock Creek to the top of the hill, where you should turn right into the National Park Service–owned parcel known as Benner's Hill. Park your vehicle at the loop.

6

Ewell Tries the Union Right Flank

STOP 24. BENNER'S HILL

Orientation

After parking, walk back down the access road until you reach the informational wayside. Facing the wayside, you will see the rooftops and church spires of the town of Gettysburg directly ahead of you. Rock Creek flows in the low ground at the base of the hill below you. To your left front, between 1,200 and 1,300 yards away, you can see the top of a blue water tower and, off to its left, a shaggy tree line; this is Cemetery Hill. Look down toward the loop to your left to see Culp's Hill, visible through the tree line.

What Happened Here?

On the afternoon of July 2, 1863, Benner's Hill anchored the left flank of the main Confederate battle line. For most of July 2 and July 3, only a thin line of skirmish-

The view from Benner's Hill toward the town of Gettysburg.

ers extended farther to your left. The hill's position within easy range of the Union positions on Cemetery Hill and Culp's Hill made it both a useful observation point and an artillery platform. The rugged terrain in the valley below, cut by chest-deep Rock Creek, made it difficult to assail the heights here and gave Lee's left flank a significant degree of security.

Lee's battle plan for July 2 called upon Ewell to demonstrate against the Union right flank on Cemetery Hill and Culp's Hill, while Longstreet launched the main effort against the Union left flank near the Round Tops. Ewell's orders required him to be prepared to act as soon as he heard the sound of Longstreet's guns. Since he had deployed the bloodied divisions of Rodes and Early in the town of Gettysburg, where they had little room to maneuver, Ewell decided that Major General Edward Johnson's fresh division (encamped behind you) would take the lead on July 2.

With Ewell's concurrence, Johnson decided to place the artillery battalion of Lieutenant Colonel R. Snowden Andrews in position along this high ground, "the only eligible hill within range," to open on the Union right flank when Longstreet launched his attack. As Andrews reported, Benner's Hill lay well within range of any Union batteries firing from Cemetery Hill or Culp's Hill, and, when deployed, nearly all the Confederate cannons participating in the bombardment "had to be crowded on this small hill, which was not in our favor."

Andrews did not command his battalion on July 2, however. He had fallen severely wounded at Winchester on the march into Pennsylvania, and the battalion went into action on July 2 under the command of its executive officer, nineteen-year-old Major Joseph W. Latimer, a former student at the Virginia Military Institute. Latimer examined the Benner's Hill area carefully and, as Andrews reported, "found great difficulty in sheltering his horses and caissons." In the end, Latimer placed his guns—with caissons, limbers, crews, and horses—in the low ground beyond the rail fence behind you until time arrived to move the guns forward to this line. Johnson understood the challenge his gunners would face. From his headquarters on the Hanover Road to your right, Benner's Hill appeared to be "directly in front of the wooded mountain [Culp's Hill] and a little to the left of the Cemetery Hill; consequently exposed to the concentrated fire from both, and also to an enfilade fire from a battery near the Baltimore road."

At approximately 4:00 P.M., Latimer ordered his guns into battery on the crest of Benner's Hill and its extension on the northern side of the Hanover Road to your right. A 10-pounder Parrott rifled gun and a 3-inch ordnance gun of Captain C. I. Raine's Lee (Va.) Battery anchored Latimer's left, back at the loop to your left. On your way to this location, you passed the position of Captain William F. Dement's four Napoleons of the 1st Maryland Artillery and Captain J. C. Carpenter's two Napoleons and two 3-inch ordnance guns of the Alleghany Battery from Virginia. To your right are the four 10-pounder Parrott rifled guns of Captain William D. Brown's Chesapeake Artillery from Maryland. Although you can see the marker and repre-

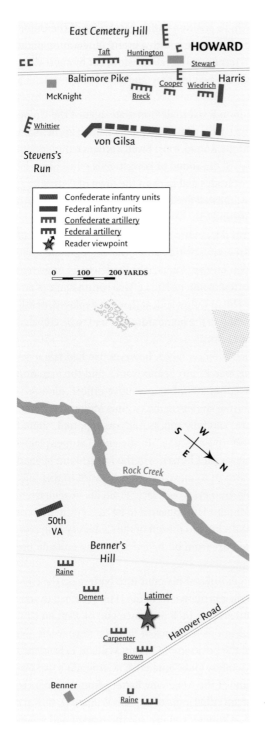

The Artillery Duel between
Benner's Hill and Cemetery Hill

sentative guns of Captain Archibald Graham's Rockbridge Artillery just beyond the Chesapeake Artillery, those guns did not fire from that position. Graham's battery, on detached service from Captain Willis Dance's battalion, was armed with four 20-pounder Parrott cannons, the heaviest field guns with the longest range that Civil War armies routinely carried into active field operations. Graham's 20-pounders— and two more guns of the same type from Raine's Lee Battery—went into position where you see cannons on the high ground just across the Hanover Road to your right. (The cannons emplaced across the road commemorate the three batteries in Lieutenant Colonel William Nelson's battalion that spent July 2 on the grounds of Pennsylvania College and deployed to this position only at the end of the fighting discussed here.)

Johnson ordered Brigadier General J. M. Jones to provide infantry support for Latimer's line. Jones immediately posted Lieutenant Colonel L. H. N. Salyer's 50th Virginia to the left of the gun line, beyond the tree line at the loop to your left. He already had posted four companies of Colonel John C. Higginbotham's 25th Virginia as skirmishers in the low ground near Rock Creek. When all had been readied, Latimer opened fire on the Union position.

At first, Latimer's men did well. Their gunnery impressed their opponents. General Hunt himself reported that the Confederate artillery "opened a remarkably accurate fire upon our batteries." Indeed, Colonel Charles S. Wainwright, commander of the I Corps artillery brigade on East Cemetery Hill—which absorbed much of Latimer's shelling—claimed that he witnessed "the most accurate fire I have ever yet seen from their artillery." But good fortune did not smile on the Confederate gunners for very long. Earlier in the day, Major Thomas W. Osborn, the chief of the XI Corps artillery on Cemetery Hill, had taken the initiative to ask Hunt "for a greater amount of artillery than we then had, as our position was finely adapted to its use." Hunt had sent him thirty-two additional guns; twelve of them engaged with Latimer's pieces. A few guns also wheeled into position on the summit of Culp's Hill. In any case, as Andrews reported, the new Union artillery line "partially enfiladed our batteries" and inflicted great damage. Both Andrews and Johnson described the artillery duel as an "unequal contest."[1]

By most accounts, the artillery fight lasted about two hours. In the end, the accuracy of the Union counterbattery fire wreaked havoc on Latimer's gun line. At least one caisson in Dement's Maryland battery exploded, and Dement himself fell wounded. Brown's Chesapeake battery lost one gun disabled, and so many cannoneers became casualties that they could only serve two of their remaining guns. Brown himself fell mortally wounded with two fractured legs; one was amputated, but he failed to rally and died on July 11.[2] As Latimer's gunners fell killed or wounded, infantrymen from Salyer's 50th Virginia stepped in. "We rendered him good service in assisting his cannoneers with their pieces," Salyer reported, losing one private killed and a lieutenant and private wounded. Latimer kept his men in line as long as the guns had ammunition to fire. Finally, the young major recommended to General Johnson that he be permitted to "withdraw the battalion, if he thought proper." Johnson ordered him to pull back, but, as the firing tapered off, one of the final Union shells mortally wounded Latimer.

The Union guns on Cemetery Hill effectively neutralized Ewell's artillery. Brigadier General William N. Pendleton, Lee's chief of artillery, admitted as much. Although he only had "partially observed" the artillery duel from high ground behind Seminary Ridge, Pendleton reported: "Massed as were the enemy's batteries on the Cemetery Hill, fronting our left, and commanding as was their position, our artillery, admirably served as it was, operated there under serious disadvantage and with considerable loss."[3] To continue carrying out Lee's orders to provide a diversion in support of Longstreet's main effort, then, Ewell had to turn to his infantry. Johnson's division, encamped in the open fields of the Daniel Lady farm behind you, prepared to attack Culp's Hill. As you return to the loop, look to your right front as you pass Carpenter's Alleghany Battery to see the top of the observation tower that crowns that height.

Who Fought Here?

C.S.A.: Engaged here were Lieutenant Colonel R. Snowden Andrews's battalion, Major Joseph W. Latimer commanding. Captain Willis Dance's Reserve Battalion from Ewell's Second Corps contributed the 20-pounder Parrotts of the Rockbridge Artillery of Lexington, Virginia.

U.S.: Among the batteries on East Cemetery Hill were Captain Michael Wiedrich's Battery I, 1st New York, from the XI Corps artillery brigade, and Captain James Cooper's Battery B, 1st Pennsylvania, and Captain Gilbert Reynolds's Battery L, 1st New York, from the I Corps artillery brigade; Reynolds had been wounded on July 1, and Lieutenant George Breck commanded the battery on July 2 and 3. Captain Greenleaf Stevens's 5th Maine Battery, under Lieutenant Edward N. Whittier, served on Stevens's Knoll in the saddle between Cemetery Hill and Culp's Hill. From the cemetery grounds, Captain Elijah D. Taft's 5th New York and Captain James F. Huntington's Battery H, 1st Ohio, both from the Artillery Reserve, participated in the bombardment of Benner's Hill. From Culp's Hill, one section of Lieutenant David H. Kinzie's Battery K, 5th U.S. Artillery, of the XII Corps artillery brigade fired on Benner's Hill.

Who Commanded Here?

Major Joseph White Latimer (1843–63), a native of Prince William County, Virginia, was only nineteen years of age at Gettysburg. He entered the Virginia Military Academy in 1859 and, when the war began, he went to Richmond with his fellow cadets to serve as a drillmaster. Assigned to the Hampden Artillery, his youthful countenance worked against him at first. "But for a solid, imperturbable earnestness with which he gave all his orders, connected with an unusual readiness and precision in the details of instruction, the officers and men would have considered it humiliating to be placed under the tuition of such a child," Captain A. R. Courtney wrote, but "on drill we paid him the utmost respect, both men and officers yielding prompt obedience to every order." Off duty, Courtney continued, "we always spoke of him as 'our little Latimer.'" Captain Courtney made a place for Latimer in his newly formed Courtney Artillery, and Latimer served in that unit until he was promoted to major and assigned to Lieutenant Colonel Snowden Andrews's battalion. He served as temporary commander of that battalion at Gettysburg, where, near the end of his bombardment

Major Joseph W. Latimer, C.S.A. (Wise)

of Cemetery Hill, a shell fragment shattered his right arm. The injured limb had to be amputated, and Latimer endured a bumpy wagon ride to Winchester to recuperate. As Lee pulled back into Virginia and Union forces approached the town, however, Latimer insisted on being moved farther south. He soon took a turn for the worse, and he died on August 1. He is buried in Harrisonburg. Even an officer so notoriously difficult to impress as Stonewall Jackson found much to admire in Latimer, asserting that "this young officer was conspicuous for the coolness, judgment, and skill with which he managed his battery, fully supporting the opinion I had formed of his high merit."[4]

Who Fell Here?

Andrews's battalion lost Major Latimer, mortally wounded, plus 4 of the 90 men in the Lee Artillery, 5 of the 90 men in the 1st Maryland Artillery, a particularly high 24 of the 91 men in the Alleghany Artillery, and 17 of the 76 men in the Chesapeake Artillery. The battalion lost 14.3 percent of its strength. The Rockbridge Artillery from Dance's battalion lost 21 of its 85 men.

On East Cemetery Hill, 13 of the 141 men in Wiedrich's Battery I, 1st New York, fell; Cooper lost 12 of his 106 men in Battery B, 1st Pennsylvania; and Reynolds's Battery L, 1st New York, lost 17 of its 124 men. On Stevens's Knoll, the 5th Maine Battery lost 23 of its 119 men. In the cemetery, Taft lost 3 of the 146 men in the 5th New York Battery, while 7 of the 99 men in Huntington's Battery H, 1st Ohio, fell killed, wounded, or captured. Kinzie's section on Culp's Hill suffered no casualties. Not all of these losses were suffered during this specific action.

Individual vignettes. On Benner's Hill, the Chesapeake Artillery—while fighting in a position described by one member of the battery as "a hell infernal"—lost an unusually high number of casualties for a battery in a single engagement. The soldier recalled the death of his commanding officer: "The Chesapeake received the most deadly evidence of that terrible duel. Our gallant Captain, William D. Brown, was the first to fall. Riding to the front of his battery, he enjoined us, for the honor of our native State, to stand manfully to our guns. The words were still upon his lips when he fell, dreadfully mangled by a solid shot."[5] Brown's remains were returned to Baltimore, where mourners at his funeral were threatened with arrest by Federal authorities.

Who Lived Here?

Christian Benner, after whose extended family Benner's Hill is named, lived with his wife Susan and two sons on a 208-acre farm just east of Gettysburg's town limits and south of the Hanover Road. One of those sons later described the use of his house as a hospital, noting that late on July 2, "the sight of the first wounded man was dreadful but it is remarkable how quickly one gets hardened to such things. In a little while I could see a man's leg sawed off, or his head sawed off, for that matter, without being disturbed." The family left the house on July 3, and when they returned on July 4, they had been "robbed of everything . . . of any value." Perhaps this helps to explain why the Benners, like many other families in the Gettysburg area, tried to make up some of their losses by salvaging items cast off by the two armies. The Quartermaster Department of the U.S. Army issued a public statement in mid-July 1863 requiring all those who picked up army property to return it. When the public generally ignored the demand, mounted patrols went from door to door to recover government property. As one army quartermaster reported on July 16, 1863: "I left here this morning, with only two Cavalrymen, to look into the state of affairs at Farm Houses. I found at Christian Benners, Guns, Blankets, Sabers, Shelter-tents &c"—and then he continued with an even longer list of finds from Benner's neighbors.[6]

What Did They Say about It Later?

Neither army carried many 20-pounder Parrott cannons into the field, so artillery-men always took great interest in their effectiveness on the battlefield. Colonel Charles Wainwright, commander of the Union I Corps artillery brigade, recalled the destructiveness of two 20-pounder artillery shells fired by the Rockbridge Artillery, both of which fell within ten yards of his position on East Cemetery Hill: "One of these shot struck in the centre of a line of infantry who were lying down behind the wall. Taking the line lengthways, it literally ploughed up two or three yards of men, killing and wounding a dozen or more. Fortunately it did not burst, for it struck so near where we were sitting that it covered us with dust. The other was a shell which burst directly under Cooper's left gun, killed one man outright, blew another all to pieces, so that he died in half an hour, and wounded the other three."[7]

Driving directions to the next stop: Return to the intersection with Hanover Road (Route 116). This is a blind intersection to your right and to your left. Carefully turn left onto Hanover Road and drive back toward the town. At the first traffic light–controlled intersection after crossing Rock Creek (0.3 miles), turn left onto Sixth Street and then right onto East Middle Street. Follow East Middle Street 0.3 miles to Liberty Street and turn left. Where the road divides in three directions, take the center road, reentering the National Battlefield property marked as Culp's Hill and East Confederate Avenue. Proceed on the one-way East Confederate Avenue 0.5 miles; just after crossing a small stone bridge where the hill slopes up sharply to the right of the road, safely pull over and park near the marker for Brigadier General J. M. Jones's brigade.

STOP 25. LOWER CULP'S HILL, JULY 2

You will visit two positions for this stop; you will have to drive to the second position.

Position 1: Johnson Attacks

Orientation

Stand in front of the marker for Jones's brigade and look up the steep slopes of Culp's Hill in front of you. Even though you cannot see Rock Creek, remember that it runs though the low ground behind you and separates Benner's Hill from Culp's Hill.

What Happened Here?

You are standing at the eastern base of Culp's Hill, the elevation that served as the pointed tip of General Meade's fishhook defense. After the sharp artillery exchange between Latimer's artillery on Benner's Hill behind you and the Union batteries on Cemetery Hill (to your right front) and Culp's Hill ahead of you, Ewell determined to follow Lee's orders and convert his demonstration into a "real attack." In this way, he hoped to divert the Army of the Potomac's attention from Longstreet's main effort against the other end of its line.

Major General Edward "Allegheny" Johnson's division of Ewell's corps had deployed on farm fields along the Hanover Road well over half a mile over your right

Jones's brigade crossed from left to right to charge up the slopes of Culp's Hill.

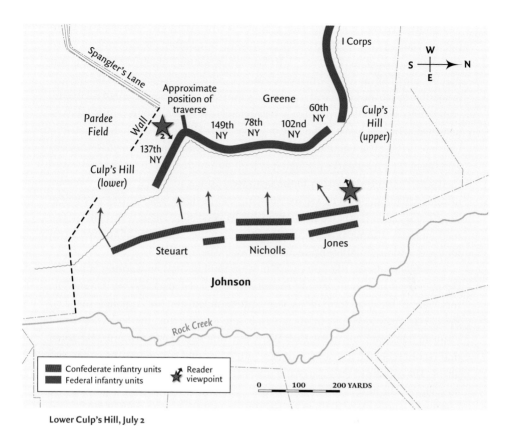

Lower Culp's Hill, July 2

shoulder during the artillery bombardment. Elements of Brigadier General John M. Jones's Virginia brigade posted on the Christian Benner farm had provided infantry support for Latimer's guns in case Union skirmishers from the Union XII Corps probed too closely. When the artillery exchange ended, Ewell ordered Johnson forward.

As Johnson described it, "I then advanced my infantry to the assault of the enemy's strong position—a rugged and rocky mountain, heavily timbered and difficult of ascent; a natural fortification." Jones's men took the right of the line, forming for battle on the other side of Rock Creek behind you and advancing toward this position. Brigadier General Francis Nicholls's Louisiana brigade—commanded this day by Colonel Jesse M. Williams—deployed on Jones's left flank, extending the Confederate line farther to your left. Rough terrain delayed Brigadier General George H. "Maryland" Steuart's mixed brigade of Virginia, Maryland, and North Carolina troops from falling in on the left flank of the Louisiana troops, but they successfully extended Johnson's line even farther to your left, beyond Nicholls's command.

Historian Harry Pfanz has made it easier to understand the confusing contemporary reports of the fighting around Culp's Hill by dividing the elevation into two parcels: the "upper" and "lower" hill. You are facing the "upper" hill, the highest part of Culp's Hill, as Jones's men confronted it. When the leaves are off the trees, it is possible to see the hill's crest, crowned by the statue of General George S. Greene, commander of the XII Corps brigade that defended it. Several hours before Johnson launched his attack, most of the XII Corps left Culp's Hill to reinforce the Union left. Greene—a West Point graduate and professional engineer in civilian life—took advantage of the breastworks his men had built during that day to make the most of their small numbers. A soldier in the 137th New York who signed himself "Viewer" informed his hometown newspaper editor: "Our position was a strong one by nature, and by noon it was made impregnable by good substantial breastworks. The men murmured some at building them, thinking they would be of no avail as on former occasions, but they proved of incalculable benefit."[1]

Jones's Virginians, the first to advance up the hill, had no warning about the strong position ahead of them. By the time they attacked, darkness was falling. The rocky terrain broke up formations. Jones fell wounded, and his Virginians made no dent in Greene's defenses. In 1864, even before Appomattox, the 60th New York's chaplain published one of the Civil War's very first regimental histories. He noted that "seven rebel officers we found dead on the ground covered by the colors and guard. The capture of these flags and prisoners shows how desperate a defense our men made. The effects of our fire were so terrible that the flags were abandoned, and the prisoners were afraid to either advance or retreat." The sight of the prisoners and trophies "greatly cheered and encouraged" the men, who "felt as though they had done a good thing."[2] For their part, Jones's Virginians soon withdrew back to the bottom of the hill to a position behind the stone wall behind you.

According to an old park photograph, the stone wall visible today at Stop 25's first position is the reconstructed breastwork of Brigadier General J. M. Jones's brigade. (*Annual Reports*)

The experience of Nicholls's Louisiana troops in attacking Greene's center regiments, the 78th and 102nd New York, on the upper hill to your left front differed little from that of Jones's Virginians. As Colonel Jesse M. Williams reported, the Louisiana brigade pushed forward until it reached a line "about 100 yards from the enemy's works, when it again engaged him with an almost incessant fire for four hours." Several efforts to pierce Greene's center "were attended with more loss than success."[3] As New Yorker John Quincy Adams informed the editor of the *Buffalo Express* after the battle, "Two brigades of Jackson's old corps, commanded by Ewell, were fighting against our small brigade, and, as they said, they were never whipped before. They had not the least idea of meeting such a terrific fire as they did, and being so horribly cut up as they were . . . if their strength had been double they would have assuredly met the same fate as the rest."[4]

Who Fought Here?

C.S.A.: Brigadier General John M. Jones's 1,520-man brigade included the 21st, 25th, 42nd, 44th, 48th, and 50th Virginia Infantry. Brigadier General Francis Nicholls's 1,104-man brigade, under Colonel Williams, included the 1st, 2nd, 10th, 14th, and 15th Louisiana Infantry. Both brigades served in Johnson's division, Ewell's Second Corps.

U.S.: The 60th, 78th, and 102nd New York of Brigadier General George S. Greene's brigade of Brigadier General John W. Geary's division, XII Corps, participated here.

Who Commanded Here?

Major General Edward Johnson (1816–73), a native Virginian, moved to Kentucky at a young age and graduated from the U.S. Military Academy with the class of 1838. He fought against the Seminoles and won two brevets for gallantry during the Mexican War. He resigned his commission on June 10, 1861, and entered Confederate service as colonel of the 12th Georgia Infantry. He became a brigadier general on December 13, 1861, and received promotion to major general on February 18, 1863. He was badly wounded in the Shenandoah valley in 1862, and when he returned to active duty with the Army of Northern Virginia for the Pennsylvania Campaign, he walked with a pronounced limp and carried a large walking stick to aid his step. This inspired one of Johnson's many nicknames: "Old Clubby." He also became known as "Allegheny" Johnson. Johnson suffered from a serious hearing loss, which frustrated him and often—as at Gettysburg—made it difficult for his staff and subordinates to work with him. Johnson's hearing problems may also help explain why, in the early morning of May 12, 1864, Hancock's II Corps surprised and overran his division's line at the "Mule Shoe" at Spotsylvania and took him prisoner. After being exchanged, he com-

Major General Edward Johnson. (USAMHI)

manded cavalry in Tennessee until he was captured a second time at Nashville. He returned to his farm in Chesterfield County, Virginia, at the war's end and died on March 2, 1873; his remains rest at Hollywood Cemetery in Richmond.

Who Fell Here?

C.S.A.: In Jones's brigade, the 21st Virginia lost 50 of its 236 men, the 25th Virginia lost 70 of its 280 men, the 42nd Virginia lost 80 of its 265 men, the 44th Virginia lost 56 of its 227 men, the 48th Virginia lost 76 of its 265 men, and the 50th Virginia lost 99 of its 240 men—for a brigade loss of 28.5 percent. Nicholls's brigade lost 39 killed and wounded in the 1st Louisiana, 62 killed and wounded in the 2nd Louisiana, 110 of the 226 men in the 10th Louisiana, 65 killed and wounded in the 14th Louisiana, and 38 killed and wounded in the 15th Louisiana. Numbers of captured and missing remain uncertain for four of these regiments; thus the brigade loss is estimated to be approximately 20.5 percent.

U.S.: Greene's losses at Culp's Hill in the regiments engaged here on July 2 and 3 include 52 of the 273 men in the 60th New York, 30 of the 198 men in the 78th New York, and 29 of the 230 men in the 102nd New York.

Individual vignettes. The breastworks that Greene's men erected undoubtedly saved many lives, but even these structures could not protect the unfortunate soldier from wounds to the head and upper body. Corporal Henry McDowell belonged to Company G of the 60th New York Infantry, on the left flank of Greene's brigade near the very crest of Culp's Hill. In the fight against Jones's Virginia brigade on the evening of July 2, a piece of shell hit the thirty-two-year-old soldier from Ogdensburgh and carried away his lower jaw. He was immediately transported to the XII Corps hospital for treatment, but the surgeons could do little for him. They kept him as comfortable as possible and no doubt tried to introduce fluids to keep him alive, but the facial artery hemorrhaged on July 13, and McDowell lost twenty ounces of blood. Corporal McDowell died on July 16 and is buried in the Soldiers' National Cemetery in grave D-66 in the New York plot.[5]

Eighteen-year-old Corporal William J. Smith served in Company K of the 1st Louisiana Infantry of Nicholls's brigade. During the advance up Culp's Hill, a bullet fractured the tibia in the lower third of his left leg. He received treatment at a field hospital until July 27, when he was able to be transferred to the U.S. Army General Hospital at Camp Letterman. Surgeon P. S. Leisenring treated the wound by placing Smith's leg in a "fracture box" to align the bones, and a "solution of lead and opium [was] applied." On August 18 the fracture box was removed, and Smith could move his limb. Surgeon W. M. Welch took over Smith's case on October 12 and discovered that the bones in his tibia had united, but ulcers around the wound site had "sloughed largely." He ordered the use of nitric acid to control the spread of infection, and he observed some temporary improvement. When Smith began to sink again, Welch used both nitric acid and bromine, but neither worked, as "the patient's system lack[ed] sufficient vitality to separate the sloughs from the living tissue." Smith also developed an "obstinate diarrhea, which baffled all treatment." Finally, Smith died on November 3, 1863, of exhaustion. His injured leg bones were removed at autopsy and sent to the U.S. Army Medical Museum by surgeon E. P. Townsend.[6]

Position 2: Greene's Defense

Orientation

Return to your vehicle and continue to follow East Confederate Avenue. On the left side of the road, you will see markers for various Confederate brigades. The only ones that concern the evening fight of July 2 are those representing the brigades of Jones, Nicholls, and Steuart. Markers for the brigades of Daniel, O'Neal, Smith, and Walker relate to the fighting here on July 3. You will learn of their experiences at Stop 30.

When you reach the stop sign at Spangler's Spring, turn right. Almost immediately, you have a choice to turn either left or right. Follow the road to your right and ascend "lower" Culp's Hill. (You will return to this area later and turn left as part of your exploration of the Culp's Hill fight on July 3.) On the highest point of lower Culp's Hill—near where yellow traffic signs warn of a very sharp left turn—park on the left side of the road in the dirt and gravel patch in front of the 29th Pennsylvania monument topped with a bronze eagle. Stand in front of that monument and face to the left. You will notice that the ground falls off sharply and then rises back up. You are looking into the swale that separates your current position on lower Culp's Hill from upper Culp's Hill ahead of you.

Now turn right and look across the park road toward a rather unusual monument—a Confederate regimental marker for the 2nd Maryland, C.S.A. During the battle, this unit actually was designated as the 1st Maryland Battalion. Notice that it is very purposefully located on the other side of a shallow ditch in front of you. That ditch extends to your right and left, from the bottom of the lower hill to the top of the upper hill, and represents the line of breastworks behind which Greene's Union defenders fought.

What Happened Here?

The line of monuments to your right leading to the base of lower Culp's Hill marks the line held by Brigadier General Alpheus Williams's XII Corps division early on July 2. However, Meade sent for Williams's men—and all but one brigade from Brigadier General John W. Geary's XII Corps division on the upper hill to your left—to assist in the repulse of Longstreet's main effort. Their departure left these breastworks empty. On the evening of July 2, as Johnson's three brigades prepared to launch their assault toward your current position, the defense of both the upper and lower Culp's Hill fell to Greene's single brigade of New Yorkers.

Greene placed three of his regiments—the 60th, 102nd, and 78th New York—from the crest of the upper hill to your left on a line that proceeded down the slope toward you. Those regiments stayed on the other side of the swale; Jones's and Nicholls's Confederates attacked that part of Greene's line. On the far side of the swale to your immediate left, Greene placed the 149th New York. Here, on this side of the swale on lower Culp's Hill, Greene deployed Colonel David Ireland's 137th New York to fill the abandoned breastworks in front of you. As Acting Adjutant Samuel B. Wheelock of the 137th New York explained on July 6, his regiment and the 149th New York now covered "a distance four times greater than [that] originally occupied by us."[7]

The 3rd North Carolina and 1st Maryland, the right-hand elements of Steuart's brigade, practically blundered into the low ground of the swale to your left front. As Steuart reported, "Our loss was heavy, the fire being terrific and in part a cross-fire" from the 149th New York on the upper hill and the 137th New York here. While

the New Yorkers exacted a high cost from the Southern infantry, other regiments of Steuart's brigade advanced against the works extending to your far right and found only a few skirmishers—or nothing at all. The small 23rd Virginia of Steuart's brigade got behind the right flank of the 137th New York—that is, into the open ground over your right shoulder—and attacked with spirit. As Colonel Ireland reported, "At this time I ordered Company A, the right flank company, to form at right angles with the breastworks." They could not hold, however, and Colonel Ireland's men pulled back with heavy losses under growing pressure from Steuart's men on front, right flank, and rear.

Colonel David Ireland, 137th New York Infantry, U.S.A. (USAMHI)

Now turn to the left and look at the swale once more. The 137th New York withdrew only to the other side of it. Some fell into Greene's line of breastworks that face to your right. But Ireland hurried many more of his men into line behind an earthen traverse—a breastwork positioned perpendicularly to the main defensive line—that faced toward where you are standing. The origin of the earthwork is not clear; Greene, always the engineer, may have ordered its construction as a defense against flank attacks against upper Culp's Hill, or it may simply have been—as he hinted in his report—an element of the emptied works of Brigadier General Thomas L. Kane's brigade that connected with his own. No physical trace of the traverse exists today, but it would have rested partway up the slope ahead of you, extending from right to left across your front and ending on the other side of the park road that rises up the hill on your left front.

Even after the 137th New York took its new position, Steuart's men continued to press their attack. Reinforcements from the I, II, and XI Corps now came to Ireland's support. These units, Greene reported, "rendered good service, being sent into the trenches to relieve our regiments as their ammunition was exhausted and their muskets required cleaning."[8] Noises in the night off to their right and rear worried some of Greene's men. They expected the Confederates to launch yet another assault. But to their great relief, they discovered instead that the rest of the XII Corps had begun to return to Culp's Hill. In the darkness, Steuart's men pulled back only slightly to the slopes of lower Culp's Hill over your right shoulder. The fighting on this front ended for now.

Who Fought Here?

C.S.A.: Brigadier General George H. Steuart's 2,121-man brigade, Johnson's division, Ewell's Second Corps, included the 1st Maryland Battalion; the 1st and 3rd North Carolina; and the 10th, 23rd, and 37th Virginia.

    U.S.: The 137th and 149th New York of Brigadier General George S. Greene's brigade, Geary's division, XII Corps, served here.

Who Commanded Here?

Brigadier General George Sears Greene (1801–99), a Rhode Islander, graduated from the U.S. Military Academy, finishing second in the class of 1823 and commissioning into the artillery. His talent for engineering, however, kept him at the Military Academy as an instructor in that department. He resigned in 1836 to work full-time as a civil engineer. He was working on the reservoir in Central Park when the Civil War broke out, and he reentered military service as colonel of the 60th New York Infantry. He became a brigadier general in April 1862 and commanded a brigade ably in 1862 and 1863. As one of his men wrote of Greene, he was "about sixty years old, thick set, five feet ten inches high, dark complexioned, iron-gray hair, full gray beard and mustache, gruff in manner and stern in appearance, but with all an excellent officer, and under a rough exterior possessing a kind heart. In the end the men learned to love and respect him as much as in the beginning they feared him."[9] After Gettysburg, Greene went west with the XII Corps, but he suffered a severe facial wound at the Battle of Wauhatchie in October 1863 and did not return to active field duty until 1865. After the war ended, he returned to the engineering profession and thrived until his death in 1899, when he was the oldest living graduate of West Point.

Brigadier General George S. Greene, U.S.A. (USAMHI)

    Brigadier General George Hume Steuart (1828–1903), a Baltimorean by birth, graduated from the U.S. Military Academy at age nineteen in 1848 as a brevet second lieutenant in the 2nd Dragoons. He had risen to the rank of captain in the 1st U.S. Cavalry when he resigned on April 19, 1861, and became lieutenant colonel of the 1st Maryland Infantry, C.S.A. Steuart received a promotion to brigadier general in March 1862. He took over the brigade he led at Gettysburg just at the start of the campaign; most of his men did not know him well. As one of his brigade surgeons quickly realized, however, "General Steuart was an excellent organizer and disciplinarian. . . and in his new position gave great attention to the physical well-being of man and beast. His camps were always models of cleanliness, and his horses and mules were always in good condition, his men well clothed, and the greatest order prevailed in everything." On May 12, 1864, like Allegheny Johnson, Steuart was captured at the "Mule Shoe" at Spotsylvania; after his exchange, he ended the war in command of the Virginia brigade led by Armistead here at Gettysburg. He lived on his farm in Anne Arundel County and remained active in the Maryland division of the United Confederate Veterans until his death.[10]

Who Fell Here?

In Steuart's brigade, the 1st Maryland Battalion lost 189 of its 400 men; the 1st North Carolina lost 151 of its 377 men; the 3rd North Carolina lost 218 of its 548 men; the 10th Virginia lost 77 of its 275 men; the 23rd Virginia lost 35 of its 251 men; and the 37th Virginia lost 54 killed and wounded, plus an unknown number of captured and missing—for a brigade loss of approximately 34.2 percent.

In Greene's brigade, the 137th New York lost 137 of its 423 men, along with 55 of the 297 men in the 149th New York. Greene's brigade suffered a total loss of 21.3 percent.

All of these units also participated in the fight on the morning of July 3; these numbers reflect casualties suffered in both engagements.

Individual vignettes. Edward J. Garrison enlisted in June 1861 in Wilmington, joining Company F of the 3rd North Carolina Infantry. Captain William Parsley, later his regimental commander, enrolled him. The twenty-one-year-old apparently showed promise as a soldier from the very start. When his company mustered in, Garrison already held the position of third sergeant. By the summer of 1862, he had been promoted to his company's first sergeant. During the Battle of Mechanicsville, the 3rd North Carolina took heavy losses; Garrison himself numbered among the wounded. When he returned to ranks, he drew the two months' pay due him—the princely sum of $40. His fiscal prospects almost immediately improved, however, because upon his rejoining his company, he received an appointment as its second lieutenant. On December 10, 1862, he was promoted to first lieutenant. On July 2, 1862, in the night attack against the 137th New York on lower Culp's Hill, First Lieutenant Edward J. Garrison was killed in action.[11]

Private John Carnine of Binghamton was among the oldest soldiers in the 137th New York Infantry. When he enlisted in Company E on August 22, he claimed to be forty-five years old. His eighteen-year-old son, Morris, enlisted the same day in the same company. The year 1863 was not kind to the Carnine family. Young Morris was captured at the Battle of Chancellorsville. Fortunately, he was paroled the next month, but the experience broke his health, and he had to be discharged from military service. His father soldiered on, however, but at Gettysburg on July 2, Private John Carnine was killed in action on Culp's Hill. Back home in New York, John's widow, Lucinda, continued to care for their fifteen-year-old daughter, but she did not apply for a pension until 1865, when she was awarded the standard $8 monthly sum. At that time, it was revealed that Lucinda was fifty-eight years old, and she produced irrefutable evidence that she and John had married on February 25, 1831. If Private John Carnine really were forty-five years old when he enlisted, then he apparently had married Lucinda when he was only thirteen! Very young soldiers usually lied about their age to reach the minimum enlistment age of eighteen; it is likely that Private John Carnine lied about his age to keep from being rejected for being too old. Private Carnine rests in the Soldiers' National Cemetery in grave B-27 of the New York plot.[12]

Who Lived Here?

Culp's Hill takes its name from the Culp (originally Kolb) family, which had owned the property on Hanover Road just outside Gettysburg since 1737. At the time of the Battle of Gettysburg, Henry Culp, the grandson of the original title holder, owned the property, which included a sturdy two-story brick house, a bank barn, a spring house, a smokehouse, and a woodshed. Their family ultimately included eight children. The location of the Culp farm relative to the fighting on the Confederate left flank on July 2 and 3, as well as the size of its barn, made its use as a hospital inevitable. One soldier certainly not treated there was Private Wesley Culp of the 2nd Virginia Infantry, who, despite the frequently told story that he was killed on Culp's Hill, almost certainly fell on skirmish duty elsewhere on the battlefield. On June 1, 1869, Henry Culp sold a thirty-one-acre tract of his land—the upper part of Culp's Hill that included the breastworks built by Brigadier General George S. Greene's New York brigade—to the Gettysburg Battlefield Memorial Association early in the effort to preserve key sites on the battlefield.[13]

What Did They Say about It Later?

Confederate Major W. W. Goldsborough, a Marylander, later recalled the following:

> Having acquired some knowledge of the country in my youth, and knowing the Baltimore turnpike was but some four or five hundred yards distant, I ordered Captain John W. Torsch to take one of his most reliable men and feel his way through the darkness until he reached the [Baltimore] turnpike, unless he encountered the enemy in the meantime. This Captain Torsch did, and reported to me that he had been so close to the turnpike that he was able to see the wagons

in motion. This satisfied me that we were not only on their flank but in the rear of the enemy's right. This information I imparted to General Edward Johnson in person a very short time after.

Johnson did nothing with that information and instead continued his frontal assaults on Greene's line rather than outflanking them. For several reasons, then, Goldsborough concluded: "But, then, General Johnson was not a Stonewall Jackson."[14] Similarly, Randolph H. McKim, who served on General Steuart's staff during the battle, realized that his brigade had come "within a few hundred yards of the Baltimore turnpike. . . . Its capture was a breach in the enemy's line through which troops might have been poured and the strong position of Cemetery Hill rendered untenable." He found entirely credible historian William Swinton's assessment that Steuart had reached "*a position which, if held by him, would enable him to take Meade's entire line in reverse.*" Unlike Goldsborough, however, Reverend McKim did not point the finger of individual blame at Johnson or any other single commander. He simply concluded: "It is only in keeping with the haphazard character of the whole battle that the capture of a point of such strategic importance should not have been taken advantage of by the Confederates."[15]

Driving directions to the next stop: Drive down the hill following the sweeping curves of Slocum Avenue. Where the road splits at the prominent statue of General John W. Geary, take the left fork (Williams Avenue). At the next stop sign (0.3 miles), turn left, then park in the turnout on your immediate right with the equestrian statue of Major General Henry W. Slocum on your left and the wayside exhibit and National Park Service sign designating Auto Tour Stop 14 on your right.

STOP 26. STEVENS'S KNOLL

Orientation

Stand in front of the informational wayside that addresses the fighting on East Cemetery Hill (Stop 27). Turn to the right and look out over the open fields.

What Happened Here?

This small knob of high ground was known locally as McKenzie's Hill for the owner of the land. It takes its current name from Captain Greenleaf Stevens, commander of the 5th Maine Battery posted here during the battle; the earthworks protecting its guns are behind you and stretch up and beyond Major General Henry W. Slocum's equestrian monument to your right. The 33rd Massachusetts of Howard's XI Corps protected the left flank of the battery; its low and very plain regimental monument is visible over your left shoulder at the intersection with the park road that runs along the base of East Cemetery Hill. To support the right flank of the battery, the Iron Brigade from the I Corps deployed on the slope to your right front; the remnant of the 24th Michigan that lost so heavily in Herbst's Woods on July 1 held the left end of the brigade line nearest the battery.

You first met Stevens's 5th Maine Battery on Seminary Ridge at Stop 13, where it formed part of the I Corps massed battery. After the withdrawal through Gettysburg late on July 1, the battery took position here. The gunners built the earthworks protecting the cannons during the night. Early on July 2, Captain Stevens fell wounded, hit by a random round from the direction of the town. Lieutenant Edward N. Whittier succeeded to command of the 5th Maine Battery for the rest of the battle.

The view from Stevens's Knoll toward the town of Gettysburg.

Lieutenant Edward N. Whittier, 5th Maine Battery, U.S.A. (USAMHI)

Late in the afternoon of July 2, because of the conformation of Culp's Hill, only the leftmost guns of the 5th Maine Battery participated in the artillery duel against Latimer's battalion on Benner's Hill. Today, tree growth makes it difficult to discern the Confederate position from this position during the summer, but when leaves are not on the trees, you may be able to spot an open ridge stretching across the middle of the thick tree line on the horizon. The exchange clearly left little impression on Whittier, who summarized the action in a single sentence: "In the afternoon, engaged at extreme range the enemy's battery."

After the artillery duel with Latimer's guns ended and the sun began to set, two brigades of Confederate infantry launched an assault on East Cemetery Hill to your left. You will explore that attack in detail at Stop 27. As part of that assault, the North Carolinians of Brigadier General Robert Hoke's brigade—under the temporary command of Colonel Isaac Avery—crossed the field in front of you, proceeding from right to left. Avery fell mortally wounded early on, however, hit in the neck by a piece of shrapnel. His brigade pressed on nonetheless through the field below, which was rocky, uneven, and cut up by stone walls. These obstacles, reported Colonel Archibald C. Godwin of the 57th North Carolina, "prevented that rapidity of movement and unity of action which might have insured success."

The Tar Heels' slow advance made them prime targets for the Maine gunners posted here. As Whittier reported, the 5th Maine Battery "enfiladed their lines, at a distance of 800 yards, with spherical case and shell, and later with solid shot and canister, expending the entire contents of the limber chests, which contained upward of 46 rounds of canister repacked from caissons."

They did not prevent the North Carolinians from reaching the Union line, however. As Godwin described, "The men now charged up the hill [to your left] with

A postwar view of East Cemetery Hill to your left taken from this position. (USAMHI-TOWER)

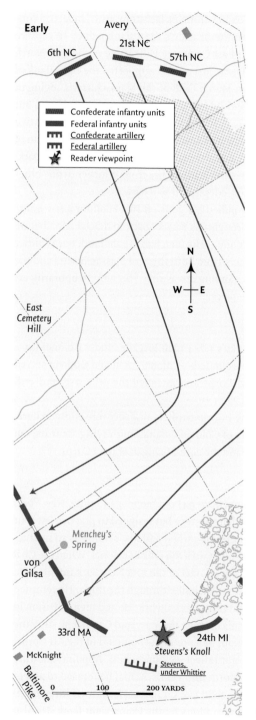

Early
Avery
6th NC
21st NC
57th NC

Confederate infantry units
Federal infantry units
Confederate artillery
Federal artillery
Reader viewpoint

N
W — E
S

East
Cemetery
Hill

Menchey's
Spring

von
Gilsa

33rd MA

McKnight

Baltimore
Pike

24th MI

Stevens's Knoll

Stevens,
under Whittier

0   100   200 YARDS

Stevens's Knoll

heroic determination, and drove the enemy from his last stone wall." Indeed, a contingent of the 6th North Carolina on the brigade's right flank helped to capture temporarily a few Union cannons on East Cemetery Hill. Some of the 57th North Carolina poured fire into the 33rd Massachusetts that supported the right flank of the 5th Maine Battery. Sergeant John March Cate of the Massachusetts regiment wrote home to his "Dearest Little Wife" on July 5: "We have had an awful fight, but We have whipped the Rebels awfully. . . . [Corporal] Jules Allen was shot dead two feet from me. [Private] Leonard Peaterson of Reading, and [Private] Wm. Meehan of Stoneham, were killed by a solid shot and were stove all to pieces (horrid)."[1] Darkness, confusion, and lack of support—not artillery fire from Whittier or any other Union battery—finally caused the Confederates to pull back.

After the fight on July 2, Whittier pulled his guns off this knoll for a few hours to refill his ammunition chests; he brought his battery back to this location before midnight, however, and prepared for July 3. His men had fought hard, but Whittier graciously acknowledged the volunteers from both the 33rd Massachusetts and the 24th Michigan who filled in for his cannoneers as they "became temporarily exhausted by the difficult service of the pieces."[2]

Who Fought Here?

C.S.A.: Brigadier General Robert Hoke's 1,244-man brigade, under Colonel Isaac Avery and—after Avery fell mortally wounded—Colonel Archibald Godwin served in Early's division of Ewell's Second Corps and included the 6th, 21st, and 57th North Carolina.

U.S.: The 5th Maine Battery of the I Corps artillery brigade were engaged here, supported by the 33rd Massachusetts of Colonel Orland Smith's brigade from von Steinwehr's division of the XI Corps and the 24th Michigan of the I Corps.

Who Commanded Here?

Major General Henry Warner Slocum (1827–94) of Onondaga County, New York, graduated from the U.S. Military Academy in 1852 but resigned to practice law four years later. Still, he maintained an interest in military affairs, serving as an instructor of artillery in the New York State Militia with the rank of colonel. When the Civil War broke out, he reentered the army as colonel of the 27th New York Infantry. He led his regiment at First Bull Run and took a bullet through the thigh. He returned to active duty as a brigadier general and commanded a brigade and then a division in the VI Corps from the Virginia peninsula through the Maryland Campaign. After the death of General Mansfield at Antietam, Slocum took command of the XII Corps. His performance at Gettysburg did not reflect well upon him. Appointed a wing commander by Meade on the march north into Pennsylvania, he refused to accept the role of tactical commander on the field late on July 1. He showed little initiative in offering options for offensive operations on the Union right flank. He also contributed little to deliberations at the "council of war" on the evening of July 2. He did complain loudly, however, in the fall of 1863 when he believed that Meade had slighted the XII Corps in his campaign and battle report. Slocum went west with his XII Corps after Gettysburg and became reinvigorated. He served well as a corps commander under Sherman during the Atlanta Campaign, the March to the Sea, and the advance through the Carolinas. He resigned in September 1865 and returned to New York, taking an active role in politics and serving in the U.S. House of Representatives for three terms as a Democrat.

Major General Henry W. Slocum, U.S.A. (USAMHI)

Who Fell Here?

C.S.A.: The casualties in Hoke's brigade will be summarized at Stop 27 in connection with their most heated combat.

U.S.: Over the course of the battle, from July 1 through July 3, the 5th Maine Battery lost 23 of its 119 men, only four of whom were killed or mortally wounded. The 33rd Massachusetts lost 45 of its 493 men in repulsing the Confederate attack on East Cemetery Hill.

Individual vignette. Private Calvin Horr, a laborer and sometime blacksmith, enlisted in Company I, 33rd Massachusetts, on August 6, 1862, in Lynnfield, Massachusetts. When he marched off to war, he left behind his wife, Mary Sullivan Horr, whom he had married in 1859, and two young children—Mary, born in April 1860, and John Elvin, born in October 1861. In late July 1863, Captain Elisha Doane, the commanding officer of Company I, wrote to Mary Horr to explain what happened to her husband near Stevens's Knoll on July 2 at Gettysburg: "He was shot in the head by a minnie ball and died in a few minutes after receiving his wound, he did not speak after he was wounded. I had him buried on the south side of the Cemitary hill near an old barn where there was three others of our regiment buried and a board with his name marked on. [It] is stuck up at the head of the grave, it was the best we could do for him." Doane gathered Horr's personal effects and sent them home to Mary; the items included "13.30 cents[,] 1 matalic cased Watch & 1 Silver Watch & 1 silk Handkerchief[,] 2 pocket Knifes & 1 watch chain." Mary Sullivan Horr was approved for a monthly pension of $8, but she gave that up in December 1864 when she remarried. Her two children, however, still remained eligible for minors' pensions, and applications were submitted in their names. They were approved for an $8 monthly pension—increased in 1866 to $10—beginning on December 5, 1864, when their mother remarried, and ending on October 18, 1877, when John turned sixteen. Captain Doane buried Horr next to Corporal Allen and Private Elijah Howe. When the Union dead were disinterred from grave sites scattered around the battlefield and brought to the Soldiers' National Cemetery, Allen, Horr, and Howe remained buried side by side in graves D-26, D-27, and D-28 in the Massachusetts plot.[3] Horr's headstone, however, reads "Calvin Howe."

Who Lived Here?

In 1860 James McKnight, a forty-two-year-old farmer, bought a five-acre plot along the Baltimore Pike for $1,200 that included this hillock. The property included a small stone house and a barn. The walls of the dark stone house can still be seen to the rear of the large white house on your left where Slocum Avenue reaches a T inter-section with the Baltimore Pike across from Evergreen Cemetery. The farm pro-vided McKnight with a home for his wife, Margaret Ann, age thirty, and their young daughter, one-year-old Jane. As the Army of the Potomac concentrated here late on July 1, McKnight reportedly stayed home to try to protect his home, but his wife and daughter joined the flood of the temporarily displaced to seek safety.[4] The barn mentioned as the final resting place of Private Calvin Horr was McKnight's barn. The McKnights did not stay on their property for very long after the battle. In April 1864 local businessman David McConaughy bought this knoll as part of the earliest efforts to preserve the Gettysburg battlefield. Its prominence and proximity to the XII Corps line on Culp's Hill made it a natural site for the location of the equestrian monument to Major General Henry W. Slocum.

What Did They Say about It Later?

The veterans of the 33rd Massachusetts on the 5th Maine's right flank held espe-cially strong memories of the battery's work on this knoll. In its regimental history, Adin B. Underwood, the former commanding officer, wrote of the evening of July 2:

> Hoke's men get up so near that the regiment starts up to use its bayonets; a rebel flag is waving almost directly over its head, when in an instant there are flashes like lightning from the muzzles of a Maine battery on the right, the roar of guns, and down drop the color and color bearer, and heaps of those brave traitors. Groans and shrieks fill the air. A fearful destruction of life! The Maine battery, Stevens', has waited with double-shotted guns till it can rake the flank of the charging column with enfilading fire, and has so mowed down an awful swath. "Good for Maine," is the shout of the Mass. men. The line in front is gone, all but the rows of dead and dying.[5]

Driving directions to the next stop: Drive forward to where the road splits and take the left fork. At the stop sign, turn right onto the Baltimore Pike (Route 97). Just over the crest of Cemetery Hill (0.3 miles), turn right into the large parking lot that is across from the Soldiers' National Cemetery and adjacent to the tall water tower. (Parking may be restricted here. If that proves to be the case, leave the lot, turn left on Baltimore Street, and park on the right, adjacent to the cemetery. Expect to feed the parking meter; parking regulations are enforced.)

STOP 27. EAST CEMETERY HILL

Orientation

Walk to the highest point on the crest of East Cemetery Hill—the equestrian monument to Major General Winfield Scott Hancock—and look across the street toward the gatehouse to Evergreen Cemetery, just as you did at Stop 1. Remember, the great value of Cemetery Hill derived from its open fields of fire; the large trees in the Soldiers' National Cemetery ahead of you, as well as the thick tree line over your right shoulder—to say nothing of the bus parking lot and blue water tower—were not part of the 1863 landscape. The major road in front of you is the Baltimore Pike, one of the Army of the Potomac's main arteries for supply, reinforcement, or withdrawal.

What Happened Here?

Both Union and Confederate generals considered Cemetery Hill to be the key terrain on the battlefield. It is perhaps somewhat surprising, then, that with the single exception of the evening of July 2, little significant combat action took place here. XI Corps troops posted on its western and northwestern slopes—the ground now covered by the Soldiers' National Cemetery to your right front, which you will visit at Stop 35—skirmished actively with Lee's men on the southern edge of Gettysburg and in the farm fields off its western slopes, but Confederate efforts to attack Cemetery Hill from the direction of the town never gained traction. The only serious effort to wrest the hill from Union hands came here on East Cemetery Hill on the evening of July 2.

Major General Winfield
Scott Hancock monument and the Evergreen
Cemetery gatehouse.

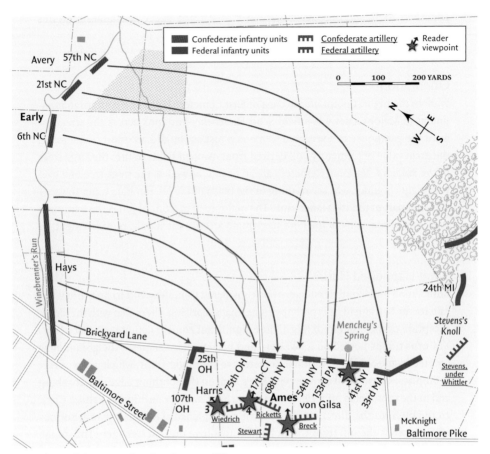

The Confederate Attack on East Cemetery Hill

Still, the profusion of monuments and cannons here shows that this hilltop rarely enjoyed quiet lulls. Late on July 1, thousands of exhausted I and XI Corps survivors arrived here, seeking their friends, their regiments, food, hospitals, and ammunition. The two prominent equestrian monuments on the hill—the one to Hancock here and, to your right, the one to Howard—recall the contentious meeting of senior commanders here late on that first afternoon. Hancock's orders to strengthen the defenses on this hill and on Culp's Hill behind you established the foundation for Meade's fishhook defense.

The best way to understand the fighting of July 2 on this ground is to break it down into its component parts. First, in addition to serving as a rallying point, East Cemetery Hill quickly became a strong Union artillery position. As part of Hancock's organizational efforts late on July 1, Colonel Charles S. Wainwright, the I Corps artillery chief, took command of the batteries here. In front of you, between

Hancock's statue and the gatehouse, are the guns of Lieutenant James Stewart's Battery B, 4th U.S. Artillery, protected by earthen lunettes and positioned to cover the approaches to the hill from the town. Now walk around to the rear of Hancock's monument and walk up to the line of cannons stretching from left to right across your front. The guns on the far left represent Captain Michael Wiedrich's Battery I, 1st New York Artillery, an XI Corps battery that spent all of July 1 here. The guns immediately in front of you represent Captain James H. Cooper's Battery B, 1st Pennsylvania Artillery, a I Corps battery whose men built their lunettes on the evening of July 1. The guns in the low ground to your right represent Captain Gilbert H. Reynolds's Consolidated Battery E and L, 1st New York Artillery, also a I Corps unit; Reynolds had fallen wounded on July 1, so Lieutenant George Breck commanded the battery in his place. Beyond Breck's battery, on a slight elevation, stand the Napoleons of Stevens's 5th Maine Battery that you saw at Stop 26. Behind Breck's battery, on the cemetery side of the Baltimore Pike, you can see the large 20-pound Parrotts of Captain Elijah D. Taft's 5th New York Battery, sent from the Artillery Reserve to strengthen this position. A second Artillery Reserve battery—Captain James F. Huntington's Battery H, 1st Ohio—also supported this position, but the gatehouse obscures your view of the guns' location.

Until 4:00 P.M. on July 2, East Cemetery Hill remained comparatively quiet, although skirmish fire took its toll. Major Joseph W. Latimer's battalion on Benner's Hill then broke that silence. Tree growth makes the crest of Benner's Hill difficult to spot. You can approximate its position, however, by locating the bluish water tower on the horizon to your far left front; the crest of Benner's Hill runs across your front to the right of and slightly below the level of the base of that tower. Immediately after the duel with Latimer, Cooper's battery in front of you was replaced by Captain R. Bruce Ricketts's Consolidated Battery F and G, 1st Pennsylvania Artillery, from the Artillery Reserve. Thus the guns ahead of you represent two batteries that served here at different times, both of which erected monuments here.

But if Latimer's cannonade was meant as a prelude to a Confederate infantry attack, nothing of consequence occurred until approximately 7:30 P.M., when the Louisiana brigade of Brigadier General Harry T. Hays and the North Carolina brigade of Colonel Isaac Avery advanced toward this position.

The best way to appreciate the East Cemetery Hill infantry fight requires you to make a circular walk that will take you to the bottom of the slope in front of you, allow you to explore the main line of the Union defense, and then return you to the top of the hill. Visitors with limited mobility or little time may wish simply to stay here at the crest and follow along as the action unfolds from right to left.

If you choose to make the terrain walk, proceed toward the stone wall to your right. A mowed path along the wall leads down to Wainwright Avenue—then called the Brickyard Lane—at the base of the hill. Look out into the open fields on the other side of the road. Across those fields, from left to right, the 6th, 21st, and 57th

North Carolina of Avery's brigade advanced from the Culp farm and wheeled toward your position. Avery's line took fire from the 5th Maine Battery on Stevens's Knoll to your right, as well as from Ricketts and Breck behind you.

You are standing where the Union defenders stood on the evening of July 2. These regiments belonged to Colonel Leopold von Gilsa's brigade, the unit that Early's Confederates had overwhelmed near Barlow's Knoll on the afternoon of July 1. Several companies of the 41st New York, von Gilsa's only fresh regiment, anchored his line to your right, while the rest of the unit deployed near the crest of the hill; the 153rd Pennsylvania, here at von Gilsa's center, divided its men the same way. The 68th and 54th New York extended von Gilsa's line to the left.

If you have made the walk down to Wainwright Avenue, proceed down the park road to your left. When you arrive at the monument to the 17th Connecticut, you have passed von Gilsa's left flank and entered the line of Brigadier General Adelbert Ames's brigade, which fought on Barlow's Knoll on July 1. Ames's men extended the XI Corps position for about another 150 yards down the lane ahead of you and then bent its line to the left, heading back up the hill perpendicular to the battle line here in the lane. Even though no large monuments mark that location, it is still worth the time to walk down the park road for 100 yards or so to appreciate the vista on your right. Today, school buildings and an athletic field fill that ground, but on July 2, 1863, these were all open fields. When Hays began his advance over this open ground, as he later reported, "my whole line became exposed to a most terrific fire from the enemy's batteries from the entire range of hills in front" of him.

If you have made the walk along Wainwright Avenue, turn around and return to the 25th and 75th Ohio joint monument. At the tree line, follow the mowed strip to the top of East Cemetery Hill to Wiedrich's battery, the first one you reach at the crest. (If you have stayed on the crest, go to the left end of the artillery line closest to the blue water tower.) Face the park road below you.

When the North Carolinians hit the base of the hill below you and to your right, the two New York regiments on von Gilsa's left flank below you broke and retreated back up the hill toward Ricketts's battery to your right. Flanking fire from some of the 41st New York and from the infantry and artillery on Stevens's Knoll slowed the Tar Heels' left flank, but it did not prevent a good number of Confederates from charging up the hill toward the batteries.

Another crisis quickly developed along the left and center of the Union line at the bottom of the hill to your front and left front. Before the fight started, Colonel Andrew Harris—in temporary command of Ames's brigade—had moved the 17th Connecticut to the extreme right of his line next to von Gilsa's left flank below you. The Connecticut regiment's move created a gap in Harris's line that nearly isolated his two Ohio units on the hillside to your left. When Hays's men hit, they quickly overwhelmed most of Harris's Ohioans. Hays reported that "few escaped, and those only in the darkness and smoke; the greater portion were no doubt made prisoners."

Along the entire base of East Cemetery Hill, only a few troops in your immediate front continued to hold.

Here on the crest, the gunners could no longer depress their muzzles low enough to fire effectively at enemy troops coming up the hill toward them. Additionally, as Hays realized, "owing to the darkness of the evening, now verging into night, and the deep obscurity afforded by the smoke of the firing, our exact locality could not be discovered by the enemy's gunners, and we thus escaped what in the full light of day could have been nothing else than horrible slaughter."

Colonel Andrew Harris, 75th Ohio, U.S.A. (USAMHI)

Here at Wiedrich's battery, the Louisiana troops rushed in among the guns. Other Louisianans and some of the 6th North Carolina from Avery's brigade charged on Ricketts's cannons to your right. As Major Samuel Tate of the Tar Heel unit reported in a letter to Governor Zebulon Vance after the fight, "75 North Carolinians of the Sixth Regiment and 12 Louisianians of Hays' brigade scaled the walls, and planted the colors of the Sixth North Carolina and Ninth Louisiana on the guns." Tate credited the artillerymen with putting up a good fight, noting that they "stood with a tenacity never before displayed by them." But, as Captain Ricketts himself reported, the Confederates "succeeded in capturing and spiking my left piece."

But Southern success was short-lived. Here in Wiedrich's battery, Major Thomas W. Osborn reported, "the cannoneers rallied with the infantry, and, seizing upon any weapons they could reach, threw themselves upon the enemy, and assisted to drive them back." In Ricketts's battery to your right, "The cannoneers fought them hand to hand with handspikes, rammers, and pistols, and succeeded in checking them." In addition to the stalwart efforts of the original defenders, the firefight on East Cemetery Hill drew immediate support from nearby commands. Right behind you, monuments to the 73rd Pennsylvania and the 134th New York of Colonel Charles Coster's brigade—as well as another marker nearby to the 27th Pennsylvania of the same brigade—represent XI Corps reinforcements sent to repulse the attackers. A low marker near the stone wall to your left salutes the service of the 106th Pennsylvania, sent here from Brigadier General Alexander Webb's brigade from the II Corps.

Complete your circle by walking back toward General Hancock's statue. Stop at the break in the stone wall just before reaching the monument and face the base of the hill once more. The regimental markers near you—including the soldier standing on top of the 7th West Virginia monument and the solid thick obelisk of the 14th Indiana—represent the most notable reinforcement of East Cemetery Hill. When noise of the fight reached General Hancock on Cemetery Ridge, he immediately sent over the fresh II Corps brigade of Colonel Samuel S. Carroll. Their advance took them directly through Evergreen Cemetery, and they arrived in the area of the gatehouse as darkness fell and while the Louisiana troops still contested possession of Wiedrich's and Ricketts's guns here. Carroll found his first glimpse of the battle-field confounding, reporting that "it being perfectly dark, and with no guide, I had to find the enemy's line entirely by their fire." The added firepower from the II Corps regiments made a difference.

Hays's and Avery's men slowly withdrew back to the edge of town. Ricketts's and Wiedrich's men retook possession of their guns. Ewell's effort to take East Cemetery Hill had come too late and with too little power to crush the key to Meade's fishhook defense. As Ames summed up the entire experience with eloquent understatement: "An attempt was made to carry the position we held, but the enemy was repulsed with loss."[1]

Who Fought Here?

C.S.A.: You met Hays's and Avery's brigades at Stop 8.

U.S.: You met Ames's and von Gilsa's brigades at Stop 8. Colonel Samuel S. Carroll's brigade of Alexander Hays's division in Hancock's II Corps included the 14th Indiana, the 4th Ohio, and the 7th West Virginia; the 8th Ohio of this brigade did not serve here. The 33rd Massachusetts of Smith's brigade in von Steinwehr's division of Howard's XI Corps also fought here. The artillery was introduced at Stop 24.

Who Commanded Here?

Brigadier General Harry Thompson Hays (1820–76), born in Wilson County, Tennessee, and raised by an uncle in Mississippi, graduated from St. Mary's College in Baltimore, Maryland. He studied law and opened a practice in New Orleans, taking time off to serve in the Mexican War in the 5th Louisiana Infantry. At the start of the Civil War, he entered Confederate service as a colonel of the 7th Louisiana Infantry, seeing action at First Manassas and in Jackson's Shenandoah Valley Campaign in 1862. Wounded in action at the Battle of Port Republic, Hays returned to duty on the day of the Battle of Antietam and continued in command of the 1st Louisiana brigade at Fredericksburg, Chancellorsville, Gettysburg, the Wilderness, and Spotsylvania. Wounded at that last battle, he subsequently drew an assignment to round up absentees in the trans-Mississippi theater, where he served until the war's end. Returning to New Orleans after the war, Hays practiced law until his death from Bright's disease (nephritis) in 1876.

Brigadier General Harry T. Hays, C.S.A. (USAMHI)

Colonel Samuel Sprigg Carroll (1832–93) was born in the District of Columbia, where his father served as a clerk for the U.S. Supreme Court. He graduated from West Point in 1856, ranking forty-fourth in a class of forty-nine cadets. After routine antebellum assignments, he became colonel of the 8th Ohio Infantry in December 1861. He served with his regiment in the Shenandoah valley in 1862 and took command of a brigade in the II Corps in the spring of 1863. He performed superbly on the evening of July 2 at Gettysburg, leading his men into a rare night fight that helped to close the breach in the XI Corps line on East Cemetery Hill. As one of his men wrote, "Our general (he is only a colonel commanding, although a graduate of West Point . . .), in the darkness and confusion, on unknown ground, and amidst a terrible fire, moved with perfect coolness, made his voice heard above the whole uproar, disposed his men with as much skill as if on familiar ground and in open day, and showed himself, as he always does, a thorough soldier, and an unsurpassed commander of men." Carroll suffered several wounds over the course of the war, the most damaging at Spotsylvania; he received his promotion to brigadier general in May 1864, shortly after receiving that injury. He retired from the U.S. Army in 1869—in part because of increasing disability brought on by his wounds—and made his home in Washington, D.C.[2]

Who Fell Here?

C.S.A.: Hays's brigade lost 67 of the 196 men in the 5th Louisiana, 61 of the 218 men in the 6th Louisiana, 58 of the 235 men in the 7th Louisiana, 75 of the 296 men in the 8th Louisiana, and 73 of the 347 men in the 9th Louisiana—for a brigade loss of 26.0 percent (some lost on July 1). Avery's brigade lost 208 of the 509 men in the 6th North Carolina, 139 of the 436 men in the 21st North Carolina, and 65 of the 297 men in the 57th North Carolina—for a brigade loss of 33.1 percent (some lost on July 1).

U.S.: Ames's brigade lost 197 of the 386 men in the 17th Connecticut, 184 of the 220 men in the 25th Ohio, 186 of the 269 men in the 75th Ohio, and 211 of the 458 men in the 107th Ohio—for a brigade loss of 58.2 percent (many lost on July 1). Von Gilsa's brigade lost 75 of the 218 men in the 41st New York, 102 of the 189 men in the 54th New York, 138 of the 230 men in the 68th New York, and a full 211 of 497 men in the 153rd Pennsylvania—for a brigade loss of 46.4 percent (much of it lost on July 1). Carroll's brigade lost 31 of the 191 men in the 14th Indiana, 31 of the 299 men in the 4th Ohio, and 47 of the 235 men in the 7th West Virginia. The 33rd Massachusetts lost 45 of its 491 men.

Individual vignettes. Alpheus S. McVicker, a single farmer from the Morgantown area, left his twenty acres to muster into military service with Company E of the 7th Virginia Infantry, U.S.A., on July 31, 1861, and soon rose to the rank of sergeant. In June 1863, when West Virginia won admission to statehood, his unit became the 7th West Virginia Infantry. While his record is silent about the circumstances of his fatal injury, Sergeant McVicker's regiment in Carroll's brigade in Hancock's II Corps served in the relief of East Cemetery Hill on the evening of July 2. During the fighting, McVicker fell badly wounded. He developed a high fever that did not respond to treatment, and he died of his injuries and the resulting feverishness on July 24. His fifty-four-year-old widowed mother, Mary, living in a "rough log house" on three acres of land near Morgantown, submitted a claim for a mother's pension in August, making her mark rather than signing her signature. Those who knew the poor quality of her late son's land affirmed that she could not expect to make money from renting it out, and she quickly won approval for her $8 monthly payment. Sergeant McVicker's remains do not rest in the Soldiers' National Cemetery; his remains can be found in the soldiers' plot in the Evergreen Cemetery on the other side of the military burial ground's iron fences.[3]

Private Horthere Fontenot, a nineteen-year-old unmarried farmer who listed his nearest post office as Flat Town, Louisiana, enlisted in Opelousas in Company F of the 8th Louisiana Infantry on March 30, 1862. He did not take well to the soldier's life, spending much time absent from ranks in the hospital. Indeed, to restore his health, the military doctors in Virginia put him on medical leave during the early months of 1863 and sent him home on furlough to Louisiana. He returned to the army and marched north into Pennsylvania. On the evening of July 2, while storming East Cemetery Hill, Private Fontenot took a bullet in the thigh. Admitted to a Confederate field hospital sometime after midnight, he proved to be too badly wounded to move when Lee's army began its withdrawal to Virginia. Thus he became a prisoner of war. Private Fontenot's wound developed gangrene, and the surgeons could not stop its spread. He died at a field hospital on July 12. Private Fontenot's records show that at the time of his death, the army owed him the relatively large sum of $253.00, but no records show any surviving family member claiming the funds.[4]

Who Lived Here?

The Confederates crossed the Henry Culp farm to assault this position, but the scene of the hardest fighting here on East Cemetery Hill took place on the property of two local residents, Peter Raffensperger and Edward Menchey. Raffensperger, a well-to-do farmer born in 1796, owned the land at the summit of the hill where Union artillerymen built lunettes around their guns; indeed, before the establishment of the Evergreen Cemetery, some locals referred to this elevation as Raffensperger Hill. Raffensperger died on June 22, 1865, so his executors acted as agents on behalf of his widow, Rebecca, to obtain compensation for all damages. As late as the 1880s, they still had under consideration with the U.S. Army quartermaster general a very specific claim for a settlement to cover a long list of items purported to have been used or destroyed by the men of General Howard's XI Corps. Ultimately, the army rejected it.

Edward Menchey owned the out lot between Raffensperger's two properties on East Cemetery Hill—roughly the strip of ground where Lieutenant Brock's guns sit—that extended to the bottom of the slope and included a spring that still bears his name. A potter by trade, he built a house in town for his wife, Mary, and his growing family; it included a built-in kiln for firing his goods. Menchey tried at least three times to obtain some type of compensation for his losses. He claimed very specifically that his property suffered greatly after "the 1st Corps took possession of Cemetery Hill, on which the crops were growing on July 1, 1863," and he accused von Steinwehr's division of appropriating forage to feed their horses. When he died in 1882, he still had an unsettled claim with the U.S. Army's quartermaster general for $661.12 to cover damage to 4 acres of corn, 2 acres of oats, 2 acres of clover and timothy, 1½ acres of wheat, and 984 feet of board fencing taken by XI Corps troops. His claim, like Raffensperger's, was rejected. David McConaughy bought Menchey's land in the fall of 1863 and Raffensperger's acres in the spring of 1864 to start the preservation of the Gettysburg battlefield.[5]

What Did They Say about It Later?

In the immediate aftermath of the battle, Southern correspondents and editors bestowed far more attention and admiration upon the Louisiana troops for their effort to storm East Cemetery Hill than they accorded Hoke's North Carolina regiments that Colonel Avery led into the battle.

Unfortunately for them, the North Carolinians practically disappeared from the history books. The Louisiana volume of the widely respected *Confederate Military History* series stated forthrightly that on East Cemetery Hill, "The summit was gained and with a rush along the whole line, Hays' men captured several pieces of artillery, four stand of colors and still more prisoners. Meanwhile, the North Carolinians, encountering stone wall after stone wall, had lost their commander, Colonel Avery, and not more than 40 or 50 were together in the last charge. The Louisianians, alone at the summit of Cemetery hill in the face of Howard's corps," stood unsupported against massive Union reinforcement and "were forced to fall back in order to a stone wall at the foot of the ridge."[6] Many accounts of postwar reunions in the 1880s featured meetings on Cemetery Hill between Union veterans and "Louisiana Tigers" who fought them there, with not a Tar Heel to be found.

Finally, Judge A. C. Avery, a kinsman of the slain Tar Heel brigade commander, determined that the controversy "be settled without further delay, by admitting that Hays' (Louisiana) and Avery's (North Carolina) Brigades are entitled to share the glory equally." To that end, he asked General Jubal Early, Hays's and Avery's division commander, for his verdict. Early replied: "Of course the Sixth North Carolina Regiment entered the works, but it was along with the rest of the Brigade. Hays' Brigade brought off four battle flags and one hundred prisoners captured from the enemy. The conduct of Hoke's Brigade, under Colonel Avery, was all that could be expected of it." He then referred Avery to the recently published Gettysburg volumes of the *Official Records of the Union and Confederate Armies* to see for himself that, despite all the storytelling and claiming of laurels, the historical record had not ignored the North Carolina brigade.

Colonel Isaac E. Avery, C.S.A., fell mortally wounded here on July 2. (Clark)

Judge Avery clearly respected Early's answer, expressing his hope that any future Louisianan "who claimed a monopoly of the honor of storming Cemetery Ridge for Louisiana will calmly examine the 'War Records' and listen to proof and reason."[7]

Driving directions to the next stop: Exit the parking lot and turn left onto Baltimore Pike (Route 97). Drive south 0.7 miles and turn right onto Hunt Avenue (the right turn prior to the traffic light ahead of you). Drive 0.5 miles and park just before the stop sign in the overflow parking lot on your right. Carefully walk across Taneytown Road to the small white house opposite the stop sign.

Day Two Conclusion

Nightfall finally ended the day's most active fighting on Thursday, July 2, but both armies spent a restless night. Field hospitals behind the lines of each army hummed with activity, as overworked surgeons made initial decisions about who might be saved by immediate medical intervention, who could wait for treatment, and, in many cases, who could not be helped at all.

Surgeon Thomas Fanning Wood of the 3rd North Carolina Infantry in Brigadier General George H. Steuart's brigade set up an aid station not far behind the line of battle at a farm near the base of Culp's Hill. Wood witnessed the exchange between Latimer's battalion and the Union guns in the cemetery, noting that "it is not easy to describe such a scene, but in this mountainous country it was grand." Casualties from Steuart's brigade soon began to arrive, and, as Wood recalled, he and his fellow surgeons "were kept busy with the wounded, day and night, until we were exhausted." He found that his own regiment, the 3rd North Carolina, "had the largest number of wounded, and the Maryland Regt. next. I administered to Col. [James R.] Herbert and Maj. [W. W.] Goldsborough of the Maryland Regt. on the field and also Genl. J. M. Jones, who were all wounded and were sent away to the rear in an ambulance." The scene replicated itself many times over behind the lines of both armies that night, as friends of the fallen attempted to find their wounded comrades who might be saved and brought them to the hospitals for care.[1] In some locations, such as in the Wheatfield or on the slopes of Little Round Top, where the rival lines rested only a few hundred yards apart, such humanitarian gestures sometimes ended in death or injury to the well-intentioned rescuers, and most such activity ceased.

General Lee and General Meade assessed their situations and counted their losses after the intense few hours of combat in the late afternoon and early evening of July 2. At his headquarters along the Chambersburg Road near the seminary, General Lee now knew that his entire Army of Northern Virginia had arrived at Gettysburg. Major General George E. Pickett's division, the last element of Longstreet's First Corps, had arrived late that afternoon and awaited orders for the next day. General J. E. B. Stuart and his cavalry also returned to the main army that afternoon; the meeting between Stuart and his commanding officer generally has been characterized as cool.

Lee did not call his corps commanders to his headquarters on the evening of July 2 to deliver their reports of the day's action in person. Nor did he solicit their input on plans for July 3. Lee already had made up his mind on that score. As he wrote in his report about the July 2 fighting, "The result of this day's operations induced the belief that, with proper concert of action, and with the increased support that the positions gained on the right [down toward the Peach Orchard] would enable the artillery to render the assaulting columns, we should ultimately succeed, and it was accordingly determined to continue the attack" on July 3. Lee continued: "The general plan was unchanged. Longstreet, re-enforced by Pickett's three brigades . . . was ordered to attack the next morning, and General Ewell was directed to assail the enemy's right at the same time. The latter, during the night, re-enforced General [Edward] Johnson with two brigades from Rodes' and one from Early's division."[2]

The Army of the Potomac adjusted its lines, too. The arrival of Major General John Sedgwick's VI Corps late in the afternoon on July 2 meant that Meade's entire army had closed on Gettysburg as well. The presence of fresh troops made it possible for Meade to strengthen his line in key areas. Elements of the V Corps, especially the 20th Maine and elements of the Pennsylvania Reserves, moved from Little Round Top to occupy Round Top after nightfall. Several brigades of VI Corps troops went into line on the southern end of Cemetery Ridge, filling the gap originally assigned to Sickles's battered III Corps. Meade sent two brigades of VI Corps troops to deploy astride the Taneytown Road behind the Round Tops facing south; if Longstreet attempted to pass around to the rear of the Round Tops on July 3—an idea he still considered—he would have found Union troops in line of battle and reinforced by artillery waiting for him. Still more VI Corps troops remained in reserve, ready to respond to any crisis.

Meade followed a different course than Lee, calling all of his corps commanders to his headquarters at the Leister house for a midnight meeting after the fighting on July 2 ended. Stop 28 will take you to the Leister house to consider the issues that General Meade and his senior subordinates discussed there.

The Third Day of Battle

July 3, 1863

The Leister house, Meade's headquarters and site of his "council of war."

7 Commanders Consider— and Reconsider—Their Options

STOP 28. MEADE'S HEADQUARTERS

Orientation

Stand on the front porch of the small white house and look out into the yard. Taney-town Road passes the left side of the house, and you are looking south. Cemetery Hill is directly behind you; this house sits at the southern base of the hill. The rise to your right is Cemetery Ridge, the main Union battle line of July 2 and 3.

What Happened Here?

Late in the evening of July 2, Meade summoned together his senior commanders. Often styled a "council of war," the meeting was not nearly as formal or its decisions as binding as the label sometimes suggests. At the time of the gathering, Meade had commanded his army for only five days, two of them locked in battle. More than anything, he needed to assess the readiness of the individual corps and the fighting spirit of his senior leaders.

Meade's "council of war" late on July 2. (USAMHI)

Little space remained in the small house once the assemblage gathered. Major General John Newton represented the I Corps, succeeding the slain General Reynolds; he replaced Doubleday, whom Meade had relieved late on July 1. Brigadier General John Gibbon and Major General David B. Birney represented the II and III Corps, respectively; both men now answered directly to Major General Winfield S. Hancock of the II Corps—also present—to whom Meade had given command authority over both organizations. General George Sykes represented the V Corps, General John Sedgwick attended for the VI Corps, and General Oliver O. Howard participated for the XI Corps. The XII Corps had two representatives present: its formal commander, Major General Henry W. Slocum, acting in his temporary assignment as wing commander; and acting corps commander Brigadier General Alpheus Williams. With the addition of Brigadier General Seth Williams, the adjutant general of the Army of the Potomac; its chief of staff, Major General Daniel Butterfield; and its chief engineer, Brigadier General Gouverneur K. Warren, the generals filled the small room. Warren, slightly wounded and exhausted from the day's exertions, soon fell asleep in the corner.

After much discussion of the events of the past two days—exchanges in which Meade largely took no active role—General Butterfield suggested a polling of the assemblage to get a sense of their views. The first question was asked: "Under existing circumstances, is it advisable for this army to remain in its present position, or to retire to another nearer its base of supplies?" As practice dictated, the junior officer present voted first, so as not to be swayed by the opinions of his superiors. Thus Butterfield recorded General Gibbon's vote: "Correct position of the army, but would not retreat." All the other generals concurred.

The second question was asked: "It being determined to remain in present position, shall the army attack or wait [for] the attack of the enemy?" Gibbon asserted that he considered the Union army "in no condition to attack," a position in which all the other senior officers generally concurred—although Howard imposed a time limit, voting to "wait attack until 4 p.m. to-morrow," and Hancock added the condition "unless our communications are cut."

The third question was asked: "If we wait [for an] attack, how long?" Gibbon voted to wait until Lee moved, but Williams, Birney, Sykes, and Sedgwick limited the waiting period to only one day. General Newton raised a concern, warning: "If we wait, it will give them a chance to cut our line." Howard took a more active position, arguing that "if [they] don't attack, attack them." "Can't wait long," Hancock advised; "can't be idle." Slocum answered all three questions the same way: "Stay and fight it out."[1] Once each officer had expressed his opinions, Meade quietly validated the group's views, saying simply: "Such then is the decision."

As the meeting wound down, Meade chatted briefly with General Gibbon, whose division held the center of the Union line on Cemetery Ridge, not far from army headquarters. "Gibbon, if Lee attacks me to-morrow it will be on your front," the

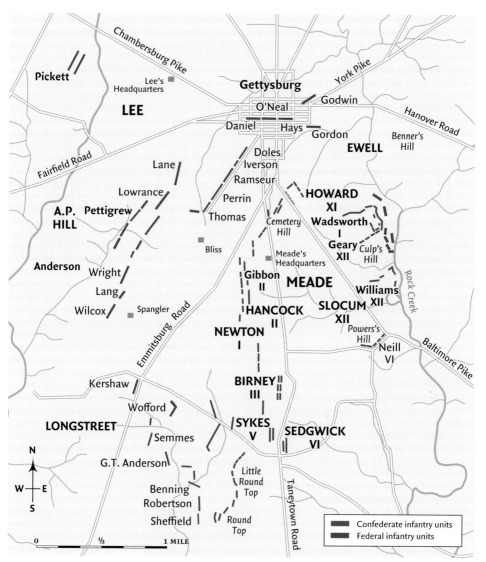

Pickett

Chambersburg Pike

Lee's
Headquarters

Gettysburg

York Pike

Godwin

Hanover Road

LEE

O'Neal

Daniel

Hays

Gordon

Benner's
Hill

Fairfield Road

Lane

Doles

Iverson

EWELL

Lowrance

Ramseur

**A.P.
HILL**

Pettigrew

Perrin

Thomas

**HOWARD
XI**

**Wadsworth
I**

Cemetery
Hill

Bliss

Meade's
Headquarters

**Geary
XII**

Culp's
Hill

Anderson

Wright

**Gibbon
II**

MEADE

Williams XII

Rock Creek

Lang

Wilcox

Spangler

**HANCOCK
II**

**SLOCUM
XII**

Emmitsburg Road

**NEWTON
I**

Powers's
Hill

**Neill
VI**

Baltimore Pike

Kershaw

**BIRNEY
III**

Wofford

LONGSTREET

Semmes

**SYKES
V**

**SEDGWICK
VI**

N

W   E

S

G.T. Anderson

Little
Round
Top

Benning

Taneytown Road

Robertson

Sheffield

Round
Top

Confederate infantry units

Federal infantry units

0   ½   1 MILE

Troop Deployments at about Midnight on July 3 at the Time Meade Convened his "Council of War"

commander said. Gibbon asked Meade why he seemed so certain. Meade pointed out that Lee had tested both of his flanks on July 2 and failed to break them; he had to try to break the center next. "Well, general, I hope he does, and if he does, we shall whip him," Gibbon assured Meade. In retrospect, it appears that Meade had divined Lee's attack plan for July 3, since Gibbon's division held that portion of the line up on Cemetery Ridge to your right front where Pickett's Charge made its deepest penetration.[2]

The Leister house became the scene of great destruction on July 3 during the Confederate early-afternoon artillery bombardment preceding Pickett's Charge. As a piece in the *New York Tribune* recounted it: "Gen. Meade's headquarters . . . received during the battle [of July 3] flying visits from thousands of monster shells, round shot, and rifle balls; but although almost every shell exploded all along the road on which the small frame building occupied by him was situated, neither himself nor any of his staff were injured. Men and horses passing along the road were torn to fragments by shells, but Gen. Meade seemed regardless of his personal safety, and was riding along the lines, attended by two orderlies."

The account illustrates quite accurately the damage caused to the Union rear area by the Confederate shelling, but it errs in two important regards. In the end, the danger forced Meade to transfer his headquarters flag to General Slocum's position at the base of Powers's Hill, and, despite the reassurance of the correspondent, Meade's staff did not escape unscathed. Another account in the same issue of the *Tribune* confirmed that "Gen. Butterfield was struck in the breast, and it is feared internally injured, by a piece of shell which exploded in the building. Lieut-Col. Joseph Dickinson of the staff had his left arm perforated by a flying fragment of shell, and it seemed a miracle that no greater damage was done to life or limb." Adjutant General Seth Williams also suffered a slight wound. Photos of Meade's headquarters taken right after the battle confirm the observation of a war correspondent who wrote that "of staff officers' horses sixteen were killed out of thirty-two in a few minutes by the enemy's shells."[3]

When Meade returned to the area after the shelling stopped, doctors already had transformed army headquarters into a field hospital, forcing the command center to move to another location down the Taneytown Road.

Who Fought Here?

Meade's staff included Major General Daniel Butterfield, chief of staff; Major General Alfred Pleasonton, chief of cavalry; Brigadier General Seth Williams, adjutant general; Brigadier General Marsena Patrick, provost marshal; Brigadier General Edmund Schriver, inspector general; Brigadier General Gouverneur K. Warren, chief engineer; Brigadier General Henry J. Hunt, chief of artillery; Brigadier General Rufus Ingalls, chief quartermaster; Colonel Henry F. Clarke, chief commissary of subsistence; Lieutenant Colonel Joseph Dickinson, assistant adjutant general; Major D. W. Flagler, chief ordnance officer; Major Jonathan Letterman, chief medical officer; Captain Lemuel B. Norton, chief signal officer; Captain George Meade Jr., aide-de-camp (and no doubt there were additional officers assigned to this duty); and Lieutenant John Edie, acting chief ordnance officer.

Who Commanded Here?

Major General Daniel Butterfield (1831–1901), of Utica, New York, enjoyed a privileged youth. The scion of a wealthy family, he graduated from Union College at age eighteen, studied law, traveled extensively, and entered the family business. When the Civil War broke out, Butterfield, without any great evidence of extensive military training, became colonel of the 12th New York Infantry. On September 7, 1861, he received a promotion to brigadier general and took command of a brigade in the V Corps. On the Virginia peninsula, he became well known throughout the Army of the Potomac for creating a system of bugle calls for his own brigade and is accorded credit for the bugle call "Taps." When General Hooker became commander of the Army of the Potomac, he named Butterfield as his chief of staff. The pressure of Lee's invasion of Pennsylvania forced a disgruntled Butterfield to continue in that position under General Meade after Hooker's relief. In many ways, he became Meade's implacable foe, allying himself with General Daniel E. Sickles to diminish Meade's reputation and achievements; Butterfield, more than anyone else, tried to portray Meade as reluctant to stand and fight at Gettysburg and claimed that Meade had ordered him to prepare instructions for a retreat. As Meade wrote to General Gibbon in the midst of this controversy and congressional hearings regarding Meade's actions at Gettysburg: "As true as there is a God in Heaven before whom I believe all men will be judged, and the secrets of this world made known I do solemnly aver I have not the remotest remembrance of having given Butterfield any such direction"; and he worried that his chief of staff, "in his hellish ingenuity to rob me of my reputation may, indeed, must, have something to go upon." But the hearings ended with no rebuke to Meade. Soon after Gettysburg, Meade replaced Butterfield, who transferred out west to rejoin Hooker. When Butterfield died in 1901, his family received permission to bury him at West Point, an honor extended to very few nongraduates.[4]

Major General Daniel Butterfield, U.S.A., Meade's chief of staff. (USAMHI)

Who Fell Here?

Butterfield, Williams, and Dickinson were wounded during the bombardment before Pickett's Charge on July 3; several orderlies also suffered shrapnel wounds. Overall, however, the headquarters component suffered extremely few casualties.

Who Lived Here?

Lydia Leister was widowed in 1859 when her husband, James, died. She bought this small ten-acre farm from Henry Bishop Sr. in 1861 for $900, and it became the new home for herself and her four children, Amos, Daniel, Mary, and Matilda. At the time, it included a one-and-a-half-story log house, a small log barn, and several outbuildings. When the Battle of Gettysburg started, only the two girls still lived at home with Mrs. Leister, and the three left the farm on July 1 to seek safety elsewhere; thus, they were not present when Lieutenant Colonel Dickinson designated Leister's home as headquarters of the Army of the Potomac. The home contained only sparse and utilitarian furnishings. A National Park Service examination of the house's furniture and layout concluded that "there was every evidence that Mrs. Leister was a good housekeeper." Mrs. Leister returned on July 5 to find complete devastation. Daniel Skelly, a local boy, passed by the farm on July 6 and recounted that, in addition to twelve to fifteen dead horses around the farm itself, "a short distance below the house there was a stone fence dividing a field. Across this was hanging a horse which had been killed evidently just as he was jumping the fence, for its front legs were on one side and the hind legs on the other." Mrs. Leister continued to occupy this house until 1888, steadily making improvements to the house and barn and even purchasing an additional tract of land from neighbor Peter Frey. Finally, in 1888 advancing age and health problems forced her to move into town with a family member. Almost immediately, the Gettysburg Battlefield Memorial Association purchased the Leister farm in May 1888 for $3,000 for incorporation into its land holdings, removed postwar alterations, and began a program of regular maintenance.[5]

What Did They Say about It Later?

John Trowbridge, a journalist, returned to Gettysburg in 1865 and interviewed Lydia Leister:

> She conceded that she lost "a heap" during the fighting. The house had been robbed by the soldiers, her stock of hay was stolen, the wheat crop was trampled, an orchard was broken down and all the fences were torn up and burned. Several shells had crashed into [her] little abode and did severe damage. Seventeen dead horses were left on her land, five of these had been burned near a peach tree which died because of the fire. She received nothing much from the government for the destruction. However, the bones of the horses were sold for 50 cents per hundred pounds and 750 pounds were collected.

She did not seem to be impressed by the fact that her house had served as the nerve center of the Army of the Potomac. As Trowbridge wrote: "This poor woman's entire interest in the great battle was, I found, centered in her own losses. That the country lost or gained she did not know nor care, never having once thought of that side of the question."[6]

Driving directions to the next stop: Turn left out of the parking lot back onto Hunt Avenue and follow it east 0.5 miles to Baltimore Pike. At the stop sign, turn right and follow Baltimore Pike south for 0.3 miles, turning left onto the National Park Service road marked for Culp's Hill. Follow this winding road 0.6 miles to Spangler's Spring near the sign designating National Park Service Auto Tour Stop 13. Park in the designated area. (Prior to leaving this location, you may wish to make use of the restroom facilities located in the small stone building that sits just west of the spring.)

STOP 29. SPANGLER'S SPRING

Orientation

Walk to the stone arch capping Spangler's Spring. Keeping the spring to your right, turn left and face the open fields. Near the top of the high hill in the distance (Powers's Hill), you should be able to spot monuments to the Union artillery batteries posted there. Baltimore Pike runs across your front at the base of that hill. The woods on your left front are McAllister's Woods. The cleared ground in your immediate front and the open slopes of Powers's Hill are outstanding examples of Gettysburg National Military Park's commitment to battlefield rehabilitation. Recently cleared of a thick growth of trees that had blocked the views entirely, the open field and hillside successfully reproduce the terrain and the lines of sight that existed in July 1863.

What Happened Here?

Until late on July 2, this entire area remained securely under Union control, since Brigadier General Alpheus Williams's division of the XII Corps occupied "lower" Culp's Hill behind you. When Major General Edward Johnson's division attacked Culp's Hill late on the evening of July 2, however, the left half of Brigadier General George H. "Maryland" Steuart's brigade advanced into this area. By then, Meade had sent Williams's entire division and most of Brigadier General John W. Geary's division of Slocum's XII Corps to the support of the Union left flank against Longstreet's main effort. Steuart's 23rd Virginia advanced into this open ground unop-

The stone arch capping
Spangler's Spring.

posed and wheeled into the tree line to your right. It surged up over the ridge of high ground you see just beyond the split in the park road and outflanked the 137th New York of Brigadier General George S. Greene's brigade defending lower Culp's Hill. This was part of the action explored at Stop 25. When the fighting ended, Steuart's men fell in line behind a stone wall on the high ground topped with the monuments behind you. Briefly, then, Spangler's Spring fell under Confederate control.

Return to the park road and walk to the grassy center of the traffic circle to your right. Face toward the same open fields you observed from Spangler's Spring itself. Even before the fighting had entirely died down on the night of July 2, the rest of the XII Corps began to return to Culp's Hill, intent on reoccupying their former positions. While some of Geary's men began to move back onto "upper" Culp's Hill off to your right and out of your line of sight, it became clear that Confederate troops now held Williams's old positions behind you on lower Culp's Hill.

Now turn around; the Indiana monument, shaped somewhat like a giant tuning fork, should be on your right. Locate the tree line on the opposite end of the open field you now face. At first light on July 3, the 2nd Virginia of the Stonewall Brigade was posted behind a stone wall there, and its men had a clear view into the field in front of you and into the open fields behind you. Steuart's brigade extended the 2nd Virginia's line up onto the high ground of lower Culp's Hill to your left front.

At daybreak on July 3, Union batteries on Powers's Hill and near the Baltimore Pike opened fire on this entire area for a brief period. In an immediate response to that abbreviated bombardment, Ewell obeyed Lee's initial orders for July 3, renewing offensive action against the right flank of the Army of the Potomac.

Now turn to your right; the Indiana monument should be to your left front. You are facing McAllister's Woods, where Colonel Silas Colgrove's brigade awaited orders. Finally, Lieutenant Snow of General Thomas Ruger's staff—Ruger served as acting commander of Williams's division and, thus, was Colgrove's immediate superior—arrived with this message: "The general directs that you advance your line immediately." Colgrove did not like the order.

Turn to your left toward the open field and the Confederate line to view the ground from Colgrove's perspective. As he explained, the open field in front of his position "was so narrow that it was impossible for me to advance more than two regiments in line. Between the enemy and our line lay the open meadow, about 100 yards in width. The enemy were entirely sheltered by the breastworks and ledges of rock. It was impossible to send forward skirmishers. The enemy's advantages were such that a line of skirmishers would be cut down before they could fairly gain the open ground that intervened. The only possible chance I had to advance was to carry his position by storming it."

For this mission, Colgrove chose his own 27th Indiana Infantry and Lieutenant Colonel Charles R. Mudge's 2nd Massachusetts, already deployed in line facing the open field. He planned for Mudge's regiment to advance toward the rocks

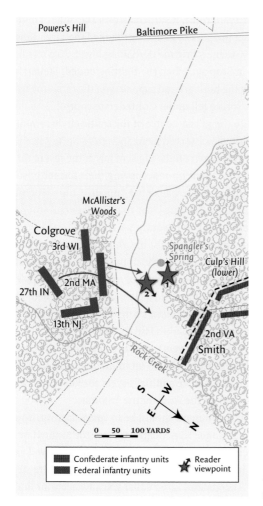

Powers's Hill

Baltimore Pike

McAllister's
Woods

Colgrove
3rd WI

Spangler's
Spring

Culp's Hill
(lower)

2nd MA

27th IN

13th NJ

2nd VA
Smith

Rock Creek

S W E N

0   50   100 YARDS

Confederate infantry units
Federal infantry units

Reader
viewpoint

**Colgrove Attacks
at Spangler's Spring**

to your left front, while the Indiana troops wheeled out into the open field and advanced toward the stone wall in front of you. "At the command, 'Forward, double-quick!,'" Colgrove reported, "our breastworks were cleared, and both regiments, with deafening cheers, sprang forward. They had scarcely gained the open ground [all around your position] when they were met with one of the most terrible fires I have ever witnessed."

Indeed, the Confederates initially held their fire. Then the remnants of Steuart's brigade, posted behind rocks and stone walls above you on your front and left front, opened a hot fire on the 2nd Massachusetts. As Lieutenant Colonel Charles F. Morse of the 2nd Massachusetts reported: "The fire while crossing the open ground was terrible, but the woods were reached and the regiment began firing." The volume

The view of the Spangler meadow and McAllister's Woods from the Confederate lines. (USAMHI-TOWER)

of fire coming from the Confederate position shredded the ranks of the 2nd Massachusetts. Mudge fell mortally wounded, and his regiment lost heavily before falling back over the open ground behind you to rally at a rock wall near the Baltimore Pike. Advancing just behind the men from Massachusetts, the 27th Indiana advanced into the open field to your right front. As Lieutenant Colonel John Fesler reported: "On arriving within about 100 yards of their position, their fire was so deadly that I was compelled to fall back to the works." There was a good explanation for the intense blast of musketry Fesler's men faced. The single regiment—the 2nd Virginia—posted behind the stone wall at daybreak had been pulled into the larger fight on upper Culp's Hill, and at least two regiments of the Virginia brigade of Brigadier General William "Extra Billy" Smith had replaced it.[1]

The fresh troops poured volleys into the 27th Indiana. The small marker in the middle of the field indicates the farthest advance of the Hoosier regiment's color guard. Finally, Colgrove himself "ordered the regiment to fall back behind the breastworks" in McAllister's Woods. Some of Smith's Virginians leaped over the wall to pursue, but Colgrove had prepared for such a possibility: "At the first fire they were completely checked, and at the second they broke in confusion and fled, leaving their dead and wounded upon the field." It may have seemed like a big fight to brigade and regimental commanders, but General Johnson summarized it this way: "A demonstration in force was made upon my left and rear. The Second Virginia Regiment, Stonewall Brigade, and Smith's brigade, of Early's division, were disposed to meet and check it, which was accomplished to my entire satisfaction."[2]

Lieutenant Colonel Charles R. Mudge, 2nd Massachusetts, killed in action on July 3. (USAMHI)

Who Fought Here?

C.S.A.: The 49th and 52nd Virginia of Brigadier General William E. "Extra Billy" Smith's brigade of Johnson's division, Ewell's Second Corps, defended the stone wall.

U.S.: Two regiments—the 27th Indiana and the 2nd Massachusetts—of Colonel Silas Colgrove's brigade, Williams's division, XII Corps, were supported in McAllister's Woods by the rest of Colgrove's brigade, the 3rd Wisconsin, the 13th New Jersey, and the 107th New York.

Who Commanded Here?

Colonel Silas Colgrove (1816–1907), a native of Steuben County, New York, was one of eighteen children. In 1837 he married and moved west to Winchester, Indiana, where he studied law and started his own practice. He became active in Republican politics on the state level, serving for a time in the Indiana House of Representatives. He began his military service as a private and quickly won election to a captaincy in the 8th Indiana Infantry, a three-month unit with which he saw his first combat at Rich Mountain in western Virginia. When the 8th Indiana mustered out of service, Colgrove became lieutenant colonel of the new 27th Indiana Regiment, which was then organizing in Indianapolis. His officers found it difficult to serve under Colgrove. In 1861 a delegation of his subordinates wrote the governor that they had "patiently submitted to insults until forbearance is beyond indurance [sic]. The regiment is now on the point of demoralization for such causes as having officers called fools, liars & threatened with a knockdown while in discharge of their duties, maltreatment of the sick & ungentlemanly treatment of old & men generally." Colgrove backed off enough to keep his commission, but twenty-seven of his officers resigned, and he never cultivated a truly effective working relationship with his subordinates. Still, he worked well enough with his superiors to be entrusted with brigade command at Gettysburg. Colgrove resigned in late 1864 and returned to Indiana, where he served as a judge, continued to practice law, and, in 1888, moved to Washington, D.C., to work at the Pension Office. When he died, his eulogists forgot his foibles in command and remembered him as "clear headed and pure hearted."[3]

Who Fell Here?

C.S.A.: Smith's Virginia regiments enjoyed the protection of the stone wall for much of the fight, but they suffered casualties in the abortive charge after the repulse of Colgrove's men. The 49th Virginia lost 100 of its 281 men, and the 52nd Virginia lost 54 of its 254 men. The 31st Virginia, which did not participate heavily in this fight, lost 59 of its 267 men. Smith's small brigade went into the battle numbering only 806 men; these casualties amount to a brigade loss of 26.4 percent.

U.S.: The 27th Indiana lost 110 of its 339 men. The 2nd Massachusetts lost Lieutenant Colonel Mudge killed and 135 more of its 316 men. The other three regiments in Colgrove's brigade suffered very light losses. Thus the brigade loss amounted to only 17.5 percent.

Individual vignettes. The *Medical and Surgical History of the War of the Rebellion* provides the case history of one J. A. Murphy, a thirty-year-old private in Company B of the 49th Virginia Infantry in Smith's brigade. On July 3 during the fighting around Spangler's Spring, a bullet hit Murphy on the right side of his scalp, without breaking the skull. At first, it did not seem to be a dangerous injury. He was put in a wagon for transport back to Virginia, but on July 6 he was captured by Union cavalry. He was sent first to Hospital No. 1 at Frederick, Maryland, for an overnight stay. While there, he accepted a parole. The following day, the provost marshal took Murphy and other parolees to Annapolis to become part of a future prisoner exchange. He did not have to wait long. Murphy arrived back in Virginia by the end of July and was admitted to a Confederate military hospital in Petersburg on August 1. On August 18, Private Murphy succumbed to a combination of chronic diarrhea and meningitis as a result of his wound. His case is unusual because it is marked by a small but crucial bookkeeping error: probably because of a flourish in the handwriting of a surgeon's clerk, the Private J. A. Murphy who found a place in the medical history of the war was in reality Private Thompson A. Murphy of Prince William County, Virginia, who had enlisted on July 1, 1861.[4]

Although he was married and had three children, Elisha Guthrie left his small town of Raglesville, Indiana, with fellow townsmen to go to Indianapolis and enlist. On September 12 he mustered in as a corporal in Company B of the 27th Indiana Infantry. He survived the regiment's early battles—including their charge through the Wheatfield at Antietam—won promotion to sergeant, and even got a furlough back to Indiana in the fall of 1862. On July 3, 1863, however, at least two Confederate bullets cut him down in the Spangler's Spring meadow. He died two days later of gunshot wounds to his right elbow and through the right side of his abdomen. Back in Raglesville, his widow, Frances, soon started the process of applying for a widow's pension, ultimately receiving the usual $8 monthly sum. In 1866 she received an additional $8 monthly to care for Laura, born in November 1852; Hetty, born in February 1857; Jackson, born in December 1860; and, finally, Lilly, born on August 3, 1863—one month to the day after her father's mortal wounding. The Raglesville Lions clubhouse displays a plaque with the names of all the men from Company B, 27th Indiana Infantry, who came from that small town; Elisha Guthrie's name can be found on the list of corporals, his rank when he first mustered in to service.[5]

Who Lived Here?

Seventy-five-year-old Abraham Spangler owned two large farms in Gettysburg, and both of them lay in the path of the hostile armies. The large farmhouse he shared with his wife, along with a daughter, a son, and a granddaughter, sat on the Chambersburg Pike northwest of town and just west of Willoughby Run on the July 1 battlefield; Davis's Mississippi brigade advanced through it. Abraham's other major property, covering 230 acres, straddled the Baltimore Pike included the key battlefield landmarks of Spangler's Spring and the Spangler Meadow, over which the 2nd Massachusetts and the 27th Indiana made their costly charge on July 3. At the time of the battle, Abraham's thirty-two-year-old son, Henry; his daughter-in-law, Sarah; and three grandchildren lived in the farm's log-and-stone house. From your second position at this stop—the one in the grassy island—the Spangler farm stands straight ahead of you along Baltimore Pike.[6]

Other properties involved in this fight include the farm of James McAllister, whose woods provided shelter to Colgrove's men before their charge. McAllister, a seventy-seven-year-old farmer, lived there with his wife, Agnes, and their seven children, ranging in age from thirty-four to sixteen. McAllister is more famous for his mill than for his farm, however. His operation on Rock Creek—his son Samuel ran it—became locally famous as a stop on the Underground Railroad; a Pennsylvania Historical Marker was dedicated near the site in 2012. Powers's Hill, the site of the high ground where several Union batteries opened up on this position, belonged to George Spangler, who owned a farm on the other side of the Baltimore Pike adjoining the property of his father. (Abraham Spangler remarried after the death of his first wife—George's mother—in 1819; thus George and Henry Spangler were half brothers.)

What Did They Say about It Later?

Considerable confusion surrounds the timing of this event. Despite the clear evidence in Colonel Colgrove's report that this engagement occurred after the firing on upper and lower Culp's Hill ended in the late morning—roughly 11:00 A.M.—the 2nd Massachusetts regimental history lists the starting time of the charge as "about 7 o'clock."[7]

Union accounts also invariably overstate substantially the strength of the opposition they faced at Spangler's Spring on July 3. One 2nd Massachusetts survivor recalled: "We found the enemy, in full force, on our right and front. . . . This was Confederate General Ewell's command, formerly commanded by Stonewall Jackson, which numbered more than seven to one of the 2nd Mass. and 27th Ind. combined."[8]

The famous story of Lieutenant Colonel Mudge's reaction to the orders to charge is not part of the original 1863 postbattle reports. In 1867 Chaplain Alonzo Quint published the 2nd Massachusetts's regimental history and related the discussion:

At about 7 o'clock, orders came to the Second, and one other regiment [27th Indiana] to advance over the meadow, and carry the enemy's position. So strange an order excited astonishment. The regiments were a handful against the mass of enemy opposite, even without any regard to their formidable position. Lieutenant-Colonel Mudge questioned the messenger, "Are you *sure* that is the order?"—"Yes."—"Well," he said, "it is murder: but it's the order. Up, men, over the works! Forward, double-quick!" With a cheer, with bayonets unfixed, without firing a shot, the line sprang forward as fast as the swampy ground would allow.[9]

Driving directions to the next stop: At the fork in the road, take the left fork, which is Geary Avenue. At the next stop sign (0.3 miles), turn left, then take the right fork in the road passing in front of the statue of General Geary. Park on the right on the gravel shoulder just beyond the Geary statue near the monument to the 29th Ohio.

STOP 30. CULP'S HILL, JULY 3

Orientation

After parking, walk to the 29th Ohio monument. Face the thick woods behind it; the park road should be behind you.

You are now on "upper" Culp's Hill. Since Henry Culp allowed his livestock to graze on these slopes, the tree growth would not have been nearly so thick or the undergrowth nearly so tangled as it is today. Confederate battle lines easily pushed forward up these slopes toward this position. Ahead of you, where the underbrush begins, you can still see the trace of the line of Union breastworks manned by the 78th, 102nd, and 149th New York Infantry of Greene's brigade when Nicholls's Louisiana brigade stormed this position on the evening of July 2.

What Happened Here?

Encouraged by the limited successes of his previous evening's assaults on "lower" Culp's Hill, Ewell spent much of the predawn hours of July 3 preparing to obey Lee's orders for an early renewal of his attack against the Union right flank. The three brigades of Johnson's division that attacked this line on the evening of July 2 still remained in line of battle in the low ground beyond the trees just in front of you; indeed, Nicholls's men had "reached a line about 100 yards from the enemy's works" ahead of you and "remained in this position during the night." To give the morning attack greater punch, however, Ewell sent reinforcements to Johnson's support. The Stonewall Brigade at first took up positions behind Steuart's men facing lower Culp's Hill across the swale to your right front. From Rodes's division, O'Neal's Alabama brigade deployed behind the Louisianans ahead of you, and Daniel's North Carolinians supported the line of Jones's Virginia brigade that faced the crest of upper Culp's Hill to your left.

The 29th Ohio Infantry monument.

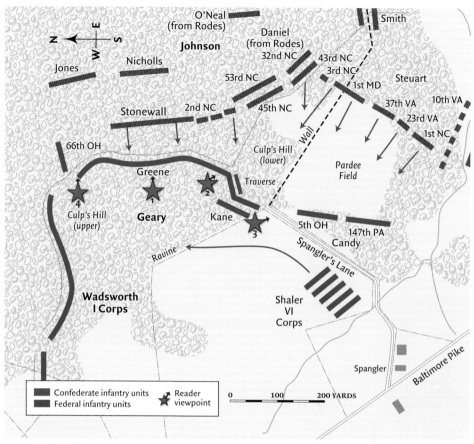

Culp's Hill, July 3

When Ewell launched the first of his early-morning attacks here, Greene's exhausted New York brigade still held this line. The first push against the crest of Culp's Hill, fortunately for the Union defenders, amounted to little. Jones's brigade apparently made little effort, and Daniel's arrival made no difference; after Daniel reconnoitered the hill, he determined that it was "so strong that it could not have been carried by any force" and awaited orders for a new assignment. Just as fortunate for the exhausted New Yorkers, the rest of their division—commanded by Brigadier General John W. Geary, whose statue stands behind you—had returned. Even before silence had fallen over the hill the previous evening, the brigades of Brigadier General Thomas L. Kane and Colonel Charles Candy had begun to filter into position on Greene's right flank at the traverse, extending and greatly strengthening the Union defensive line along a ridge of ground over your right shoulder. You will visit that site shortly.

Sunrise brought Greene's men even more help. Ewell's first push on July 3 in your immediate front proved to be far more aggressive than the effort against other portions of the Union line. Since his front still remained comparatively quiet, Candy sent four of his six regiments—the 7th, 29th, and 66th Ohio as well as the 28th Pennsylvania—to support Greene's line where needed; the monument to the 29th Ohio to your left represents one of Candy's units. Greene received additional help from the three regiments of Brigadier General Henry H. Lockwood's small brigade, just recently attached to the XII Corps during the Army of the Potomac's march to Gettysburg. The monuments to the 150th New York and the 1st Maryland Potomac Home Brigade up the slope to your left—you will see them as you drive up to the crest—commemorate their actions here. As General Geary reported of Lockwood's command: "This brigade composed almost entirely of untried troops . . . rendered efficient service."

Now turn around and face the park road. General Geary's statue should be to your left front. At about 8:00 A.M., still more Union reinforcements arrived. Brigadier General Alexander Shaler's brigade from the VI Corps reported in to bolster the Union line on upper Culp's Hill and "took a sheltered position in the rear of a piece of woods, beyond which the action was then progressing." The line of monuments across the road—each bearing the Greek cross insignia of the VI Corps—represent these fresh regiments; through the trees, you can see the low ground they used for shelter.

The senior Union officers then developed a process to make the best use of the growing number of troops on the hill. Turn around and once more face the main Union battle line at the tree line. With ready reinforcements now available, when a XII Corps regiment behind the breastworks here ran low on ammunition, it simply swapped places with one of Shaler's fresh and fully-supplied VI Corps commands—or one of Lockwood's, Kane's, or Candy's regiments—waiting under cover behind you. The protection of the breastworks paid off in the preservation of lives; the soldiers faced their greatest risks during their brief exposure to Confederate fire as they switched position in or out of the front line.

Brigadier General Alexander Shaler, U.S.A. (USAMHI)

The arrangement worked quite effectively. First Sergeant Ambrose Henry Hayward of the 28th Pennsylvania explained this to his father in a letter a few weeks later: "[We were] soon ordered to releive [sic] the 29th Ohio of our brigade who were in action in the entrenchments. [W]e were in action 3 hours, during which time I fired 65 rounds of Amunition. [T]his is more than I have used in any battle. I often had to wait for my rifel [sic] to cool, ram[m]ing the ball home with a stone. We were releived by the 1st Md Regt. (Home Brigade)."[1]

By midmorning, Jones's Virginians and Nicholls's Louisiana brigade, both greatly reduced by casualties and exhaustion, pulled back to the base of the hill.

By necessity, fresher Confederate units took the lead. The Stonewall Brigade from Johnson's division now shifted to its right to launch a series of attacks against your front. According to the commander of the 149th New York, "The enemy again furiously attacked us. His charges were the most impetuous and his fire terrific. Twice was our flag shot down, and a rebel first sergeant, in a brave attempt to capture it, fell within 2 feet of the prostrate banner, pierced with five balls." Color Sergeant William C. Lilly won official notice for splicing the broken staff together to keep the flag flying. The Confederates paid a high price for their aggressive attacks. "Our regiment has only 66 men left," a member of the Stonewall Brigade wrote to his sister afterward, "and the whole division suffered proportionally through the folly of our hard fighting Johnson. . . . Three or four times did he throw our gallant band against powerful breastworks and Yankees without number each time mowing them down."[2]

Now turn to the right and walk down the slope toward the low ground of the swale, stopping at the monument to the 137th New York. Continue to face downhill. The monument's position roughly indicates the location of the traverse where the regiment successfully repulsed Confederate attacks the previous evening. Although no physical evidence of the traverse remains, it would have extended across your front to your right roughly at a ninety-degree angle from the original line of breastworks on your left, continuing across the road to your right and ending somewhere near where the ground descends into a ravine.

Turn to your right, cross the road, and locate the short, square monument to the 29th Pennsylvania on a rock at the lip of the ravine. Stand on that rock and face to the left toward the open field across the park road that cuts across your front. In walking to this position, you have followed the approximate trace of the traverse, and now you are standing in the line occupied by Kane's small Pennsylvania brigade when it returned to Culp's Hill the previous evening. The two regiments under Colonel Candy that were not sent to support Greene's line—the 600 men of the 5th Ohio and the 147th Pennsylvania—held the line on the high ground of the Abraham Spangler farm across the ravine to your right; you can see their monuments to the right of the park road below you. This part of lower Culp's Hill is known as "Pardee Field" in honor of Lieutenant Colonel Ario Pardee Jr., commander of the 147th Pennsylvania.

While Kane and Candy returned to Greene's support late on July 2, Steuart's North Carolinians, Marylanders, and Virginians spent the night beyond the tree line visible to your left along the high ground at the top of Pardee Field. Of the three brigades General Johnson sent into action against Culp's Hill the previous evening, only Steuart's stalwarts remained fully engaged in the fight by midmorning on July 3. As they prepared to attack, they moved up to a stone wall at the tree line at the top of Pardee Field. Artillery fire from Powers's Hill and the Baltimore Pike, combined with heavy volleys from the Union infantry in their front, quickly stopped most of Steuart's regiments. Only the 1st Maryland continued its advance across

Reunion of the 147th and 28th Pennsylvania of Candy's brigade that fought near Pardee Field on July 3. (USAMHI)

Pardee field. During that charge, as Steuart reported, they "suffered very severely, and, being unsupported, wavered, and the whole line fell back." Kane observed that the 1st Maryland's "dead lay mingled with our own" and acknowledged that "it cannot be denied that they behaved courageously."

Now backtrack to your former position near the 137th New York's monument, but face the trees on the main battle line rather than the swale. Daniel's North Carolinians were supposed to advance in concert with Steuart's charge, but they delayed. When they finally moved forward, Steuart's attack was nearly over. Without any other enemy forces to distract the attention of the Union infantry, the Tar Heels absorbed countless volleys of musketry. They fought at close quarters. Daniel even claimed that his men drove the Union line "from a portion of their works in front of my center and right," while his 45th North Carolina utilized the swale to your right to open up a "destructive fire . . . for five minutes upon a crowd of the enemy who were disorganized and fleeing in great confusion." The arrival of Union reinforcements once again shifted the advantage, however, and as Geary reported, the heavy fire that poured in by regiments closing in on the swale from the brigades of Greene, Candy, and Kane inspired a number of Confederates to "wave white flags, handkerchiefs, and even pieces of paper, in preference to meeting again that fire which was certain destruction."[3] Major Benjamin Watkins Leigh of Johnson's staff rode into the maelstrom on horseback, demanding that the surrendering soldiers cease and desist. A blast of Union gunfire quickly felled him. To hasten the withdrawal of Daniel's and Steuart's men and the rest of Johnson's command, Colonel Archibald L. McDougall's brigade from Williams's division pressed forward from its early-morning position near the Baltimore Pike to retake its trenches on lower Culp's Hill. Williams finally got back his breastworks.

Brigadier General George H. "Maryland" Steuart, C.S.A. (USAMHI)

The fighting for Culp's Hill on July 3 ended in costly defeat for the Confederates. As Colonel George Cobham of the 111th Pennsylvania described the scene to his brother on July 4: "The slaughter was terrible on their side, and we have not all escaped. All around me as I write, our men are busy burying the dead. The ground is literally covered with them, and the blood is standing in pools. It is a sickening sight."[4] Union burial crews reported the interment of between 900 and 1,500 Confederate dead in trench graves at the bottom of the hill. By the time the fighting ended at this front, Ewell's men had fought the XII Corps and its reinforcements for nearly seven hours. The intense fighting convinced Robert E. Lee to reevaluate his initial July 3 intentions to continue the previous day's effort to press the Union flanks. His revised plan became known to history as "Pickett's Charge."

Return to your vehicle and turn right at the stop sign to make a brief stop at the very peak of upper Culp's Hill. Stand in front of the statue of General Greene and look in the direction that he is pointing. Jones's Virginia brigade attempted to scale these slopes on the evening of July 2, and the 60th New York in the entrenchments a few yards down the slope in front of you easily stopped them. When Jones's men tried again on the morning of July 3, the 66th Ohio arrived from Candy's brigade, filed down the slope to your left front, faced to the right, and outflanked the Virginians. Major Joshua G. Palmer of the 66th Ohio fell mortally wounded in the firefight, but his Buckeyes guaranteed the security of Greene's left flank until the fight ended.

Who Fought Here?

C.S.A.: In addition to the three brigades of Johnson's division previously introduced—those of Jones, Nicholls, and Steuart—Brigadier General James A. Walker's 1,323-man Stonewall Brigade, which included the 2nd, 4th, 5th, 27th, and 33rd Virginia Infantry, participated in this fight. Daniel and O'Neal from Rodes's brigade first appeared at Stop 5 and fought here with greatly reduced numbers.

U.S.: In addition to Greene's brigade previously introduced, the fighting on July 3 at Culp's Hill drew in most of the remainder of Geary's division of Slocum's XII Corps, including Brigadier General Thomas L. Kane's 700-man brigade, which included the 29th, 109th, and 111th Pennsylvania Infantry, and Colonel Charles Candy's 1,798-man brigade, which included the 5th, 7th, 29th, and 66th Ohio as well as the 28th and 147th Pennsylvania Infantry. Brigadier General Henry H. Lockwood's 1,818-man provisional brigade, not yet assigned to a division in Slocum's XII Corps, included the 1st Maryland Eastern Shore; the 1st Maryland, Potomac Home Brigade; and the 150th New York Infantry. Colonel Archibald McDougall's 1,835-man brigade that entered the fray at the end included the 5th and 20th Connecticut, the 3rd Maryland, the 123rd and 145th New York, and the 46th Pennsylvania Infantry.

Brigadier General Alexander Shaler's 1,769-man brigade, Wheaton's division, Sedgwick's VI Corps, included the 65th, 67th, and 122nd New York and the 23rd and 82nd Pennsylvania Infantry.

Who Commanded Here?

Brigadier General Alpheus Starkey Williams (1810–78), born in Connecticut and educated at Yale University, opened a law office in Detroit in the mid-1830s. He became active in all manner of public-service activities, from running a newspaper to serving as postmaster of Detroit. He gained military experience as the lieutenant colonel of Michigan volunteers during the Mexican War. When the Civil War broke out, he already served as a brigadier general in state service, so on August 9, 1861, he obtained a commission at that same rank in Federal service. He served in the Shenandoah valley in the spring of 1862, and his command became part of the Army of the Potomac's XII Corps just before Antietam. He did well in division command at Chancellorsville and Gettysburg, and he even served temporarily in corps command on several occasions after the XII Corps transferred to the western theater in late 1863. He long resented that his division did not receive due credit for its contributions at Gettysburg. He wrote to his daughter that General Geary "gets all the credit for the operations on the right during the morning of July 3rd, and myself, who spent a sleepless night in planning the attack, and my old division commanded by Gen. Ruger, which drove the Rebs from their double line of entrenchments, are not alluded to. Save me from my friends!" For unknown reasons, he never received a permanent assignment at the corps level. After the war, he returned to public service, and he died in Washington in December 1878 while serving his second elected term as a member of the U.S. House of Representatives from Michigan. His wartime letters, published as *From the Cannon's Mouth,* offer very useful insights into XII Corps affairs.[5]

Brigadier General John White Geary (1819–73) of Mount Pleasant, Pennsylvania, attended Jefferson College (now Washington and Jefferson College) until his father's death forced him to return home. Geary taught, clerked, studied law and engineering, and served as lieutenant colonel and colonel of the 2nd Pennsylvania Infantry in the Mexican War. He then moved to California and became the first mayor of San Francisco and later served as territorial governor of Kansas during its contentious path to statehood. He reentered military service in 1861 as colonel of the 28th Pennsylvania Infantry. Wounded on several occasions, he became a brigadier general on April 25, 1862, and served in brigade and then division command in the XII Corps through Gettysburg. Modesty did not rank among Geary's most notable personal traits. As he wrote to his wife on July 4: "Yesterday I had the honor to defeat Gen Ewell's Corps (formerly Jackson's). They attacked my command at 3 oclock A.M. and we fought until ½ past 11. The result was I repulsed his command. . . . The whole fight was under my control, no one to interfere." He went west and took command of a division in the XX Corps that absorbed his old unit, and he served ably on the "March to the Sea" and as military governor of Savannah. When he returned to Pennsylvania, Geary was elected governor as a Republican, even though he had supported the Democratic Party in his earlier political activity. He served two terms, and he died almost immediately upon leaving office in 1873.[6]

Who Fell Here?

C.S.A.: In the Stonewall Brigade, the 2nd Virginia lost 25 of its 333 men, the 4th Virginia lost 137 of its 257 men, the 5th Virginia lost 58 of its 345 men, the 27th Virginia lost 48 of its 148 men, and the 33rd Virginia lost 70 of its 236 men—for a brigade loss of 25.5 percent. For the casualties in Jones's, Nicholls's, and Steuart's brigades, see Stop 25. For Daniel's and O'Neal's losses, see Stop 5.

U.S.: Kane's small brigade of Geary's division lost 98 of its 700, for a brigade loss of 14.1 percent. Candy's brigade also suffered comparatively lightly, losing 140 of its 1,798 men for a brigade loss of 7.7 percent. Lockwood's provisional brigade—briefly engaged near the Trostle farm on July 2 and here on July 3—lost 194 of its 1,818 men; the 1st Maryland (Eastern Shore) lost 104 of that total. Colonel Archibald McDougall's brigade participated in only the last part of the July 3 fight on lower Culp's Hill and lost only 78 of its 1,835 men.

Shaler's brigade from the VI Corps arrived in timely fashion to support the XII Corps at the breastworks. It lost only 79 of its men for a brigade loss of 4.0 percent.

Individual vignettes. Charles Longworth, a paper hanger from Philadelphia, mustered into Company D of the 28th Pennsylvania Infantry on July 6, 1861, with the rank of corporal. By the time he marched to Gettysburg, he was a sergeant. In the fighting on Culp's Hill, his regiment from Candy's brigade rushed to the support of the original defenders. Early in the day, Longworth suffered a gunshot to the leg. In a letter dated July 17, First Sergeant Ambrose Henry Hayward described to his father how he had "helped carry Sergt Longworth of[f] the field after we had been releived [sic] the first time. [T]his makes 4 Sergts we have had wounded in the leg." Sergeant Longworth died of his wounds in the XII Corps hospital on July 14. Back in Philadelphia, Longworth's aging parents, sixty-two-year-old Margaret and seventy-six-year-old Henry, mourned the loss of their son and their sole means of support. Margaret was illiterate and Henry an invalid, so for at least five years before his enlistment, Charles had provided wholly for their needs, paying the rent on their small house on Cauffman Street and buying their food and clothing. In March 1864 Margaret was approved for an $8 widow's pension. The elderly couple—both still alive in 1876—continued to have dealings with the Pension Office in an effort to improve their circumstances.[7]

Beale Duvall Hamilton came from Anne Arundel County, Maryland. Like many Marylanders with Southern sympathies, he went to Richmond to enlist in the Confederate army, joining Company C of the 2nd Maryland Battalion. He spent nearly two months in a Staunton, Virginia, hospital from November 1862 until January 11, 1863, but he still apparently impressed his officers with his soldierly qualities sufficiently to win a promotion to corporal. During the attack on Kane's lines on July 3, Corporal Hamilton was wounded in the right shoulder and in both legs. He fell into Union hands and received his initial medical treatment at a XII Corps hospital. Surgeon W. S. Tusford of the 27th Indiana attempted a excision of the damaged sections of Hamilton's right humerus and a resection of the remaining bone, but the effort failed. Corporal Hamilton died on July 22, 1863. His case is registered on the "Condensed Summary of One Hundred and Forty-five Fatal Primary Excisions of the Shaft of the Humerus for Shot Injury" in the *Medical and Surgical History of the War of the Rebellion*, but Hamilton is carried on the list as a member of the 1st Maryland Union Infantry.[8]

No matter how one looks at it, tragedy dogged George G. and Anne Watkins Lowry's life together. They married in May 1851 in Berlin, Maryland. On July 3, 1853, a son, George Thomas Lowry, was born, but he died the next day. On August 17, 1857, Margaret Virginia arrived; she died on September 14, 1861. Just a few months earlier, on February 13, 1861, Anne had given birth to another daughter, Sarah. Just after Christmas in December 1861, George enlisted in Company K of the 1st Maryland, Potomac Home Brigade, designated primarily for home defense. At first, his service proceeded smoothly. But then young Sarah died on November 7, 1862. Even then, Ann was carrying their fourth child, Mary, who was born—and died—on June 20, 1863. Two weeks later, at the breastworks on Culp's Hill on July 3, as his command replaced a unit that had exhausted its ammunition, Private George G. Lowry took a bullet in the right lung. His comrades took him to a field hospital, but he died two days later. Anne now faced life with an empty home and an $8 widow's pension. Private Lowry rests in grave C-1 of the Maryland plot.[9]

Who Lived Here?

"Upper" and "lower" Culp's Hill, of course, belong to Henry Culp. Pardee Field and the surrounding area were part of Abraham Spangler's farm.

What Did They Say about It Later?

During the fall of 1863, when General Meade wrote his report on the Battle of Gettysburg, he lacked full accounts of the XII Corps action. General Slocum, the corps commander, took his role as wing commander during the battle quite seriously, and he submitted a report "of the operations of the Twelfth Corps, and such other troops as were placed under my command" that covered his corps' action in a very general way. Acting XII Corps commander General Alpheus Williams, who reverted back to division command when Meade abandoned the wing organization after the battle, did not feel he should write a corps report, either.

Not surprisingly, when Meade's report was published, General Slocum found it entirely unsatisfactory. On December 30 he wrote an extended complaint to Meade—enclosing a letter from Williams that outlined specific errors in the report—to urge him to revise it and set the record straight.

> Your report is the official history of that important battle, and to this report reference will always be made by our Government, our people, and the historian, as the most reliable and accurate account of the services performance by each corps, division, and brigade of your army. If you have inadvertently given to one division the credit of having performed some meritorious service which was in reality performed by another division, you do an injustice to brave men and defraud them of well-earned laurels. It is an injustice which even time cannot correct. That errors of this nature exist in your official report is an indisputable fact.

Indeed, Meade had made errors. He wrote of Lockwood's brigade as belonging to the I Corps. He credited Geary's entire division for the defense of Culp's Hill, rather than Greene's lone New York brigade, and Slocum made it clear that "the failure of the enemy to gain entire possession of our works was due entirely to the skill of General Greene and the heroic valor of his troops alone." Meade had named Brigadier General Frank Wheaton's brigade rather than Shaler's men as the VI Corps reinforcements. Most of all, Slocum demanded fairness for General Williams. "Although the command of the Twelfth Corps was given temporarily to General Williams by your order," Slocum pointed out, "and although you directed him to meet at the council with other corps commanders, you fail to mention his name in your entire report, and in no place allude to his having any such command." Meade also had failed to note the fact "that more than one corps was at any time placed under my command, although at no time after you assumed command of the army until the close of this battle was I in command of less than two corps."

Meade graciously received Slocum's complaints: "I very much regret that any injustice should have been done in my official report of the battle of Gettysburg to any part of the Twelfth Corps or any officer in it. I do assure you most sincerely that nothing was further from my intentions, and that what has occurred was the result of accident and not of design." He promised to make an official statement of revisions to his report. Meade followed through, correcting all of these issues in an official addendum to his report on February 25, 1864.[10]

Few XII Corps veterans forgot the snub, however. Among the monuments on lower Culp's Hill, the distinctive monument of the 123rd New York stands out. Clio, the muse of history, sits atop a pedestal, recording truth in her ledger.

Driving directions to the next stop: Drive straight down the hill from the observation tower past the equestrian statue of General Slocum. Where the road divides, take the left fork. At the T intersection with Baltimore Pike (Route 97), turn right and drive 0.7 miles, passing over Cemetery Hill into the town. At Middle Street (Route 116 West), turn left at the traffic light and drive 0.7 miles to Seminary Ridge and West Confederate Avenue. Turn left onto West Confederate Avenue and drive another 0.7 miles. Park on the right in the designated parking spaces near the North Carolina monument and the sign designating National Park Service Auto Tour Stop 4.

STOP 31. ORGANIZING THE ASSAULT AGAINST THE UNION CENTER

Orientation

Stand in front of the North Carolina monument and look out across the open fields ahead of you. You have returned to Seminary Ridge, the main Confederate battle line on July 2 and July 3. During those two days, Lieutenant General A. P. Hill's Third Corps filled the fields on the reverse slope of this ridge behind you, and the cannons and markers representing the batteries in Hill's artillery battalions line the park road on which you have been traveling. The key terrain of Cemetery Hill is the tree-covered high ground to your left front. Monuments lining Cemetery Ridge—the long shank of Meade's fishhook defense—cross the horizon to your right front. Emmitsburg Road cuts across your front at the base of Cemetery Ridge. About one-third of the way across the valley in front of you, note the scrubby area that marks the wartime location of the Bliss barn and house that changed hands several times as sharpshooters and skirmishers from both armies sought its cover for a clear view of enemy lines and a bit of protection from hostile fire.

What Happened Here?

The duration and intensity of the fighting on Culp's Hill convinced Lee that Meade must have strengthened his flanks. Lee discussed options with his second in command, General Longstreet, and it was clear from the start that the two men contin-

The North Carolina monument on Seminary Ridge.

ued to hold quite different ideas about the most appropriate course of action. While Lee had planned for a renewed assault on both flanks, Longstreet, in his report, made clear that he had prepared for a different approach. "Our arrangements were made for renewing the attack by my right," he wrote, "with a view to pass around the hill [Round Top] occupied by the enemy on his left, and to gain it by flank and reverse attack. This would have been a slow process, probably, but I think not very difficult." When Lee made clear that he now intended to focus on a penetration of the Union center, Longstreet objected. While he did not relate the details of their discussion in his battle report, he did state forthrightly that the proposed attack by "Pickett's, Heth's and part of Pender's divisions" covered great distance "under the fire of the enemy's batteries, and in plain view," and thus "seemed too great to in-sure great results, particularly as two-thirds of the troops to be engaged in the as-sault had been in a severe battle two days previous." Lee stuck with his revised plan nonetheless.

After he decided to attack the Union center on Cemetery Ridge, Lee made four additional decisions about its execution. First, concerned about the impact that massed Union artillery fire would have on the ranks of his assault force, he opted to saturate the crest of Cemetery Ridge in your immediate front with a preattack bombardment by his own batteries. Lee's exterior lines offered few advantages, but he planned to take full advantage of something they did possess: the ability to lay a converging fire on a small area in the enemy's line. He already may have contemplated the benefits of such action in support of his initial plan to hit the Union flanks even before he decided to assault the center of the enemy line. Briga-dier General William N. Pendleton, Lee's chief of artillery, reported: "By direction of the commanding general, the artillery along our entire line was to be prepared for opening, as early as possible on the morning of the 3d, a concentrated and destruc-tive fire, consequent upon which a general advance was to be made."

Second, Lee decided upon the target area for the assault. Look straight ahead to Cemetery Ridge and locate the tall obelisk on the ridgeline. The large clump of trees to its left is the famous "copse of trees" that Lee personally selected as the target for the July 3 attack. It is also entirely possible that Lee meant to target all the visible trees in that area of Cemetery Ridge, including not only the clump of trees but also Ziegler's Grove to its left. When the bombardment started, Confederate artillery shells rained down all along the ridgeline and damaged Union batteries all along the crest in the Union center, suggesting that the artillerymen fired toward an area rather than simply at a single point. The Third Corps artillery battalions under the command of Majors William T. Poague, William J. Pegram, David McIntosh, and John Lane served on this portion of Seminary Ridge.

Lee's third decision—which is the primary reason for your stopping in this lo-cation—involved the composition of the attacking force. As Longstreet rightly ob-served, Major General George E. Pickett's 5,500-man division, Lee's only major fresh

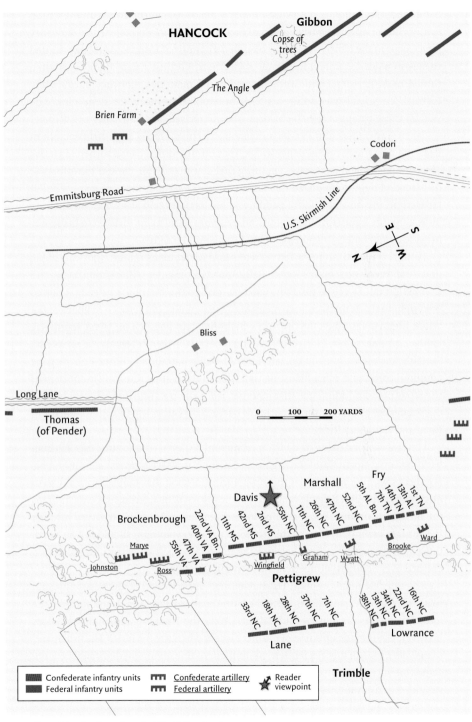

HANCOCK

Gibbon

Copse of trees

The Angle

Brien Farm

Codori

Emmitsburg Road

U.S. Skirmish Line

N E S W

Bliss

Long Lane

Thomas (of Pender)

0   100   200 YARDS

Fry

Marshall

Davis

1st TN
13th TN
14th TN
7th TN
5th AL Bn.
52nd NC
47th NC
26th NC
11th NC
55th NC
2nd MS
42nd MS
11th MS
2nd VA Bn.
40th VA
47th VA
55th VA

Brockenbrough

Ward

Brooke

Marye

Graham   Wyatt

Johnston   Ross   Wingfield

Pettigrew

7th NC
37th NC
28th NC
18th NC
33rd NC

16th NC
22nd NC
34th NC
13th NC
38th NC

Lane

Lowrance

Trimble

Confederate infantry units   Confederate artillery   Reader viewpoint
Federal infantry units   Federal artillery

Organizing the Assault against the Union Center

341

command remaining, certainly would play a major role in the attack on the Union center. Since Longstreet convinced Lee that it would be inadvisable to use the entire First Corps in the effort—the badly bloodied divisions of Hood and McLaws needed to stay in place to protect the Army of Northern Virginia's right flank—Lee then turned to A. P. Hill's Third Corps for additional manpower for the attack. While Pickett's Virginians have secured a place in national memory, the same cannot be said for these troops of the Third Corps who comprised over half of the attack force.

Since Anderson's and Pender's divisions of Hill's Third Corps held sectors of Lee's main line here on Seminary Ridge, the commanding general turned to Heth's division, positioned in reserve. On July 3 that command still showed the effects of its extended fight that opened the battle on July 1. Late that first day, a spent bullet hit Heth in the head, but extra padding in his hatband had absorbed much of the blow. Still, the injury forced him to hand over command of his division to his senior brigade commander, Brigadier General J. Johnston Pettigrew.

Pettigrew placed Archer's Tennesseans and Alabamians on the right end of his line. Archer was now on his way to Baltimore as a prisoner of the Union army, and Colonel Birkett D. Fry of the 13th Alabama took command of the brigade. Look to your right to the Tennessee state memorial. Lieutenant Colonel S. G. Shepard of the 7th Tennessee described the order in which the regiments fell in: "First Tennessee on the right; on its left, Thirteenth Alabama; next, Fourteenth Tennessee; on its left, Seventh Tennessee, and, on the left, Fifth Alabama Battalion."[1] When Fry's brigade advanced into these open fields, its right flank rested approximately in the area of the stout post-and-rail fence that emerges from the tree line immediately behind the Tennessee monument and continues out into the open field toward Emmitsburg Road and Cemetery Ridge.

Pettigrew's succession to division command required him to turn over his own badly battered North Carolina brigade to Colonel James Keith Marshall. Among his regiments was the remnant of the 26th North Carolina that tangled with the 24th Michigan of the Iron Brigade on July 1; according to its quartermaster, only perhaps 216 men of its original 800 remained in ranks on July 3. Marshall deployed his men to Fry's left, essentially placing them behind you over your right shoulder. The North Carolina memorial sits here because the left of Marshall's Tar Heel brigade likely crossed over Seminary Ridge very close to this location.

Brigadier General Joseph R. Davis remained in command of the Mississippi and North Carolina brigade that opened the battle against Cutler's men and suffered the loss of many prisoners in the railroad cut. Unlike the other brigades in this division, however, Davis made up some of his July 1 losses when the fresh 11th Mississippi rejoined his ranks on July 2; a modern monument to this regiment, dedicated in 2000, stands on the west side of the park road behind you. Davis's regiments formed on Marshall's left and advanced straight ahead and slightly to the left of your present position.

Colonel John M. Brockenbrough's small Virginia brigade stood on Davis's left flank. Gettysburg was the colonel's first battle in brigade command—its previous commander recently fell at Chancellorsville—and he had shown on July 1 that he was not quite up to the task. When they started their advance, they pressed through the open fields to your left, heading toward the ground now covered by the modern housing development.

Noting the thinness of Pettigrew's ranks and the number of lightly wounded men who had returned to duty in these four brigades, Lee assigned the North Carolina brigades of Brigadier Generals James H. Lane and Alfred Scales from Pender's division as a support. Like Pettigrew's command, these two brigades had fought on July 1. Lane still commanded his brigade, but artillery fire from Wainwright's I Corps guns near the seminary had wounded Scales badly; Lieutenant Colonel William L. J. Lowrance—the senior surviving field officer in the entire brigade—had succeeded to command. Pender himself had fallen mortally wounded late on July 2, so Lee assigned command of these two brigades to Major General Isaac R. Trimble, a veteran commander without a current troop assignment. Lowrance's North Carolinians formed its battle line approximately 200 yards behind Fry and Marshall over your right shoulder, and Lane's men were about 200 yards behind Marshall and Davis behind you. Brockenbrough's weak brigade received no extra support whatever.

The fourth and final decision Lee made before the charge centered on the designation of a commander to execute his orders. He chose the man who least wanted that authority: Lieutenant General James Longstreet. In justifying his request to be relieved of the assignment, Longstreet pointed out that only Pickett's 5,500 men came from his own First Corps. The Third Corps troops that Lee had just assigned to the assault outnumbered those contributed by his own corps. Thus he suggested that the responsibility be given to A. P. Hill. Lee did not accept his entreaty. Longstreet's critics have made much of this action, but his lapse of professionalism was short-lived. As he admitted in a letter to his uncle just three weeks later: "General Lee chose the plans adopted; and he is the person appointed to choose and to order. I consider it a part of my duty to express my views to the commanding general. If he approves and adopts them, it is well; if he does not, it is my duty to adopt his views, and to execute his orders as faithfully as if they were my own."[2]

Who Fought Here?

You met the four brigades of Heth's division at Stops 2, 3, 11, and 12. You met the two brigades from Pender's division at Stop 13

Four of the Third Corps's artillery battalions participated in the Confederates' preassault bombardment. Major John Lane's battalion was composed of Companies A, B, and C of the Sumter Battalion of Georgia. Major William T. Poague's battalion included the Albemarle (Va.) Artillery, the Charlotte (N.C.) Artillery, the Madison (Miss.) Light Artillery, and Capt. J. V. Brooke's Virginia Battery. The Danville (Va.) Artillery, the Hardaway (Ala.) Artillery, the 2nd Rockbridge (Va.) Artillery, and Capt. Marmaduke Johnson's Virginia Battery made up Major David G. McIntosh's battalion. Major William J. Pegram's battalion included the Crenshaw (Va.) Battery, the Fredericksburg (Va.) Artillery that fired the first cannon shots on July 1, the Letcher (Va.) Artillery, the Pee Dee (S.C.) Artillery, and the Purcell (Va.) Artillery.

Who Commanded Here?

Major General Isaac Ridgeway Trimble (1802–88), born in Culpeper County, Virginia, graduated from the U.S. Military Academy in 1822. After ten years of army service, he resigned to enter the railroad construction business. He joined the Confederate army in May 1861 and put his engineering skills to work around Norfolk. On August 9, 1861, he received a commission as a brigadier general and gained a reputation for aggressiveness on the battlefield until he suffered a serious wound at Second Manassas. While recuperating, he rose to major general. The Pennsylvania Campaign marked his return to active duty, but he accompanied the Army of Northern Virginia as a supernumerary general officer without a designated command until Lee gave him the two North Carolina brigades of Pender's division assigned to the assaulting column for the July 3 attack on the Union center. Trimble lost a leg in the charge, and he remained a Union prisoner until February 1865; he held no further field command. Trimble took up his pen after the war in an effort to correct "the numerous misrepresentations, errors and omissions" in Southern accounts of the battle. Claiming a uniquely close relationship to Lee—he described his communications with the general as written with "the freedom of an old acquaintance"—he purported to introduce Lee's unarticulated thoughts about his goals for the Pennsylvania Campaign into public discourse. Blaming "adverse circumstances; disobedience of orders by his commander of cavalry, and want of concerted action and vigorous onset among his corps commanders at critical moments in the assaults of each of the three days," Trimble pointed the finger of blame at Generals Stuart, Ewell, Rodes, and Longstreet by name for defeating Lee's "reasonable expectations" for victory.[3]

Major General Isaac R. Trimble, C.S.A., lost his leg in battle on July 3. (USAMHI)

Brigadier General James Johnston Pettigrew (1828–63), born in Tyrrell County, North Carolina, entered the University of North Carolina at the age of fifteen and achieved a remarkable scholastic record in his four years there. He then studied law and traveled in Europe, where he learned to speak and write French, German, Italian, and Spanish and to read Greek, Hebrew, and Arabic. Returning to the United States, he was elected to the South Carolina legislature in 1856. As a militia colonel, he was present for the firing on Fort Sumter and soon won election as colonel of the 12th South Carolina Infantry. He accepted a commission as a brigadier general in Confederate service to rank from February 1862. Pettigrew saw action in the Peninsula Campaign, and he fell wounded and was captured at Seven Pines in late May 1862. Exchanged two months later, he commanded the defenses of Petersburg and served in North Carolina. He and his brigade were assigned to Heth's division, A. P. Hill's Third Corps, for the Gettysburg Campaign, and he temporarily commanded the division on July 3. Although he survived the Battle of Gettysburg, Pettigrew was mortally wounded on July 14 while commanding the rear guard as Lee's army crossed the Potomac River back into Virginia. He died near Bunker Hill, Virginia, three days later, and his remains were taken home to North Carolina for burial.

Brigadier General J. Johnston Pettigrew, C.S.A., fell wounded on July 3 and died of a second wound suffered on the retreat to Virginia. (USAMHI)

Who Fell Here?

The infantry losses will be detailed at the culmination of Pickett's Charge at Stop 33. Hill's Third Corps artillery battalions that fought along this line lost 179 of their 1,475 soldiers, with some of these casualties suffered on July 1. "We interred our dead decently," wrote Major John Lane, "and brought every wounded man of the battalion across the Potomac."

Individual Vignettes. Private William J. Bartley enlisted in Staunton, Virginia, on August 1, 1861, and became a member of a battery that became best known as the Second Rockbridge Artillery. A soldier's life held little appeal for Bartley, and at some point in 1862, he simply left ranks and returned home to his wife, Charity. During the war, the Davis administration occasionally announced limited amnesties to encourage deserters to return to ranks without facing the standard penalty for desertion in the face of the enemy: execution by firing squad. Bartley apparently returned to his battery in early 1863. He soon learned, however, that he still had to accept a lesser punishment for his unauthorized absence. In short order, Private Bartley was court-martialed, found guilty, and sentenced to pay a fine of $24. Bartley remained in ranks after that incident, and he served with the Second Rockbridge Artillery in Major David McIntosh's battalion at Gettysburg. The soldier who had tried to run away from the war had the war come to him in its most lethal manifestation: he was killed in action by Union counterbattery fire on July 3, 1863.[4]

Lieutenant William H. Pool of the 11th Mississippi Infantry wrote a vivid description of the impact of one artillery shell in the ranks of Davis's brigade during the bombardment:

In the hottest of the cannonading I heard a shell strike in the right of the reg't. & turning over, as I lay upon my back, I looked just in time to witness the most appalling scene that perhaps ever greeted the human eye. Lt. Daniel Featherston, of Co. "F.," from Noxubee County, was the unfortunate victim. He was a large man—would have weighed perhaps Two Hundred pounds. He was lying on his face when the shell struck the ground near his head, &, in the ricochet, entered his breast, exploding about the same time & knocking him, at least ten feet high, & and not less than twenty feet from where he was lying.

Daniel A. Featherston, a native South Carolinian, enlisted in the Noxubee Rifles in Macon, Mississippi, on April 25, 1861. A mechanic in his midtwenties, he apparently thrived on army life. He received a promotion to corporal on April 21, 1862, and, after Antietam, his company elected him second lieutenant. The 11th Mississippi did not participate in the fighting during the opening phases of the battle on July 1, so Lieutenant Daniel Featherston became the first soldier in his regiment to die at Gettysburg. Many more soon would join him on the regimental casualty list.[5]

Who Lived Here?

The land on which you now stand belonged to David McMillan. Born in 1798, McMillan bought forty acres of land along Seminary Ridge in 1838 and built the house that still sits on a two-acre, privately owned tract (known as an inholding) surrounded by Gettysburg National Military Park property; you passed the white McMillan house on the left side of West Confederate Avenue just before you reached this stop. McMillan dabbled in a number of occupations; he was a surveyor, a teacher, and a pioneer in fruit growing in Adams County. On July 1, as Reynolds's I Corps left the Emmitsburg Road to march cross-country toward the Chambersburg Road, they crossed McMillan's fields; to facilitate their movement, McMillan took his axe and chopped down his own fences. On July 2 the McMillans left their farm; David actually watched part of the fight from Little Round Top. When they returned to the farm on July 8, they found nineteen shell holes in the walls and roof of his house. All the furnishings and household goods were gone; only an eight-day mantel clock remained, still ticking on its shelf over the fireplace.[6]

The scrubby growth of small trees about one-third of the way across the field in front of you marks the site of the William Bliss farm. Elwood Crist's study of this fight remains the most reliable source of information about this small piece of a very large battle. The fighting around the farm cost the Union army approximately 357 men and the Confederate army about 473 men. Evidence of the importance of this fight to those who participated in it can be seen in the bas-reliefs on the monuments to the 12th New Jersey and the 106th Pennsylvania Infantry during your visit to Cemetery Ridge at Stop 33.

William Bliss, a native of Massachusetts born in 1799, married Adeline Carpenter in 1823 and immediately started a family. Life brought both blessings and sorrows. The couple enjoyed the arrival of several children but then experienced the tragedy of losing several of them to illness at young ages. After a long stint of living and working in western New York, William and Adeline moved to Gettysburg in 1856 and bought their fifty-three-acre farm—complete with house, barn, and orchard— from Alexander Cobean on April 7, 1857. Bliss added a bit more acreage before the Civil War broke out, and he, his wife, and two adult daughters lived on the farm; his second grandchild was born there, too. The destruction of his farm during the battle, of course, meant that everything Bliss had worked for all his life literally had gone up in smoke. He sold off the remnants of his holdings to Nicholas Codori in 1865 and returned to New York. During the postwar years, Bliss submitted multiple damage claims for the burning of his farm. He set his losses at $3,256.08. Unfortunately, at the time of his death in August 1888, he had not received a cent in payment. His heirs continued to press the claim into the early twentieth century, also without success. As with so many other cases at Gettysburg, destruction of property due to the "operation of war" did not qualify for compensation of any sort.[7]

What Did They Say about It Later?

In the postwar years, Longstreet made clear on many occasions his opposition to launching the charge against the Union center on July 3. In an article for the *Philadelphia Times*'s "Annals of the War" series, he wrote about the morning of that day:

> Fearing that he was still in his disposition to attack, I tried to anticipate him, by saying: "General, I have had my scouts out all night, and I find that you still have an excellent opportunity to move around to the right of Meade's army, and maneuvre him into attacking us." He replied pointing with his fist, "The enemy is there, and I am going to strike him." I felt then that it was my duty to express my convictions; I said: "General, I have been a soldier all my life. I have been with soldiers engaged in fights by couples, by squads, companies, regiments, divisions, and armies, and should know, as well as any one, what soldiers can do. It is my opinion that no fifteen thousand men ever arrayed for battle can take that position," pointing to Cemetery Hill. General Lee, in reply to this, ordered me to prepare Pickett's Division for the attack. I should not have been so urgent had I not foreseen the hopelessness of the proposed assault. I felt that I must say a word against the sacrifice of my men; and then I felt that my record was such that General Lee would or could not misconstrue my motives. I said no more, however, but turned away.[8]

Longstreet also criticized Lee for putting him in command of the charge: "He knew that I did not believe that success was possible; that care and time should be taken to give the troops the benefit of positions and the grounds; and he should have put an officer in charge who had more confidence in his plan. Two-thirds of the troops were of other commands and there was no reason for putting the assaulting forces under my charge." In his memoirs, published in the 1890s, Longstreet went a step further, fundamentally challenging Lee's veracity. He rejected entirely the accuracy of Lee's battle report for July 3, in which his commander had written: "Longstreet . . . was ordered to attack the next morning, and General Ewell was ordered to attack the enemy's right at the same time." Longstreet argued that this statement was "disingenuous": "He did not give or send me orders for the morning of the third day, nor did he reinforce me by Pickett's brigades for morning attack. . . . I found a way that gave some promise of results"—although he did not explain where he planned to go—"and was about to move the command, when he rode over after sunrise and gave his orders."[9]

Just as Lee's Virginia supporters condemned Longstreet during the postwar years for his alleged recalcitrance on July 2, they launched similar attacks on him for his opposition on July 3. Jubal Early, for one, contended that "the officer who was entrusted with the conduct of the attack . . . has no right to complain that the charge was hopeless from the beginning. It was his own conduct that contributed to make it so."[10]

Longstreet found few Southern advocates during the postwar years who willingly defended him in print, but some proved bold enough to do so. Major G. Moxley Sorrel, who served on Longstreet's staff at Gettysburg, admitted that Longstreet "failed to conceal some anger" and showed "apparent apathy in his movements," which "lacked the fire and point of his usual bearing on the battlefield." But in his final assessment of his commander's performance on July 3, Sorrel wrote: "While Longstreet by no means approved the movement, his soldierly eye watched every feature of it. He neglected nothing that could help it and his anxiety for Pickett and the men was very apparent."[11]

Driving directions to the next stop: Drive forward 0.3 miles to the large Virginia monument on your left. Park on the right side of the road near the sign designating National Park Service Auto Tour Stop 5.

8

The High-Water Mark?

STOP 32. PICKETT'S CHARGE

You will visit two positions at this site. To reach the second position, you will have to walk several hundred yards over slightly irregular terrain.

Orientation

Stand in front of the Virginia monument and look eastward into the open fields. On the skyline directly ahead of you, you will see Union monuments atop Cemetery Ridge, the main battle line of the Army of the Potomac. Once again, identify the large obelisk that looks much like the Washington Monument and the large cluster of trees to its left, the historic "copse of trees." The single large tree to the left of the copse of trees marks the point where the stone wall protecting the Union infantry makes a ninety-degree turn to the east (toward the horizon) and then turns left again. The area between the copse of trees and that single individual tree is the area best known as "the Angle" where "Pickett's Charge" penetrated the Union line. The evenly spaced individual trees on the skyline to the left of the copse of trees marks the site of the orchard at Ziegler's Grove. The small white farm buildings to the left of the orchard mark the site of the Brien farm. The road that angles across your front, more than halfway across the field, is Emmitsburg Road; the red buildings of the Nicholas Codori farm on your right front rest on the far side of the road.

The Virginia monument.

Position 1: The Artillery Bombardment

What Happened Here?

It is essential that you understand from the start that the fields immediately in front of you are not those over which Major General George E. Pickett's Virginia division made its famous assault on the Union center. This Virginia memorial stands here simply to mark the general location from which Lee observed the assault and rode out to rally and comfort the survivors.

To your right front, follow the asphalted walkway out into the field to the informational wayside next to several artillery pieces. If you previously had difficulty locating the famous copse of trees, simply look down the barrel of the cannon closest to the wayside; the copse appears to touch the left side of the muzzle.

From this position, you can gain greater understanding of the Army of Northern Virginia's preattack cannonade. The cannons here at the wayside represent the position of a portion of Major William T. Poague's battalion from A. P. Hill's Third Corps during the bombardment. You can visualize Hill's artillery line by mentally pushing forward into this field the line of cannons you have passed along West Confederate Avenue so far. Hill's guns that took part in the cannonade were, as General Pendleton reported, "well placed."

Now look to your right front and locate the red barn and white house of the Daniel Klingel farm on Emmitsburg Road. In front of the Klingel farm, on this side of the road and the white fences that line it, you can see a slight ridge of ground. On that rise, which extends well to the right toward the Peach Orchard, Longstreet's I Corps artillery rolled into line. Their position allowed them to lay an enfilading (or angled) fire around the copse of trees capable of inflicting more damage than Hill's guns emplaced here could produce with frontal fire alone. But they could not do so with impunity; Longstreet's gun line also came under the fire of Union artillery on southern Cemetery Ridge and Little Round Top. Still, when General Pendleton visited the nearly sixty guns along the First Corps artillery line off to your right earlier in the day, he reported: "In the posting of these [cannons] there appeared little room for improvement, so judiciously had they been adjusted."

Unfortunately, from this position you cannot see the positions of any of Ewell's Second Corps guns, but their contributions to the great bombardment were minimal. Their batteries had exhausted much of their ammunition earlier in the day supporting the fight on Culp's Hill, and several commanders complained of defective shells. Colonel J. Thompson Brown, the Second Corps artillery chief, makes no mention at all in his report about his guns' participation in the cannonade.

At approximately 1:00 P.M., after two signal shots fired by Captain M. B. Miller's battery of the Washington Artillery from Longstreet's line to your right front, Pendleton reported that "our guns in position, nearly one hundred and fifty, opened fire along the entire line from right to left, salvos by battery being much prac-

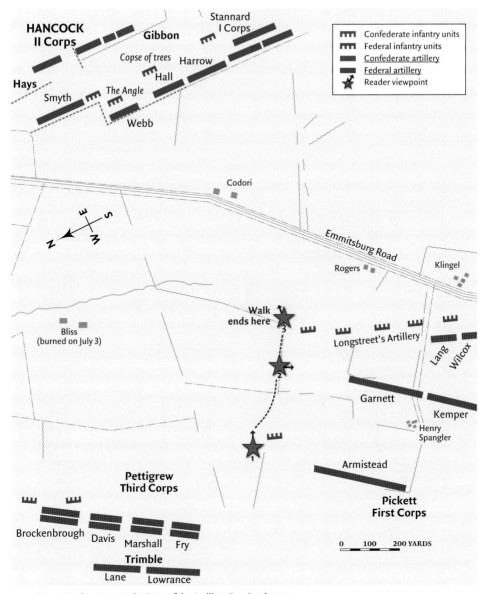

HANCOCK
II Corps

Gibbon

Stannard
I Corps

Hays

Copse of trees   Harrow

Hall

The Angle

Smyth

Webb

Codori

Confederate infantry units
Federal infantry units
Confederate artillery
Federal artillery
Reader viewpoint

N E
W S

Emmitsburg Road

Rogers   Klingel

Walk
ends here
3

Longstreet's Artillery

Lang Wilcox

Bliss
(burned on July 3)

2

Garnett

Kemper

Henry
Spangler

1

Armistead

Pettigrew
Third Corps

Pickett
First Corps

Brockenbrough Davis

Marshall   Fry

0   100   200 YARDS

Trimble

Lane Lowrance

Troop Deployments at the Start of the Artillery Bombardment

ticed. . . . So mighty an artillery contest has perhaps never been waged, estimating together the number and character of guns and the duration of the conflict." He estimated the average distance between his guns and their targets to be approximately 1,400 yards. Most battery and battalion commanders specifically described a measured, deliberate fire that was designed to ensure accuracy and to conserve ammunition.

Confederate artillery officers filled their reports with superlatives to describe the bombardment. Colonel H. C. Cabell on Longstreet's line considered it "far, very far, exceeding any cannonading I have ever before witnessed." Captain E. M. Brunson, commanding a reserve battalion in the Third Corps, asserted that "the artillery fight was one of the most terrific on record, and never were guns served more splendidly, and never did men behave more heroically, than the artillerymen did in that memorable battle of the 3d." If success that day had relied upon the artillery, Brunson added, the Battle of Gettysburg would be listed on "the resplendent roll of victories that have heretofore marked the career of the Army of Northern Virginia."[1]

Longstreet had placed West Point–educated Lieutenant Colonel Edward Porter Alexander, one of his artillery battalion commanders, in command of the First Corps guns on July 3. In so doing, he chose not to rely upon his command's most senior artilleryman, Colonel J. B. Walton, who was not a professional soldier. Even before the cannonade began, Alexander received an unexpected message from Longstreet: "If the artillery fire does not have the effect to drive off the enemy . . . I would prefer that you should not advise Gen. Pickett to make the charge. I shall rely a great deal on your good judgment to determine the matter & shall expect you to let Gen. Pickett know when the moment offers." Alexander realized that Longstreet had tried to shift much of the responsibility for ordering the charge from his own shoulders to those of his subordinate. Alexander replied, "I will only be able to judge of the effect of our fire on the enemy by his return fire," and he raised a more serious concern: "If, as I infer from your note, there is any alternative to this attack it should be carefully considered before opening our fire, for it will take all the artillery ammunition we have left to test this one thoroughly."

At the height of the bombardment, from his own artillery line to your right, Longstreet observed some of the exchange of fire, watching intently and noticing that "the enemy put in fresh batteries about as rapidly as others were driven off." He believed that "we must attack very soon, if we hoped to accomplish anything before night." But Alexander and other artillerymen realized they were running low on ammunition. At "exactly" 1:25 P.M., Alexander sent a message to Pickett: "If you are coming at all, come at once, or I cannot give you proper support, but the enemy's fire has not slackened at all. At least eighteen guns are still firing from the cemetery itself." Just ten minutes later, Alexander sent a second message to Pickett: "For God's sake come quick. The 18 guns are gone. Come quick or I can't support you." When Longstreet learned of the ammunition shortage, he wanted to delay the assault long enough to refill the chests, but he soon learned that this could not be done in a timely way. "Frequent shell endangering the First Corps ordnance train in the convenient locality I had assigned it," Pendleton reported, so he moved it farther to the rear. As Longstreet wrote in his official report: "The order for this attack, which I could not favor under better auspices, would have been revoked if I felt that I had that privilege." But Lee had made his wishes clear. When Pickett looked to Longstreet for orders to advance, all the corps commander could do was nod in assent.[2]

Who Fought Here?

In addition to the four battalions of A. P. Hill's Third Corps artillery to which you were introduced at the previous stop, the following battalions of Longstreet's First Corps artillery formed a line to your right and right front to participate in the bombardment on July 3. Major James Dearing's battalion included the Fauquier (Va.) Artillery, the Hampden (Va.) Artillery, the Richmond Fayette Artillery, and Blount's Virginia Battery. Lieutenant Colonel Alexander's battalion included the Ashland (Va.) Artillery, the Bedford (Va.) Artillery, the Brooks (S.C.) Artillery, the Madison (La.) Light Artillery, Parker's Virginia Battery, and Taylor's Virginia Battery. Colonel H. C. Cabell's battalion was composed of Battery A, 1st North Carolina Artillery; the Pulaski (Ga.) Artillery; the 1st Richmond (Va.) Howitzers; and the Troup (Ga.) Artillery. The First, Second, Third, and Fourth Companies of the Washington (La.) Artillery comprised Major Benjamin F. Eshelman's battalion.

Who Commanded Here?

Brigadier General William Nelson Pendleton (1809–83), born in Richmond, graduated fifth in the U.S. Military Academy's class of 1830. He left the army after three years and entered the Episcopal ministry, becoming rector of Grace Church in Lexington, Virginia. When the Civil War broke out, he immediately became captain of the Rockbridge Artillery and its four cannons, nicknamed "Matthew, Mark, Luke, and John." His West Point ties likely helped to elevate him rapidly to colonel of artillery on General Joseph E. Johnston's staff and won him a promotion to brigadier general on March 26, 1862. When Robert E. Lee took command of the Army of Northern Virginia on June 1, 1862, he retained Pendleton as his chief of artillery, but Pendleton rarely served as its operational commander; as the war went on, his duties increasingly revolved around administrative and logistical concerns rather than battlefield deployment. On the rare occasions—such as at Gettysburg on July 3—when Lee really needed an officer of Pendleton's rank to coordinate the preassault artillery bombardment in order to make the best possible use of all available guns, Pendle-

Brigadier General
William N. Pendleton,
C.S.A. (USAMHI)

ton proved incapable of doing so. As Confederate artilleryman E. Porter Alexander observed, the artillery chief "was too old & had been too long out of army life to be thoroughly up to all the opportunities of his position. But I never knew that Gen. Lee himself fully appreciated it."[3]

Lieutenant Colonel Edward Porter Alexander (1835–1910), born in Washington, Georgia, graduated from West Point in 1857, ranking third in a class of thirty-eight. Second Lieutenant Alexander resigned from the U.S. Army in May 1861 to enter Confederate service as a captain of engineers. In his initial assignments, he served as a signal officer for General Beauregard at First Manassas and sent the message that alerted the Confederate forces to General Irvin McDowell's effort to turn their left flank. He became chief of ordnance for the Army of Northern Virginia and helped to develop a Confederate signal corps. Promoted to lieutenant colonel of artillery in December 1861 and colonel of artillery a year later, he commanded one of five artillery battalions in Longstreet's First Corps, seeing action at Fredericksburg and Chancellorsville. After commanding his battalion actively on July 2, Alexander received orders from Longstreet on July 3 to plan and organize the First Corps's portion of the artillery bombardment preceding the attack against the Union center best known as Pickett's Charge. After Gettysburg, Alexander continued to command artillery units in Longstreet's First Corps, eventually becoming corps chief of artillery. He saw action at Chickamauga and Knoxville in the west before receiving a promotion to brigadier general in February 1864 and returning to Virginia for the fighting at the Wilderness, Spotsylvania, Cold Harbor, and Petersburg. Seriously wounded at Petersburg, he returned to the army in time to make the last march to Appomattox Court House. Even before the war's end, Alexander was recognized as the most accomplished artillerist in the Army of Northern Virginia. After the war, Alexander led an equally distinguished career as a professor of engineering, a railroad president, and a rice planter. His *Military Memoirs of a Confederate*, published in 1907, remains one of the best personal accounts of the war. Edward Porter Alexander died in Savannah in April 1910.

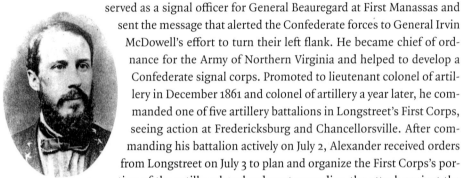

Lieutenant Colonel Edward Porter Alexander, C.S.A. (USAMHI)

Who Fell Here?

In Longstreet's First Corps, Dearing's battalion lost 29 of its 419 men, Alexander's battalion lost 139 of its 576 men, Cabell's battalion lost 52 of its 378 men, and the Washington Artillery lost 30 of its 338 men.

Individual vignettes. Private Henry Redeau, a clerk who worked in New Orleans, traveled through Mobile, Alabama, in late May 1863. There he crossed paths with Lieutenant Colonel Michael Nolan, a fellow resident of New Orleans and a senior officer in the 1st Louisiana Infantry, who was on his way home on a recruiting trip. Somehow, Nolan managed to convince Redeau to enlist, and on May 30, 1863, the young man became a private in the Third Company of the Washington Artillery. Redeau was only seventeen years old. He proceeded directly to Virginia and joined his new command on June 9 at the start of the march north to Pennsylvania. On July 3, during the bombardment, Redeau was killed by Union counterbattery fire. The printed form listing the eastern theater's major battles in his file contains only a single handwritten entry: a K for "killed" after the name of the only battle in which he fought. He served only long enough to get his $50 enlistment bounty; he never received any other pay for his brief service. Coincidentally, Lieutenant Colonel Nolan rejoined his 1st Louisiana just before the Battle of Gettysburg and fell dead on the slopes of Culp's Hill on the evening of July 2, less than twenty-four hours before Redeau died.[4]

Confederate artillery fire drew Union counterbattery fire. Shots that went long invariably fell among the infantrymen, already deployed to advance when the firing ceased. Company B of the 3rd Virginia Infantry, a unit raised around Norfolk, lay in position behind Dearing's battalion; on July 3 this decidedly undersized unit counted only three commissioned officers and twelve enlisted men present for duty. During the bombardment, wrote a chronicler, "Lieutenant [Robert] Guy was killed as was also Private Joshua Murden. Private Walter Leggett was wounded, six of the others were overcome by heat, so that only six were in condition to advance when the order was given."[5] Guy, a mechanic, had enlisted in Portsmouth, Virginia, on April 20, 1861, as the company's second sergeant; after promotion to first sergeant in September 1861, he won election to second lieutenant on January 1, 1863. A Union artillery shell tore off Guy's shoulder, and he died on July 4. Private Murden, a mechanic born in Princess Anne County, also enlisted in 1861 and went into the July 3 battle as the regimental color-bearer. His commanding officer, Colonel Joseph C. Mayo, later wrote about how readily Murden fell into ranks, demonstrating "as fine a type of true soldiership as ever stepped beneath the folds of the spotless stars and bars," only to fall "stark and stiff, a hideous hole sheer through his stalwart body, and his right hand closed in a death grip around the staff of that beautiful new flag which to-day for the first and last time had braved the battle and the breeze."[6]

Who Lived Here?
The fields to your immediate front are part of the Nicholas Codori farm. The fields to your left beyond the post-and-rail fence mostly belonged to William Bliss.

What Did They Say about It Later?
Several questions relating to the bombardment demonstrate just how difficult it can be for a historian to reconstruct events of long ago. In a highly charged event that threatens life and limb, individual perception and perspective shape what one remembers afterward.

In stressful situations, for instance, the passage of time can take on a fluidity that makes it seem to speed up or slow down, depending on circumstances. This proved to be true during the cannonade. Major Benjamin Eshelman of the Washington Artillery, focused on keeping his gun crews firing, reported that thirty minutes elapsed between the first signal shot and the advance of the infantry. On the other hand, Colonel James Mallon of the 42nd New York, his men lying in wait on the forward crest of Cemetery Ridge, believed that the cannonade lasted every bit of four hours. His corps commander, General Hancock, reported that it lasted "an hour and forty-five minutes." General Meade—as well as Henry J. Hunt, the Union artillery chief; General Howard of the XI Corps; and General Gibbon of the II Corps division in the target area, along with his brigade commanders, Generals Alexander S. Webb and William Harrow and Colonel Norman J. Hall—reported that the bombardment began at about 1:00 P.M. and ended at about 3:00 P.M., providing a foundation for the traditionally accepted time span of two hours. General Lee reported a bombardment two hours in length. His artillery chief, General Pendleton, reported that the cannonade started at 1:00 P.M., but he made no specific reference to its duration.[7]

How many Confederate cannons took part? General Pendleton estimated the number to have been "nearly one hundred and fifty." General Hunt, in his report, estimated the number of guns "bearing on our west front at from one hundred to one hundred and twenty." Hancock offered an estimate of between "one hundred and fifteen to one hundred and fifty." But Corporal J. L. Bechtel of the 59th New York wrote on July 6 with great confidence that he endured the fire of exactly "113 guns for one hour and a half" and suffered only a bruised heel.[8]

How effective was the bombardment? Major Dearing reported that "the firing on the part of my battalion was very good, and most of the shell and shrapnel burst well. My fire was directed at the batteries immediately in my front, and which occupied the heights charged by Pickett's division. Three caissons were seen by myself to blow up and I saw several batteries of the enemy leave the field." Captain Charles A. Phillips of the 5th Massachusetts Battery commented, on the other hand, that "viewed as a display of fireworks, the rebel practice was entirely successful, but as a military demonstration, it was the biggest humbug of the season." Colonel Hall provided this colorful assessment: "The experience of the terrible grandeur of that rain of missiles and that chaos of strange and terror-spreading sounds, unexampled, perhaps in history, must ever remain undescribed, but can never be forgotten by those who survived it."[9]

Surprisingly, perhaps, Colonel Alexander made no comment at all in his report about the effectiveness of the bombardment, its start or end time, or its duration. In his postwar recollections, however, he admitted: "I had, at first, taken no very special thought as to how long I would let the fire continue, before telling Pickett to go. Some 20 to 30 minutes I supposed would be about right. Not shorter than 20, for the longer the time the more punishment the enemy would have. But not longer than

30, because they had a long charge, & I must allow plenty of time for them to cover the distance within the hour. For I did not like to use up more ammunition than that would consume before having the crisis of the matter determined."[10]

Position 2: Pickett's Charge

Orientation
Stand in front of the cannon next to the wayside. Look to your left toward the North Carolina monument you visited at Stop 31.

What Happened Here?
All of Pettigrew's men formed to your left and rear, on the reverse slope of Seminary Ridge. Trimble's men fell into ranks about 200 yards behind behind them. Recall that Colonel Fry's—formerly Archer's—Tennesseans and Alabamians held the right of Pettigrew's line, no closer to your current position than the nearest post-and-rail fence line to your left that heads out across the field. As Lieutenant Colonel S. G. Shepard of the 7th Tennessee confirmed, "There was a space of a few hundred yards between the right of Archer's brigade and the left of General Pickett's division when we advanced . . . they not being an exact continuation of each other." It would be up to staff officers to carry commanders' orders to senior subordinates in an effort to maintain some semblance of order.

Now look to your right into the swale of low ground and locate the red barn and buildings associated with the Henry Spangler farm. That is where Pickett's Virginians deployed. Follow the mowed path along the post-and-rail fence in front of you straight ahead for about 300 yards. As you walk, note the unevenness of the ground and how quickly your surroundings change. Keep asking yourself four key questions: (1) Who can see me here? (2) Who cannot see me here? (3) What can I see? (4) What can't I see? The answers will change as you cross higher ground or dip into lower ground. Proceed forward until you reach the first fence line that stretches off to the left. You should now be even with the Spangler farm buildings in the low swale off to your right. Once again, consider your four questions and notice how the terrain shapes your answers.

Now turn to the right and face the Spangler farm buildings. View the map on page 358 to appreciate fully the troop deployments around the farm. A dirt lane passes from the Emmitsburg Road, going from left to right through the complex of farm buildings, back into the tree line and well into the Confederate rear area. Early that morning, Pickett's men left their camps and followed that lane from right to left up into the grounds of the Spangler farm. The house and barn presented obstacles to an advance, so Garnett's and Kemper's men marched past the farm buildings and deployed in front of them—just to the left of the structures as you look at them. Garnett's men went into line of battle to the left of the lane and perpendicular to it,

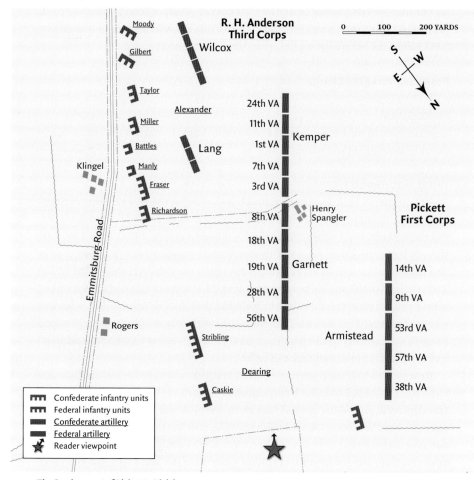

The Deployment of Pickett's Division

their line extending toward you and filling about half the space between your current position and the farm buildings. Kemper's five regiments went into their line of battle to the right of the lane and extending south, well beyond the buildings. Notice that the open ground in front of the lines of Kemper and Garnett to your left front rises up, giving the infantry a certain amount of protection from enemy artillery fire. (The remnants of Lang's Florida brigade and Wilcox's Alabama brigade deployed on that slope in front of Kemper's line.) Armistead's brigade formed its line behind Garnett's men, but they did not march through the Spangler farm complex to go into position. They lay instead behind the low ridge of ground, visible to your right front and forward of Seminary Ridge's tree line.

When Garnett and Kemper began their advance, they did not start by marching directly up the slopes in front of them. The report of Captain William W. Bentley of the 24th Virginia in Kemper's brigade left the clearest explanation of the way in which Pickett's men advanced. "The first movement was by the left flank . . . and then by the front," he wrote, describing a path that would have brought Garnett and Kemper's initial advance northward toward you before moving "by the front," or to your left, toward the Union line. By so doing, they took advantage of the cover offered by the rising ground in their front. Apparently, they did this several times. "We moved alternately by the front and by the left flank," Bentley continued, as they crossed the field and positioned themselves to hit the Union line at the designated point of attack: the copse of trees.

Turn to the left and face toward the Union line. Walk forward until the fence line on your right ends. Nearby, you will see a marker commemorating the service of the 1st Massachusetts skirmish line on July 2. The closest Union skirmishers to your current position on July 3, however, waited in the bed of the Emmitsburg Road in front of you. While you are in this location, take the time once again to consider your four questions. Immediately ahead of you, a mowed path roughly follows the direction of the advance of the left half of Garnett's brigade as it moved toward the Emmitsburg Road. Notice the angle the path takes as Garnett's brigade continued to use the cover provided by the rolling terrain and the orchard. Where the path crosses the rise to your left front, Garnett's men were only about thirty yards from the fences lining the road. They still had not fired a shot, and, except for some scattered musketry from Union skirmishers from Stannard's Vermont brigade, they had met little resistance.

When Garnett's men reached the top of the rise to your left front, however, several important changes occurred. First, they came into clear view of Union batteries near the copse of trees. To this point, those guns fired solid shot and shrapnel, but now they began to switch to canister—the ultimate antipersonnel weapon of the artillery. Note, too, that Pickett's left flank and Pettigrew's and Trimble's right flank likely saw each other now; this had not been possible earlier in the advance. Colonel Shepard of the 7th Tennessee offers one of the most precise commentaries about the relative position of the two elements at this point in the assault, reporting that "as we advanced, the right of our brigade and the left of General Pickett's division gradually approached each other so that by the time we had advanced a little over half of the way, the right of Archer's touched and connected with Pickett's left." At the top of that rise to your left front begins the real killing zone of Pickett's Charge.

Look to your right. As Garnett's men moved forward along the mowed path—and Armistead's brigade followed behind them much of the way—Kemper's men pressed forward across the fields to your right. Note the rolling nature of the terrain that Kemper's men crossed and, once again, consider the four questions. There were many times during Kemper's advance, too, when the ripples in the terrain, the Codori farm buildings, and fences and orchards gave the Virginians good protection. But one particular sight likely unnerved Pickett's men—and especially those in Kemper's brigade. In front of the far tree line to your right front, General Hunt formed an artillery line of at least six batteries during the early morning of July 3. It was not there the previous day when Wilcox, Lang, and Wright crossed over these same fields. The Union gunners could not resist the easy target that Kemper's men presented, but none of Pickett's men were safe from its fire. Major Joseph R. Cabell of the 38th Virginia in Armistead's brigade reported specifically about the "severe enfilading fire from the right" and the struggle to maintain their lines through the "grape and canister [that] were poured onto us from the right and front."[11]

As the assault force neared the Emmitsburg Road fences in front of you, Pettigrew's and Trimble's men prepared to cross them to your left. Garnett's men crossed ahead of you, most of them breaking to the left of the Codori farm buildings. Kemper's men crossed the road and climbed the fences to your right front. We will pick up the culmination of Pickett's Charge from the Union perspective at Stop 33.

Who Fought Here?

Major General George E. Pickett's 5,473-man division, Longstreet's First Corps, included the 1,459-man brigade of Brigadier General Richard B. Garnett, which included the 8th, 18th, 19th, 28th, and 56th Virginia Infantry; James L. Kemper's 1,634-man brigade, which included the 1st, 3rd, 7th, 11th, and 24th Virginia Infantry; and Lewis A. Armistead's 1,950 men of the 9th, 14th, 38th, 53rd, and 57th Virginia Infantry. The remnants of Brigadier General Cadmus M. Wilcox's 8th, 9th, 10th, 11th, and 14th Alabama Infantry and Colonel David Lang's 2nd, 5th, and 8th Florida—all badly battered on July 2 in their attack on the southern portion of Cemetery Ridge—prepared to advance to Pickett's support, if needed.

Who Commanded Here?

Major General George Edward Pickett (1825–75), born near Richmond, graduated last in the U.S. Military Academy's class of 1846. He saw service with the 8th U.S. Infantry in Mexico, forging lasting bonds in combat with fellow Southerner James Longstreet, with whom he stormed the defenses of Chapultepec. He served routine frontier duty in Texas, but in 1859 he made a name for himself by standing up for American claims to the San Juan Islands in a border dispute with Canada over ownership of land around the Puget Sound. He resigned his captaincy in the U.S. Army in 1861 and received a commission as a colonel in the Confederate army; he then won a promotion to brigadier general in January 1862. Seriously wounded in brigade command at the Battle of Gaines Mill during the Seven Days Battles, Pickett did not return to active duty until after the Maryland Campaign. With a promotion to major general in October 1862, he took command of a division in Longstreet's First Corps. Only three of his five brigades marched

Major General
George E. Pickett,
C.S.A. (USAMHI)

north into Pennsylvania in the summer of 1863, but he and they won lasting fame on July 3, when the Richmond press began calling their attack on the center of the Union line "Pickett's Charge." Much of Pickett's modern reputation still rests on a carefully crafted image nurtured by his young wife, LaSalle Corbell Pickett, whom he married shortly after Gettysburg. She considered her efforts to clear Pickett's name necessary since her "Soldier" had many detractors in the postwar years who tried to paint him as a coward, as a drunk, or merely as so inept that he let Robert E. Lee down not only at Gettysburg but also late in the war at Five Forks, where his lines crumbled under the Union assault that finally broke the Petersburg line and led to Appomattox a week later.

Brigadier General Lewis Addison Armistead (1817–63) came from a military family; both his father, Brevet Brigadier General Walker Keith Armistead, and his Uncle George—commander of Fort McHenry when Francis Scott Key wrote "The Star Spangled Banner" during the War of 1812—served for years in the U.S. Army in the early history of the Republic. Born in New Bern, North Carolina, Armistead attended West Point but did not graduate, his poor academic record as well as excessive demerits ending his cadetship. Commissioned directly from civilian life, Armistead saw significant combat during the Mexican War and then endured incredible personal tragedy, including the loss of two wives and two children to disease, a near-fatal disease of his own, and the loss of his family home. These misfortunes combined to turn him into a "misanthropic loner" by the time of the Civil War. He resigned his captaincy in the 6th U.S. Infantry in May 1861 and became colonel of the 57th Virginia Infantry. His promotion to brigadier general followed on April 1, 1862, as did a wound at Antietam. On July 3 his brigade deployed in the second line of Pickett's formation, and Armistead pleaded with his superiors to be allowed to advance in the first line—and not for the first time.

Brigadier General Lewis A. Armistead, C.S.A., was mortally wounded on July 3. (USAMHI)

He had done the same on previous occasions, such as at Malvern Hill, but not all of his men appreciated it. As one lieutenant wrote home afterward: "Armistead cares nothing for the men. He is full of saying 'go on boys' but has never said 'come on' when we are going into a fight." As it turned out, his position in the second line made him the only one of Pickett's three brigade commanders to breach the Union line at the Angle. He fell mortally wounded and died on July 5; his friends buried him in St. Paul's churchyard in Baltimore.[12]

Brigadier General James Lawson Kemper (1823–95) graduated from Washington College in 1842, practiced law, and engaged in politics throughout the antebellum years. He served briefly as a captain of Virginia volunteers in the Mexican War, and that experience, plus his presidency of the board of visitors of Virginia Military Institute, won him a commission as colonel of the 7th Virginia Infantry in

1861. Of Swedish ancestry, "a sturdy, martial breed of Norseman," Kemper "did not belie his lineage." Noted for his gallantry at Williamsburg and Fair Oaks, he won promotion to brigadier general on June 3, 1862, and served temporarily—and ably—in division command during the fall of 1862 while wounded superiors recuperated. On July 3, 1863, his brigade comprised the right flank of Pickett's line. Not far from the stone wall, Kemper fell with a bullet through the thigh. His men rescued him from capture on the field, but he became a prisoner a few days later when his condition did not allow him to be removed to Virginia with other Confederate wounded. Although later exchanged, Kemper was unfit for further field duty—surgeons had amputated his wounded leg—and he served in administrative positions until war's end. He resumed his political career with avidity, serving as the governor of Virginia from 1874 to 1877 "with a fidelity and ability which sustained the best traditions of the Commonwealth," although he became embroiled in political turmoil centered on the state debt. The experience exhausted him, and "he never left the shades of private life."[13]

Brigadier General James Lawson Kemper, C.S.A., lost a leg in Pickett's Charge on July 3. (USAMHI)

Brigadier General Richard Brooke Garnett (1817–63), a Virginian, graduated from the U.S. Military Academy in 1841. He did not serve in the Mexican War, but he served in a wide range of assignments until he resigned his commission in May 1861. He won early promotion to brigadier general on November 14, 1861, and commanded the Stonewall Brigade at the start of Stonewall Jackson's Shenandoah Valley Campaign. Jackson preferred charges against Garnett for retreating without orders at Kernstown, but he was never actually tried. Instead, he languished without an assignment until after Jackson's death, when the Army of Northern Virginia began its march into Pennsylvania. Determined to shake any hint of cowardice that might darken his reputation, Garnett rode his horse into the charge against the Union center on July 3, despite orders for officers to advance dismounted; an injured leg rendered that option impossible, and Garnett simply refused to stay behind. As one of his men recalled: "Never had our brigade been better handled. . . . There was scarcely an officer or man in the command whose attention was not attracted by the cool and handsome bearing of General Garnett, who, totally devoid of excitement or rashness, rode immediately in rear of his advancing line." Near the Angle, Garnett disappeared in a blast of Union musketry and artillery fire. General Hunt, the Union artillery commander, later claimed to have identified Garnett among the dead in front of the Angle, but his remains apparently became mixed in with the rest of Pickett's dead; thus, he likely rests with them on Gettysburg Hill at Hollywood Cemetery in

Brigadier General Richard B. Garnett, C.S.A., was killed in action on July 3. (USAMHI)

Richmond. Garnett remains one of the most mysterious of all the Confederate generals. The photographic image that is generally identified as his may, in fact, depict his cousin, fellow Confederate Brigadier General Robert Selden Garnett, killed in action in 1861.[14]

Who Fell Here?

You will learn about the casualties in Pickett's division in greater detail at Stop 33.

Individual vignettes. During the advance, a bullet hit twenty-four-year-old Corporal William Thomas Lancaster of Company F, 3rd Virginia Infantry, in the squamous portion of the right temporal bone and lodged there. His comrades could not remove him from the field, and stretcher bearers took him to a field hospital where surgeons removed the bullet and had him sent to the Seminary Hospital for further treatment. On July 20 they deemed him stable enough for travel and transferred him to the West's Building Hospital in Baltimore. When admitted, Lancaster showed signs of irritation, "as his wound was painful, and his sleep at night disturbed." The surgeons continued to apply cold-water dressings to the wound, but on August 1, Lancaster began to experience short periods of delirium accompanied by a weak but rapid pulse. He developed "obstinate diarrhea." On August 4 his delirium became increasingly more constant, and on August 9 he fell into a stupor. "Insensibility followed," noted the surgeon, and Corporal Lancaster died at about 5:00 P.M. on August 10. An autopsy discovered that the bullet had caused a three-by-two-inch fracture that involved several bones, the fragments of which caused a "disorganization of the brain" in the region of the injury but left the other portions of the brain "healthy." Assistant Surgeon Brooks preserved Corporal Lancaster's skull, and it became pathological specimen 1720 in the surgical section of the Army Medical Museum.[15]

Also during the July 3 charge, Sergeant William H. Gaskins of Company K, 8th Virginia Infantry, took a bullet in the sole of his right foot that exited from the top of the foot. Gaskins fell too close to the Union line to be taken back to a Confederate aid station. Thus he became a Union prisoner and, ultimately, entered the general hospital at Camp Letterman. His wound refused to heal, and on August 1 surgeons removed his right foot just above the ankle. He did not rally. Abscesses formed around the stump, and he suffered from diarrhea. The surgeons applied astringents and provided a nourishing diet, tonics, and stimulants, and by early September, Gaskins had begun to improve. On about October 30, however, the surgeons discovered severe necrosis in the portion of Gaskins's leg bone closest to the stump, and on November 4 they removed six inches of the diseased bone. Sergeant Gaskins died from the trauma the next day. Surgeon E. P. Townsend sent the necrotic segment of his leg bone, showing the "very extended ravages of disease," to the Army Medical Museum, where it became Specimen 1962.[16]

Who Lived Here?

Although most maps of the Gettysburg battlefield identify the buildings in the swale as the Henry Spangler farm, Spangler and his family did not reside here on July 3. He had purchased the farm in 1862, but he and his wife, Sarah, continued to live with their family in a house near Culp's Hill on the Baltimore Pike owned by his father. Spangler rented out this 152-acre farm to a father and son, Nicholas and Jacob Eckenrode, who lived here at the time of the battle with Sarah Eckenrode, Nicholas's wife. In a damage claim, Jacob explained what happened to the Spangler farm: "A Union officer directed him to leave with his family because of the danger from the battle. He left on July 2 leaving all his property except [three] horses and a colt which he left at a neighbor's for safety. He returned July 5th and found the barn containing the threshing machine and farming implements burned to the ground, the growing crops thoroughly destroyed, the four [horses] carried off and the horses captured by the rebels." He claimed damages worth $1,407.00. The quartermaster general's office entirely rejected his claim in unusually specific language: "This locality was embraced in the battlefield and was the scene of hard fighting. Kemper's Brigade of Pickett's Division, Longstreet's Corps formed on this land for the charge on the third day of July. It is clear that this is a claim for damage & depredation for which the United States is not responsible. None of the property was taken or used by the United States."[17]

What Did They Say about It Later?

The Civil War saw many frontal assaults by large numbers of troops. Some of them—such as the Confederate attack at Gaines Mill or the Union assault at Missionary Ridge—succeeded. Others—including Pickett's men at Gettysburg, Hood's Confederates at Franklin, or Burnside's troops at Fredericksburg—failed. But very few such attacks have earned a name that in itself has become iconic. How did "Pickett's Charge" achieve fame when all of these other assaults did not? Pickett's men did not name it. Northern press coverage of the battle almost never mentioned Pickett by name. The Richmond newspaper community, however, had little choice but to give the assault extensive coverage. Pickett's men represented the hometown heroes, and their heavy losses in the final major action at Gettysburg required a much higher degree of narration, analysis, and demand for accountability than any other single episode in the battle. Richmond editors gave their readers in Tidewater and Piedmont Virginia, many of whom had kinsmen in Pickett's ranks, exactly what they wanted. One early account set the tone. Pickett's men advanced "as coolly and deliberately as if forming for dress parade." The "crowning glory of those patriot heroes was achieved in the assault upon the iron-clad crest of Gettysburg," and "the bravery and patriotism of that blood-stained and scar-honored division" could best be measured by the length of its casualty lists.

In July 1863, Virginia readers heartily endorsed the sentiments that flowed from the pen of "T," who wrote: "From the time men first met men in deadly strife, no more unflinching courage was ever displayed by the veteran troops of the most martial people than the battle of Gettysburg witnessed in the determined valor of Pickett's division." The writer lamented their heavy losses: "See that shattered arm, that leg shot off; that headless body, and here is the mangled form of a young and gallant Lieutenant, who had braved the perils of many battles." He understood he could not assuage the grief of all those who had lost sons, husbands, brothers, fathers, and friends. He knew "many a Virginia home will mourn the loss of some noble spirit, yet, at the name of Pickett's division, and the battle of Gettysburg, how the eye will glisten, and the blood course quicker, and the heart beat warm, as among its noble dead is recalled the name of some cherished one."[18] Over time, Pickett's men found themselves endowed with a reputation as "the flower of Lee's army." As a postwar journalist intoned: "Greece has her Marathon, Sparta her Thermopylae, Europe her Waterloo, America her Bunker Hill, but the Confederacy has her charge of Pickett's division."[19]

Interestingly, the Virginians themselves started a controversy that certainly did not shed glory on Pickett's division. That matter centered on Pickett's whereabouts during the charge. Immediately after the war, and while Pickett remained alive, no one made an issue of his activities on July 3. In early postwar discussions, Longstreet himself had placed Pickett at the Codori farm, an appropriate location from which he could control the fight of his division. Then, in November 1894, allegations of professional misconduct surfaced. Major Kirkwood Otey of the 11th Virginia published an accusation in a Richmond newspaper that stunned many Virginians: "Whoever will take the trouble to make inquiries will find that there is an underground rumor, narrative, or whatever you may call it, that General George E. Pickett did not take part in the immortal performance of his division" on July 3. Otey related that he had been wounded in the attack, and when he went to the rear to tend to his injury, he stopped at the "whiskey wagon" for some "Confederate chloroform" and saw "two officers of General Pickett's staff (their names can be furnished if desired)," each holding a tin cup and awaiting their turn for a drink. Otey did not state that Pickett was there; he simply suggested that the presence of the staff officers "naturally suggested that General Pickett might be in the neighborhood."[20]

For approximately fifteen years, other Virginians with a personal or political grudge against Pickett picked up the theme, casting aspersions on the general's character and bravery—if not outright accusing him of an excessive fondness for alcohol. Pickett's wartime staff rallied to his defense, of course. His orderly Thomas Friend announced that no "base slanderers" would "take one laurel from the crown of Gen. George E. Pickett, as long as his Soldiers and his Soldiers' Children live."[21] In time, Pickett's friends overwhelmed his accusers with a literary counterattack, but the legacy of this brief flurry of accusations and defenses still colors some Gettysburg literature today.

Driving directions to the next stop: Drive south on the one-way West Confederate Avenue 0.6 miles to the intersection with Millerstown Road. Turn left and drive 0.3 miles to the intersection with Emmitsburg Road. Cross over Emmitsburg Road and drive another mile on Wheatfield Road to the stop sign at Sedgwick Avenue. Turn left onto Sedgwick Avenue and drive on this one-way road 1.2 miles past the Pennsylvania monument. Park in the designated parking spaces on the right near the distinctive monument to the 42nd New York Infantry crowned by a large wigwam and Native American warrior.

STOP 33. THE UNION REPULSE OF PICKETT'S CHARGE

A full appreciation of the events at this important stop requires breaking the action into four separate phases.

Orientation

Across the road from where you parked, you will see a monument that looks like a large open book. The cluster of trees behind it is the famous "copse of trees." The "Angle" is the open area to the right of the copse. Close to the road, between you and the copse, you will see two cannons flanking the monument to Captain Andrew Cowan's 1st New York Battery. Stand at his left cannon and face in the direction it is pointing.

Position 1: The Artillery Bombardment

What Happened Here?

Lee intended for his great artillery bombardment to silence the Union artillery here on the crest of Cemetery Ridge. As you look to your right and your left, the guns in place on this side of the road generally represent the batteries of Hancock's II Corps emplaced here when the bombardment began. In the low ground to your left rest the guns of Captain James M. Rorty's Battery B, 1st New York Artillery. To your right, on the grass inside the Angle, Lieutenant Alonzo H. Cushing's Battery A, 4th U.S. Artillery, held the line. To Cushing's right, placed at the left edge of the park road, Captain William A. Arnold's Battery A, 1st Rhode Island Artillery, served. Al-

The view beyond Captain Andrew Cowan's 1st New York Battery monument.

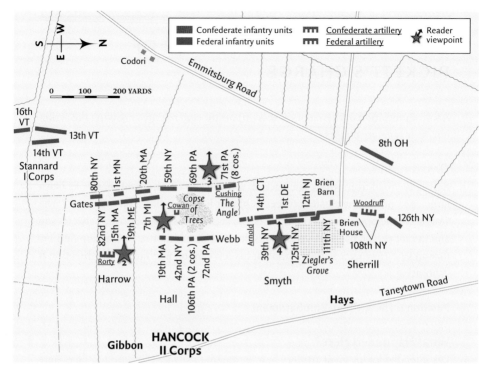

The Union on Cemetery Ridge

though you cannot see it from your present position, Lieutenant George A. Woodruff's Battery I, 1st U.S. Artillery, extended the II Corps artillery line just beyond the white buildings of the Brien farm to your right. Lieutenant T. Fred Brown's Battery B, 1st Rhode Island Artillery, originally filled the position where you are currently standing.

Now look to your left to the white-domed Pennsylvania monument. Beginning the evening of July 2 and continuing into the morning of July 3, General Hunt established a strong massed battery on the crest of southern Cemetery Ridge. It extended from the area of the Pennsylvania monument southward to the George Weikert farm. (You visited this general location at Stop 23.) By General Hunt's assessment, and including these II Corps cannons here, there were "on the western crest line seventy-five guns, which could be aided by a few of those on Cemetery Hill" and Little Round Top.

When the Confederate cannonade began, the infantry in line in front of you simply hunkered down as best they could to protect themselves from the shelling. Captain Henry L. Abbott explained to his father right after the battle how the men of the 20th Massachusetts survived: "The thin line of our division against which it [the bombardment] was directed was very well shielded by a little rut they lay in &

in front of our brigade by a little pit, just one foot deep & one foot high, thrown up hastily by one shovel, but principally by the fact that it is very difficult to hit a single line of troops, so that the enemy chiefly threw over us with the intention of disabling the batteries & the reserves."[1] The infantrymen likely were not the Southern gunners' primary targets, however; Lee wanted the cannonade to destroy the II Corps batteries. As Captain John Hazard, commander of the II Corps artillery brigade, reported: "The batteries did not reply at first, till the fire of the enemy becoming too terrible, they returned it till all their ammunition, excepting canister, had been expended; then they waited for the anticipated infantry attack."[2]

When the shelling finally ceased, these II Corps batteries had suffered significant losses in horses and men; several caissons of ammunition exploded, and Captain Rorty was dead. Brown's battery posted here had to be replaced, and Cowan's 1st New York Battery wheeled into the front line just in time to participate in the repulse of Pickett's men. Monuments to many of the batteries that arrived to reinforce this position during this action also sit along the crest of Cemetery Ridge, most of them placed on the other side of the road behind you.

Who Fought Here?

The individual batteries named in the text served in the front line during the bombardment and through most of the repulse.

Who Commanded Here?

Brigadier General Henry Jackson Hunt (1819–89), born in Detroit, was the son and paternal grandson of Regular Army officers. He graduated from West Point in 1839, ranking nineteenth in a class of thirty-one. During the Mexican War, he earned two brevets for gallantry while serving in the field with an artillery battery, and he quickly established himself as one of the Army's top specialists in that combat arm. Indeed, he served on the army's three-man board charged with revising its light artillery tactics, and its report became the foundation for the system used by both the Union and Confederate armies during the Civil War. A battery commander in the war's early months, Hunt spent the winter of 1861–62 training the Army of the Potomac's artillery reserve; his outstanding service at Malvern Hill won him a promotion to brigadier general in September 1862. He served with distinction as the Army of the Potomac's chief of artillery under Major Generals George B. McClellan and Ambrose Burnside, but a disagreement with Major General Joseph Hooker reduced his authority until Meade restored it just before Gettysburg. In June 1864 Lieutenant General Ulysses S. Grant expanded Hunt's duties to include all siege operations around Petersburg. After Appomattox, Hunt reverted to his prewar rank of lieutenant colonel and retired

Brigadier General Henry J. Hunt, U.S.A. (USAMHI)

as a colonel in 1883. He became governor of the Soldiers' Home in Washington, D.C., and is buried in its cemetery.

Who Fell Here?

In the II Corps Artillery Brigade, Rorty's Battery B, 1st New York, lost Rorty and 26 of his 117 men; Arnold's Battery A, 1st Rhode Island, lost 32 of its 117 men; Brown's Battery B, 1st Rhode Island, lost 28 of its 129 men; Woodruff's Battery I, 1st U.S. Artillery, lost Woodruff and 24 of his 112 men; and Cushing's Battery A, 4th U.S. Artillery, lost Cushing and 38 of his 126 men. A number of infantry volunteers also fell while assisting the artillerymen during the fight. Cowan's 1st New York Battery that entered the main battle line here lost 12 of its 103 men.

Individual vignette. Edward Peto immigrated to the United States in November 1856, leaving from Liverpool with his new wife, Jemima, to start a new life. The twenty-eight-year-old laborer and his wife lived near Auburn, New York, when the Civil War broke out, and in October 1861 he enlisted as a private in Captain Andrew Cowan's 1st New York Battery that arrived at the center of Hancock's II Corps line near the copse of trees as the great bombardment ended. During the repulse of Pickett's Charge, a Confederate shell hit Private Peto in the abdomen, killing him instantly. In later years, Captain Cowan used Peto's death to discount the credibility of another Gettysburg account that claimed Lieutenant Cushing had been "disembowled" by a shell but was able to "grab his intestines" and keep on fighting until a bullet through the mouth killed him. "One of my men, Private Edward Peto, was struck there by a shell," Cowan wrote, and it "almost severed his body above his hips, as would likely have been the case had Lieut. Cushing also been hit by a shell in the abdomen." Twenty-seven-year-old Jemima Peto applied for a widow's pension, but she ran into difficulty since she possessed no records of her marriage to Edward in the parish church at Corydon in Surrey, England, where the Irish-born couple wed shortly before their departure for the United States. She finally received approval for her $8 monthly payment in December 1864.[3]

Who Lived Here?

The open fields beyond the stone wall in front of you are part of the Nicholas Codori farm, but much of the land on the crest of Cemetery Ridge here belonged to Peter Frey, a prosperous farmer. His home sits along the Taneytown Road behind you, and his barn became an important II Corps aid station on July 2 and 3. Surgeon Francis Wafer of the 108th New York described the impact of the shelling: "The outbuildings, fences and fruit trees were completely torn to pieces . . . [and] the roof of the house was torn up and the stone wall broken in one place & the stones thrown upon the floor. . . . It soon became impossible to do much" for the wounded.[4] The famous copse of trees belonged to Peter Frey.

What Did They Say about It Later?

On July 3 both Generals Hunt and Hancock claimed authority over the artillery on the II Corps line. Hunt ordered all battery commanders on Cemetery Ridge to cease their counterbattery fire during the bombardment to save ammunition to repulse the Confederate infantry. Hancock, on the other hand, ordered the batteries along this portion of the line that belonged to his II Corps to keep firing to bolster troop morale. Victory at Gettysburg did not settle the disagreement; a literary war between the two men and their friends extended well into the 1880s. General Hunt once asserted: "Had my instructions been followed here . . . I do not believe that Pickett's division would have reached our lines." One of Hancock's staff officers retorted: "Winfield S. Hancock did not read his commission as constituting him a major-general of infantry [only], nor did he believe that a line of battle was to be ordered by military specialists. He knew that by both law and reason the defense of Cemetery Ridge was intrusted to him, subject to the actual, authentic orders of the commander of the Army of the Potomac, but not subject to the discretion of one of General Meade's staff officers."[5]

Position 2: Pickett's Advance on Harrow and Hall

Orientation

Walk to the base of the obelisk commemorating the U.S. Regular Army to your left. Face the large red barn of the Codori farm. As you look directly across the valley, the large white Virginia monument that you visited at Stop 32 stands out against the trees of Seminary Ridge. As you look to your left front, on the other side of Emmitsburg Road, the top of Henry Spangler's large red barn marks the deployment site of Pickett's division.

What Happened Here?

You are standing at the left center of the line of Brigadier General John Gibbon's division in Hancock's II Corps. The prediction that Meade had made to Gibbon at the "council of war" the previous evening—that if Lee attacked on July 3, he would hit here—was about to become reality. The line of monuments to your left represent the regiments in Brigadier General William Harrow's brigade. The line of monuments to your right front represent the regiments in the brigade of Colonel Norman J. Hall.

After the cannonade ended, the attention of Harrow's and Hall's men shifted to their left front. They saw Kemper's brigade advance over the rise of high ground in front of the Spangler farm and then, just as quickly, disappear into a dip of low ground. Then they saw them appear a second time, now much closer to the Emmitsburg Road and to the left of the Codori farm. The Union artillery line to your left also saw the right flank of Kemper's line quite clearly, and Hunt ordered those guns to open on the Virginians. Still, Hunt reported that "the enemy advanced magnificently, unshaken by the shot and shell which tore through his ranks."

As Kemper's men crossed the double set of post-and-rail fences that lined both sides of the Emmitsburg Road, their advance angled across Harrow's front (and your left front) from left to right. They continued their movement across Hall's front (and your right front) as well, heading toward the copse of trees. As Hall described the action to your right front: "The perfect order and steady but rapid advance of the enemy called forth praise from our troops, but gave their line an appearance of being fearfully irresistible." Nonetheless, he "caused the Seventh Michigan and the 20th Massachusetts Volunteers to open fire at about 200 yards." The rest of Hall's men held their fire until the Virginians were "within 100 yards, some regiments waiting even until but 50 yards." When they opened fire, "there was but a moment of doubtful contest in front of the position of this brigade." As the Virginians cleared Harrow's front entirely and moved increasingly away from Hall's front toward the copse, some soldiers along this portion of the Union line launched into premature celebration. The soldiers of the 20th Massachusetts ahead of you, Captain Abbott reported, "were feeling all the enthusiasm of victory, the men shouting out, 'Fredericksburg,' imagining the victory as complete everywhere else" as it was in front of Hall's position.[6] But the Virginians continued to press forward.

Who Fought Here?

The Union defenders here included the 1,346-man brigade of Brigadier General William Harrow that included the 19th Maine, the 1st Minnesota, the 15th Massachusetts, and the 82nd New York Infantry; the brigade already had suffered significant losses in its July 2 fight against R. H. Anderson's division. Colonel Norman J. Hall's small 922-man brigade that included the 19th and 20th Massachusetts, the 7th Michigan, and the 42nd and 59th New York also had taken part in the fight of the previous day. Elements of Colonel Chapman Biddle's brigade of Newton's I Corps, especially the 80th New York, under Colonel Theodore Gates, fought on Harrow's left flank on July 3.

Who Commanded Here?

Brigadier General John Gibbon (1827–96), a Philadelphian by birth, grew up in North Carolina; three of his younger brothers served in Confederate gray. Gibbon graduated from the U.S. Military Academy in the middle of the class of 1847. Gibbon's antebellum career followed a typical pattern—service in Mexico and against the Seminoles in Florida—but he also spent significant time as an artillery instructor at West Point. That assignment led him to publish The Artillerist's Manual in 1860, and it became an important reference work for soldiers in both the Union and Confederate armies. When the Civil War broke out, Gibbon first served as a divisional chief of artillery, but after his promotion to brigadier general in May 1862, he took command of a brigade of midwestern infantry, drilling and attiring them in the uniform of the U.S. Regulars; this command became famous as the "Iron Brigade" that fought in Herbst's Woods on July 1. At Gettysburg, he commanded a II Corps division in the center of the Union line on Cemetery Ridge, where Pickett's Charge briefly penetrated the line. Gibbon fell wounded in its repulse. He returned to the army for the Overland Campaign and finally received command of the XXIV Corps in the Army of the James in January 1865. One of Meade's staff officers described him as "steel-cold General Gibbon, the most American of Americans, with his sharp nose and up-and-down manner of telling the truth, no matter whom it hurts." Gibbon did not retire from the U.S. Army until 1891 after a long postwar career on the western frontier. General Gibbon is buried at Arlington National Cemetery.[7]

Brigadier General John Gibbon, U.S.A., was wounded in action on July 3. (USAMHI)

Who Fell Here?

C.S.A.: Kemper fell badly wounded; he was captured during the Confederate withdrawal and admitted to the Seminary Hospital, where he lost his wounded leg to amputation. In Kemper's brigade, the 1st Virginia lost 113 of its 209 men, the 3rd Virginia lost 128 of its 332 men, the 7th Virginia lost 149 of its 335 men, the 11th Virginia lost 146 of its 359 men, and the 24th Virginia lost 163 of its 395 men—for a brigade loss of 50.5 percent. Among the regimental field officers, Colonel Lewis B. Williams of the 1st Virginia, Lieutenant Colonel Alexander Callcote of the 3rd Virginia, and Colonel Waller Tazwell Patton of the 7th Virginia were killed in action or mortally wounded.

U.S.: The regiments in Harrow's brigade fought hard on both July 2 and July 3. The 19th Maine lost at least 28 of its 65 killed or mortally wounded on July 3 alone. The 15th Massachusetts lost at least 15 of the regiment's 35 dead on July 3. The 1st Minnesota absorbed its greatest loss on July 2 but still lost 3 of its 79 killed or mortally wounded on July 3. The 82nd New York lost at least 24 of its 58 dead on July 3, as well. Overall, the brigade loss reached 57.1 percent. Colonel Hall's men also fought on both July 2 and 3. In the 19th Massachusetts, at least 11 of the unit's 15 dead lost their lives on July 3. The 20th Massachusetts lost 31 of its 43 dead on July 3. The 7th Michigan lost Lieutenant Colonel Amos Steele on July 3 and 15 more of its 25 dead that day. The 42nd New York lost 20 of its 26 killed on July 3. The 59th New York lost 7 of its 12 dead on July 3. Overall, Hall's brigade loss reached 40.9 percent. Colonel Gates's 287-man 80th New York from the I Corps suffered most of its 170 casualties on July 1, but at least 10 of its 39 dead were killed as a result of the July 3 combat.

Individual vignette. George Joeckel of Roxbury mustered in to Company B of the 20th Massachusetts Infantry on August 28, 1861. The twenty-five-year-old soldier left behind his widowed mother, Barbara, and four younger siblings—Elizabeth, fifteen; Barbara, thirteen; Jacob, eleven; and Helen, nine—with a promise that he would continue to provide for them from his army pay, just as he had contributed his wages to their support before he enlisted. His tent mate later attested that Joeckel regularly sent home $10 of his monthly pay. Joeckel proved to be a good soldier, and in December 1862 he won a promotion to sergeant for gallantry at the Battle of Fredericksburg. A raise in pay accompanied that promotion, and from that day forward, he increased his monthly contribution to his family's support to $13. He likely added a bit more a few months later when he became Company B's first sergeant. On July 3, as Pickett's men neared the front of Hall's brigade, First Sergeant Joeckel suffered a gunshot wound through the head that killed him instantly. Back in Roxbury, with four children to feed, Barbara Joeckel did not have time to grieve. She began the process of applying for a mother's pension as early as July 17. While the pension process for so many widows and bereaved mothers took six months or longer, Barbara Joeckel's application won approval by October 1863. First Sergeant Joeckel's remains rest in the Soldiers' National Cemetery in grave A-12 of the Massachusetts plot.[8]

Who Lived Here?

You are still standing on land owned by farmer Peter Frey and looking out over the fields of the Nicholas Codori farm.

What Did They Say about It Later?

Wartime press coverage of Pickett's Charge still colors our images of that event today. Writing for the *Richmond Enquirer*, Jonathan Albertson asserted:

> I have never seen since the war began (and I have been in all the great fights of this army) troops enter a fight in such splendid order as did this splendid division of Pickett's. . . . On presses Pickett's brave Virginians, and now the enemy open upon them, from more than fifty guns, a terrible fire of grape, shell and canister. On, on they move in unbroken line, delivering a deadly fire as they advance. Now they have reached the Emmetsburg [*sic*] road, and here they meet a severe fire from heavy masses of the enemy's infantry, posted behind the stone fence, while their artillery, now free from the annoyance of our artillery, turn their whole fire upon this devoted band. Still they remain firm. Now again they advance; they storm the stone fence; the Yankees fly; the enemy's batteries are, one by one, silenced in quick succession as Pickett's men deliver their fire at the gunners and drive them from their pieces. I see Kemper and Armistead plant their banner in the enemy's works; I hear their glad shout of victory.[9]

Even Northern journalists sensed they had witnessed something extraordinary, even though they tended to include far less detail in their tactical descriptions. As one described the charge: "About fifty yards in front of our batteries was a stone wall, turning from our centre in a southwesterly direction, behind which laid several of our regiments, picking off the enemy as they advanced up the slope of the hill. Notwithstanding the terrible fire poured into their ranks from our guns, so impetuous was the charge of the rebels that they drove our men from their position, and were advancing upon our batteries, several of which they captured."[10]

Position 3: Breakthrough at the Angle

Orientation

Walk forward to the line of monuments in front of you, turn to the right, and pass the markers to the 20th Massachusetts and 7th Michigan, noting especially the monument of the 59th New York. Just past the copse of trees, you will reach the distinctive monument to the 72nd Pennsylvania Infantry, topped by a bronze statue of a soldier swinging his rifle like a club. Stand in front of it and face Emmitsburg Road. Note the stone wall running across your front at your feet. Look down the wall to your right; at the large monument to the 71st Pennsylvania near the single large tree, the wall makes a sharp turn to the right (east) until it almost intersects with Hancock Avenue behind you. Just before it reaches the road, it resumes a northward course parallel to the road. The open space immediately behind you, bounded by the stone wall to your front and right, became known simply as "the Angle."

What Happened Here?

Continue to face Emmitsburg Road. You are now standing in the line of Brigadier General Alexander S. Webb's brigade of Gibbon's division. Since all four of his Pennsylvania regiments came from the City of Brotherly Love, the army generally referred

The view beyond the 72nd Pennsylvania Infantry monument.

Cemetery Ridge looking west from Webb's position. (USAMHI)

to Webb's command as the Philadelphia Brigade. On July 3 the 69th Pennsylvania held the left front of the brigade, marked by the obelisk and the ten small company markers attached to each other by chains to your left; the 71st Pennsylvania held the wall to your right. The 72nd Pennsylvania deployed in a second line, near the road behind you; most of the 106th Pennsylvania served on detached duty elsewhere and was not present for this fight. The guns of Cushing's battery were deployed behind you.

Soldiers in the Philadelphia Brigade probably had the best view of the entire attack known as Pickett's Charge. When they looked to your right front, they had a clear view of the advance of Pettigrew's and Trimble's lines, their right flank seemingly headed directly toward the Angle. Off to your left front, however, the rapid approach of Pickett's men toward this position presented a more immediate threat. As Captain William Davis of the 69th Pennsylvania reported: "Onward they came, and it would seem as if no power could hold them in check. Our troops, with few exceptions, met them bravely, but still they came."

Webb reported that once Pickett's men crossed the fences at the Emmitsburg Road, they "formed in the hollow in our immediate front several lines of battle" and pressed forward. Union artillery fire had slackened. Captain Hazard recounted that "half the valley had been passed over by them before the guns dared to expend a round of the precious ammunition remaining on hand." But now the guns opened up once more. A badly wounded Cushing rolled his three remaining pieces up to the wall to your immediate right and joined in. Hundreds of Virginians fell or fell back, but the remainder closed the gaps, dressed their ranks, and continued to push forward toward your position. As Major C. R. Fontaine of the 57th Virginia reported: "In passing over the field in front of the enemy's batteries the regiment lost nearly a third of [its] number in killed and wounded."[11]

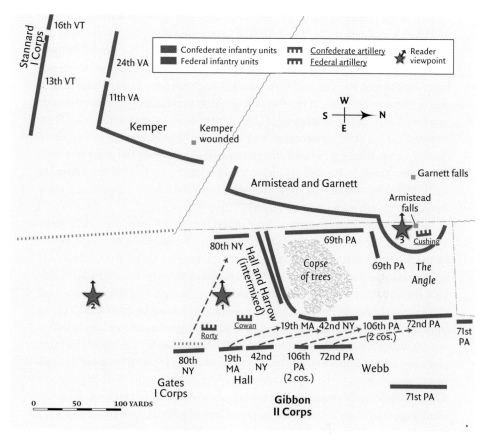

Pickett's Division Pierces the Union Line

By the time Pickett's men neared the wall, they had narrowed their front to just a few hundred yards, stretching from here at the Angle to a point to your left beyond the far end of the copse of trees. The advancing line stopped approximately twenty-five yards in front of you and fired a volley at the defenders all along this portion of the Union line. Cushing's guns and Webb's Philadelphians returned fire. In the close-range exchanges, Garnett and Cushing both fell dead, and now, for the first time, the Confederates advanced on the run. They breached the Union line in two places.

The smaller gap opened up to your left, at the juncture of Webb's and Hall's brigades, in the area of the 59th New York monument that you passed on your way to this position. As Captain Andrew Cowan of the 1st New York Battery reported: "I fired my last charge of canister, many of the rebels being over the defenses and within less than 10 yards of my pieces." The effect of his fire was "greater than I could have anticipated." The Virginians on his front "broke and fled in confusion," and Union infantry from Hall's brigade sealed the breach.[12]

The larger breach occurred roughly in the area where you now stand. A cluster of Pickett's regimental flags lined the wall here, rising and falling as the 69th and 71st Pennsylvania struggled with the Virginians. After a brief but violent struggle, the 71st Pennsylvania broke for the rear, Cushing's guns fell silent, and Confederate troops surged into the Angle. The breakthrough happened so suddenly that, as Major Fontaine reported, "a number of [Union] prisoners threw themselves within our lines" and "in the excitement of the moment were ordered to the rear."[13] Armistead, his hat upon his sword, at the head of an unknown number of Virginians, quickly widened the gap, while hundreds more kept up a heavy fire at the rock wall. Lieutenant Frank A. Haskell of Gibbon's staff wrote to his brother soon after the battle that as he watched the line at the Angle break, he felt that "the fate of Gettysburg hung upon a spider's single thread!"[14]

But the Union troops quickly rallied. Colonel Dennis O'Kane of the 69th Pennsylvania to your left ordered his five right companies—the five companies represented by the five small linked posts closest to you—to redeploy to face the Confederates pouring into the Angle, while his left flank continued to fire forward at Pickett's men near the wall. Hall and Harrow hurried their men through the copse of trees itself and toward the Angle. As O'Kane and his lieutenant colonel both fell dead, Hall reported, "the enemy was rapidly gaining a foothold; organization was mostly lost; in the confusion commands were useless." Hall relied upon the "officers of [his] staff and a few others, who seemed to comprehend what was required" to move his regiments to and through the copse to Webb's assistance.[15] On the crest of Cemetery Ridge, Webb's 72nd Pennsylvania in the brigade's second line initially made no forward motion to come to the aid of their brothers in arms. Haskell himself ordered the regiment to charge, but they did not move until he ordered its color sergeant forward with the colors, shouting: "Let the Rebels see it close to their eyes once before they die." The sergeant obeyed, but a Confederate bullet quickly felled him. With Webb offering personal encouragement, the color-bearer's enraged comrades became a "maddened load [of] men, arms, smoke, fire, a fighting mass" that reached the wall, where "flash [met] flash" and "a moment ensue[d] of thrusts, yells, blows, shots and undistinguishable conflict."[16] Armistead fell mortally wounded in the melee, and those with him also fell, became prisoners, or rushed back over the wall.

Now leaderless, and with no supports in sight, the surviving Virginians could do no more. Three regiments of Brigadier General George J. Stannard's Vermont brigade of the I Corps advanced into the open fields to your left front to hit Pickett's disorganized men at the wall. "Our right flank was entirely exposed," reported Colonel Joseph Mayo of the 3rd Virginia, who gave credit to the 24th and 11th Virginia for refusing their line to confront the new threat; if they had not done so, Mayo asserted, "the enemy would have penetrated our rear."[17] The fighting continued; both Hancock and Gibbon fell wounded. But the Virginians' time had run out. Since the 13th, 14th, and 16th Vermont regiments of Stannard's brigade now blocked their way back to the Henry Spangler farm where they had started, the Virginians simply proceeded straight across the fields to Seminary Ridge. The prominent Virginia monument you saw at Stop 32 stands where Lee met his retreating countrymen and told them, "It is all my fault."

After the Vermonters did all they could do against Pickett's flank, they received orders to about-face and head south. In the fields to your far left, in front of the Pennsylvania monument and Hunt's massed batteries, the Vermonters and the artillery combined to repulse quite bloodily the remnants of Wilcox's Alabamians and Lang's Floridians—the only reinforcements that made any significant effort to come to Pickett's direct support. No more followed.

Who Fought Here?

The primary Union defenders here belonged to the 1,224-man brigade of Brigadier General Alexander S. Webb and included the 69th, 71st, 72nd, and 106th Pennsylvania; most of the 106th Pennsylvania, however, served on detached duty elsewhere on the field at this time. Many of Hall's and Harrow's men rushed up from their positions to assist in the action here, as well, and the nine-month men of the 13th, 14th, and 16th Vermont of Stannard's brigade from Newton's I Corps—troops that saw their first combat action on July 2—also contributed to the results here on July 3.

Who Commanded Here?

Brigadier General Alexander Stewart Webb (1835–1911), a New York City native, graduated from the U.S. Military Academy in 1855 as a brevet second lieutenant of artillery. After a brief stint fighting the Seminoles in Florida, he returned to West Point to teach mathematics. Webb served primarily on staff duty for the first two years of the Civil War. He took over the famed Philadelphia Brigade on June 23, 1863, the same day he received his promotion to brigadier general. He had never led infantry in battle before Gettysburg. On July 3 Webb commanded from the front, leading the 72nd Pennsylvania forward to seal the breach made by Pickett's men at the Angle. He suffered a slight wound in the fighting and ultimately was awarded the Medal of Honor for his efforts. Webb fell wounded again at Spotsylvania in May 1864 and returned only in January 1865 to become Meade's chief of staff. As one of Meade's staff officers described Webb: "He is very jolly and pleasant, while, at the same time, he is a thorough soldier, wide-awake, quick and attentive to detail. In fact, I believe him much better for the place than Gen. H[umphreys, Meade's former chief of staff]. . . . My only objection to General Webb is that he continually has a way of suddenly laughing in a convulsive manner." He retired from the army in 1870 and served as president of

Brigadier General Alexander S. Webb, U.S.A., was awarded the Medal of Honor for his leadership of the Philadelphia Brigade on July 3. (USAMHI)

the College of the City of New York for thirty-three years. General Webb is buried at West Point.[18]

Who Fell Here?

C.S.A.: In Garnett's brigade, the general himself fell dead on the field of battle. His remains were never identified. Among his regiments, the 8th Virginia lost 178 of its 193 men for a 92.2 percent loss—the highest of the battle. The 18th Virginia lost 245 of its 312 men, the 19th Virginia lost 151 of its 328 men, the 28th Virginia lost 182 of its 333 men, and the 56th Virginia lost 189 of its 289 men—for a brigade loss of 65.0 percent. Among the field officers, Lieutenant Colonel John Ellis of the 19th Virginia, Colonel Robert C. Allen and Major Nathaniel Wilson of the 28th Virginia, and Colonel William D. Stuart of the 56th Virginia were killed in action. In Armistead's brigade, the general fell mortally wounded and died on July 5. Among his regiments, the 9th Virginia lost 177 of its 257 men, the 14th Virginia lost 250 of its 422 men, the 38th Virginia lost 194 or its 356 men, the 53rd Virginia lost 213 of its 435 men, and the 57th Virginia lost 249 of its 476 men—for a brigade loss of 55.6 percent. Among the brigade's field officers, Major John Owens of the 9th Virginia, Colonel James Gregory Hodges and Major Robert Poore of the 14th Virginia, Colonel E. C. Edmonds of the 38th Virginia, and Colonel John Bowie Magruder and Major Benjamin Wade of the 57th Virginia were killed here.

U.S.: In Webb's Philadelphia Brigade, the 69th Pennsylvania lost Colonel O'Kane, Lieutenant Colonel Martin Tschudy, and 135 more of its 284 men; the 71st Pennsylvania lost 98 of its 261 men; and the 72nd Pennsylvania lost 192 of its 380 men. The 106th Pennsylvania lost 64 of its 280 men, mostly in action away from this location. The percentage loss for the three Pennsylvania regiments that fought here on July 2 and 3 reached nearly 46.2 percent. In Stannard's brigade, the 13th Vermont lost 123 of its 636 men, the 14th Vermont lost 107 of its 647 men, and the 16th Vermont lost 119 of its 661 men—for a brigade loss of 18.0 percent.

Individual vignette. Private John Farren, a resident of Jersey City, mustered in to Company C of the 72nd Pennsylvania Infantry on August 10, 1861. On July 3, 1863, a Confederate bullet hit him in the right shoulder, lodging in the head of the humerus. Surgeon Henry Janes approved his transfer to the Mower Hospital in Philadelphia on July 7. There, surgeon J. Hopkinson reported that on July 22, Farren was operated on; a four-to-five-inch vertical incision was made down his upper arm to allow the doctor to access the head of the humerus. "During the manipulation," however, "the head snapped from the shaft. The end of the shaft was then sawn off, and the head of the bone removed," a process called excision. The surgeons held the rest of the humerus to the shoulder bones with "silver wire sutures and adhesive strips, and dressed [the wound] with compresses dipped in iced water." The following day, Farren ran a fever and suffered from constipation, and his pulse reached

120 beats per minute. After he was administered a laxative, he seemed to rally. By July 24 he "rest[ed] very easily, slept well during the night by taking a quarter of a grain of sulphate of morphia," and his "appetite [was] good." For over a month, Farren's condition seemed to improve. In early September, however, he began to complain of "having chills through the night," and his wound began once again to discharge from the shoulder very copiously. Still, he lived until September 27. His friends claimed his remains for burial near his home. Farren's excised humerus, with the bullet still embedded, was contributed to the Army Medical Museum by assistant surgeon J. H. McClellan.[19]

Who Lived Here?
You are still standing on Peter Frey's property. Some maps of the period show the fields in your front as belonging to P. A. Small, a businessman from nearby York, Pennsylvania.

What Did They Say about It Later?
Colonel Hall saw something special in the fight here at the Angle. As he reported after the battle: "The decision of the rebel commander was upon that point; the concentration of artillery fire was upon that point; the din of battle developed in a column of attack upon that point; the greatest effort and greatest carnage was at that point; and the victory was at that point."[20] In time, Northern war correspondents described the event in phrases and imagery that became iconic in themselves. As Charles Carleton Coffin of Boston later wrote of "the thin blue line" of Union defenders that repulsed the grand Confederate assault: "How inspiring the moment! How thrilling the hour! It is the high water mark of the Rebellion,—a turning point of history and of human destiny!" William Swinton, a noted New York journalist, saw in the repulse of the charge the start of the South's ultimate defeat, noting that, with the repulse, "the star of the Confederacy, reaching the zenith, turned by swift and headlong plunges toward the nadir of outer darkness and collapse."[21] John B. Bachelder, who oversaw the initial layout of the battle lines and the first efforts to interpret the historic events that transpired on the battlefield, fully embraced the notion; the bronze book near the copse of trees was Bachelder's own idea.

Although the "high-water mark" notion has become a staple element of many Gettysburg narratives, the idea recently has drawn serious challenge from modern historians who question the battle's broader strategic importance. Since the Civil War continued for nearly two more years, and the two armies combined lost far more casualties after this battle than in all those before it, it is more difficult to view Gettysburg as the clear start of the path leading to the Confederacy's inevitable defeat. As historian James M. McPherson has asserted: "Gettysburg is not important primarily as the high water mark of the Confederacy, but as the place where this nation, under God, shall have a new birth of freedom."[22]

Position 4: Pettigrew's Attack on Hays's Line

If you wish, you may return to your vehicle and move it up the road to the white buildings of the Abraham Brien farm before resuming your exploration of Pickett's Charge.

Orientation

Locate the equestrian monument to General Meade, the only figure on horseback in this area of the battlefield. Stand in front of it and look out over the fields over which Pettigrew's and Trimble's Confederates charged. General Meade's headquarters, which you visited at Stop 28, is in the low ground directly behind you.

What Happened Here?

When the stone wall that created the Angle reached Hancock Avenue by Arnold's battery to your left front and then began to parallel the road across your front, you crossed over from Gibbon's sector of the II Corps line to that of Brigadier General Alexander Hays. Like Gibbon's men, Hays's three brigades saw significant action on July 2. Colonel Thomas A. Smyth's brigade, in line along the wall directly in front of you, had participated in the fight for control of the Bliss farm, halfway across the field to your right front. Colonel George Willard's New York brigade—with Colonel Eliakim Sherrill now in command after the unit's July 2 fight against Barksdale's Mississippians—formed on Smyth's right flank. Except for the 8th Ohio on the skirmish line, Hays's third brigade under Colonel Samuel S. Carroll remained on East Cemetery Hill, where it helped to restore the XI Corps line the previous evening.

Walk down to the stone wall just across the road ahead of you. Notice that because the battle line here rests much farther up the slope of Cemetery Ridge, Gibbon's more-advanced position to your left combined with the smoke of battle to obscure much of Pickett's advance from Hays's men. Indeed, Lieutenant John F. Dent of the 1st Delaware was the only officer on Hays's line to describe the "united attack of the Pickett and Pender [actually Pettigrew] columns," with Pickett "moving on us in an oblique direction from the left, the Pender column moving on us in an oblique direction from the right," and both converging on his front.

The Alabamians, Tennesseans, Mississippians, North Carolinians, and Virginians under Pettigrew and Trimble advanced straight across the fields toward your position. As Hays described it: "Their march was as steady as if impelled by machinery, unbroken by our artillery, which played upon them a storm of missiles."

The troops that assaulted Smyth's brigade at this section of the wall probably included some of Fry's Tennesseeans and Alabamians, but most came from Marshall's brigade of North Carolinians. As Colonel Smyth reported: "My men were directed to reserve their fire until the foe was within 50 yards, when so effective and incessant was the fire from my line that the advancing enemy was staggered, thrown

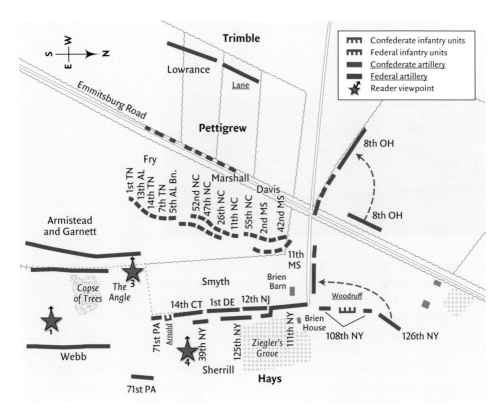

Hays's Repulse of Pettigrew and Trimble

into confusion, and finally fled from the field, throwing away their arms in their flight." Most of his men, however, opened fire well before the Confederates got that close. Major John T. Jones of the 26th North Carolina reported that "within about 250 or 300 yards of the stone wall . . . we were met with a perfect hail-storm of lead from their small arms." Nonetheless, Fry and Marshall tried to push forward, Jones claiming that "many had reached the wall" before Smyth's volleys pushed them back. Fry was wounded and captured, Marshall was killed, and Pettigrew himself suffered a minor wound in action against this front.

Now walk up the road to your right until you reach the white buildings marking the Brien farm. Face the open fields once more. Behind these stone walls, Colonel Sherrill's New York brigade confronted Davis's Mississippians and North Carolinians; Sherrill fell mortally wounded.

The fate of Davis's brigade illustrates well the intensity of the fighting on Sherrill's front. When the attack began, Brockenbrough's small Virginia brigade held the left flank; but first it had been delayed, and then, according to Colonel Robert M. Mayo of the 47th Virginia, it "met a flanking party of the enemy," halted, and ended

Cemetery Ridge looking north along the line of Hays's division. (USAMHI)

up engaging "ten times our number."[23] Their absence left Davis's men vulnerable to "a most galling fire of musketry and artillery" from behind the stone wall and artillery fire from the massed batteries on Cemetery Hill that "so reduced the already thinned ranks that any further effort to carry the position was hopeless." The 592-man 11th Mississippi had not participated in the brigade's fight on July 1; all 312 men on its Gettysburg casualty list fell on July 3.

Continue to walk along Hancock Avenue past the Brien farm until you reach the guns of Woodruff's battery on the right of the park road. The North Carolinians under Brigadier General James H. Lane in the second line under Trimble angled to the left to strengthen Pettigrew's weakening left flank. General Lane reported that his men "opened with telling effect, repeatedly driving the cannoneers from the pieces, completely silencing the guns in our immediate front." Lieutenant Woodruff fell mortally wounded at his battery posted near here. Lane claimed that his men "advanced to within a few yards of the stone wall" near this location. But then his men, too, became exposed to the fire of the the 8th Ohio of Carroll's brigade. The large regimental monument resting on the far side of Emmitsburg Road from this position recognizes the contributions of the Ohioans. "Our fire was poured into their flank with terrible effect," Lieutenant Colonel Franklin Sawyer reported, adding that "the whole mass gave way, some fleeing to the front, some to the rear, and some through our lines, until the whole plain was covered with unarmed rebels, waving coats, hats, and handkerchiefs in token of a wish to surrender."[24] Trimble received a bad wound in the leg, and Lane's and Davis's survivors fled back to Seminary Ridge.

Who Fought Here?

The Union defenders here included two of the three brigades belonging to Brigadier General Alexander Hays's Third Division of Hancock's II Corps. Colonel Thomas A.

Smyth's 1,069-man brigade included the 14th Connecticut, the 1st Delaware, the 12th New Jersey, and the 108th New York Infantry. Colonel Eliakim Sherrill's brigade included the 39th, 111th, 125th, and 126th New York Infantry; all of these regiments suffered heavily on July 2, including the loss of their original brigade commander, Colonel George Willard.

Who Commanded Here?

Brigadier General Alexander Hays (1819–64), born in Franklin, Pennsylvania, left Allegheny College in his senior year to accept an appointment to West Point. Despite his outstanding preparation, he graduated near the bottom of the class of 1844. Assigned to the infantry, Hays won a brevet for gallantry during the Mexican War, but he soon gave up military life. He tried the iron business, prospected for gold in California, and returned east to build bridges in his home state. He reentered the army at the start of the Civil War, soon obtaining the colonelcy of the 63rd Pennsylvania Infantry. He served ably until he was wounded at Second Manassas, and he won promotion to brigadier general on September 29, 1862. When he returned to active duty, he became commander of a brigade of New York troops derisively called the "Harpers Ferry Cowards" for their surrender to the Confederates during the Maryland Campaign. With discipline and a great deal of personal leadership, he helped to turn that unit into a reliable command, as the performance of Willard's brigade on July 2 and 3

Brigadier General Alexander Hays, U.S.A. (USAMHI)

clearly demonstrated. Hays led a division in Hancock's II Corps at Gettysburg, and he commanded from the front, always visible to his men during the repulse of Pettigrew's charge against his line on July 3. A New York correspondent described watching Hays in action: to the "streaming tail" of his horse he ties "a Rebel flag that drags ignominiously in the mud, [while] he dashes along our lines now rushing out into the open field, a mark for a hundred sharpshooters, but never touched. . . . I reckon him the grandest view of my life. I bar not Niagara [Falls]." Conducting himself in a similar fashion on May 5, 1864, Hays led his brigade into the tangles of the Wilderness, where a Confederate bullet killed him. His remains rest in Allegheny Cemetery in Pittsburgh.[25]

Who Fell Here?

C.S.A.: The brigades in Pettigrew's division all fought on July 1, and it is not always easy to differentiate July 1 casualties from those suffered on July 3. Still, it is apparent that these brigades paid a heavy price here. In Fry's brigade, its original commander (Archer) was captured on July 1, and when Colonel Fry fell wounded on July 3, he shared the same fate. His brigade lost 684 of its 1,197 men for a 57.1 percent loss. Pettigrew's brigade lost Colonel Marshall, its commander on July 3, and a total of

1,619 of its 2,580 men for a 62.8 percent loss. Davis's brigade lost 1,225 or more of its 2,305 men for a brigade loss of at least 53.1 percent. Brockenbrough's small brigade fell back early in the fight and lost only 214 of its 972 men, for a loss of 22.0 percent. In Trimble's command, Scales's brigade under Lieutenant Colonel Lowrance lost 704 of its 1,351 men, for a 52.1 percent loss. Lane's brigade lost 792 of its 1,734 men, for a 45.7 percent loss. On July 3 these commands, like Pickett's division, lost heavily in senior regimental commanders, including Lieutenant Colonel David Humphries of the 2nd Mississippi, Colonel Hugh Miller of the 42nd Mississippi, Major George Clark of the 34th North Carolina, Major Owen Brown of the 37th North Carolina, and Colonel James Keith Marshall and Major John Q. Richardson of the 52nd North Carolina.

U.S.: Smyth's brigade lost 360 of its 1,069 men during the entire battle, for a brigade loss of 33.7 percent. A number of them fell in action around the Bliss farm. Willard's brigade lost both Colonel Willard and Colonel Sherrill, his successor, and 714 of its 1,508 men, many of whom fell on July 2. The 8th Ohio of Carroll's brigade lost 102 of its 209 men—an unusually high percentage (48.8 percent) for a unit that fought mostly on the skirmish line throughout the battle.

Individual vignette. Private Andrew J. Dildine mustered in with Company A of the 8th Ohio Infantry on June 22, 1861, leaving behind his young son, William, not quite two years old. Young William had been born out of wedlock during the summer of 1859—the exact date remains unclear—but Dildine and Augusta Myers, William's mother, went before a local justice of the peace and took their marriage vows on October 6. The marriage did not go smoothly, and Dildine's departure for the war did not help matters. In the fall of 1862, Augusta took the unusual step of filing for divorce. She accused Dildine of "the Several acts of extreme cruelty and gross neglect of duty." For his part, Dildine's representatives countered that Augusta had abandoned young William, a likely possibility given that Private Dildine's father clearly served as William's legal guardian. In any case, the judge granted the divorce and permitted Augusta Myers Dildine to resume using her maiden name. On July 3, during the repulse of Pickett's Charge, Private Dildine fell mortally wounded and died the next day. In August 1863 his father submitted an application for a pension for a minor child, and, in due course, William began to receive an $8 monthly payment, effective on the date of his father's death and ending on July 21, 1875, his sixteenth birthday. Private Dildine's remains rest in grave F-3 in the Ohio plot.[26]

Who Lived Here?

The prominent white house and barn here belonged to Abraham Brien, an African American man born in Maryland and just over sixty years old at the time of the battle. He first appears as a resident of Gettysburg on the 1840 census, when he was listed as a thirty-eight-year-old man with a wife and five children. He outlived at least two wives before he married Elizabeth in the 1850s. He purchased twelve acres of land, divided into two parcels, south of Gettysburg in 1857 from James A. Thompson; this parcel along the Emmitsburg Road included a small building on the road itself plus a house and barn located where you see them today. The second parcel fronted on the Taneytown Road. At the time of the battle, Brien had divided his Taneytown Road parcel into three fields and planted wheat, barley, and grass for hay. He also maintained a small orchard and usually kept at least one horse and one cow. Brien filed damage claims for $1,028 but appears to have received only $15 to cover the cost of hay consumed by U.S. Army horses. After the war, Brien worked at a hotel in town. He died on May 30, 1879, and rests in the Lincoln Cemetery, the town's historically black burial ground.[27]

What Did They Say about It Later?

Pettigrew's and Trimble's men long resented their treatment at the hands of the wartime Richmond press. In an account of the July 3 charge, one correspondent glowingly described Pickett's advance and then continued:

> Let us now look after Pettigrew's division. Where are they now? While the victorious shout of the gallant Virginians is still ringing in my ears, I turn my eyes to the left [your front], and there all over the plain, in utmost confusion is scattered this strong division. Their line is broken; they are flying, apparently panic stricken, to the rear. The gallant Pettigrew is wounded, but he still retains command, and is vainly striving to rally his men. Still the moving mass rushes pell mell to the rear. Pickett is left alone to contend with the hordes of the enemy now pouring in upon him on every side.[28]

A soldier in Wright's Georgia brigade offered a similar account: "I see Pickett still vigorously pushing on, dealing a deadly fire at every step. The enemy fall back from his front—they take shelter behind the stone wall—still Pickett advancing. On the left Pettigrew's line wavers—it pauses—all is lost—it falls back—it runs. . . . Helter-skelter, pell-mell, here they come. But one thought seems to actuate them all, and that is to gain a safe place in the rear."[29]

To contradict such criticism, a writer calling himself "Deo Vindice" accused the editors of the *Richmond Enquirer* of printing "facts . . . which are so grossly untrue that we cannot allow them to pass uncorrected." In response to descriptions that labeled Pettigrew's and Trimble's men as the supports that failed to come to the Virginians' aid, he wrote: "Our position on that bloody day was in the front line, *supporting* no one; we being on the left of Gen. Pickett and our line but a continuation of his, and advancing as far and as gallantly as did his division." He blamed sloppy journalism for much of the misperception, noting that "there is but little information to be gained from so long a range as an eminence in the rear, and for copper-distilled, unadulterated facts, one must be in closer proximity, though, perhaps, less consistent with personal safety."[30]

The conflict continued—and even became far more heated—in the postwar years. Advocates for Pettigrew's and Trimble's men despised the name "Pickett's Charge," preferring "Longstreet's Assault" or, at the very least, the "Pickett-Pettigrew-Trimble Assault." The monuments on this front to the 11th Mississippi and the 26th North Carolina are modern manifestations in support of the wartime claims of Pettigrew's division that each of these units advanced farther up the slope of Cemetery Ridge than did any of Pickett's men, that they fought longer, and that they left the field last. As William R. Bond asserted in 1888, striking a theme that still resonates in parts of the former Confederacy today: "Longstreet's assault on the third day at Gettysburg, or what is generally, but very incorrectly known as 'Pickett's Charge,' has not only had its proper place in books treating of the war, but had been more written about in newspapers and magazines than any event in American history. Some of these accounts are simply silly. Some are false in statement. Some are false in inference. All in some respects are untrue."[31] In any case, the last major infantry action in the Battle of Gettysburg was over.

Driving directions to the next stop: Drive forward 0.3 miles to the next stop sign. Turn left, then turn right at the next stop sign, entering Steinwehr Avenue (Business Route 15). Follow this avenue 0.5 miles to Baltimore Street. Turn left onto Baltimore Street (Business Route 15 North). Drive 0.5 miles to the traffic circle in the center of town. Drive one-quarter of the way around the traffic circle and enter York Street (Route 30 East). At the second traffic light, bear to the left, following York Street/York Road (still Route 30 East) 2.6 miles to the Cavalry Field Road intersection with York Road. Turn right onto Cavalry Field Road and drive 0.7 miles to Hoffman Road. Cross over Hoffman Road and drive 0.2 miles. After the road makes a sharp right turn onto Gettysburg National Military Park property, proceed to the second turnout on the right and park near the metal tablet commemorating Breathed's battery of Beckham's Horse Artillery Battalion that has no cannons positioned with it.

STOP 34. EAST CAVALRY FIELD

Orientation

Stand to the right of the metal tablet and look out over the open fields. You may well have to look very closely, but the tall white monument to Custer's Michigan Cavalry brigade stands out against the greenery to your right front. You will visit there shortly, but it will give you a good point of reference for the narrative that follows.

What Happened Here?

On July 3 Brigadier General David M. Gregg received orders to take his division to "the point of intersection of the Gettysburg and Hanover turnpike with the road which ran in rear of the right of our line of battle," the Low Dutch Road. The Low Dutch Road connected the Hanover Road to the Baltimore Pike, one of Meade's two main arteries for men, supplies, communication, and retreat. From your current position, Hanover Road runs across your front behind the Michigan Cavalry Brigade monument. While you cannot see the important intersection of Hanover Road with the Low Dutch Road from here, it is on a line to your slight left front behind the far tree line. When Gregg arrived with his lead brigade under Colonel John B. McIntosh, he received orders to "make a demonstration against the enemy." Initially unbeknownst to Gregg, however, Major General James Ewell Brown "Jeb" Stuart had moved on this same area on orders from Lee. As Stuart acknowledged in his report, Lee wanted control of this ground not only because it "render[ed] Ewell's left entirely secure" but also because it "commanded a view of the routes leading to the enemy's rear." A collision loomed.

You are standing on Cress's Ridge, the high ground on which Stuart deployed his cavalry. His horse artillery batteries, and the Louisiana Guard Artillery detached

The view past the marker for Breathed's battery.

from Ewell's Second Corps to support Stuart, took position on this ridge. They dueled with Union batteries deployed on a low ridge in front of the Hanover Road and Low Dutch Road intersection. Stuart brought four brigades with him, numbering approximately 6,600 men. Brigadier General Fitzhugh Lee's cavalry brigade, deployed to your left, and Brigadier General Wade Hampton's brigade, here on the left center of the line, were Stuart's largest units, numbering nearly 3,700 men. To your right, Brigadier General W. H. F. Lee's brigade—under the temporary command of Colonel John Chambliss—held the right center, and Brigadier General A. G. Jenkins's Virginians—led on July 3 by Lieutenant Colonel Vincent Witcher—formed the right of Stuart's line.

The fight between the rival horsemen developed in three phases. Phase I began around the Rummel farm, the prominent buildings of which sit in the low ground to your right front. Witcher's men and some of Chambliss's troopers, all dismounted, advanced toward the farm buildings, intent on using them for cover. To Stuart's clear displeasure, Witcher's men were supplied with only ten rounds of ammunition. Stuart admitted, however, that for a while, they fought "with decided effect."

Return to your vehicle and follow the park road until you reach the large monument to the 1st New Jersey Cavalry on your left. There is no turnout here, so carefully pull off to the side of the road far enough to permit other vehicles to pass. Stand in front of the monument and look toward the Rummel farm buildings. Although the trees block your view, Hanover Road is to your left. The key intersection with the Low Dutch Road is well over your left shoulder.

As the dismounted Confederates moved forward toward the Rummel farm— and your position—Gregg ordered Colonel McIntosh to deploy his men to meet them. This action initiated Phase II. McIntosh reported: "I immediately placed the First New Jersey Cavalry, under command of Major [Myron H.] Beaumont, well to the right [north] of the road leading to Gettysburg." The Jerseymen took position here, using the farm lane on your right for cover. They began to take fire immediately and returned it vigorously.

Gregg did not know how strong a threat he faced. Fortunately for him, he had readily available support. Brigadier General George A. Custer's Michigan brigade from Kilpatrick's division already held the key Low Dutch Road intersection when Gregg arrived, but Custer had received orders to depart and had pulled back his men to leave. Realizing that a defeat here would be "productive of the most serious consequences," Gregg ordered Custer to stay, and Custer, "fully satisfied of the intended attack, was well pleased to remain."

Custer's willingness to stay allowed McIntosh to send immediate reinforcements to the 1st New Jersey Cavalry here. Dismounted troopers from the 3rd Pennsylvania and 1st Maryland Cavalry regiments soon arrived, and small groups of them pushed forward in a loose skirmish line to take on Witcher's men near the barn. As the firefight grew in intensity, Custer sent forward his 5th Michigan Cavalry. The men

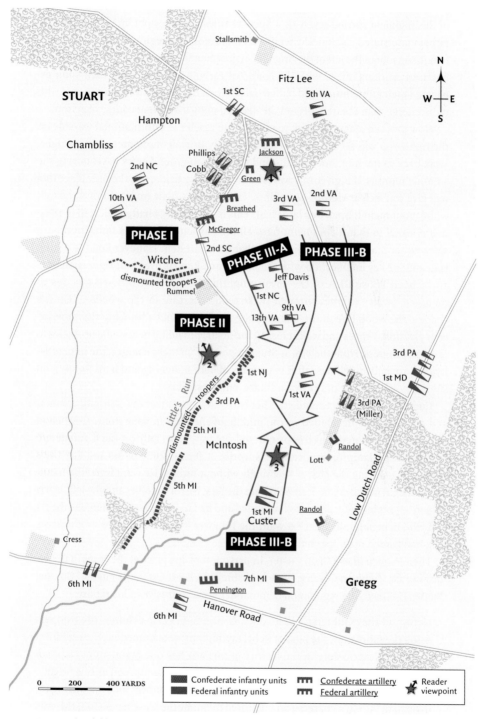

N
W—E
S

STUART

Stallsmith

Fitz Lee

1st SC

5th VA

Hampton

Chambliss

Phillips

Jackson

Cobb

Green

2nd NC

2nd VA

10th VA

3rd VA

Breathed

PHASE I

McGregor

2nd SC

PHASE III-A   **PHASE III-B**

Witcher

Jeff Davis

dismounted troopers

Rummel

1st NC

9th VA

PHASE II

13th VA

3rd PA

1st MD

1st NJ

1st VA

3rd PA
(Miller)

3rd PA

5th MI

McIntosh

Randol

Lott

5th MI

Little's Run

dismounted troopers

3
1st MI
Custer

Randol

Cress

PHASE III-B

6th MI

7th MI

Gregg

Pennington

6th MI

Hanover Road

0   200   400 YARDS

| | Confederate infantry units | | Confederate artillery | | Reader viewpoint |
| | Federal infantry units | | Federal artillery | | |

East Cavalry Field

of this regiment carried seven-shot Spencer rifles, and they put up a good fight. In rather understated fashion, Custer merely reported: "The regiment was dismounted to fight on foot of the left of the brigade. Major [Noah] Ferry was killed." As the deep boom of cannons mixed with the sound of carbine fire, Witcher's men soon exhausted their ammunition and pulled back. When the Union troopers pursued with more energy than Stuart expected, he decided upon a different course of action.

Now proceed along the park road until you reach the informational wayside on the right. You will see the tall Michigan Cavalry Brigade monument to your right. Walk back to the monument and stand on the high ground at its base; during the summer months, if high corn covers the surrounding fields, it is the only place that will give you a clear view of key points. Look to your right front and find the tall, white monument topped by a large ball. This is the Cavalry Shaft, dedicated in 1884; it is unusual in that it commemorates all the participants in this fight from both sides rather than a specific Union unit that took part in it. Hanover Road is behind you, and the key intersection with the Low Dutch Road is over your right shoulder.

To open Phase III-A of the cavalry fighting here, Stuart ordered a series of mounted cavalry charges through these fields, starting in the woods of Cress's Ridge—the wood line in the distance ahead of you—and advancing right toward your position. Fences and walls crossed the fields, providing occasional obstacles to forward progress. Nonetheless, as Stuart reported, "in these charges, the impetuosity of those gallant fellows, after two weeks of hard marching and hard fighting on short rations, was not only extraordinary, but irresistible."

Custer mounted his 1st and 7th Michigan Cavalry to meet the charging column, and a sharp clash developed in the middle of the field in your front. Confusion reigned as more mounted troops entered the fray, especially on the Confederate side. General Hampton reported his surprise at seeing some of his and Fitz Lee's regiments entering the charge seemingly without orders. He went into "the hand-to-hand fight which ensued" to "extricate the First North Carolina and the Jeff. Davis Legion" of his brigade, but he fell wounded and had to leave the field. Finally, the 1st and 7th Michigan pulled back toward the Hanover Road. It appeared as if Stuart's men had gained the upper hand.

Then to open Phase III-B, Custer, in person, took his place at the front of the reforming 1st Michigan Cavalry, drew his sabre, and led them in the charge. Colonel Charles H. Town, the regimental commander, waxed effusive in his report:

> Nobly did the "Old First" do its duty. Charging in close column, the troopers using the sabre only, the host of Rebel myrmidons were immediately swept from the field. Never before in the history of this war has one regiment of National cavalry met an entire brigade of Confederate cavalry, (composed as this brigade was of regiments, each of which equaled in point of numbers the First Michigan) in open field—in a charge—and defeated them. By the blessing of God, this was

done by the First Michigan. The enemy were not only defeated, but they were driven from the field in great confusion.

By contrast, and again with uncharacteristic modesty, Custer simply reported that the 1st Michigan Cavalry "charged in close column upon Hampton's brigade, using the sabre only, and driving the enemy from the field, with a loss to this regiment of 6 officers and 80 men."[1]

In his report, Gregg also acknowledged the special contributions of the 3rd Pennsylvania Cavalry to Union success here. During the early part of the fight, when Colonel McIntosh had sent some of the 3rd Pennsylvania's men to fight as dismounted skirmishers near the Rummel farm, the rest remained with their horses in the woods to your right front, just beyond the Cavalry Shaft monument. There, Captain William Miller watched as Hampton's and Fitz Lee's men charged across his front. Although he had been told to hold his position, he saw an opportunity he could not ignore. He ordered his troopers forward to hit the enemy's flank. Their unexpected appearance disrupted the momentum of Stuart's attacking column and contributed materially to its ultimate repulse. Miller won the Medal of Honor for his display of initiative.

Stuart pulled his scattered regiments back to Cress's Ridge and then withdrew to rejoin Robert E. Lee's main force. Gregg successfully held the key intersection of Hanover Road and the Low Dutch Road, effectively ending any real threat to the Union rear area and its essential routes of communication and supply.

Who Fought Here?

C.S.A.: Brigadier General Wade Hampton's 1,751-man brigade included the 1st North Carolina, the 1st and 2nd South Carolina, Cobb's (Ga.) Legion, Phillip's (Ga.) Legion, and the Mississippians of the Jeff Davis Legion. Brigadier General Fitzhugh Lee's 1,913-man brigade included the 1st Maryland Cavalry along with the 1st, 2nd, 3rd, 4th, and 5th Virginia Cavalry. Brigadier General W. H. F. Lee's 1,173-man brigade, under Colonel John Chambliss, included the 2nd North Carolina and the 9th, 10th, and 13th Virginia Cavalry. Jenkins's 1,126-man brigade under Lieutenant Colonel Vincent Witcher included the 14th, 16th, and 17th Virginia Cavalry Regiments and the 34th and 36th Virginia Cavalry Battalions. Five batteries of horse artillery accompanied Stuart's force; the Louisiana Guard Artillery from Ewell's Second Corps was attached for this action.

U.S.: Colonel James B. McIntosh's 1,311-man brigade from Brigadier General David M. Gregg's division in Pleasonton's Cavalry Corps included the 1st Maryland, the 1st New Jersey, the 1st and 3rd Pennsylvania, and the Purnell Legion. Colonel J. Irvin Gregg's 1,263-man brigade of Gregg's division included the 1st Maine, the 10th New York, and the 4th and 16th Pennsylvania Cavalry. Brigadier General George A. Custer's 1,924-man Michigan brigade from Brigadier General H. Judson Kilpatrick's division in Pleasonton's Cavalry Corps included the 1st, 5th, 6th, and 7th Michigan Cavalry. Several horse artillery batteries—including Battery E, 1st U.S. Artillery; Battery M, 2nd U.S. Artillery; and the 3rd Pennsylvania Heavy Artillery—were on the field, as well.

Who Commanded Here?

Major General James Ewell Brown Stuart (1833–64), a Virginian by birth, graduated from the U.S. Military Academy at West Point in 1854. His weak chin—not then hidden by a beard—inspired the nickname "Beauty." Stuart spent much of his antebellum army career with the 1st U.S. Cavalry in Kansas. While on leave in Washington, D.C., in 1859, he accompanied Lieutenant Colonel Robert E. Lee to Harpers Ferry and carried to abolitionist John Brown the colonel's demand that he surrender. Stuart resigned his commission in 1861 and became colonel of the 1st Virginia Cavalry. He quickly gained a reputation both for his boldness and for his astute assessments of enemy capabilities; his effective intelligence gathering during his "ride around McClellan" in June 1862 forged a strong bond between Stuart and Lee. Controversy still swirls around Stuart's actions leading up to Gettysburg; his broad orders gave him latitude to follow the geographical course he took, but nonetheless, he failed to carry out his most important requirement to keep Lee informed of Union troop dispositions and movements. Stuart arrived at Gettysburg on the afternoon of July 2 to a cool reception from Lee. Still, on July 3 he readily climbed back into the saddle to protect the army's left flank, with the possibility of turning it into an offensive operation against the Union rear should circumstances permit. His efforts that day did not redeem him in the eyes of many of his fellow Confederate generals—and succeeding generations of critics—many of whom listed him among those most responsible for the defeat of the Army of Northern Virginia at Gettysburg. Stuart fell mortally wounded on May 11, 1864, shot out of his saddle by one of Custer's Michigan cavalrymen during a skirmish at Yellow Tavern. He died the next day. As a Northerner wrote of him after the war: "In Stuart the Confederacy had a natural leader of cavalry. Daring, cool, eminently a man of resources in an emergency, full of the spirit of adventure, young, gay, handsome, a fine horseman, he carried into the somewhat prosaic operations of our civil war not a little of the chivalrous spirit of former times."[2]

Major General J. E. B. Stuart, C.S.A., Robert E. Lee's cavalry commander. (USAMHI)

Brigadier General David McMurtrie Gregg (1833–1916), born in Huntingdon, Pennsylvania, graduated from the U.S. Military Academy in 1855 and received a commission as a brevet second lieutenant of dragoons. Serving in California when the Civil War began, he did not return east until early 1862 to accept the colonelcy of the 8th Pennsylvania Cavalry. He served well enough during the 1862 campaign season to receive a promotion to brigadier general on November 29 and, in the spring, command of a cavalry division. He continued in that role until February 3, 1865, when, without offering an explanation, he resigned from the army and returned to civilian life. He did not turn his back on his wartime experiences, however. He penned several insightful articles that triggered an element of controversy about the July 3 cavalry fight east of Gettysburg on July 3. "On a fair field, there was another trial between two cavalry forces," Gregg wrote, "in which most of the fighting was done in the saddle, and with the trooper's favorite weapon—the sabre. Without entering into the details of the fight, it need only be added, that Stuart advanced not a pace beyond where he was met; but after a severe struggle which was only terminated by the darkness of night, he withdrew, and on the morrow, with the defeated army of Lee, was in retreat to the Potomac." It did not take long for Stuart's chief of staff, H. B. McClellan, to remind Gregg publicly that "the last charge in the cavalry battle at Gettysburg was made by the Southern cavalry." Gregg's men responded immediately. One wrote that, in Gregg, Stuart "had 'a Roland for his Oliver,' and in a fair fight, in an open field, with no surprise on the one side or the other, he was, in plain language simply defeated in all that he undertook to accomplish."[3]

Brigadier General David McMurtrie Gregg, U.S.A., in his mature years. (USAMHI)

Brigadier General George Armstrong Custer (1839–76), born in New Rumley, Ohio, grew up in Michigan and entered West Point in 1857. He graduated last in his class in June 1861 from a combination of poor academics and a lengthy list of demerits. Until June 1863, he served largely on staff duties, a situation that brought him into close contact with general officers on a regular basis and fit well with his energy and initiative. On June 29, 1863, just a few days before the Battle of Gettysburg, the first lieutenant received a promotion to brigadier general, one of three very junior officers to enjoy such a rapid rise in rank. (The other two, Wesley Merritt and Elon Farnsworth, also fought at Gettysburg, the latter falling dead in a skirmish on another part of the field on July 3.) Although he did not serve in Gregg's division, Custer appreciated the growing threat on the Union right flank and remained in place to pro-

Brigadier General George A. Custer, U.S.A. (USAMHI)

vide essential support. Even officers such as the 3rd Pennsylvania Cavalry's William Brooke-Rawle, who believed that Custer took for "himself and his Michigan brigade alone, the credit which, to say the least, others were entitled to share," could not resist describing the critical moment when the young general saw the front ranks of the 1st Michigan Cavalry hesitate. Custer "waved his sabre and shouted, 'Come on, you Wolverines!' and with a fearful yell, the First Michigan rushed on, Custer four lengths ahead." Custer ended the war as a major general but reverted to lieutenant colonel of the 7th U.S. Cavalry in 1866. He, with approximately 266 of his command, famously fell in battle with Lakota and Cheyenne warriors at Little Bighorn on June 25, 1876; his remains rest at West Point.[4]

Who Fell Here?

C.S.A.: As these figures show, cavalry combat—while perhaps more colorful than infantry fighting—generally results in far fewer casualties. During its mounted charges, Hampton's large command lost 100 men, for a brigade loss of 6.4 percent. The estimated 95 casualties in Fitz Lee's brigade amounted to a brigade loss of approximately 5 percent. In W. H. F. Lee's brigade, the loss of roughly 56 troopers equated to a brigade loss of 4.8 percent. Over the course of its very active involvement around Gettysburg—not merely on July 3—Jenkins's brigade suffered quite lightly, with its loss reaching 1.6 percent. Horse artillery losses remain unknown.

U.S.: McIntosh's brigade lost a light 2.7 percent of its strength, most of it in the 3rd Pennsylvania, which lost 21 of its 335 men in action here. Colonel J. Irvin Gregg's brigade, mostly serving on picket duty, suffered a loss of only 1.7 percent. In Custer's brigade, which faced the most severe combat here, the 1st Michigan lost 73 of its 427 men; the 5th Michigan lost 56 of its 646 men, mostly near the Rummel barn; the 6th Michigan lost 28 of its 477 men, mostly on the retreat over the next few days in July; and the brigade's newest regiment, the 7th Michigan, lost 100 of its 383 men. Custer's brigade lost 13.3 percent, a very high percentage for this kind of unit. Battery E, 1st U.S. Artillery, had no losses; but Battery M, 2nd U.S. Artillery, lost 1 of its 117 men.

Individual vignettes. Thirty-five-year-old William G. Conner had lived a full life, even before the outbreak of the Civil War. Born on April 5, 1826, in Adams County, Mississippi, he showed such academic promise that his parents hired a special tutor to prepare William and his younger brother, Lemuel, for a college education at Yale. William graduated as the salutatorian of the class of 1845. He returned to Mississippi, got married, and started a family that eventually expanded to include six children. He studied law but devoted most of his energies to running his cotton plantation; he owned at least 271 slaves. Tragedy struck in 1857, when his wife died. Conner left the children under the care of his extended family and took some time to travel in Europe. When the Civil War broke out, he enlisted in the Adams Troop on May 18, 1861, in Natchez. Part of the only body of Mississippi cavalrymen sent to Virginia, his company mustered into Confederate service in Lynchburg on June 26, 1861, and became Company A of the Jeff Davis Legion. The company soon elected Conner first lieutenant and then captain, admiring his leadership style. The first company commander behaved like a martinet, one of his soldiers complained, but "Lieutenant Conner although more strict is far more popular for he is what Martin never was, nor I fear can be—a gentleman." On the Virginia Peninsula in the spring of 1862,

Conner fell into Union hands near Williamsburg on May 4; he was exchanged and returned to the Jeff Davis Legion on August 9. On March 17, 1863, Conner received a promotion to the rank of major and command of the legion. During the mounted charges on July 3, he fell dead on the field of battle. In the melee, no one was certain about their major's fate. In the end, a captured Union lieutenant confirmed the bad news.[5]

Phillip H. Hill mustered in as a private in Company E, 5th Michigan Cavalry, on August 27, 1862, in Detroit. The twenty-six-year-old from Armada, Michigan, left behind his Canadian-born wife, Clara Tripp Hill, age twenty-three, and their two young children, Hannah and James, both under the age of three. Hill became a good soldier and earned a promotion to corporal. During the fighting around the Rummel barn on July 3, Corporal Hill suffered a severe gunshot wound through the right lung, and he at first seemed simply to disappear, his name listed among his regiment's "missing" in the early casualty returns. But he did not remain missing for long; he actually had been removed to a field hospital, where he died the following day. Corporal Hill's remains rest in the Soldiers' National Cemetery in grave F-9 of the Michigan plot. Back in Michigan, Clara began the process of applying for a widow's pension. Her Canadian birth complicated the verification of some of her personal information, but her most difficult task centered on proving that she was, in fact, the mother of Hannah. A "practicing physician" had delivered young James, but Hannah had been delivered by a midwife, who had to supply an affidavit that she had attended the birth. In the end, Clara received her $8 monthly widow's pension and later received $2 monthly increases for both Hannah and James that lasted until their sixteenth birthdays.[6]

Who Lived Here?

John and Sarah Rummel bought their farm, the site of the most intense cavalry fighting, at a sheriff's auction in 1845. They paid a little less than $700 for the working farm of at least 123 acres that included a large barn, a log house, a smokehouse, a spring house, and room for blacksmithing equipment and wagons. During the fighting of July 3, Witcher's Confederate cavalrymen took over the Rummel barn and knocked out some of the boards to make firing slits. During the clash, the barn was damaged by intense musketry fire, and artillery shells hit both the barn and the log house. After the armies left, at least thirty dead horses dotted Rummel's fields. A popular guidebook published in the 1930s related that

> Mr. Rummel, the owner of part of the cavalry field, who assisted in removing the dead, found a Unionist and a Confederate who had cut each other down with their sabres, lying with their feet together, their heads in opposite directions and the blood-stained sabre of each still tight in his grip. At another point he found a Virginian and a Pennsylvanian who fought on horseback with their

sabres until they finally clinched and their horses ran from under them. Their heads and shoulders were severely cut, and their fingers, though stiff in death, were so firmly imbedded in each other's flesh that they could not be removed without the aid of force.

Rummel submitted a damage claim for only $219.95, but the Federal government disallowed it, claiming that the Confederates did the damage that the farmer specified on his application.[7] Only the barn is a Civil War–era structure; the house is a postwar building.

What Did They Say about It Later?

Luther Trowbridge, a senior Michigan cavalryman, offered a scenario that he hoped would resolve the sectional disagreement over battle honors in the East Cavalry Field:

> There has been much dispute as to who occupied the field after the fight was over. Stuart and his officers claim they drove the Union forces from the field. On the other hand, Gregg, McIntosh, Custer and their officers maintain that they remained master of the field, even of that portion occupied by the Confederates at the beginning of the fight. McIntosh claims that after the fight he established his picket lines in the woods where Hampton and Lee had massed their forces in the morning. . . . It is, however, a matter of small moment who had actual physical possession of the field. It is the opinion of the writer that neither side actually occupied that portion of the field where the fight took place, but that each retired to the positions occupied by them at the beginning of the fight.

But Trowbridge's effort to calm the waters likely failed when he summarized: "One thing must be admitted by all, and that is that Stuart attempted to turn the flank of Meade's army, and that he failed to do it; and further, that he was prevented from doing it by the good generalship of General Gregg, in forcing the fighting, and the hard fighting of the brave men under his command."[8]

An important note on cavalry fighting at Gettysburg. Two additional cavalry actions took place on July 3 on the southern end of the battlefield. One element centered on the advance of Brigadier General Wesley Merritt's brigade northward on the Emmitsburg Road to threaten the Confederate right flank. The second stop, just south of Round Top, centers on the near-simultaneous advance of Brigadier General Elon J. Farnsworth's brigade of horsemen. Do not consider these two fights to be unimportant because they do not receive the same level of detailed description as the East Cavalry Field fight.

If you drive south on U.S. 15 (Emmitsburg Road) for a mile beyond the park road that leads to the fields of Longstreet's main effort on July 2, you will pass Alexander

Currens's stone house on the right of the road and his farm fields, where G. T. Anderson's Georgia brigade deployed to protect the right flank of the Army of Northern Virginia. After passing a bowling alley and campground on your left, look for the distinctive regimental monument to the 6th Pennsylvania Cavalry—also known as "Rush's Lancers," commemorated by the presence of lances on the marker—on the left side of the road. This marks the advanced position of Merritt's skirmishers as they advanced toward the Confederate line through which you have just driven. A short distance ahead, just where you begin to drive down a steep slope, look carefully to your left for an open grassy area with a few visible monuments. There are no turning or designated parking areas for visitors here, but you may pull over carefully to explore this field and the woods behind it, where a number of substantial monuments salute the U.S. Regular cavalry regiments that fought in the fields through which you drove. This area was the launching point for Merritt's advance and the position of his horse artillery. Most of the action—mostly skirmishing between dismounted Union troopers and Georgia infantry—took place between this location and the Currens house. The fighting ebbed and flowed across these fields for several hours, but Merritt's men made no serious threat to the security of the Confederate right flank. Merritt himself had little to say about the details of the clash, but its duration is worth attention: "I marched with the brigade about 12 m. to attack the enemy's right and rear, and annoy him, which the battle was progressing on the right [near Culp's Hill]. . . . This fight lasted about four hours (some time after the cannonading had ceased on the right)."[9] Merritt's brigade reported a loss of only forty-nine men.

To explore the area of Farnsworth's Charge from the scene of Merritt's fight, drive north on U.S. 15, make a sharp right turn onto South Confederate Avenue, and proceed beyond the Alabama monument to the designated parking spots in the low ground where the open fields enter the thick wood line. Of all the tactical actions that comprise the Battle of Gettysburg, probably no individual episode outstrips Farnsworth's Charge for generating modern-day controversy. The traditional narrative includes a heated exchange between Brigadier General H. Judson Kilpatrick and one of his brigade commanders, Elon J. Farnsworth. As one mid-1880s account noted: "Farnsworth spoke with emotion: 'General, do you mean it? Shall I throw my handful of men over rough ground, through timber, against a brigade of infantry?' Kilpatrick said: 'Do you refuse to obey my orders? If you are afraid to lead this charge, I will lead it.'" Farnsworth led the charge, of course, taking his men into this substantially more rocky and undulating terrain than that through which Merritt's men had advanced. Here the 1st Vermont, the 5th New York, the 1st West Virginia, and the 18th Pennsylvania Cavalry confronted the Texas Brigade and some of Law's Alabamians. Farnsworth died in the ensuing charge.

While some still accept the veracity of the traditional narrative, others recently have challenged a number of key elements of the story. Some see less of a confrontation between the two generals and describe the exchange simply as "the two generals in conference." The exact ground over which Farnsworth's men charged has become an increasingly contentious matter, as well. As additional acreage was added to the battlefield, veterans from a number of units pushed for the movement of their regimental monuments from their initial sites to new locations closer to their actual fight. For this reason, the relocation of the 5th New York Cavalry's marker from a site much farther up the western slope of Round Top to its current position on the knoll to the right of your parked car has raised questions about where the regiment actually fought.[10] The nature of Farnsworth's death—was he killed by Confederate bullets, or did he die by his own hand rather than surrender?—still stirs debate. Indeed, Farnsworth's Charge offers us a stark reminder that we can never know with certainty everything that happened, even on a field as well-studied as Gettysburg.

Driving directions to the next stop from the vicinity of the Michigan Cavalry Brigade monument: Drive forward on Gregg Avenue 0.3 miles, following the road to the right and then to the left. At the intersection with the Low Dutch Road, turn right and drive 0.5 miles to the four-way intersection with Hanover Road. Turn right onto Hanover Road and drive 3.0 miles back toward the town. You will cross under Route 15 and over Benner's Hill. At the bottom of the hill, after crossing Rock Creek, turn left at the first traffic light onto Sixth Street and then right onto East Middle Street. Drive west on East Middle Street 0.6 miles past Baltimore Street to Washington Street. Turn left onto Washington Street and follow it south 0.7 miles, crossing over Steinwehr Avenue and entering Taneytown Road. The Soldiers' National Cemetery will be on your left. Vehicles are prohibited from entering the cemetery. Park toward the top of Cemetery Hill in the large parking area on the right side of Taneytown Road opposite the cemetery. While you are in the cemetery, you may wish to make use of the restroom facilities, which are in a small red-brick building at the east end of the cemetery adjacent to Baltimore Street.

STOP 35. THE SOLDIERS' NATIONAL CEMETERY

Orientation

When you enter the National Cemetery, proceed straight ahead, stopping to examine the monument to the Gettysburg Address on your right if you wish. Please understand that this marker is *not* located on the site where President Lincoln delivered his powerful message.

Follow the road through the cemetery that takes you closest to the black iron fence that separates the Soldiers' National Cemetery from the community's Evergreen Cemetery, which you learned about at Stop 1. Remember that these would have been open fields during the battle; the decorative plantings, the large trees, and the stone walls surrounding you all represent elements of late nineteenth-century cemetery design.

What Happened Here?

Along the right side of the road through the Soldiers' National Cemetery you will notice a line of monuments, each flanked by two cannons. These markers represent the Union artillery line of the XI Corps—reinforced by the batteries that General Hunt sent from the Artillery Reserve—emplaced to defend the western crest of Cemetery Hill on July 2 and July 3. Occasionally, through breaks in the trees to your

The Taneytown Road entrance to the Soldiers' National Cemetery.

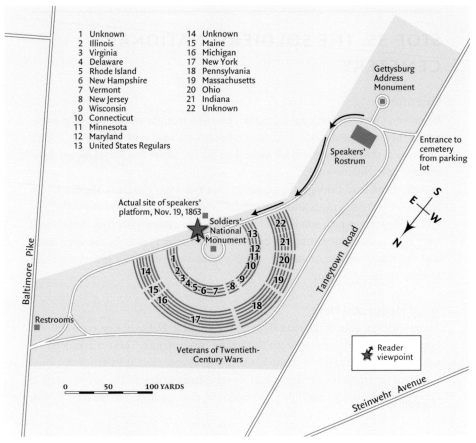

The following is the legend from the map:

1 Unknown
2 Illinois
3 Virginia
4 Delaware
5 Rhode Island
6 New Hampshire
7 Vermont
8 New Jersey
9 Wisconsin
10 Connecticut
11 Minnesota
12 Maryland
13 United States Regulars
14 Unknown
15 Maine
16 Michigan
17 New York
18 Pennsylvania
19 Massachusetts
20 Ohio
21 Indiana
22 Unknown

Gettysburg Address Monument

Entrance to cemetery from parking lot

Speakers' Rostrum

Actual site of speakers' platform, Nov. 19, 1863

Soldiers' National Monument

Taneytown Road

Baltimore Pike

Restrooms

Veterans of Twentieth-Century Wars

Reader viewpoint

Steinwehr Avenue

0   50   100 YARDS

The Soldiers' National Cemetery

left, you can see well beyond the cemetery to the targets of the gunners here: the lines of Rodes's and Pender's divisions and the Confederate batteries on Seminary Ridge and around the Seminary itself. On July 3 the gun crews swung these cannons obliquely to the left to fire on Pettigrew's advance. In combination with the guns on East Cemetery Hill that you saw at Stop 27, this line became part of one of the Army of the Potomac's largest massed batteries in the entire war.

Proceed to the large Soldiers' National Monument on your left and face it. For years, visitors learned that this monument marked the site of the platform from which Lincoln delivered his Gettysburg Address on November 19, 1863. As the nearby informational wayside explains, however, recent research has proved that the authentic location rests on the other side of the iron fence within the boundary of the town's Evergreen Cemetery. The stirring events of that day inspired an annual commemoration called Remembrance Day, still held in Gettysburg each November.

Who Fought Here?

At the time of the battle, this ground lay within the lines of the XI Corps of the Army of the Potomac.

Who Commanded Here?

Major General O. O. Howard commanded the XI Corps.

Who Fell Here?

No close combat action took place on this sector of Cemetery Hill. The comparatively small number of Union soldiers who fell here likely were victims of Confederate artillery or the bullets of sharpshooters and skirmishers posted in houses on the edge of town or in the fields to the west.

Who Lived Here?

Shortly after the battle, Pennsylvania governor Andrew Gregg Curtin appointed Gettysburg attorney David Wills to serve as his agent to carry out the requirements of an 1862 state law to provide for the care of the commonwealth's wounded soldiers and burial of its soldier dead. The sheer number of the slain overwhelmed the community, and while Wills offered several suggestions for their burial, perhaps even in Gettysburg's Evergreen Cemetery, he finally pushed for the establishment of a separate soldiers' cemetery. On March 24, 1864, Governor Curtin signed the articles of incorporation. Before that date, of course—on November 19, 1863—he had visited Gettysburg for the formal dedication ceremonies during which President Abraham Lincoln delivered "a few appropriate remarks."

In time, many of the Union dead found their final resting place in the Soldiers' National Cemetery. (USAMHI)

The Soldiers' National Cemetery rests on seventeen acres, most of which had been covered with crops at the time of the battle. Wills had to deal with five individual owners to purchase the land on which the cemetery sits. One of these men was John Weirich, a local tanner who lived with his family in town and used his out lot on the west side of Cemetery Hill to grow wheat, corn, and forage for his animals. Although he received payment for the purchase of his land, he—and, after his death in 1883, his family—still submitted damage claims for the crops and the fencing destroyed on his Cemetery Hill property. The Weirichs asked for little in their final claim to the U.S. Army's quartermaster general's office, submitting a request for only $250 for the destruction of fencing, corn, wheat, and oats. Since "the lot of the Claimant now part of the National Cemetery was occupied by the Union troops," they hoped to tie their losses to the needs and use of the Army of the Potomac. Like so many other Gettysburg residents, however, the Weirichs received a rejection.[1]

What Did They Say about It Later?

Face the Soldiers' National Monument once more. The cornerstone of this monument was laid in 1865, and large crowds gathered for its formal dedication in 1869. As you can see, the graves are laid out around it in concentric semicircles. The dead from each state and the U.S. Regulars are buried within individual plots, both officers and enlisted men lying together. A single marker at the head of each plot identifies the state and the number of its soldiers buried there. Within the state plots, each grave is marked with the soldier's name, his rank (a name without a rank indicates that the soldier was a private), the letter of his company, and the number of his regiment. Graves marked as "unknown" within state plots are the final resting place of

A semicircle of newly set gravestones on Cemetery Hill. Note the openness of the terrain in the background. (USAMHI)

soldiers whose remains were found buried next to or among identified dead from a specific state or, in some cases, individual sets of remains that bore some kind of state identification, perhaps a belt buckle or uniform buttons. The rows of square stones grouped in plots on each end of the semicircle mark the graves of soldiers who could not be identified at all.

Each grave contains the remains of a soldier with his own story to tell, of course. Use the markers at the head of each plot to identify the state it represents, then seek the graves of some of the soldiers whose stories you read at various stops.

Individual vignettes. Private Richard Titterington of New York City enlisted in Company G of the 82nd New York, leaving behind his wife, Isabella, whom he had married in April 1850, and his four children. On the Emmitsburg Road on July 2, he fell severely wounded, and he died the following day. Isabella now had to care for John, age eleven; James, about to turn six; Joseph, age four and a half; and Anna, only three. She applied for a widow's pension in August 1863, but she was not approved for her $8 monthly pension until November 1864. The long delay may have been caused by a lack of verification of her husband's death in battle. Whoever buried Titterington's remains failed to provide full identification; when his body was brought to rest in the Soldiers' National Cemetery, only portions of his name could be discerned. Thus, the grand schematic of the graves at the cemetery originally labeled his grave simply as "_____d _____ngton" and identified it simply as a New York Volunteer without a regimental designation. Isabella finally won approval of her widow's pension and the $2 additional monthly pay for each of her dependent children until each reached the age of sixteen. Private Titterington's remains rest in grave B-117 in the New York plot; his name still is not fully restored.[2]

Although he is buried in the Pennsylvania plot, Private Eli T. Green is not a Pennsylvanian. He did not even serve in the Army of the Potomac. In reality, he rests here due to an administrative error. Eli T. Green enlisted in Clarksville, Virginia, on May 12, 1861, at age twenty-two, becoming a soldier in Company E of the 14th Virginia Infantry. A saddler by trade, Green served reliably—most of the time. Only one glaring incident appears on his record: a twenty-day absence without leave in May 1863. On July 3, during Pickett's Charge, a bullet hit Private Green in the right arm below the elbow. After the repulse of the charge, Union stretcher bearers removed him to a I Corps hospital, where a surgeon amputated his arm above the elbow. Surgeons transferred Green to Letterman Army Hospital on August 7, where he died of his wounds on August 15. A transcription error during his burial changed 14th "VA" to 14th "PA" and, as a consequence, Private Green fills grave D-61 in the Pennsylvania plot.[3]

Finally, as you circle around to the cemetery road behind the largest semicircles of graves, you will notice more rows of graves marked by the standard vertical marble markers supplied by the U.S. government. Since the Soldiers' National Cemetery is part of the National Cemetery System, these graves are the final resting place of Americans who fought—and, in many cases, died—in twentieth-century conflicts. If you look closely, you can find the final resting places of servicemen who fell on such important dates in American military history as Pearl Harbor's December 7, 1941, and D-Day's June 6, 1944. In the single and double rows of graves toward your entrance to the cemetery, and in the area behind the Lincoln speech monument you saw near that gate, you can find the graves of a number of local men who fell in Vietnam. Clearly, not all of the military history in this cemetery relates to the Civil War.

The Aftermath JULY 4, 1863, AND BEYOND

The Consequences of Victory: General Meade,
the Army of the Potomac, and the North

On July 4, occasional skirmishing broke a tense silence. General Meade issued a congratulatory order to praise his army's stout defense. At the same time, however, he also forbade his artillery from firing the traditional Independence Day salute. He did not want the Confederates to interpret it as the start of another attack.

Late in the day, the heat and humidity building over the last few days triggered heavy thunderstorms. Surgeons often set up field hospitals near creeks for a ready water supply, and now they, their stewards, and lightly injured soldiers tried to pull the more badly wounded men to higher ground for safety. Some soldiers, immobilized by their wounds, drowned before rescuers could move them. Under the cover of darkness and the heavy rain, Lee pulled back Ewell's Second Corps from its positions around Culp's Hill and consolidated his forces along Seminary Ridge. By the morning of July 5, Union patrols from Cemetery Hill entered the town of Gettysburg and found that most of Lee's men had gone.

Word of Lee's withdrawal triggered elation throughout the North. Loyal Union editors offered celebratory headlines bearing such glad tidings as "The Rebellion Receives Its Death Sentence," "The Victory Complete," and "The Decisive Battle of the War Fought Here." The *Philadelphia Inquirer* trumpeted: "Waterloo Eclipsed!" "The success of General Meade not only [broke] the power, the prestige and the hopes of the great rebel army of the East," but it also dispelled "the clouds and darkness which lately overshadowed us," wrote a New York editor, adding that he saw in Lee's defeat "the cheering light of the dawning of our national deliverance."[1] News of the fall of Vicksburg arriving almost simultaneously sent loyal Northerners into unprecedented euphoria.

But Lee's army still represented a dangerous threat, and it still remained on Northern soil. As Lee pulled his battered forces away from Gettysburg toward Maryland and the crossings of the Potomac River, he utilized two different routes. The Army of Northern Virginia's infantry and artillery—Lee's combat power— marched on the Fairfield Road, heading southwest toward the Monterrey Gap and, from there, toward Hagerstown and on to Williamsport to use a ford and pontoon bridges to cross the Potomac. Approximately 5,000 Union prisoners marched with this column, guarded by the survivors of Pickett's division, some of whom wondered if their selection for such unpopular duty represented a punishment for their failure on July 3. Lee also organized a second column, the famous wagon train of wounded that extended for an estimated seventeen miles, and sent it northwest out of Gettysburg on the Chambersburg Road—the same road where the two armies had traded the opening shots of the battle. Under the protection of Brigadier General John Imboden's cavalry, the wagons filled with wounded men followed a route that took them through Cashtown and Greencastle and then on to Hagerstown, Williamsport, and the river.

Meade fully intended to contest Lee's withdrawal. Even before the battle ended, his cavalry began to probe the Army of Northern Virginia's flanks and rear. Now the Union horsemen followed closely on the heels of both Confederate columns and clashed frequently with Southern troopers protecting them. Union cavalry liberated many Northern prisoners and captured hundreds of wounded and unwounded Confederates. While Meade's cavalry pressed forward aggressively, however, the Army of the Potomac's seven corps of infantry and artillery spent most of July 4 and 5 gathering their wounded and burying their dead. Meade sent elements of Sedgwick's VI Corps down the Fairfield Road to harass Lee's retreating column on July 5, but the troops halted just a few miles west of Gettysburg when G. T. Anderson's Georgia brigade put up a minor show of resistance. Meade then decided not to follow Lee closely with his infantry and risk ambush in the mountain gaps; instead, he would take the Army of the Potomac directly south from Gettysburg into Maryland, turn west through Turner's and Fox's Gaps—familiar scenes of fighting during the 1862 Antietam Campaign—and then perhaps intercept and destroy Lee's army.

Meade wanted a decisive end to the campaign, and no one shared that desire more than President Lincoln. Buoyed by news of Grant's great victory at Vicksburg, Lincoln expressed his growing dissatisfaction with Meade's seeming inaction. He objected to what he deemed to be a defensive tone in Meade's congratulatory order to his army that simply could not provide inspiration for an energetic pursuit. It did not help Lincoln's mood to learn that Major General William H. French—who commanded a significant body of Union troops in Maryland at the same time Meade fought his battle in Pennsylvania—reported the transit of Lee's first train of wounded over the Potomac "without saying why he does not stop it, or even intimating a thought that it ought to be stopped." Concerns over French's initial inaction and then Meade's lack of initiative nearly convinced Lincoln that his generals had decided "to cover Baltimore and Washington, and to get the enemy across the river again without a further collision."[2]

Lincoln had reason to be frustrated. Opportunity beckoned. Even before he arrived at Williamsport, Lee learned that the recent rains had raised the water level at the ford he planned to use, and, moreover, enemy action had destroyed his pontoon bridge at nearby Falling Waters. When Lee's columns all reached the river by July 10, they had no way to pass large numbers of troops across it safely. Thus Lee ordered his exhausted survivors to construct a strong line of breastworks outside the town and be prepared to make a stand. The slow advance of Meade's infantry gave the Confederates all the time they needed to complete their work.

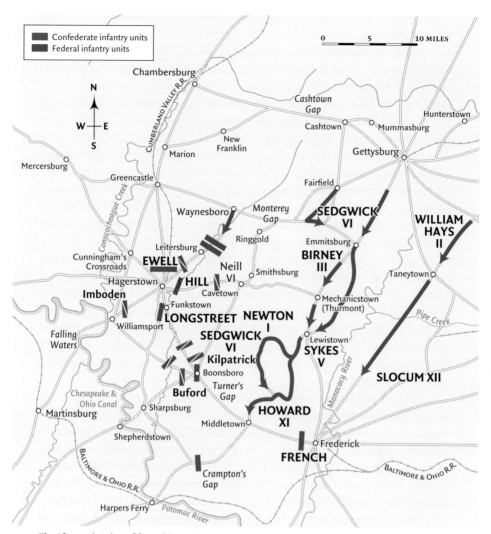

The Aftermath: July 4, 1863, and Beyond

The situation infuriated Lincoln. Halleck had forwarded to Meade Lincoln's note of July 7—written just after the president had received word of Vicksburg's surrender—which asserted: "If General Meade can complete his work, so gloriously prosecuted thus far, by the literal or substantial destruction of Lee's army, the rebellion will be over." Halleck reminded Meade frequently over the next few days of Lincoln's desire to see the war end with the destruction of Lee's army in Maryland.[3] A stung Meade offered to resign if the commander in chief did not approve of his course of action, but Halleck assuaged his wounded pride. By July 12, Meade's vanguard arrived near Williamsport and found Lee's men in battle array behind their formidable earthworks. Meade called his corps commanders together yet again to consider their options. While an attack on those works appeared to be a great opportunity to end the war, General Howard asserted that such an action might result in a Pickett's Charge in reverse. It had begun to rain hard again, and Meade delayed his proposed attack from July 13 until July 14, hoping for better weather. Lee reported, however, that during the brief delay, "a good bridge was completed," with "new boats having [been] constructed and some of the old recovered." The Army of Northern Virginia crossed the Potomac safely on the night of July 13.[4]

No Northerner rued that development more than President Lincoln. "I do not believe you appreciate the magnitude of the misfortune involved in Lee's escape," the president wrote to General Meade, adding, pointedly: "Your golden opportunity is gone and I am distressed immeasurably because of it."[5] Lincoln never sent this letter to the general, but it is not difficult to appreciate his frustration, especially in the aftermath of his army's successes at Gettysburg and Vicksburg.

But any realistic hope that the two recent Union victories presaged a quick end to the war soon evaporated. Within a week, some regiments from the victorious Army of the Potomac reversed course. Instead of marching southward, they arrived by train in New York City to put down violent anticonscription riots. Just two weeks after Gettysburg, the promising start of Union operations near Charleston suffered a serious reverse when the attack on Fort Wagner failed at high cost, including the loss of a significant number of African American soldiers belonging to the 54th Massachusetts Infantry.

Indeed, it took several weeks for the North just to learn of the high cost of its victory at Gettysburg. In a preliminary accounting, Meade's Army of the Potomac had lost 3,155 soldiers killed in action, 14,529 wounded—including perhaps as many as 2,000 who would die of their injuries over the next weeks and months—and 5,365 captured or missing.[6] Those numbers equated to 24.5 percent of the Union soldiers engaged in the battle. Despite it all, however, Meade appreciated what he had accomplished. As he listed his achievements in his official report, dated October 1, 1863, he stated that the Army of the Potomac successfully achieved "the defeat of the enemy at Gettysburg, his compulsory evacuation from Pennsylvania and Maryland and withdrawal from the upper Shenandoah and in the capture of 3 guns, 41 standards and 13,621 prisoners and 24,978 small arms."[7] In strictly military terms, that was impressive in itself.

Many of Meade's subordinates and much of the nation at large, however, failed to appreciate just how well he had fought this battle. He had made effective use of his superior numbers and interior lines to shuttle troops from quiet sectors to crisis points, most obviously in his support of Sickles on July 2. He not only maintained an army reserve—Sedgwick's VI Corps—but also used it to good effect, as his deployment of Shaler's brigade to Culp's Hill showed. He sought buy-in—but not permission—from his subordinates to continue the fight after July 2. And he did it all within his first week in army command. A practical man in many ways, Meade realized from the start that the public adulation he enjoyed immediately after Gettysburg would not last: "My success at Gettysburg has deluded the people and the Government with the idea that I must always be victorious," and that such good feelings would "be dissipated by any reverse that I should meet with."[8]

Meade's assessment proved to be entirely true. Although he remained commander of the Army of the Potomac until the end of the war, he led a force that changed dramatically in the months after Gettysburg. Nearly every regiment in Meade's army needed to refill thin ranks, and initial allotments of raw conscripts arrived in August and September 1863 to replace experienced veterans who now filled hospital beds or soldiers' graves. During the winter of 1863–64, the War Department invited all the army's three-year regiments raised in the late spring and summer of 1861 to "veteranize" and serve for the duration of the war; over forty of the Army of the Potomac's experienced regiments that served at Gettysburg opted to disband rather than see the conflict through to the end. Most unpopular of all, Reynolds's I Corps and Sickles's III Corps had suffered such heavy losses in July 1863 that just before the start of active operations in the spring of 1864, Meade ordered the two units to be disbanded. The survivors of the I Corps regiments became a division in the V Corps, and Sickles's III Corps veterans found themselves reassigned to Hancock's II Corps.

On a more personal note, during the spring of 1864, Meade faced a strong challenge to his authority and professional reputation. The Joint Committee on the Conduct of the War convened hearings to investigate Meade's command decisions at Gettysburg, and the general suffered the indignity of having to defend his actions in a victorious cause.[9] Even though the opening of the spring 1864 campaign brought an end to the sideshow, Meade's fortunes continued to founder. Lieutenant General Ulysses S. Grant, the new general in chief of the U.S. Army, kept him in command of the Army of the Potomac, but then he almost instantly shoved Meade into history's shadows by deciding to accompany that army into the field until its final victory at Appomattox in April 1865. Meade languished there for nearly a century until modern historians reevaluated his performance and found him and his decisions worthy of much more positive attention.

The Consequences of Defeat: General Lee, the Army of Northern Virginia, and the South

The results of the three-day battle at Gettysburg confronted Lee and the Army of Northern Virginia with the unfamiliar experience of defeat. The casualty lists for Lee's army were shocking enough. Medical Director Lafayette Guild reported on July 29, 1863, that the Army of Northern Virginia lost 2,592 killed, 12,709 wounded, and 5,150 captured or missing—for a total loss of 20,451.[10] Those numbers accounted for 32.4 percent of Lee's engaged strength. While he lost no corps commanders,

Lee lost the services of several key division commanders, most notably the mortally wounded Pender and the badly injured John Bell Hood. He also had lost four veteran brigade commanders killed or mortally wounded—Armistead, Garnett, Semmes, and Barksdale—and he lost Pettigrew in the retreat. Many of his regiments never recovered from the loss of field officers and company-grade commanders at Gettysburg. Lee himself offered his resignation to Jefferson Davis, who immediately rejected it.

The South at large learned of—and reacted to—the defeat of its primary army quite differently from the way in which Northerners experienced the euphoria of victory. While the results of the fighting at Gettysburg became common knowledge throughout the North by July 6, Southern editors could not get timely and accurate news for days. Gettysburg was Lee's first major battle fought well beyond ready telegraph range of Richmond, the journalistic heart of the Confederacy. As late as July 8, a Richmond editor felt confident in writing: "We feel as well assured that General Lee, if he has met the enemy in a pitched battle, has inflicted a terrible defeat upon them, as we do that we are living, breathing, sentient beings."[11] Until July 10, fully a week after the battle, Richmond newspapers continued to predict victory in Pennsylvania, based on fragmentary reports from Northern newspapers about Union reverses on July 1.

It took until at least July 10 for the first credible reports of Lee's defeat to appear in Richmond newspapers. As the news spread throughout the Confederacy, Southerners seemed incredulous. Few seemed willing to credit the Army of the Potomac for putting up a good fight. If the Army of Northern Virginia failed to win, someone in its own ranks had to be responsible for the defeat and should be held accountable. But who deserved the blame? For the next month, Richmond newspapers teemed with critiques of the campaign, scrutinizing a number of senior Confederate leaders and their commands. Cavalry commander Jeb Stuart took much blame for the absence of his command at key moments in the campaign. Others pointed to Ewell for his failure to take Cemetery Hill on July 1. Heth's division, commanded by Pettigrew on July 3, became the scapegoats for the devastation suffered by Pickett's division in their grand charge against the Union center; indeed, Richmond newspapers writing for a Virginia audience used the phrase "Pickett's Charge" by the third week of July. Editors even questioned the merits of some of Lee's own decisions. The historical debate over the causes of the Confederate defeat at Gettysburg rests heavily, but not exclusively, upon the Richmond press reports of July 1863.[12] Most interesting, perhaps, is the fact that General James Longstreet did not become a primary target of the Richmond editors in July 1863; his transformation into "Lee's tarnished lieutenant" occurred after Lee's death in 1870.

Like Meade, Lee thought well beyond the public rumblings. Lee, too, evaluated his accomplishments during his Pennsylvania Campaign. He submitted two detailed campaign reports, one dated July 31, 1863, and the other written in January

1864. In his first report, Lee offered a set of goals he had hoped to accomplish by moving his army north of the Potomac River. Lee's claims may seem fairly modest and eminently reasonable. They may also be considered somewhat self-serving, since he drafted them after the battle, when he had to justify the high cost of his efforts with some positive evidence of accomplishment.

In any case, his first stated objective included "the relief of the Shenandoah Valley from the troops that had occupied the lower [northern] part of it during the winter and spring, and, if practicable, the transfer of the scene of hostilities north of the Potomac." In this regard, modern historian Kent Masterson Brown argues, the Pennsylvania Campaign was an unqualified success. "That Lee's campaign into Pennsylvania was a foraging expedition carried out on an immense scale, and that it succeeded in bringing back to Virginia the enormous stores and herds of livestock that it did, was never understood by Southern civilians or newspaper reporters," Brown asserts, but "the campaign may well have furnished enough meat, fodder, and stores to extend the life of the army of Northern Virginia until the harvests in the Southern seaboard states could be used."[13]

Lee also hoped to "strike a blow at the army then commanded by General Hooker," but even if he failed in that effort, he hoped that his northward advance might still compel the Union army "to leave Virginia, and, possibly to draw to its support troops designed to operate against other parts of the country." Lee did not specify which parts of the Confederacy he hoped to relieve in this way, but Suffolk, in Virginia, and not Vicksburg out west had demanded much of his recent attention. In any case, Lee did not point out that his campaign actually failed to alleviate pressure in southeastern Virginia.

Lee hoped as well that, by moving the Confederate army north, "the enemy's plan of campaign [in Virginia] for the summer would be broken up, and part of the season of active operations would be consumed in the formation of new combinations," or plans started from scratch. Lee can claim modest success in this case, since the next major military action in Virginia did not occur until May 1864. Other than these stated goals, he merely looked for "other valuable results" that "might be attained by military success."[14] Lee's report downplays or omits entirely a host of reasons that modern military historians usually cite as his campaign goals, including such notions as turning Northern public opinion against the war or the Lincoln administration, setting up the decisive battle that would force the Union to sue for peace, capturing Harrisburg or Philadelphia, or even securing Pennsylvania's hard coal reserves.

Indeed, Lee's report left many wartime military analysts entirely unimpressed. His first account appeared in the public press across both the North and the South by late summer. William Conant Church, editor of the *Army and Navy Journal*, soon published a pointed and highly critical evaluation of the report. "We cannot discover in General Lee's operations after entering Maryland and Pennsylvania the proofs of any well-conceived military project," Church wrote.[15] Even if he accomplished all of the items he listed in his report, Lee never explained how they served a larger purpose; in particular, he did not explain how he hoped his incursion into Pennsylvania might contribute to securing the Confederacy's independence. Nor did he explain why he decided to stay and fight after July 1; why he rejected reasonable alternatives, such as the possibility of maneuvering to fight Meade in a position of his own choosing; or even why he chose a battlefield that imposed upon him exterior lines that put his numerically inferior army at a disadvantage against Meade's larger force. All of Church's points still merit consideration. Although the Northern editor did not comment specifically upon Lee's command style, it, too, deserves attention. The general himself seemed slow to appreciate that what had worked well with Longstreet and Jackson did not work nearly as effectively with Hill and Ewell. Lee had given his experienced subordinates a welcome degree of freedom to design and execute their own plans to accomplish a common goal. Hill and Ewell, on the other hand, had served until recently as subordinates to commanders who had given them very specific orders that required little initiative or decision making on their parts.

And so the war went on. In September 1863 Lee begrudgingly did what he refused to do in May and June: he sent Longstreet's Corps to the western theater, where it won laurels at Chickamauga and then lost them in east Tennessee. After Grant became general in chief in March 1864, concentration of effort became the hallmark of Union operations, each of its scattered armies latching on to the nearest enemy forces and tying them down so the Confederates could not use their interior lines to shift troops to threatened sectors. Grant's Overland Campaign and Petersburg siege, as well as Sherman's advance from Chattanooga to Atlanta in the spring and early summer of 1864 and beyond, showed a tenacity and perseverance previously unseen in Union military operations. While Lee in Virginia and Generals Joseph Johnston and then Hood in Georgia organized stout defenses against the Union offensives, the losses incurred over the final twenty-one months of the war after Gettysburg substantially exceeded the loss of soldiers' lives in the war's first twenty-six months.

Meanwhile, Back in Gettysburg . . .

Even before the rival armies departed, Gettysburg and environs became a large hospital. Hundreds of houses, shops, and barns provided shelter to wounded soldiers in the immediate aftermath of the battle. After the fighting ended, Union army surgeons developed a more systematic approach to handling mass casualties. After army engineers rebuilt the railroad bridge over Rock Creek, doctors sent the lightly and moderately wounded soldiers to hospitals in York, Harrisburg, Baltimore, Philadelphia, and even New York City. Ultimately, all of the seriously wounded who could not be evacuated were sent to the massive U.S. Army general hospital at Camp

Letterman on the York Road east of Gettysburg. The Camp Letterman hospital remained open through mid-November.

In addition to medical care, the great numbers of wounded required massive amounts of food, as well as bandages, blankets, and clothing. Hungry Confederate soldiers had stripped bare most of the food stocked in the residents' pantries. A Wisconsin man named Taylor wrote to a friend in Washington, D.C., on July 9 about a visit to a Gettysburg hospital where many soldiers from his home state lay wounded. "They are almost starving," he wrote, adding: "At first I had to buy bread at any price." As contributions flowed in from nearby communities, many local residents freely dipped into stocks of food they successfully hid from the invaders. Taylor publicly thanked Mrs. Dr. Horner, "who must think the world of all the Badgers," for she had supplied "wines, jellies, bread, butter, tea, sugar, in fact, anything and everything that could in any manner add to the comfort of our boys." Not all who cared for the wounded spoke well of local residents' generosity, however. Some condemned local farmers for extorting high cost for hay, rides, food, and even a place to sleep in a shed. Within a few days, the Christian Commission arrived to satisfy many of the wounded soldiers' needs, and later in the month, Virgil Cornish of Connecticut reported that "hospital supplies are now abundant," praising the commission for "doing a good work."[16]

The dead—both the soldiers and the four-legged beasts who had fallen in battle with them—had to be buried. Many regiments buried their own dead if they controlled the ground on which they fought, but the Union dead of July 1 remained unburied behind Confederate lines for several days before their comrades could reach them. Many Confederates who died at the Angle or on the slopes of Little Round Top or Culp's Hill could not be retrieved by their comrades. Many of them lay unburied when the two armies left the battlefield. It fell to prisoners and to locals to complete the job, initially burying the dead where they fell. Work parties piled up dead horses and mules, doused them with kerosene, and torched them, creating clouds of greasy, black smoke that lingered for days. Peppermint oil or camphor, dabbed under the nose, provided at least a little relief from the stench. Inevitably, the burial parties missed some of the dead. A week after the battle, a visitor described a field "where the conflict raged fiercest" that contained "about forty dead horses . . . within a space of one hundred yards, and on the adjoining field are the bodies of about a dozen rebels, some of them presenting the most frightful and ghastly appearance."[17] In 1872 Southern women's groups raised funds to disinter the Confederate remains from Gettysburg's trench graves for shipment back to cemeteries in Richmond, Raleigh, Charleston, and Savannah.

It did not take long for Gettysburg to take on a special aura that it has never quite escaped. The residents of Gettysburg themselves started the process of transforming the battleground to a national shrine even before 1863 ended. Local resident David McConaughy started the Gettysburg Battlefield Memorial Association to preserve the battlefield and purchased key plots of land on Cemetery Hill, Little Round Top, and Culp's Hill within the first year after the battle. Gettysburg attorney David Wills led the local effort to create a burial ground for the Union dead, purchasing ground on Cemetery Hill next to Evergreen Cemetery for that purpose.

Abraham Lincoln contributed to Gettysburg's special place in national memory when he visited the town as it still recovered from the battle's destructive forces to deliver his Gettysburg Address. At the dedication of the Soldiers' National Cemetery on November 19, 1863, Lincoln committed the United States to "a new birth of freedom" under a strong federal union, secured by the sacrifice of thousands of men who "shall not have died in vain." An Ohio resident who attended the dedication ceremonies described them as "solemn and imposing," and he took solace in knowing that "here sleep loved ones from every State in the Union . . . and here are laid those also from every civilized land and nation." He declared the president's address to be "noble words; fitly spoken." At the time, 1,188 of the Union dead had been reinterred in the Soldiers' National Cemetery from their graves on the battlefield or at the field hospitals; thousands more would follow.[18]

Gettysburg's death toll included local residents, as well. Most visitors to Gettysburg learn the story of Jennie Wade, the only civilian death caused by enemy fire on July 3, but few hear about the tragic demise of Edward McPherson Woods, age three, who died on July 5 from a gunshot inflicted accidentally by his five-year-old brother who mishandled a loaded weapon he found on the battlefield. Indeed, as one early visitor wrote, "the battlefield for miles around is covered with rifles, bayonets, blankets, cartridge boxes, clothing, &c, &c., and thousands of dollars worth of it are carried off daily by those visiting the scene of the conflict."[19] The market for souvenirs of the great battle proved lucrative, and men offered cash to local children for all the bullets, bayonets, and artillery shells they found. Missteps could prove lethal. During the next few years, over a dozen residents and visitors to Gettysburg died or suffered grievous injury from mishandling unexploded artillery shells.[20]

The Gettysburg Battlefield Memorial Association made little progress in preserving the actual acreage of battlefield during the 1870s, but the important work of historical documentation continued. Beginning in the late 1860s, John B. Bachelder—generally acknowledged as the first "official" historian of Gettysburg—invited veterans from both armies to return to the battlefield to help him mark the positions and movements of various commands. In time, especially during the 1880s and until his death in 1894, when veterans finally returned in great numbers to erect and dedicate their monuments, Bachelder served as the association's authority on the marking of the battle lines and the approval of the site, design, and wording on each of the memorials placed on the battlefield. The following year, General Sickles—then a Democratic congressman from New York—introduced the legislation that created Gettysburg National Military Park. When the bill passed, the association handed over administration of the park to the War Department; the Department of the Interior's National Park Service took it over in 1933.[21]

Few of those who survived those days in July 1863—whether military or civilian—forgot the experience. Union veterans returned to Gettysburg for reunions of their regiments or annual encampments of the Grand Army of the Republic. In time, Confederate veterans returned, too. The first reunion that brought together blue and gray veterans on the exact ground where they fought each other occurred at Gettysburg in July 1887, when the Pickett's Division Association met the Philadelphia Brigade survivors at the Angle. But the men who wore the gray returned by the thousands for the golden anniversary of the battle in 1913 for a massive celebration of national reconciliation. Reunions of Civil War veterans continued until 1938, when 1,800 of them attended the seventy-fifth anniversary ceremonies that included the unveiling of the Eternal Light Peace Memorial on Oak Hill.

Why did these men come? Indeed, why do we still come to view these fields and woodlots? When the 68th Pennsylvania came to dedicate its monument in the Peach Orchard in 1888, the orator summarized the veterans' sentiments about Gettysburg's signal importance—not just for them, but for all Americans: on these fields, just as "the armies of the Union and the armies of the Rebellion [came] together," ultimately, it falls to "the people north and south, east and west" to "make for all time to come this republic that Lincoln died for, a government of the people, by the people, and for the people."[22]

Even if modern scholarship has eroded the validity of the battle as the single most decisive "turning point" of the war—other events have their proponents, including the Battle of Antietam, which provided Lincoln with the opportunity to an-

Veterans of the 68th Pennsylvania visit their monument in the Peach Orchard. (USAMHI)

nounce the Emancipation Proclamation and broaden the Union's war aims; and the presidential election of 1864, which returned Lincoln to the White House and guaranteed there would be no brokered peace—popular memory still accords Gettysburg's fields, farms, hills, and woods a special place. As another veteran noted, the landscape itself had become "majestic" in its own right. "The theater and the play were well matched," he asserted, adding: "On those commanding heights, and sheltered by those now silent groves, stretched out in grim and deadly opposition the gathered hosts of kindred yet warring men. Here, as at Marathon, as at Cannae, as at Waterloo, destiny brought two great causes together and bade them struggle for the mastery of the world and the guidance of the future."[23] We hope you draw inspiration from those who followed their conscience and their flags to what the 20th Maine's Colonel Joshua Chamberlain called "these deathless fields."

Acknowledgments

The inspiration for this field guide owes everything to the vision and persistence of David Perry, the University of North Carolina Press's crack editor in chief. He saw the utility in making the substance of our battlefield programs accessible to a wide audience and convinced us to accept his challenge. While we wish him a wonderful retirement, we will miss him immensely. We thank him for rallying the full support of the Press's exceptional editorial staff behind this project, and we are especially happy to thank Jay Mazzocchi, our masterful copyeditor, who kept us roughly on time and always on target.

During the preparation of this guide, we have enjoyed the active support of a number of individuals we now wish to thank. Kurt Vossler provided essential research support into the damage claims records at the Adams County Historical Society and worked through large portions of the *National Tribune* in search of veterans' accounts about Gettysburg. Wayne Motts, former director of the Adams County Historical Society, gave us unparalleled access to his collections in the early phases of our work. Denise Bussard Doyle opened up the cupola of the Seminary Ridge Museum to allow us to take photographs only two days after the removal of trees that had obscured for a century the vista enjoyed by Generals Buford and Reynolds on July 1, 1863. We thank Janice Pietrone for "test-driving" our stops and offering very useful advice. At Gettysburg National Military Park, John Heiser and Scott Hartwig provided essential logistical and informational support. At the U.S. Army Heritage and Education Center (USA-HEC), Jack Giblin, Rich Baker, Molly Bompane, Rodney Foytik, and Gary Johnson worked to complete a large photo order quite expeditiously. This project has benefited from the total support of Tom Hendrix, director of the U.S. Army Military History Institute—now an element of USAHEC—and Mike Perry, director of the Army Heritage Center Foundation. Since the Military History Institute has played a significant role in the careers of both authors, we are pleased to commit a portion of the proceeds of this book to its support.

Karen Luvaas deserves a special thank-you for her stalwart efforts to work through the military records of the individual soldiers who fell at Gettysburg and the pension claims submitted by their widows and mothers. She clearly inherited the enthusiasm and skill for historical research of her father, Jay Luvaas, and this work is all the richer for her contributions to it.

We both profusely thank Barbara Vossler for her frequent and numerous contributions to this effort. These range from computer maintenance to far more than her fair share of the care and feeding of "General Reynolds" and the rest of the Simmental cattle herd at Mountain View Farm. We could not have done this without her.

Photo Credits

Uncredited photos are by the authors; all others are provided by one of the following sources.

Annual Reports: Gettysburg National Military Park Commission, *Annual Reports to the Secretary of War, 1893–1901* (Washington, D.C.: Government Printing Office, 1901).

Chamberlin: Thomas Chamberlin, *History of the One Hundred and Fiftieth Regiment Pennsylvania Volunteers Second Regiment, Bucktail Brigade* (Philadelphia: F. McManus Jr. & Co., 1905).

Clark: Walter Clark, ed., *Histories of the Several Regiments and Battalions from North Carolina in the Great War, 1861–65,* 5 vols. (Raleigh, N.C.: E. M. Uzzell, 1901).

USAMHI: Military Order of the Loyal Legion of the United States Photograph Collection, U.S. Army Military History Institute, U.S. Army Heritage and Education Center, Carlisle, Pa.

USAMHI-TOWER: Tower Gettysburg Album, U.S. Army Military History Institute, U.S. Army Heritage and Education Center, Carlisle, Pa.

Wise: Jennings Cropper Wise, *The Long Arm of Lee; or, The History of the Artillery of the Army of Northern Virginia* (Lynchburg, Va.: J. P. Bell, 1915).

President William Howard Taft visits McPherson's Ridge, May 13, 1909. (USAMHI)

Notes

Abbreviations

ACHS Adams County Historical Society, Gettysburg, Pa.
CSR Civil War Compiled Service Record, National Archives, Washington, D.C.
CV *Confederate Veteran*
GM *Gettysburg Magazine*
GNMP Gettysburg National Military Park
NT *National Tribune*
NYH *New York Herald*
OR U.S. War Department, *War of the Rebellion: A Compilation of the Official Records of the Union and Confederate Armies*, 128 vols. (Washington, D.C.: Government Printing Office, 1880–1901)
PR Pension Records for Union Soldiers, National Archives, Washington, D.C.
SHSP *Southern Historical Society Papers*

Introduction
1. Mary Johnston, "Gettysburg," *Atlantic Monthly* 110 (July 1912): 1.
2. Edwin B. Coddington, *The Gettysburg Campaign: A Study in Command* (New York: Charles Scribner's Sons, 1968), 7.
3. Clifford Dowdey and Louis Manarin, eds., *The Wartime Papers of Robert E. Lee* (New York: Bramall House, 1961), 430.
4. Ibid., 434–35.
5. Ibid., 438.
6. Hotchkiss quoted in Coddington, *The Gettysburg Campaign*, 8.
7. Captain George Hillyer, *My Gettysburg Battle Experiences*, comp. and ed. Gregory A. Coco (Gettysburg, Pa.: Thomas Publications, 2005), 9.
8. OR, vol. 27, pt. 1, 35.
9. OR, vol. 27, pt. 2, 316.
10. For General Order No. 72, see OR, vol. 27, pt. 3, 912–13; for General Order No. 73, see ibid., 942–43.
11. OR, vol. 27, pt. 1, 60.
12. George Gordon Meade, ed., *The Life and Letters of George Gordon Meade, Major General, United States Army*, reprint ed. (Baltimore: Butternut and Blue, 1994), 2:11.
13. OR, vol. 27, pt. 1, 61.
14. Meade, *Life and Letters of General George Gordon Meade*, 2:30.

How to Use This Book
1. Theodore Ditterline, *Sketch of the Battles of Gettysburg, July 1–3, 1863* (New York: C. A. Alvord, 1863), 5.
2. Graduate Mary Kendlehart quoted in William A. Frassanito, *Early Photography at Gettysburg* (Gettysburg, Pa.: Thomas Publications, 1995), 2; Daniel Alexander Skelly, *A Boy's Experiences during the Battle of Gettysburg* (Gettysburg, Pa.: self-published, 1932), 10; Tillie Pierce Alleman, *At Gettysburg; or, What a Girl Saw and Heard of the Battle* (New York: W. Lake Borland, 1889; Butternut and Blue reprint, 1994), 10.

3. "Details of Wednesday's Battle," *New York Times*, July 6, 1863; "From Gen. Lee's Army," *Richmond Examiner*, July 13, 1863.

4. "Our Army Correspondence," *Richmond Daily Dispatch*, July 13, 1863.

5. John W. Busey and David G. Martin, *Regimental Strengths and Losses at Gettysburg*, 4th ed. (Hightstown, N.J.: Longstreet House, 1982).

6. "The New Commander," NYH, June 29, 1863; Theodore Lyman, *Meade's Headquarters, 1863–1865: Letters of Colonel Theodore Lyman from the Wilderness to Appomattox*, ed. George R. Agassiz (Boston: Atlantic Monthly, 1922; reprint ed., Salem, N.H.: Ayer, 1987), 25; George Gordon Meade, ed., *The Life and Letters of George Gordon Meade, Major General, United States Army*, reprint ed. (Baltimore: Butternut and Blue, 1994), 1:v, 2:11–12.

7. Gary W. Gallagher, ed., *Fighting for the Confederacy: The Personal Recollections of General Edward Porter Alexander* (Chapel Hill: University of North Carolina Press, 1989), 91–92.

8. "25 Years After," NT, July 12, 1888.

9. "Ignorance of the War," NT, December 13, 1888.

10. O. B. Curtis, *History of the Twenty-Fourth Michigan of the Iron Brigade*, reprint ed. (Gaithersburg, Md.: Olde Soldier Books, 1988), 424.

11. *Richmond Dispatch*, July 8, 1863.

Stop 1

1. John B. Bachelder, *Gettysburg: What to See, and How to See It* (New York: Lee, Shepard and Dillingham, 1873), 44.

2. OR, vol. 27, pt. 1, 702, 748, 722.

3. Gary W. Gallagher, ed., *Two Witnesses at Gettysburg* (St. James, N.Y.: Brandywine Press, 1994), 40–41; Forbes quoted in Gregory A. Coco, *A Strange and Blighted Land: Gettysburg, the Aftermath of a Battle* (Gettysburg, Pa.: Thomas Publishing 1994), 10; Emmet Crozier, *Yankee Reporters, 1861–1865* (New York: Oxford University Press, 1956), 353.

4. "Experience during Battle," *Gettysburg Compiler*, July 26, 1905; Peter Thorn Damage Claim, ACHS.

5. Gary W. Gallagher, ed., *Fighting for the Confederacy: The Personal Recollections of General Edward Porter Alexander* (Chapel Hill: University of North Carolina Press, 1989), 232.

6. "Gen'l O. O. Howard's Personal Reminiscence of the War of the Rebellion," NT, November 27, 1884.

7. Major Joseph G. Rosengarten, "General Reynolds' Last Battle," *Annals of the War* (Philadelphia: Press of the Times, 1879), 62; Samuel P. Bates, *The Battle of Gettysburg* (Philadelphia: T. H. Davis and Company, 1875), 75; Edwin B. Coddington, *The Gettysburg Campaign: A Study in Command* (New York: Charles Scribner's Sons, 1968), 302–3.

8. NT, July 8, 1886; NT, July 2, 1888.

Stop 2

1. OR, vol. 27, pt. 2, 637; OR, vol. 27, pt. 1, 934; OR, vol. 27, pt. 2, 646; OR, vol. 27, pt. 1, 924, 934. This note includes citations to all of the OR reports used in this section.

2. Quoted in Harry W. Pfanz, *Gettysburg—The First Day* (Chapel Hill: University of North Carolina Press, 2001), 36–37.

3. David L. Ladd and Audrey J. Ladd, eds., *The Bachelder Papers: Gettysburg in Their Own Words* (Dayton, Ohio: Morningside Press, 1994), 1:201–2.

4. "Gen. Henry Heth," CV 7 (1899): 569–70.

5. CSR, Henry C. Rison.

6. See, for instance, David G. Martin, *Gettysburg July 1* (Conshohocken, Pa.: Combined Publishing, 1995), 68–69, 79.

7. Edward McPherson Files, ACHS; James J. Daugherty, "A History of the McPherson Farm at Gettysburg," *GM* 26 (2002): 20–44.

8. Abner Hard, M.D., *History of the Eighth Cavalry Regiment Illinois Volunteers, during the Great Rebellion*, reprint ed. (Dayton, Ohio: Morningside Bookshop, 1996), 256–57.

9. Samuel P. Bates, *The Battle of Gettysburg* (Philadelphia: T. H. Davis and Company, 1875), 58–59.

Stop 3

1. *Richmond Enquirer*, August 14, 1863.

2. Ibid.

3. OR, vol. 27, pt. 1, 244, 267; OR, vol. 27, pt. 2, 646; OR, vol. 27, pt. 1, 274. This note includes citations to all of the OR reports used in this section.

4. NYH, July 3, 1863; *Harrisburg Evening Telegraph*, July 3, 1863.

5. For a discussion of the problem of determining Archer's casualties in this opening fight, see Marc Storch and Beth Storch, "'What a Deadly Trap We Were In': Archer's Brigade on July 1, 1863," *GM* 6 (1992): 25–27.

6. George H. Otis, *The Second Wisconsin Infantry*, reprint ed. with introduction by Alan D. Gaff (Dayton, Ohio: Morningside Press, 1984), 88, 283.

7. CSR, Jacob W. Pickett.

8. John Herbst affidavit, June 1, 1863, ACHS.

9. OR, vol. 27, pt. 2, 637.

10. E. T. Boland, "Death of Gen. Reynolds," NT, May 20, 1915.

Stop 4

1. Undated and unidentified digitized postbattle newspaper clipping at dmna.ny.gov/historic/reghist/civil/infantry/147thInf/147thInfCWN1.pdf (accessed August 17, 2012).

2. OR, vol. 27, pt. 1, 281–82.

3. OR, vol. 27, pt. 2, 649.

4. [Dear friends at home] from C. A. Watkins, July 24, 1863, quoted in R. L. Murray, *Letters from Gettysburg: New York Soldiers' Correspondence from the Battlefield* (Wolcott, N.Y.: Benedum Books, 2005), 34.

5. Undated and unidentified digitized postbattle newspaper clipping at dmna.ny.gov/historic/reghist/civil/infantry/147thInf/147thInfCWN1.pdf (accessed August 17, 2012).

6. OR, vol. 27, pt. 1, 359.

7. Undated and unidentified digitized postbattle newspaper clipping at dmna.ny.gov/historic/reghist/civil/infantry/147thInf/147thInfCWN1.pdf (accessed August 17, 2012).

8. CSR, James C. Knott.

9. "Fighting Them Over," NT, March 20, 1884.

10. "The 76th New York," NT, July 28, 1887.

11. "Battle of Gettysburg," NT, August 25, 1887.

12. New York Monuments Commission, *Final Report on the Battlefield of Gettysburg* (Albany: J. B. Lyon, 1900), 3:995–96.

13. H. C. Matrau to Aunt Sarah, August 12, 1863, in *Letters Home: Henry Matrau of the Iron Brigade*, ed. Marcia Reid-Green (Lincoln: University of Nebraska Press, 1993), 60–61.

14. Joseph J. Hoyle, *"Deliver Us from This Cruel War": The Civil War Letters of Lieutenant Joseph J. Hoyle, 55th North Carolina Infantry* (Jefferson, N.C.: McFarland and Company, 2010), 126.

15. OR, vol. 27, pt. 1, 276.

16. Rufus R. Dawes, *Service with the Sixth Wisconsin Volunteers*, reprint ed. (Dayton, Ohio: Morningside Press, 1996), 161–62.

17. *Medical and Surgical History of the War of the Rebellion* (1876; reprint ed., Wilmington, N.C.: Broadfoot Publishing Company, 1991), 8:578.

18. CSR, J. Martin Adkins.

19. *Encyclopedia and Contemporary Biography of Pennsylvania* (New York: Atlantic Printing Company, 1898), 3:44.

20. "The Capture at the Railroad Cut," NT, September 1, 1910.

Stop 5

1. OR, vol. 27, pt. 2, 444, 553, 579–80, 554. This note includes citations to all of the OR reports used in this section.

2. William H. Runge, ed., *Four Years in the Confederate Artillery: The Diary of Private Henry Robinson Berkeley* (Richmond: Virginia Historical Society, 1991), 50.

3. OR, vol. 27, pt. 1, 310–11.

4. *Fayetteville Observer*, July 27, 1863.

5. *Southern Illustrated News*, July 4, 1863.

6. Walter Clark, ed., *Histories of the Several Regiments and Battalions from North Carolina in the Great War, 1861–65*, reprint ed. (Wilmington, N.C.: Broadfoot Publishing Company, 1996), 2:239.

7. Haskell Monroe, ed., "The Road to Gettysburg: The Diary and Letters of Leonidas Torrence of the Gaston Guards," *North Carolina Historical Review* 36 (1959): 514–15.

8. ACHS, *Farms at Gettysburg—The Fields of Battle*, compiled by Timothy H. Smith (Gettysburg, Pa.: Thomas Publications, 2007), 9.

9. Clark, *Histories of the Several Regiments and Battalions*, 2:235, 239.

10. Robert J. Wynstra, *The Rashness of That Hour: Politics, Gettysburg, and the Downfall of Confederate Brigadier General Alfred Iverson* (New York: Savas Beattie, 2010), 333. See also the very insightful work of Gary Kross, "That One Error Fills Him with Faults: General Iverson and His Brigade at Gettysburg," *Blue and Gray Magazine* 12 (February 1995): 22–24, 48–53; and Robert K. Krick, "Three Confederate Disasters on Oak Ridge: Failures of Brigade Leadership on the First Day at Gettysburg," in *The First Day at Gettysburg: Essays on Confederate and Union Leadership*, ed. Gary W. Gallagher (Kent, Ohio: Kent State University Press, 1992), 129–37.

11. Frederick W. Hawthorne, *Gettysburg: Stories of Men and Monuments* (Gettysburg, Pa.: Association of Licensed Battlefield Guides, 1988), 27.

Stop 6

1. "War Diary of Captain Robert Emory Park, Twelfth Alabama Regiment," SHSP 26 (1898): 13.

2. OR, vol. 27, pt. 1, 307; OR, vol. 27, pt. 2, 592; OR, vol. 27, pt. 1, 310. This note includes citations to all of the OR reports used in this section.

3. PR, Margaret E. Price for Private Francis J. Price.

4. CSR, John Preskitt; "War Diary of Captain Robert Emory Park," 13.

5. ACHS, *Farms at Gettysburg—The Fields of Battle*, compiled by Timothy H. Smith (Gettysburg, Pa.: Thomas Publications, 2007), 10.

6. *Pennsylvania at Gettysburg: Ceremonies at the Dedication of the Monuments Erected by the Commonwealth of Pennsylvania* (Harrisburg, Pa.: Wm. Stanley Ray, 1904), 1:483.

Stop 7

1. Wheeler to his Grandfather and Aunt, July 24, 1863, quoted in Guy Breshears, *Loyal Till Death: A Diary of the 13th New York Artillery* (Bowie, Md.: Heritage Books, Inc., 2003), 186–87.

2. OR, vol. 27, pt. 1, 728; OR, vol. 27, pt. 2, 597, 603; OR, vol. 27, pt. 1, 754. This note includes citations to all of the OR reports used in this section.

3. Breshears, *Loyal Till Death*, 186.

4. "War Diary of Capt. Robert Emory Park, Twelfth Alabama Regiment," SHSP 26 (1898): 12–13.

5. Digitized newspaper clippings found at dmna.ny.gov/historic/reghist/civil/war/infantry /157thInf/157thInfCWN.htm (accessed August 15, 2012).

6. Ibid.; *Medical and Surgical History of the War of the Rebellion* (1876; reprint ed., Wilmington, N.C.: Broadfoot Publishing Company, 1991), 9:229

7. CSR, William R. Butler.

8. Gettysburg Daily website, wp.beta.gettysburgdail.com/?p=148 (accessed September 30, 2012).

9. David A. Heagey Damage Claim File, ACHS.

10. New York Monuments Commission, *Final Report on the Battlefield of Gettysburg* (Albany: J. B. Lyon, 1900), 3:1058–60.

Stop 8

1. *Philadelphia Press*, July 4, 1863.

2. OR, vol. 27, pt. 1, 728; OR, vol. 27, pt. 2, 492; OR, vol. 27, pt. 1, 742; OR, vol. 27, pt. 2, 582; OR, vol. 27, pt. 1, 712–13. This note includes citations to all of the OR reports used in this section.

3. Captain William H. Harrison to Mother, ca. July 1863, quoted in Gregory C. White, *"This Most Bloody and Cruel Drama": A History of the 31st Georgia Volunteer Infantry* (Baltimore: Butternut and Blue, 1997), 94.

4. OR, vol. 27, pt. 1, 718.

5. NYH, July 3, 1863.

6. OR, vol. 27, pt. 1, 720.

7. The veracity of this story still inspires controversy. Harry W. Pfanz, *Gettysburg—The First Day* (Chapel Hill: University of North Carolina Press, 2001), 248–49, repeats much of this story but does not make reference to the postwar reunion.

8. CSR, Joseph R. Haden.

9. Edward Marcus, ed., *A New Canaan Private in the Civil War: Letters of Justus M. Silliman, 17th Connecticut Volunteers* (New Canaan, Conn.: New Canaan Historical Society, 1984), 42, 44, 47–48.

10. Friends of the National Parks at Gettysburg, *The Gettysburg Battlefield Farmstead Guide* (Gettysburg, Pa.: Friends of the National Parks at Gettysburg, 2000), 11.

11. ACHS, *Farms at Gettysburg—The Fields of Battle*, compiled by Timothy H. Smith (Gettysburg, Pa.: Thomas Publications, 2007), 12.

12. Ibid., 12.

13. "Fighting Them Over," NT, March 19, 1885.

14. *Report of the Gettysburg Memorial Commission* (Columbus, Ohio: Nitschke Bros. Press, 1887), 72.

15. G. W. Nichols, *A Soldier's Story of His Regiment (61st Georgia)* (N.p., 1898), 116.

Stop 9

1. OR, vol. 27, pt. 1, 728, 721, 755; OR, vol. 27, pt. 2, 486. This note includes citations to all of the OR reports used in this section.

2. *Philadelphia Press*, July 4, 1863.

3. *Medical and Surgical History of the War of the Rebellion* (1876; reprint ed., Wilmington, N.C.: Broadfoot Publishing Company, 1991), 11:79.

4. PR, Lucy J. Heath for Ebenezer Heath.

5. Mark H. Dunkelman and Michael J. Winey, "The Hardtack Regiment in the Brickyard Fight," GM 8 (1993): 20.

6. New York Monuments Commission, *Final Report on the Battlefield of Gettysburg* (Albany, N.Y.: J. B. Lyon Company, 1900), 3:1051–52.

7. Photograph in Civil War Centennial, Adams County File, ACHS.

Stop 10

1. OR, vol. 27, pt. 1, 301; OR, vol. 27, pt. 2, 587; OR, vol. 27, pt. 1, 297. This note includes citations to all of the OR reports used in this section.

2. "War Diary of Captain Robert Emory Park, Twelfth Alabama Regiment," SHSP 26 (1898): 13.

3. Charles Barber to "Wife and Children," July 8, 1863, in *The Civil War Letters of Charles Barber, Private, 104th New York Infantry*, ed. Raymond G. Barber and Gary E. Swinson (Torrance, Calif.: Gary E. Swinson, 1991), 135.

4. OR, vol. 27, pt. 1, 290.

5. OR, vol. 27, pt. 1, 295–96.

6. NYH, July 19, 1863.

7. A. R. Small, *The Sixteenth Maine Regiment in the War of the Rebellion* (Portland, Maine: B. Thurston and Company, 1886), 127.

8. CSR, Jacob A. Massey.

9. Charles E. Davis Jr., *Three Years in the Army: The Story of the Thirteenth Massachusetts Volunteers* (Boston: Estes and Lauriat, 1894), 228.

10. *Maine at Gettysburg: Report of Maine Commissioners Prepared by the Executive Committee*, reprint ed. (Gettysburg, Pa.: Stan Clark Military Books, 1994), 47.

Stop 11

1. Quoted in Thomas Chamberlin, *History of the One Hundred and Fiftieth Regiment Pennsylvania Volunteers, Second Regiment, Bucktail Brigade* (Philadelphia: F. McManus Jr. and Company, 1905), 120. Weber was wounded in the arm near the shoulder and never rejoined the 150th Pennsylvania.

2. OR, vol. 27, pt. 1, 329. OR, vol. 27, pt. 2, 566; OR, vol. 27, pt. 1, 330; OR, vol. 27, pt. 2, 574, 567. This note includes citations to all of the OR reports used in this section.

3. Chamberlin, *History of the One Hundred and Fiftieth Pennsylvania*, 121.

4. *Medical and Surgical History of the War of the Rebellion* (1876; reprint ed., Wilmington, N.C.: Broadfoot Publishing Company, 1991), 9:228.

5. John Lipscomb Johnson, *The University Memorial: Biographical Sketches of Alumni of the University of Virginia Who Fell in the Confederate War* (Baltimore: Turnbull Brothers, 1871), 413–16.

6. Walter Lord, ed., *The Fremantle Diary* (New York: Capricorn Books, 1954), 204.

7. Chamberlin, *History of the One Hundred and Fiftieth Pennsylvania*, 129–30.

8. *Pennsylvania at Gettysburg: Ceremonies at the Dedication of the Monuments Erected by the Commonwealth of Pennsylvania* (Harrisburg, Pa.: Wm. Stanley Ray, 1904), 2:696.

Stop 12

1. OR, vol. 27, pt. 1, 268; OR, vol. 27, pt. 2, 639, 643; OR, vol. 27, pt. 1, 274, 279–80, 268. This note includes citations to all of the OR reports used in this section.

2. O. M. Curtis, *History of the Twenty-Fourth Michigan of the Iron Brigade*, reprint ed. (Gaithersburg, Md.: Olde Soldier Books, 1988), 188.

3. *Fayetteville Observer*, July 20, 1863.

4. OR, vol. 27, pt. 1, 327, 315; OR, vol. 27, pt. 2, 638; OR, vol. 27, pt. 1, 266. This note includes citations to all of the OR reports used in this section.

5. Survivors' Association, *History of the 121st Regiment Pennsylvania Volunteers* (Philadelphia: Burk and McFetridge Company, 1893), 46.

6. Charles D. Walker, *Biographical Sketches of the Graduates and Eleves of the Virginia Military Institute Who Fell during the War between the States* (Philadelphia: J. B. Lippincott and Company, 1875), 436–38.

7. Curtis, *History of the Twenty-Fourth Michigan of the Iron Brigade*, 35, 40, 43, 160, 189.

8. PR, Lucinda Potter for Corporal Elkanah Sulgrove.

9. CSR, Cleveland Coffey, Thomas Milton Coffey, and William S. Coffey.

10. OR, vol. 27, pt. 1, 317, 320; Harry W. Pfanz, *Gettysburg—The First Day* (Chapel Hill: University of North Carolina Press, 2001), 79.

11. Michigan Monuments Commission, *Michigan at Gettysburg, July 1st, 2nd, and 3rd, 1863. June 12th, 1889* (Detroit: Winn and Hammond, 1889), 118, 123.

12. [Jaquelin Marshall Meredith], "The First Day at Gettysburg," SHSP 24 (1896): 185, 187.

Stop 13

1. OR, vol. 27, pt. 1, 355, 356; OR, vol. 27, pt. 2, 670, 662; OR, vol. 27, pt. 1, 323. This note includes citations to all of the OR reports used in this section.

2. *Philadelphia Press*, July 4, 1863.

3. Blake McKelvey, ed., *Rochester in the Civil War*, Rochester Historical Society Publication, no. 22 (Rochester, N.H.: Rochester Historical Society, 1944), 129.

4. Ezra J. Warner, *Generals in Gray* (Baton Rouge: LA: Louisiana State University Press, 1959), 235.

5. CSR, George Ouzts and James Ouzts.

6. George Henry Mills, *History of the 16th North Carolina Regiment in the Civil War*, reprint ed. (Hamilton, N.Y.: Edmonston Publishing, 1992), 36–37; CSR, John B. Ford.

7. PR, Sarah Bush, mother of Private Duane S. Bush, 80th New York Infantry.

8. Lutheran Theological Seminary Archives, *Report of the Chairman of the Faculty, August 11, 1863*.

9. ACHS, Charles P. Krauth letter to Aunt Jane, July 9, 1863.

10. Varina D. Brown, comp., *A Colonel at Gettysburg and Spotsylvania* (Columbia, S.C.: The State Company, 1931), 80, 84. At Gaines's Mill, on June 27, 1862, the 1st South Carolina Rifles—also called Orr's Rifles—suffered one of the highest rates for any regiment in the entire war.

Day One Conclusion

1. NYH, July 3, 1863.

2. *Philadelphia Inquirer*, July 8, 1863.

3. Ibid.

4. Quoted in Philip Hatfield, *The Rowan Rifle Guards: A History of Company K, 4th Regiment, North Carolina State Troops, 1857–1865* (Lexington: University Press of Kentucky, 2011), 208.

5. OR, vol. 27, pt. 2, 445.

6. OR, vol. 27, pt. 1, 252, 704.

7. OR, vol. 27, pt. 2, 318.

Stop 14

1. OR, vol. 27, pt. 1, 482, 507, 517; OR, vol. 27, pt. 2, 617.

2. Lydia Minturn Post, ed., *Soldiers' Letters from Camp, Battle-field, and Prison* (New York: Bunce and Huntington, 1865), 260.

3. Douglas Southall Freeman, *Lee's Lieutenants: A Study in Command* (New York: Charles Scribner's Sons, 1944), 3:202.

4. Norman E. Rourke, ed., *I Saw the Elephant: The Civil War Experiences of Bailey George McClelen, Company D, 10th Alabama Infantry Regiment* (Shippensburg, Pa.: Burd Street Press, 1995), 40–41; CSR, William F. Carter, Clark L. Harmon, Thomas Mackey, and Silas B. Street.

5. Quoted in R. L. Murray, *Letters from Berdan's Sharpshooters* (Wolcott, N.Y.: Benedum Books, 2005), 131–33.

6. Claims of Samuel Pitzer, No. 2231, from the Border Claim File, Samuel Pitzer, File 14 CF-79, GNMP.

7. "The 3d Me. at Gettysburg," NT, October 13, 1927.

8. "Berdan's Reconnaissance," NT, July 12, 1888.

9. Harry W. Pfanz, *Gettysburg—The Second Day* (Chapel Hill: University of North Carolina Press, 1987), 102.

Stop 15

1. OR, vol. 27, pt. 2, 318, 366–67, 375, 429.

2. Quoted in Carol Reardon, *"I Have Been a Soldier All My Life": Gen. James Longstreet, CSA* (Gettysburg, Pa.: Farnsworth House, 1997), 10.

3. See Carol Reardon, "The Valiant Rearguard: Hancock's Division at Chancellorsville," in *Chancellorsville: The Battle and Its Aftermath*, ed. Gary W. Gallagher (Chapel Hill: University of North Carolina Press, 1996), 147.

4. ACHS, *Farms at Gettysburg—The Fields of Battle*, compiled by Timothy H. Smith (Gettysburg, Pa.: Thomas Publications, 2007), 28; James Warfield Claim File, ACHS.

5. William Swinton, *The Campaigns of the Army of the Potomac*, reprint ed. (New York: Smithmark, 1995), 340.

6. J. A. Early, "Reply to General Longstreet's Second Paper," SHSP 5 (1878): 270–71, 280.

7. James Longstreet, "Lee in Pennsylvania," in *The Annals of the War* (Philadelphia: Philadelphia Weekly, 1879), 434.

8. James Longstreet, "The Mistakes of Gettysburg," *The Annals of the War* (Philadelphia: Philadelphia Weekly, 1879), 632.

Stop 16

1. For Sickles's testimony and additional analysis, see Bill Hyde, ed., *The Union Generals Speak: The Meade Hearings on the Battle of Gettysburg* (Baton Rouge: Louisiana State University Press, 2003), 40–44.

2. OR, vol. 27, pt. 1, 116.

3. Quoted in Hyde, *The Union Generals Speak*, 45.

4. W. C. Storrick, *Gettysburg: The Place, the Battles, the Outcome* (Harrisburg, Pa.: J. Horace McFarland Company, 1932), 90–91.

5. ACHS, *Farms at Gettysburg—The Fields of Battle*, compiled by Timothy H. Smith (Gettysburg, Pa.: Thomas Publications, 2007), 20, 21, 27.

6. Excerpted from Wm. Emory Sherfey, *The Sherfey Family in the United States, 1751–1948*, copied and annotated by Robert L. Brake, April 1974, ACHS.

7. Abner Doubleday, *Chancellorsville and Gettysburg*, reprint ed. (New York: The Blue and the Gray Press, n.d. [1882]), 178.

8. Henry J. Hunt, "The Second Day at Gettysburg," in *Battles and Leaders of the Civil War*, reprint ed. (New York: Castle Books, 1956), 3:311.

Stop 17

1. E. M. Law, "The Struggle for 'Round Top,'" in *Battles and Leaders of the Civil War: Retreat from Gettysburg*, reprint ed. (New York: Castle Books, 1956), 318–19.

2. J. B. Hood, *Advance and Retreat: Personal Experiences in the United States and Confederate States Army*, reprint ed. (Lincoln: University of Nebraska Press, 1996), 56, 58, 59.

3. OR, vol. 27, pt. 1, 518–19; OR, vol. 27, pt. 2, 392, 395, 404.

4. Brian Craig Miller, *John Bell Hood and the Fight for Civil War Memory* (Knoxville: University of Tennessee Press, 2010), 48.

5. "General E. M. Law at Gettysburg," CV 30 (1922): 50.

6. John C. West, *A Texan in Search of a Fight* (Waco, Tex.: Press of J. S. Hill and Company, 1901), 87; CSR, Joe C. Smith.

7. Russell C. White, ed., *The Civil War Diary of Wyman S. White, First Sergeant, Company F, 2nd United States Sharpshooters* (Baltimore: Butternut and Blue, 1991), 161–62, 174; *Portsmouth Journal of Literature and Politics*, September 5, 1863.

8. ACHS, *Farms at Gettysburg—The Fields of Battle*, compiled by Timothy H. Smith (Gettysburg, Pa.: Thomas Publications, 2007), 30.

9. White, *The Civil War Diary of Wyman S. White*, 164.

Stop 18

1. OR, vol. 27, pt. 1, 202, 600.

2. William Swinton, *Campaigns of the Army of the Potomac*, reprint ed. (New York: Smithmark, 1995), 346–48; Samuel P. Bates, *The Battle of Gettysburg* (Philadelphia: T. H. Davis, 1875), 117; Abner Doubleday, *Chancellorsville and Gettysburg*, reprint ed. (New York: The Blue and the Gray Press, n.d. [1882]), 168–69; Henry J. Hunt, "The Second Day at Gettysburg," in *Battles and Leaders of the Civil War: Retreat from Gettysburg*, reprint ed. (New York: Castle Books, 1956), 3:307–9.

3. Oliver Willcox Norton, *The Attack and Defense of Little Round Top* (New York: Neale, 1913), 312.

4. OR, vol. 27, pt. 1, 616–17.

5. OR, vol. 27, pt. 2, 412; John C. West, *A Rebel in Search of a Fight* (Waco, Tex.: Press of J. S. Hill and Company, 1901), 94–95.

6. OR, vol. 27, pt. 2, 391; online at dmna.ny.gov/historic/reghist/civil/infantry/44thInf/44thInfCWN2.pdf (accessed September 7, 2012).

7. Online at dmna.ny.gov/historic/reghist/civil/infantry/140thInf/140thInfCWN5.pdf (accessed September 7, 2012).

8. CSR, John Taylor Darwin; CSR, Reuben Franks; Jeffrey D. Stocker, ed., *From Huntsville to Appomattox* (Knoxville: University of Tennessee Press, 1996), 208.

9. PR, Lydia M. Webb for Sanford O. Webb; "At Gettysburg," NT, August 25, 1892.

10. For an interesting examination of the evidence relating to the 16th Michigan's performance at Gettysburg, see Kim Crawford, *The 16th Michigan Infantry* (Dayton, Ohio: Morningside Press, 2002). The quotation can be found on page 365.

11. Quoted in ibid., 368.

12. Livermore diary, July 2, 1863, in *With a Flash of His Sword: The Writings of Major Holman S. Melcher, 20th Maine Infantry*, ed. William B. Styple (Kearny, N.J.: Belle Grove Publishing Company, 1994), 77.

13. *OR*, vol. 27, pt. 2, 393. All quotations from Chamberlain's report come from *OR*, vol. 27, pt. 1, 622–25.

14. CSR, Barnett H. Cody; William C. Oates, *The War between the Union and the Confederacy and Its Lost Opportunities* (New York: Neale, 1905), 226.

15. *Medical and Surgical History of the War of the Rebellion* (1876; reprint ed., Wilmington, N.C.: Broadfoot Publishing Company, 1991), 8:504, 509.

16. Tillie Pierce Alleman, *At Gettysburg; or, What a Girl Saw and Heard of the Battle* (New York: W. Lake Borland, 1889; Butternut and Blue reprint, 1994), 43–44; J. A. Curran, "Billings at Gettysburg," *New England Journal of Medicine* 269 (1963): 24.

17. Quoted in Styple, *With a Flash of His Sword*, 77–78, 83–84.

18. Ellis Spear, "The Left at Gettysburg," NT, June 12, 1913.

Stop 19

1. For interesting early Devil's Den lore, see Garry E. Adelman and Timothy H. Smith, *Devil's Den: A History and Guide* (Gettysburg, Pa.: Thomas Publications, 1997), 7–11.

2. *OR*, vol. 27, pt. 1, 510, 513, 526; *OR*, vol. 27, pt. 2, 393, 394, 415.

3. William Styple, ed. *Our Noble Blood: The Civil War Letters of Major General Regis de Trobriand* (Kearney, N.J.: Bellegrove, 1997), 88.

4. J. B. Polley, *Hood's Texas Brigade: Its Marches, Its Battles, Its Achievements*, reprint ed. (Dayton, Ohio: Morningside Books, 1976 [1910]), 225.

5. John Rozier, ed., *The Granite Farm Letters: The Civil War Correspondence of Edgeworth and Sallie Bird* (Athens, Ga.: University of Georgia Press, 1988), 118.

6. Ibid., 115–17, 120; CSR, Everard Culver, Joseph Dickson, William H. Hardwick, Montgomery Harrison, Lovick Pierce, James E. Medlock, James T. Middlebrook, Jasper Boyd, Dawson McCook, and James R. Reynolds.

7. PR, Abigail Toothaker for John A. Toothaker.

8. Adelman and Smith, *Devil's Den*, 5.

9. W. F. Perry, "The Devil's Den," CV 9 (1901): 161–62.

10. Polley, *Hood's Texas Brigade*, 168–70.

Stop 20

1. Quoted in Captain George Hillyer, *My Gettysburg Battle Experiences*, comp. and ed. Gregory A. Coco (Gettysburg, Pa.: Thomas Publishing, 2005), 39.

2. Online at dmna.ny.gov/historic/reghis/civil/infantry/63rdInf/63rdInfCWN.htm (accessed August 18, 2012).

3. *OR*, vol. 27, pt. 1, 379–81, 386, 389, 400–401, 522, 607–8, 610–11, 645, 653; *OR*, vol. 27, pt. 2, 368, 400–401. This note includes all of the quotations cited in this section from *OR* reports.

4. W. J. Andrews, "'Tige' Anderson's Brigade at Sharpsburg," CV 16 (1908): 579.

5. Ezra J. Warner, *Generals in Gray* (Baton Rouge: Louisiana State University Press, 1959), 171; Guy R. Everson and Edward H. Simpson Jr., eds., *"Far, Far from Home": The Wartime Letters of Dick and Tally Simpson, Third South Carolina Volunteers* (New York: Oxford University Press, 1994), 226.

6. William B. Styple, ed., *Our Noble Blood: The Civil War Letters of Major-General Regis de Trobriand* (Kearny, N.J.: Belle Grove Publishing Company, 1997), 116.

7. J. W. Muffly, ed., *The Story of Our Regiment: A History of the 148th Pennsylvania Volunteers* (Des Moines, Iowa: Kenyon Printing Company, 1904), 577, 603.

8. CSR, William Messer Pritchett.

9. Gilbert Frederick, *The Story of a Regiment, Being a Record of the Military Services of the Fifty-Seventh New York State Volunteer Infantry* (Chicago: C. H. Morgan, 1895), 191.

10. ACHS, *Farms at Gettysburg—The Fields of Battle*, compiled by Timothy H. Smith (Gettysburg, Pa.: Thomas Publications, 2007), 3, 33; Federal Claim Files for George Rose (214-938), John Rose (214-937), and Francis C. Ogden (214-918), GNMP; *Adams Sentinel and General Advertiser*, August 7, 1866.

11. Ronald H. Moseley, ed., *The Stilwell Letters: The Story of Our Regiment; a Georgian in Longstreet's Corps, Army of Northern Virginia* (Macon, Ga.: Mercer University Press, 2002), 184–85.

12. Robert Laird Stewart, *History of the One Hundred and Fortieth Regiment Pennsylvania Volunteers* (Philadelphia: Franklin Bindery, 1912), 426–27.

Stop 21

1. OR, vol. 27, pt. 1, 499, 505, 882; OR, vol. 27, pt. 2, 430.

2. "Barksdale-Humphreys Mississippi Brigade," *CV* 1 (1893): 206.

3. CSR, William R. Oursler and Robert A. Oursler.

4. *Pennsylvania at Gettysburg: Ceremonies at the Dedication of the Monuments Erected by the Commonwealth of Pennsylvania* (Harrisburg, Pa.: Wm. Stanley Ray, 1904), 1:356–57, 393–94, 545.

Stop 22

1. James I. Robertson Jr., *The Civil War Letters of General Robert McAllister* (New Brunswick, N.J.: Rutgers University Press, 1965), 332–33.

2. John G. Barrett, ed., *Yankee Rebel: The Civil War Journal of Edmund DeWitt Patterson* (Knoxville, Tenn.: University of Tennessee Press, 2004), 116.

3. Colonel David Lang to Brigadier General E. A. Perry, July 19, 1863, reprinted in Francis P. Fleming, *Memoir of Capt. C. Seton Fleming, of the Second Florida Infantry, C.S.A.* (Jacksonville, Fla.: Times Union Publishing House, 1884), 65.

4. OR, vol. 27, pt. 1, 501, 532, 533, 543, 551, 554, 566; OR, vol. 27, pt. 2, 618, 631.

5. Theodore Lyman, *Meade's Headquarters, 1863–1865: Letters of Colonel Theodore Lyman from the Wilderness to Appomattox*, ed. George R. Agassiz (Boston: Atlantic Monthly, 1922; reprint ed., Salem, N.H.: Ayer, 1987), 7, 73.

6. Edward N. Thurston, "Memoir of Richard H. Anderson, C.S.A.," SHSP 39 (1914): 148.

7. "Gettysburg," NT, January 29, 1891; "Batteries F and K, 3d U.S. Artillery," NT, March 23, 1916.

8. CSR, Rudolphus H. McClellan.

9. Quoted in Harry W. Pfanz, *Gettysburg—The Second Day* (Chapel Hill: University of North Carolina Press, 1987), 137; *Daniel Klingel Farmhouse—Historic Structure Report*, prepared by Oehrlein and Associates, May 10, 2010, Klingel Farm Folder, archives of GNMP.

10. *The Press* (Philadelphia, Pa.), July 4, 1888; historical note submitted by John Heiser on August 10, 2000, Rogers Farm File, archival record V2–7/258230, GNMP.

11. Peter Trostle Farm File and Catherine Trostle Farm File, GNMP.

Stop 23

1. NYH, July 5, 1863.

2. Online at dmna.ny.gov/historic/reghist/civil/infantry/126thInf/126thInfCWN05.pdf (accessed on September 14, 2012).

3. *Baltimore Sun*, July 10, 1863.

4. Online at dmna.ny.gov/historic/reghist/civil/infantry/126thInf/126thInfCWN05.pdf (accessed on September 14, 2012).

5. Quoted in Richard Moe, *The Last Full Measure: The Life and Death of the First Minnesota Volunteers* (New York: Henry Holt and Company, 1993), 271. "Sergeant" quoted in Moe, *Last Full Measure*, 267; see also 269–71.

6. OR, vol. 27, pt. 1, 317, 371, 425, 443; OR, vol. 27, pt. 2, 618–19. This note includes all of the quotations cited in this section from OR reports.

7. General Francis A. Walker, *General Hancock* (New York: D. Appleton, 1897), 147.

8. Brian Leehan, *Pale Horse at Plum Run: The First Minnesota at Gettysburg* (Minneapolis: Minnesota Historical Society Press, 2002), 170, 174.

9. PR, Mary A. Cobb for Byron Welch (Cobb).

10. John Day Smith, *The History of the Nineteenth Regiment of Maine Volunteer Infantry* (Minneapolis, Minn.: Great Western Printing Company, 1909), 98.

11. Andrew E. Ford, *The Story of the Fifteenth Regiment Massachusetts Volunteer Infantry* (Clinton, Mass.: Press of W. J. Coulter, 1898), 269–70.

12. OR, vol. 27, pt. 1, 419, 422, 423, 427; OR, vol. 27, pt. 2, 629, 632.

13. Gary W. Gallagher, ed., *Fighting for the Confederacy: The Personal Recollections of General Edward Porter Alexander* (Chapel Hill: University of North Carolina Press, 1989), 255.

14. Bertram H. Groene, ed., "Civil War Letters of Colonel David Lang," *Florida Historical Quarterly* 54 (1976): 340–41, 354–64.

15. CSR, Thomas M. Albert.

16. George Weikert Farm File, William Patterson Farm File and Nicholas Codori Farm File, GNMP.

17. William Cowan McClellan to Thomas Joyce McClellan, July 4, 1863, in *Welcome the Hour of Conflict: William Cowan McClelland and the 9th Alabama*, ed. John C. Carter (Tuscaloosa: University of Alabama Press, 2007), 237.

18. New York Monuments Commission, *Final Report on the Battlefield of Gettysburg* (Albany: J. B. Lyon Company, 1900), 2:886.

19. NYH, July 5, 1863.

Stop 24

1. OR, vol. 27, pt. 1, 233, 358, 748–49; OR, vol. 27, pt. 2, 504, 543–44.

2. CSR, William Dawson Brown.

3. OR, vol. 27, pt. 2, 352, 544, 539.

4. Charles D. Walker, *Biographical Sketches of the Graduates and Eleves of the Virginia Military Institute Who Fell during the War between the States* (Philadelphia: J. B. Lippincott, 1875), 328–34.

5. W. W. Goldsborough, *The Maryland Line in the Confederate Army, 1861–1865* (Baltimore: Guggenheimer, Weil and Company, 1900), 324–25.

6. Gregory A. Coco, *A Vast Sea of Misery: A History and Guide to the Union and Confederate Field Hospitals at Gettysburg* (Gettysburg, Pa.: Thomas Publications, 1988), 115; Christian Benner Damage Claim, ACHS; Captain W. Williard Smith to Brig. Gen. M. C. Meigs, July 16, 1863, GNMP File V4-18.

7. Allan Nevins, ed., *A Diary of Battle: The Personal Journals of Colonel Charles S. Wainwright, 1861–1865*, reprint ed. (Gettysburg, Pa.: Stan Clark Military Books, n.d. [1962]), 243.

Stop 25

1. Online at dmna.ny.gov/historic/reghist/civil/infantry/137thInf/137thInfCWN.htm (accessed on August 18, 2012).

2. Richard Eddy, *History of the Sixtieth Regiment New York State Volunteers* (Philadelphia: self-published, 1864), 261.

3. OR, vol. 27, pt. 1, 856, 861; OR, vol. 27, pt. 2, 504, 513.

4. Online at dmna.ny.gov/historic/reghis/civil/infantry/78thInf/78thInfCWN.htm (accessed on August 18, 2012).

5. *Medical and Surgical History of the War of the Rebellion* (1876; reprint ed., Wilmington, N.C.: Broadfoot Publishing Company, 1991), 8:351.

6. Ibid., 12:436.

7. Online at dmna.ny.gov/historic/reghist/civil/infantry/137thInf/137thInfCWN.htm (accessed August 18, 2012).

8. OR, vol. 27, pt. 1, 856, 857, 866; OR, vol. 27, pt. 2, 510.

9. Quoted in John D. Cox, *Culp's Hill* (New York: Da Capo, 2003), 51.

10. Donald B. Koonce, ed., *Doctor to the Front: The Recollections of Confederate Surgeon Thomas Fanning Wood, 1861–1865* (Knoxville: University of Tennessee Press, 2000), 93.

11. CSR, Edward J. Garrison.

12. PR, Lucinda Carnine for Private John Carnine.

13. Henry Culp Farm File, GNMP.

14. W. W. Goldsborough, *The Maryland Line in the Confederate Army, 1861–1865* (Baltimore: Guggenheim, Weil, and Company, 1900), 104–5.

15. "Steuart's Brigade at the Battle of Gettysburg—A Narrative by Rev. Randolph H. McKim, D. D., Late First Lieutenant and Aide-de-Camp, Confederate Army," SHSP 5 (1878): 295.

Stop 26

1. Jean M. Cate, ed., *If I Live to Come Home: The Civil War Letters of Sergeant John March Cate* (Pittsburgh: Dorrance Publishing Company, 1995), 104.

2. OR, vol. 27, pt. 1, 361; OR, vol. 27, pt. 2, 484. This note includes all of the quotations cited in this section from OR reports.

3. PR, Mary Sullivan Horr for Calvin Horr.

4. McKnight Farm File, ACHS.

5. Adin B. Underwood, *The Three Years' Service of the Thirty-Third Mass. Infantry Regiment, 1862–1865* (Boston: A. Williams and Company, 1881), 130.

Stop 27

1. OR, vol. 27, pt. 1, 457, 713, 715, 718, 749, 894; OR, vol. 27, pt. 2, 480, 484, 486.

2. Stephen W. Sears, ed., *Mr. Dunn Browne's Experiences in the Army: The Civil War Letters of Samuel W. Fiske* (New York: Fordham University Press, 1998), 111.

3. PR, Mary McVicker for Alpheus S. McVicker.

4. CSR, Horthere Fontenot.

5. Federal Claim Files for Peter Raffensperger and Edward Menchey, ACHS; *Gettysburg Times*, December 28, 1989.

6. Clement A. Evans, ed., *Confederate Military History*, vol. 10, *Louisiana*, reprint ed. (Secaucus, N.J.: Blue and Gray Press, n.d.), 260.

7. Walter Clark, ed., *Histories of the Several Regiments and Battalions from North Carolina in the Great War, 1861–65* (Raleigh: R. M. Uzzell, 1901), 1:357–59.

Day Two Conclusion

1. Donald B. Koonce, *Doctor to the Front: The Recollections of Confederate Surgeon Thomas Fanning Wood, 1861–1865* (Knoxville: University of Tennessee Press, 2000), 106–7.

2. OR, vol. 27, pt. 2, 320.

Stop 28

1. *OR*, vol. 27, pt. 1, 73.

2. This exchange appears in a number of variant forms. This version comes from George Gordon Meade, ed., *The Life and Letters of George Gordon Meade, Major General, United States Army* (New York: Charles Scribner's Sons, 1913), 2:97.

3. *New York Tribune*, July 6, 1863.

4. John Gibbon, *Recollections of the Civil War* (New York: Putnam's, 1928), 187.

5. Lydia Leister Farm File, GNMP; Daniel Alexander Skelly, *A Boy's Experience during the Battles of Gettysburg* (Gettysburg, Pa.: Daniel Alexander Skelly, 1932), 21.

6. John T. Trowbridge, "The Field of Gettysburg," *Atlantic Monthly* 16 (November 1865): 616–24.

Stop 29

1. Smith left no report since he resigned his commission soon after Gettysburg. Colonel John S. Hoffman wrote a confusing report that suggests that only the 49th and 52nd Virginia served behind the stone wall against which the 27th Indiana advanced. He makes no mention of the 31st Virginia, Smith's remaining regiment.

2. *OR*, vol. 27, pt. 1, 813–15, 817; *OR*, vol. 27, pt. 2, 308, 505.

3. Wilbur D. Jones, *Giants in the Cornfield: The 27th Indiana Infantry* (Shippensburg, Pa.: White Mane, 1997), 47–48, 57, 252.

4. *Medical and Surgical History of the War of the Rebellion* (1876; reprint ed., Wilmington, N.C.: Broadfoot Publishing Company, 1991), 7:76; CSR, Thompson A. Murphy.

5. PR, Frances Guthrie for Elisha Guthrie; for a photo of the clubhouse plaque, see Jones, *Giants in the Cornfield*, 106.

6. Abraham Spangler Farm File, GNMP.

7. Alonzo H. Quint, *The Record of the Second Massachusetts Infantry, 1861–65* (Boston: James P. Walker, 1867), 180.

8. Lyman Richard Comey, ed., *A Legacy of Valor: The Memoirs and Letters of Captain Henry Newton Comey, 2nd Massachusetts Infantry* (Knoxville, Tenn.: University of Tennessee Press, 2004), 132.

9. Quint, *The Record of the Second Massachusetts Infantry*, 180.

Stop 30

1. Hayward to Father, July 17, 1863, in *Last to Leave the Field: The Life and Letters of First Sergeant Ambrose Henry Hayward, 28th Pennsylvania Volunteers*, ed. Timothy J. Orr (Knoxville: University of Tennessee Press, 2010), 160.

2. Ted Barclay to Sister, July 8, 1863, in *Letters from the Stonewall Brigade: Ted Barclay, Liberty Hall Volunteers*, ed. Charles W. Turner (Berryville, Va.: Rockbridge Publishing Company 1992), 90.

3. *OR*, vol. 27, pt. 1, 681, 829, 830, 847, 868; *OR*, vol. 27, pt. 2, 511, 513, 523, 526, 568, 569.

4. Colonel George Cobham to brother Henry, July 4, 1863, in *Martial Deeds of Pennsylvania*, by Samuel P. Bates (Philadelphia: T. H. Davis and Company, 1873), 448.

5. Milo M. Quaife, ed., *From the Cannon's Mouth: The Civil War Letters of General Alpheus Williams* (Detroit: Wayne State University Press, 1959), 271–72.

6. William A. Blair, ed., *A Politician Goes to War* (University Park, Pa.: Penn State University Press, 1995), 98.

7. PR, Margaret Longworth for Sergeant Charles Longworth; Orr, *Last to Leave the Field*, 161.

8. CSR, Beale D. Hamilton; *Medical and Surgical History of the War of the Rebellion* (1876; reprint ed., Wilmington, N.C.: Broadfoot Publishing Company, 1991), 10:683; Robert J. Driver Jr., *First and Second Maryland Infantry, CSA* (Bowie, Md.: Heritage Books, 2003), 430.

9. PR, Anne W. Lowry for George G. Lowry.

10. OR, vol. 27, pt. 1, 120–21, 763–65, 770.

Stop 31

1. OR, vol. 27, pt. 2, 351, 359, 636, 645, 647.

2. J. Longstreet to A. B. Longstreet, July 24, 1863, quoted in General James Longstreet, "Lee in Pennsylvania," *Annals of the Civil War* (Philadelphia: Times Publishing Company, 1879), 414.

3. Isaac Ridgeway Trimble, "The Battle and Campaign of Gettysburg," SHSP (1898): 17.

4. CSR, William J. Bartley.

5. CSR, Daniel A. Featherston; Ellen Sheffield Wilds, transcriber, *Far from Home: The Diary of Lt. William H. Peel, 1863–1865* (Carrollton, Miss.: Pioneer Publishing, 2005), 64.

6. David McMillan Farm Damage Claim, ACHS.

7. Elwood W. Crist, *The Struggle for the Bliss Farm at Gettysburg, July 2nd and 3rd, 1863*, 2nd ed. (Baltimore: Butternut and Blue, 1994), 104–8, 114–21; OR, vol. 27, pt. 1, 454, 465.

8. Longstreet, "Lee in Pennsylvania," 429.

9. James Longstreet, *From Manassas to Appomattox: Memoirs of the Civil War in America*, reprint ed. (Secaucus, N.J.: Blue and Gray Press, 1984), 387–88.

10. General J. A. Early, "Reply to General Longstreet's Second Paper," SHSP 5 (1878): 284–85.

11. G. Moxley Sorrell, *Recollections of a Confederate Staff Officer*, ed. Bell Irvin Wiley, reprint ed. (Wilmington, N.C.: Broadfoot Publishing, 1991), 157, 163.

Stop 32

1. Gary W. Gallagher, ed., *Fighting for the Confederacy: The Personal Recollections of General Edward Porter Alexander* (Chapel Hill: University of North Carolina Press, 1989), 254–55, 259; James Longstreet, *From Manassas to Appomattox: Memoirs of the Civil War in America*, reprint ed. (Secaucus, N.J.: Blue and Gray Press, 1984), 392.

2. OR, vol. 27, pt. 2, 352, 360, 376, 678.

3. Gallagher, *Fighting for the Confederacy*, 336.

4. CSR, Henry Redeau. In some sources, his surname is spelled "Rideau."

5. John W. H. Porter, *A Record of Events in Norfolk County, Virginia, from April 19th, 1861, to May 10th, 1862, with a History of the Soldiers and Sailors of Norfolk County, Norfolk City, and Portsmouth Who Served in the Confederate States Army or Navy* (Portsmouth, Va.: W. A. Fiske, 1892), 54.

6. CSR, Robert Guy; CSR, Joshua Murden; Joseph C. Mayo, "Pickett's Charge at Gettysburg," SHSP 34 (1906): 330–31.

7. OR, vol. 27, pt. 1, 117, 239, 373, 417, 420, 428, 437, 451; OR, vol. 27, pt. 2, 318, 435.

8. OR, vol. 27, pt. 1, 239, 258; OR, vol. 27, pt. 2, 308, 352; J. L. Bechtel to Miss Connie, July 6, copy at GNMP.

9. Letter of Captain C. A. Phillips, July 6, 1863, quoted in *History of the Fifth Massachusetts Battery* (Boston: Luther E. Cowles, 1902), 652; OR, vol. 27, pt. 1, 437.

10. Gallagher, *Fighting for the Confederacy*, 254.

11. OR, vol. 27, pt. 2, 352, 359, 360, 619, 999; *Supplement to the Official Records of the Union and Confederate Armies*, vol. 5, pt. 1, serial no. 5 (Wilmington, N.C.: Broadfoot Publishing Company, 1995), 308, 316, 317, 331, 332.

12. Wayne E. Motts, *Trust in God and Fear Nothing: Lewis A. Armistead, CSA* (Gettysburg, Pa.: Farnsworth House Books, 1994), 4, 12–14, 40.

13. "The Southern Cause," SHSP 30 (1902): 367.

14. Robert K. Krick, "Armistead and Garnett: The Parallel Lives of Two Virginia Soldiers," in *The Third Day at Gettysburg and Beyond*, ed. Gary Gallagher (Chapel Hill: University of North Carolina Press, 1994), 96, 98, 121–22.

15. *Medical and Surgical History of the War of the Rebellion* (1876; reprint ed., Wilmington, N.C.: Broadfoot Publishing Company, 1991), 7:203.

16. Ibid., 12:530.

17. Jacob Eckenrode Damage Claim, ACHS; *Gettysburg Compiler*, July 25, 1931; "Henry Spangler House Historic Structure Report," 1989, GNMP.

18. Quoted in Carol Reardon, *Pickett's Charge in History and Memory* (Chapel Hill: University of North Carolina Press, 1997), 54.

19. Quoted in ibid., 155.

20. *Richmond Times*, November 7, 1894.

21. Quoted in Reardon, *Pickett's Charge in History and Memory*, 159.

Stop 33

1. Henry Abbott to Father, July 6, 1863, in *Fallen Leaves: The Civil War Letters of Major Henry Livermore Abbott*, ed. Robert Garth Scott (Kent, Ohio: Kent State University Press, 1991), 186.

2. OR, vol. 27, pt. 1, 238, 480, 437.

3. PR, Jemima Peto for Edward Peto; Andrew Cowan, "Recitals and Reminiscences," NT, November 12, 1903.

4. Quoted in Gregory A. Coco, *A Vast Sea of Misery: A History and Guide to the Union and Confederate Field Hospitals at Gettysburg* (Gettysburg, Pa.: Thomas Publications 1988), 63.

5. See the exchange between Hunt and Walker in "General Hancock and the Artillery at Gettysburg," in *Battles and Leaders of the Civil War*, ed. Robert U. Johnson and Clarence Clough Buel (New York: Century, 1888), 3:385–87.

6. OR, vol. 27, pt. 1, 239, 439, 445.

7. Theodore Lyman, *Meade's Headquarters, 1863–1865: Letters of Colonel Theodore Lyman from the Wilderness to Appomattox*, ed. George R. Agassiz (Boston: Atlantic Monthly, 1922; reprint ed., Salem, N.H.: Ayer, 1987), 107.

8. PR, Barbara Joeckel for First Sergeant George Joeckel.

9. "The Battle of Gettysburg," *Richmond Enquirer*, July 23, 1863.

10. *Harrisburg Daily Telegraph*, July 7, 1863.

11. *Supplement to the Official Records of the Union and Confederate Armies*, vol. 5, pt. 1, serial no. 5 (Wilmington, N.C.: Broadfoot Publishing Company, 1995), 340.

12. OR, vol. 27, pt. 1, 428, 431, 480, 690.

13. *Supplement to the Official Records*, 340.

14. Frank A. Haskell, *The Battle of Gettysburg* (Madison: Wisconsin History Commission, 1908), 119.

15. OR, vol. 27, pt. 1, 439.

16. Haskell, *Battle of Gettysburg*, 129–30.

17. *Supplement to the Official Records*, 316.

18. Lyman, *Meade's Headquarters*, 307.

19. *Medical and Surgical History of the War of the Rebellion* (1876; reprint ed., Wilmington, N.C.: Broadfoot Publishing Company, 1991), 10:540.

20. OR, vol. 27, pt. 1, 441.

21. Charles Carleton Coffin, *Four Years of Fighting* (Boston: Ticknor and Fields, 1866), 297; and William Swinton, *The Twelve Decisive Battles of the World* (New York: Dick and Fitzgerald, 1867), 311.

22. James M. McPherson, *Hallowed Ground: A Walk at Gettysburg* (New York: Crown Publishers, 2003), 138.

23. *Supplement to the Official Records*, 414.

24. OR, vol. 27, pt. 1, 462; OR, vol. 27, pt. 2, 650, 666.

25. Quoted in Wayne Mahood, *Alexander "Fighting Ellick" Hays* (Jefferson, N.C.: McFarland, 2005), 117.

26. PR, William S. Dildine for Andrew J. Dildine.

27. Abraham Brien Farm File, GNMP.

28. "The Battle of Gettysburg," *Richmond Enquirer*, July 23, 1863.

29. *Richmond Dispatch*, July 28, 1863, and widely reprinted.

30. *Richmond Enquirer*, August 7, 1863.

31. William R. Bond, *Pickett or Pettigrew? An Historical Essay* (Scotland Neck, N.C.: W. L. L. Hall, 1888), 9.

Stop 34

1. OR, vol. 27, pt. 1, 956, 998, 1050; OR, vol. 27, pt. 2, 697–99, 725; *Supplement to the Official Records of the Union and Confederate Armies*, vol. 5, pt. 1, serial no. 5 (Wilmington, N.C.: Broadfoot Publishing Company, 1995), 257–58.

2. John C. Ropes, "Major General James Ewell Brown Stuart," *Papers of the Military Historical Society of Massachusetts* (Boston: The Society, 1895), 10:157.

3. D. M. Gregg, "The Union Cavalry at Gettysburg," *Annals of the War* (Philadelphia: Times Publishing Company, 1879), 379; J. Edward Carpenter, "Gregg's Cavalry at Gettysburg," *Annals of the War*, 527, 533.

4. William Brooke-Rawle, "The Right Flank at Gettysburg," *Annals of the War*, 470, 481–82.

5. CSR, William G. Conner; Donald A. Hopkins, *The Little Jeff: The Jeff Davis Legion, Cavalry, Army of Northern Virginia* (Shippensburg, Pa.: White Mane Books, 1999), 19, 156; Nathaniel Cheairs Hughes Jr., *Yale's Confederates: A Biographical Dictionary* (Knoxville: University of Tennessee Press, 2008), 44–45.

6. PR, Clara Tripp Hill for Corporal Phillip Hill.

7. W. C. Storrick, *Gettysburg: The Place, the Battles, the Outcome* (Harrisburg, Pa.: J. Horace McFarland Company, 1932), 108; Rummel farm, online at www.gettysburg.stonesentinels.com/Places?Rummel.php (accessed on October 6, 2012).

8. L. S. Trowbridge, "The Cavalry on the Gettysburg Campaign," *War Papers* (Detroit: MOLLUS Commandery of Michigan, 1893), 17.

9. OR, vol. 27, pt. 1, 943, 992.

10. OR, vol. 27, pt. 1, 993. Many quotations about the postwar controversies can be found in Andie Custer, "The Kilpatrick-Farnsworth Argument That Never Happened," *GM* 28 (2003): 101–16; and Custer, "John Hammond's 'Mis-stake': How a Misplaced Wooden Stake Altered the History of Farnsworth's Charge at Gettysburg," *GM* 30 (2004): 98–113. For another strongly argued study that reaches very different conclusions about the Farnsworth fight, see Eric J. Wittenberg, *Gettysburg's Forgotten Cavalry Actions* (Gettysburg, Pa.: Thomas Publications, 1998), especially chapters 2 and 3.

Stop 35

1. John Wierich Damage Claim, ACHS.

2. PR, Isabella Titterington for Richard Titterington; Commonwealth of Pennsylvania, *Report of the Select Committee Relative to the Soldiers' National Cemetery* (Harrisburg, Pa.: n.p., 1864), 68.

3. CSR, Eli T. Green.

The Aftermath: July 4, 1863, and Beyond

1. See Carol Reardon, *Pickett's Charge in History and Memory* (Chapel Hill: University of North Carolina Press, 1997), 41–42; NYH, July 6, 1863.

2. Roy P. Basler, ed., *The Collected Works of Abraham Lincoln* (New Brunswick, N.J.: Rutgers University Press, 1953), 6:318.

3. Ibid., 6:319.

4. OR, vol. 27, pt. 2, 323.

5. Basler, *The Collected Works of Abraham Lincoln*, 6:328.

6. OR, vol. 27, pt. 1, 168–72.

7. OR, vol. 27, pt. 1, 118.

8. George Gordon Meade, ed., *The Life and Letters of George Gordon Meade, Major General, United States Army* (New York: Charles Scribner's Sons, 1913), 2:133.

9. For the most comprehensive coverage of these hearings, see Bill Hyde, ed., *The Union Generals Speak: The Meade Hearings on the Battle of Gettysburg* (Baton Rouge: Louisiana State University Press, 2003).

10. OR, vol. 27, pt. 2, 346.

11. *Richmond Dispatch*, July 8, 1863.

12. See Reardon, *Pickett's Charge in History and Memory*, 51–61; *Richmond Dispatch*, August 1, 1863

13. Kent Masterson Brown, *Retreat from Gettysburg: Lee, Logistics, and the Pennsylvania Campaign* (Chapel Hill: University of North Carolina Press, 2005), 389.

14. OR, vol. 27, pt. 2, 305.

15. *Army and Navy Journal*, October 10, 1863.

16. "Wisconsin Wounded at Gettysburg," *Milwaukee Daily Sentinel*, July 27, 1863; "Our Sick and Wounded at Gettysburg," *Connecticut Courant* (Hartford), August 1, 1863.

17. "Our Wounded at Gettysburg," *New York Evening Post*, July 10, 1863.

18. "Dedicating of the National Cemetery," *Greene County Journal* (Xenia, Ohio), November 27, 1863.

19. "Our Wounded at Gettysburg," *New York Evening Post*.

20. Travis W. Busey and John W. Busey, *Union Casualties at Gettysburg: A Comprehensive Record* (Jefferson, N.C.: McFarland, 2011), 3:1368.

21. For the best study of this transformation, see Jim Weeks, *Gettysburg: Memory, Market, and an American Shrine* (Princeton, N.J.: Princeton University Press, 2003).

22. *Pennsylvania at Gettysburg: Ceremonies at the Dedication of the Monuments Erected by the Commonwealth of Pennsylvania* (Harrisburg: Wm. Stanley Ray, 1904), 1:399.

23. "The Battle's Lesson," NT, May 28, 1885.

Index

Cemetery Hill, 311; on July 1, 100, 119, 147, 152–53; fighting on July 2, 176, 274–5, 299–304; as key battleground, 25–29, 299

Cemetery Ridge: fighting on approaches to, on July 2, 176, 258–64; on July 3, 308, 313, 367–88

Chamberlain, Col. Joshua Lawrence: biographical sketch of, 206–7; at Little Round Top, 198, 204–7, 418

Chamberlin, Maj. Thomas, 127

Chambliss, Col. John, 390

Chapman, P. G., 55

Christian Commission, U.S., 104, 415

Christie, Col. Daniel, 75

Church, Pvt. Jonathan B., 63

Church, William Conant, 413–14

Clark, Maj. George, 386

Clarke, Col. Henry F., 316

Clifford, Pvt. John, 254

Coan, Cpl. Elisha, 209

Coates, Capt. Henry C., 264

Cobean, Samuel, 94

Cobham, Col. George, 333

Coddington, Edwin B., 32

Codori, Nicholas and Elizabeth, farm of: on July 2, 176, 239, 248, 266, 271; on July 3, 347, 349, 355, 359, 365, 370–73

Cody, Lt. Barnett H., 207–8

Coffey, Pvts. Cleveland, Thomas Milton, and William S., 140

Coffin, Charles Carleton, 29, 381

Colgrove, Col. Silas: biographical sketch of, 324; on July 3, 321–24, 326

Colvill, Col. William, 259, 263

Comstock, Sgt. Samuel, 104

Connecticut regiments: 5th, 334; 14th, 283; 17th, 97, 100, 101, 104, 105, 302, 305; 20th, 334

Conner, Lt. Col. Freeman, 200

Conner, Maj. William G., 396–97

Cooper, Capt. James H., 127, 129, 136, 143, 278, 280, 301

Cooper, Lt. Thomas W., 139

Cornish, Virgil, 415

Coster, Col. Charles R.: biographical sketch of, 109–10; brigade of, 28, 107–9, 303

Coulter, Sgt. William J., 268

Courtney, Capt. A. R., 279

Cowan, Capt. Andrew, 367, 369–70, 377

Craig, Col. Calvin A., 250

Crawford, Brig. Gen. Samuel W., 231

Cress's Ridge, 389–90, 392

Crippen, Sgt. Benjamin, 130–31

Cromwell, Maj. James, 217, 220

Cross, Col. Edward E., 228, 232, 234

Crounse, L. L., 10

Culp, E. C., 105

Culp, Henry and Anna, 291, 306, 328, 336

Culp, Pvt. Wesley, 291

Culp's Hill: as factor in planning for July 2, 176, 195, 264, 275; on July 1, 152; on July 2, 282–85, 287–89, 320; on July 3, 320–21, 328–38

Culver, Pvt. Everard, 220

Culver, Lt. Thomas, 220

Cummins, Col. Robert, 136, 138

Currans, Alexander, 398–99

Curtin, Andrew Gregg, 4, 14, 403

Cushing, Lt. Alonzo H., 17, 367, 369, 376–77

Custer, Brig. Gen. George A.: biographical sketch of, 395–96; on July 3, 390, 392–93, 398

Cutler, Brig. Gen. Lysander: biographical sketch of, 61–62; on July 1, 49, 50, 59–61, 80, 145, 342

Dana, Capt. Amasa E., 46

Dance, Capt. Willis, 275, 278

Daniel, Brig. Gen. Junius: biographical sketch of, 128; on July 1, 71, 123–26, 144–45; on July 3, 287, 328–29, 332–33

Darwin, Sgt. John Taylor, 202

Davis, Capt. James T., 91

Davis, Jefferson, 1, 3, 16, 62, 412

Davis, Brig. Gen. Joseph R., 324; biographical sketch of, 62; brigade of, on July 1, 41–42, 57–61, 65–66; brigade of, on July 3, 342, 383–85

Davis, Capt. William, 376

Dawes, Lt. Col. Rufus R., 65–68

Day, Col. Hannibal, 231–32, 234

Dearing, Maj. James, 353–56

Delaware regiment, 1st, 382, 385

Dement, Capt. William F., 275, 277

Dent, Lt. John F., 382

De Trobriand, Col. Regis: biographical sketch of, 234; brigade of, 179, 225–28, 232, 234, 243

Devil's Den: Sickles advances to, 179, 184; origin of name, 211; fight on July 2, 211–18

Devin, Col. Thomas, 58–59, 87

Devoe, Pvt. William H., 236

Dickinson, Lt. Col. Joseph, 316–17

Dickson, Pvt. Joseph C., 220

Dildine, Pvt. Andrew J., 386

Dilger, Capt. Hubert, 89–91

Ditterline, Theodore, 9

Doane, Capt. Elisha, 297

Dobke, Lt. Col. Adolphus, 81

Doles, Brig. Gen. George P.: biographical sketch of, 83; brigade of, 91–92, 95, 97–99, 104–5

Doubleday, Maj. Gen. Abner, 136, 314; biographical sketch of, 52; as critic of Meade, 182–83; on July 1, 49–50, 65–66, 79–80, 87, 122, 132, 143, 153–55; on July 2, 269; postwar writings of, 182–83, 196–97

DuPont, Commodore Samuel, 1

Durham, Cpl. Gabriel B., 45

Earl, Pvt. William N., 110

Early, Maj. Gen. Jubal A.: biographical sketch of, 102; criticisms of Longstreet, 348; on July 1, 69, 79, 97, 308; postwar writings of, 307

Eason, Cpl. J. H., 91

East Cemetery Hill, fighting on July 2, 293–94, 299–304

Eckenrode, Jacob, Nicholas, and Sarah, 364

Edie, Lt. John, 317

Edmonds, Col. E. C., 380

Eisenhower, Dwight D., 164, 272

Ellis, Col. A. VanHorn, 212, 216–17, 220

Ellis, Lt. Col. John, 380

Eshelman, Maj. Benjamin F., 353, 356

Eternal Light Peace Memorial, 69, 75, 77, 123, 417

Evergreen Cemetery, 25–29, 31, 403, 416

Ewell, Lt. Gen. Richard S.: on advance into Pennsylvania, 4, 6, 12; biographical sketch of, 73–74; blamed for defeat, 412; on July 1, 46, 69–70, 152–53; on July 2, 275, 282; on July 3, 308, 321, 328–29

Excelsior Brigade and Field, 180, 240, 244, 248, 253

Fairchild, Col. Lucius, 49

Fairfield, George, 68

Farley, Capt. Porter, 197

Farnham, Lt. Col. Augustus B., 116

Farnsworth, Brig. Gen. Elon J., 398–401

Farren, Pvt. John, 380–81

Featherston, Lt. Daniel A., 346

Ferry, Maj. Noah, 392

Fesler, Lt. Col. John, 323

Flagler, Maj. D. W., 317

Florida regiments: 2nd, 252–53, 269, 360; 5th, 252–55, 269, 360; 8th, 252–53, 267, 269–70, 360

Fontaine, Maj. C. R., 376, 378

Fontenot, Pvt. Horthere, 306

Forbes, Edwin, 29

Ford, Lt. John B., 149–150

Forney, John Swope and Mary, 75, 82, 119

Forster, Capt. Robert M., 235

Fowler, Lt. Col. Douglas, 97

Fowler, Col. Edward B., 66, 68

Francine, Col. Louis, 245

Franks, Pvt. Rufus B., 202

Fremantle, Lt. Col. A. J. L., 130

French, Maj. Gen. William H., 408

Frey, Peter, 370, 381

Friend, Thomas, 365

Friends of the National Parks at Gettysburg, 104–5

Fry, Col. Birkett D.: brigade of, 53, 342–43, 357, 380–81; wounded and captured, 382–83, 385

Gamble, Col. William, 40–41, 43, 48,

Garnett, Brig. Gen. Richard B.: biographical sketch of, 362–63; brigade of, 12, 356, 357–59, 377–78; death of, 52, 377, 380, 412

Garrison, Lt. Edward J., 290

Gaskins, Sgt. William H., 363

Gates, Col. Theodore, 373

Geary, Brig. Gen. John W.: biographical sketch of, 334–35; on July 2, 269, 287, 320; on July 3, 321, 329–33, 337

Georgia regiments: 2nd, 215–16, 218, 220; 2nd Battalion, 269–70; 3rd, 269–70; 4th,

Livingston, Lt. Manning, 254
Lockwood, Brig. Gen. Henry H., 330, 334, 337
Longstreet, Lt. Gen. James: biographical sketch of, 170–71; critics of, 19, 102, 173–74, 348; evaluations of, 19, 102, 348, 412, 414; on July 1, 155; on July 2, 167, 187; on July 3, 308, 339–43, 352–53; on march into Pennsylvania, 5–6, 12; postwar writings of, 165, 173–74, 347–48
Longworth, Sgt. Charles, 335–36
Louisiana regiments: 1st, 285–86, 354; 2nd, 285–86; 5th, 100, 304–5; 6th, 100, 304–5; 7th, 100, 304–5; 8th, 100, 304–6; 9th, 100, 303–5; 10th, 285–86; 14th, 285–86; 15th, 285–86; Louisiana Guard Artillery, 100, 389–90, 393; Madison Artillery, 353; Washington Artillery, 350, 352–54
Lowell, Capt. Oliver H., 118–19
Lowrance, Lt. Col. William L. J., 343, 386
Lowrie, Lt. J. B., 139
Lowry, Pvt. George G., 336
Lumpkin, Lt. Col. Samuel P., 103
Lutheran Theological Seminary, 9, 119, 137, 142–50
Lutz, Capt. John M., 100
Lyman, Adj. H. H., 64
Lyman, Lt. Col. Theodore, 14–15, 43, 252, 373, 379
Lyons, Pvt. B. F., 220

Mackenzie, Lt. Ranald, 195–97
Mackey, Pvt. Thomas, 163
Madill, Col. Henry J., 242–43
Magruder, Col. John Bowie, 380
Mahler, Col. Francis, 103
Mahone, Brig. Gen. William, 270
Maine regiments: 3rd, 29, 159, 161–62, 164–65, 242–43, 245; 4th, 212, 214, 216, 218, 220–22; 16th, 116–19, 137; 17th, 225–26, 230, 232, 253; 19th, 266–70, 372–73; 20th, 198, 204–8, 310; 1st Cavalry, 393; 2nd Battery, 59, 61, 62, 64; 5th Battery, 142, 278–79, 293–94, 296–98, 301–2
Mallon, Col. James, 355
Malone, Pvt. John, 253
Maloney, Pvt. Patrick, 50

Mansfield, Maj. John, 50, 133
Marks, Pvt. W. Edwin, 164
Marshall, Col. James Keith: brigade of, 342–43, 382–83; death of, 383, 385, 386
Maryland regiments, C.S.A.: 1st Cavalry, 393; 1st Maryland Artillery, 275, 277, 279; 2nd Battalion (1st Battalion at time of battle), 287–90, 309, 331–32, 336; Chesapeake Artillery, 275, 277, 279–80
Maryland regiments, U.S.A.: 1st Maryland Eastern Shore, 334–35; 1st Potomac Home Brigade, 330, 334, 336; 3rd, 334; 1st Cavalry, 390, 393; Purnell Legion Cavalry, U.S.A., 393
Massachusetts regiments: 1st, 248, 252–53, 255, 259, 359; 2nd, 321–23, 326–27; 11th, 252–53; 12th, 73, 81, 84; 13th, 113–19; 15th, 268–270, 372–73; 16th, 252–53, 255; 19th, 263, 269–70, 372–73; 20th, 269–70, 368, 372–73, 375; 32nd, 227, 230; 33rd, 293, 296–98, 305; 54th, 508; Battery C, 3rd Artillery (Walcott), 231; 5th Battery, 353; 5th Battery (Phillips), 240, 243, 356; 9th Battery (Bigelow), 240, 243
Massey, Pvt. Jacob A., 119
Matrau, Pvt. Henry, 65–66
Maxwell, Pvt. Charles N., 161–62
Mayo, Col. Joseph C., 355, 378
Mayo, Col. Robert M., 383–84
McAllister, James, Agnes, and Samuel, 326
McAllister, Col. Robert, 248
McAllister's Woods, 320–24
McCandless, Col. William, 231, 234
McClean, Moses, farm of, 81, 83, 85, 89, 91, 94, 113, 115, 119
McClelan, Pvt. Bailey George, 163
McClellan, Maj. Gen. George B., 16
McClellan, H. B., 395
McClellan, Cpl. Rudolphus Henry, 254–55
McClellan, Pvt. William Cowan, 272
McConaughy, David, 307, 415–16
McCook, Pvt. Dawson, 221
McCreary, Samuel, 221
McDaniel, Maj. H. D., 226
McDougall, Col. Archibald L., 333–34
McDowell, Cpl. Henry, 286
McFarland, Lt. Col. George F., 136, 146

Seddon, James A., 3

Sedgwick, Maj. Gen. John, 14, 29, 310, 314, 408, 410

Seeley, Lt. Francis W., 248, 251

Sellers, Maj. Alfred, 115

Seminary Ridge: on July 1, 136–37, 142–50; on July 2, 159–62; on July 3, 337, 400

Semmes, Brig. Gen. Paul J.: brigade of, 169, 230, 232, 235, 237; death of, 230, 235, 237, 412

Shaara, Michael, 47, 209

Shaler, Brig. Gen. Alexander, brigade of, 330, 334–35, 337, 410

Shefferer, Christian, 172

Sheffield, Col. James, 187

Shehan, Pvt. Jeremiah, 254

Shepard, Lt. Col. S. G., 42, 50–51, 342, 357, 359

Sherfy, Jacob, 221

Sherfy, Joseph and Mary, home of, 166, 181–82, 239–40, 242–43, 245–47

Sheridan, Maj. Gen. Philip H., 14, 102

Sherman, Maj. Gen. William T., 14, 73, 414

Sherrill, Col. Eliakim, 262, 382–83, 385–86

Shryock, George, 31

Sickles, Maj. Gen. Daniel E., 255, 315; biographical sketch of, 180–81; as critic of Meade, 14, 178–79, 182–83; deploys to Emmitsburg Road ridge, 159, 161, 169, 177–78; during the postwar years, 64; wounded, 247, 250; writes legislation to establish military park, 416–17

Sigel, Maj. Gen. Franz, 92, 99

Silliman, Pvt. Justus M., 104

Simons, Chap. Ezra D., 272–73

Skelly, Daniel, 10, 316

Slentz, John, 46

Slocum, Maj. Gen. Henry W., 14, 255, 293; biographical sketch of, 296–97; at council of war, 314; on July 1, 153; 312, 334–35

Slyder, John, farm of, 184, 187, 190–91, 214

Small, Maj. Abner, 119–20

Small, P. A., 381

Smith, Capt. James A., 211–14

Smith, Lt. James J., 228

Smith, Lt. Joe C., 189–90

Smith, Lt. Col. Maurice T., 63

Smith, Col. Orland, 28, 296

Smith, Brig. Gen. William "Extra Billy," brigade of, 287, 323–24

Smith, Pvt. William J., 286

Smyth, Col. Thomas A., brigade of, 382–83, 385

Snyder, Conrad, 31

Soldiers' National Cemetery: establishment of, 25, 416; tour of, 401–6; vignettes of soldiers buried there, 63, 67, 140, 203, 208, 254, 265–66, 286, 290–91, 297–98, 336, 373–74, 405

Soldiers' National Monument, 402, 404

Sorrel, Maj. G. Moxley, 348

South Carolina regiments: 1st, 146–47, 149; 2nd, 243, 245; 3rd, 227, 232, 245; 7th, 227, 232; 8th, 243, 245; 12th, 146–47, 149; 13th, 146–47, 149; 14th, 146–47, 149, 151; 15th, 227, 232; 1st Cavalry, 393; 2nd Cavalry, 393; 3rd Battalion, 243; 1st (Orr's) Rifles, 149; Brooks Artillery, 353; Pee Dee Artillery, 43, 344

Southern Historical Society, and its *Papers*, 102, 173

Southern Illustrated News, 74

South Mountain, Battle of, 74

Spangler, Abraham, 325–26, 331, 336

Spangler, George, farm of, 104, 326

Spangler, Henry and Sarah, farm of, 239, 326, 357–58, 364, 371, 379

Spangler's Spring, stop at, 319–27;

Spear, Maj. Ellis, 210

Speed, Capt. William J., 139

Stannard, Brig. Gen. George J., 378, 380

Staub, Catherine Codori, 272

Steele, Lt. Col. Amos, 373

Steuart, Brig. Gen. George H.: biographical sketch of, 289–90; on July 2, 283, 288–90, 309, 320–21, 328; on July 3, 328, 331–33

Stevens, Lt. Col. George H., 50

Stevens, Capt. Greenleaf T., 142, 278, 293, 301

Stevens's Knoll, 293–98, 301–2

Stevens's Run, 108, 111

Stewart, Lt. James, 125, 129, 143, 301

Stikeleather, Pvt. John, 152

Stillwell, Pvt. William, 237

Stone, Col. Roy: biographical sketch of, 127–28; brigade of, 64, 122–27, 129, 137, 143–44, 146–47